PERSONAL FINANCIAL MANAGEMENT

PERSONAL FINANCIAL MANAGEMENT

MARK R. GREENE
Distinguished Professor
of Risk and Insurance
University of Georgia

ROBERT R. DINCE
Professor of Banking
and Finance
University of Georgia

Published by

F50   **SOUTH-WESTERN PUBLISHING CO.**

CINCINNATI   WEST CHICAGO, ILL.   DALLAS   PELHAM MANOR, N.Y.   PALO ALTO, CALIF.

Copyright © 1983
by South-Western Publishing Co.
Cincinnati, Ohio

Book Production: The Book Department, Inc.

Cover Photo: Ferro Corporation, Cleveland, Ohio

Library of Congress Catalog Card Number: 82–50576

ISBN: 0–538–06500–1

1 2 3 4 5 6 7 8 D 0 9 8 7 6 5 4 3

Printed in the United States of America

CONTENTS

PREFACE

The authors' goals in writing this text are several. Foremost is to fill the need for an up-to-date treatment of personal finance, which not only reflects the changes made under the Economic Recovery Tax Act of 1981, but also incorporates the realities of continuing high taxes, inflation, and interest rates in our economy. These conditions influence personal financial planning in a very direct way; they cannot be handled as "side issues."

The text will provide the student with (1) an appreciation of the need for financial planning, (2) a working knowledge of how to carry out effective financial planning, (3) a knowledge of risk management and the use of insurance in protecting income and assets in an efficient way, (4) an understanding of how to accumulate property through investments, (5) the ability to coordinate income and assets into a comprehensive program that takes the planner through all stages of the family life cycle, and finally (6) an introduction to retirement and estate planning.

Emphasis throughout this text is given to applying knowledge to practical, consumer-oriented problems in personal financial planning. The end-of-chapter cases enable the student to apply this knowledge to "real-life" situations. Additionally, the text includes topics of current interest, such as zero coupon bonds and universal life insurance, which appear with regularity in the financial press.

The text should prove to be valuable to both business and nonbusiness majors. For the nonbusiness major, this will probably be the only classroom exposure to personal financial management topics. For the business major, the text will serve as an interesting introduction to areas that will be studied in more depth in subsequent courses. Also, most business majors will not take all of the individual courses whose topics are introduced here.

In writing this book we have tried to avoid "talking down" to the reader. All terms believed to be "technical" are defined the first time they are introduced. A glossary is provided for subsequent reference. The reader is shown how to use the interest tables as an aid in solving finanacial problems. Learning objectives appear at the beginning of each chapter and a list of suggested readings appears at the end of the text.

In addition to solutions to the end-of-chapter questions and cases, the instructors' manual contains the purpose, outline, learning objectives, summary, new terms, and teaching suggestions for each chapter. A wealth of multiple-choice questions for testing purposes are also included.

Many individuals have contributed to the development of this book. We would like especially to thank Professors Mark Hanna and Scott Bauman, who contributed Chapters 12 and 13. To all of the others who helped and offered valuable criticism of the manuscript, we extend our thanks and appreciation, all the while accepting final responsibility for the text.

Mark R. Greene
Robert R. Dince
Athens, Georgia

CHAPTER

CHAPTER 1

INCOME AND EXPENDITURE PLANNING

LEARNING OBJECTIVES

In studying this chapter, you will learn:

The meaning of financial planning;

How stages in your life cycle affect the nature and extent of your planning goals;

How to make a financial plan;

How to set up a simple budget system;

How to develop and utilize records needed for planning;

Why taxes should motivate you toward better planning;

Some guides to efficient spending.

The basis of successful personal financial management is effective planning in regard to income and expenditures. The alternative—unfortunately, the technique used by most individuals—may be described as the "hit-or-miss" approach to decisions about how to spend income, use credit, purchase insurance, make investments, and handle other financial matters. All too often the "hit-or-miss" method means that individuals will not have funds available when they are needed to accomplish certain goals. Frustration brought on by the lack of adequate funds for reaching financial goals can lead to personal unhappiness. A way to overcome this problem is to make an effort to plan effectively and realistically.

GOALS OF FINANCIAL PLANNING

What are the goals of financial planning? The answer depends on what you want out of life, on what stage in life you are in, and on whether your objective is to be accomplished in the short run or over a period of years. A basic assumption in this book is that you want to acquire things that require financial planning—for example, economic security, a home for your family, and sufficient resources to obtain education, to pursue hobbies, to build an estate, and to purchase needed goods and services.

We usually learn about the need for planning very early in life. Even though young people tend to think in terms of very brief periods and to set short-term goals, they soon realize that without some advance thinking and planning they cannot acquire the things they want. Thus, a teenage student planning to go on an outing the following week must make commitments ahead of time to somehow obtain the necessary funds and perhaps to make arrangements for taking along a companion at added cost. As we get older, planning tends to become a lengthier process. For example, college-bound students must usually plan at least a year or longer for being admitted to college and for earning money for tuition and other expenses.

Life-Cycle Approach

Goals for financial planning vary according to the tasks to be accomplished. The tasks, in turn, depend on many factors relating to one's personal circumstances. In personal financial management it is convenient to work with the "life-cycle approach," although the life-cycle stages may not be applicable to every individual. Stages in the life cycle (see Exhibit 1–1) include

EXHIBIT 1–1
Role of Life-Cycle
Stages in
Planning Goals

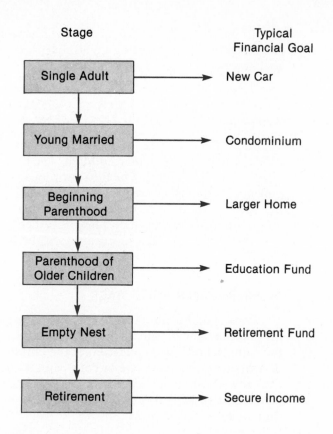

Stage	Typical Financial Goal
Single Adult	New Car
Young Married	Condominium
Beginning Parenthood	Larger Home
Parenthood of Older Children	Education Fund
Empty Nest	Retirement Fund
Retirement	Secure Income

(1) the single-adult stage, (2) the young-married stage, (3) the beginning-parenthood stage, (4) the parenthood stage with older children, (5) the parents-alone, or "empty nest," stage, and (6) the retirement stage.

SINGLE-ADULT STAGE

Perhaps the most important stage in the life cycle, single adulthood, is the stage during which basic habits become firmly rooted for a lifetime. If one establishes sound systems of budgeting for income and expenditures and of keeping records, one sets a foundation for better performance of these functions in later years. Of particular importance is practice in keeping adequate records to support personal income tax deductions.

Common tasks requiring adequate financial planning in the single-adult stage include purchasing appropriate insurance and saving to establish a household and to pay for career training. Each of these tasks requires money and planning. For example, if a young adult wishes to have an apartment, a financial commitment is necessary. An income sufficient to pay the rent on the apartment is required, as is a savings fund for furniture, apartment decoration, and other household items. Action to obtain credit or other types of borrowing is also necessary. Once the financial plan is set, the young adult can reach the goal of setting up an independent household. Seldom is this goal attainable unless financial planning precedes it.

YOUNG-MARRIED STAGE

Many young married persons begin to make plans for the not-so-distant future, when they will have children. The expanded family will perhaps require a larger dwelling, which in turn means that the family must have a previously established credit record. At this stage, young families should also pay special attention to the need for adequate life and health insurance. If young marrieds can develop plans together for achieving these goals, the chances of the marriage succeeding will be increased greatly.

BEGINNING-PARENTHOOD STAGE

Once children are added to a family, new tasks requiring financial planning are also added. Parents must address the problem of providing funds for the care, training, and education of the children. Budgets may also have to be structured to enable one or both parents to upgrade their education and thus advance their careers. Planning is also needed to offset educational expenses and possible reductions in income if one person leaves a job for further study.

PARENTHOOD STAGES WITH OLDER CHILDREN

This stage frequently involves development of an estate plan, a will, and other plans to distribute one's property. Common tasks include more mature versions of tasks identified in earlier stages—for example, building educational funds, increasing career training, expanding living quarters, establishing a more adequate program of insurance, developing adequate plans for investment of excess savings, and making initial plans for retirement and estate building.

EMPTY-NEST STAGE

After the children have moved out, the parents' tasks are again altered. One task may be relocating to obtain smaller living quarters or to be nearer to the children. This stage involves planning more seriously for retirement needs. One of the parents may also consider reentering the work force, which may involve additional training or education.

RETIREMENT STAGE

Tasks during this stage are largely shaped by accomplishments during the previous stages. Insurance and annuity programs need to be completely reviewed, and basic changes in one's insurance program may be necessary. Old policies may be cashed in or altered. In addition, increased budgets for travel may be arranged, and changes may be made to reflect different housing and transportation needs.

ADVANTAGES OF FINANCIAL PLANNING

Considering the tasks to be accomplished at various stages in the life cycle, what are the main advantages and purposes of financial planning? With advance planning, you can accomplish the following tasks:

1. You will be able to satisfy more goals without sacrificing current wants.
2. You will not spend all your income immediately and thus be left without cash until your next paycheck arrives.
3. You will achieve some control over your own affairs and will not become completely dependent on other people or on society.
4. You and your family will be protected against losses beyond your control through adequate insurance protection.
5. You will be able to meet your responsibilities to others, including members of your own family.
6. You will have a much better chance to achieve the personal satisfaction and happiness that derives from a sense of accomplishment.
7. You will know more about resources available to you, such as employee benefits, social insurance, and tax-qualified savings plans.
8. You will become more aware of your priorities—that is, the goals most important and least important to you.

A FINANCIAL PLANNING GUIDE

The essential steps in modern financial planning are as follows:

1. Analyzing current and future needs for funds;
2. Identifying and budgeting the resources to meet these needs;
3. Protecting assets and income against unknown contingencies;
4. Estate planning through the coordination of resources to provide adequate retirement income and to preserve your wealth for dependents by minimizing the effect of inflation and taxes.

"I think that sound financial planning will be the key to a long, successful relationship, my dear."

The Bettman Archive, Inc.

Step 1: Analyzing Needs

The analysis of current and future needs can be broken down into a statement of (1) current needs for self-maintenance or family maintenance and

(2) needs for future projects. For example, a listing of current living expenses may dictate that an individual has a minimum outgo of $1,000 a month. However, obtaining a home or a car or living in a better apartment may require a total outgo of $2,000 a month. In this case, current savings should be considered. If savings are minimal, the individual has a $1,000-a-month deficit. Until a plan is made to cover this deficit, future needs will remain unsatisfied. Pursuing Step 1 to completion establishes financial needs and forces clarification of financial goals.

Step 2: Identifying and Budgeting Resources

Step 2 establishes a plan for obtaining the resources to meet any deficits discovered in Step 1. The most common method of obtaining the needed resources is to learn what amount of savings would be required to meet the gaps noted in Step 1, and how long it would take to accumulate the necessary amount. Savings can be accumulated in a variety of ways, not the least of which is to reduce planned expenditures or to buy economically. The savings realized by minimizing taxes is an important source of additional funds.

Step 3: Protecting Assets and Income

Many individuals ignore this step because the need for protecting accumulated savings or assets isn't always obvious. Most people take the attitude that losses due to such things as auto accidents or fires will not affect them personally; such random events are always thought to occur "to the other fellow." Yet a plan for protecting assets is essential in personal financial planning.

Step 4: Estate Planning

Estate planning involves accumulating resources and making plans for retirement for yourself and your dependents as well as for the distribution of property after your death. Estate planning is more difficult in an economy characterized by high inflation and heavy income and estate taxation. Inflation makes it difficult to determine how much to save to meet future needs and how to accumulate the savings. Estate planning is discussed in detail in Part IV.

FACTORS AFFECTING INCOME

As noted above, an essential step in financial planning is carefully identifying the sources of income you have or expect to have in the future. From this income, all expenditures must be made in the long run. Of course, borrowing is possible in situations where expenditures must exceed income. Eventually, however, the borrowing must be repaid. Thus, your income sets your life-style and serves as the base from which to make financial plans.

Income must be judged not only by its size but by its stability. Some occupations provide unstable sources of income. The quality, or stability, of income is a necessary consideration in a financial plan. If the income is subject to interruption by bad weather (as in the case of farmers) or by a strike (as in the case of industrial labor union workers), the possibility of interruption must be taken into account in any financial plan. As we will learn later, insurance can assist in making an income more stable, since certain types of losses that interrupt income—accidents or illnesses, for example—can be insured against.

Income in the United States is not distributed evenly in proportion to family units. For example, the top 20 percent of families receive approximately 40 percent of the country's total income, while the income of about 15 percent of the population is below poverty level. As shown in Exhibit 1–2, about 19 percent of all U.S. households receive under $10,000 a year, while only 6.7 percent receive over $50,000. Several factors influence the size, distribution, and stability of income. These factors include a worker's educational level, occupation, age, sex, and geographical location, as well as the inflation and taxability of the income.

EXHIBIT 1–2
Distribution of Income, U.S. Households, 1980

Income Bracket	Percentage of Households Falling in Each Bracket
Under $ 5,000	6.2
$ 5,000–$ 9,999	12.7
$10,000–$14,999	14.2
$15,000–$19,999	14.0
$20,000–$24,999	13.7
$25,000–$34,999	19.7
$35,000–$49,999	12.8
$50,000 and over	6.7
Total	100.0
Median Income	$21,023
Mean Income	$23,974

Source: U.S. Department of Commerce, Bureau of Census, *Consumer Income*, Series P–60, No. 127 (March, 1981), p. 14.

Income and Education

A positive correlation exists between higher income and higher education. The average income of college graduates is about 1.5 times the average
income of high school graduates. For example, in 1977 the average annual
income of college graduates was slightly over $25,000, compared to $16,000
for high school graduates. These data should not be interpreted to mean that
it is always necessary to have a college education to obtain a relatively good
income; many individuals in jobs that do not require college educations
(especially the skilled trades) earn more than the average college graduate.

Income and Occupation

A person embarking on a program of personal financial planning can
estimate future income on the basis of data that show average incomes in
different occupational groups in various parts of the country. By an appropriate
choice of a career, a person can maximize potential lifetime income. Average
incomes of different occupational groups are shown in Exhibit 1–3. Note that
some occupations not only have higher beginning salaries but also offer greater
opportunity for achieving a relatively larger final salary (three times the beginning salary, in the case of attorneys). Relatively little room for salary increases
seems to characterize occupations such as file clerk, secretary, and job analyst.

Data show that 58 percent of all college graduates become professional
and technical workers. About 18 percent become managers, 7 percent enter
sales work, 5 percent take up blue collar occupations, and the remainder enter

EXHIBIT 1–3
Average Salary
by Occupation,
March 1981

Occupation	Annual Mean Salaries		Ratio of Average Top Salaries to Average Beginning Salaries
	Beginning	Top Level	
Accountant	$16,529	$43,754	2.7
Attorney	22,477	56,958	2.5
Buyer	16,202	30,583	1.9
Job analyst	16,940	28,718	1.7
Personnel director	27,848	53,914	1.9
Chemist	18,092	48,845	2.7
Engineer	21,712	56,828	2.6
Computer operator	10,869	20,796	1.9
File clerk	8,423	11,691	1.4
Personnel clerk	10,777	20,079	1.9
Secretary	12,947	19,615	1.5

Source: *National Survey of Professional, Administrative, Technical, and Clerical Pay, March 1981* (Washington,
D.C.: USGPO, 1981), pp. 11–12.

"Challenging jobs open up for college graduates."

other fields, such as service, farm, and clerical occupations.[1] Because of the increasing numbers of college graduates in recent years, competition for jobs has increased. Average earnings of college graduates compared to high school graduates have declined somewhat, and some occupations that require a college degree—most areas of teaching, for example—are overcrowded. Still, college training is a distinct advantage for most workers, and average incomes and job challenges tend to be greater for college graduates than for people without college training.

---

1. U.S. Department of Labor, *Occupational Outlook for College Graduates*, Bulletin 2956 (Washington, D.C.: USGPO, 1978), p. 23.

Income and Age, Sex, and Location

Income tends to vary with a worker's age and sex. The longer a person has been working in a particular field, the higher his or her income tends to be. Women tend to earn less than men, even in the same occupation, partly because many women have only recently entered some occupations and lack seniority, experience, and educational background. In some cases women have been discriminated against because of their sex and their lack of bargaining position. Evidence exists that such discrimination is diminishing, partly because of federal legislation requiring equal pay for equal work.

Income also tends to vary according to geographical region; some areas of the country enjoy considerable income superiority over other areas. For example, the average per capita income in southeastern states is generally about 80 percent of the average per capita income in northern and western states. The purchasing power of income also varies regionally. As shown in Exhibit 1–4, total annual living costs in 1979 in different cities varied considerably; the highest living cost was recorded in Anchorage, Alaska, and the lowest in Oklahoma City, Oklahoma. Note that a family living on $18,000 in Oklahoma City could have saved $2,723, while the same income would have put an Anchorage family $3,029 in debt.

EXHIBIT 1–4
Total Annual
Living Costs,
Selected U.S.
Cities, 1979

City	Total Annual Living Cost
Anchorage, Ala.	$21,029
Little Rock, Ark.	15,851
Santa Ana, Calif.	19,839
Wilmington, Del.	17,196
Albany, Ga.	16,789
Boise, Idaho	18,053
Waukegan, Ill.	19,624
Pontiac, Mich.	18,365
Northeast New Jersey	19,484
Albany, N.Y.	16,654
Raleigh/Durham, N.C.	16,430
Canton, Ohio	18,179
Oklahoma City, Okla.	15,277
San Antonio, Tex.	15,694
Olympia, Wash.	17,405

Note: Data apply to a family of four earning $18,000, living in a six-room house, and driving a compact car.

Source: *Family Weekly* (January 27, 1980), p. 21. Reprinted by permission of *Family Weekly*, copyright 1980, 641 Lexington Avenue, New York, N.Y. 10022.

Income and Inflation

In making estimates of income, one should consider the factor of inflation, particularly for planning that exceeds a period of one year. In recent years inflation in the United States has been running at approximately 9 percent to 11 percent annually. A tabulation of the effect of inflation is given in Exhibit 1–5. Observe that if you start out with an income of $1,000 a month, a 10 percent rate of inflation means that within three years you must earn $1,331 per month—and within five years $1,610 per month—just to "stay even." Moreover, **progressive income tax rates** mean that a higher dollar income is subjected to proportionately higher taxes that effectively reduce buying power. Unless your income keeps pace with inflation and increased taxes, your living standard will tend to fall—a fact that has important implications on financial planning. In the Economic Recovery Tax Act of 1981, Congress mandated changes in the income tax system that help alleviate the problem. After 1984, income tax brackets, the zero bracket amount, and personal exemptions (see Chapter 9) are to be adjusted for inflation based on changes in the consumer price index.

EXHIBIT 1–5   Effect of Inflation on Monthly Income of $1,000

Inflation Rate	Income Needed to Keep Pace with Inflation after:			
	3 Years	5 Years	8 Years	10 Years
0%	$1,000	$1,000	$1,000	$1,000
5	1,158	1,276	1,477	1,628
7	1,225	1,402	1,718	1,967
10	1,331	1,610	2,143	2,593
12	1,404	1,762	2,475	3,105
15	1,520	2,011	3,059	4,045

Source: Calculated by the authors.

To gain further insight into the effects of inflation, consider the cost of typical goods and services, each of which is rising at different rates. Exhibit 1–6A gives estimates of levels to which these items may rise by the end of the century; Exhibit 1–6B gives estimates of earnings in white collar and blue collar jobs during the same time period. In light of such predictions, the need for financial planning becomes more apparent.

Income and Uneven Flows

In financial planning one must recognize that income does not always flow evenly from month to month. Bonuses, for example, are often paid at

EXHIBIT 1–6A   Cost Estimates of Future Goods and Services

Item	Cost in Past Years		Compounded Rate of Increase	Cost Assuming Same Rate of Increase	
	1962	1979		1989	1999
35-foot cabin cruiser	$22,500	$59,700	6.3%	$109,978	$202,599
One-family house	19,300[a]	68,300	8.8	158,748	368,975
Chevrolet Impala 4-door	2,529	5,828	5.4	9,861	16,685
Annual college cost[b]	980	2,230	5.3	3,738	6,264
Two-week London vacation for 2	893	1,508[c]	3.3	2,086[c]	2,887[c]
Refrigerator-freezer	470	530	0.7	568	609
Medical bills	468[d]	1,070	7.1	2,125	4,219
Annual Social Security deduction	150	1,403	15.0	3,561[e]	6,770[e]
Man's wool suit	130	238	3.9	349	512
Auto insurance premium	87	250	6.8	483	932
Monthly electric bill	8	30	8.6	68	156
Prime-rib dinner	4.65	10.95	5.5	18.70	31.94
Haircut	1.00	3.50	8.2	7.70	16.93
Paperback novel	.95	2.60	6.5	4.88	9.16
Movie ticket	.81	2.46	7.2	4.93	9.88
Gasoline per gallon	.31	.79	6.0	1.41	2.53
Hamburger (McDonald's double)	.28[a]	.80	7.2	1.60	3.21
Pizza (slice)	.15	.70	10.1	1.83	4.80
Hershey bar	.05	.25	10.6	.68	1.88
Daily newspaper (N.Y. Times)	.05	.20	9.1	.48	1.14
First class postage stamp	.04	.15	8.6	.34	.78

[a]1963 data.   [b]For state resident.   [c]Assumes Laker Airways fare.   [d]1966 data.
[e]Amounts set by legislation in effect.

Sources: Bureau of the Census, Bureau of Labor Statistics, Chris-Craft, Edison Electric Institute, General Motors, Hart, Schaffner & Marx, Hershey Foods, Indiana University, McDonalds, Motion Picture Assn. of America, Publishers Weekly, State Farm Ins., Whirlpool Corporation.

year's end, and dividends from investments arrive quarterly. Unless irregular income flows are budgeted, they are likely to be "squandered" when they become available. In the same manner, unless unusual outflows are budgeted, one is likely to need access to expensive credit in order to meet obligations.

EXHIBIT 1–6B   Estimates of Future Earnings

Earnings	Earnings in Past Years		Compounded Rate of Increase	Earnings with Same Rate of Increase	
	1962	1979		1989	1999
In-house Attorney					
Gross earnings	$16,440	$42,318	6.1%	$76,502	$138,302
After-tax earnings	12,872	30,113	5.5%	41,860	56,878
After-tax adjusted for inflation	29,577	30,113		23,155	17,404
After-tax earnings as % of gross	78%	71%		55%	41%
Production worker					
Gross earnings	$ 5,021	$13,850	6.5%	$25,998	48,802
After-tax earnings	4,420	11,795	6.3%	19,698	30,615
After-tax adjusted for inflation	10,156	11,795		10,494	8,688
After-tax earnings as % of gross	88%	85%		76%	63%

Assumptions: Married taxpayer, joint return, two dependent children, standard deduction, no change in 1979 tax structure for subsequent years, gross earnings less net tax liability, state and local income taxes (assuming the same proportion of state and local taxes to federal taxes), Social Security tax for 1989 and 1999 from legislation in effect.

Source: *Forbes* (July 11, 1979), p. 108.

PLANNING INCOME AND EXPENDITURES: BUDGETING

Financial planning requires an estimate of monthly needs and resources. A good place to start is to make careful estimates of present expenditures by examining checkbook stubs or by keeping sales receipts for a month or two to learn exactly where income is currently being spent. Although financial planning must be tailored to individual needs, average budgets used by others may be of some help. For general information on what others spend, reference can be made to aggregate statistics reported by governmental agencies. A sample of such a budget is found in Exhibit 1–7, which shows average spending in 1980 for four-person urban families. The data depict three representative living standards (low, medium, and high) applied to a thirty-eight-year-old husband, a wife working only at home, and two children—a boy, thirteen, and a girl, eight. It is assumed that each family has an average inventory of clothing, house furnishings, and major durables such as appliances and automobiles. The data do not try to show minimum amounts

EXHIBIT 1–7   Average Annual Budgets for Four-Person Urban Families, Autumn 1980

| | Budget Level | | | | | |
| | LOW | | MEDIUM | | HIGH | |
	Amount	% of Total	Amount	% of Total	Amount	% of Total
Total budget	$14,044	100%	$23,133	100%	$34,408	100%
Total family consumption						
Food	$ 4,321	31	5,571	24	7,024	20
Housing	2,608	19	5,106	22	7,747	22
Transportation	1,160	8	2,116	9	2,751	8
Clothing	907	6	1,292	6	1,888	5
Personal care	352	3	471	2	668	2
Medical care	1,298	9	1,303	6	1,359	4
Other family consumption	597	4	1,109	5	1,829	5
SUBTOTAL	$11,243	80	$16,968	74	$23,266	66
Miscellaneous expenditures (gifts, contributions, insurance)	583	4	957	4	1,610	5
Social Security and disability payments	881	6	1,427	6	1,608	5
Personal income taxes	1,337	9	3,781	16	7,924	23
TOTAL	$14,044	100%	$23,133	100%	$34,408	100%
MONTHLY AVERAGE	$ 1,170		$ 1,928		$ 2,867	

Note: Percentages calculated do not add to 100% due to rounding.

Source: U. S. Department of Labor, Bureau of Labor Statistics, *Monthly Labor Review* (August, 1981), p. 56.

on which a family could survive, nor do they indicate how specific families do or should spend their incomes.

Budgets vary greatly, depending on income and living standards. Total living costs also vary considerably—as much as 10 percent—according to geographical area. As shown in Exhibit 1–7, the high-budget family may spend 60 percent more on food than the low-budget family; nevertheless, food costs for the high-budget family are only about 20 percent of their total budget, compared with 31 percent of the low-budget family's expenses. Medical care may cost about the same amount in dollars for the three types of families represented, but the relative importance of medical costs is much higher for the low-budget family (about 9 percent of the total budget) than for the high-budget family (about 4 percent of the total budget). On the other hand, personal income taxes consume nearly three times more of the total budget of a high-income family than of a low-income family (23 percent versus 9 percent).

In the development of a personal financial plan or budget, all numbers should be tailored to individual life-styles, incomes, and spending needs. Exhibit 1–7 provides only general indications, or "ball park" figures, which might serve as a starting point for checking one's own spending needs against those of others.

Steps in the Budgeting Process

The following steps should be observed if the budgeting process is to be successful:

1. Establish the financial goals to be accomplished.
2. Estimate total monthly income for the planning period(s).
3. Estimate outlays under several headings, such as monthly fixed payments, irregular or seasonal payments, variable day-to-day items, and amounts to be set aside for major purchases or longer-term goals.
4. Set up a system for keeping and analyzing records to show how well goals are being reached.

SETTING FINANCIAL GOALS

Establishing a set of goals is the starting point in financial planning. Recognizing explicit goals will help you decide which ones should receive priority. Setting goals will also motivate you to carry your financial plan to completion, since you will be readily able to see the value of planning.

Goals can be stated in several ways—in general or specific terms, in long-term or short-term contexts, and in maximum or minimum bases. It is sometimes helpful to work from general to specific goals. For example, a general goal might be "to achieve financial independence" or "to have a high yet secure standard of living." In specific terms, the first goal might be "to have a debt-free home and enough income to live comfortably in retirement." The second goal might be stated more specifically as "eating out once a week, having maid service, driving a luxury car, making regular savings for retirement, and providing adequate insurance protection against catastrophes."

If goals are stated in terms of time periods, they might appear in your planning records as follows:

Long-term (10–30 years):

1. Provide for retirement.
2. Set aside funds for children's education.

Intermediate-term (2–10 years):

1. Save for vacation abroad.
2. Save for new auto or for home down payment.
3. Set aside three months' salary as an emergency fund.

Short-term (1 year):

1. Purchase new washer or dryer.
2. Set aside funds for auto, life, or health insurance premiums.
3. Pay off installment debt on old car.

Using such a framework for planning helps ensure that longer-term projects will not be forgotten or pushed aside to satisfy more immediate desires. Without a financial plan, for example, it would be easy to use up a car-replacement fund to pay for a summer vacation or for some other impulse purchase less practical than the original plan.

The financial outlays necessary for given goals may be expressed either as lump sums or as monthly outlays that will accumulate to a given sum at a given interest rate over a given time period. Suppose, for example, that you want to budget for a new car in three years. The car costs $8,000 in today's dollars. You assume that new-car costs are rising 10 percent a year and that interest returns of 8 percent can be earned on a savings fund in a tax-exempt investment. The first step is to discover the amount to which $8,000 will accumulate at 10 percent in thirty-six months. Reference to 10 percent interest tables (see Appendix A-1) shows that $1.00 invested at 10 percent interest grows to $1.331 in three years. Thus, $8,000 will grow to $10,648—the price of the new car—after three years. To determine how much must be saved each year to accumulate this sum, refer to Appendix A–2, which shows that annual deposits of $.308 are necessary to accumulate $1.00 of desired savings after a three-year period at 8 percent interest. To accumulate $10,648 by the end of the third year, you must save $3,280 annually ($.308 × $10,648 = $3,280). Similar procedures should be followed for budgeting outlays to meet other goals.

ESTIMATING INCOME

The next step in personal financial planning is to make an estimate of when the income from each source will be available. For example, you may develop a simple schedule like the one in Exhibit 1–8. If potential variation in, or uncertainty about, income exists, a range of estimates may be made that includes highest to lowest figures. For longer-term planning (more than two years), upward revisions in salaries and wages for anticipated adjustments due to inflation or promotions can be incorporated in the budget.

In making these estimates, keep in mind that a budget is a plan and a guide, not a forecast. You should expect periodically to revise advance esti-

EXHIBIT 1-8   Estimated Income for 19–

Source	Amount	Payable
Salaries		
Husband	$____	Monthly
Wife	$____	Monthly
Interest on S & L account	$____	Monthly
Dividends from 100 shares of XYZ stock	$____	Jan. 15, Apr. 15, July 15, Oct. 15
Wages from extra job in summer	$____	June 30, July 30, Aug. 30
Year-end bonus from work	$____	Dec. 15
Anticipated birthday gifts from parents	$____	Aug. 23, Oct. 10

mates to fit reality as the reality emerges over time. Records should be kept in such a way that necessary changes or adjustments can be made easily. In this way the budget can be an efficient instrument that gives the planner real control over the financial future.

ESTIMATING OUTLAYS

Estimating expenses, as well as comparing actual expenses each month with planned expenses, is the heart of the budgeting process. Those who have not previously engaged in budgeting can derive some notion of what they spend for various items by examining check records for two or three months, setting up different categories of expenses, and adjusting these items for known outlays not appearing in the check records.

Easiest to estimate are regular fixed expenses, such as rent, mortgage installments, and utilities. Seasonal or quarterly payments for taxes, insurance, gifts, and tuition are also relatively easy to estimate. Amounts to be set aside for future needs, such as the purchase of an automobile, are also determinable with considerable certainty.

Most difficult to estimate and control are daily expenditures for personal maintenance, such as food, clothing, medicine, and recreation. The amount spent on these items may vary considerably from month to month; unless careful records are kept and attempts are made to control these costs, the whole budget may fail. The key to adequate management of these items is a simple system to facilitate proper classification and recording of daily personal expenses.

RECORD SYSTEMS

Two basic types of records are necessary for adequate financial control:

1. A budget plan, a statement of the overall plan of income and outlay;

2. A budget record book, a record of original expenditures, by type, as they are made.

To illustrate how to develop both types of records, consider a hypothetical case, simplified for ease of understanding. The case involves a newly married couple, Joe and Karen Brown. Both work, they have no children, and they drive one car. Joe earns $12,000, and Karen, $14,400. They have an apartment and wish to save $5,000 for a down payment on a condominium. Costs of life and health insurance and retirement plans are fully paid by their respective employers. The Browns have $3,000 in their savings account for emergencies and wish to add $50 a month to this account.

The Budget Plan. The Browns' initial budget is shown in Exhibit 1–9. Since the Browns' estimated outlays are $84 a year (or $7 a month) higher than their estimated income, they need to reduce anticipated outlays by this amount to have a balanced budget. The Browns decide to reduce deposits to the reserve fund by $7 a month. This reduction is shown in Exhibit 1–10, on page 24.

The Budget Record Book. The Browns decide to set up a simple system to record and monitor expenditures as they are made. Therefore, they purchase a loose-leaf notebook with columnar paper and establish a column heading for each type of expenditure.

Records for the month of January are illustrated in Exhibit 1–10. Entries are usually made once or twice a week. As the Browns spend money, a hand notation on a slip of paper or a retail store receipt is placed in a cardboard box on the kitchen desk. These original records, together with checkbook notations, are classified, entered, totaled monthly, and compared with the budget allowance each month.

If the Browns find they are spending more or less than is budgeted, the record book tells exactly where the surplus or the deficit exists. If there is a deficit, the Browns can decide whether to reduce spending, borrow, or draw on savings to cover it. If there is a surplus, the Browns can decide whether to use the excess for other items, to save it for emergencies, or to add to their long-term account for purchase of a condominium.

For the month of January, the Browns spent $20 less than the amount budgeted. This $20 was allocated to the reserve fund column and added to the "amount available" row for February. If there had been a deficit, an equal amount could have been deducted from the reserve fund. If the reserve fund is exhausted by a monthly deficit, the Browns must decide whether to borrow or to transfer funds from the savings account or the condominium fund.

A major advantage to this method of recording expenses is that it conveys prompt information that provides financial planners with a continuous indication of how they are doing. On any given day it is a simple matter to total the balances across the columns and to compare them with the total budget for that month. If expenditures are running higher than planned,

EXHIBIT 1-9   Typical Initial Budget Plan

Estimated Income	Annual	Monthly
Karen	$14,400	$1,200
Joe	12,000	1,000
Bonus, paid in December		
Karen	1,440	120
Joe	1,200	100
Total	$29,040	$2,420

Estimated Expenditures	Annual	Monthly
Long-term needs	—	—
Intermediate-term needs		
Set aside for down payment on condominium in 5 years, assuming 8% interest	$ 816	$ 68
Short-term needs		
Reserve fund	600	50
Food	6,000	500
Housing (rent, utilities, etc.)	6,000	500
Transportation (gas, fares)	1,800	150
Clothing	1,800	150
Personal care (medical and insurance costs)	2,400	200
Miscellaneous	1,800	150
Payroll deductions		
Social Security	1,946	162
Income taxes	5,962	497
Total	$29,124	$2,427

necessary adjustments can be made promptly. For example, if borrowing becomes necessary, the required amount can be arranged well in advance, thus preserving one's good credit standing.

Note that the Browns have budgeted all their estimated income, including bonuses that will not be paid until December. Unless they pay attention to uneven cash inflows and cash outlays, problems may arise in meeting expenses that precede the inflow of funds budgeted for them. To handle this problem the Browns may decide to prepare a supplemental statement for their budget plan showing income and outgo in terms of monthly data. Such a statement is shown in Exhibit 1-11.

The Browns' total income in December is $4,840 (regular salaries of $2,200 plus $2,640 in bonuses). They wish to use the bonus to make deposits to their savings plan for down payment on the condominium ($816), to deposit $600 for the reserve fund, and to spend $1,224 (or $102 a month) for other items in their budget throughout the year. Their monthly budget is adjusted to reflect these facts. The deficits in the first eleven months are to be met from savings.

Without a budget plan, the Browns might have been tempted to squander the December bonus on nonessentials, only to be forced into borrowing or undue scrimping on other items they wish to enjoy later.

EFFICIENT SPENDING

Many problems in personal financial management result from imbalance between spending and income. People usually complain about "lack of sufficient income"; in many cases, however, the real problem stems from inefficient spending, waste, and money spent without regard to priorities.

Tax Implications of Efficient Spending

A problem related to inefficient spending arises from failure to realize that the old adage "A penny saved is a penny earned" is not exactly true. In most cases, because of income taxes, a penny saved is equal to perhaps two pennies earned. Consumers would be more inclined to shop carefully if they recognized that by buying in such a way that they saved $10 on a purchase, they actually had "saved" $20.

Why is it true that $10 saved may be equal to $20 earned? Consider the way income taxes operate. Married persons filing jointly are taxed according to a scale that in 1981 was as follows:

(1) Taxable Income	(2) Tax Rate on Excess over Col.1
$ 3,400	14%
5,500	16%
7,600	18%
11,900	21%
16,000	24%
20,200	28%
24,600	32%
29,900	37%
35,200	43%
45,800	49%
60,000	54%

EXHIBIT 1–10   Budget Record Book

	1 Food		2 Housing		3 Transportation		4 Clothing		5 Personal Care	
	Spent	Budget Under (Over)	Spent	Budget Under (Over)	Spent	Budget Under (Over)	Spent	Budget Under (Over)	Spent	Budget Under (Over)
	DAY		DAY		DAY		DAY		DAY	
January	1	500		500		150		150		200
		Balance		Balance		Balance		Balance		Balance
	3 50	150	1 100	100	7 20	130	8 25	125	8 45	155
	7 125	325								
	15 50	275	15 120	(20)	16 25	105	2 125	0	13 40	115
	22 75	200			20 50	55			19 50	65
	30 150	50			28 50	5			30 80	(15)
January totals	450	50	520	(20)	145	5	150	0	215	(15)
February budget		500		500		150		150		200
Available on February 1		550		480		155		150		185

6 Miscellaneous		7 Reserve Fund		8 Savings for Condominium		9 Social Security		10 Income Taxes		11 Total	
Spent	Budget Under (Over)	Spent	Budget Under (Over)	Spent	Budget Under (Over)	Spent	Budget Under (Over)	Spent	Budget Under (Over)	Spent	Budget Under (Over)
DAY		DAY		DAY		DAY		DAY		DAY	
	150		43		68		162		497		2,420
	Balance		Balance		Balance		Balance		Balance		Balance
7 70	80			3 68	0						
20 70	10										
30 10	0										
		30 43	9			31 162	0	30 550	0		
	150	43	0	68	0	162	0	550	0	2,400	20
	150		43		68		162		497		2,420
	150		63		68		162		497		2,420

EXHIBIT 1-11   Typical Monthly Budget Plan

Month	Income	Outgo	Surplus (Deficit)	
			Monthly	Cumulative
January	$ 2,200	$ 2,302	$ (102)	$ (102)
February	2,200	2,302	(102)	(204)
March	2,200	2,302	(102)	(306)
April	2,200	2,302	(102)	(408)
May	2,200	2,302	(102)	(510)
June	2,200	2,302	(102)	(612)
July	2,200	2,302	(102)	(714)
August	2,200	2,302	(102)	(816)
September	2,200	2,302	(102)	(918)
October	2,200	2,302	(102)	(1020)
November	2,200	2,302	(102)	(1122)
December	4,840	3,718	1122	0
Total	$29,040	$29,040	—	0

If a husband and wife together have a taxable income of $24,600, for example, the "extra" earnings (over $24,600) are taxed at 32 percent for federal income tax purposes. Furthermore, in most states they would also pay another 6 to 11 percent as state income tax. Their **marginal tax rate,** as it is called, may easily be 40 percent or more. It is the marginal tax rate that counts, not the average taxes, which are usually much less than 40 percent of total income. Families with taxable incomes of $35,200 may be in the marginal tax bracket of 50 percent (43 percent federal plus 7 percent state).

If you can earn an extra $20, you can keep only about 60 percent, or $12, since the extra $20 is taxed at the marginal rate of 40 percent, amounting to a tax of $8. Similarly, saving $12 on some purchase is the equivalent of earning an extra $20. Saving is thus rewarded under the tax system. It is usually much easier to save $12 than it is to earn an extra $20.

Saving is frequently possible without sacrificing essential quality. For example, buying food in case lots may save 10 percent on the price applicable to individual packages. If you pay $20 for a case of canned goods and thus save $2, you have $20 invested, but your "return" on the investment is 10 percent, tax free. If you consume two cases a year, your return is 20 percent annually, tax free. If your marginal tax rate is 50 percent, this return is equivalent to a taxable investment returning 40 percent annually. In contrast, many savers are obtaining only 10 to 12 percent on savings, and this return is usually fully taxable.

In another example, consider the return on insulating your house. An expenditure of $1,000 not only may be tax deductible (costing only $500 after taxes if your marginal tax rate is 50 percent) but may save, say, $200 a year in costs of heating and air conditioning. Thus, you have a chance to earn 40 percent tax free (200/500 = .40) on your $500 investment—an amount equivalent to an 80 percent return on taxable investments. Even leaving aside personal enjoyment to be derived from having a more comfortable home, why should the homeowner leave funds in a 12 percent savings account (6 percent after taxes) when an 80 percent return is available?

Spending Hints

The following list provides other examples of how money can be saved without sacrificing quality:

1. Purchase discounted gasoline if possible. Most experts agree that such fuel is indistinguishable from advertised gas.
2. Make phone calls "station-to-station," never "person-to-person." Use direct dialing and call on weekends or after 11 P.M. if possible.
3. Have your doctor prescribe "generic" rather than brand-name drugs; the only difference is the price. All aspirin, for example, is substantially the same.
4. Consider buying good used cars instead of new ones. Used cars cost, on the average, 30 to 50 percent less to drive (see Exhibit 1–12). After five years your per mile cost of driving is about half the amount it was when the car was new. Radial tires, which increase gas mileage by 5 to 7 percent, can further reduce car costs.
5. In purchasing groceries, take advantage of weekend sales or specials, where savings of 1 to 20 percent are possible.

EXHIBIT 1–12
Cost of Driving a Used versus a New Compact Car, 1981

Age in Years When Purchased	Purchase Price	% Saved on Price	Cost in Cents per Mile	% Saved
New	$6,454	—	43.73	—
1	5,292	18	39.79	9
2	3,356	48	30.55	30
3	1,872	71	24.49	44
4	1,355	79	22.30	49
5	1,033	84	21.87	50

Note: Data are based on three years of use at 10,000 miles a year. Cost per mile includes average repairs, national average repair prices, and a 5% sales tax.

Source: Reprinted by courtesy of *Consumer Views*, published by Citibank, Vol. 12, No. 4 (April, 1981).

6. For home repairs, obtain competitive bids from at least three contractors.
7. Buy car insurance with higher deductibles. You may save $100 a year by purchasing $200 deductible collision insurance rather than $100 deductible. That is, you save $100 by giving up $100 of additional coverage for each accident; you are ahead unless you have more than one accident a year.
8. Use a bank that does not charge for writing checks. Even better, have your payroll check deposited in an account that pays interest on the balance until checks actually clear. Although the interest is taxable, earning interest is still better than getting nothing or having to pay for the privilege of writing checks.
9. Save electricity by routinely turning off lights in unused rooms. Turn off heating and air conditioning vents to unused rooms. Close closets. Use an electric blanket on winter nights rather than turn up the thermostat.

SUMMARY

1. Successful personal finance management requires effective planning. Financial goals should be established and written down as a basis for this planning.
2. Financial goals will vary according to your stage in the life cycle. Perhaps the main advantage of financial planning is to increase greatly the chance that your goals will be achieved.
3. Financial planning involves four main steps: analyzing your financial needs, identifying resources to meet these needs, protecting assets and income against contingencies, and estate planning.
4. Many factors affect your "real" income, such as your education, where you live, what occupation you select, your age, your sex, and the inflation rate as it affects the items you buy. The financial planner should consider as many of these factors as possible in setting forth estimated resources to meet financial goals.
5. Budgeting income and outgo is the heart of financial planning. Budgets can be simple or complex, but they must always be tailored to your personal circumstances and adjusted frequently. Using "average" budgets may be helpful in the beginning. The simpler the record-keeping system, the better and the more likely it will be to help you in controlling your finances.
6. A powerful motive for controlling expenditures is the effect of marginal income tax rates on wage earners. A penny saved on a purchase may, because of taxes, be equivalent to two pennies earned. Furthermore, in many cases you can save on expenditures without sacrificing much, if any, quality.

REVIEW QUESTIONS

1. Why is it that "long term" for one person may be "short term" for another? Support the statement with a financial planning example.

2. What are the stages in the "financial life cycle"? Give examples of goals typical of each stage.

3. (a) What are the main advantages of financial planning? (b) Can you think of any disadvantages?

4. What are the principal steps in financial planning?

5. Discuss whether budgeting is more important for people with low incomes than for people with high incomes.

6. How do (a) education, (b) age, (c) occupation, and (d) geography tend to affect one's income?

7. One of the purposes of progressive income taxes is to bring about a more even distribution of income. With reference to Exhibit 1–2, discuss to what extent this effort has succeeded.

8. How much will 12 percent inflation affect your income and living costs: (a) within 5 years? (b) within 10 years? (See Exhibits 1–5 and 1–6.)

9. If incomes and prices rise at equal rates, does this not solve most of the problems that inflation causes in personal financial planning? (See Exhibit 1–6.)

10. Suggest reasons for the fact that, as income rises, the percentage of income budgeted for food and medical care should normally decline while the percentage budgeted for housing should rise. (See Exhibit 1–7.)

11. Discuss to what extent you should try to involve your entire family in the budgeting process.

12. If you were to set up a budget, (a) what "long-term" goals would you establish? (b) what intermediate-term goals? (c) what short-term goals? Give examples and indicate how much of your income you would allocate to each item.

13. Cite examples of how you have saved money recently without sacrificing significant quality in items you have purchased.

14. Why is the consideration of marginal income tax rates an important consideration in economizing on purchases?

CASE PROBLEMS

I. The Need for Financial Planning

The following letter was written by a high school alumnus:

12 Spring Avenue
Centreville, USA 00006
March 1, 1979

Dear Teacher:

You once asked us to let you know what happened to us after leaving good ol' Faber High. And now seemed as good a time as any to do it. Lately, I've been trying to figure out how high school prepared me for the "real world."

You used to tell us to *plan* before we spend. I didn't want to then, but the exercises you put us through did teach me something I've used. (Just wish my first husband had learned it, too.)

I moved to the city right after graduation and got a job as a secretary. Also got an apartment which was too expensive, so I found a roommate in the office. (*Sharing* expenses was one of your pet themes.) Unfortunately, that arrangement lasted only three months. But just before Jennie moved out Joe and I decided to get married, and he helped pay the rent. (Sharing again.)

But after a while, Joe started drinking and spending money like there was no tomorrow—*without any planning.* So we split after a few months.

When I lived alone I had problems trying to stay within a budget, so I tried making my own clothes. I also tried to cut down on food in order to save, but I got sick and then I was in a car accident. You told us all about insurance and how important it is to be protected by it. But did I listen? No. I figured I was young and healthy. Besides, I wanted to save as much money as possible, so when my employer offered life and health insurance to me for a small fee, I refused it.

I got so lonely living by myself that I decided to marry Brant. We had a fancy wedding and we thought things were going well. But now we're head-over-heels in debt, thanks to *installment* buying, which you also warned us about.

I never paid much attention when you talked about *financial planning and high-pressure salesmanship* or how to use *community resources*—banks, tax advisers—to help with financial problems.

I surely hope your students are paying more attention to you than I did. Are you still teaching about financial planning or have you given up?

Sincerely,

Susie Chapman

Susie Chapman

Source: American Council of Life Insurance, and Health Insurance Institute, *Teaching Topics*, Vol. 28, No. 1 (Spring, 1979), p. 2.

QUESTIONS

1. How does the above letter illustrate the need for financial planning? (Were goals set? Were all the steps in planning recognized?)

2. Make a list of three rules you believe Susie Chapman should follow. Explain your reasons.

II. The Effect of Inflation on Various Life-Styles

Not everyone is affected equally by inflation. Consider the personal CPIs (Consumer Price Indexes) of the five families listed below, each of whom experienced changes in living costs for the year ending in April 1980. Note that the CPI probably went up less than the national average if a person (1) lived in a moderate climate, (2) walked to work, (3) allocated more of the budget to food and clothing than average families (large families often do), or (4) bought a used car as the major purchase of the year. The CPI probably went up more than the national average if a person (1) commuted by car and spent more than the average consumer on gasoline, (2) bought a new house and took out a big, high-rate mortgage, or (3) lived in an old, uninsulated house in the northern United States and used oil heat.

FAMILY	PERSONAL CPI % CHANGE 4/79–4/80
1. Secretary, income about $12,000. Has an apartment in Manhattan that takes a disproportionate share of her income. She is single, 25. No car. Housing and food account for two-thirds of total expenditures. Keeps a tight budget otherwise.	8.1%
2. Junior professional family in late 20s. No children. Income about $25,000. Wife works part-time. Rent	10.1

an apartment in Atlanta. Own one late-model car. Like to dine out and travel.

3. Two-earner young family. One child who attends public school. Both parents in early 30s. Husband a manager, wife a reporter. Combined income about $44,000. Live in their own home in a New York suburb, bought in 1979. Two cars.   16.4

4. Husband and wife in late 30s with two young children. Husband a middle manager. Income about $35,000. Drives to work. Wife does not work outside the home. They bought a new home in San Francisco suburbs in 1975. Have a large mortgage. They use oil heat, have two cars.   12.6

5. Executive and wife in late 50s. Income about $55,000. Have older home in Westchester County, New York, with mortgage substantially amortized. Heat and cook with natural gas. Own one car, fairly new and gas-efficient. One child in private school, another in college. Wife active in local politics. Enjoy theatre, sports.   10.5

OFFICIAL AVERAGE—all U.S. urban families   14.7

New York–Northeastern N.J. average   11.9

Atlanta average   13.8

San Francisco–Oakland average   16.6

Source: Reprinted by courtesy of *Consumer Views,* published by Citibank, Vol. 11, No. 6 (June, 1980).

QUESTIONS

1. Why was Family 1 apparently less affected by inflation than families 2, 3, 4, and 5?

2. Was your own family affected by inflation last year, to a greater or to a lesser degree than the general rate of inflation? Suggest possible reasons.

III. Preparing a Budget

Develop a simplified one-month budget of income and expenditure for your family, similar to that devised for Joe and Karen Brown. Does your budget balance? If not, how would you recommend that any surplus or deficit be handled?

CHAPTER 2

CREDIT AND BORROWING

LEARNING OBJECTIVES

In studying this chapter you will learn that:

Installment credit has become the dominant form of credit for financing consumer durables in the United States;

Banks are the major providers of single-payment loans, which are the cheapest form of credit;

In addition to banks, other financial institutions, such as savings banks, savings and loan associations, credit unions, and life insurance companies, are also providers of consumer credit;

Lenders use ability to repay as the major determinant of granting credit;

Collateral is used to strengthen the credit and reduce the lender's risk;

Federal laws make it illegal for any lender to hinge a credit decision on race, religion, age, sex, or marital status;

Federal law requires lenders to display prominently the annual percentage rate (APR) and the money costs of the credit;

Borrowers must be told why their credit has been turned down and given the right to inspect their credit reports;

Inflation gives the economic advantage to borrowers.

Modern life is continually split between our folk consciousness that "savings is next to godliness" and the never-ending media blitz enticing us to buy and buy, borrow and borrow. Instead of equating borrowing with irresponsibility, as did past generations, Americans today see credit as an essential part of their lives. Even the economists have altered their definitions to take the sin out of debt; they measure borrowing as "negative" savings and the repayment of the principal as "savings."

An indicator of the importance of credit is the fact that interest on personal debt is the second-largest deduction on income tax returns; it is larger than donations to charity and health expenditures. Only state and local taxes are larger deductions than interest on personal debt.

AMERICAN CREDIT USAGE

Consumers use credit for various reasons: to improve real estate, to buy cars and other consumer durables, to go on vacation, and to buy incidentals at department stores. As Exhibit 2–1 shows, the amount of consumer credit outstanding has grown at a rapid rate. However, when total outstanding credit is compared with disposable consumer income (the source of payment), the rise is less worrisome. The proportion of debt to disposable personal income has not changed materially in the last ten years; it has remained at about 20 to 24 percent at any one time.

Credit has become so all-pervasive that most of us cannot conceive of an economy where credit is severely limited or unavailable. Exhibit 2–1 shows that in terms of total consumer credit relative to **disposable income** (income received by individuals less personal taxes), credit use has remained stable from 1970 to 1981. Consumer credit from 1950 to 1981 increased more than thirteen times in absolute numbers and approximately doubled as a percentage of disposable income. The volume of retail sales in the United States today is closely related to the volume of credit extended to consumers. The old idea of saving before consumption, while not totally dead, is barely breathing. Indeed, the "buy now, pay later" concept has changed the consumption/savings pattern in the United States so that personal savings as a percentage of national income has fallen from 7.7 percent in 1970 to 4.1 percent in 1980.

EXHIBIT 2-1   Consumer Credit, 1950–1981 (in billions of dollars)

	1950	1960	1970	1975	1978	1979	1980	1981
Total credit outstanding	$ 31.5	$ 66.6	$150.1	$ 235.8	$ 351.6	$ 396.3	$ 409.2	$ 428.1
Installment loans	$ 15.5	$ 45.1	$105.5	$ 172.4	$ 273.6	$ 312.0	$ 313.4	$ 333.4
Percent distribution								
Auto	39%	40%	34%	33%	37%	37%	38%	38%
Credit card	—	—	—	9%	17%	18%	17%	18%
Other	61%	60%	61%	58%	46%	45%	45%	44%
Total	100%	100%	100%	100%	100%	100%	100%	100%
Noninstallment loans	$ 16.0	$ 21.5	$ 44.6	$ 64.4	$ 78.0	$ 84.3	$ 95.8	$ 94.7
Percent distribution								
Banks	23%	42%	43%	43%	46%	47%	48%	48%
Other	77%	58%	57%	57%	54%	53%	52%	52%
Total	100%	100%	100%	100%	100%	100%	100%	100%
Total disposable income	$262.5	$360.0	$735.8	$1,190.9	$1,462.9	$1,641.7	$1,821.7	$2,015.8
Percent total credit outstanding to disposable income	12%	18%	20%	20%	24%	22%	22%	21%

Source: *Federal Reserve Bulletin* and *Statistical Abstract of the United States*, various issues. March 1982.

FORMS OF CONSUMER CREDIT

Credit is created whenever the seller of goods transfers the possession of goods to the buyer in return for a money claim. Charge accounts, retail store and bank credit cards, and gasoline company credit cards are examples of forms of retail credit.

Charge Accounts

One of the simplest forms of consumer credit is the old-fashioned **charge account.** A retail store extends credit to the customer for thirty days; in turn, the customer is expected to pay within ten days of the receipt of the bill. Charge accounts of this type usually have no explicit interest charge, such as 1-1/2 percent a month, for unpaid balances. Rather than charge interest, merchants often limit further use of the charge account until some substantial reduction of the account occurs.

Some retailers extend credit with a small discount if payment is made within ten days of receipt of the bill. A discount earned for prompt payment is not truly a reduction in price. More accurately, not earning the discount results in a penalty premium being added to the sales price. The premium can be quite expensive in terms of simple interest. For example, standard credit terms are often 2/10, net 30. That is, a 2 percent discount is offered if the bill is paid within ten days of receipt of the invoice, after which the net (total) price is due by the thirtieth day. These terms convert into a simple interest rate of 36 percent per annum.[1]

Although the profit margin on retail sales is large enough to allow "free credit," in the past some stores have advertised lower prices in return for cash. Some well-known retailers who led this movement were J. "Cash" Penney, R. H. Macy, and the large supermarket grocery chains. However, to meet competition, most of these retailers have altered their "cash-only" policies. Penney's was the last major retailer to end its cash-only policy and offer credit. Penney's customers owed the company $2.5 billion in 1980, and 41 percent of the stores' sales were made on credit. While credit for groceries is increasingly rare, some of the major chains now offer their customers the right to use bank charge cards for grocery purchases.

After 1970 the trend in retail credit began to shift again. The customer expected to shop for some sort of a "discount" and to receive credit as well. Such credit is now often supplied by a third party, the credit card company. Where once the open charge account was a fairly standard way of doing business throughout the United States, it is becoming less widely used except for merchants selling high-cost luxury goods.

Credit Cards

The major change in credit during the last twenty-five years has been the rapid growth in the number and use of **credit cards.** There are three kinds of cards: the company card, the bank card, and the credit company card. An excellent example of a **company card** is the gasoline card, which permits the cardholder to charge a certain brand of gasoline wherever that brand is sold. Company or private cardholders are usually expected to pay for billings within a stated period (usually twenty-five days from the date of the bill). Interest is charged on unpaid balances, but the cardholder is expected to reduce the balances to zero unless the company specifically allows the cardholder longer

---

1. Determined by solving the equation $2/20 = X/360$, where X is the annual equivalent simple interest rate. If the buyer does not pay in 10 days, the charge is 2% for the use of the credit for an additional 20 days. There are eighteen 20-day periods in a year ($360/20 = 18$). Thus, if the borrower fails to take the discount, the loss is equivalent to losing 2% eighteen times a year, or 36% per year.

"Would you be interested in a job with our collection department?"

periods to pay for such items as tires and batteries. Customers who do not pay for the gasoline as agreed face confiscation of their cards.

Bank cards (such as Visa or Master Card) provide credit to the consumer by allowing the cardholder to use the card in retail establishments throughout the world. The card is provided by either a local bank or a bank seeking to extend its market by issuing cards nationally. The issuing bank receives a small percentage of the retail sale from the merchant when the cardholder makes a credit purchase. As opposed to a private card, which is issued to encourage cardholders to use a specific product, a bank card is not tied to any retailer or any product. If the cardholder does not pay the total bill, interest is charged on the unpaid balance. Calculation of this unpaid balance varies from one issuer to another.

The third form of card, the **credit company card**, is issued by private companies such as American Express, Carte Blanche, and Diners Club. Like bank cards, credit company cards are not tied to one seller. But unlike balances on most credit cards, the total unpaid balance on these cards must be paid monthly for the card to remain usable. Since little or no interest is charged to the cardholder, these companies collect almost all their income from the merchant.

All credit cards operate on the assumption that cardholder applicants are carefully screened and that applicants are deemed credit-worthy up to some predetermined limit. For example, a student with a part-time job might have a credit card with a **line of credit** of $300, but the student's mother, a well-established businesswoman, might have a line of credit of $2,500. The typical credit card charges no interest if the total balance is paid off within 25 or 30 days of receipt of the bill. Private credit card companies such as American Express charge their holders an annual "membership" fee; this practice is being increasingly copied by issuers of bank cards.

At one time issuers of bank cards, in an attempt to get established and to build their volume, sent out cards while doing little or no screening of applicants. As a result, many people who were poor credit risks received cards; other people, who had no desire for cards, also received them. Congress has since made it illegal for a bank to provide a credit card that has not been applied for.

The typical card company charges the merchant an average of 3.5 percent of the billed amount. This charge varies with the volume of charges and the average size of the charge. Stores may offer a discount for cash (check), but retailers must make this fact clear to all buyers. Retailers may not charge more than the regular price to customers who use credit cards.

DEBIT CARDS

The latest wrinkle in charge cards is the **debit card.** This card does not involve any credit; it is a means of transferring payment from the buyer to the seller without writing a check. For example, suppose you have an account with the West Bank of the Mississippi and hold a Visa debit card. You go to the local K-Mart and buy five dollars' worth of nuts and bolts. Instead of charging, paying cash, or writing a check, you use your new debit card. The process is identical to the standard credit card procedure except that the amount of the bill is debited to (deducted from) your bank account immediately. The bank receives the same fee from the merchant that it would receive for a credit card transaction and avoids the expense of handling a check; the cardholder avoids the annoyance of waiting in line to have a check authorized.

REVOLVING CREDIT

The type of credit issued by bank credit cards and many department stores is called **revolving credit.** As long as the customer maintains the account by paying the minimum amount required monthly, the account remains open and further charges may be made up to the predetermined maximum limit. The minimum monthly payment keeps the account current and in good standing. Revolving credit is very convenient for the borrower. With a department store credit card, one may buy anything from a bathing suit to a grand piano. With a national or a bank credit card, one may make purchases of goods and services from New York to Los Angeles, and often in foreign countries, and receive one consolidated bill at the end of the month. For credit limits over $200, most bank credit cards specify a minimum monthly payment of 5 percent of the outstanding balance or $10, whichever is higher. In cases where the cardholder exceeds the predetermined credit line, the bank's credit department will review the status of the credit before approving the excess, or **overline.** If the account is current, an overline of as much as 20 percent of the established line is usually approved.

LOST OR STOLEN CARDS

A cardholder's risk is limited to $50 if the card is lost or stolen. In case of a lost card, the cardholder must notify the card issuer within sixty days after the card is lost in order not to be responsible for any unauthorized charges. After notification, the cardholder is responsible only for the first $50, even if the card is illegally used up to the authorized credit limit. The same $50 limit applies to debit cards and to **EFT cards.**[2] In the case of EFT cards, the bank must be notified within two days after the loss for the $50 limitation to apply.

FINANCE CHARGES ON CREDIT CARDS

The maximum amount of interest the lender can charge the borrower who uses a credit card is determined by state **usury laws.**[3] While federal law overrides state interest ceiling laws for many types of interest, it does not override state limits for most consumer credit. State interest rate limitations caused Citibank of New York, the second-largest bank in the United States, to shift its credit card operation from New York to South Dakota. Some credit card issuers feel that one way to bolster income in the face of state usury law limits is to charge an annual membership fee.

---

2. EFTS (electronic funds transfer system) refers to a plastic card issued by banks and other financial institutions that permits the user to receive money from an automated teller machine. The card also permits deposits and certain forms of funds transfers through use of the machine. Certain systems also permit the use of these cards at retail establishments. These **point of sale terminals** (POS terminals) transfer funds immediately from the buyer's bank account to the merchant without requiring that a check be drawn.

3. State usury laws are a vestige of ancient beliefs that interest is somehow immoral and should be regulated. These laws limit the interest rates the borrower can be charged for small loans and home mortgages. Business loans and personal loans over some minimum amount are usually exempted from usury laws.

The standard arrangement for credit issued under a bank charge card allows the cardholder to pay off a new balance with no interest due if payment is made within twenty-five days of the billing date. The traditional retail store rarely charged interest if a buyer was slow in payment. The modern credit card issuer, whether a bank, a store, or a major credit card company, is more realistic; the issuers realize that people are often unable to pay in thirty days and yet do not need extended installment credit. Rather, they need temporary financing that they can repay in a lump sum. Interest of 1-1/2 percent a month on the unpaid balance is a standard charge.

The unpaid balance is calculated in several ways. The standard procedure is to pay interest on a weighted average balance of credit outstanding. The weighted average outstanding balance on which the interest is calculated is usually different from the month-end outstanding balance. Under the Fair Credit Act of 1969, the lender must explain fully how the interest is calculated. Exhibit 2–2 shows an actual credit card bill, which portrays a typical situation. Mr. Davis owes $358.46 and has a preauthorized credit limit of $1,900. All the bills charged by Davis and received by Visa through November 13, 1981, are shown on the bill. If he pays the total balance of $358.46 within twenty-five days (November 13–December 9), he will not owe any additional interest. If he makes any payment greater than the $18 minimum, his account will be current. His previous balance was $542.39; he paid $250 on account and had additional charges of $57.84, and the bank charged him $8.23 in finance charges.

The finance charge of $8.23 for the month is equal to the average daily balance ($548.85) times the monthly interest rate (1.5 percent, or $8.23). Another method of calculating interest owed is to multiply the interest rate of 1.5 percent times the outstanding balance due last month ($542.39); the interest owed under this procedure would be $8.14. This method gives no credit for any payments or charges made during the month.

Credit and Merchandising

The types and terms of credit offered by merchants are as varied as the types of goods they sell and the customers to whom they cater. In most cases stores offer terms similar to the bank's. While the terms of a department store credit card might be identical to a bank's terms, the store would tend to reduce credit standards somewhat to obtain more credit customers. The store is dealing with the **gross margin** between its cash costs of making the sale and the retail selling price, while the bank's profit consists only of the discount charged the merchant plus the customer's interest charge on the unpaid balance. Stores selling "big-ticket" items such as furniture, pianos, jewelry, appliances, and stereo equipment are apparently engaged as much in the business of credit as in retailing. By being able to borrow at attractive com-

EXHIBIT 2-2   Bank Card Bill

C & S CHARGE ACCOUNT SERVICE

A DIVISION OF
THE CITIZENS AND SOUTHERN BANKS

AMOUNT ENCLOSED **$**

You may avoid additional
FINANCE CHARGE
by paying the NEW BALANCE
by this date

Max Davis
300 Main Street
Athens, GA 30606

CLOSING DATE	ACCOUNT NUMBER	NEW BALANCE	MINIMUM PAYMENT	PAYMENT DATE
11 13 81	4327542012078	358 46	18 00	12 09 81

TO INSURE PROMPT CREDIT: MAKE CHECK PAYABLE TO THE CITIZENS AND SOUTHERN BANK. RETURN THIS PORTION OF STATEMENT WITH PAYMENT, AND MAKE SURE ADDRESS ON BACK SHOWS IN WINDOW OF ENCLOSED ENVELOPE.

106100001063277 43275420120781 080035846000180016

DETACH HERE – RETAIN THIS COPY FOR YOUR RECORDS

CLOSING DATE	ACCOUNT NUMBER	CREDIT LIMIT	DIRECT TELEPHONE INQUIRIES TO	PAYMENT DATE
11 13 81	4327542012078	1900	1-404-231-7641	12 09 81

PLEASE SEND INQUIRIES TO CITIZENS AND SOUTHERN BANK, P.O. BOX 4614, ATLANTA, GA. 30302, INCLUDING YOUR ACCOUNT NUMBER AND TELEPHONE NUMBER WITH ALL CORRESPONDENCE. THIS STATEMENT IS CONSIDERED CORRECT UNLESS INQUIRY IS RECEIVED WITHIN 60 DAYS OF DATE MAILED.

You may avoid additional
FINANCE CHARGE
by paying the NEW BALANCE
by this date

REFERENCE NUMBER	POSTING DATE	PURCHASE DATE	DESCRIPTION	AMOUNT
4141001027UA6AUFWJ	1028	1017	THE COUNTRY STORE WESTON VT	21 49
4327001104 5A94T6TX	1104	1020	BAKER'S MUSIC SHOP ATHENS GA	24 91
4341001105UA7P3KGH	1106	1101	ATLANTA ARTS ALLIANCE ATLANTA GA	11 44
4327001113006068 45	1113		PAYMENT RECEIVED, THANK YOU	250 00 CR

REPORT LOST OR STOLEN CARDS IMMEDIATELY

NOTICE: SEE REVERSE SIDE FOR IMPORTANT INFORMATION.

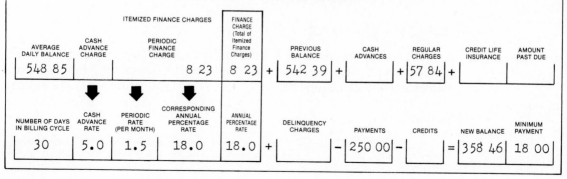

mercial rates from financial institutions, the store can relend at higher rates to fairly weak credit risks.

In states where usury laws limit the amount earned on credit, the credit transaction often shows up in the inflated price of the merchandise. "Easy credit" is almost always synonymous with expensive credit or expensive goods. As long as merchants disclose to the buyer the rates charged and observe the limits of state usury laws and the disclosure requirements of the federal government, they may charge any interest rate.

Single-Payment Bank Loans

One of the simplest forms of consumer credit is the single-payment bank loan. The borrower arranges a loan from a bank and agrees to repay in thirty, sixty, or ninety days or in any one of a variety of maturities up to several years. The loan is for a given amount and is usually for a specific purpose (e.g., a vacation, a medical bill). The interest charged is **simple interest**— that is, interest paid on the unpaid balance.[4] The borrower is almost invariably a depositor of the bank. The bank typically provides such loans to its depositors based on their ability to repay, which is usually determined by the amount and stability of their income.

BORROWER COLLATERAL

In addition to ability to repay, the bank sometimes provides credit on the basis of **collateral**, especially when the loan is large in comparison to the borrower's ability to repay. Collateral refers to property of value pledged to the lender in case the borrower is unwilling or unable to repay the loan. Pledging means that the lender has the right to seize the property in case of borrower default. The collateral used for single-payment loans is usually a readily marketable asset, such as stocks or bonds, which serves as security for the loan. Bankers do not demand collateral on personal loans unless the size of the loan requires the bank to protect itself against excessive risk. The banker uses the collateral not as the basis for granting the loan but as extra protection against the risk of default.

BORROWER CHARACTER

The borrower's character is an additional consideration for granting a loan. Character can mean many things, but in credit it usually refers to a prior demonstration of willingness to repay a debt. This definition is the basis of

---

4. Compare simple interest to **add-on interest**, the standard method of computing interest on installment loans, where the interest is calculated on the total balance, even though the borrower repays the principal in installments.

the many stories that circulate about the person who pays cash for everything and never borrows; then at some crucial point the person cannot get credit because no credit history exists. This story is always based on the fact that the applicant has not demonstrated credit-worthiness to the bank. A young adult might well be advised to establish credit by borrowing from a bank occasionally and repaying the loan with interest. The interest charge could be likened to the annual charge American Express levies on its cardholders—a kind of entry fee to the "brotherhood" of good credit risks.

BORROWER RISK

Single-payment credit, because it is always stated in terms of simple interest, is one of the cheapest forms of credit available to borrowers. For this reason it is more difficult to secure than other forms of credit. Banks usually do not extend loans of this type to borrowers who do not meet rigorous standards of credit risk. A bank might make a loan to a borrower on the collateral of a car for many reasons: the extra security of the collateral, a higher effective interest rate, the guarantee of the dealer, or the deposit balances of the dealer. However, the same borrower might be rejected for an unsecured personal loan in the same amount.

Sometimes the banker and the borrower have an informal understanding that the single-repayment note will, in fact, become a form of an installment note. For example, a person borrows $1,000 for ninety days. It is understood that the note will be reduced by a partial payment on the renewal date, at which time the balance will be renewed for another ninety days. This method provides for flexibility in repayment. Very often borrowers do not have incomes that permit payment of a regular monthly installment. However, irregular income such as a bonus check can permit substantial reduction of the note in a designated month.

Installment Loans

As we saw in Exhibit 2–1, installment credit is today the dominant form of personal and consumer credit in the United States; it accounted for 77 percent of all outstanding credit to individuals in 1981. The concept is simple: a loan is given or a purchase is made (in the case of a purchase, the net amount loaned is the principal sum less any down payment). Interest throughout the life of the loan is calculated either on the total initial balance (add-on interest) or on the unpaid balance. Equal monthly installments, which will retire the outstanding debt within a specified period, are determined. Within the maximum terms permitted by the lender, the borrower selects the number of installments that will result in an affordable monthly payment.

For example, suppose a borrower needs $5,000 to finance a new car and has a before-tax income of $25,000. At 15 percent **APR** the monthly payment over three years would be $173.33, or 8.3 percent of total income (see Exhibit 2–3).[5] If the borrower would like to lower the monthly payment, he or she can borrow the same amount at the same interest rate over four years. The monthly payment for four years would drop to $139.15, or 6.7 percent of monthly income. Lowering the monthly payment means that the total amount of interest paid rises from $1,239.76 to $1,679.38, an increase of 25 percent. Exhibit 2–3 gives some examples of payments for two, three, and four years at 15 percent APR.

In the case of a purchase of a consumer durable (such as a piano, typewriter, or automobile), the form of the note is usually a **conditional sales contract,** which keeps legal title in the hands of the lender. When the final payment is made, the title is automatically transferred to the borrower and the loan is canceled. The term *conditional sales contract* means that transfer of title to the goods is conditional upon the buyer's making all payments as

EXHIBIT 2–3   A Sample Form for Alternate Shopping Disclosures Assuming New-Car Financing at 15% APR

Loan Term (in months)	Amount Financed	Monthly Payment	Total Payment	Finance Charge (dollar amount the credit will cost)
24	$5,000	$242.43	$5,818.40	$ 818.40
	6,000	290.92	6,982.08	982.08
	7,000	339.41	8,145.84	1,145.84
36	5,000	173.33	6,239.76	1,239.76
	6,000	207.99	7,487.71	1,487.71
	7,000	242.66	8,735.66	1,735.66
48	5,000	139.15	6,679.38	1,679.38
	6,000	166.98	8,015.26	2,015.26
	7,000	194.82	9,351.13	2,351.13

Note: The amount financed is the amount of credit provided, figured by taking the cash price of the car, subtracting the down payment (including any trade-in) and any finance charge paid at the time of purchase, and adding other items to be financed, such as insurance. If they so request in writing, buyers have the right to receive a written itemization of the amount financed before the purchase is completed.

Total payment is the amount paid if all payments are made as scheduled. Total payments plus the down payment and trade-in equals the total sale price (including interest charges) of the car bought on credit. The new car will serve as security for repayment.

If any payment is more than ten days late, the buyer must pay a late charge of $5. The buyer who pays off early is entitled to a refund of some of the finance charge. The installment sales agreement contains more information on the effects of early payment, default, and nonpayment of the lender's right to accelerate the debt.

---

5. APR is the federally required statement (Regulation Z) of the annual percentage rate of interest being charged. Truth in lending requires that any creditor (lender) must tell the borrower the APR and the total dollars paid to use the credit. These dollar charges include interest, service charges, and credit-related insurance premiums.

agreed. Perhaps the English term for this contract—"hire-purchase"—is more descriptive; it implies that one hires the product by paying a rent that results in purchase when the final payment is made.

Exhibit 2–4 is an example of a consumer installment transaction. Our hypothetical borrowers, Max and Linda Davis, borrow $4,925 to buy a used Chevrolet Camaro. They pay $75 credit life, which will pay off the note in case of premature death of one of the borrowers. They will be responsible for thirty-six monthly payments of $173.33 before the car is fully paid for. The note has been written in clear language with little or no "legalese."

The Davises have the good sense to read the loan document completely before signing it. One peculiar phrase attracts their attention; it is located in the middle of the note in the paragraph headed "Prepayment of Whole Note." If they pay off the note before the three years are up, they must follow the **rule of 78s** (see Exhibit 2–5), which is often a source of trouble and misunderstanding between borrowers and lenders. Suppose, for example, that after making seventeen payments the Davises decide to pay off the note on the eighteenth payment. They assume they have paid the bank half of the total $6,239.76, or $3,119.88, and therefore owe $2,500 less the usual insurance. But at this point, the rule of 78s comes into play. Under the rule the interest is not allocated on a straight-line basis, which would mean that half of the interest would be paid when the note had been paid over half the period. Rather, the interest is calculated for refund purposes on a proportional basis, which means that for the first month the borrower pays a proportion of the total interest owed ($1,239.76), equal to $36/36 + 35 + \ldots + 1 = 666$. The amount of interest, instead of being $1/36$ (2.7 percent of the total, is $36/666$ of the total, or 5.4 percent. This form of calculation is called the sum-of-the-years'-digits method. Thus, instead, of being able to pay off the bank with a payment of $173.33 plus half of the remaining balance of $2,500, the Davises actually owe the bank $2,802.33 because the interest was not equally allocated over each payment; a higher proportion was allocated during the early period of the loan. Although monthly payments were equal, a higher proportion of the early payments was allocated to interest and less to principal. While every financial institution does not follow this rule—credit unions, for example, charge only on the unpaid balance—most do.

INTEREST CHARGES ON INSTALLMENT LOANS

A major technical problem in installment lending is the calculation of the interest rate. The problem is of such moment that it has resulted in the passage of the Truth-in-Lending Act. In addition, almost every state has either a small-loan law or a usury law that regulates maximum interest rates. While many mathematical and financial elements complicate the issue of the actual rate of interest in any given loan contract, the major problem stems from the mathematical approximation of the actual annual percentage rate (APR).

EXHIBIT 2–4
Sample
Installment
Note

C&S   19-4150-0 Rev. 7-80

Consumer Installment Note   Note Number _141414_   Date _DECEMBER 20,_   19 _81_

In this note, the words I, me, mine and my mean each and all of those who signed it. The words you, your and yours mean _THE CITIZENS AND SOUTHERN NATIONAL BANK, ATHENS, GEORGIA_ _____
                                                    BANK
TERMS OF REPAYMENT: I promise to pay you _SIX THOUSAND, TWO HUNDRED THIRTY-NINE AND 76/100_ _____ Dollars
($ _6,239.76_). I'll pay this sum at one of your branches in _____ **consecutive monthly installments**
of $ _173.33_ each and one (balloon) payment of $ _____. Payments will be due on the _____
day of each month, starting _____.

Here's a breakdown of my loan:
1. Amount of the loan $ _4,925.00_
2. Property insurance   _____
3. Other charges (specify)   _____
                                                 _____
4. Credit life insurance   _75.00_
5. Credit disability insurance   _____
6. Amount financed (1+2+3+4+5) $ _5,000.00_
7. FINANCE CHARGE   _1,239.76_
8. Total of Payments (6+7)   _6,239.76_
   ANNUAL PERCENTAGE RATE _____ _15_ %

INSURANCE: Credit Life or Credit Disability Insurance is not required to get this loan. However, the premiums can be a part of this note. A statement regarding this insurance is found on the reverse side of this note. I do ☐ do not ☐ have to maintain property insurance on the property covered by the Security Section for its full insurable value. If I do have to maintain this insurance, I can buy it from a person of my choice, and I agree to the terms of the Statement of Property Insurance on the other side of this note.

☐ Credit Life Insurance is requested at a cost of $ _75.00_ for the term of the loan
☐ Credit Disability Insurance is requested at a cost of $ _____ for the term of the loan
☐ Loan not eligible for Credit Life Insurance
☐ Loan not eligible for Credit Disability Insurance
☐ Credit Life Insurance is declined
☐ Credit Disability Insurance is declined
Date _12/20/81_   Signature _Max Davis_ _____   Date of Birth _12/21/54_
                              (Borrower to be insured)

PREPAYMENT OF WHOLE NOTE: While I don't need to pay more than the fixed installments, I have the right to prepay the whole outstanding amount of this note at any time. If I do, you will refund the unearned FINANCE CHARGE. You will figure the unearned FINANCE CHARGE by applying the Rule of 78's method to the difference between the FINANCE CHARGE and an acquisition charge of $ _____. I understand that refunds of less than $1.00 will not be made.
LATE CHARGE: If I am more than 10 days late in paying an installment, I promise to pay a late charge of 5% of the overdue installment, but no more than $5.
SECURITY: To protect you if I fail to pay this note or any other debt I may owe you now or at a later time, I give you a security interest in:

1979 CHEVROLET CAMARO (SERIAL #123-456789)
_____
_____

and all proceeds thereof including without limitation any return or unearned insurance premiums. I also transfer and convey to you any and all balances, deposits and accounts of mine now or hereafter with you, and agree that upon any default under this note you may apply my balances, deposits and accounts to the payment of this note or of any other debt I may owe you. I understand that even after this note has been fully paid, you may retain any security interest I have given you to protect you from my failure to pay any other debt I may owe you.
DEFAULT: I'll be in default:
1. If I don't pay on time any installment on this note or on any other debt I owe you; or
2. If anyone else tries by legal process to take any money of mine in your possession; or
3. If I default on any other agreement I have with you; or
4. If you, acting in good faith, believe that the prospect of payment or performance under any of my agreements with you has been impaired.
You can then demand immediate payment of the balance of this note minus that part of the FINANCE CHARGE which has not been earned computed using the pro rata method.
DELAY IN ENFORCEMENT: You can delay in enforcing any of your rights under this note without losing them.
IRREGULAR PAYMENTS: You can accept late payments or partial payments, even though marked "payment in full," without losing any of your rights under this note.
COLLECTION COSTS: If I'm in default under this note and you demand full payment, I agree to pay you interest on the amount at 9% per year. If you collect this note by referring it to an attorney at law, I also agree to pay attorney's fees equal to 15% of the principal and interest due.
JOINT AND SEVERAL LIABILITY: I understand that along with any other signer of this note, I will be jointly and severally liable to you for the repayment of the note, and that therefore you may collect the entire amount due under the note from me, without first trying to collect from anyone else who has signed the note.

Signed, sealed and delivered by the Borrower, who acknowledges receipt of a completely filled-in copy of this note.
300 MAIN ST., ATHENS, GA _____   _Max Davis_ _____ (Seal)
Address   Borrower
(SAME) _____   _Linda Davis_ _____ (Seal)
Address   Borrower

EXHIBIT 2–5   Rule of 78s

> The name "rule of 78s" comes from the sum of the number of months making up one year's payments. Thus 12 + 11 + 10 + . . . + 1 = 78. In the case of three years' payment, the sum of the digits is equal to 666. The proportion of interest allocated during the first period is equal to 36/666, the second is equal to 35/666, and so on. The sum of the percentages for the first eighteen payments for a thirty-six-month contract at an annual percentage rate of 15% is 77.4%.
>
> | | |
> |---|---:|
> | Total interest owed | $1,239.76 |
> | 77.4% of the above | 959.57 |
> | Total payments made after 18 months ($173.33 × 18) | 3,119.94 |
> | Less insurance for 18 months (1/2 × $75) | 37.50 |
> | Balance | 3,082.44 |
> | Less interest allocated | 959.77 |
> | Principal repaid | 2,122.67 |
> | Principal owed ($4,925.00 − $2,122.67) | 2,802.33 |
>
> A generalized procedure for finding the proportion in any one month is as follows: The numerator is equal to the number of installments owed less the number paid (i.e., 36 − 18 = 18). The denominator is equal to (number of periods plus 1) times (number of periods/2). Thus, 36 + 1 × 36/2 = 666.
>
> Thus, the portion of total interest repaid during the first period is equal to 36/666, or 5.4%.

Lenders formerly used slightly misleading advertising in which the borrower was told that loans were available at low bank rates of "6 percent add-on." The law now requires that any rate advertised must state what the interest rate is in APR terms. Similarly, any loan contract must have a clear statement of the actual dollar charge for the loan as well as the APR rate. Single-payment loans, mortgage loans, credit union loans, and revolving-credit loans (such as those made through credit cards) are calculated at simple interest.

When a borrower repays a note by installments and the finance charge is calculated on the total balance of the loan, mathematical problems develop. To standardize the procedure, the Federal Reserve has calculated a set of standard tables that give the APR for every conceivable set of rates and maturities. Every provider of credit in the United States must conform to the Truth-in-Lending Act and to the Federal Reserve tables. Hand-held business calculators can be used to determine APRs.

Small-loan acts or usury laws, in effect in almost every state, typically set maximum interest rates for installment nonbusiness loans. However, in recent years inflation in the United States has raised interest rates to the point where the old ceilings are inoperative—that is, market rates have surpassed ceiling rates.

Regulation Z of the Federal Reserve Board implements the **Truth-in-Lending Act.** This law requires creditors to disclose (1) finance charges on all the costs associated with receiving the credit; (2) annual percentage rates (APRs), which impose a standard way of calculating annual interest charges so that a borrower can compare APRs among lenders; and (3) various terms and conditions associated with the credit offering. The law also allows a borrower to rescind a credit contract within three business days if the loan is secured by the borrower's home.

LIFE INSURANCE ON INSTALLMENT LOANS

All lenders offer, as a regular service, life and health insurance to cover installment loans. The borrower pays a premium (invariably a stated percentage of the amount borrowed) that will purchase enough insurance to repay the lender in case of the borrower's death or disability. This insurance is a form of life insurance or disability insurance issued by a licensed insurer. The premium must cover the varied classes of risk represented by all the borrowers.

Under the credit regulations of the Federal Reserve Board (Regulation Z), the lender must specifically identify the insurance costs. The borrower must volunteer to buy the insurance and sign a statement that is an application to buy the insurance. Most banks offer the insurance without requiring the borrower to purchase it as a condition of obtaining credit. However, as the quality of the borrower's credit declines, the pressure to buy the insurance usually increases. The amount of profit made by the lender increases if the buyer purchases insurance on the installment note. In most cases the person taking the credit application for the installment note is also the legal agent for the insurer.

Commissions on insurance are often substantial, perhaps as great as the agent's salary. Credit life insurance not only protects the lender against the possibility that the borrower will be unable to repay because of death or disability; it also relieves the borrower's estate of any financial responsibility for outstanding installment loans. Most institutions charge between 0.5 percent and 1 percent of the loan amount for life and disability insurance on the loan. Credit unions provide life insurance on loans without extra charge.

Nonbank Credit

Personal loans may come from sources other than banks. These sources include savings and loan associations, mutual savings banks, credit unions, life insurance companies, and finance companies.

SLA'S AND MSB'S

The increased powers allowed to savings and loan associations (SLAs) and mutual savings banks (MSBs) have allowed these institutions to compete with commercial banks in issuing personal loans. For example, in 1980 savings and loan associations were permitted to make installment loans to individuals for home improvements. Since the passage of the **Financial Institution Deregulation Act** in 1980, a savings and loan association or a mutual savings bank may make consumer loans for any purpose in amounts up to 20 percent of the institution's total assets. Before the passage of the act, SLAs regularly loaned money on the collateral of their own passbooks or savings certificates. Now even these restrictions have been lifted, and the SLAs can make loans unrelated to the passbook or certificate.

CREDIT UNIONS

Another source of credit is the **credit union,** usually formed by a group of people with some element in common—perhaps employees of the same firm. Credit unions offer federally insured savings accounts and relatively low-cost loans to members. The credit union usually charges member borrowers a flat rate from 1 to 1-1/2 percent of the monthly unpaid balance of the loan.

LIFE INSURANCE COMPANIES

Perhaps the single least expensive source of personal credit is a type of loan made by life insurance companies against the cash reserves built up by the policyholder. In a **whole life policy**, the insured pays a premium payment that may be considered to serve two purposes: (1) it provides the pure insurance that covers the risk of mortality, and (2) it builds a cash reserve. Life insurance companies guarantee policyholders the right to borrow against these cash reserves at some guaranteed rate, usually 8 percent. Since the rate is often less than market rates of interest, it is often advantageous for the consumer to use this source of credit. Most observers believe that a policy loan is, strictly speaking, not a loan but rather a reduction in the amount of insurance in force, since there is no requirement that the policyholder repay the loan. In the case of the policyholder's death, the company uses the proceeds of the policy to pay off the loan and any accumulated interest.

FINANCE COMPANIES

An important source of personal and installment loans are consumer finance companies, which specialize in small loans to individuals for the purchase of consumer durables or for the repayment of existing bills.

Finance companies are second only to banks in the volume of consumer credit extended. These companies are generally of two types. The first, **consumer finance companies,** are general-purpose companies that extend loans for many reasons, most often to customers who want to acquire consumer durables. Well-known consumer finance companies are Household Finance and Beneficial Finance. The second type of company is the manufacturer-related **sales finance company**—for example, General Motors Acceptance Corporation (GMAC), which almost exclusively finances General Motors auto dealers and their customers. Both types of companies generally have excellent credit standing; they borrow money from commercial banks at wholesale rates and relend to consumers at higher rates.

Small-loan companies lend relatively small amounts of money repayable on an installment basis. Most of these companies are regulated by the states under the **Uniform Small-Loan Law,** which permits fairly high interest rates to cover the costs of making many small loans. Typically the law permits small-loan companies to lend up to $5,000 and permits interest rates as high as 3-1/2 percent a month (42 percent a year APR). The growth of small-loan companies is the result of efforts to eliminate "loan sharks," unlicensed lenders who charge elevated and usually illegal rates. Nevertheless, it is difficult to eliminate exploitive loan practices. In many cases high charges are leveled on the poorest members of society, who usually borrow small amounts.

LENDING TERMS

Not so many years ago most financial institutions did not lend to the general public for purposes of personal and consumer credit. Only the finance companies provided loans to individuals. Credit was so limited that large automobile companies such as General Motors developed wholly owned subsidiaries such as General Motors Acceptance Corporation to provide installment loans to the ordinary citizen. The excellent credit experience of these companies, as well as the profits involved, drew banks and other financial institutions into the field. To make consumer lending as risk-free as possible, lenders have developed a number of techniques, some of which are discussed in the sections that follow.

Collateral

Financial institutions usually take collateral as security for loans made to purchase consumer durables. Very often consumer finance companies require borrowers to put up cars, household goods, or the equity in their homes as collateral for loans. Salable collateral provides extra protection to the lender in case the borrower is unable to pay as agreed. The possibility of losing collateral maintains pressure on the borrower to repay.

Cosigning and Endorsement

Many lenders use the devices of **cosigning** and/or **endorsement** as additional methods of improving or securing the credit. The most onerous form of guaranty is the cosigning of a note. Both signers are equally responsible for payment, and the lender may move against either signer. If the first signer is in default, the lender may immediately turn to the cosigner for payment. In the case of endorsement, the person who endorses or guarantees the loan is not liable for payment until the lender has exhausted all normal remedies for payment by the borrower. Banks are traditionally hesitant to make loans on the strength of an endorsement. Even a millionaire who lends endorsement to better a poor relative's borrowing ability is often reluctant to pay the relative's debt when no personal benefit is to be derived from doing so. A common use of endorsement is the case of a minor child borrowing to buy a first automobile. The bank often will not make—or in some states is legally prohibited from making—the loan without the endorsement of a parent.

Financial institutions often attempt to reduce their risk by insisting that both husband and wife sign the note. This procedure is followed in anticipation of financial difficulties associated with divorce. For example, suppose the husband buys a car and takes a note on the car; later husband and wife are divorced. In the divorce settlement the husband assigns his interest in the car to his wife, who did not sign the note. The title to the car is still clouded by the conditional sales contract, on which the husband may no longer care to make payments. If the bank had the wife cosign the note in the first place, the bank's right to loan repayment would be assured. However, there is a very fine line here. A lender who insists on a wife's cosigning as a condition of granting the credit is violating the Equal Credit Opportunity Act. The wife cosigns only if she has a financial interest in the loan or in the purpose of the loan.

Balloon Loans

Generally speaking, borrowers tend to be less conscious of loan costs than of credit availability. **Balloon loans** have been commonly used to tailor loans to the borrowers' ability to repay. With this type of loan the borrower makes monthly payments insufficient to retire the principal during the life of the loan. The large final (balloon) payment becomes the basis for refinancing the loan for a new, extended installment period. Balloon notes have had an unfortunate reputation in American consumer protection circles because of the large dollar amounts of interest potentially owed by the borrowers. But in periods of high interest rates and credit shortages, balloon loans become more respectable and more widely used. The point to remember is that under the Truth-in-Lending Act the lender must reveal the true (APR) costs of the loan;

the credit decision is left to the lender, and the willingness to sign the contract to the borrower.

Term of the Loan

Credit losses from the various forms of installment credit are quite low, averaging less than 1 percent of outstanding credit. For large amounts, the borrower usually makes a down payment that reduces the loan to the approximate wholesale value of the collateral. Payments are set so that the remaining balance is roughly in line with the depreciated value of the collateral. Thus, a borrower can get a longer contract on a new car (forty-eight months is not exceptional) as opposed to a used car (thirty months is a common maximum).

The more expensive the item purchased, the longer the contract; thus, twelve-year terms on mobile homes are not unusual. The longer contract brings the monthly payment into a range the buyer can afford. For example, a $7,000 auto loan with a 13 percent APR finances out to $232.50 a month for thirty-six months, as compared to $184.34 a month for forty-eight months. The forty-eight month borrower pays $478.32 more in interest but reduces each payment by 21 percent.

OTHER CONSIDERATIONS

Years ago it was common practice in small towns with two banks to refer to one bank as the "Methodist bank" and the other as the "Baptist bank." For a lender to select risks on the basis of their religious beliefs, their hair color, or their sex is now illegal under federal law. In any case, most such practices had already been disappearing under competitive pressure.

Federal credit laws have two major aspects. The first is the truth-in-lending concept, which we have already discussed. Under the law the two major points that must be revealed to the borrower are (1) the finance charge and (2) the annual percentage rate (APR). The APR is considered important by consumers because it prevents add-on interest and permits the borrower to compare credit costs regardless of the dollar amounts of these costs or the length of time over which the payments are to be made.[6] Both the finance charge and the APR must be prominently displayed on the form used to secure credit.

---

6. Add-on interest may be illustrated by a loan offered at, say, 10% "add-on." The borrower will pay $100 for the use of $1,000 for a year, repaying the note at the rate of $91.67 a month. The APR is actually 17.98%.

"Now, Clark, when the bank says you have to cosign, remind them of the Equal Credit Opportunity Act."

The Bettman Archive, Inc.

When a home is used to secure credit, the law requires that the lender give the borrower three days to think it over and possibly cancel the transaction. This "cooling-off period" must be granted to all borrowers, even if they do not want it.

The other major thrust of federal legislation is the **Equal Credit Opportunity Act**, which states that a credit application cannot normally ask sex, age, race, color, religion, or national origin. In addition, a spouse cannot be asked to cosign or endorse a loan unless he or she is going to share equally in the proceeds of the loan. Thus, if Max Davis wanted a car for his own business, the bank could not insist that Linda Davis cosign. For real estate loans the law requires the lender to ask about each of the above-listed characteristics to permit federal monitoring of compliance with nondiscrimination policies, but the lender cannot use any of these data as a factor in evaluating the credit.

Essentially, the lender must analyze the credit on two major bases. First, the credit and employment histories are very important. Does the potential borrower repay current and past obligations? Does the borrower pay on time?

Assuming that the borrower is an "AA" credit (a person who pays "as agreed"), the granting of credit rests on the ability to repay. Here the creditor is allowed to consider factors such as age. For example, a sixty-five-year-old borrower facing retirement is not quite the same risk as a forty-five-year-old borrower with the same income. However, the lender cannot discriminate solely on the basis of age.

Lenders must also be particularly careful not to discriminate on the basis of the borrower's sex. In past years many financial institutions did not view the income of a working wife in the same way they viewed the husband's income. They argued that (1) the wife was working only for "money" and not for a career, (2) she would become pregnant and want to stay home and rear the children, and (3) she had interests more important to her than work. Now lenders must consider women on the same basis as men in credit-granting decisions. Women's incomes cannot be weighted differently or discounted. The lender may consider only the previous employment record of the woman.

After analysis of credit history and employment history and consideration of factors such as collateral and endorsers, the granting of credit is simply a question of the disposable income relative to the anticipated payment. A typical financial institution, after ascertaining all the credit and employment history, would analyze ability to repay as illustrated in Exhibit 2–6. The net disposable income relative to the monthly payment is the ultimate test of whether the credit should be granted.

Approval or Denial of Credit

Within thirty days after an application for credit is completed, the creditor must notify the applicant whether the application has been approved or disapproved. It is almost inconceivable that a lender would take one month to approve a credit.

If the application is denied, the creditor must give the applicant in writing the following information:

1. A statement of the action taken;
2. A statement of the applicant's rights;
3. The name and address of the federal agency enforcing compliance with the various federal credit laws;
4. The reason for denial or a notice that the lender will give the reason to the applicant only upon written request.

EXHIBIT 2–6
Determination of
a Credit
Applicant's Net
Disposable
Income

Income and Deductions	Amount
Combined monthly gross income	$3,000
Less payroll deductions	1,300
Less 50% of gross income minus payroll deductions (for food, clothing, medical bills)	850
Adjusted net income	850
Less fixed monthly obligations (rent, other payments, debt)	500
Net disposable income	$ 350

Credit Rating

Under the **Fair Credit Reporting Act** borrowers have the right to see and correct, or at least comment on, their credit files. Suppose the credit applicant is told the requested credit is denied because the credit rating is poor. In this case the applicant has the right to see the credit history.

Credit bureaus are required to follow reasonable procedures to ensure that the credit information is accurate. However, mistakes may occur. Erroneous data, misinterpreted data, or credit files of another person may get confused with the credit file in question. When the aggrieved person disputes the accuracy of what is contained in the credit file, the credit bureau must investigate and modify or remove any incorrect statements.

If reinvestigation does not resolve the problem, the applicant has the right to submit a statement of no more than 100 words explaining why the file is inaccurate. This statement must be supplied by the credit bureau to all creditors performing a credit check. The amendment or the correction must also be sent to any potential creditor who has requested the credit file within the previous six months. If the file was requested by a potential employer, the amended file must be sent to every potential employer over the previous two years.

CREDIT AND INFLATION

Debtors have an obvious advantage in periods of inflation. Payments for goods are fixed at the time of purchase. During a time of serious inflation the prices of goods rise, and incomes used to purchase goods or to service debt rise as well. When the borrower arranges a loan to buy goods, the amount borrowed and the terms of borrowing remain fixed. The borrower's income usually rises with inflation, but the money cost of the debt remains fixed.

These circumstances thus give a double advantage to buying and borrowing now and to saving less. Once people become convinced that inflation is permanently built into economic life, buying and borrowing may be expected to continue at an even more rapid rate. Government efforts to restrict credit and to encourage savings may become a permanent part of the future economic environment with which the personal financial planner will have to deal. The problems of inflation and its effect on personal finance are discussed in more detail in Chapter 3.

SUMMARY

1. The use of credit has grown steadily in the United States but has leveled off as a percentage of income in the last ten years. Installment credit has become the dominant form of retail credit.
2. Banks are the major providers of single-payment credit. This type of credit is relatively cheaper but typically given only to the best credit risks. Installment credit is the dominant form of credit for financing consumer durables such as automobiles and household goods. All interest now must be specified in annual percentage rate (APR) terms.
3. Other providers of personal credit are life insurance companies as well as SLAs and MSBs. Traditional lenders also include credit unions and personal finance companies.
4. Lenders often use collateral as a means of strengthening the quality of credit. However, ability to repay is the real determinant of credit quality.
5. Federal law now makes it illegal for any lender to discriminate between borrowers. Lenders cannot allow race, religion, age, sex, or marital status to affect their credit decisions.
6. Inflation has given the economic advantage to borrowers but has also penalized savers.

REVIEW QUESTIONS

1. Discuss why consumer debt, which has risen sharply since 1970, has made it more difficult for consumers to repay their debts.

2. A fuel oil dealer bills you $100 on payment terms of 1/10, net 30. Would it pay you to borrow the money from the bank at 12 percent simple interest to pay the bill within the discount period?

3. Banks and department stores both grant credit on a ''revolving'' basis. Why can stores be more lenient than banks in approving credit?

4. If a bank can secure its loan with good collateral, should the bank make the loan? Discuss.

5. The interest on installment loans is traditionally quoted two different ways: (1) "add-on," (2) unpaid balance. Contrast the two methods.

6. Credit life insurance insures the lender against nonpayment of a loan in the case of the untimely death of the borrower. Does the borrower also benefit from purchase of credit life? Discuss.

7. Small-loan companies typically lend small amounts at high interest rates. Do they exploit the borrower? If not, how can these loans be justified?

8. Joe, the neighborhood loan shark, offers to lend Bob $5 if he will repay $6 seven days later. How much interest is Joe charging for the loan on an annualized basis?

9. Are loans issued over a longer period advantageous to the borrower?

10. Why is inflation "beneficial" to a borrower?

11. (a) What are the advantages of a bank-issued credit card? (b) Can you think of any disadvantages?

12. What are the major sources of personal credit other than banks and finance companies?

13. Why does the use of the rule of 78s bother borrowers?

14. What two things must be revealed to a potential borrower in the financing statement?

15. What is the law as it applies to a working wife when she applies for credit in her own name?

CASE PROBLEMS

I. Financing Alternative

Jim and Marcia are newlyweds who are trying to furnish their apartment. They do the best they can by "borrowing" pieces from their families and scouting yard sales, but they still need to buy about $2,000 worth of furniture. If they borrow at Jim's credit union, they will pay 1.6 percent a month on the unpaid balance or $128.76 a month for eighteen months. The bank will lend them $2,000 for twelve months, and they will have to pay $181.46 a month. The store offers to sell them the furniture at no interest if they pay $666.67 a month for three months. What should they do?

II. Borrowing on Life Insurance

Frank, a bachelor, has just come out of the hospital after recuperating from injuries received in a motorcycle crash. He cannot go back to work for another two months. He gets $80 a week sick pay and owes $1,000 to various creditors. He has a $20,000 life insurance policy with a cash surrender value of $5,000 and a right to borrow against the cash value at a rate of 8 percent. What should he do?

III. Financing Alternatives and Establishing Credit

Mimi, a recent university graduate, gets a good job with a salary of $15,000 a year. She needs a reliable car for her work. She can get a new Chevy Citation for $8,000. If she buys the car, the company will pay her an $850 rebate, which she can use for the down payment. The dealer offers her a forty-two month contract at $254.72 a month (APR of 20 percent). Her father suggests that she visit his bank and arrange for a two-and-a-half year renewable note at a 15 percent rate; the note is to be repaid in ten quarters. Her father will have to sign the note. What do you recommend?

CHAPTER 3

PERSONAL SAVINGS, INFLATION, AND TAXES

LEARNING OBJECTIVES

In studying this chapter you will learn:

> The steps to follow in developing a savings plan;
>
> Why some traditional savings principles should be questioned because of inflation and taxes;
>
> The basic causes of inflation;
>
> The characteristics of major savings methods;
>
> The value of deposit insurance;
>
> Why NOW accounts should be analyzed carefully;
>
> How returns vary on different savings media;
>
> How inflation and taxation affect savings media.

Personal savings the difference between current income and outgo, are necessary for effective money management as well as for national capital formation. Savings are a measure of personal wealth. The absence of savings spells eventual financial hardship and potentially excessive use of credit for most people. The existence of some regular savings, even if the amount is small, gives a measure of financial independence. Savings provide a financial cushion against hardship on "rainy days," a margin for budgetary error, and a visible measure of one's progress in building a fund for some purchase.

Without a plan, budget, or other financial control, most people will accumulate little, if any, permanent savings. Not surprisingly, most people live from "hand to mouth" since doing so requires much less discipline than does setting aside regular amounts for future spending needs. In this chapter we examine how one can save more effectively, regardless of income, in an environment characterized by high inflation and heavy taxes.

GOALS OF SAVING

A savings plan will have a greater chance of success if specific goals are written down and studied in the light of other needs. For example, Joe and Karen Brown, the couple whose finances we examined in Chapter 1, might state their current goals as follows:

To accumulate a down payment on a condominium;
To provide a reserve for emergencies and to avoid the use of credit for daily expenses;
To pay for a vacation.

Later on, if children arrive, new goals may be added:

To build an education fund;
To move to a larger home.

As the children grow up and leave home, still new goals may emerge:

To supplement their retirement income;
To make gifts to grandchildren.

Goals of saving may vary greatly, depending on one's stage in the financial life cycle. In the early stage spending needs are usually high and income is relatively low. Saving money at this stage is difficult but nonetheless important. Later on, when income rises, spending needs tend to decline and saving becomes easier.

Successful savings plans depend on the saver's willingness to define needs in such a way as to give some priority to future needs rather than to devote one's resources entirely to current desires. To create funds for future needs, you should evaluate short-term "needs" very carefully. Ask questions such as the following: Is this item or service I am about to buy really necessary? Is it worth more than the new car I want in the future? Can I eliminate a weekly dinner out in favor of a meal at home and obtain just as much satisfaction?

When setting goals for savings, you must differentiate between long-term and short-term needs; otherwise savings plans will be relatively restricted, and longer-term goals will tend to be pushed aside in favor of short-term goals. Some people may argue that saving for long-term goals does not make sense in an inflationary environment, since inflation tends to destroy the value of dollars accumulated. To some extent this is true, but certain counter-arguments can be advanced and will be discussed later in this chapter. If you save for a longer-term goal, the amount that must be saved is less than the total cost of the goal because your savings fund earns interest. For example, if Joe and Karen Brown need $5,000 for the down payment on a condominium, they need to save only $4,082 ($68.05 a month for sixty months); the difference is supplied by interest earnings (assumed to be 8 percent a year in this example).

CONSIDERATIONS IN ESTABLISHING A SAVINGS PROGRAM

The steps in developing a successful savings plan are as follows:

1. Establish definite goals for savings and determine the amount you wish to set aside regularly to meet these goals.
2. Place the savings allocation in your budget and pay yourself *first*, not after other expenses have been met. Some savers find it helpful to have a portion of their check sent directly to a thrift institution or to have the employer make regular purchases of savings bonds on their behalf through payroll deductions. Other savers understate their tax exemptions and later file for a tax refund (not the best way, but effective for some).
3. Decide the most effective ways (media) for accumulating regular savings. Consider the following factors: safety, yield, taxes, inflation, convenience, and liquidity.

Safety

The first criterion for selecting a savings medium should be safety of principal since, unless your money is reasonably secure, the entire plan may fail.

Most people seldom wish to take too much risk in their savings plans, even though the returns are usually less as safety levels rise, and vice versa.

Yield

Yield is the financial return earned on savings or investments. On savings, yield is expressed as a percentage rate of interest. The interest on savings is important, especially for longer-term savings. In the illustration cited in Chapter 1, for example, if Joe and Karen Brown receive only 5 percent rather than 8 percent interest on their savings, they must save $73.52 rather than $68.05 a month for five years to accumulate $5,000. In other words, they must save a total of $4,411 rather than $4,082, or an additional $329. Yet most financial advisers would agree that safety should not be sacrificed for a higher yield of a few percentage points.

Sometimes savings investments offer nearly identical degrees of safety but differing yields. Obviously, you should prefer the higher yield if safety and other factors are roughly the same. For example, in 1980 U.S. Government Series EE savings bonds yielded 8.0 percent, while equally safe U.S. Treasury bonds yielded about 11.25 percent. Interest on Series EE bonds is deferred for income taxes until the bonds are cashed, while treasury bond interest is taxable currently. Series EE bonds must be held for nine years to yield 8 percent; otherwise they yield only about 6 percent. Treasury bonds are taxed and fluctuate in price from day to day, which introduces some market risk if you sell them prior to maturity. But if your savings plan calls for a ten- or eleven-year holding period, you could increase your after-tax yield by about 60 percent by buying treasury bonds (or shares in investment companies that buy treasury bonds) rather than buying Series EE bonds.

Taxes

Income taxes are an important factor in personal financial management. Most savings plans are fully subject to income taxes in amounts that vary according to your tax bracket. The higher your income, the higher the applicable tax rate. The tax rate applicable to successively higher tax brackets is known as the **marginal tax rate.** Thus, if you can earn 8.0 percent interest on a taxable savings account and are at the 40 percent marginal tax rate, you net only 4.8 percent after taxes [$.08 - .40(.08) = .048$] on your savings. You may obtain more than 4.8 percent on a municipal bond, where the interest is tax-exempt. This return is nearly as safe as bank interest, but since bond prices rise and fall, you are subject to some uncertainty as to the amount you will receive when you cash in your bond. The higher your tax bracket, the more advantageous it is to invest savings in tax-sheltered media. In recent years Congress has authorized many ways to save money without paying current income taxes.

Inflation

Inflation has a significant effect on the yield and on the "real" value of your savings. If inflation rises during the savings period, the purchasing power of your fund will decline. Furthermore, if your savings are in the form of a bond, and to obtain cash you must sell the bond before it matures (comes due), you may suffer a loss. As inflation increases, new savers demand higher interest returns on their money as a reward for refraining from current spending. Therefore, the value of older bonds issued at lower interest rates declines. For example, assume that you have invested your savings in $1,000 bonds paying 6 percent, or $60 a year. Two years later, because of inflation, current bond buyers are getting 8 percent, or $80 a year. If you sell your bond before it matures, a buyer would pay you only enough so that the $60 interest payment on your old bond would yield the buyer 8 percent on the investment. Your bond's price would thus be reduced to $750 (60/750 = .08). Thus inflation creates considerable risk for savers unless they hold bonds until maturity, when they are worth **face value** (the amount printed on the bond certificate). One way to overcome losses due to inflation is to purchase short-term bonds whose date of maturity corresponds to the time you will be needing the money. This will prevent losses on the sale of bonds but will not overcome the loss in purchasing power of the proceeds. For example, if you were saving $8,000 for a new car and after five years inflation had caused the car's price to rise to $10,000, your savings plan would have been inadequate.

Convenience

Savings plans should be as convenient and as automatic as possible. The denomination of savings instruments should be small enough to accommodate the amount you want to save each month. You should be able easily to make deposits (perhaps by mail or through payroll savings) and withdrawals (possibly by telephone). Easy-to-read reports on your savings account should be available regularly, particularly in the case of long-term savings in media such as mutual funds.

Liquidity

High liquidity of savings means you can obtain your savings in cash without delay; **low liquidity** means you must wait to obtain your money, are subject to withdrawal penalties, and may have to sell your investment at a loss to realize funds. Saving money in a passbook account at a bank gives high liquidity but relatively low yield; in general you must sacrifice some liquidity for higher yields. Money invested in a house, for example, generally has low liquidity but may yield much more than other kinds of investments.

TRADITIONAL SAVINGS PRINCIPLES

Traditional savings principles may need to be reexamined in the light of high inflation and heavy income tax rates. Financial advisers have traditionally counseled people according to the following principles:

1. Borrow and use credit sparingly; if you must borrow, borrow over as short a term as possible and repay early if possible. Borrowing is actually "negative savings" and should be minimized.
2. Never sacrifice safety for yield in your savings plan.
3. Have at least three months' salary (six months' is better) in a liquid savings fund for emergencies before you make an investment such as a home purchase.

Using Credit Sparingly

The principle of avoiding credit, while still valid in some circumstances, may not be entirely advantageous. One might believe that avoiding credit should be especially important during periods in which borrowing costs escalate considerably. Consider, however, the effect of inflation. The real cost of borrowing is the **nominal cost** of interest less the inflation rate. That is, if you must pay 12 percent interest when inflation is running at 10 percent, the "real" cost to you is only 2 percent. For example, say you borrow $10,000 for a piece of property and pay 12 percent interest. After one year inflation has raised the replacement cost of the property by 10 percent, or to $11,000. By borrowing, you have paid $11,200 ($10,000 plus $1,200 interest) and you are able to use the property immediately. Thus, the real cost of financing the property is $200 ($11,200 − $11,000), or 2 percent for the year.

Consider next the effect of income taxes. If your marginal tax rate is 25 percent, the after-tax cost of interest is not 12 percent, but rather 9 percent [.12 − .25(.12) = .09]. In the case of the property purchase cited above, the tax-adjusted real cost of interest is negative. You have paid only 9 percent for financing property that has risen 10 percent in value and thus have gained 1 percent on your investment. Even if you now sell the property and pay a tax on your profit, you are still even and your financing costs are zero. The final after-tax result is calculated as follows:

Sales price of property	$11,000
Purchase price	10,000
Gross gain	1,000
Tax[1]	100
Net gain before financing costs	$ 900
Less financing cost:	
Gross interest, $1,200,	
less value of tax	
deduction of $300	
(.25 × $1,200)	900
After-tax cost of financing	$ 0

Because of inflation and income taxes, it may pay you to reconsider the traditional taboo against credit. In many cases borrowing will have a negative real cost, not a positive cost. Of course, borrowing for items not needed, or borrowing for items whose real value may be declining, would not be wise. Yet you may ask: Why defer needed purchases when I may actually gain by making purchases now?

Safety versus Yield

Consider the second traditional savings principle: not sacrificing safety for yield. The real question is, what is "safe"? For example, few would recommend storing cash because the practice is "safe." By storing cash you forgo interest on the savings; you must also find a safe place for storage and might risk loss by fire or theft. Finally, cash would decline in value because of inflation. Therefore, should you save in a 5-1/4 percent passbook savings account, which is safe because it is protected by deposit insurance of up to $100,000 by the Federal Deposit Insurance Corporation?

Because of taxes and inflation, the 5-1/4 percent passbook account may produce a negative yield. If your marginal tax bracket is 40 percent, after taxes the 5-1/4 percent is reduced to slightly over 3 percent. After inflation of 10 percent, the 3 percent becomes − 7 percent. Is the safety of the 5-1/4 percent account worth losing 7 percent on your money? Many people, faced with these

---

1. In 1980 only 40 percent of the gain was subject to tax. Since in this example it is assumed that the taxpayer is in the 25 percent bracket, the tax paid is one-fourth of the amount subject to the tax ($1,000 × .40 + .25), or $100 (see Chapter 9 for further explanation of how such gains are taxed).

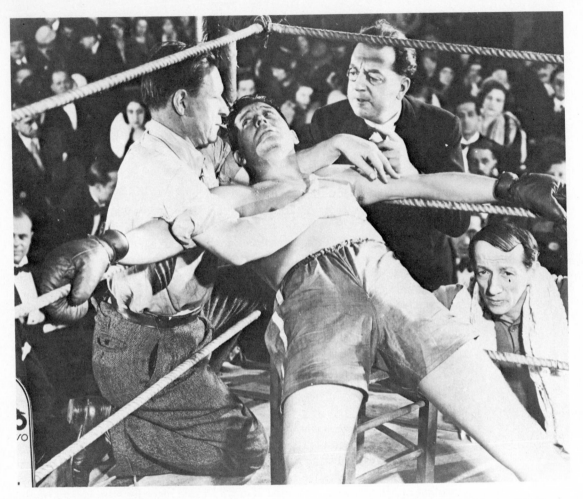

"Now remember what we told you—get out there and quit sacrificing safety for yield."

The Bettman Archive, Inc.

facts, seek a higher yield at some sacrifice of safety, liquidity, and convenience. Many modern savings instruments, such as tax-exempt bond funds or money market funds, offer good yields with only modest sacrifices in other areas.

Emergency Savings

The third traditional savings principle, accumulating at least three months' salary as an emergency fund, should also be reexamined. At 1980 salary levels of $1,500 a month, for example, three months' salary might be between $4,000 and $5,000. This guideline is probably not realistic for most people. In fact, statistics show that few families accumulate substantial liquid savings or maintain programs to save regularly, even for such short-term plans as one-year Christmas savings. The combination of inflation and income taxes makes substantial liquid savings very difficult to accumulate.

A "rule-of-thumb" guideline, furthermore, is not appropriate for many individuals. A more realistic way to determine the size of a desirable emergency fund is to examine your budget carefully and estimate the size of monthly deficits in cash flow that may require drawing on reserve funds to avoid debt. The size of an emergency fund varies according to one's circumstances. If you have very even cash flows of income and expenditures throughout the year, you will need an emergency fund much smaller than would be necessary if your income was irregular (such as commission income from sales). To advise a person to have an emergency fund of three months' salary is possibly to overstate the required level for some and to understate it for others.

One factor that reduces the need for extensive liquid emergency funds is the greater availability of insurance programs. Through individual life, health, property, and liability insurance, employer-sponsored security plans, and social insurance programs, most individuals have considerable protection against financial loss from random perils such as accidents, sickness, unemployment, premature death or disability, fire, or windstorm (see Part II for further information on insurance).

Thus, many traditional savings guidelines are not appropriate today as valid generalizations. You should attempt to overcome the income tax "bite" by saving through methods that offer either tax-exempt or tax-deferred income. The problems created by inflation can be partially overcome if you seek to maximize returns by means consistent with other objectives such as safety and convenience (see Part III for information on how investments can help you achieve financial goals).

INFLATION AND SAVINGS

Since 1950 inflation in the United States has increased at the compounded annual rate of 9.3 percent. However, since 1970 consumer debt has been remarkably stable as a percentage of disposable income. As inflation increases, wages generally rise. Inflation aids debtors since their payments remain fixed while their incomes rise.

The following statistics give some impression of how serious inflation is. In 1970 the average wage earner made $119.46 a week. In 1980 average weekly wages were $232.75, a 95 percent increase. But in terms of purchasing power, the 1980 wages purchased only $94.15 worth of goods and services—a decrease in real income of 21 percent. Despite wage increases, the economic position of the typical wage earner has worsened.

Causes of Inflation

Inflation is an economic disease caused by the creation of too much money relative to the supply of goods and services. When government and the banking system create too much money relative to available goods, prices rise. Since rising prices entail rising wages, rising profits, and rising interest rates, a sick economy looks and even feels good to many. It is, however, an illusion.

Most of us are on a treadmill. As prices go up, our wages and salaries also go up. Overall, we stay in some sort of balance. But inflation is unfair; some of us fall off the treadmill. Inflation picks its victims quite randomly. For example, inflation pushes up the price of housing so severely that young adults entering the housing market cannot afford the down payment or the monthly payments. Houses in Los Angeles, for instance, cost ten times more than they did twenty years ago; therefore, young adults entering the housing market cannot afford to buy houses similar to the ones their parents bought twenty years earlier.

Essentially, inflation means that economic resources shift away from people who cannot afford higher prices toward people whose incomes rise directly with inflation. Those who can stay even do not mind inflation; those who do not have the power to stay even suffer severely. Anyone who does not have sufficient economic or political power to bargain for cost-of-living adjustments will lose in the inflationary process.

Inflation is always a monetary process; it occurs because the government prints money or permits the banking system to increase the supply of money more quickly than the nation is able to produce goods. Inflation has become "inevitable" because of government's unwillingness to balance the budget and to restrain spending. When a deficit occurs and the nation accommodates the gap through either increased bank credit or creation of new money by the central bank or treasury, inflation results. The cause of inflation is the creation of new money, not rising prices.

The monetary process that creates inflation is not clearly understood by the general public, by the Congress, or even by some economists. Rising prices do not cause inflation; they are the result of inflation. One example of government "misunderstanding" of the cause-and-effect relationship was the Carter administration's blaming U.S. inflation on OPEC (Organization of Petroleum Exporting Countries), an international cartel that attempts to control petroleum output and prices. In the face of steadily increasing world demand for oil, OPEC controlled the supply simply by raising oil prices. Since no near substitutes for oil exist, the rest of the world had to pay the price. But rising oil prices do not cause inflation, any more than rising prices of mink coats cause inflation. If a seller of a scarce commodity can exploit the market, the price rises because of the creation of an artificial or a real shortage. But if steak prices rise and chicken prices do not, one whose income is fixed tends to eat less steak and more chicken.

Because our economy is so dependent on oil, oil producers have a "bigger dipper." To alleviate the problem, the government puts "more water" (money) into the pot. But since no new goods or services have been added, the prices of everything rise and inflation results.

If it is all that simple, why can't we just stop the inflationary process? The answer is that controlling the money supply without controlling total spending makes for a situation beyond our present capabilities. The political consequences of controlling inflation and spending are quite severe and are probably unacceptable in the short run. Effective anti-inflation measures produce high unemployment, high interest rates, and housing shortages. Inflation is an economic sickness for which no quick or palatable economic cure is acceptable in a democracy.[2]

Savings and Their Placement

Persistent inflation and its negative effects on savings have produced many changes in how and where savers place their surplus monies. Inflation has tended to increase interest rates, but many traditional types of savings were subject to regulations that prevented institutions from rewarding savers with the higher rates. The changes wrought by inflation culminated in the Interest Deregulation Act of 1980, which legalized the payment of interest on demand deposits through the approval of negotiable order of withdrawal (NOW) accounts. The act also eliminated many of the differences between banks and thrift institutions. The most important philosophical change has been recognition of the rights of savers to a market rate of interest instead of a severely regulated rate.

The old regulations kept interest rates down to prevent undue competition between financial institutions and, very importantly, to keep the cost of funds down—particularly for home mortgage borrowers. As inflation became more of a problem, policymakers saw that inflation was discouraging the national propensity to save. One obvious solution was to permit financial institutions to pay a market rate of interest, which would partially compensate for the erosion in the value of money.

---

2. Many observers point out that inflation is unknown in the Soviet bloc. Rigid price controls prevent any manifestations of inflation as we know it. But while prices don't rise, there are long lines in front of food stores, and buying a car (for cash only) may mean a two- or three-year wait. Lines and shortages are manifestations of Soviet inflation.

Savings Institutions

As inflation has radically changed economic conditions in recent years, the traditional forms of savings have also changed. To set up your savings program, you must understand both the various types of savings institutions and the savings arrangements they offer.

Exhibit 3–1 shows the extent to which savers use the various types of financial institutions, which are described in detail in the following subsections. Certain institutions have grown more rapidly than others. Banks have lost market shares relative to credit unions and savings and loan associations (SLAs), while money market mutual funds have had much growth.

EXHIBIT 3–1   Savings Deposits in Various Financial Institutions, 1960–1980

	Number in 1980	Assets (in billions)						% Change for Assets 1960–1980
		1960	1970	1975	1978	1979	1980	
Commercial banks	14,390	$66.8	$ 98.8	$160.7	$220.9	$207.8	$208.7	212.4
Savings & loan associations	4,246	62.1	146.6	285.7	431.0	470.2	489.0	687.4
Mutual savings banks	463	36.4	72.1	110.6	142.7	145.1	148.6	308.2
Credit unions	21,751	5.0	9.2	33.1	53.7	56.2	60.6	1,112.0
Money market funds	na	na	na	3.6	10.3	43.6	90.1	na

Source: *Federal Reserve Bulletin*, 1960–1980; annual reports, Federal Deposit Insurance Corporation.

COMMERCIAL BANKS

Commercial banks provide a wide range of savings contracts for individuals. They offer everything from passbook accounts to fixed-rate certificate contracts with up to eight-year maturities.

Savings plans at banks and other depository institutions are of two types. The first is the **passbook savings account,** where interest is paid on balances left in the bank and is withdrawable at any time. (Technically, the bank or thrift institution has the right to delay payment on a passbook for thirty days, but no insured institution has invoked this privilege in recent years.) Interest rates are lowest on passbook savings. Under Regulation Q, the section of the law that allows the Federal Reserve's Board of Governors to set maximum rates of interest, the maximum rate of simple interest that could be paid by a bank in 1980 was 5-1/4 percent. The actual interest rate depends on how often the interest is compounded. A common practice is to compound interest daily. While most banks pay interest on passbook accounts from the day of deposit to the day of withdrawal, the bank legally can pay interest on the minimum balance or on the average balance left on deposit. Before opening an account, you should determine the actual method of interest computation, because daily compounding of interest is more favorable than the other methods.

Prior to 1981, checking accounts could receive no interest. Beginning in January 1981, most financial institutions were allowed to offer a form of checking account called the **NOW account,** on which interest is paid. Additionally, the interest differential (one-quarter of 1 percent) that savings banks are allowed to pay over commercial banks will be phased out by 1986.

SAVINGS AND LOAN ASSOCIATIONS

The major purpose of SLAs is to provide a place to pool community savings and to make them available primarily for home mortgages. SLAs provide a variety of insured savings plans primarily aimed at the nonbusiness saver. With some exceptions SLAs do not offer checking accounts. Effective January 1981, all SLAs had the option of providing NOW accounts, but some elected not to do so.

MUTUAL SAVINGS BANKS

One of the oldest forms of financial institutions in the United States is the **mutual savings bank** (MSB). These institutions, organized to provide a safe place for small savings deposits, are heavily concentrated in the northeastern and mid-Atlantic states. They are organized as mutuals—that is, they are legally owned by depositors, not by stockholders. They are controlled by a board of directors whose major goals are the safety of the depositors' money and a commitment to the general economic welfare of the community. Unlike SLAs, MSBs have no historical role as providers of funds for local mortgage markets. Generally their lending powers have been much wider; they are permitted to invest in all forms of government and corporate bonds, mortgages on private single-family homes, and general mortgages on apartment buildings and offices. While their operations are generally quite conservative, the fact that they have not been restricted to one form of lending has allowed them to attract depositors by offering a broad range of customer services.

Mutual savings banks have been the leaders of the movement among savings institutions to offer demand deposits in competition with commercial banks. Because of their wide offerings of savings and demand deposit accounts (NOW accounts), they have been viewed as "department stores" of financial services for the small depositor. Under the Financial Institutions Deregulation Act of 1980, MSBs, like all savings institutions, have been empowered to make loans to individuals of up to 20 percent of total bank assets. Mutual savings banks are more generalized lenders and investors than are savings and loan associations, but their deposit liabilities are quite similar.

CREDIT UNIONS

As Exhibit 3–1 shows, one of the fastest-growing thrift institutions in the United States is the **credit union.** In 1980 there were over 21,000 such organizations. The distinguishing characteristic of a credit union is that its depositors are linked together by some element—usually a common employer, union membership, or association membership. Credit unions are mutual organizations owned by depositors. Most credit unions have federal insurance on their deposits. While many offer various types of time certificates, they generally specialize in a passbook form of savings account that usually pays a higher rate than is offered on similar passbook accounts by competing thrift institutions. Borrowers must be credit union members before they can qualify for loans. Credit unions have very low costs of administration since employers and unions subsidize their operations by providing free office space, or by approving payroll deductions for making savings or repaying loans.

MONEY MARKET FUNDS

One of the newest forms of savings institutions is the **money market fund** A money market fund pools the funds of individual savers and invests in large-denomination money market instruments such as short-term notes issued by banks, large corporations, and governments. Money earns interest by the day and is withdrawable at any time. Most funds offer investors the privilege of writing checks against their balances. The right to draw checks is usually limited in some manner—for example, allowing checks only over some given amount or limiting the number of checks that can be drawn per time period. As of June 1982, there were almost $200 billion in assets in money market funds, with approximately $150 billion in the form of funds catering to small investors. Interest paid equals the average return on the investment portfolio less the costs of administration. The interest rate is determined each day. The fund makes no guarantee that the investor will receive a certain interest rate over some specified period of time. Neither is the principal guaranteed. Money market funds carry no government deposit insurance, nor does any capital of the sponsoring firm back up the assets of the fund. If some economic calamity were to occur, the losses, if any, would have to be absorbed by the savers. However, since these funds hold mainly U.S. Treasury securities and the negotiable certificates of deposit of major insured U.S. banks, the risk of losing principal is minimal.

Deposit Insurance

In the depression that began in 1930, a bank crisis resulted in a "bank holiday"; over four thousand commercial banks closed in 1933. The crisis led to the creation in 1934 of the Federal Deposit Insurance Corporation

(FDIC). The essential function of the FDIC is to insure bank deposits and depositors against loss. The total insurance fund of $10 billion is less than 1 percent of all domestic deposits, but the existence of the insurance fund rather than its size, as well as its right to borrow from the U.S. Treasury, provides the basis for its safety.[3] In other words, once an account is insured, the possibility that the depositor will be unable to withdraw account balances is eliminated. Before the creation of the FDIC, the fear of such a possibility might have caused a bank to fail when many depositors, simultaneously attempting to withdraw their accounts, created a "bank run." The bank would have been unable to convert its loans and investments into cash fast enough to satisfy its panic-prone depositors and would have had to close.

The 1980 limit of FDIC insurance stands at $100,000 per account. Thus, you and your spouse can insure as much as $300,000 in one bank if each of you has an individual account and both have a joint account. No distinction is made among demand or time deposits, certificates, or any other domestic deposits. Similar insurance plans cover savings and loan associations and credit unions. All insured financial institutions must prominently display the fact that they have insurance and must feature the insurance in their advertising.

Savings in the United States

Households are the major net suppliers of funds to business and government. Approximately 75 percent of all funds provided to the net borrowers—government and business—are provided by households, and one-third of that amount can be traced to household holdings of time deposits and savings deposits in financial institutions. Even though Americans are not "big" savers as compared, for example, to the Japanese, American households provide the bulk of financial funds for other American institutions.

PASSBOOK ACCOUNTS

A passbook savings account allows you to deposit funds in the bank or thrift institutions and to receive interest from the day of deposit to the end of the interest period or to the day of withdrawal. Interest will usually be compounded on some basis, but the maximum interest that can be paid is fixed by the Federal Reserve on a simple interest basis. For example, if a savings and loan association says it pays the maximum passbook rate allowed by law (in 1981, 5.5 percent), it pays the equivalent of 5.65 when compound-

---

3. Insurance covers only domestic deposits. Similar government-sponsored insurance plans cover savings and loan deposits, mutual savings banks, and credit unions.

ed daily.[4] Usually the financial institution will pay interest on the passbook deposit up to the day of withdrawal, though it is not required to do so by law. Under Regulation Q, thrift institutions are permitted to pay an interest rate 1/4 percent higher than that paid by banks on all savings forms other than the various term money market certificates.

NOW ACCOUNTS

For years various Congresses and presidential administrations have pondered the problem of the structure of the U.S. financial system. One proposal that has continually appeared in all the studies and recommendations has been the idea of making thrift institutions more like banks. One way to make SLAs and MSBs more "bank-like" is to permit them to offer checking accounts. These special accounts, called NOW (Negotiable Order of Withdrawal) accounts, were finally permitted by the Interest Deregulation Act of 1980.

Simply stated, a NOW account is a savings account that pays interest and also permits the depositor to write checks against the account. Since the financial institution sets the conditions (although the maximum rate is set by the Board of Governors of the Federal Reserve System under Regulation Q), there are many different account plans. A few institutions offer the NOW account with no minimum balance; others, predominantly banks, require a minimum account balance of $1,500. Some permit an unlimited number of checks to be written; others limit the number of free checks to fifteen or twenty a month. Credit unions offer a variety of the NOW account, called a **share draft,** which requires the institution to insist on not returning the canceled share draft (check) to the depositor. This practice is called **truncation** and is an obvious cost benefit to the financial institution. Some financial institutions other than credit unions have followed this lead and now offer NOW accounts only if the depositor will accept truncation.

For years the standard banking approach to demand deposits was to calculate what minimum balance was needed to compensate the bank for allowing an individual to draw unlimited numbers of checks against the bank. Depending on the bank's desire to compete for consumer deposits and on its cost structure, varying minimum balances were imposed. These balances could be as low as $100 in a small bank and as high as $2,500 in large wholesale banks that did not want to encourage small accounts. In return for the minimum balance, the bank offered a free checking account. For example, suppose the minimum balance was $500 and you wrote twenty-five checks a month. In keeping $500 in the account, you lost about $2.19 a month in

---

4. Compounded daily, the rate is 5.6536; quarterly, the rate is 5.6144. At 5.5% in ten years, $100 will equal $173.32 compounded daily, as compared to $172.67 compounded quarterly.

interest ($500 times the passbook rate of 5.4 percent). In return you received free checking, which was worth about $2.50 ($.10 times twenty-five checks).

Now suppose that the same bank offered a NOW account that included free checking plus 5.25 percent interest on the minimum balance of $1,000. In such an account you would earn $4.32 a month in interest on the minimum balance of $1,000. However, if you let the balance slip below $1,000, a service charge of $5 would be imposed to cover the first fifteen checks written, and there would be an additional $.25 fee for each check after the fifteenth. Thus, if you wrote twenty-five checks you would pay $7.50 under a NOW account if the minimum required balance was not maintained. These charges would more than offset the interest earnings and might make it advantageous for you to retain the regular account carrying free checking for a $500 balance. Alternatively, you could deposit the extra $500 (which would otherwise be kept in the NOW account) in a money market fund earning 14 percent interest, which would give you $5.33 in interest a month. Using this procedure, you would obtain free checking plus $5.33 a month. By comparison, in the NOW account you would obtain free checking plus $4.32 a month but would run the risk of paying $7.50 if the balance fell below $1,000. All in all, the comparison is difficult to make and depends on the ease with which you can maintain a minimum balance, on the number of checks written, on how much interest could be earned in higher-yielding liquid assets such as money market funds, and on the convenience of using the NOW account.

COMPARING TERMS AND YIELDS AMONG SAVINGS MEDIA

The typical yield received in various types of savings accounts in May 1982 is shown in Exhibit 3–2. None of the yields shown on the various certificates or on the money market fund are fixed, because they are determined by changing money market conditions. Further, the other yields are **ceiling rates** (maximum rates), and the financial institution might want to pay less than the maximum if competitive conditions warrant.

The Federal Reserve Board has set some penalties if the saver cashes in a savings certificate before maturity. The penalty on a six-month certificate mandates that the saver owes the financial institution three months' interest at the rate originally contracted, regardless of when the certificate is cashed. Suppose you bought a six-month certificate for $10,000 at the rate of 12 percent per annum, and circumstances required you to cash the certificate sixty days after you had bought it. You would owe the institution $300 ($10,000 × .12 × 3/12), which would be deducted from your $10,000. If you liquidated the certificate in four months, you would forfeit three months' interest ($300) and would receive one month's earnings ($100). If you purchased a thirty-month certificate, the forfeit would amount to six months' interest.

If you have any doubt about your ability to keep a certificate until maturity, you should carefully consider your options. For example, you might want

EXHIBIT 3-2   Typical Interest Rates Available to Savers, May 5, 1982

Institution	NOW Account	6-Month Certificate of Savings	30-Month Certificate of Savings
Commercial bank	5.25%	13.030%	13.50%
Mutual savings bank	5.25%	13.030%	13.85%
Savings & loan association	5.25%	13.030%	13.85%
Credit union	8.00%	13.75 %	14.35%
Money market fund			
Ready assets	12.45%	na	na
CMA	12.06%	13.38 %	na

Note: The 6-month certificate required a $10,000 minimum; the 30-month certificate, a $100 minimum.

Source: Survey by the authors.

to put your money in a money market fund, which does not charge penalties for early withdrawal. Or you might use passbook accounts, which do not have substantial penalties for early withdrawal.

The six-month certificate is issued with a minimum amount of $10,000 and in multiples of $1,000 over the minimum. Thirty-month certificates are issued in minimum amounts of $100 and in multiples of $100.

SAVINGS BONDS

The U.S. government traditionally has provided an alternative channel for savings dollars. Two selling points of Series E and Series H bonds have been that they are a means of direct payroll savings and are a simple way for individuals to purchase government debt instruments directly. Since November 1980, **Series EE bonds** have been offered at a minimum $50 denomination face value; they accrue interest at a rate of 8 percent, compounded annually. The saver pays $25 for the $50 bond, which matures in nine years. Buyers of U.S. savings bonds have another option; they can purchase **Series HH bonds,** which pay interest directly to the bondholder semiannually at the guaranteed annual rate of 7.5 percent.

Perhaps the most interesting facet of savings bonds is their tax position. The buyer of Series EE savings bonds has the option of paying or not paying the tax as the interest accrues. In addition, at maturity the holder of Series EE bonds can convert them to Series HH bonds without paying any taxes on the accrued interest—a potentially valuable option, since the saver will be able to postpone paying tax on the interest until retirement, when one's taxable income usually falls. Interest on a government bond has another tax advantage: Under the Constitution states are not permitted to tax federal government debt instruments.

Taxation of Savings

The interest on most savings media is fully subject to federal and state income taxes, although in some cases (e.g., savings bonds) the tax may be postponed until a later year. **Municipal bonds** are an exception to this rule; interest is exempt from federal income taxes and also exempt from state income taxes for residents of the state in which the bond is issued. Savers living in states other than the state of issue must pay state income tax on interest received on municipal bonds. As we will see in Part II, interest accruing on certain types of life insurance policies is tax-deferred (not exempt) until the policy is surrendered for its cash value.

Other types of savings plans—principally those in which the saver is setting aside funds for retirement—are also subject to deferred taxes on amounts deposited as well as on interest and dividends paid during the savings period. Examples are the Keogh plans authorized under the Employees' Retirement Income Security Act (ERISA) for the self-employed, and individual retirement accounts (IRAs). Savers with long-term goals, such as supplementing retirement income, should give careful consideration to the advantages offered by tax deferral. Even if, after retirement, the saver is in the same or in a higher tax bracket, total returns will be considerably greater under a tax-deferred savings program than under one that is not tax-deferred; interest has been earned on funds that otherwise would have been paid in taxes during the income-earning years.

Effective in 1982, Congress has also authorized individual taxpayers to deduct up to $100 ($200 for a family filing jointly) of qualifying common stock dividends. Thus, some additional tax incentive is being given to encourage more savings (see Chapter 9 for further information). Yet, since interest is deductible for income taxes, the tax system also tends to encourage going into debt rather than saving. For example, the interest deductible on a home mortgage encourages home ownership with maximum levels of mortgage indebtedness. If a typical loan can be floated for an interest rate of about 15 percent, the after-tax cost for a buyer in the 40 percent bracket is only 9 percent. Since prices tend to escalate more quickly than the after-tax cost of interest, going into debt may be more advantageous than trying to save the purchase price of an article.

ALL SAVERS CERTIFICATES

One of the newest savings instruments is the **all savers certificate** (ASC), authorized by Congress in the summer of 1981. The ASC has a one-year maturity, and the interest rate is tied to the average (one-month) yield of one-year-maturity U.S. Treasury bills. The amount paid is 70 percent of the treasury bill rate and is exempt from federal income tax. The exemption limit is set at $1,000 per taxpayer ($2,000 for a married couple filing jointly). The

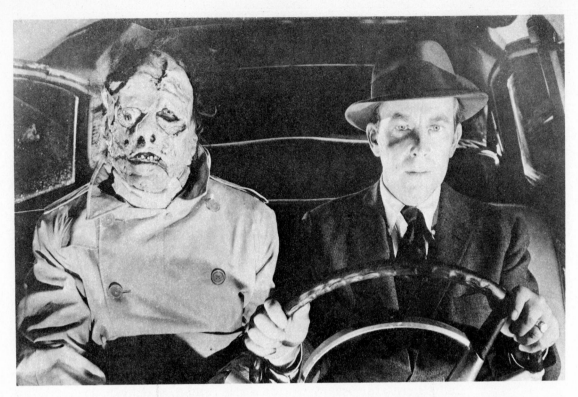

"If I were in your condition, Fred, I wouldn't worry about opening an IRA account."

The Bettman Archive, Inc.

taxpayer may receive this exemption only once during the legislative life of this special instrument, which expires in 1986.

It is extremely difficult to analyze the value of the ASC to an individual depositor, since the real yield is based on the depositor's tax bracket. The higher the depositor's income, the higher the effective yield. For example, suppose the one-year treasury bill rate was 12 percent, and the ASC yield rate was 8.4 percent (70 percent of 12 percent). If you were in the highest marginal rate bracket and paid 50 percent in taxes, the ASC would have a taxable equivalent yield of 16.8 percent (.084 ÷ .50). But if you were only in the 20 percent bracket, the taxable equivalent yield would only be 10.5 percent, which is hardly different from the after-tax yield of the treasury bill you might have bought directly.

Savers have not rushed to buy this new instrument; the tax exemption has apparently not been important enough to draw savers in large numbers to a certificate paying 70 percent of the market rate of interest. Perhaps the loss of liquidity and the substantial interest penalty for early withdrawal also have influenced savers' perception of the ASC's value.

Indexation of Savings

Some countries, particularly those in South America that suffer from high rates of inflation, encourage savings by a process known as **indexation.** The details of indexation vary considerably among countries, but the procedure generally works as follows: You are guaranteed a basic return (e.g., 6 percent) on a savings account made by a qualifying institution. If inflation runs at 6 percent or less during the year, you earn 6 percent on the account. If inflation runs at 25 percent, your account is credited with the basic interest rate plus the inflation rate, or a total of 31 percent. In this way the government assumes the purchasing power risk and effectively removes one barrier to savings. Savers are encouraged to lay aside funds, which add to the pool of money available for investment in the country and thus help the economy to become more productive. A stronger economy, in turn, helps reduce inflation.

Neither indexation nor any other automatic adjustment of savings account interest for inflation has yet been tried in the United States, although reverse procedures have been employed. That is, the government has traditionally set a limit on the amount of interest banks and other savings institutions could pay on savings accounts. In 1980, for example, the limit payable on NOW accounts was 5.5 percent; banks could not pay more, even if they were willing and able to do so. To the extent that inflation exceeds the allowable bank limits, savers are penalized. The penalty has varied with the inflation rate, but in recent years, with inflation at around 11 percent, the penalty for savings has averaged about 5.5 percent annually. As we have noted, however, legislation has been passed to phase out government limitations on amounts that institutions may pay on savings.

SUMMARY

1. Because of rapid changes in the economic environment, savers must pay greater attention to developing sound plans for personal savings.
2. Major considerations in planning for savings include selection of savings media and consideration of safety of principal, yield, liquidity of savings, inflation protection, and income taxes. A sound plan establishes definite goals for savings and allows for savings to be deposited on a regular basis.
3. Traditional guides for savings and borrowing may not be appropriate under modern economic conditions; their validity should be re-examined.
4. An examination of the basic causes of inflation, which are not well understood, suggests that easy or quick remedies for the "inflation disease" are not likely. Thus, long-term savings and borrowing plans

should take inflation into account. Specifically, the likelihood of continuing inflation means that you must select media with regard for their ability to enlarge total returns under inflation and to shelter savings from income taxes as much as possible. Borrowing (negative savings) may make more economic sense in periods of inflation than at other times.

5. Financial regulations that formerly restricted interest returns payable in various savings media have been relaxed. Differences that formerly existed between such media as bank savings accounts, savings and loan accounts, and other types of savings are now blurred. Yet choices about where to make liquid savings do exist. One of the more popular of the newer media is the money market fund, a mutual fund of high-yield but liquid securities that usually pays much higher interest than is available elsewhere.

6. Beginning in 1981, commercial banks and savings and loan associations were permitted to pay interest on checking accounts (called NOW accounts). To avoid penalties and charges for writing checks, you must maintain a substantial minimum balance in the NOW account, a factor that may negate the value of this type of account when compared to a traditional checking account, which offers free checking for a relatively small minimum balance.

7. Deposit insurance to protect you against failure of a savings institution is available in all savings media (except money market funds). Thus, the risk of losing your principal is minimal also. With money market funds because of the nature of their investments, however, various restrictions may subject you to loss of interest or to other penalties for withdrawal of savings before maturity.

8. U.S. savings bonds, while paying a relatively low interest rate, offer you an opportunity to defer income taxes otherwise levied on interest being earned currently. Other forms of savings also offer tax deferral, but in general, federal and state income taxes are levied on savings as ordinary income, a factor you should consider when comparing savings to other forms of investments.

9. Unlike some countries the United States does not offer indexation of savings accounts for inflation protection.

REVIEW QUESTIONS

1. Discuss why savings goals are related to the life-cycle concept outlined in Chapter 1.

2. (a) Do you agree that some people will save part of their income whether or not they have a definite goal, while other people will never save anything, regardless of their income level, even if they have a definite goal?

   (b) Reconcile this statement with the theory that unless you have a definite goal the likelihood of completing a successful savings program is greatly diminished.

3. (a) Considering the three steps of a savings program, why is it usually necessary for you to "pay yourself first"?
   (b) Suggest various ways of "paying yourself first."

4. Which of the six factors to be considered in making savings should receive highest priority: safety, yield, taxes, inflation protection, convenience, or liquidity?

5. If inflation is 12 percent a year and interest rates on savings are 12 percent, what is the "real" rate of return on your funds?

6. Discuss Question 5 in view of your marginal income tax bracket. Assume the following brackets:
   (a) 25 percent;
   (b) 40 percent;
   (c) 50 percent.

7. June Gomez owns a treasury bond bearing a nominal interest rate of 10 percent. She paid $1,000 for the bond.
   (a) If, in the following year, interest rates rise to 12 percent, what will happen to the price of June's bond?
   (b) How could June avoid the risk of loss from fluctuating interest rates?

8. Do you think that the interest paid on savings accounts and bonds should vary with the rate of inflation? Discuss.

9. (a) How has the U.S. government encouraged savings and discouraged savings through tax legislation?
   (b) On balance, do you believe that the net effect of government influence on interest returns has been to encourage or to discourage savings? Why?

10. Is interest that is tax-deferred preferable to interest that is taxed currently? Why or why not?

11. A financial adviser states: "Your child will be entering college in 1998. Give her a tax-free gift of $6,000 a year now for one or two years. Put the proceeds in a money market fund and let assets accumulate at her low-income-bracket rate. You won't need a lawyer, since most states have minor-custodian acts." Assume that the parents are in the 38 percent marginal tax bracket and can earn 8 percent in the money market fund.
   (a) Consult Appendix A–1 and determine how much $6,000 will accumulate to in eighteen years at 8 percent and at 5 percent [8% − (8% × .32)].
   (b) Discuss whether the adviser's plan is sound.

12. "Inflation occurs because prices are rising." Do you agree? Why or why not?

13. A NOW account enables the individual to combine a savings account and a checking account.
   (a) What advantages do you see in a NOW account?
   (b) Can you identify any disadvantages?

14. (a) What are the major U.S. institutions that you, as a saver, can use?
    (b) Which institutions are growing the most rapidly? (See Exhibit 3–1.)

15. Why has government deposit insurance helped alleviate the possibility of financial panic in the United States?

16. (a) What important advantage do U.S. savings bonds have over other forms of savings?
    (b) In your opinion, is this advantage important?

CASE PROBLEMS

I. Alternate Methods of Home Financing

Robert Pilchic is a "set-up" man in a diesel engine plant in Cleveland, Ohio, and makes $25,000 a year. He makes an extra $5,000 a year working weekends as a mechanic for an emergency truck repair service. His wages contain a union-negotiated, annual automatic cost-of-living increase. This increase has averaged 8 percent a year over the last few years. His wife Elsie works in a sewing plant and makes $9,000 a year. The Pilchics live with their three children in a small rented house in an older area. Elsie has become increasingly unhappy with the schools and wants the children to go to a better school that will help prepare them for college.

The Pilchics are quite frugal and have managed to save $15,000 during their twelve-year marriage. This money is kept in a passbook account at the local savings and loan. On Sundays they have been looking at suburban houses. They can move into a new subdivision, four-bedroom house for $89,500. If they take an 80 percent mortgage, they can secure a mortgage at 13 percent for thirty years with monthly payments of $792.04. Another possibility is a thirty-year FHA mortgage with a 10 percent down payment but with an interest of 14-1/2 percent. Monthly payments would be $986.38. They have also read an ad in the newspaper that offers a 12 percent mortgage, 15 percent down, for thirty years with a variable rate that can increase no more than 1 percent a year, with a maximum increase of 5 percent overall. The monthly payment would be $782.52 now; if interest rates continue to rise, the monthly payment could rise to a maximum of $1,084.58 under the variable rate plan. The closing costs of $2,700 are identical for all mortgages. What would you recommend the Pilchics do? (Hint: Their combined incomes put the Pilchics in a 37 percent income tax bracket. Mortgage interest is a tax-deductible expense; during the first year, interest will constitute 97 percent of the monthly payments.)

II. Determining the Best Return on Cash Reserves

Bob and Molly Bloom have retired and are now living in Sarasota, Florida. Their needs are well covered by their pensions and by Social Security. They have $15,000, which they keep as a cash reserve. Half is in a 5-1/2 percent passbook account, and the other half in a bank checking account. They realize that their handling of the cash reserve is "lazy" and that they ought to do something about it. Their bank offers a 5.25 percent NOW account. They can buy $10,000 six-month certificates of deposit (CDs) from the SLA for a yield of 14 percent. Newspapers and television heavily advertise money market funds that offer free checking (for amounts greater than $500) and a current 16 percent interest rate. Before making up their minds they hear a radio advertisement for a small SLA about four miles away that offers a free NOW account for a $50 minimum balance and a 5 percent yield. Which alternative would you recommend to the Blooms?

III. Savings Bonds as an Investment

A financial commentator found it hard to believe that anyone "smart enough to save $5,000 could be dumb enough to invest in 7 percent U.S. savings bonds." The commentator then presented a list of comparable savings media with yields that ranged from – 6.6 percent (a tax-exempt municipal bond) to 13.4 percent (a money market fund).

QUESTIONS

1. Respond to the writer's statement.

2. List some other investments and their current savings yield in addition to those mentioned above.

CHAPTER 4

PRINCIPLES OF RISK MANAGEMENT AND INSURANCE

LEARNING OBJECTIVES

In studying this chapter, you will learn:

A sound way to approach the problem of handling personal risks;

The value of insurance as well as of other methods of handling risk;

The meaning of risk, probability, perils, and hazards;

How better to analyze risks and understand insurance;

The requisites of insurable risks;

The major types of insurance contracts, companies, and agents;

The distinction between insurance and gambling;

How to compare insurance policies;

What to expect from insurance agents;

How to save money on insurance;

Some common errors in personal risk management.

A basic element of success in personal financial planning is the protection of assets and income against random losses from various perils. Failure either to recognize the possibility of such losses or to develop plans to meet risks results in poor financial planning. You may strive for many years to build a home, to save money for a new car, or to train for your career, and a single catastrophe can wipe out all your efforts. With an appropriate plan for protection against catastrophe, however, the economic impact of the loss may be wholly or partially offset so that you may still succeed in realizing your long-term financial goals.

In recent years a new approach to the management of personal risks has greatly improved the likelihood of success in protecting assets and income against unexpected loss. Termed **risk management,** this approach differs in several ways from the traditional way of managing personal risk. Before discussing risk management, however, let us examine the main elements of the traditional approach.

TRADITIONAL APPROACH TO HANDLING RISKS

The traditional approach to the management of personal risk is to buy insurance from commercial insurers. Some types of insurance must be "sold" to the prospect, who is otherwise unaware of the need. Other types might be purchased because they are required as a condition of obtaining a loan for, say, a house or a car. The buyer generally makes little or no independent effort to determine needs or to shop among different insurers for the best contract or the lowest price. Normally the buyer gives no thought to the financial soundness of the insurer issuing the contract or to problems that may arise in proving losses once they occur. The buyer does not usually analyze the effect of clauses in the policy that may restrict coverage, reduce loss recoveries, or exclude various sources of loss. Thus, the buyer may often be "insurance poor" because the value of insurance is not fully appreciated.

The most important weakness of the traditional way of handling risk is that it focuses mainly on insurance, whereas better ways of handling risk may exist. Insurance agents will not usually attempt to assist you in identifying and handling risks for which no insurance contracts are designed. For example, if your house is subject to flood but your agent cannot or does not sell a flood insurance policy, the agent will not discuss flood perils with you. Consequently, your property may remain unnecessarily exposed to loss.

The traditional approach to insurance buying is to accept a policy from the first agent with whom you deal and to pay whatever price is asked. There are very large differences in insurance prices in almost all lines of coverage, and yet the typical purchaser is not aware of them and tends not to shop among different agents for the best price. Even if you ask the agent for competitive quotes from different insurers, the agent may obtain the quotes from insurers represented in the agent's office. Therefore, you have no assurance that the quotation obtained is the lowest or the best quote available, simply because no one agent represents all insurance companies.

To purchase appropriate insurance, you must understand the policy's conditions, exclusions, and coverage. The traditional approach to insurance buying is to turn this responsibility over to an agent and to trust the agent's judgment. However, not all agents are equally qualified, and even a well-qualified agent may not completely understand your particular needs and resources. Moreover, many individuals deal with several agents and thus give no single agent a chance to take a comprehensive view of the buyer's insurance problems. You should at least know enough to ask pertinent questions about insurance coverage, exclusions, and pricing structure.

RISK MANAGEMENT

The risk management approach, considerably broader than the traditional approach, involves the procedures illustrated in Exhibit 4–1. First you must recognize the existence of various risks and measure their financial impact. Next you should develop alternative courses of action for handling the serious and the nonserious risks you face. For example, upon recognizing a "serious" risk, you can insure it, transfer it under an agreement with another person (not necessarily an insurer), avoid the risk altogether by conducting your affairs in an alternative manner, reduce the impact of the risk through effective loss-control methods, or simply "run" the risk in the full knowledge that you are doing so.

Identifying Risks

Consider the risks introduced when you become the owner and driver of a new automobile. Using the traditional approach, you might phone your insurance agent and say, "I just bought a new car; can you please cover me?" If the agent agrees, you consider the matter closed. With the risk management approach, however, you try to consider all the risks you face because you own and drive a new car: (1) risk of collision loss; (2) risk of all other loss except collision (e.g., theft, falling objects, flood, and fires); (3) liability to third parties because of bodily injury or damage to others' property stemming from negligent driving; (4) medical or funeral expenses stemming from

EXHIBIT 4–1   The Risk Management Process

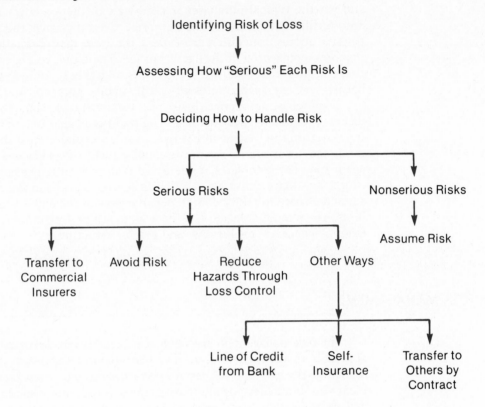

an accident to you or your passengers; (5) loss of income to you or your passengers because of disability arising from an accident; (6) cost of towing and labor stemming from a breakdown; (7) cost of renting a car if yours is stolen or disabled by an accident; and (8) cost of hiring extra help to perform household chores in case you are disabled by an accident.

Assessing Risks

Once the different risks have been identified, the "seriousness" of each must be assessed. Some risks may already be covered by other types of insurance or by other resources; some risks need to be given high priority, others less. For example, the losses that may result from negligence in a car accident can be extremely large; they generally require first priority in the insurance plan. Collision losses, on the other hand, are normally limited to the value of the automobile; if you are driving a five-year-old car, the costs of insuring for collision may be excessive when compared to the maximum amount you could collect under the coverage. This risk might be considered nonserious, and you may choose to assume it personally.

Handling Risks

The next step in the risk management process is to decide how to handle each risk. If insurance is to be used for part of the risks, the type of policy, the quality of the insurer and the agent, the price of coverage, and other factors must be analyzed.

INSURING RISK

Once you have decided to obtain insurance, you should select from among at least three competitive insurers' bids. In buying **physical damage insurance,** you may decide to assume part of the risk by accepting a substantial deductible amount, whereas you may decide to seek million-dollar limits for liability coverage. You may choose not to purchase some available coverages, such as towing and labor, because the losses (even if they should occur) may be too low to require being met by much advance planning. In selecting an agent, you should inquire among friends or financial advisers about the qualifications and service records of various agents. Once your agent proposes coverage with a given insurer, you should check the financial rating of the insurer or ask the agent to make a report on the insurer's past performance in settling claims.

AVOIDING RISK

Risk avoidance, as the name suggests, involves avoiding situations that produce risk. In the case of automobile insurance, you might simply decide not to drive a car but to take public transportation instead. This approach to handling risk is difficult at best in modern society, since many risks simply cannot be avoided. For example, being a pedestrian involves risks that can hardly be avoided unless you become a recluse and never leave the house. However, risk avoidance can frequently be employed in some matters; for example, you may decide to rent a house rather than to own one and thereby avoid the risk of home ownership.

REDUCING HAZARDS

Reduction of hazards in the matter of car ownership can be accomplished by purchasing less expensive cars and thereby reducing the cost of insuring against collision and other physical damage losses. Using safety features such as seat belts or taking courses in driving safety are other ways to reduce hazards; they may result in reduced insurance costs. Taking precautions when driving (e.g., observing speed limits) can also help you to avoid insurance premium penalties that otherwise would be imposed because of too many traffic citations.

OTHER METHODS

An additional method of handling risk is to plan a credit line at the bank to meet a loss that might occur. In other words, you assume the risk of loss but make plans to restore the asset or to pay a claim through borrowing, if necessary. Advance planning makes it easier to get credit when credit is needed.

Another method of risk handling is self-insurance. Under self-insurance you expect to pay for any losses personally and may allocate funds from a savings account to do so. This method may be used when the cost of insurance is too high or when insurance is unavailable. You may also transfer risk to others by contract—for example, you may lease (rather than own) a house or car; in these cases the owner of the property must purchase insurance or otherwise bear the risk of loss.

Risk management is a careful and scientific way to deal with the risks to which you and your property are subject. To implement this approach, you must devote much more time and effort to risk planning than is usual with the traditional approach. The rewards, however, make the extra time and effort worthwhile.

BASIC RISK CONCEPTS

Understanding certain basic concepts of risk and risk management will make it easier to make better decisions in managing personal finances. The concepts of risk, risk aversion, probability, the law of large numbers, and insurance as a means of transferring risk are discussed in the following subsections.

Risk

Risk must be distinguished from concepts such as hazard, peril, and probability. **Risk** is the uncertainty as to whether economic loss will be incurred. Two types of risk, pure and speculative, should be distinguished (see Exhibit 4–2). In risk management we are generally referring only to **pure risk,** which, if it occurs, will produce a loss rather than a gain. **Speculative risk** involves acts that could produce either a loss or a gain (e.g., investing in a given stock). The investing decision involves the risk of loss, but investing is usually not considered a part of risk management because investing is undertaken main-

EXHIBIT 4–2
Classification of
Risk

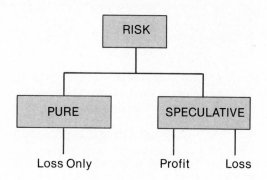

ly for gain, not to offset a possible loss. Handling an event such as a liability suit or a fire involves only pure risk; if the event materializes, it produces only a loss.

Risk Aversion

Most people consider risk undesirable. They will pay to avoid it or to reduce its impact on their lives. To illustrate, consider which choice you would make in the following situation: You are offered two jobs. The first is considered a steady job with relatively little room for salary advancement, but once you are employed, you have almost no chance of being discharged. The second job has considerable opportunity for salary advancement, but you know that the firm hires several people with the idea of retaining only a few of the best and discharging the remainder within a year or two. The second job pays a 25 percent greater beginning salary than the first job.

If you indicate a preference for the first job, you are exhibiting a tendency toward risk aversion. Various studies have shown that a majority of individuals would lean toward the first job rather than take a chance on being discharged from the second job, even though the salary of the latter is higher (see Exhibit 4–3).

Consider a second situation: A government inspector tells you that you run a fifty-fifty chance of suffering total loss of your house from subsidence because of its location over an abandoned coal mine. You can avoid the loss by paying a substantial fee to a firm employed by the government to move your house to a safe location. The government will help finance the moving fee over a long period of years at low interest rates. Would you incur the expense or run the fifty-fifty chance of suffering total loss of the house?

If you decide to pay the moving fee rather than to chance losing your house, you can be considered somewhat risk-averse. This situation is not unlike the thousands of decisions people make every year when they purchase insurance against various perils such as fire, explosion, and windstorm,

EXHIBIT 4-3

Are You a Risk Taker or a Risk Averter?

Circle (a), (b), or (c).

1. Assume that you have a mortgage on your home. Which of the following strategies is most appealing to you?
   (a) Continue making monthly mortgage payments, paying off the loan on schedule.
   (b) Prepay the mortgage as quickly as possible to save interest costs.
   (c) Refinance the loan and use the cash for some other investment or expenditure, such as a vacation home.

2. You have $50,000 available for investing. Which of the following investments would you select?
   (a) A savings account.
   (b) Income-producing real estate.
   (c) An oil-drilling partnership.

3. You are considering the purchase of a new car. In all likelihood it will be:
   (a) Smaller and more economical than your present one.
   (b) A conventional, standard-sized car with a wide assortment of optional features.
   (c) A sports car emphasizing style, speed, or performance.

4. If you were betting on a horse race, which wager would you make?
   (a) Bet on the "favorite," even though your winnings would be relatively small.
   (b) Select a horse that has a good chance of winning and will return a moderate amount if it does win.
   (c) Pick a "long shot" in hopes of making a "killing."

5. You are considering an employment change. What condition appeals most to you?
   (a) Joining a well-established firm and performing work similar to what you are now doing.
   (b) Associating with a newly formed organization in a newly created position for which you'll need training.
   (c) Going into business for yourself.

6. If you were considering a new job, which of the following circumstances would you select?
   (a) Little chance for higher salary but virtual assurance of permanent employment.
   (b) A moderately higher salary combined with better employment assurance.
   (c) A chance for a much higher salary but considerable risk of being fired.

Scoring: Give yourself 3 for each question you marked (a), 4 for each (b), and 5 for each (c). Scores between 18 and 20 show high risk aversion; between 28 and 30, high willingness to take risk. A score of 24 is average.

except that the payment made to transfer risk is lower. Insurance premiums are usually only a small fraction of the total possible loss.

Probability

Probability is the chance that a given event will occur—for example, the 50 percent chance of getting heads in the flip of a coin. In the field of risk management, probability usually refers to the chance that a given event causing a loss will occur. Probability of loss may be estimated subjectively or may be based on statistical evidence of past losses. Note that probability is different from risk, which has to do with the uncertainty of an event. In Exhibit 4–4, for example, the probability of drawing a black ball (having a loss) is 10 out of 100, or 10 percent. The risk, on the other hand, is the chance that less than or more than 10 balls will actually be drawn—that is, that the loss will be something other than 10 percent.

EXHIBIT 4–4
Risk and Probability

KEY
Loss - Drawing black ball

No loss - Drawing white ball

LONG RUN
Probability of Loss - 10%

Probability of No Loss - 90%

RISK
Chance that loss will be something other than 10%

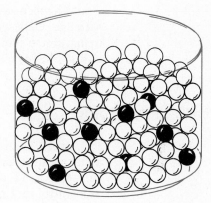

Law of Large Numbers

A powerful natural law helps clarify the basis of risk management and is employed by insurance companies to help them predict aggregate losses. The **law of large numbers** says that as you gather a larger and larger group of objects under your control, each subject to a given probability of loss, it is more and more likely that the actual losses observed will equal the probability number predicted. Thus, as the number of objects exposed to loss increases, the variations in losses decline; hence the risk declines. If you have

1,000 houses under your management, and each house is subject to a probable loss by fire of 1 percent, you may expect that total fires per year will be 10 (1,000 × .01 = 10). However, the actual number of fires may be 9, 11, or some other number. You cannot be sure there will be exactly 10. If instead of 1,000 houses, you have 100,000 houses, and the probability of 1 percent still exists, you may expect to have 1,000 fires. The variation from 1,000, however, will be much less, relatively speaking, than when only 10 fires were expected. This lower relative variation is a way of saying that the risk of having a much greater loss than anticipated is less if you have more objects under your control.

Since most individuals do not have a large enough number of objects to make the law of large numbers work, the attendant risk is much greater to an individual than to a group. Most individuals seek ways to reduce the risk or to handle it so as to eliminate any adverse financial impact.

Note that the central problem in risk management is to reduce risk and its impact. If we knew for certain that a loss was going to occur, there would be no uncertainty and hence no risk. Probability of loss would be 100 percent. The techniques of risk management would not be needed since the loss would happen and there would apparently be nothing we could do except suffer it. Once your house catches fire, it is too late for insurance. Risk management requires the planning of expected losses and the assessment of risk so that plans can be made in advance.

Perils and Hazards

A **peril** is an event whose occurrence can cause a loss. We commonly insure against various perils such as fire, flood, or windstorm. **Hazards,** on the other hand, are conditions that affect the probability of losses and the probability that perils will occur. For example, the southeastern section of the United States is subject to atmospheric hazards that can produce the peril of a tornado. The factor causing the loss is the tornado, not the atmospheric conditions giving rise to the tornado. We can do relatively little about perils, but we can and do influence hazards. A substantial part of risk management has to do with **loss-control activities,** which are aimed at reducing the severity of losses and the likelihood of occurrence of the corresponding perils.

Insurance

Insurance is a method of transferring risk. The insurer combines objects exposed to loss in such a way that the insurer's total claims become predictable within narrow limits. Thus, total risk to the insurer is reduced. Insurance is generally in the form of a contract between two parties, usually (but not necessarily) in writing, under which one party (the insurer) agrees to pay a loss of the other party (the insured) if some specified peril or other contingency happens during a stated time period. Insurance must meet the requirements of a legal contract: A consideration called a **premium** must be paid, the agreement must have a legal purpose, it must be made by legally competent parties, and the parties must give mutual consent. Insurance is often distinguished from other contracts under which risk is transferred because it involves loss sharing, usually through creation of a fund from contributions of a group. Out of this fund payments are made to group members who suffer losses.

INSURANCE AS A METHOD OF HANDLING RISK

Most individuals use all the methods of risk handling (illustrated in Exhibit 4–1) in various combinations. However, people rely heavily on insurance in most cases because it is often the safest, most economical, and most effective method of handling serious risks. Various statistics reveal, for example, that most families have at least some life insurance and some hospital-medical coverage. Estimates by the American Council of Life Insurance showed that two out of every three persons were insured by life insurance companies in 1980 and that over 80 percent of the adult population was covered by health insurance of some type.[1]

Requisites of Insurable Risk

Before you can fully understand insurance, you must examine the requirements for insurability. Most of the requirements flow from the law of large numbers, discussed above. For effective insurance coverage, all the objects should to a reasonable degree meet the conditions illustrated in Exhibit 4–5.

LARGE NUMBERS

The number of objects in the insured group should be large enough to enable the insurer to make good predictions as to the occurrence of losses. If the number is too small, losses may vary significantly from year to year—that is, the risk will be high. The objects should also be reasonably homo-

---

1. *1981 Life Insurance Fact Book* (Washington, D.C.: American Council of Life Insurance, 1981), p. 17; and *Source Book of Health Insurance Data, 1978-79* (Washington, D.C.: Health Insurance Institute, 1980), p. 7.

EXHIBIT 4–5
Requisites of
Insurable Risk

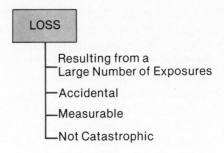

EXHIBIT 4–5
Requisites of
Insurable Risk

geneous in nature; otherwise the dollar amounts of loss claims may vary significantly. For example, an insurer will not consider private residences and commercial buildings as one homogeneous group to be rated as "buildings," because these two types of structures are subject to entirely different hazards.

ACCIDENTAL LOSSES

The insured loss should be accidental and unintentional. Loss should occur randomly; otherwise there would be no uncertainty and hence no risk to insure. For example, if losses are under the control of the insured, they would tend to occur whenever it was to the financial advantage of the insured to make a claim. Therefore, losses caused by a deliberate act of the insured, such as arson, are excluded from coverage. Likewise, if a person is sick, it is too late to purchase medical insurance for that sickness because there is no uncertainty about the loss. Thus, health insurance policies usually have a clause eliminating any claims that stem from some preexisting condition. If the insurers were to cover such claims, the premiums paid by all insureds would have to be much larger. This could be uneconomical for the insured, since the premiums might exceed the cost of paying directly for the loss.

MEASURABLE LOSSES

The insured loss should also be measurable. That is, the loss must be definite in regard to time and place. Insurance contracts usually are very specific about how losses will be determined and measured; otherwise it would be difficult to know just how much should be paid on the claim. One of the greatest difficulties in determining proper insurance rates is the difficulty in determining what losses will be. For example, in liability insurance the ultimate loss is often not determined until an extensive jury trial takes place several years later. It may also take a jury trial to determine the value of "pain and suffering," for which the insurer must respond. If you insure your car against physical damage, the insurer's loss adjustment process must determine the value of "comparable" vehicles to make an appropriate allowance for depreciation. If you have spent a great deal of money fixing up

"Some risks are just not insurable."

The Bettman Archive, Inc.

your car with special equipment or restoring an antique model car, you must make the insurer aware of the special values exposed to loss so that if loss occurs, the insurer will respond accordingly.

DIVERSIFICATION OF OBJECTS

The objects of insurance should not be subject to **simultaneous destruction**—that is, to a catastrophic loss. For example, if all the objects to be insured are contained in a single area, they may be subject to simultaneous loss by a peril such as fire or flood. The principles of insurance depend significantly on adequate diversification or dispersal of insured objects so that losses will occur randomly, as discussed above. Insurers know that fires may occur randomly, but they assume that not all the property covered by a given insurer will be destroyed by a single fire. Thus, insurers will limit underwriting so that not too many objects are unduly concentrated in a given area or are of a given type.

Requisites for the Insured

From your standpoint as a purchaser of insurance, certain requisites for insurability should also be observed. First, the potential loss must be high enough to warrant protection—that is, the loss must be "serious." Obviously, what is serious to one person may not be serious to another. A rich man might not purchase insurance on his automobile, but insurance might be advisable for a student whose only asset is a car; its destruction would mean financial hardship.

A second requisite is that the likelihood (probability) of loss must not be so high that the premium becomes prohibitive. If the probability of loss exceeds 50 percent, the insurer might charge a basic premium equal in the long run to the value of the insured property. The insurer does so to allow for losses and for **loading** (the cost of doing business). It would not be economical to "trade dollars" with an insurer under these circumstances. For every dollar you gave the insurer in premiums, you would expect in the long run to recover no more than a dollar in lost property—a fruitless exercise at best.

Insurance and Gambling

Is purchasing insurance a form of "betting" with an insurer? Actually, insurance is the opposite of gambling since under an insurance contract you are covering a risk that already exists; in gambling a new risk is created that did not exist before. The very act of gambling creates a risk, whereas insurance merely attempts to transfer an existing risk to someone else. Legally you must be able to demonstrate an **insurable interest** in the subject of the insurance— that is, you must show that you would suffer an economic loss if the insured item were destroyed. For example, you must demonstrate ownership of your car to collect for its loss through physical destruction or theft. Without this requirement you could take out an insurance policy on your neighbor's car and then hope for its sudden destruction. Again, if you were not required to demonstrate an insurable interest, nothing would prevent you from taking out several contracts on one piece of property and collecting in full from each of them when a loss occurred. Under these circumstances insurance would indeed be a gambling contract.

Indemnity

Under the principle of **indemnity,** you may be reimbursed for an amount not exceeding the actual cash value of the lost property. For example, if your five-year-old car is stolen, you will not be indemnified for a new model but only for a comparable car as revealed by reference to the current used-car market. In other words, depreciation will be considered in loss settlements unless the contract waives this provision by offering what is called **full replacement coverage.** The principle of indemnity does not apply to life insurance policies, which are called **valued policies**—that is, they pay off in case of death for the amount stated on the face of the policy.

TYPES OF INSURANCE

Insurance has been classified in many ways. A useful way to view the field is to divide contracts into two general classes: personal insurance and property-liability insurance. **Personal insurance** includes all contracts that have to do with your life and health—life insurance, annuities, retirement income policies, hospital-medical expense policies, disability income policies, and the like. **Property-liability insurance** includes all contracts written on your property or on your legal liability arising out of the use of property—for example, homeowner's contracts and automobile insurance.

Another way to classify insurance is to determine whether it is issued by private insurers or by government agencies. Data reveal that in the United States about half of all insurance is written by government agencies, and the other half is written by private insurers. Much government insurance is compulsory and serves various social objectives. It includes Social Security (old age, survivors, disability, and health insurance, or OASDHI), unemployment insurance, and workers' compensation insurance, which is written for occupational injuries. Most private insurance is voluntary and includes most types of personal and property-liability contracts.

TYPES OF INSURERS

Private insurance is written by two main types of insurers or carriers: stocks and mutuals. **Stocks** are corporations owned by stockholders who have purchased the stock to obtain a return or profit. **Mutuals** are corporations owned by the policyholders. A mutual insurer has no "profits" as such. Any excess earnings from underwriting insurance or from investments are added to surplus or distributed to the owners in the form of dividends proportional to the premiums paid by the policyholders. Because of the absence of a profit element, it would be logical to believe that insurance is cheaper when purchased from a mutual insurer instead of from a stock insurer. Most students of the subject, however, have detected little difference in price between the different legal forms of organization of the insurer. Factors such as management efficiency, underwriting skill, and investment gains are more significant in determining the ultimate price of insurance.

Insurers are frequently organized in groups, or fleets, under a single corporation, or **holding company**, which offers all types of insurance "under one roof." Actually, the holding company coordinates the activities of separate insurance corporations, each of which specializes in some line of coverage. For example, one of the largest U.S. stock groups, the Aetna Life and Casualty Insurance group, operates approximately ten separate insurers, each of which specializes in a given line or in a given territory. Separate subsidiaries are normally organized to write coverage in foreign countries.

At one time mutual insurers enjoyed predominance in the life and health insurance field, while stocks dominated property-liability insurance. However, it can no longer be said that one type of insurer dominates the other, though most of the very large life insurers tend to be mutuals. There are approximatley 1,800 life and health insurers and 2,900 property-liability insurers operating in the United States, although most insurance business is written by relatively few (approximately 100) companies.

REGULATION OF INSURERS

Insurance is regulated mainly at the state level by persons known as **insurance commissioners**. An important reason for insurance regulation is consumer protection. All aspects of insurer operations are regulated: pricing, agency practices, financial solvency matters, claims practices, and contract provisions. Although the federal government has some regulatory authority over insurers, mainly in the area of antitrust and fair business dealings, most immediate regulatory control is exercised by the state insurance commissioners. Most state insurance departments maintain divisions or sections to receive consumer complaints and to act on them. Most complaints concern insurer handling of claims and insurer pricing methods. Each insurer operating in a given state must be "admitted"—that is, the insurer must meet the state's legal requirements.

INSURANCE DISTRIBUTION METHODS

Insurers usually distribute policies through three main marketing channels. First, licensed agents and brokers, who are "independent" insofar as they are not owned by the insurer, may be authorized to represent an insurer in a specified territory. This system has been called the **independent agency system**, or **American agency system.** Second, insurers distribute policies through agents who are company employees and usually represent one insurer. This system has been called the **direct writing system**, or **exclusive agency system.** Prominent examples of insurers using this system are Allstate Insurance Company and State Farm Insurance Company. Third, insurers rely on direct contact with policyholders through the mails. Under this method offers to buy and sell insurance are conducted exclusively by mail or telephone, and no sales agents as such are employed. Consumer service is provided by company employees at home or in a regional office. Some insurers employ more than one channel of distribution.

Insurers who use independent agents believe this system best serves the overall interests of both the insurer and the consumer. One agent may represent several insurers and thus be able to offer a variety of packages of coverage and prices. Many independent agents are also **brokers**, legal representatives of the insurance buyer who contacts the insurance "market" (insurance companies) to find appropriate coverage on the buyer's behalf. It may be argued that this arrangement better serves the buyer's needs by providing more unbiased service, since the broker has no incentive to favor one insurer over another.

Direct writing companies, which have tended to specialize in auto and homeowner insurance, claim that they can offer insurance at lower cost because of lower commissions paid to their agents and the greater efficiency made possible by the mass processing of policies. Direct mail insurers make similar claims. Since they pay no commissions, their prices can be even lower than those of direct writers. However, direct mail insurers tend to specialize in one or two lines and usually have fairly strict underwriting requirements so that not everyone can take advantage of their special services and prices.

MANAGING INSURANCE PROGRAMS

From the viewpoint of the insurance consumer, insurance management involves several steps:

1. Deciding on the form of coverage;
2. Selecting agents, brokers, and insurers;
3. Negotiating for prices and coverage;

4. Analyzing ways to reduce insurance costs (including selecting insurance deductibles);
5. Seeing that terms of insurance contracts are complied with;
6. Handling loss settlements in negotiations with adjusters;
7. Designing and maintaining adequate records of coverage and other data necessary to collect for losses.

The following subsections show how to incorporate these steps into an effective program of insurance management.

Product, Price, and Service Comparisons

Not all insurers and agents are alike in the service, quality, or type of product they offer. Large variations exist, and you must establish a firm idea of your own requirements before attempting to manage an insurance program effectively. Perhaps the first principle of insurance buying is to make comparisons among insurers and agents to establish an idea of what constitutes the best combination of product and service available at a given time.

Second, you should realize that you can negotiate with insurers and agents. The insurance policy or services of the agent are not "set" and impervious to change. Many available endorsements and policy amendments can vary the terms of coverage to meet individual needs. Since prices vary considerably and are often subjectively determined, competitive bidding is advisable for most buyers, even small buyers.

Reducing Insurance Costs

Insurance costs can usually be reduced by several different methods. You should select the lowest costs compatible with considerations such as adequacy of coverage, safety of the insurer, and availability of the agency for service. The judicious selection of deductibles can be a great cost saver. A **deductible clause** eliminates from coverage small losses that are almost certain to occur and hence are very expensive to insure. The insurer grants a reduction in premium for your accepting the deductible, and this reduction increases as the size of the deductible rises. However, the rate of increase becomes less as the deductible grows larger; you must select a proper cutoff point. For example, increasing a deductible from $50 to $100 in automobile collision coverage may save you $25 a year. Increasing the deductible from $100 to $200 may save an additional $25. But the premium may be reduced perhaps only 5 percent or 10 percent for a deductible above $500. Your willingness and ability to bear losses up to $500 should be considered (see Exhibit 4–6).

Another way to reduce the cost of insurance is to use certain contract provisions or to accept certain conditions of coverage. For example, elimina-

EXHIBIT 4–6
Possible Savings
in Premium with
Larger
Deductibles

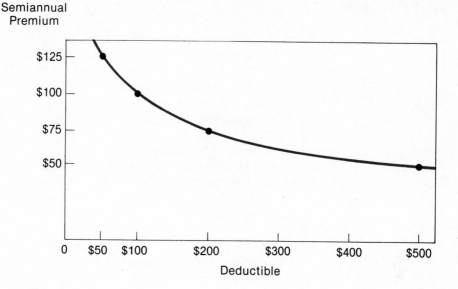

tion of unneeded coverages, such as towing and labor in auto insurance, will save substantial sums. In establishing the insurable value of a private house, the value of the land or the underground utilities need not count, since they will not be lost (or paid for) in the event that the house burns. These reductions in the face amount of the policy will reduce the premium.

Insurance costs can also be reduced by buying in quantity or by negotiating a contract to cover a period longer than one year. Automobile insurance premium reductions are often given under the heading of "fleet" discounts when you insure more than one car under a single policy; insuring as few as two or three automobiles can produce savings.

You can also utilize one type of policy for the first portion of a loss and another type of policy for losses in excess of the limits of the first policy. For example, liability insurance may be purchased in connection with the homeowners policy, and for excess coverage another liability policy, known as an **umbrella liability policy,** may be added.

Insurance costs can often be reduced by changing the type of property covered, if it is possible to make such changes before the insurance is purchased. For example, insurance rates are considerably lower on brick homes than on wooden homes, yet the costs of building a brick home may not vary substantially from the costs of building an entirely frame house. Obviously, such a decision must be made before the house is constructed. A similar situation applies to the purchase of an automobile. Most people purchase cars without considering the insurance costs, but a "souped-up" car will cost much more to insure than will a standard model. Practicing risk management by giving consideration to the insurance costs is one way to save money.

Cost Comparisons

There are at least three ways to compare costs of insurance policies: (1) direct comparison of the gross premiums, (2) comparison of the gross premium less any estimated dividends, and (3) comparison of operating efficiencies of the insurer. Since many mutual companies pay dividends and stock companies generally do not, you must consider dividends in many cost comparisons. An **insurance dividend** is a partial return of premium and is not considered taxable income in the manner that a dividend on capital stock would be. Dividends in insurance are usually estimated, not guaranteed. Dividends can be estimated from past records of the insurers offering them. Dividends are particularly common in the life insurance field, where they may amount to as much as 20 percent of the gross premium. Dividends are declared annually and may be received in cash or used to purchase additional coverage.

Dividends frequently reflect the operating efficiency of the insurer. The greater the operating efficiency, the higher the dividend, and hence the lower the ultimate cost of the insurance.

The operating efficiency of property-liability insurers may be determined by a comparison of losses and expenses. Insurers usually try to keep losses low by careful selection of the subjects they insure. Insurers may trim expenses by selling directly to customers without paying commissions to agents. If you qualify, you can often reduce insurance costs by dealing directly with insurers whose strict standards you must satisfy before you are accepted for coverage (e.g., you may have to be a nonsmoker). Dealing with "direct writing" insurers, which avoids or reduces selling costs, may result in savings.

Insurers also may keep losses and expenses low by thorough training of agents, careful loss adjusting, and computerized office management. These measures ultimately benefit policyholders by providing insurance at the least possible cost consistent with adequate coverage and service.

Financial Solvency and Stability

It does not do you much good to purchase insurance coverage if the insurer becomes insolvent and unable to pay any claims. Hence, you should consider the financial stability of the insurer. It is often assumed that state regulation of the insurance industry guarantees the financial solvency of the insurer. Unfortunately, this assumption is not always justified; data show continual insolvencies and bankruptcies that result in losses to policyholders. Fortunately, some of these losses have been met by funds known as **guarantee insolvency funds,** which are set up in most states for consumer protection purposes.

A gauge of the financial stability and solvency of an insurer may be obtained from the financial rating provided by the insurance service called *Best's*

Reports. Each insurer is rated as excellent (A or A +), very good (B +), fairly good (C +), or fair (C). Most analysts recommend avoiding insurers with a C or C + rating. If an insurer is not rated, this means that data are not adequate or that the company is too new for full analysis. You should be careful about assigning business to nonrated insurers.

What to Expect from Agents

Most buyers deal through agents, who receive a commission that varies from 10 to 20 percent or more of the premium, depending on the line of coverage. In purchasing property-liability insurance, you are entitled to the following services from your agent: (1) analysis of your exposures to loss, (2) engineering analysis of hazards you face, (3) advice on which risks to assume and which to insure, (4) recommendations on the amount and type of insurance for each peril, (5) forms tailored to meet your particular needs, (6) selection of the best insurer at the lowest price, including an analysis of insurer solvency, (7) continuous consultation and analysis of loss-prevention activities that might qualify you for lower rates, and (8) assistance in obtaining fair claim adjustments in case of loss.

Life insurance commissions may reach 100 percent or more of the first year's premium. Agents are expected to earn these commissions by tasks such as the following: (1) analyzing the customer's needs for coverage, (2) recommending and explaining different policies, (3) coordinating the customer's life insurance policies with each other and with other resources such as Social Security and employer-paid pensions, and (4) helping the beneficiary obtain a proper settlement in case of death of the insured.

Price Comparisons in Life Insurance

Some problems related to selecting life insurers should receive particular attention. Many life insurance contracts are **participating**—that is, they offer dividends to the policyholder. Dividends can vary greatly, and you should carefully estimate their probable size. A special problem in comparing life insurance contracts stems from the fact that many contracts are purchased with various kinds of **riders,** or amendments, that cause coverages of losses to differ. When making a price comparison, you should be certain that the two policies contain the same coverage.

Dividends

Participating life insurance contracts contain provisions for paying dividends to the policyholders (though the dividends are not guaranteed). The

"I can get you a cheaper rate on your policy if you can just stand up."

dividends are based on the insurer's experience with three basic factors: the mortality rates, the interest earned, and the overhead, or loading. Dividends will be larger as mortality rates decrease, interest earnings rise, and loading charges decline. Some life insurers cater to special classes of persons expected to have lower mortality rates; these insurers may also have higher interest earnings or lower expenses and therefore will tend to offer life insurance at lower rates. Some insurers offer more efficient distribution systems, less agency service, or both as a way of reducing the cost of their contracts. You must consider each of the three determinants of cost to select those life insurers whose product will cost least.

Exhibit 4–7 provides an estimate of the premiums and dividends of ten major life insurers in the United States from 1960 to 1980. The gross premium minus the dividend and the final cash value is the so-called net cost to the consumer. In the exhibit, the net cost is expressed in dollars per thousand of face amount of the contract. Net costs as originally projected vary from a – $34.94 to a + $.15 per thousand dollars per year. In regard to actual net costs, the ranks of the companies tended to change somewhat. In the period from 1960 to 1980, however, the actual net cost was generally lower than the projected net cost.

The data in Exhibit 4–7 may lead you to believe that life insurance has been provided at little or no net cost. However, such an assumption ignores the interest element on advanced payments made for life insurance. Insurance cannot be provided free, as the traditional net cost method of comparing life insurers might suggest. The negative net cost figures result from the fact that

EXHIBIT 4–7   Projected and Actual Dividends and Costs of Insurance per $1,000 Coverage, 1960–1980

Insurer	20-Year Premiums	20th-Year Cash Value	Projected			Actual		
			20-Year Dividends	Net Cost	Net Cost Rank	20-Year Dividends	Net Cost	Net Cost Rank
State Farm	$480.80	$381.75	$ 98.90	$ .15	10	$169.67	$(70.62)	1
Massachusetts Mutual	475.00	362.44	125.85	(13.29)	7	163.09	(70.53)	2
Central Life, Iowa	470.60	362.44	132.02	(23.86)	3	176.67	(68.51)	3
Lutheran Mutual	467.40	363.75	138.59	(34.94)	1	170.65	(67.00)	4
Mutual of New York	475.80	388.00	100.52	(12.72)	8	148.14	(64.34)	5
National Life, Vermont	477.40	370.00	124.08	(16.68)	5	151.03	(63.41)	6
John Hancock	471.80	380.83	107.17	(16.20)	6	153.25	(62.28)	7
Standard Insurance	497.40	372.00	132.89	(7.49)	9	187.67	(62.27)	8
Union Mutual	473.60	363.00	139.33	(28.73)	2	172.68	(62.08)	9
Connecticut Mutual	477.80	370.83	126.61	(19.64)	4	167.83	(60.86)	10
Average	476.76	371.50	122.60	(17.34)	·	166.07	(65.19)	
Ratio: Average Dividends/Average Premiums			.26			.35		

Note: Based on ordinary whole life policy for a male aged 35.
Net cost = 20-year premium minus 20th-year cash value minus 20-year dividends.
Projected net cost ranking refers to rank among these ten companies; actual net cost rank refers to rank of these companies in a survey of 71 leading life insurers.

Source: *Best's Review, Life Edition* (February, 1981), pp. 54–61.

the insurance companies do not reflect interest earnings on these funds in their comparisons. For example, assume you can earn 10 percent interest on money that you save. If you pay $100 for life insurance, you are giving up $10 a year that you would otherwise earn. Assume that the insurer earns the $10 instead, and that the cost of providing insurance is $5 a year. At the end of the year the insurer is in a position to return $105 to you. You have enjoyed insurance protection, and you get back $5 more than you paid. Does this mean that your protection has been "free"? No, because you have, in effect, received a reduced interest rate (5 percent instead of 10 percent), and your "real" cost of insurance has accounted for the difference.

Differences in "cost" that reflect the interest factor are recognized in what is termed the **interest-adjusted cost** of life insurance. Using interest-adjusted cost as a measure often produces rankings different from those in Exhibit 4–7. Most people do not realize how greatly life insurance costs can vary.

INSURANCE AND SAVINGS

The relationship of insurance to personal savings is significant. In many ways insurance can be viewed as a supplement to, and in part as a substitute for, savings. Instead of setting aside money to meet an unknown contingency, you buy insurance. Thus, insurance is in a sense a substitute for the savings fund insofar as the fund was designed to meet a given contingency. The advantage of insurance over a savings fund in meeting contingencies is twofold: First, full protection is afforded from the time insurance is purchased; under the savings method you must accumulate a fund before adequate protection exists. Second, in the event that two losses occur consecutively, insurance protection still exists; with the savings method the fund might be exhausted after the first loss, and you would be unprotected against subsequent loss.

The insurance method may be not only more efficient and secure but also less expensive. Consider the typical savings objective of accumulating funds for a "rainy day." Many financial advisers believe that three, four, or even six months' salary is necessary for the proverbial rainy day. The practical difficulties of accumulating such an amount were explored in Chapter 1. It may be helpful to examine precisely what a "rainy day" implies. If you are referring, for example, to the fact that you may be ill and unable to earn a salary during a given time period, insurance is a more economical alternative than attempting to accumulate a savings fund. On the other hand, a savings fund for various other emergencies is still a good idea. You must plan on insuring yourself against specified contingencies and saving for other types of emergencies for which insurance is not appropriate.

COMMON ERRORS IN PERSONAL RISK MANAGEMENT

Some of the most common errors in personal risk management are covered in the following subsections.

Failure to Recognize Exposure to Loss

Most planners do not systematically approach the problem of finding areas in which they are exposed to loss and making plans to meet such risks. People tend naturally to look at the positive side of things and not to consider what could go wrong. They tend to think, "It cannot happen to me." Frequently an individual will purchase insurance against some contingency only after a neighbor or close friend has suffered a loss.

Underinsurance

Insurance buyers frequently fail to purchase enough coverage or allow insured limits to remain unchanged, even though the value of the object exposed to loss may have greatly increased. For example, a home may have increased in value two or three times since the original insurance was placed and a fire or other loss would find the individual seriously underinsured. A person who is underinsured is inadvertently assuming risk, when the risk could be much more economically transferred to an insurer. In another example, national surveys reveal that most people fail to carry enough liability insurance. Yet liability loss is one of the most serious losses.

Errors in Insurance Coverage

Common examples of insurance coverage errors are failure to consider the economy of using deductibles and purchasing two policies on the same risk when it is impossible to collect from both policies. Another coverage error is to arrange insurance for a nonserious loss but leave a serious risk of loss uncovered—for example, a buyer may purchase collision insurance on an old car but ignore the liability risk, purchasing only minimum limits of bodily injury coverage when for only a slightly higher premium much more adequate bodily injury coverage could be purchased.

Organizational Errors

People commonly employ several insurance agents for a program of insurance protection. Such a procedure is probably not in the insured's best interest, because no one agent has an overall view of the needs and resources of the insured. Giving all one's insurance business to one or two agents gives each agent a financial incentive to do a good job. Purchasing coverage from several agents greatly increases the probability of duplication of coverage or gaps in coverage.

Many people also fail to understand what service to expect from the agent. They may believe that the agent will obtain "necessary" coverage, but no list of risks is ever actually drawn up and agreed upon. It is wise to have such an understanding in writing—for example, a letter from the agent outlining services and procedures.

Failure to Review Risk Management Programs

The task of handling risk is a continuous one and requires frequent review. Many people tend to install an insurance program and leave it undisturbed for many years. They use the same agents and insurers and renew the same coverage regardless of whether lower prices or better coverage is available elsewhere.

Failure to Consider Loss Control

Large savings in insurance premiums are frequently possible by adopting loss-prevention methods or by reducing hazards among groups of insured objects. For example, in many automobile rating systems even a single accident will increase your insurance premium substantially and may result in cancellation. You thus pay for the accident not only initially but many times through higher insurance premiums. More careful attention to safe driving could pay large dividends.

SUMMARY

1. Risk management, an improved way to recognize and handle risks, has several advantages over more traditional methods. These advantages include possibly significant savings on insurance, coverage of risks that cannot economically be handled by insurance, consideration of all important risks, reduction of losses, and avoidance of common errors in personal risk handling.
2. Basic concepts in risk management include risk, risk aversion, probability, the law of large numbers, perils, hazards, and insurance. Insurance is the most widely used tool of risk management. Basic elements of

insurance include requisites of insurable risks, insurable interest, and the principle of indemnity.

3. Insurance regulations provide the consumer with some measure of protection. Insurance commissioners in each state supervise pricing, contract terms, methods of distribution, and the financial solvency of insurers.

4. The steps in managing an insurance program successfully include making valid comparisons of insurance products and their prices, analyzing elements of insurer cost and efficiency, studying financial ratings of insurers, and dealing with insurance agents and brokers.

5. You should use insurance as a supplement to, and to some extent as a substitute for, savings. Proper use of insurance can reduce the need for saving for certain contingencies and thus release funds for other uses.

6. Many common errors in personal risk management can be avoided by following the suggestions made in this chapter. Among the errors are failure to shop for insurance, failure to approach risk management systematically, underinsurance, overinsurance, failure to consider proper use of deductibles, failure to use methods of loss control, and failure to evaluate the risk management program on a regular basis.

REVIEW QUESTIONS

1. Contrast the traditional approach to managing personal risk with the risk management approach. Which is the broader concept? Why?

2. How can the various ways of handling risk be illustrated in the question of how to handle the risk of owning a home? In your answer, identify what you believe to be the major risks of home ownership. (See Exhibit 4–1.)

3. How does probability differ from the following concepts:
   (a) risk;
   (b) hazards;
   (c) perils.

4. Why does risk tend to decrease as the number of objects exposed to loss increases?

5. Explain the basic requisites of insurable risk.

6. A writer states: "The price—the premium—you pay for automobile insurance is based mainly on the number of dollars spent by insurance companies to pay claims resulting from automobile accidents. The more accidents you and your friends have, the higher the cost of claims and the higher the cost of your insurance."
   (a) Which method of handling risk does the above statement illustrate?
   (b) On what other factors besides claims are auto insurance prices based?
   (c) What do you believe might be the significance of the reference to "your friends" in the last sentence of the quotation?

7. An insurance company brochure states: "The only sure way to establish the amount of insurance needed on a dwelling that is not newly constructed is to have a local appraiser or contractor make an appraisal of the property. The value of the land should be disregarded when estimating the value for insurance purposes."
   (a) How does the above statement illustrate the steps in risk management? (See Exhibit 4–1.)
   (b) Why should the value of the land be disregarded in setting the amount of insurance?

8. An insurer offering homeowners insurance advises: "Premium credits are allowed in many states if the dwelling is protected by an approved burglar alarm, fire alarm, or sprinkler system. Currently our dividend is 35 percent, payable at the end of the policy year for homeowners and tenants."
   (a) What method of risk management is being illustrated in this statement?
   (b) Is the type of dividend referred to the same as one that might be promised on a share of common stock?
   (c) Would insurance dividends constitute taxable income to the policyholder? Why or why not?

9. An informational guide for consumers purchasing auto insurance, published by the state insurance division of Connecticut, states in part: "It is best to contact several agents or companies for quotations. Differences in rates can be due to competition between companies, different classification systems, and variations in different companies' loss experience. Rates must be filed with the Department, but are not subject to approval before they are used. Some of the most important facts affecting rates are territory, age, sex, marital status, amount of driving experience, and car usage (business or pleasure). Most companies use safe-driver plans, giving discounts for the absence of traffic accidents and violations. Discounts may be available for multiple-car ownership, driver training, good student credits, having a compact car, improved bumpers, and driving in carpools."
   (a) For financial planners approaching risk from a risk management standpoint, list ways suggested by this statement to reduce the cost of handling auto ownership risk.
   (b) Which methods of risk management are recognized in the insurance division's statement?

10. A writer states: "A broker also sells insurance. Generally a broker does not represent an insurance company and therefore cannot make a commitment on behalf of any company." Criticize this statement. Does it tell the whole truth?

11. An article states: "Today, spurred by inflation and a widespread tendency of jurors to err on the side of injured plaintiffs, jury awards of several hundred thousand dollars in liability cases excite little comment. Fifteen years ago there was only one liability verdict of $1 million or over a year, but by 1977 juries were handing out such verdicts on the average of once a week."
   (a) Utilizing Exhibit 4–1, suggest a method of handling the risk described in the article.
   (b) Why would assumption, or self-insurance, not be feasible in view of the facts stated in the article?

12. The life insurer quotes the "net cost" of life insurance (ordinary life plan for a male, age 25) as follows:

20-year premium	$400
Less cash value, end of 20 years	(300)
Less sum of 20 years dividends	(110)
Net cost	$ (10)

The agent explains that since the policyholder gets back more money ($10) than was paid in, the life insurance protection for twenty years actually costs nothing.
(a) Criticize the agent's conclusions.
(b) What alternative method is available to measure the cost of life insurance?
(c) Which method is best?

13. Is insurance a substitute for savings? Why or why not?

14. Identify each of the common errors in risk management discussed in the text. Why are they "errors"?

15. A study comparing personal security expenditures in the United States over the period 1960 to 1978 concluded that for each $10 in income, expenditures for financial security (mainly private insurance and Social Security) totaled $1.12 in 1978 and $.85 in 1960—an increase of 32 percent.
(a) Do these figures support the conclusion that risk aversion is increasing in the United States?
(b) What other factors might have accounted for part of the increase?

16. Do you view yourself as risk-averse? Give examples of some recent financial activity that (a) supports your conclusion. (b) does not support it. (If you don't know whether you are a risk-taker or a risk-averter, take the quiz in Exhibit 4–3.)

CASE PROBLEMS

I. Dirty Tricks

The Pennsylvania insurance commissioner published and distributed a consumer bulletin titled "How to Spot Insurance Rip-offs: Thirty Dirty Tricks Forbidden by Pennsylvania Law." The bulletin stated: "If you can't get the answer or the help you need from your insurance company or agent, contact the nearest office of the Pennsylvania Insurance Department for free professional help." Among the "thirty dirty tricks" listed in the bulletin were the following:

1. Misrepresenting the dividends to be received on any insurance policy or misrepresenting the dividends previously paid on policies;
2. Misrepresenting an insurance policy as shares of stock;

3. Making misleading statements encouraging policyholders to lapse, give up, or exchange a policy;

4. Promising or paying rebates or special considerations not specified in the contract to encourage a customer to buy an insurance policy;

5. Failing to acknowledge or act promptly on written or oral communication relating to claims;

6. Not attempting in good faith to provide prompt, fair, and equitable settlement of claims in which the company's liability has become reasonably clear;

7. Forcing policyholders to go to court to recover amounts due under an insurance policy by offering substantially less than the amounts due and eventually recovered by lawsuits;

8. Attempting to settle a claim for less than the amount to which a reasonable person would have believed he or she was entitled on the basis of advertising material accompanying an application;

9. Canceling or refusing to renew a policy (if it has been in force at least sixty days) without good reason or without informing the policyholder of the specific reason.

QUESTIONS

1. For each of the above, indicate why, from the viewpoint of the policyholder, the particular practice might be damaging or unfair. Also, indicate from your personal experience to what extent insurers engage in the practice.

2. How do the "dirty tricks" listed above illustrate the need for the regulation of insurance companies and agents?

II. Insurance Tips

The Wall Street Journal contained the following report:

Insurance Tips

Accountants at the firm of Deloitte Haskins & Sells have drawn up a list of insurance tips for their executive clients. Here are the suggestions:

1) Avoid flight insurance. Life-insurance coverage can be purchased most efficiently as part of a well-thought-out plan. That makes flight insurance—which is "very expensive," the accountants say—unnecessary.

2) When you rent a car, consider *not* accepting the rental company's offer to waive its claim on you for any collision damage under the $300 or so deductible. The collision-damage waiver will cost you $2 or so a day. Especially if your own personal automobile insurance has a low deductible, the accountants say, you should forgo the waiver and keep your $2. "Many (personal automobile) policies," the accountants say, "will pay the difference between the rental deductible and the deductible on your own policy."

3) Mortgage and other loan insurance, taken out to pay the balance of a loan if the borrower dies, often costs more than con-

ventional decreasing-term life insurance. For one thing, you are often buying the loan insurance with borrowed money, and paying interest on it. Consider conventional term insurance instead.

4) Credit-property insurance, to cover any loss on property you have bought on credit, may merely unnecessarily duplicate coverage in your homeowner's insurance policy.

5) Cancer insurance usually covers in-hospital costs only, although many cancer patients incur large, uncovered costs outside a hospital. Moreover, other medical in-

surance may already cover most of the in-hospital costs that cancer insurance aims to protect you against.

6) To buy hospital-indemnity insur-ance—providing fixed daily payments while you are in the hospital—may not be such a good idea for the Medicare patients to whom such insurance is often sold. For one thing, Medicare does pay the first 60 days in the hospital, after a small deductible. For another, the additional coverage you can purchase through Medicare is usually less expensive than hospital insurance.

Source: Reprinted by permission of *The Wall Street Journal* (October 22, 1979), p. 48. © Dow Jones & Company, Inc. (1979). All rights reserved.

QUESTION

1. Do the suggestions above conform to sound principles of risk management? Why or why not?

III. The Cost of Life Insurance

A comparison of life insurance costs in 1981 for selected insurers revealed the following facts about the cost of an ordinary life policy of $10,000 for a male aged 25, which is held ten years.

Insurer	Ten Premiums	Total Dividends	Cash Value	Net Cost	Interest-Adjusted Payments Index
Acacia Mutual	$131.40	$11.82	$88.00	$31.58	$12.11
Bankers Life of Iowa	103.80	20.16	80.00	3.64	8.60
John Hancock Mutual	125.21	25.69 7.21[a]	101.00	7.21	10.16
State Farm Life	159.00	37.24 4.45[a]	88.98	28.33	12.56

[a]Termination dividend.
Note: Net cost equals premiums minus dividends minus cash value.

The interest-adjusted payments index is based on the 5 percent interest-adjusted method. Under this method annual premiums and dividends are accumulated at 5 percent interest. Accumulations are then subtracted from accumulated premiums and the result divided by the accumulation of $1 a year for ten years at 5 percent ($13.207). Similar procedures are followed for other periods.

Source: *1981 Best's Flitcraft Compend* (Oldwick, N.J.: A.M. Best Co., 1981).

QUESTIONS

1. Which method of comparing life insurance costs is most valid: comparing gross premiums, net cost, or interest-adjusted payments index costs?

2. Which insurer offered the lowest cost?

CHAPTER 5

LIFE AND HEALTH INSURANCE

LEARNING OBJECTIVES

In studying this chapter, you will learn:

Why you should understand life and health insurance;

The differences between the major types of life and health insurance;

How to decide how much life insurance you should purchase;

The meaning of major clauses and endorsements in life and health insurance policies;

How to analyze the "buy term and invest the difference" argument;

How to compare life insurance costs;

Some guides to buying life and health insurance;

The advantages of buying life and health insurance under group plans rather than individual plans.

Personal financial security requires advance planning for catastrophes that can cause loss of life or of health. Premature death can cause great hardship to one's dependents if planning has not been done or if insurance or other risk management devices are not a part of the plan. Loss of health may necessitate large outlays for medical expenses as well as deprive the family of part or all of its income. Such losses may well exceed those caused by premature death.

This chapter analyzes ways in which you can provide, through private insurance, for possible losses resulting from premature death, sickness, or accident. (Social insurance is discussed in Chapter 7.) We will examine the major types and uses of life and health insurance, how life insurance is treated under various tax rules, how to understand the major provisions of the insurance contracts, how much and what types of insurance to buy, investment aspects of life insurance, and how to obtain the advantages of group insurance coverage.

PROBABILITY OF LOSS

What is the probability of losing one's life at any given time? Mortality tables used by life insurance companies provide the basis on which aggregate estimates are made. Mortality tables are based on death statistics of large segments of the population during specified time periods. For example, the table in general use in the United States, called the Commissioners Standard Ordinary (CSO) Table, is based on deaths recorded by insurers during the years 1950 to 1954 (see Exhibit 5–1). Note that the probability of death, quite small at young ages, rises rapidly with age; the likelihood of death at age 50 is nearly five times that at age 20. The mortality table extends to age 100. As may be expected, life insurance premiums rise rapidly with age, corresponding to rising death rates. The cost of life insurance is considered prohibitive for most buyers after age 65. Since women outlive men by an average of about seven years, life insurance rates are generally lower for women than for men at the same age.

Life expectancies have been rising in the United States because of better living conditions and better health care. For example, the life expectancy at birth of a white male in 1900 was only 48.2 years, compared with about 70 years in 1976. The greater likelihood that a young person will live to an old age enhances the need for financial planning to provide support during the retirement years. Death rates in 1977 were less than half the death rates in 1915. Life insurance premiums have also decreased to reflect this fact.

EXHIBIT 5-1
Probability of
Death at Various
Ages

Age	Number of Deaths per 1,000	Expectation of Life (in years)
20	1.79	50.37
25	1.93	45.82
30	2.13	41.25
50	8.32	23.63
65	31.75	12.90
75	73.37	7.81

Source: Commissioners Standard Ordinary Table, 1958, *1981 Fact Book of Life Insurance* (Washington, D.C.: American Council of Life Insurance, 1981), pp. 108–109. This source also provides information of other mortality tables in use.

Much of the improvement in life expectancy has been due to medical advances in controlling diseases of the young. Less improvement is due to progress in curing diseases of the old. About 70 percent of all deaths in the United States result from heart disease and cancer. Accidents, while much publicized in newspapers and other media, actually cause only about 6 percent of all deaths.

Losses from Ill Health

Financial loss resulting from health problems can be divided into two general categories: payment for medical care and the loss of income during illness. Both types of losses are very serious. Estimates placed the cost of medical care expenditures in the United States in 1977 at about $163 billion, and the loss of income from illness at about $81 billion; together, these losses accounted for about 16 percent of national income. Furthermore, health care costs have been rising faster than other living costs.

Leading risks to good health are heart conditions, arthritis, back impairments, hypertension, visual impairments, and musculoskeletal disorders. Like death rates, the diseases that cause most loss of health are associated with higher age levels. Accidents produce 22 percent of the conditions that become severely disabling. Most accidents occur either on the job or in a moving vehicle. Women are more likely than men to report chronic illness, but men have more accidents than women.

One out of six individuals between the ages of twenty and sixty-four has been disabled for three months or longer. In a 1972 survey of 106 million people, nearly half reported chronic conditions or impairments that were not actually disabling but had the potential of becoming so. At the time of the 1972 survey, an average of 7 percent of the adults surveyed were so severely disabled that they could not work regularly.

"Most accidents occur on the job."

The Bettman Archive, Inc.

Losses due to poor health or premature death are ideal objects of insurance because relatively small numbers of people suffer these losses at any one time. Since such losses are often severe when they do occur, individuals usually cannot pay health care expenses without some outside help or without insurance. Health care costs can be shared by many individuals through insurance so that no unsupportable burden falls on any single person or group.

LIFE INSURANCE

Life insurance is a method of creating a fund or an income for the protection of your dependents or for other beneficiaries in case of your premature death. It operates by employing the **principle of loss spreading** to meet a risk or contingency one cannot usually predict or afford. It is put into effect by a legal contract arranged so that all members of a group pay a small amount (a **premium**) in return for a promise that a much larger sum (the **face amount**) will, when they die, be paid to their beneficiaries.

Types of Life Insurance Policies

There are three basic types of life insurance contracts: term, whole life, and endowment. The three types of contracts can be combined in different ways and with different endorsements to form innumerable other plans of life insurance. They all pay the beneficiary the face amount stated on the policy (usually in $1,000 units) if the insured's death occurs while the contract is in force. The proceeds can be paid in a lump sum or in installments. Proceeds are free of federal income taxes since they are considered compensation for a loss.

TERM LIFE INSURANCE

Term life insurance is designed solely for death protection and provides no cash values or savings element. It generally covers limited periods and does not extend for the entire life of the insured. The need for protection is considered "temporary." Typical contracts offer coverage for one, five, ten, or twenty years, although "term-to-age-65" is not uncommon. At the end of the time period, the policy is usually renewable for another, similar period without medical examination or other evidence of insurability. The premium on renewal is always higher because the insured is older (see Exhibit 5–2).

The amount of death protection may be "level" with an unchanging face amount of protection during the term of the policy, or the amount may be decreasing steadily. The premium payable, however, is even throughout the term of the policy. Such policies are commonly called **decreasing term policies.** They are often issued to provide coverage for declining balances of home mortgages, so that if an insured homeowner dies, there is just enough life insurance to pay off the mortgage balance. Another use of decreasing term policies is in connection with family income policies, discussed later in this chapter. Term life insurance is the least expensive of all forms of life insurance because it provides no allowance for a savings element.

WHOLE LIFE INSURANCE

As the name suggests, **whole life insurance** includes contracts providing coverage over the entire life of the insured. The protection need is "permanent"; the policies are designed for costs such as funeral expenses or taxes, where payments must be made regardless of the date of death. All whole life

EXHIBIT 5–2
How Premiums
Change with
Age (Yearly
Renewable Term
Life Insurance)

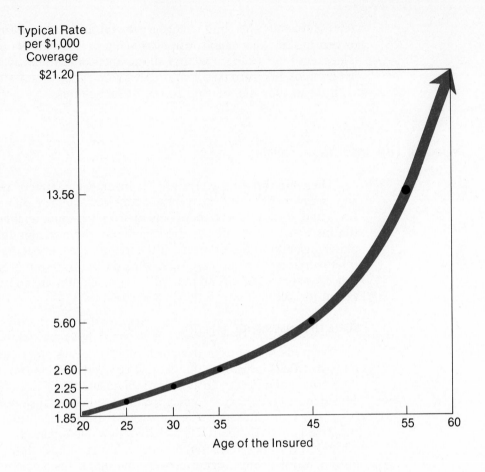

Typical Rate
per $1,000
Coverage

Age of the Insured

policies contain a savings element—that is, the policy accumulates a cash value that increases with the length of time the policy is held. On the death of the insured, the face amount of the policy is paid to the beneficiaries. The premium is higher for whole life insurance than for term and is level in amount.

The most common form of whole life insurance is **ordinary life,** in which the savings element is relatively small at first but eventually builds to the full face amount of the policy at maturity (i.e., at insured's age 100). Premiums are set so that they continue for the entire life of the insured. Other forms of whole life insurance, which are discussed later in this chapter, are "life-paid-up-at-65," 20-payment life, 30-payment life, and "single-premium life" (i.e., the insured makes a single premium payment and no further premiums are due; coverage continues indefinitely for the face amount of the contract.)

The cash value of a whole life policy may be borrowed, and the loan does not have to be repaid. In case of the insured's death, the insurer deducts any policy loan, plus accumulated interest, from the death proceeds of the policy.

Whole life thus may be viewed as a long-term savings vehicle as well as a source of insurance protection. As shown in Exhibit 5–3, for example, the insured has accumulated savings of $577 by age sixty-five in a $1,000 ordinary life policy issued at age twenty.

EXHIBIT 5–3

Structure of Whole Life Insurance (Ordinary Life Issued to a 20-Year-Old Male, Annual Premium $11.32)

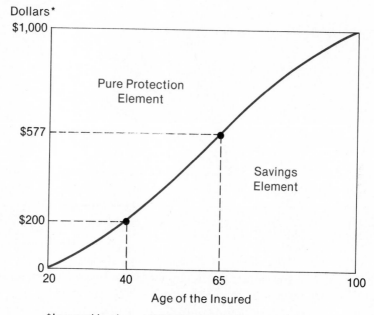

*Insured is also entitled to dividends.

ENDOWMENT LIFE INSURANCE

Endowment life insurance is a combination of savings and insurance—essentially an insured savings plan. If you die before the endowment period has expired, the face amount of the policy is payable to your beneficiary. Thus, if you fail to live long enough to complete your savings goal, the insurer completes it for you. The premium is relatively high, intended mainly for the savings element. The amount of pure insurance is relatively low and diminishes rapidly over the life of the policy. Exhibit 5–4 compares the savings element of term-to-65, ordinary life, 20-payment life, and 20-year endowment. Note that, if you die, the insurer pays the face amount in all three cases to your beneficiary; if you live, the insurer returns the savings element to you in the proportions shown. The 20-year endowment, which matures for its face value ($1,000) in twenty years, has the greatest savings element, whereas term-to-65 has no savings element. The other policies fall between these two extremes.

EXHIBIT 5–4

Comparison of
Savings Elements
in Life Insurance

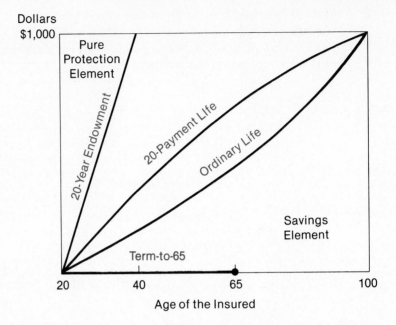

Exhibit 5–5 shows that the essential differences among life insurance forms relate to the degree of savings element present and to the period of years over which the pure protection element exists. Premium rates depend on these factors as well as on the age and health of the applicant.

PACKAGE LIFE INSURANCE POLICIES

Package life insurance contracts are combinations of basic types of life insurance to meet specialized needs. A common example is the **family income policy,** a combination of decreasing term insurance and ordinary (whole life) insurance. As the name suggests, the policy is designed to provide a large amount of protection when children are young and to replace the family income lost through the death of the insured. The contract is issued in two parts—a base policy, usually whole life insurance, and a supplemental contract known as a decreasing term rider. (A **rider** is a written amendment changing the terms of coverage or the price of a policy.) The decreasing term rider is commonly expressed as so many units of income at $10 a unit. Thus, the policy might contain $10,000 basic whole life coverage together with 10 units of decreasing term insurance, which would provide $100 a month to the beneficiary for a specified period of years (frequently twenty years). If the insured had purchased $100,000 worth of insurance with 100 units of decreasing term insurance and had died almost immediately, the widow or other beneficiary would receive $1,000 a month (100 units × $10) for twenty years, and at the end of this period, $100,000, either in cash or in installments. If the insured

EXHIBIT 5–5   Features of Basic Types of Life Insurance

Term insurance:	Issued for a specified term, such as 5 or 10 years, or until age 65. Has no savings element, no cash or loan values. Lowest gross premium of the three. Protection is generally unavailable after advanced ages (above 65) except at very high premiums. Suitable for "temporary" protection.
Whole life insurance:	Can remain in force for life or as long as the insured desires. Has a savings feature with cash values that build up over time. Premium is considerably higher than term contracts because of the savings element. Premium usually remains level throughout the insured's life. Suitable for long-term needs, including needs that exist at older ages. Frequently called "permanent" insurance.
Endowment insurance:	Essentially a savings plan combined with a pure protection element. Premiums are the highest among the three types. Contract is generally written for a limited term, such as 10 or 20 years, or until the insured reaches a specific age, such as 65. Policy matures for its face value at the end of the term. Used frequently for savings plans for specific purposes, such as meeting children's college expenses.

died after five years, the income would be paid for the remaining fifteen years of the twenty-year period, followed by the $100,000 payment. After such a policy has been in force fifteen years, the term rider has only five years left to run; it expires at the end of twenty years with no cash value. However, the insured may retain the $100,000 base policy as long as desired.

An advantage of a family income policy is that it provides a large amount of pure protection for the family at a relatively modest cost, since term insurance is much cheaper than whole life insurance. Yet the insured may also choose to keep the base policy and enjoy life insurance protection in retirement years.

Another popular package policy is known as a **modified life policy.** Premiums are arranged so that they are smaller than average for the first five or ten years of the contract and are larger for the remaining years of the contract. Premiums are set by combining term insurance with the whole life policy so that the insured pays more than the cost of pure term at the issue age but less than the cost of whole life insurance.

Another commonly used package is the **family group policy,** in which each member of the family is insured for a different amount. The head of the family normally obtains the most coverage, and insurance on the spouse and children is limited to a smaller amount. For example, if the owner of the policy is covered for $100,000, the spouse and children may each have $20,000 coverage. The plan may be on either a term or a whole life basis, but coverage on family members is usually term insurance that can be converted to permanent insurance.

Premium Payment Plans

Life insurance may be purchased annually in level (equal) payments or as a single premium. Level payments are the most common. When whole life insurance is arranged so that premium payments are due throughout the life of the insured, it is called ordinary life insurance. However, whole life insurance may be arranged so that the contract is "paid up" in ten or twenty years or at some given age, such as "paid-up-at-65." These are called **limited payment whole life policies.** If you purchase 20-payment life, for example, no further premiums are due after twenty years, but the full face amount of the policy remains in force until your death or until you surrender the contract for its cash value.

Endorsements

Life insurance policies may be written with several different kinds of **endorsements,** which extend the coverage or change the amount of coverage of the basic policy. An example is the **waiver-of-premium rider.** This rider states that if you are permanently or totally disabled, no further premiums need be paid on the basic contract; yet the amount of coverage under the basic policy, including any buildup of cash values, remains undisturbed.

The **disability income rider** carries the waiver-of-premium idea a step further. If you become totally and permanently disabled, a monthly indemnity of $5 or $10 is paid for each $1,000 face amount of insurance in effect. The disability income becomes effective after a four-to-six-months' waiting period. A common requirement is that disability must occur before some stated age, often fifty-five or sixty. The income continues as long as you remain totally and permanently disabled, but not beyond the maturity date of the policy or age sixty-five, whichever comes sooner. At age sixty-five the coverage generally provides that the basic life insurance policy will become paid up and no further premiums will be due.

Another frequently used endorsement is known as the **double indemnity rider.** This coverage provides that twice the face amount of the policy will be paid if your death is accidental. Many policies define "accidental" rather technically, however, so you must not assume that *any* accidental death will result in double payment of benefits. The charge for the double indemnity rider is not high (about $1.25 for each $1,000 face amount of insurance), since accidents are not a leading cause of death.

Need for Life Insurance

A useful way to think about life insurance needs is to determine whether they are permanent or temporary. Permanent needs would be those for which cash is required whenever you die, no matter how far in the future that may be. Examples would be the cost of paying for your funeral or paying off accumulated debts, estate and income taxes, and monthly household bills. Another permanent need would be to provide life insurance for your surviving spouse or other relatives.

Temporary needs are needs that last only for specified periods of time. One example would be life insurance protection needs during the time of an outstanding debt, such as a home mortgage. Another example would be income to meet family expenses while your children are still dependents.

Some individuals use life insurance to meet a savings need, such as accumulating money for college or for retirement. The use of life insurance as a savings vehicle has limitations that are explored later in this chapter.

HOW MUCH INSURANCE

Life insurance should be purchased to meet some specific need or set of needs. The first step is to state these needs in concrete terms—for example, $5,000 to meet funeral expenses, $20,000 for college funds for the children, $50,000 to pay off a home mortgage, and $1,000 a month for eighteen years for family living expenses. The second step is to determine the extent of assets or other resources available to meet these needs if you should die. The third step is to compare the results of the first two steps; if needs exceed existing resources, you should consider purchasing insurance to fill the gaps.

The amount of life insurance you require can be determined by a process life insurance agents call **programming**. Most agents will assist you in developing a complete program, or plan, of your existing resources and future life insurance needs. Programming involves expressing income needs in terms of amounts needed currently to produce a predetermined amount of planned income in the future.

A specific function of life insurance is to replace family income in the event of your premature death. During the programming process, your present income and the proportion of this income that needs replacement must be stated. Factors to be considered include number of dependents, income taxes, and other resources—for example, Social Security. A major life insurer has developed a guide that considers these factors (see Exhibit 5–6). Using the exhibit, we can see that a family head, age thirty, who earns $12,000 a year, is covered by Social Security, and has two children to support would need life insurance equal to about five times annual income, or $60,000, to replace 75 percent of the lost income after taxes. If $25,000 of protection is available from an employer-paid group life insurance policy, the thirty-year-old would need to supply only the balance, $35,000, from individually purchased policies.

Through programming, a careful estimate of your individual needs for life insurance can be ascertained. Savings elements of permanent life insurance policies can be planned to supplement income needs at retirement.

EXHIBIT 5-6   Life Insurance Needs Factors

Gross Annual Income	Income Multipliers for Various Ages					
	30	35	40	45	50	55
$ 7,500	5.3	6.2	7.3	8.5	7.9	5.6
9,000	5.1	6.0	7.0	8.1	7.8	5.5
12,000	5.0	5.8	6.7	7.9	7.6	5.4
15,000	4.9	5.7	6.7	7.9	7.4	5.3
20,000	4.9	6.5	7.4	8.1	7.3	5.2
30,000	7.4	8.2	8.4	8.3	7.2	5.1
40,000	8.4	8.7	8.6	8.2	6.9	4.9
60,000	9.0	8.9	8.4	7.8	6.5	4.6

Note: Insurance proceeds required, expressed as multiples of gross income, to replace 75% of earnings after income taxes, from date of death to age 65, assuming Social Security survivor's income based on two children born at insured's age 26 and 29.

Source: Adapted from literature developed by Bankers Life of Iowa.

Programs should be revised every three to five years to adjust to changes in family composition, income levels, inflation, and income tax rates.

Clauses in Life Insurance Contracts

Many contractual provisions, or **clauses,** enable you to gain a clearer understanding of the scope or the limitations of life insurance protection. Most of these clauses protect the interests of the insured.

INCONTESTABLE CLAUSE

The **incontestable clause** states that if the policy has been in force for a given period—often two years—and if the insured has not died during that time, the insurer may not refuse to pay the proceeds, cancel the policy, or contest the contract except for nonpayment of premiums. For example, suppose Jack lies about his health when he applies for insurance, stating that he has not seen a doctor for medical treatment in the previous five years. Six months later Jack dies of a heart attack. The insurer investigates and discovers that Jack had been under a doctor's care for three years. Since the death occurred within two years of the application, the insurer may refuse to pay the face value of the policy because of the fraud. But, had the death occurred after the two-year period, the insurer would have had to pay the face amount of the policy, regardless of the misstatement. The legal justification for this clause is the protection beneficiaries need after the death of the insured has made it impossible for the beneficiaries to defend against the insurer's refusal to pay, since the insured cannot testify.

SUICIDE CLAUSE

The **suicide clause** states that if the insured commits suicide within two years of issuance of the policy, the insurer may deny liability. After two years, suicide is not a defense against paying the proceeds.

REINSTATEMENT CLAUSE

If a life insurance policy lapses for nonpayment of premium, the **reinstatement clause** says that the insured may reinstate the policy within a period of three to five years upon presenting evidence of insurability. Frequently it is more desirable for an insured to reinstate a policy than to acquire a new contract, because an old policy may have more desirable provisions and be more economical than a new policy.

GRACE PERIOD CLAUSE

The **grace period clause** gives the insured an extra thirty days in which to pay a premium before lapse takes place. In effect, the extra thirty days is a period of free insurance. Once the policy has lapsed (i.e., the premium has gone unpaid beyond thirty days after due date), a special application must be made and evidence of good health presented before the policy can be reinstated.

AUTOMATIC PREMIUM LOAN CLAUSE

The **automatic premium loan clause** is available so that, if an insured inadvertently fails to pay a premium, the company will automatically borrow the necessary premium from whatever accumulated cash values the policy may have. In this way the protection will be continued as long as the policy has cash value sufficient to pay the premiums.

MISSTATEMENT OF AGE CLAUSE

If an applicant misstates his or her age to get a lower premium, the **misstatement of age clause** allows the amount of coverage to be adjusted when proof of age is given, usually at the time of the insured's death. For example, if a premium that should have been $30 was actually $25 because the insured wrongly stated his or her age to obtain coverage at a reduced rate, the insurer will pay only 25/30 (5/6) of the death proceeds otherwise payable.

SPENDTHRIFT TRUST CLAUSE

Most states grant the life insurance owner an exemption from claims of creditors to the extent of the death proceeds or cash values that exist. In this way financial obligations of the insured are not allowed to wreck the income security of life insurance beneficiaries. To extend further protection to the beneficiaries of life insurance, the insured may attach what is called the **spend-**

thrift trust clause, under which creditors cannot attach beneficiaries' life insurance proceeds to satisfy debts beneficiaries may have accumulated. As long as the funds retain their identity as life insurance proceeds, they may not be attached by the beneficiary's creditors. The insured, however, must request that the spendthrift clause be attached to the policy.

DIVIDEND OPTIONS

Many policies provide for **dividends**, which in reality are a partial return of the premium paid by the insured (see Chapter 4). Dividends on life insurance may be returned to the policyholder in the form of cash, or the policyholder may use them in the following ways: (1) use as paid-up additions of coverage, (2) leave with the insurer at interest, or (3) use them to reduce premiums otherwise due on the policy. An advantage of using dividends to purchase additional insurance is that insurance purchased in this way is not subject to many of the loading charges applicable to new contracts of coverage. Chief among loading costs on new contracts are commissions paid to insurance agents.

Insurance purchased with dividends requires no medical examinations or other evidence of insurability. The new coverage purchased may also have a cash value that can be borrowed.

LOAN VALUES

On life insurance policies that accumulate a cash savings, the insured may at any time borrow the cash values at a stated rate of interest that usually does not exceed 8 percent. By borrowing on cash values, the insured can keep the original life insurance policy in force undisturbed. Borrowing cash values of life insurance may be economical because market rates of interest are frequently higher than rates of interest available on life insurance policies. Moreover, while you are using money borrowed from a life insurance policy and are paying interest on it, the insurer is crediting your account with the interest and dividends it pays all policyholders on savings in life insurance contracts. Thus, while you may be paying the insurer 8 percent on a life insurance loan, the insurer could be crediting your policy with 5 percent or 6 percent. The net cost of the loan would be the difference between these two rates, perhaps 2 or 3 percent. In many cases the interest cost of borrowing on life insurance is also an income tax deduction, which makes the net borrowing cost even lower. At the death of the insured, outstanding loans are deducted from the proceeds of the policy.

SETTLEMENT OPTIONS

You may receive the cash value of life insurance, or you may elect to have the death proceeds paid either in a lump sum or in installments. The ways in which life insurance proceeds are paid are called **settlement options**.

In addition to the lump-sum option, you may select (1) a fixed-period option, (2) a fixed-amount option, (3) an interest option, or (4) a life-income option.

Under the **fixed-period option** you may direct the insurer to pay proceeds in installments over a set time period, such as five or ten years. No extra charge is made for this service. Under the **fixed-amount option** you may direct the insurer to pay a set sum, such as $500, for as long as the proceeds last.

Under the **interest option** the insurer would hold the proceeds of the policy and pay an interest income to the beneficiary. The beneficiary could retain the right to withdraw the principal as needed. The interest option is frequently used when the proceeds of the policy are intended as an emergency fund, when interest is required to supplement family income, or when the beneficiary wishes to retain the principal in a safe place until it is needed.

Under the **life-income option** the proceeds may be left as an annuity to guarantee the beneficiary a life income, with or without any minimum number of guaranteed installments. A frequent use of the life-income option is to supplement a retirement pension available to the beneficiary from other sources, such as Social Security or an employer-paid plan. The advantage of a life-income option is that the insurance proceeds can be spread out to meet a need—for example, providing a life income to the surviving spouse, with payments ceasing at his or her death. The insurer retains control and guarantees payment of the amount of the annuity.

Settlement options are a valuable way to extend life insurance to accomplish the goals for which it was intended. The insurer makes no additional charge for the use of settlement options. By viewing life insurance proceeds in terms of the income it will provide rather than as a lump sum, you can keep sight of what is generally the purpose of life insurance—to restore a lost income.

NONFORFEITURE OPTIONS

If you wish to stop paying premiums on a permanent life insurance policy, you may select from among three **nonforfeiture options:** cash value, paid-up insurance of a reduced amount, and extended term. After a given period of years, for example, a $1,000 whole life policy might have a cash value of $200. This $200 is available in a lump sum if you desire. Alternatively, you may use the $200 to convert the policy to a new, paid-up contract with, perhaps, $750 as its face amount. You may also select the **extended-term option,** under which the original $1,000 of face amount of protection is maintained for several years without further premiums. Each life insurance contract has a table stating the values under each nonforfeiture option.

Frequently life insurers will employ the extended-term option unless you specifically select another one. Thus, if you cease paying premiums on a policy with a cash value, the policy may remain in effect for its full face value for a stated number of years. In some cases people have died with such policies in force, and the surviving spouse has believed that the policy expired some years ago, when the insured ceased making premium payments. Careful examination of old policies may reveal that they are still good under the extended-term option.

Life insurers do not usually make payments on policies of clients who have died unless an application is made by the beneficiary or by the manager of the deceased's estate. Unclaimed sums eventually revert to the government. However, if the policy is in force under an extended-term option, it eventually expires because the cash value has been used to purchase term insurance on the life of the insured. You should make certain that beneficiaries know of the existence of all life insurance policies so that they can follow proper claims procedures.

Premium Comparisons

A comparison of a typical insurer's premium charges per $1,000 of coverage under various life insurance plans is given in Exhibit 5–7. Note that at age twenty-one, whole life insurance costs about 3.3 times as much as five-year renewable term and about 58 percent as much as 20-payment life. Thus, the purchaser can obtain much more death protection under term insurance than under whole life insurance. Of course, there is no accumulating cash or loan value on the term plan. On the whole life plan, for each $1,000 of face amount issued at age twenty-one, there would be a cash or loan value of nearly $200 after twenty years.

EXHIBIT 5–7   Life Insurance Premiums on Nonparticipating Policies per $1,000 Face Amount for a Male

Age	Renewable Five-Year Term	Whole Life	20-Payment Life	20-Year Endowment	Endowment at Age 65
21	$ 3.58	$11.78	$20.19	$44.31	$ 15.49
30	3.80	15.67	25.00	44.84	22.39
35	4.45	18.63	28.50	45.60	27.69
45	11.08	27.56	37.00	49.00	47.27
55	18.40	41.88	49.58	57.19	105.50

Note: Nonparticipating means that no dividends are payable.

Source: *Best's Flitcraft Compend, 1980* (Oldwick, N.J.: A.M. Best Co., 1980).

The true costs of life insurance contracts are difficult to compare for three reasons: (1) For policies paying dividends (i.e., participating), dividends may vary from what is projected; (2) final costs depend on the time value of money, as measured by interest rates, and actual interest rates may differ considerably from those assumed; (3) not all contracts offer identical provisions. In spite of these difficulties, the intelligent buyer of life insurance may compare the interest-adjusted cost index for different insurers (see Chapter 4) and select the insurer with the lowest cost index.

THE "BUY-TERM-AND-INVEST-THE-DIFFERENCE" ARGUMENT

Some financial planners prefer to use term life insurance for protection needs and to use other media for savings needs. The justification is the fact that one can obtain a higher return on savings than on life insurance. However, funds accumulating in life insurance policies are not subject to income tax during the savings period, though they are subject to eventual taxation if cash values exceed the amount saved. But most life insurance policies do not produce cash values higher than the sum of the premiums, which include an allowance for death payments as well as for savings. Thus, the savings element in life insurance may be said to be tax-sheltered.

In spite of the tax shelter, the savings returns from life insurance are lower than those from other methods of savings. In 1980, for example, a saver could obtain about 7 percent on municipal bond funds with short-term maturities. The bonds were completely tax-exempt and about as safe and as liquid as savings in life insurance contracts.

To illustrate, assume you are a male, aged twenty-five, considering two savings plans—Plan A and Plan B. Plan A is to purchase a whole life policy, nonparticipating, with a premium of $12.69 per $1,000 and with a guaranteed cash value of $225 per $1,000 in twenty years. Plan B is to purchase twenty-year reducing-term insurance costing $2.69 per $1,000 and to save the difference ($10 a unit) in a tax-exempt municipal bond fund at 8 percent interest. The term insurance coverage reduces $50 a year from its initial face amount and expires in twenty years. Each plan will provide approximately the same estate protection if you die within twenty years. Your cash outlay is $12.69 a year under both Plan A and Plan B. The available savings per $1,000 after twenty years are as follows:

Plan A

20-year guaranteed
  cash value: $225.00

Plan B

Value of savings after 20 years:
  $12.69 (whole life premium) − $2.69 (term premium)
  × $45.76 ($1 a year for 20 years at 8% compound interest) = $457.60

The buy-term-and-invest-the-difference plan illustrated in Plan B has produced savings of $457.60, compared with $225.00 produced by the whole life insurance in Plan A. Of course, the insurance coverage under the whole life policy will still be in effect after twenty years; the term policy must be renewed at a higher rate if the plan is to be continued.

INVESTMENT LIFE INSURANCE

Because more consumers today appreciate the buy-term-and-invest-the-difference argument, in recent years life insurers have introduced new policies designed to increase the investment returns available to the life insurance buyer—for example, variable life and universal life policies. In **variable life policies** part of the premium is invested in a portfolio of common stocks selected to help the investor overcome the long-run effects of inflation, which reduce the value of the investment. A variable life policy is described in Exhibit 5–8. In **universal life policies** part of the premium is invested in money market funds to obtain a high rate of interest return (see Chapter 13). An example of a universal life policy is shown in Exhibit 5–9.

Distribution Methods

Life insurance is sold through individual sales agents and through group insurance methods.

INDIVIDUAL AGENTS

Individual sales agents usually represent just one insurer, although they may also serve as brokers to sell other insurers' policies. Agents can help you program insurance and offer valuable advice and counsel. The individual agent can tailor coverage to your personal needs and circumstances. Agents are paid on commission; they receive perhaps half of the first year's premium and a 5 percent renewal commission annually for ten years.

GROUP INSURANCE

Most businesses and other employers provide life insurance on a group basis for their employees. Frequently the coverage is purchased and paid for entirely by the employer. The amount of protection is often a multiple of your salary (e.g., twice your annual wages). Group life insurance is a valuable addition to your personal financial security.

Group life insurance is on a term basis. Thus, it provides no cash values. You are eligible regardless of health conditions. If you should leave your job, you are eligible to convert your group life insurance protection to an individual policy, usually within thirty days. If you doubt whether you are insurable for individual life insurance policies, you should take action immediately to convert group insurance to an individual contract. You are not eligible to pur-

EXHIBIT 5-8 Variable Life Insurance

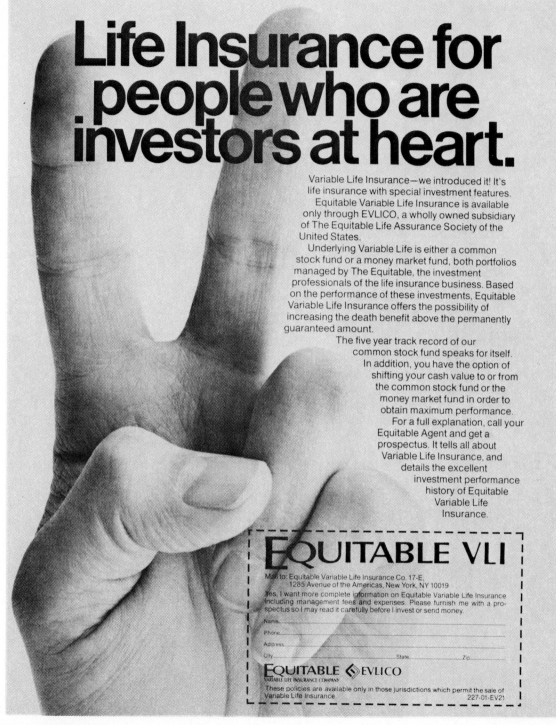

Source: Equitable Variable Life Insurance Company

EXHIBIT 5-9   Universal Life Insurance

The Hartford announces The Solution.[SM]

Now you can get life insurance that earns a current 12% on cash value buildup.

That's right, 12%.

The Solution is The Hartford's revolutionary universal life insurance policy. It gives you the permanent lifetime protection and tax advantages* of traditional Whole Life. And it currently earns a competitive 12%** on cash value.

The Solution is flexible, too. As your needs change, you can increase or decrease the amount of protection, raise or lower premium payments, and add or remove insureds. You can also choose from a wide range of payout options.

The Solution is truly responsive to today's consumer needs. It is a sophisticated product specifically designed to give people with substantial resources the financial protection and flexibility their situation requires. That makes it an ideal financial and estate-planning vehicle.

The Solution is a prime example of the highly praised "Universal Life" concept. "Universal Life" is the name given to a new type of life insurance policy–epitomized by The Solution–that has been hailed as a breakthrough by leading financial periodicals.

Find out more about this remarkable new life insurance policy. For a free booklet on The Solution, call toll free or mail the coupon today. Or contact an independent agent who represents The Hartford.

"The 'universal' policy grows in popularity."
The New York Times

"If you tried to invent the ideal policy, it might closely resemble universal life."
Money Magazine

*Rulings have been requested from the IRS on income tax treatment.

**This current interest rate is guaranteed for the first policy year. Thereafter, the rate may rise or fall periodically based on the anticipated business environment.

YOUR Independent Insurance AGENT SERVES YOU FIRST

Source: The Hartford Insurance Company

chase life insurance in excess of the insurance you carried under the group policy.

People frequently maintain group insurance coverage in reduced amounts after retirement. Thus, if you had $25,000 of group life insurance protection while employed, you might be entitled to retain $12,500 in coverage during your retirement.

Guides to Buying Life Insurance

1. Life insurance should not be purchased simply because you believe that "a little bit of life insurance is a good thing." You should determine precisely how much life insurance you need and for what purpose. Buy no more insurance than will cover the specific needs you have identified.

2. Favor temporary contracts (and mainly term insurance) for temporary needs. Consider permanent contracts (generally whole life) for permanent needs. Since most needs of young buyers are temporary (e.g., for the family-raising period), such buyers should generally favor term insurance because a great deal more coverage can be purchased for the same dollar amount that would be spent on whole life or endowment coverages.

3. Avoid buying life insurance policies with too many options or endorsements. Double indemnity riders, for example, may not be worth their cost, even though the cost appears nominal. The same applies to disability income riders. Accident insurance may be purchased more economically on specially designed contracts.

4. Avoid purchasing life insurance if your main objective is to save money. Savings policies are not designed essentially as savings vehicles. The savings element in these contracts exists to provide for the payment of level premiums throughout your life. Excesses paid in the early years (above the cost of pure term protection) help meet the higher costs of protection in later years. The savings element thus is incidental. Better vehicles than life insurance exist for long-term savings.

5. Shop carefully for life insurance; large variations exist in the cost of different contracts.

6. Choose an agent who will render service in addition to selling the policy and filling out the application. Professional agents are generally willing to help you determine what your needs are and to program life insurance proceeds to fill these needs efficiently. Favor agents who have the designation CLU (chartered life underwriter) or who have earned other types of professional recognition. You are paying a substantial commission for agents' services, and qualified agents charge no more than unqualified ones.

7. To facilitate collection on life insurance proceeds, have proof of your age available when application is made and when your beneficiaries make claims.

8. Make sure your life insurance policies and other papers are available for beneficiaries when needed. Keeping life insurance policies in safe deposit boxes is not wise, because on the death of the insured, safe deposit boxes are closed and their contents are not available for some time. Life insurance policies should be readily available (e.g., in your desk), and their location should be specified. Life insurance proceeds are payable directly to beneficiaries; they are excluded from the judicial proceedings required for other items in your estate.

9. Be sure to name beneficiaries of life insurance policies carefully so that the proceeds will go to those for whom you intend them. **Contingent beneficiaries** (secondary beneficiaries) should also be named in case the primary beneficiary is deceased at the time of your death. If you have not named a secondary beneficiary, individuals other than those for whom you may have intended the proceeds might benefit.

HEALTH INSURANCE

Health insurance indemnifies (pays) you for expenditures you make for medical and hospital care and for loss of income resulting from accident or sickness. Such losses can be financially devastating. Insurance is an ideal method of planning for such contingencies. If you rely on savings or personal assets to meet these costs, your entire financial plan might fail because of recurrent losses that exhaust your savings before a new fund can be built up. Health insurance will cover losses on a continuous basis. Unfortunately, health insurance is not always complete. The following discussion will help you sort out various means of providing adequate protection against health losses.

Extent and Types of Health Insurance

There are five general types of health insurance: (1) hospitalization, (2) surgical expense, (3) regular medical expense, (4) major medical expense, and (5) disability income insurance. In addition, special coverages (e.g., for dental expenses) are available on a group basis.

HOSPITALIZATION INSURANCE

Hospitalization insurance indemnifies you for necessary hospital expenses, including room and board, nursing care, laboratory fees, use of the operating room, and certain medicines and supplies.

SURGICAL INSURANCE

Surgical insurance provides for indemnity for doctors' fees for all procedures involving surgery. Surgical insurance is of two general types. One type allows a specific amount for a given operation (e.g., $200 for an appendectomy or $25 for a tonsilectomy). The second type indemnifies on a "usual, customary, and reasonable charge" (UCR) basis. That is, the policy will pay whatever expense is deemed reasonable, customary, and usual in the community in which the doctor performs the service. Charges above the UCR level must be paid by the patient.

REGULAR MEDICAL INSURANCE

Regular medical insurance indemnifies you for physicians' services for other than surgical procedures. It provides allowances for physicians' visits at home or in the hospital and for office calls. Regular medical is usually written as part of another type of health insurance, not as a separate contract.

MAJOR MEDICAL INSURANCE

Major medical insurance is designed to cover very large or catastrophic medical expenses on a "blanket" basis with relatively few limitations. Frequently the policy limits are $50,000, $100,000, or higher and contain a deductible (often $100) applicable for any one calendar year's expenses. Major medical is also written with a coinsurance percentage deductible (e.g., 20 percent), which requires the insured to pay a specified percentage of the bill above the flat dollar deductible.

DISABILITY INCOME INSURANCE

Disability income insurance provides for periodic payments when you are unable to work because of illness or accident. Two general classes exist: short-term and long-term coverage. Short-term coverage usually extends for six months; long-term up to age sixty-five. Both contracts usually contain a waiting period (e.g., one month) before the insured starts receiving payments. A disability is usually defined as a condition that prevents you from carrying on your usual occupation. In long-term policies after a period of time (e.g., two years), the definition of disability is extended to include any condition that prevents you from carrying on *any* occupation for which you are qualified by education, training, or experience. Benefits per period may be higher for short-term coverage than for long-term coverage. Coverage for accidents may differ from coverage for sickness. Sometimes disability insurance contracts are coordinated with other types of similar policies and with Social Security or workers' compensation coverages (see Chapter 7). A clause in the contract limits your total benefits from all similar policies to some reasonable percentage of the income you earned before you were disabled. Clauses of this nature are called **coordination-of-benefits clauses.**

DENTAL INSURANCE

Dental insurance, a type of policy introduced fairly recently in the United States, covers dental expenses such as cleaning, X-rays, oral examinations, fillings, extractions, dentures, bridgework, root canal therapy, orthodontics, and other dental procedures. Dental insurance is normally offered as a group insurance policy.

The relative importance of the preceding types of insurance may be judged from the data in Exhibit 5–10, which shows the number and percentage of people covered by various kinds of health insurance in the United States. Note that hospital, surgical, and regular medical expenses are the most frequently covered risks. The number of persons covered by disability income insurance and by dental insurance is still relatively small. Part of the explanation for the low percentage for private disability income insurance is that this protection is provided through the Social Security system. The fact that dental insurance is still relatively new accounts for its small market share.

Group versus Individual Policies

Health insurance policies may be issued individually or to groups. Most health insurance premiums are issued on a group basis. Group benefits have been growing steadily, while individual coverage has been declining. For example, in 1978 approximately 87 percent of all health insurance benefits paid were under group contracts.[1] Group health insurance predominates for the following reasons:

1. Group insurance generally provides more generous levels of benefits than are possible under individual contracts.
2. Group insurance is available at a lower unit cost.
3. Group insurance has been more actively promoted than individual policies. Both government and organized labor have urged group insurance as a major employee benefit.
4. Group insurance has had considerable publicity as a result of various social insurance programs and legislative requirements. For example, in 1973 Congress passed legislation encouraging the development of health maintenance organizations (HMOs), which resemble group clinics designed to offer health insurance protection on a group basis.

ADVANTAGES OF GROUP INSURANCE

Some of the advantages of group insurance contracts include lower administrative costs, freedom from adverse selection, reduced acquisition ex-

---

1. *Source Book of Health Insurance Data, 1978-1979* (Washington, D.C.: Health Insurance Institute, 1982), p. 22. Percent calculated.

EXHIBIT 5–10
Persons Covered
by Private Health
Insurance, 1978

Type of Insurance	Number of Persons (in millions)	Percentage of U.S. Population, 1976
Hospital expense	181	82%
Surgical expense	172	78%
Regular medical (physician expense)	164	75%
Major medical expense	142	65%
Disability income		
Short-term	70	32%
Long-term	19	9%
Dental	60	27%

Note: Percentages are based on U.S. population of 220,000,000.

Source: *Source Book of Health Insurance Data, 1979–1980* (New York: Health Insurance Institute, 1980), p. 12.

penses, and exemption from certain taxes that characterize other kinds of insurance. If you receive a group insurance benefit from an employer, for example, you are not required to pay income taxes on the value of this benefit. If you purchase coverage individually, however, payment would have to be made with after-tax dollars. Because federal and state income taxes amount to a large percentage of personal income, the savings are substantial and have led to increased use of group insurance as a method of paying health expenses. Another benefit of group insurance is that employers frequently provide services such as payroll deductions for premium payments.

Insurer losses tend to be lower under group contracts because the covered individuals are organized for a purpose other than obtaining insurance. If you are well enough to go to work, presumably you are well enough to be eligible for group insurance without special medical examination. Applicants for individual health insurance, on the other hand, frequently have health problems more likely to cause insurer losses, which lead to increases in the cost of premiums.

MAJOR GROUP INSURERS

Some notion of the relative size of group health insurers is provided in Exhibit 5–11, which shows benefits paid by three major types of insurers. Commercial insurers such as life insurance companies account for almost half of the total benefits paid under private insurance plans, and Blue Cross–Blue Shield pays out nearly as much. Independent plans (e.g., private group clinics, union plans, and health maintenance organizations) make up the balance of the payments.

Blue Cross–Blue Shield organizations are nonprofit groups organized in the early 1930s to offer hospital insurance nearly at cost for individuals and groups willing to prepay coverage. Blue Cross–Blue Shield organizations have

EXHIBIT 5–11
Benefit Payments
of Private Health
Insurance Plans,
1978

Insurer	Benefits (in billions)	Percentage of Total Payments
Blue Cross–Blue Shield and other plans[a]	$24.4	48%
Insurance companies		
Group policies	22.9	45%
Individual policies	3.5	7%
Total	$50.8	100%

[a]Includes commercial, union, private group clinic, and dental service plans.

Source: *Source Book of Health Insurance Data, 1979–1980* (Washington, D.C.: Health Insurance Institute, 1980), p. 24.

expenses of less than 10 percent of premium dollars paid and are exempt from most taxation. Blue Cross offers hospital insurance, and Blue Shield offers a surgical plan in cooperation with the companion Blue Cross group. Practically all Blue Cross–Blue Shield coverage is on a group basis, but the organizations also offer individual plans for persons transferring between groups or leaving a group and needing continued individual coverage.

Blue Cross is noted for the fact that insurance coverage is on a "service basis"—that is, you are entitled to a semiprivate room in a hospital and to all attendant services and costs without additional charge. If you want a private room, you must pay extra. Even if the price of a hospital room goes up, you are protected and will receive service without dollar limitation for room and board. Most Blue Cross plans are limited to 120 days a year in the hospital, whereas commercial insurance plans often extend to 365 days. Nearly all Blue Cross hospital plans have no deductible amount, while commercial insurance usually is sold with some type of dollar deductible.

In contrast to Blue Cross plans, commercial coverages offered by life insurance companies are issued with dollar limits for the services they cover. For example, a commercial insurance plan might cover all costs of hospital room and board up to $150 or $200 a day. Anything extra would be paid by the patient. Similarly, hospital services (e.g., use of the operating room or anesthesia) usually are limited by some dollar amount.

The newest type of group insurance is that offered by health maintenance organizations (HMOs), a type of group hospital clinic. The differences between HMOs, Blue Cross–Blue Shield, and commercial insurance are the following:

1. HMOs stress regular health care, early diagnosis and treatment, and disease prevention. Coverage is prepaid, and visits are unlimited. HMOs attempt to minimize the costs of medical care by preventing serious illnesses from developing.

2. HMOs control costs by providing doctors with incentive to perform efficient treatment. HMOs also attempt to reduce the length of hospital stays

and frequently employ physicians on a salaried basis; thus, doctors would have no incentive for assigning patients to a hospital, since the possibility of receiving greater fees for doing so is removed.

3. HMOs employ a variety of medical specialists, including nurses, pharmacists, and mental health personnel, on the same premises to treat the patient on the day of the visit. Under commercial insurance the patient must often seek care from different specialists in separate locations.

4. Under the HMO Act of 1973, the HMO must be offered as an alternative to a commercial insurance plan if there is an HMO in a community. Thus, although enrollment is voluntary, employers are required to offer the alternative if it is available. This requirement frequently results in competition between HMOs and commercial insurers and may tend to keep costs lower. Most HMOs offer coverage with fee schedules and monthly costs similar to those of Blue Cross–Blue Shield and of commercial insurers.

Significant Contract Provisions in Individual Health Insurance Coverage

You can be a better buyer of individual health insurance if you understand the major provisions of the policies. The following subsections define the limitations of coverage, what conditions must be satisfied, how deductibles work, and other important aspects of insurance.

ACCIDENT VERSUS SICKNESS

Two general types of health insurance contracts exist—those covering accidents only, and those covering both illness and accidents. In an accident-only contract, the insurance shopper should avoid restrictive wording such as *accidental means* in favor of the term *accidental injury*. Accident-only contracts typically are further restrictive to mean only travel accidents. Such policies are generally less expensive, but they should be avoided in favor of accident contracts that are not so restrictive.

Policies covering both illness and accident are generally preferable, although they cost more than accident-only policies. These contracts restrict the definition of illness, frequently excluding mental disease, tuberculosis, childbirth and pregnancy, dental treatment, intentionally self-inflicted injuries, attempted suicide, preexisting illnesses, cosmetic surgery, losses recoverable through workers' compensation, and war and aviation losses.

Some types of contracts offer coverage only for certain types of illness, such as cancer. Coverage limits under these policies are relatively large (e.g., $50,000), and premiums are modest. Such policies contain many limitations and should be studied carefully.

"Podiatrist fees are collectible under some health insurance plans."

The Bettman Archive, Inc.

PERSONS COVERED

As a buyer of health insurance, you should look carefully to see who the policy covers. Some policies are restricted only to the named insured, while others cover your dependents. If dependents are covered, their benefits may or may not be equal to yours.

RECURRING LOSSES

You should also check to see how a period of loss is defined in the policy. If you are ill and enter the hospital, are discharged, and later return to work only to be rehospitalized for the same illness, has a new period of eligibility begun? What is a "spell of illness"? The definition makes a difference, because policies generally limit the number of days a person is eligible for hospitalization. If the policy contains a recurrent disability clause, the contract will specify that hospital reentry must be owing to an entirely new set of causes or that some period of time (e.g., one to six months) must elapse between hospitalizations for a second period of disability to be considered a new period of entitlement. In group insurance, the recurrent disability clause is quite favorable to the insured, who usually need only return to work to be entitled to a new period of eligibility.

ELIGIBLE HOSPITALS

The policy also defines what constitutes an eligible hospital. Frequently institutions such as clinics, nursing homes, sanitariums, or rest homes are not defined as hospitals, and eligibility therefore does not exist for such institutions.

CANCELABILITY AND RENEWABILITY

The policy spells out under what conditions a health insurance policy can be canceled by the insurer. May it be canceled midterm, before the end of the usual one-year policy period? Is it subject to not being renewed if you have had a poor health record during the policy period? Ideally, policies should be noncancelable and guaranteed renewable. Such policies are sometimes more expensive, but you definitely need the protection afforded by the broader terminology.

DISABILITY INCOME POLICIES

Policies that pay an income to someone who is disabled should be examined carefully to see how the term *disability* is defined. Some policies do not consider you disabled unless you are unable to perform any of your normal duties or the duties involved in any occupation. Other policies state that you must only be unable to perform your regular occupation. The latter wording is clearly preferable; under the former wording an engineer, for example, could be denied benefits if the insurer could claim she was well enough to sell pencils on the street. Frequently these contracts indicate that for the first two to five years you must be unable to perform your regular occupation. After that period you must be unable to perform *any* occupation for which you are reasonably qualified by education, training, and experience. Thus, a dentist who has suffered the loss of a hand may be able to collect full disability benefits for two years. After two years benefits would be denied on the grounds that the dentist could sell dental supplies or perform other administrative work, even though he could not perform regular dental services.

DEDUCTIBLES AND ELIMINATION PERIODS

Health insurance policies frequently contain two types of deductibles. The first, a **flat dollar deductible**, is subtracted from any loss before payment is made under the policy. The second, a **coinsurance deductible**, is a percentage that must be borne by the insured. This percentage is applied to all loss claims above the flat dollar deductible. For example, if you have a major medical policy covering $10,000 of loss, and you suffer a $5,000 loss, how much could you collect under a typical wording? The typical policy might contain a $100 flat deductible and a 20 percent coinsurance deductible. Under its terms you would collect 80 percent of $4,900 ($5,000 − $100), or $3,920. Exhibit 5–12 provides a further illustration of how deductibles work. The purpose of deductibles is to give you some incentive to control and minimize losses.

Another form of deductible in health insurance contracts is known as an elimination, or waiting, period. An **elimination period** specifies that no benefits will be payable during the first month or two for any physical conditions or illnesses the insured had at the time the policy went into effect. This wording defines a preexisting illness. So long as the illness does not cause a loss within the elimination period, it is covered. A waiting period begins to apply after the disability occurs. Found in loss-of-income policies, the elimination period means that you must wait a specified period of time (e.g., thirty days) before your disability income commences.

EXHIBIT 5–12
How Deductibles
Work in Health
Insurance

Hypothetical loss from auto accident (hospital and doctor expense)	$25,000
Paid by basic insurance coverage (no deductible)	9,900
Subtotal	$15,100
Flat dollar deductible under Major Medical	100
Subtotal	$15,000
20% coinsurance deductible under Major Medical	3,000
Balance paid by Major Medical	$12,000
Summary Insurance pays ($9,900 + $12,000)	$21,900
You pay ($3,000 + $100)	3,100*
Total	$25,000

*Some policies contain a maximum limit, such as $1000, above which the policyholder need not pay in any single year.

INCONTESTABILITY

Most individual health insurance contracts contain a clause that limits the right of the insurer to deny claims after a certain time period has elapsed. Known as the **time-limit-on-certain-defense clause,** the restriction requires that after a two-year period, no misstatements made by the applicant (except for fraudulent statements) may be used to void coverage. Neither may any preexisting condition be used to void coverage after the policy has been in force for two years.

Special Group Health Insurance Conditions

Coverage under group health insurance differs in some respects from coverage under individual health insurance. Some of the differences are as follows:

1. Group policies are not cancelable as far as an individual is concerned unless the insurer cancels the entire group contract. As far as the individual is concerned, the policy is guaranteed renewable and noncancelable.
2. The definition of disability is broader in group policies, which only require that you be unable to perform the regular duties of your occupation for the first five years. Benefits are available during periods of hospitalization.
3. Group insurance is usually restricted to nonoccupational accidents and illnesses because occupational injuries are normally covered under state workers' compensation laws.
4. Group insurance is usually subject to experience rating, under which the rate may vary periodically as the employer's loss experience varies.
5. All employees are covered in a group plan, regardless of health conditions. If you are well enough to be employed, you are eligible for coverage. In addition, you may be able to secure benefits unavailable from individual policies (e.g., dental coverage).

Guides to Buying Health Insurance

1. Most individual health insurance policies give you a ten-day "free look" at the policy and the right to a full refund if you are not satisfied. Take advantage of this and read the policy carefully before finally accepting it.
2. Check the policy's renewability and cancelability provisions, the waiting period, and the exclusions for various types of illnesses. Make sure these exclusions are not damaging to you.

3. Know whether the policy covers you on a worldwide basis. If you are restricted to illness only when in the United States or Canada, and then suffer illness while you are traveling in Europe or Japan, you may as well not have had health insurance at all.

4. Know whether the policy covers your spouse or other dependents if you should die, and whether the policy is available to survivors at a reduced premium.

5. Know whether the policy covers your dependent children until they reach age twenty-three and are still in school. Some policies limit coverage to children up to ages eighteen or twenty-one. See if your policy gives dependents the right to continue health insurance on an unrestricted basis once they become independent.

6. Know whether your policy covers preexisting conditions. If it is restricted, will the restriction be damaging to your case?

7. Examine the policy to see how the coverage is expressed. Choose a policy that offers limits of coverage on a per disability basis. Some policies limit coverage to some maximum amount and then allow no further coverage. It is possible for you to have several disabilities, and the maximum limit should apply to each. If the policy does not contain per disability coverage, it should restore coverage to the original amount once a loss has been paid.

8. Avoid accumulating several different policies covering separate types of illnesses or accidents. Instead, purchase one comprehensive policy if possible. Having a single policy eliminates the chance of purchasing duplicating or overlapping coverage.

9. Don't forget to purchase disability income insurance. Disability is probably the most severely underinsured health peril. Coverage should be equal to 60 or 70 percent of your current income. Check with your employer to see how long your salary would continue if you should become ill or disabled, and then purchase a disability income policy with a waiting period equal to the period of time that your employer provides sickness coverage. In this way, your full salary will continue for a while, and you can then go on disability with no lapse in income. Consider available disability coverage under Social Security, workers' compensation, and the employer's retirement plan before deciding on the amount and type of private disability coverage.

Health Insurance and Sex Discrimination

It is illegal under most state laws for health insurers to discriminate on the basis of age, sex, or marital status. For example, a law in Florida prohibits an insurer from denying coverage to females who are employed solely at home, if similar coverage is offered to males. Insurers cannot deny coverage under group policies to the husbands of female employees when dependent coverage is available to the wives of male employees. Insurers cannot deny disability income policies to employed women when coverage is offered to men similarly employed. Insurers may not treat complications of pregnancy differently from any other illness or sickness covered under the policy; nor can insurers offer women lower monthly maximum benefits than are paid to men in the same classification under a disability income policy.

SUMMARY

1. Through life and health insurance you can transfer many of the most important risks you face. Risks include the uncertainty about loss of income or about expenses arising out of poor health or premature death. The insurance method of dealing with these risks is, for all practical purposes, the only efficient way available, since most people cannot handle substantial losses individually.

2. Life insurance policies are of three basic types: whole life, term, and endowment. Whole life policies are used mainly for permanent insurance needs; term policies, for temporary needs; and endowments, for savings purposes. Life insurers have developed many combinations of policies and endorsements to fit individual circumstances, including family income policies, decreasing term riders, and family group policies.

3. Life insurance can be arranged so that you pay the premiums over varying periods. For example, you can pay a single sum or pay over five-, ten-, twenty-year or longer periods. You can alter the payment period by paying up a policy before its maturity. Premiums are lowest for term insurance and highest for endowments; the cost of whole life premiums falls between these two.

4. The amount of life insurance needed is found by determining the amount required for some particular purpose—for example, providing an income to a widow, paying children's college expenses, or paying off a mortgage. Consideration should be given to factors such as income taxes, availability of resources like Social Security, and the number and ages of dependents. Programming is a process of formally outlining life insurance needs and other resources.

5. Life insurance contracts contain certain important clauses—for example, the incontestable, the spendthrift trust, and the suicide clauses. They also contain reinstatement provisions and clauses governing grace periods, misstatement of age, automatic premium loans, and dividends.

6. Life insurance may be paid off at the insured's death or at the insured's surrender of the policy. Payment may be made in a lump sum or in installments over a fixed period or over the lifetime of the insured. Proceeds may be left with the insurer to accumulate interest. If you wish to stop making premium payments, available cash values may sometimes be utilized to keep the policy in force. These provisions

help you to retain the value of the life insurance and to utilize it most effectively.

7. Many people choose term insurance, which is less expensive than whole life insurance, because they believe they can invest the difference between premiums more effectively than can the life insurer. In recent years insurers have responded by offering universal life and variable life contracts, which permit the life insurance buyer to obtain a greater rate of return.

8. Major kinds of health insurance include policies covering hospital expense, surgical expense, physicians' expenses, major medical costs, disability income loss, and dental expense.

9. Health insurance is offered on both individual and group policies. Group policies are more widely used. Suppliers of health insurance include commercial life and health insurers, which offer reimbursement in dollars for covered expenses, and Blue Cross–Blue Shield organizations, which mainly offer group contracts providing services. The newest type of health coverage provider is the health maintenance organization (HMO). HMOs stress preservation of good health and provide medical services through contracts with participating physicians.

10. In purchasing individual health insurance policies, you should give special attention to clauses that define renewability of coverage, deductibles and elimination periods, losses, and excluded conditions. In general, conditions governing individual health policies are more restrictive than conditions governing group insurance contracts.

REVIEW QUESTIONS

1. Explain why life and health losses are ideally suited for handling through the insurance mechanism.

2. Explain which types of life insurance policies you would select to cover the following:
   (a) Expenses arising out of the insured's death (funeral costs, taxes, and current debts);
   (b) Funds to supplement family income during the child-raising period.

3. List the three basic types of life insurance and their distinguishing features.

4. Does the double indemnity rider double the amount of life insurance coverage? Why or why not?

5. How should you determine the amount of life insurance to buy?

6. Use Exhibit 5–7 to answer the following questions:
   (a) How much life insurance protection is needed by a forty-year-old earning $30,000 annually?
   (b) How should this result be adjusted?

7. (a) Explain the incontestable clause and the suicide clause.
   (b) How do these clauses protect beneficiaries?

8. Why are life insurance dividends and death proceeds not subject to income tax?

9. Explain the uses of settlement options in life insurance.

10. A life insurance agent presented a policy to a thirty-year-old that carried a $500 annual premium and a face amount of $10,000. The twenty-year cash value of $9,000, plus estimated dividends of $4,000, amounted to about $13,000. The agent stated: "Now, if this plan only helped you accumulate $10,000, it would be a great plan, wouldn't it?" Compare the plan to one under which the thirty-year-old purchases $10,000 of twenty-year term insurance at $30 a year and saves the difference, $470 a year, in a savings plan paying an after-tax rate of return of 8 percent.

11. (a) What are the major types of health insurance?
    (b) Which is the most widely used and the least widely used?

12. Maria is gainfully employed in freelance editorial work at home. Her earnings are important to the total family budget. When she applied for disability income insurance, she was denied a policy, although the same company had sold a disability income policy to her brother, a freelance photographer who works out of his home. In your opinion, does the company's refusal to grant the policy constitute unfair discrimination based on sex or employment status?

13. June is a teacher, and her husband is a self-employed mechanic. June wanted to name her husband as a dependent to qualify him for the group health insurance offered to her in the private school where she teaches. The insurer refused coverage, even though male teachers at the school had no problems insuring their wives under the group policy. Would such a prohibition be illegal under antidiscrimination laws in most states?

14. A certain disability insurer made the following claims about its contract. Explain why each claim is either favorable or unfavorable to the insured.
    (a) Coverage under the basic policy can continue beyond ages sixty-five through seventy-two at no increase in rates if the insured continues to be gainfully employed on a full-time basis.
    (b) Benefits are payable in addition to any other form of insurance also available to the insured, such as workers' compensation, veterans' compensation, or Social Security benefits.
    (c) A new disability is defined as one separated from the original disability by a period of at least six months' continuous work by the insured on a full-time basis. Each new disability is subject to its own elimination and maximum benefit periods.
    (d) House confinement is not necessary for a person to collect disability income insurance. Coverage continues even if the insured flies privately or publicly or travels abroad.

(e) Total disability from accidental injury does not have to occur within any specified number of days from the date of the accident to qualify as a claim for accident.

(f) Preexisting conditions will not disqualify an insured for coverage if the conditions do not appear for a two-year period after the policy has been in force.

(g) Disability owing to war, pregnancy, childbirth, and miscarriage is not covered.

15. (a) Suggest reasons why group insurance is frequently priced lower than individual insurance.

(b) Are there any limitations to group insurance that the buyer should keep in mind?

16. John Jones has an individual health insurance policy on which he has paid the first premium. He enters the hospital on the day the second premium becomes due. Under most health insurance policies must John pay his premium, or is it waived during an illness?

17. What is a typical definition of "long-term disability," and why is the definition important to the insured?

CASE PROBLEMS

I. The Straight Facts about Life Insurance

Listed below are statements on life insurance. Alongside each statement is the comment of a life insurance agent.

"Agents' commissions are usually higher on the straight life policies, so they may prefer to sell you this type of coverage."

"I like to think most agents prefer to sell what is best for the prospect. As far as commissions are concerned, straight life does pay a higher commission initially, but it pays only one first-year commission. With many companies, when a five-year term policy is sold, it pays a first-year commission initially and additional first-year commissions each time the policy is renewed. With this arrangement, the agent is better compensated by selling term."

"Find out if you are eligible for group insurance. You can save from 15 to 40 percent by taking advantage of a group plan."

"You will get the cash value of the policy when you reach an age specified in the contract."

"If you live long enough, the cash value you collect will be greater than the total premium you have paid. You will, however, have less profit than if you had purchased term insurance and put the difference in a savings account."

"You can borrow against the cash value of your insurance policy, but you still have to pay the interest."

"The cost of group insurance depends on the average age of the group. If you are in your twenties and are part of a group where the average age is forty, you will pay more for group insurance than you would if you purchased the coverage individually."

"You can obtain the cash value of the policy any year you want."

"In most dividend-paying policies, you will collect more cash than premiums paid at the end of the twelfth policy year. Naturally you would receive more had you made deposits with a bank instead of an insurance company, but how much would the bank have paid in the event of the depositor's death after the first deposit? And in the event of disability of the depositor, how many deposits would the bank make for the disabled depositor?"

"When you borrow, on what assets *don't* you have to pay interest? If you borrow on your savings passbook, you pay interest. If you borrow on your auto or home, you pay interest. If you borrow on securities, you pay interest."

"Most agents who sell life insurance are clearly aware that what is best for the prospect is best for them, be it term insurance, straight life, or anything else."

QUESTIONS

1. For each of the above statements, indicate with reasons whether you agree or disagree.

2. Do you agree with the agent's concluding comment? Why or why not?

II. Life Insurance—How Much and What Type

The following text is excerpted from an article in *Business Week*.

LIFE: A $100,000 MINIMUM
Plan More Coverage in Your Middle Years

If you have children to educate and a mortgage to pay off, figure on $100,000 of life insurance as a rock-bottom minimum today. Build from there—most likely you will need a lot more protection.

Ordinary life insurance builds up cash value—money you can borrow against in a pinch at a low rate; money you can draw on after retirement as your need for insurance wanes. But more people rely now on term insurance for their middle years, when the need for protection is greatest. Term is relatively cheap—sometimes cheaper than your own company's group plan insurance. Or you may want an endowment (insurance plus a fixed income after retirement) if your company is one of the many that have dropped their pension plans since the new pension reform law took effect earlier this year. You can invest up to $1,500 tax-free in an endowment through one of the new individual retirement accounts (IRAs) created by the new law.

As an insurance tie-in to the retirement annuity, many insurers give you an option to buy a substantial amount of term life insurance at a premium rate about 20 percent under the regular rate. At forty, you can buy up to $150,000 in one-year term coverage, renewable to age seventy, on the strength of your $1,500 IRA annuity.

Term Coverage. If you just want more life insurance, check your own company's group plan first. A typical arrangement is for the company to provide insurance equal to one year's salary and to offer the option of buying coverage equal to one-and-one-half or two years' salary at an average rate of $7.20 per $1,000 a year. "But don't assume that the group rate is the cheapest," cautions Gordon Collins, an insurance specialist with Chase Manhattan Bank in New York. "It depends on your age."

At thirty-five, an extra $70,000 in group insurance would cost $500 a year at the $7.20 rate. Term insurance, bought independently, would cost only $250. That would increase to $300 at forty, but your premium would not reach $500 until your forty-eighth birthday. But check with your company before you do anything. The $7.20 rate is average; the range is from about $6 to $8 per $1,000. And some companies pay 20 percent to 40 percent or more of any additional insurance you buy through the group plan, cutting your cost way down. Remember that with company group insurance your choice at retirement is to drop it or convert to ordinary life at high cost.

Ordinary life has some benefits. However, the same $70,000 in coverage at thirty-five would cost $1,500. But you can combine ordinary and term life in a single contract and bring the cost down. If you combine $20,000 in ordinary life and $50,000 in twenty-year term, the annual premium would be $560, with a cash value of $6,800 at age fifty-five.

Source: *Business Week* (November 17, 1975), pp. 130–132.

QUESTIONS

1. Evaluate the advice given in the first paragraph. How should you determine how much life insurance to buy?

2. What are the advantages of term coverage over ordinary life or endowments? The disadvantages?

III. The High Cost of Medical Care

The *Wall Street Journal* reported the following data as "typical" medical costs.

Typical Medical Costs, September 1980

Metropolitan Area	Hospital Room (semiprivate, one day)	Office Visit (general practitioner)	Surgeon's Fee (simple appendectomy)
New York	$270	$35	$900
Chicago	254	20	680
Ann Arbor, Mich.	240	20	475
San Jose, Calif.	170	21	720
Denver	165	16	510
Baltimore	135	25	470
Kansas City, Mo.	125	17	380
Fort Lauderdale, Fla.	106	20	520
Houston	100	18	550
Lexington, Ky.	78	14	450

QUESTIONS

1. Suggest reasons for the regional differences observed in the above data.

2. In your opinion are typical health losses severe enough to require some risk-handling device other than assumption of risk by an individual? Discuss.

CHAPTER 6

AUTOMOBILE AND HOMEOWNERS INSURANCE

LEARNING OBJECTIVES

In studying this chapter, you will learn:

Why automobile and homeowners insurance are vital tools for effective personal financial management;

What important exposures to loss arise from ownership of an automobile or a home;

What is covered and what is not covered by homeowners and auto insurance;

The main factors affecting the cost of property insurance;

Ways to reduce the cost of insurance;

How to get coverage if you are turned down by an insurer;

The main differences between various types of homeowners policies;

The "best buy" among homeowners policies;

What kinds of losses are paid under homeowners insurance.

Successful personal financial management requires adequate protection of your assets. For most owners of homes and automobiles, the best way to protect themselves against various threats to their assets is to have adequate insurance coverage. Automobile and homeowners insurance account for most of the premium dollars spent by consumers (see Exhibit 6–1). Insurance costs are a significant portion of the total costs of maintaining homes and cars.

EXHIBIT 6–1
Purchases of Property and Liability Insurance by Individuals, 1980

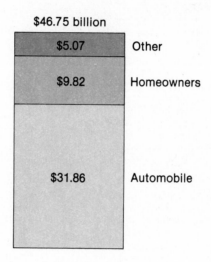

$46.75 billion

$5.07 — Other

$9.82 — Homeowners

$31.86 — Automobile

Source: Based on data provided by A.M. Best Company in *Insurance Facts*, 1981–82 ed. (New York: Insurance Information Institute, 1981), p. 20.

AUTOMOBILE INSURANCE

Because operating an automobile gives rise to losses that few individuals can pay out of current income, insurance coverage has emerged as the only practical way of providing for such losses (see Exhibit 6–2). Through insurance the loss can be spread in such a way that the risk is not an intolerable burden on any one person. Automobile insurance is the largest single type of property and liability insurance sold in the United States; it accounts for about 40 percent of all nonlife premiums collected. In the period from 1970 to 1979, automobile insurance premiums more than doubled. Costs of operating an automobile have been significantly increased by rising insurance costs (see Exhibit 6–3).

EXHIBIT 6–2   Auto Insurance Coverage Reported by U.S. Car Owners, 1981

By Age Group	Total U.S.	18–29	30–39	40–49	50–59	60 & Older
Have insurance	92%	86%	93%	97%	95%	95%
Do not have insurance	8%	14%	7%	3%	5%	5%
By Place of Residence		Total U.S.	Urban	Suburban	Rural	
Have insurance		92%	92%	95%	88%	
Do not have insurance		8%	8%	5%	12%	

Source: *Insurance Facts*, 1981–82 ed. (New York: Insurance Information Institute, 1981), p. 11.

EXHIBIT 6–3   Cost of Operating an Automobile, Cents per Mile

	Vehicle Cost Depreciated	Maintenance Accessories Parts & Tires	Gas & Oil (Excluding Taxes)	Garages Parking & Tolls	Insurance	State & Federal Taxes	Total Cost Per Mile
Standard size	6.3¢	5.5¢	5.6¢	3.2¢	2.4¢	1.6¢	24.6¢
Compact size	5.2¢	4.8¢	4.9¢	3.2¢	2.3¢	1.3¢	21.7¢
Subcompact size	3.8¢	4.1¢	4.1¢	3.2¢	2.2¢	1.1¢	18.5¢

Source: Federal Highway Administration, U.S. Department of Transportation, as published in *Insurance Facts*, 1981–82 ed. (New York: Insurance Information Institute, 1981), p. 41.

Losses from Automobile Accidents

Four major types of losses occur as a result of auto accidents (see Exhibits 6–4 and 6–5).

1. Bodily injury and death;
2. Physical damage loss to one's automobile, including theft;
3. Liability to others for negligent operation of the automobile;
4. Loss of income and loss of use of the automobile.

Insurance is available against each of these types of losses, and claims costs are rising steadily (see Exhibit 6–6).

BODILY INJURY AND DEATH

Each year in the United States approximately 52,000 deaths and 5 million injuries result from auto accidents. In 1980 approximately 24 million accidents were reported; with 140 million drivers registered in the United States, the chance of having an accident is about one in six. Motor vehicle accidents cause over half of all accidental deaths in the United States—nearly four times

EXHIBIT 6–4
Possible Losses
from Auto
Accidents

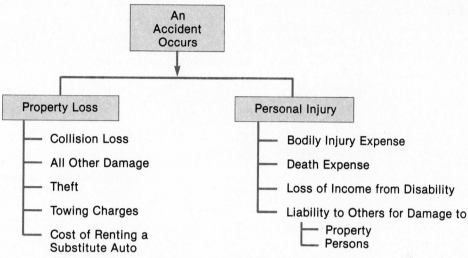

as many as occur on the job and twice as many as occur at home.[1] Excessive speed and driving under the influence of alcohol and drugs are major causes of accidents.

Statistics reveal that youthful drivers are involved in a disproportionate number of accidents. For example, in 1980 drivers under age twenty constituted about 10 percent of all drivers but had 16.8 percent of all accidents and 15.8 percent of all fatal accidents. In contrast, drivers between ages thirty-five and thirty-nine constituted 9.5 percent of all drivers but had only 7.3 percent of all accidents and 7 percent of all fatal accidents (see Exhibit 6–7). These statistics reveal why insurance premiums for youthful drivers are high in comparison with the rates charged to older drivers.

COLLISION

In 1981 about 12 percent of all vehicles reported collision losses, with an average loss per claim of slightly over $1,000. Collision losses tend to vary according to the size and type of automobile; full-sized cars cost considerably more to repair than intermediate or compact cars. However, subcompact cars were responsible for a larger average loss payment than were many larger automobiles; subcompacts are more susceptible to collision loss when they are driven on highways amidst larger vehicles.

THEFT

Theft of automobiles, although high, has been declining in recent years in proportion to the number of cars on the road. Over 1,100,000 automobiles

---

1. *Insurance Facts*, 1981–1982 ed. (New York: Insurance Information Institute, 1981), p. 54.

EXHIBIT 6–5

U.S. Traffic
Accident Trends
Since the 1970s

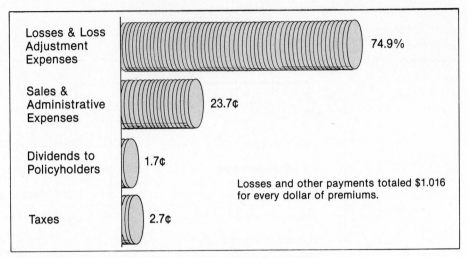

Losses & Loss Adjustment Expenses   74.9%

Sales & Administrative Expenses   23.7¢

Dividends to Policyholders   1.7¢

Taxes   2.7¢

Losses and other payments totaled $1.016
for every dollar of premiums.

Source: *Insurance Facts,* 1981–82 ed. (New York: Insurance Information
Institute, 1981), p. 54.

EXHIBIT 6–6

Countrywide
Average Paid
Claim Costs,
Liability
Insurance,
Private Passenger
Cars

Year	Bodily Injury	Property Damage
1971	$1,852	$346
1972	1,926	355
1973	2,125	375
1974	2,472	397
1975	2,646	445
1976	2,583	490
1977	2,890	544
1978	3,123	622
1979	3,559	715
1980	4,010	787

Notes: Costs are for all limits combined and include all loss adjustment expenses. Dollar
averages exclude Massachusetts (for all years) and most states that have no-fault
automobile insurance laws.

An apparent decline in 1976 in the amount of the average paid bodily injury claim
is the result of an adjustment resulting from a change in the data base, and does not
necessarily reflect an improvement in the claims experience. The revised data base has
been applied to all claims figures for 1976 and succeeding years, but not to the figure
for earlier years.

Source: Insurance Services Office, as published in *Insurance Facts,* 1981–82 ed. (New York: Insurance Information
Institute, 1981), p. 56.

EXHIBIT 6–7   Accidents by Age of Drivers, 1980

Age Group	Number of Drivers	% of Total	Drivers in All Accidents	% of Total	Drivers in Fatal Accidents	% of Total	Accident Involvement Rate	
							All[a]	Fatal[b]
Under 20	14,300,000	9.8	5,000,000	16.8	10,800	15.8	35	76
20–24	17,400,000	11.9	5,900,000	19.8	14,200	20.8	34	82
25–29	17,500,000	12.0	4,400,000	14.8	9,700	14.2	25	55
30–34	16,800,000	11.5	3,500,000	11.7	8,300	12.2	21	49
35–39	13,900,000	9.5	2,200,000	7.3	4,800	7.0	16	35
40–44	11,700,000	8.0	1,900,000	6.4	4,700	6.9	16	40
45–49	11,400,000	7.8	1,600,000	5.3	3,800	5.6	14	33
50–54	11,700,000	8.0	1,300,000	4.4	2,900	4.2	11	25
55–59	10,100,000	6.9	1,300,000	4.4	2,600	3.8	13	26
60–64	7,500,000	5.2	900,000	3.0	2,200	3.2	12	29
65–69	6,400,000	4.4	1,000,000	3.4	1,700	2.5	16	27
70–74	4,400,000	3.0	300,000	1.0	1,200	1.8	7	27
75 and over	2,900,000	2.0	500,000	1.7	1,400	2.0	17	48
Total	146,000,000	100.00	29,800,000	100.0	68,300	100.0	20	47

[a]Drivers in all accidents per 100 drivers in each age group.
[b]Drivers in fatal accidents per 100,000 drivers in each age group.

Source: National Safety Council, as published in *Insurance Facts*, 1981–82 ed. (New York: Insurance Information Institute, 1981), p. 55.

were stolen in 1980[2]—that is, 1 in every 145 vehicles on the road, as compared with 1 in every 123 in 1969. Automobile thefts are much more frequent in populous states such as New York and California. Automobile theft losses cost approximately $3 billion annually in the United States.

LIABILITY

Approximately two-thirds of all claims paid by automobile insurers are for liability losses; the remaining one-third stem from collision and from other physical damage to cars. If you are at fault in an accident, you may be held liable not only for the physical loss of the other driver's car or property but also for medical expenses, loss of income, and even "pain and suffering" of the other driver, as determined by a court of law. These claims may total hundreds of thousands of dollars. Courts are becoming more willing to assess large damages for negligent operation of vehicles, and such losses are rising more rapidly than any other type of claim.

---

2. Ibid., p. 65.

Source: Business Insurance (November 9, 1981), p. 24.

LOSS OF INCOME

If you are disabled in an automobile accident and are unable to work, your income may be cut off. Without insurance protection, you might be unable to pay living costs for you and your family. Economic costs (including lost income) associated with traffic accidents amounted to $56 billion in 1979—nearly three times as much as costs totaled ten years earlier.

Basic Automobile Insurance Coverages

Basic types of insurance against losses arising out of the ownership and operation of automobiles are as follows:

1. Liability insurance, including bodily injury and property damage liability;
2. Health insurance for medical payments coverage, accidental death and dismemberment coverage, and personal injury coverage under no-fault laws;
3. Coverage of physical damage to the automobile, including collision and comprehensive;
4. Miscellaneous coverages for uninsured motorists, for towing and labor costs, and for rental reimbursement.

LIABILITY INSURANCE

Perhaps the most important type of coverage offered under the typical automobile policy is protection in case you are found negligent and, hence, liable for losses that others suffer because of bodily injury or property damage. Known as **bodily injury and property damage liability insurance**, this coverage usually has certain limits. For example, $25/$50 limits would pay $25,000 for loss from bodily injury liability for any one person, or $50,000 for all persons involved in any one accident. Property damage liability is usually expressed as a single limit, such as $5,000 or $10,000, for any one accident.

Legal liability, also called **tort liability**, may result if a court finds that you were to blame for an accident. A legal finding of **negligence** implies that you failed to exercise the degree of care required under the circumstances. Typical examples would include driving too fast, running a stop sign or a red light, or failing to yield to oncoming traffic while making a left-hand turn. If you were found negligent and had no insurance, you could be forced to sell your home and all your property, and your wages could be garnered for many years to satisfy court judgments. Under most circumstances liability claims cannot be eliminated even if you declare bankruptcy. Liability insurance pays defense costs, including the cost of court bonds, in addition to any liability judgments awarded. Thus, liability insurance is considered almost a necessity in modern society.

Property damage liability arises not only from striking another person's automobile, but also from running into a house, over a lawn, or into a telephone pole or building. For example, you may be to blame in a highway accident where a large truck loaded with valuable cargo is overturned. The resulting loss is considered property damage liability and might result in a very large claim—much larger than the typical limits carried in property damage liability insurance. Your only hope is to have coverage sufficient to meet such a claim.

HEALTH INSURANCE

The typical automobile insurance policy covers various health insurance losses. **Medical payments insurance**, for example, pays medical claims made by you, your passengers, or others riding in your car. Medical payments also cover you and your family as pedestrians if you are injured by another car. This coverage pays for all reasonable medical expenses incurred within a one-year period from the date of the accident. If death results, the insurance also covers funeral expenses. Payment is made regardless of who is at fault in the accident.

Some insurers offer **accidental death and dismemberment insurance**, under which a lump sum is paid if you are accidentally killed while driving an automobile or if you are struck by another car. The policy usually pays a portion of the principal amount if you lose an arm, a leg, or an eye. The policy may also cover a weekly or monthly disability income if you should become totally disabled as a result of an automobile accident.

In about one-half of the states, "no-fault laws" require that insurers offer a type of coverage called **personal injury protection (PIP)**. To some extent PIP coverage duplicates medical payments insurance. However, PIP protection also includes a loss of income allowance for individuals who are disabled temporarily as a result of an automobile accident. PIP coverage pays regardless of fault. It covers the costs of wages of individuals hired to per-

"Negligence implies that you failed to exercise the degree of care required under
the circumstances."

form essential home services formerly performed by an injured family
member—for example, a spouse who was not working for an independent
income.

Both medical payments and PIP are limited according to the amount purchased. Limits for medical payments are frequently $500 or $1,000 for each
individual. Medical payments coverage up to $10,000 a person is available.
PIP coverage limits can rise to $50,000 or more.

Medical payments and PIP protection differ from bodily injury liability
coverage in that they apply to you and to guests in your car, not to third parties in another car or to pedestrians, both of whom are protected by bodily
injury liability coverage.

PHYSICAL DAMAGE INSURANCE

The two major types of insurance that cover physical damage loss to your
automobile are collision insurance and comprehensive insurance. **Collision**

insurance is the coverage on losses to your vehicle as a result of its striking another vehicle or object, or as a result of turning over, running off the road, or other type of moving accident. **Comprehensive insurance** covers all other types of losses to your car, including theft. For example, if a flying rock breaks your windshield, the loss would be paid under comprehensive. Comprehensive will include any noncollision peril—for example, fire, theft, glass breakage, flood, falling objects, missiles, explosions, earthquakes, windstorms, water, vandalism, malicious mischief, or damage caused by the car's striking a bird or an animal. Excluded from comprehensive coverage would be losses due to wear and tear, engine failure, radiator leakage, or other mechanical difficulties. A major reason for your carrying comprehensive is the protection it affords against theft.

Both collision and comprehensive insurance are usually sold with a deductible amount that applies to each loss. Collision deductibles, for example, range from $100 to $500. A typical deductible for comprehensive insurance is $50. The purpose of these deductibles is to eliminate small claims; they effect substantial rate reductions in your premium payment. If you finance your automobile, most finance companies or banks require collision and comprehensive insurance as a condition for making a loan.

One advantage of having collision insurance in addition to property damage liability is that if another car runs into you and its driver is liable, you can make an immediate claim against your own insurer for collision loss reimbursement. If your insurance includes a deductible, your insurer will pursue the claim against the insurer of the liable third party. Upon making collection, your insurer will restore the deductible to you. If you have no collision coverage, you may not be reimbursed immediately because legal delays in the settlement process may slow collection against the other party.

MISCELLANEOUS COVERAGES

Three miscellaneous coverages are a part of the typical automobile insurance policy. The first is the **uninsured motorist endorsement (UME)**. Most states require this endorsement. UME applies mainly to bodily injuries (in a few states it also applies to property damage) for which an uninsured motorist or hit-and-run driver is legally liable. Thus, if you are struck by a hit-and-run driver and incur a bodily injury, you may make a claim against your own insurer for the loss. Various levels of liability limits for UME are specified in each state.

Another coverage is available to meet the expenses of towing and labor. **Towing and labor coverage** provides indemnity when your automobile is disabled and you must incur expenses towing it in for repairs. Usually the limits of liability under this coverage are relatively small (e.g., $25).

If your car is involved in an accident and you must rent a substitute vehicle, **rental reimbursement coverage** pays the expense, subject to limits ranging from $10 to a maximum of $300 a day. Rental reimbursement insurance imposes a forty-eight-hour waiting period before reimbursement begins.

Some Facts about Automobile Coverage

The typical automobile insurance policy is long and complex. Individuals often fail to make claims because they do not realize that certain losses are covered under their policies. The following are examples of little-known coverages included in a typical policy.

1. You are covered if you are driving someone else's car with permission. The same coverage applies to other members of your family.
2. Anyone living in your household on a permanent basis is covered while driving your automobile, as is anyone driving it with your permission. In most cases, these individuals are also covered while driving with permission other cars not owned by you.
3. You are covered even if the suit made against you is fraudulent, false, or groundless. Liability insurance in automobile coverage is frequently called **defense insurance** because of this feature.
4. If you are involved in an accident and someone in the other car is injured, your bodily injury liability insurance will pay for first aid and other medical expenses to the injured party, regardless of whether you are ultimately held liable for the accident. This coverage is in addition to the general liability limits of your policy.
5. Your liability policy will respond to court costs, costs of appeal bonds, and other legal expenses involved in a suit, in addition to the liability limits for which you are covered. Frequently defense costs are more expensive than the actual costs of liability judgments.
6. If you are hit and injured by another vehicle, your own medical payments coverage will respond. You need not make a claim against the driver of the other car to collect. The same coverage applies to members of your family.
7. Although your home may not be insured against flood or earthquake damage, your automobile is.
8. Automobile coverage applies whether you own or lease the car.
9. Your policy covers pickup trucks or panel trucks if they are not customarily used in your occupation or profession.
10. Your policy gives automatic protection on newly acquired vehicles for thirty days. After thirty days you must notify your insurer to obtain coverage.
11. If you carry certain limits of liability required in your state and you are driving in another state with higher limits, your policy automatically protects you for the higher limits.

Exclusions and Limitations of Automobile Coverage

Several types of losses are excluded by your personal automobile policy. They are listed as follows:

1. If you are using your car for hire as a taxi or a bus, your coverage is suspended. This exclusion, however, does not usually apply to "share-a-ride" arrangements to and from work.

2. Any losses you cause intentionally are excluded. Thus, if you deliberately run into and destroy your neighbor's dog, the resulting liability to your neighbor would not be covered.

3. If the loss arises from war, coverage is suspended.

4. You are only covered for private passenger automobiles, not for commercial vehicles, motorcycles, or snowmobiles. Separate coverage for business use must be purchased for these vehicles.

5. Trailers are not covered automatically as "cars." Physical damage losses to an office, a store, or a display or passenger trailer are excluded unless you have paid an extra premium for specific coverage. However, your liability coverage is not affected if you haul a trailer.

6. Coverage on nonowned automobiles is not as broad as coverage on owned automobiles. You should check the terms of your policy on this point. If two policies cover the same loss, the policy covering the insured vehicle must usually pay first, and any excess losses will be paid by other policies. Thus, if you are driving your neighbor's car, your own collision insurance policy will apply as excess coverage, if necessary, over the coverage owned by your neighbor.

7. If you fail to report a loss promptly, or if you fail to take action to save and preserve your property from further loss at the time of an accident, you may not be able to collect at all. Your insurance contract requires you to take all steps to prevent further loss and to prove the amount of your loss within a specified time period.

8. Your coverage does not apply to anyone in the automotive business— for example, a service station employee who uses your car while it is being serviced or repaired. Such individuals must have their own protection.

9. Unless your policy is so written, it will not cover cars made available or furnished for your regular use—for example, a car provided by your employer. Your employer's insurance would give you protection in this situation.

10. The policy excludes certain types of automobile property from physical damage loss. For example, unless you pay an extra premium, the loss of car tapes, records, or other devices is usually not covered, nor is the loss of citizen band radios.

11. Unless the loss is due to another covered peril (e.g., theft or collision), the policy excludes damage from wear and tear, freezing, elec-

trical breakdown, or road damage to tires. Thus, if you have a flat tire or if your engine freezes in the winter, your policy will not usually pay.

12. The policy limits payment to the cost of repairing or replacing property of a "like kind and quality." In other words, the coverage is on an "actual cash value" basis. For example, if it costs $3,000 to repair a car worth only $2,000, the insurer's maximum payment will normally be the lower figure. If you have an antique or customized automobile, you may add an endorsement that sets a specific policy limit, such as $5,000 or $10,000.

Other Provisions of Automobile Policies

If a loss occurs, you should notify your agent or your insurer as soon as practicable. If your car is stolen, you must also notify the police. You must cooperate with the insurer in investigating or defending any claim or suit against you. The insurer also requires that you submit a proof of loss to show that you personally suffered the loss in the amount claimed.

You must also take reasonable steps after a loss to protect your automobile and its equipment from further damage. For example, if after an accident you leave your car unlocked by the side of the road and a thief later removes the contents of the car, you may not be able to collect on the contents because you failed to lock your car or take other steps to protect it.

During the first sixty days the insurer can cancel your policy for any reason. After sixty days, the insurer can cancel only for nonpayment of premium unless certain conditions are present; for example, the insurer can cancel if your driver's license has been suspended or revoked.

Your policy contains a **subrogation clause** that gives your insurer the right to pursue liable third parties for your loss. If you are in a collision and someone else is responsible, you can collect under your collision coverage, but your insurer has the right to attempt to recover this payment from the third party who was responsible for the damage. The insurer's subrogation rights are limited to the amounts the insurer has paid you. If you have suffered losses in excess of the amount you can collect from your insurer, you may pursue liable third parties for the additional claims.

Your policy generally provides coverage only while you are driving in the United States or Canada. If you travel outside these countries—for example, if you drive in Mexico—special coverage must be arranged.

Some policies cover certain personal property against limited perils—for example, fire or lightning. Other policies exclude all loss of personal property carried in the automobile.

Automobile Insurance Premiums

Automobile insurance premiums depend on a number of factors—for example, the cost of repairing damages on your particular type of vehicle, labor rates and medical costs in your community, insurer overhead, and your community's experience in regard to liability judgments (see Exhibit 6–8).

Premiums vary considerably, depending on the type and limits of coverage. A sports car will usually carry a greater premium rate for similar coverage than will a standard automobile. The amount of the deductible you select has an important effect on the premium. The age of the car and whether you have obtained a discount for insuring two or more cars are additional factors affecting premiums.

EXHIBIT 6–8

Where the Premium Dollar Goes: Experience of the Property/ Casualty Insurance Business in 1980

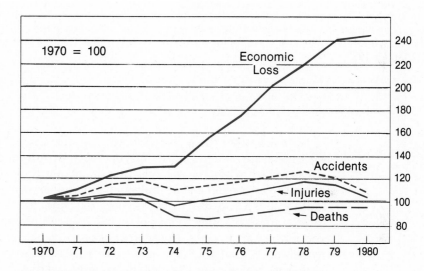

Source: Based on data provided by A.M. Best Company in *Insurance Facts,* 1981–82 ed. (New York: Insurance Information Institute, 1981), p. 14.

Automobile insurance costs less if you accept higher deductibles. For example, you can save about 45 percent of the premium cost of $100 deductible insurance by accepting a $500 deductible (see Exhibit 6–9). Some older cars probably should not be insured at all for collision or comprehensive since the loss of such a car might not be a financially serious blow.

On the other hand, you can double your limits of bodily injury liability from $25,000 to $50,000 for only a 20 percent increase in premium. The premium for $100,000 of bodily injury liability is only one-third higher than the premium for $25,000 limits. These premium dollars may be well spent; liability damages can easily exceed basic limits required by law, and a larger damage award could be a crippling blow to your finances.

EXHIBIT 6-9   Automobile Prices and the Cost of Insurance, 1982

| | | Cost of Physical Damage Insurance | | | |
| | | Comprehensive | | Collision | |
Automobile	New Car Price	No Deductible	$50 Deductible	$100 Deductible	$500 Deductible
Ford Escort	$ 5,518	$ 34	$27	$ 85	$ 47
Chevrolet Citation	6,754	34	27	85	47
Oldsmobile Cutlass					
Brougham	9,900	66	53	127	70
Buick Electra	11,713	66	53	127	70
Cadillac Seville	23,500	101	81	190	105

Note: Rates apply to a twenty-six-year-old male with no traffic violations in the previous five years, driving less than twenty miles to and from work in Marietta, Georgia (a suburb of Atlanta), 1982.

Source: Allstate Insurance Company.

In most states the highest rates are usually charged to young, unmarried males who are owners or principal operators of automobiles. Although these rates are high when the policy is first taken out, they are scaled down as the driver becomes older and acquires more driving experience. A premium credit is allowed if a youthful driver is going to school some distance from home. Most states have safe-driver plans under which points are assessed against you if you are involved in accidents or receive traffic citations. A "clean" record means that you have not been involved in any accident in which you have been at fault, nor have you been convicted of a serious traffic law violation for three years. If either or both of these things have happened to you, points are assessed against you. Higher rates accompany higher point totals.

Special discounts are usually given if your car or truck is being used in farming. If you have completed a driver education course, you may also be eligible for a reduced rate of up to 25 percent. If you use your car only to drive to and from work or school each day, you will be charged a lower premium than if you drive your car as part of your work.

Not all automobile insurance policies are the same. For example, the contract called the **family auto policy (FAP)** offers more deluxe features and fewer exclusions than the type of policy known as the **personal auto policy (PAP)**. The latter may offer more restricted coverage and less flexibility than the former, but you may be able to save substantial sums by purchasing the PAP. Many large insurers develop their own policy contracts, which you must study individually to learn just what coverage is included.

Automobile Insurance and the Law

Four major types of state laws affect you as an automobile driver: assigned risk plans, financial responsibility laws, no-fault laws, and laws requiring an uninsured motorist endorsement (UME). Almost all states have assigned risk plans and financial responsibility laws; about half of the states have no-fault laws. Nearly all states require inclusion of the UME.

A basic purpose of automobile insurance laws is to increase the chance that motorists who suffer losses in automobile accidents will be able to collect from negligent parties or from their own insurers. Financial responsibility and UME laws are based on the doctrine of negligence (also called tort liability), while no-fault laws eliminate the requirement of negligence up to stated dollar limits of loss.

ASSIGNED RISK PLANS

Nearly every state has an **assigned risk plan** under which a person who applies for automobile insurance and is rejected may still be able to get coverage. Under assigned risk plans the risk of insuring people who have been rejected is shared equally among all automobile insurance companies operating in the state. The premium for a case of assigned risk may be somewhat higher and the coverage more limited than under regular policies, but at least some amount of insurance is available.

FINANCIAL RESPONSIBILITY

Financial responsibility laws require you to carry liability insurance or to maintain other proof of financial responsibility for a given period (usually three years) in case you are involved in an accident. If you are not able to offer either insurance or other evidence of financial responsibility after an accident, your driver's license will be suspended and you will be unable to drive legally. Note that financial responsibility laws do not require insurance coverage as a prior condition of driving. However, once you have had a loss or an accident, you must be able to demonstrate financial responsibility. The weakness of these laws is that they provide no assurance that all drivers will have liability coverage before they drive. Thus, motorists have little protection against the hit-and-run or the stolen-car driver, or against motorists driving illegally without insurance. Studies show that many uninsured motorists operate on U.S. highways.

NO-FAULT LAWS

To correct some of the weaknesses of financial responsibility laws and to speed compensation for highway accidents, approximately half of the states have passed **no-fault laws** under which insurance is usually compulsory (see Exhibit 6–8). Most no-fault laws provide that in the event of a serious acci-

"Hey, Dad, does this mean we'll have to go into an assigned risk pool?"

The Bettman Archive, Inc.

dent, or if total losses exceed a certain dollar amount known as a "threshold" (at least $500), you may make a claim directly against your own insurer without showing proof of negligence or fault on the part of either driver. Only if the accident produces "serious" losses, or if these losses exceed the threshold level, do the general principles of tort liability and negligence apply. Losses under no-fault laws include medical expense and loss of income, but, except in ten states, not physical damage to the vehicle.

Studies show that in states with no-fault statutes, over 40 percent of the potential liability claims have been eliminated; the injured person is paid by the driver's own insurer on a no-fault basis. In no-fault states more individuals were able to collect something for their losses than were individuals in states without no-fault laws. In states without no-fault, delays, costs, and other difficulties involved in bringing liability action to court were probably instrumental in preventing injured persons from either making claims or collecting their losses.

Exhibit 6–10 provides a summary of financial responsibility laws, as well as required limits of liability under these laws, in various states as of 1981. For example, in Alabama auto insurance is not compulsory, but if you purchase coverge, you need limits of "10/20/5" to satisfy provisions of the state's financial responsibility law. That is, state law requires a minimum of $10,000/$20,000 bodily injury coverage and $5,000 property damage liability coverage. Thus, if you are involved in an accident in which the court awards a $12,000 damage judgment to one passenger and $8,000 of bodily injury damage to a second passenger, the policy will pay $10,000 for the first loss and $8,000 for the second, or a total of $18,000. You would be required to pay $2,000 to the first passenger because you had inadequate limits of liability. Thus, it is wise to carry more than the minimum required limits.

No-fault laws are classified in Exhibit 6–11. Some states require liability and PIP coverage and also have restrictions prohibiting drivers from suing under tort liability. For example, the state of Georgia has a $500 "threshold" of loss, which prohibits negligence suits unless losses exceed $500. Assume that driver *A* suffers bodily injury losses of $400 as a result of an accident in which driver *B* is at fault. *A*'s $400 loss would be paid under *A*'s personal injury protection, and *A* would have no right to sue *B* for additional amounts—for example, for "pain and suffering"—since the loss was under the threshold limit. If the loss had been $1,000 (exceeding the threshold of $500), *A* not only would have been able to recover $1,000 under personal injury protection, but also could have brought a much larger damage suit against *B* for pain and suffering. Six states have passed laws requiring "first-party benefits" (PIP coverage) to be optional The nine states that do not restrict the right to sue have not really adopted the no-fault principle.

HOMEOWNERS INSURANCE

The most widely used method of transferring the risks associated with owning or occupying a home or apartment is an insurance "package" known as a homeowners program. **Homeowners insurance** is a combination of coverages formerly sold separately at much higher total costs. Homeowners insurance costs are modest—about 3 percent of average housing expenses (see Exhibit 6–12). Under these packages you may obtain insurance against perils such as fire, windstorm, explosion, theft, liability, and medical payments.

EXHIBIT 6–10
Financial
Responsibility
Laws and
Required Limits
of Liability

State	Compulsory	Required Limits
Alabama	No	10/20/5
Alaska	No	25/50/10
Arizona	No	15/30/10
Arkansas	No	25/50/15
California	Yes	15/30/5
Colorado	Yes	15/30/5
Connecticut	Yes	20/40/5
Delaware	Yes	10/20/5
Dist. of Columbia	No	10/20/5
Florida	No	10/20/5
Georgia	Yes	10/20/5
Hawaii	Yes	25/unlim./10
Idaho	Yes	10/20/5
Illinois	No	15/30/10
Indiana	No	15/30/10
Iowa	No	15/30/10
Kansas	Yes	25/50/10
Kentucky	Yes	10/20/5
Louisiana	No	5/10/5
Maine	No	20/40/10
Maryland	Yes	20/40/10
Massachusetts	Yes	10/20/5
Michigan	Yes	20/40/10
Minnesota	Yes	25/50/10
Mississippi	No	10/20/5
Missouri	No	10/20/2
Montana	No	25/50/5
Nebraska	No	15/30/5
Nevada	Yes	15/30/5
New Hampshire	No	20/50/25
New Jersey	Yes	15/30/5
New Mexico	No	15/30/5
New York	Yes	10/20/5
North Carolina	Yes	25/50/10
North Dakota	Yes	25/50/10
Ohio	No	12.5/25/7.5
Oklahoma	Yes	10/20/10
Oregon	Yes	15/30/5
Pennsylvania	Yes	15/30/5
Rhode Island	No	25/50/10
South Carolina	Yes	15/30/5
South Dakota	No	15/30/10
Tennessee	No	10/20/5
Texas	No	10/20/5

State	Compulsory	Required Limits
Utah	Yes	15/30/5
Vermont	No	20/40/10
Virginia	No	25/50/5
Washington	No	25/50/10
West Virginia	No	20/40/10
Wisconsin	No	15/30/5
Wyoming	No	10/20/5

Source: *Insurance Facts,* 1981–82 ed. (New York: Insurance Information Institute, 1981), p. 71.

EXHIBIT 6–11
U.S. No-Fault Laws and Requirements

I. Compulsory PIP coverage and liability insurance

   A. States restricting lawsuits[a]

Colorado (1974)	Michigan (1973)
Connecticut (1973)	Minnesota (1975)
Georgia (1975)	New Jersey (1973)
Hawaii (1974)	New York (1974)
Kansas (1974)	North Dakota (1976)
Kentucky (1975)	Pennsylvania (1975)
Massachusetts (1971)	Utah (1974)

   B. States not restricting lawsuits

      Delaware (1972)
      Maryland (1973)
      Oregon (1972)

II. Compulsory liability, no restrictions on lawsuits, optional PIP coverage

      South Carolina (1974)

III. Optional liability and PIP coverage, no restrictions on lawsuits

Arkansas (1974)	Texas (1973)
New Hampshire (1971)	Virginia (1972)
South Dakota (1972)	

IV. Optional liability, compulsory PIP, some restrictions on lawsuits

Florida (1972)	Puerto Rico (1970)

[a]Nevada repealed a law of this type, effective 1980. Florida and Puerto Rico also abolished compulsory liability insurance but retained PIP coverage on a compulsory basis.

Source: *Insurance Facts,* 1981–82 ed. (New York: Insurance Information Institute, 1981), p. 72.

EXHIBIT 6-12
Composition of
Median Monthly
Housing Expense

Item	1979	1977	Increase	1977-1979 of Total
Mortgage payment	$401	$273	$128	85%
Real estate taxes	58	54	4	3%
Utilities	75	60	15	10%
Hazard insurance	16	13	3	2%
Total	$550	$400	$150	100%

Source: U.S. League of Savings Associations, as published in *Insurance Facts,* 1981–82 ed. (New York: Insurance Information Institute, 1981), p. 41.

Coverage under a Homeowners Policy

The typical homeowners policy has the following seven parts:

Coverage A: Dwelling	$15,000 (minimum)
Coverage B: Other structures	10% of Coverage A
Coverage C: Unscheduled personal property	50% of Coverage A
Coverage D: Additional living expenses (loss of use)	20% of Coverage A
Coverage E: Comprehensive personal liability	$25,000 (limit may be increased)
Coverage F: Medical payments to others	$500 per person (higher limits are available)
Physical damage to property of others (voluntary property damage)	$250

To illustrate, consider the home of Don and Mary Adams, which they have just purchased for $80,000. They would like to insure the home for 80 percent of the amount it cost, or $64,000. Thus, Coverage A would be in the amount of $64,000. Coverage B (other structures) would be $6,400 and would cover loss to such structures as garages or tool sheds. Coverage C would provide $32,000 of coverage on all items of personal property—for example, furniture, clothing, tools, money, and other property. (Some property is subject to lower limits of coverage.)

The policy would automatically provide $12,800 of limits on Coverage D (additional living expense). This type of coverage applies if the house is damaged by an insured peril and the occupants must move to a hotel or to other temporary quarters and thus incur higher-than-normal living expenses.

For example, if they must pay $1,000 a month to live in a hotel and normal house payments are $400, they could collect $600 a month under Coverage D.

Under Coverage E, Don and Mary would also have $25,000 of liability insurance, which would apply in case someone brought suit against them for damages incurred while on their property. For example, if a guest slipped on a polished floor and Don and Mary were legally liable, the comprehensive personal liability coverage would pay any resulting liability claims. The policy automatically provides at least $500 in medical payments coverage to guests or other persons on the insured's property. Medical payments coverage under the homeowners program differs from medical payments coverage under automobile insurance because the former does not apply to the homeowner or to the family members, whereas automobile medical payments apply to the driver and to all passengers. Finally, the homeowners policy pays up to $250 for loss of others' property for which Don and Mary are responsible—for example, theft of a borrowed lawnmower. Proof of legal liability for such losses is not required. In summary, the amount of coverage Don and Mary would have under their $64,000 policy is as follows:

Coverage A	$64,000
Coverage B	6,400
Coverage C	32,000
Coverage D	12,800
Coverage E	25,000
Coverage F	500
Voluntary property damage	250
Total	$140,950

Types of Homeowner Policies

Seven different types of homeowners policies have been designed to fit the differing needs of buyers (see Exhibit 6–13). The differences among the policies are described in the following subsections.

HO–1

Known as the basic coverage, Homeowners–1 offers protection against a limited list of perils—for example, fire, lightning, windstorm, hail, explosion, riot, civil commotion, aircraft, nonowned vehicles, smoke, vandalism and malicious mischief, theft, and glass breakage. Losses from these perils may be limited in the amount of coverage. For example, glass breakage is limited to $50, and loss of trees, shrubs, and other plants is limited to $500 or 5 percent of the policy amount, whichever is less.

EXHIBIT 6-13   Perils Against Which Properties Are Insured under the Various Homeowners Policies

Basic HO-1	Broad HO-2	Special HO-3	Renter's HO-4	Compre-hensive HO-5	Condo-minium HO-6	Older Home HO-8	Perils
■	■	■	■	■	■	■	1. Fire or lightning
■	■	■	■	■	■	■	2. Loss of property removed from premises endangered by fire or other perils*
■	■	■	■	■	■	■	3. Windstorm or hail
■	■	■	■	■	■	■	4. Explosion
■	■	■	■	■	■	■	5. Riot or civil commotion
■	■	■	■	■	■	■	6. Aircraft
■	■	■	■	■	■	■	7. Vehicles
■	■	■	■	■	■	■	8. Smoke
■	■	■	■	■	■	■	9. Vandalism and malicious mischief
■	■	■	■	■	■	■	10. Theft
■	■	■	■	■	■	■	11. Breakage of glass constituting a part of the building
	■	■	■	■	■		12. Falling objects
	■	■	■	■	■		13. Weight of ice, snow, sleet
	■	■	■	■	■		14. Collapse of building(s) or any part thereof
	■	■	■	■	■		15. Sudden and accidental tearing asunder, cracking, burning, or bulging of a steam or hot water heating system or of appliances for heating water
	■	■	■	■	■		16. Accidental discharge, leakage or overflow of water or steam from within a plumbing, heating or air-conditioning system or domestic appliance
	■	■	■	■	■		17. Freezing of plumbing, heating and air-conditioning systems and domestic appliances
	■	■	■	■	■		18. Sudden and accidental injury from artificially generated currents to electrical appliances, devices, fixtures and wiring (TV and radio tubes not included)
		■		■			All perils except flood, earthquake, war, nuclear accident and others specified in your policy. Check your policy for a complete listing of perils excluded.

■ Dwelling and Personal Property (HO-1, HO-2, HO-6, HO-8)

□ Dwelling only (HO-3, HO-5)

■ Personal Property only (HO-4)

*Included as a peril in traditional forms of the homeowners policy; as an additional coverage in the simplified (HO-76) policies.

Source: Insurance Information Institute

HO-2

Homeowners–2, also called the broad form, is similar to HO–1 except that the list of perils insured is somewhat broader, and the definition of covered perils is somewhat more liberal. For example, in HO–1 smoke damage is limited to smoke from a faulty heating or cooking unit connected to a chimney. The policy excludes smoke from fireplaces. HO–2 contains a broader definition of smoke, and the only restriction is that the smoke loss must be sudden, accidental, and not due to agricultural smudging or to industrial operations. Thus, accidental smoke damage from a fireplace would be covered. HO–2 also covers perils not mentioned in HO–1—for example, falling objects, weight of ice and snow, collapse of buildings, freezing of plumbing, damage from electrical currents, explosion of heating systems, and accidental discharge of water.

HO–3

Homeowners–3, sometimes called the special form, provides all-risk coverage on the dwelling itself. Coverage on personal property within the residence is the same as in HO–2 (i.e., named perils). **All-risk coverage** on the dwelling means that if a loss is not excluded on this form, it is covered. Thus, HO–3 gives your dwelling considerably better protection than do HO–1 and HO–2.

HO–4 RENTERS

Homeowners–4 is a special type of policy designed for people who do not own a residence but who are renting an apartment or a home. HO–4 enables you to insure your personal property on a broad-form basis (same basis as HO–2) and still obtain the other advantages of the homeowners program.

HO–5 COMPREHENSIVE

Homeowners–5 is the most comprehensive type of coverage you can buy. Not only is the dwelling on an all-risk basis, but so are personal property items. As might be expected, comprehensive coverage is considerably more expensive than other forms.

HO–6 CONDOMINIUM OWNERS

Homeowners–6 for condominium owners offers coverage similar to HO–4, except that this policy is designed for condominiums. A condominium owner technically does not own the building but owns all the air space inside a given unit. The wording of HO–6 is adjusted to fit the particular legal status of the condominium owner.

HO–8

Homeowners–8 is a policy designed to meet the needs of owners of older buildings that have been remodeled and would have replacement costs high in comparison with replacement costs for similar homes. A major difference between HO–8 and the other forms is that the coverage is on an actual cash value (ACV) basis and not on a replacement cost basis.

Personal Property Coverage

All forms of homeowners insurance cover unscheduled personal property to a limit of 50 percent of the coverage on the dwelling. In the case of Don and Mary Adams, $32,000 of personal property coverage would exist on a face amount of $64,000. "Personal property" would include items such as jewelry, television, clothing, furniture, currency, guns, bicycles, shoes, and carpets—in short, anything of value of a personal nature. Personal property located at another insured residence, such as a vacation house, is also covered up to $1,000 or 10 percent of the coverage at the main residence (Coverage C). If Don and Mary Adams had a vacation house, they would have an additional $3,200 of coverage for personal property located at that residence. If Don and Mary had a daughter at college who was considered a permanent resident of their house, the $3,200 of coverage would apply to property damaged by an insured peril in the daughter's room at college. For example, theft of a stereo set or of clothing would be covered.

EXCLUSIONS AND LIMITATIONS ON PERSONAL PROPERTY COVERAGE

Certain types of property are excluded from coverage under homeowners insurance, and special limits of liability exist on other types of property. Excluded property includes animals; motorized vehicles such as motorcycles, golf carts, and snowmobiles (although motorized lawnmowers and Rototillers are covered); sound equipment in an automobile; aircraft and parts; property of roomers, boarders, or other tenants; property rented to others, such as furniture in a rental house; property pertaining to a business; and any property separately described and insured, such as cameras, watches, or rings.

The following dollar limits of coverage generally apply: $100 on money; $500 on securities; $500 on water craft, including trailers and outboard motors; $500 on trailers not used with water craft; $500 on theft of jewelry, watches, furs, or precious stones; $1,000 on theft of silverware, goldware, or pewter; and $1,000 on theft of guns. These limits mean that you should probably buy separate coverage on valuables such as coin and stamp collections, sterling silver sets, and securities if they are kept in your home. Since the $500 limit on jewelry, watches, and furs is an aggregate and not a per item limit, you will probably need additional coverage if you have substantial amounts invested in these items. For example, if your spouse has a $200 watch, an $800 fur coat, and several semiprecious stones, $500 would probably not be adequate coverage. You should therefore obtain special policies to cover such items.

ADDITIONAL PROTECTION UNDER PERSONAL PROPERTY COVERAGE

In addition to the protection already mentioned, your homeowners policy also covers the following items: (1) the cost of removing debris following damage by an insured peril, (2) repairs incurred in protecting your property from further loss following an insured peril, and (3) loss of trees, shrubs, and plants (up to $500 for any one item). In the case of trees and shrubs, the loss must be due to an insured peril; windstorm loss is excluded.

Charges for services performed by a fire department are covered, as is loss of property that has been removed and kept in another location to protect it from an insured peril. For example, if you take your furniture out during a fire and store it in a nearby garage where it is damaged by water, the loss would be covered under your homeowners policy.

Also covered are losses due to forgery of your signature on a credit card or to your accepting counterfeit money. For example, if you accept an altered check or a counterfeit twenty-dollar bill, the loss would be covered up to a limit of $500.

Limitations on Coverage

Your homeowners coverage is suspended if the building in question is vacant for more than thirty days. Loss owing to leakage of water from plumbing, heating, or air conditioning systems over a period of time is excluded, but sudden water loss is covered. Losses due to earth movement, flood, war, negligence on the part of the insured in protecting the property from further loss, and spoilage are excluded. Losses due to birds; vermin; insects; domestic animals; settling and cracking of pavement, patios, or foundations; and other types of "inherent vice" or wear and tear are also excluded.

While property is off the premises of the insured, some additional restrictions apply. For example, theft of trailers or campers is not covered while they are away from the insured's premises. Neither is loss of water craft or their furnishings. Thus, if you lose an outboard motorboat that you have left at the lake, the loss is not covered under your homeowners policy. Property stolen from your automobile is excluded from theft coverage unless the car was locked and marks of forcible entry were visible. Theft coverage does not apply to property in a residence that you rent to others or in an unoccupied summer home.

Extensions of Coverage

You can extend the coverage under your homeowners policy by adding specific kinds of endorsements. For example, you can insure earthquake coverage subject to a $250 deductible or to 2 percent of the amount of insurance on Coverage A. Coverage of losses from sinkhole collapses (sudden settlement or collapse of the earth supporting a house) can be insured by endorsement. You can also obtain an "inflation guard" endorsement under which your policy limits are raised by a certain percentage every three months; your coverage thus continues to be adequate to meet the rising costs of replacement.

Homeowners policies can also contain a mortgagee clause that protects the lender. Thus, the mortgagee (lender) does not have to incur the extra expense of a separate policy covering its own interest.

UMBRELLA LIABILITY

You may feel uncomfortable with the relatively low limits of liability applicable on homeowners insurance. Therefore, you may choose to purchase what is called an **umbrella liability policy,** which allows limits of $1 million or more for any one incident. Such a policy is considered coverage in excess of the coverage you have in your basic homeowners policy; consequently, umbrella liability is rather inexpensive and gives protection against catastrophe in the event of loss for which you are held personally liable.

FLOOD

Flood losses are excluded in homeowners policies, but such losses can be covered separately through a program sponsored by the federal government, provided that you live in an eligible community. Flood is defined as inundation of normally dry land, overflow of inland or tidal waters, or unusual and rapid accumulation of runoff or surface waters from any source. Flood insurance also includes inundation from mudslides. If a heavy rainstorm caused your street sewers to back up, flood your basement, and cause loss to property you keep there, the flood insurance policy would cover the loss. Your insurance agent can handle the details of obtaining federally sponsored flood insurance.

Deductibles and Coinsurance

The homeowners policy is written with a flat dollar deductible (usually $50 or $100) applicable to any one loss. The purpose of the deductible is to eliminate small claims and the relatively high costs of settling such claims.

In addition to a flat dollar deductible, the homeowners policy contains a **coinsurance clause** that requires you to carry coverage equal to or exceeding 80 percent of the replacement cost of your home. If you do not meet this requirement, your recovery at the time of loss might be less than full replacement cost. In no case, however, will your recovery be less than the actual cash value (ACV) of the loss—that is, the loss after adjustment for depreciation has been subtracted from the replacement cost.

For example, suppose your house has an estimated life of forty years and a replacement cost of $100,000. The house is twenty years old and is considered 50 percent depreciated. If the roof burns and a new one costs $10,000, how much will you collect? You can collect the full replacement cost of the roof if you are carrying coverage that equals at least 80 percent of the value of your house, or $80,000. If you are carrying a lesser amount—say, $60,000—you can collect only 60/80, or three-fourths of the loss ($7,500).[3] In no case would you collect less than the fully depreciated value of the burned roof. In this case, since the house is 50 percent depreciated, presumably the roof would be subject to depreciation of half of its new value, or $5,000. Thus, even if you had allowed your total coverage to slip to only 10 percent of the replacement cost, or to $10,000, you would still be able to collect $5,000 in actual cash value for the loss of your roof.

Since most people need the protection afforded by being able to replace any damaged portion of a house or property without deduction for depreciation, you would probably be practicing wise risk management by maintaining coverage equal to the 80 percent replacement cost mandated by the coinsurance clause. Alternatively, you could add a replacement-cost endorsement to your policy.

Premium Cost

Exhibit 6–14 shows differences in annual premium costs under various homeowners policies. The rates shown are based on a deductible of $100; however, premium credits of approximately 10 percent are allowed if you choose a $250 deductible. Deductibles will save you money in the long run; rate credits are greater if you live in an area where you are likely to have few or no claims.

Examples of Covered Losses

A number of unusual occurrences are covered by the typical homeowners policy. The following list includes some examples.

1. A strong drain flush containing sulfuric acid spills on a hardwood floor and ruins a large section. The floor needs replacement.
2. A frightened animal stampedes into the side of your house and causes substantial damage to the siding.

---

3. The formula for determining the amount collected when the coinsurance clause is not met is as follows:

$$\text{Loss paid} = \frac{\text{Insurance carried}}{\text{Insurance required}} \times \text{Loss, where}$$

insurance required is 80% of the full cost of replacing damaged property with like quantity and quality of materials.

EXHIBIT 6-14
Annual Premium
Costs of Various
Homeowners
Policies, 1981

Amount of Insurance	Annual Premium			
	HO-1	HO-2	HO-3	HO-5
$20,000	$118	$124	$130	$166
30,000	144	150	158	203
40,000	169	177	186	240
50,000	185	194	204	263

Note: Rates are based on a brick residence in a class 2 territory in Atlanta, Georgia. Each policy includes a $100 deductible.

3. You fall through the living room ceiling while you are in the attic attempting to make repairs.
4. Digging in the yard, you cut a telephone wire and damage piping to an air conditioner.
5. While on a trip, you lose a suitcase and its contents.
6. A burglar breaks up the inside of your house with a heavy metal instrument.
7. Your careless smoking starts a fire in your apartment. Your landlord's insurer pays the landlord's loss but brings a legal action against you under the policy's subrogation rights.

Consumer Caveats

1. To collect in full for partial losses, insure your property for at least 80 percent of its replacement cost. You should have your property appraised regularly to make sure that the 80 percent requirement is being met.

2. Make an inventory of your household possessions, particularly of expensive items. Your inventory should show what the original cost was, as well as where and when you purchased each item. Original bills of sale or receipts are helpful in proving claims. So that you won't forget any items, take snapshots of each room in your house. Some people use a movie camera to make photographic records of personal property. In the event of loss, the photographs can help to prove what property you owned. Keep the photographs in your safe deposit box or in another location away from your house.

3. If you have valuable items such as jewelry, furs, coin collections, and stamp collections, have them appraised and scheduled separately according to their current value. You can then protect these items with a scheduled personal property endorsement on your homeowners policy.

4. Consider increasing the liability limits applicable to your policy. You may find that an umbrella liability policy is both economical and comprehensive.

5. Accept a $50 or $100 deductible on your homeowners policy. You will probably save money in the long run.

6. Consider purchasing decreasing term life insurance, which will protect your home if you die before the mortgage is paid off. Also consider a mortgage disability income policy, which will cover mortgage payments if you become sick and unable to work.

7. Probably the "best buy" among homeowners plans is HO–3. An HO–3 policy costs somewhat more than an HO–1 or HO–2, but it provides all-risk coverage on your dwelling.

SUMMARY

1. You are subject to several types of losses if you own or operate an automobile. Losses include personal injury or death, loss of income, loss of the automobile from collision or theft, and liability to others for property damage or personal injury. The only practical way for most people to handle these risks is through insurance.

2. Automobile insurance covers four major areas: your liability to others, physical damage to your car, medical expense and resulting income loss, and miscellaneous items such as uninsured motorist coverage, towing and labor costs, and rental reimbursement.

3. Under the terms of a typical automobile insurance policy, you can obtain protection against the following costs: *(a)* costs incurred while driving nonowned cars; *(b)* costs incurred to defend any suit against you arising out of the use of the car, whether or not the suit is false or fraudulent; *(c)* costs of any court judgments handed down against you; *(d)* costs incurred through the loss of your car from almost any cause; and *(e)* costs incurred while driving anywhere in the United States or Canada.

4. Your private automobile policy does *not* cover the following: *(a)* intentionally caused losses; *(b)* commercial vehicles; *(c)* losses that you fail to report promptly; *(d)* cars supplied to you by others for your regular use; *(e)* personal property carried in your car; *(f)* damage due to depreciation, freezing, or electrical failure; *(g)* replacement of your car with a new car (depreciation is applied when claims are adjusted).

5. You can save on automobile insurance rates by *(a)* accepting deductibles, *(b)* driving safely, *(c)* taking driver education, *(d)* shopping among insurers, *(e)* driving standard model cars rather than sports cars or other specialized vehicles.

6. Laws affecting you as owner and operator of a car usually require you to either carry insurance or demonstrate financial responsibility for any personal injury loss to others for which you may be found liable. About half of the states allow settlement of automobile accident disputes on a no-fault basis under specified conditions.

7. Insurance is available in a single policy that gives broad protection against most losses arising out of home occupancy. Homeowners insurance applies all-risk or named-peril protection to the dwelling and its contents. Homeowners insurance also covers additional living expenses incurred as a result of a loss, personal liability, medical payments to others, and loss of others' property, whether or not you are liable.

8. Probably the best policy for the average homeowner is HO–3, although more comprehensive forms are available at higher cost. The main difference between HO–2 and HO–3 is that the latter provides all-risk coverage on the dwelling, while the former covers the dwelling only for a list of specified perils. Special policies are available for renters, owners of condominiums, and owners of older, remodeled buildings. You can also obtain coverage to meet a variety of special perils such as earthquake and flood. Homeowners insurance also offers coverage on a full-replacement-cost basis if you carry coverage equal to or exceeding 80 percent of the replacement cost of your home.

REVIEW QUESTIONS

1. (a) What major types of losses are associated with ownership and use of automobiles?
    (b) On which type of loss are the most claims paid?

2. Is driving experience a useful variable in assessing fair rates for auto insurance? Why, or why not?

3. June is held liable in a car accident. She carries liability limits of 10/20/5. Losses are as follows: $8,000 for bodily injury to X, $22,000 for bodily injury to Y, $1,000 for bodily injury to Z, and $6,000 for damage to the other car. How much will June's policy pay on the losses?

4. James drives a $10,000 Datsun 280-Z with full auto insurance coverage. Under which of the typical coverages will the following losses be paid:
    (a) $1,500 for repair of a damaged fender?
    (b) $3,000 for repair of a neighbor's house into which James ran when he entered the wrong driveway?
    (c) $500 in medical bills for injuries he suffered following the accident?
    (d) $1,000 in loss of income during time he spent in the hospital?

5. You are struck by a hit-and-run driver.
    (a) What portion of your automobile coverage would most likely apply to bodily injury loss?
    (b) What portion would apply to a bent door on your car?

6. Why is coverage for "towing and labor" not generally recommended?

7. If you loan your car to a friend and the friend damages it, would your collision insurance cover the loss? Why, or why not?

8. You leave your fur coat in the back of your car, lock the car, and go shopping. When you return, the coat is gone and the window of your car is broken.
   (a) Under which policy would you seek recovery, your automobile policy or your homeowners policy?
   (b)) How would you seek recovery if you had not locked your car when you left for the shopping trip?

9. You drive into Mexico from the border in Tijuana, near San Diego, California. While driving in Mexico, you hit a tree.
   (a) Are you covered under your automobile policy? Why, or why not?
   (b) Would you be covered for the same circumstances if you had been driving in Canada?

10. Harold is driving his car in a state whose no-fault law sets a $1,000 threshold. He is involved in an accident in which $800 of medical claims and income loss is incurred by the other driver. Harold is uninjured. Both drivers have PIP coverage and other coverage required under their state's no-fault laws. In addition to his $800 loss, the other driver attempts to sue Harold for $5,000 for "pain and suffering." Will this suit be permitted? Why, or why not?

11. (a) What is the difference between a financial responsibility law and a no-fault law?
    (b) Which law is considered the best solution to the problem of the uninsured motorist?

12. If Joanne has a homeowners policy with limits of $50,000, what other coverage does she automatically have under a typical form?

13. Why is HO–3 generally recommended over both HO–1 and HO–2?

14. Mary owns a $50,000 house, which she insures for $25,000 under HO–3. If a fire partially damages the roof, which will cost $2,000 to repair, how much can she collect?

CASE PROBLEMS

I. Automobile Insurance

A has $10/$20 bodily injury coverage and $5,000 property damage coverage on the personal auto policy, along with comprehensive, $100 deductible collision, and $500 medical payments. A is involved in an accident with B, and A is found negligent. No-fault insurance does not exist in the state in which A lives.

QUESTIONS

1. Will A's policy cover damages to B in the amount of $11,000 and to B's wife, Mary, in the amount of $9,000?

2. Will *A*'s policy cover a $500 hospital bill for injuries to *A* and a $5,000 loss due to "pain and suffering"?

3. Will *A*'s policy pay $40 to allow *A* to rent a substitute car for three days?

4. Will *A*'s policy cover the vacation trailer he was towing (damaged to the extent of $500) as well as *B*'s vacation trailer (damaged to the extent of $1,000)? (*B* has $100 deductible collision coverage on his own car.)

5. If it had been found that *A* had not been negligent, how would you answer questions 2, 3, and 4?

II. Homeowners Insurance

Mr. Chen has a homeowners broad form policy (HO–2) with the following coverages (assume that a $50 flat deductible is in force for Section I coverages):

Section I:	(1) Dwelling	$50,000
	(2) Appurtenant private structures	5,000
	(3) Unscheduled personal property	25,000
	(4) Additional living expense	10,000
Section II:	(5) Personal libility: bodily injury or property damage	50,000
	(6) Medical payments to others	$500/25,000
	(7) Damage to property of others	$250/person

QUESTIONS

For each of the following losses, tell whether the loss is covered by Mr. Chen's HO–2 policy and if so, for how much. Explain which part of the policy is applicable to the loss.

1. Draperies are damaged by smoke from a defective heater. Repair cost, $95.

2. Cash in the amount of $175 is stolen from a desk drawer.

3. A $200 camera is stolen from the back seat of the insured's open car at a drive-in theater while the passengers are buying refreshments.

4. Fire damage to the front porch costs $2,000 to repair. It is determined that, because of the age of the dwelling, $500 of depreciation applies to the loss. It would currently cost $10,000 to replace the porch.

5. The insured leaves some windows open in his house while he is away for the evening. A heavy rainfall causes $350 damage to carpets, drapes, and furniture.

6. The insured pays $500 to rent a hotel room for a month while repairs to his house are being made after a fire. His normal house payments are $300.

7. A stereo set valued at $250 is stolen from the dormitory room in which the insured's son (a resident of the insured's household) lives while he is away at school.

8. The insured spills ink on his guest's suit coat. Cost of replacement, $80.

9. A fire caused by the insured spreads to his neighbor's house. The neighbor receives a liability judgment of $20,000 against the insured.

10. The insured is sued by a trespasser who injured himself on a rusty fence post. The insured wins the suit, but his defense costs $5,000.

11. On the golf course, the insured's sixteen-year-old daughter tees off before the golfers in front have moved sufficiently far ahead. Her golf ball strikes one of the golfers in the face and causes partial loss of sight. Judgment against the girl is $70,000. Cost of defense is $10,000.

CHAPTER 7

SOCIAL SECURITY

LEARNING OBJECTIVES

In studying this chapter, you will learn:

What the four major programs are under Social Security;

What benefits are available under Social Security for covered workers and their dependents;

What you must do to be eligible for Social Security;

How Social Security benefits may be coordinated with private plans for financial security;

What Social Security will cost you and your employer;

How to judge the financial soundness of Social Security;

Ways to get the most out of Social Security;

What is included in state government programs of social insurance—for example, workers' compensation and temporary disability programs.

The United States has provided an extensive network of government insurance at both state and federal levels. Established in 1935 and commonly known as Social Security, this insurance actually comprises not one program, but several. Each provides a specific set of benefits that should be carefully coordinated with your other financial security programs. Because most social insurance programs are compulsory, you are paying for them through taxes even if you are not currently a recipient of their benefits. Thus, you should understand these benefits thoroughly and know how to obtain them.

NATURE OF FEDERAL SOCIAL SECURITY

Commonly called OASDHI (old age, survivors', disability, and health insurance), the federal Social Security program is financed by a payroll tax shared equally by employees and their employers.[1] In addition to OASDHI, federal and state governments operate an unemployment insurance program and a welfare program under which income and medical expense grants are made to needy persons, regardless of whether they are insured under any formal program of coverage. Analysis of unemployment insurance and welfare programs is outside the scope of this text. (If you follow the principles of personal finance herein outlined, you probably will not need to be concerned personally with either program.)

Certain basic differences exist between social insurance programs and private insurance programs. Unlike private insurance, social insurance is issued without evidence of a specific policy or contract. Provisions are governed by state or federal laws and regulations issued by the agencies that administer the programs. Since these regulations often change, you should check periodically with the administrators of social insurance programs to be aware of the latest details affecting your coverage and benefits.

Most social insurance programs require that you be attached to the labor force—that is, you must be employed or have been employed in an occupation subject to the particular social insurance program. Most social insurance programs allow for only the minimum benefits one needs to survive; they do not attempt to replace all of a person's lost income or all the other losses a person may suffer from insured events. Thus, you should not expect to "get rich" from social insurance programs.

Unlike private insurance benefits, benefits under social insurance are set in advance; you have little choice of varying levels of benefits. For example,

---

1. In this discussion OASDHI is used synonymously with Social Security, although different rules, procedures, and tax rates apply to each section of the program.

you are not allowed to purchase additional death benefit allowances from Social Security. Also, most social insurance programs are compulsory so that risk is sufficiently spread and so that all covered workers contribute to the costs. Lastly, many social insurance benefits are conditional upon your meeting certain qualifications. For example, you must have a qualified dependent to benefit from survivorship allowances under OASDHI.

In sum, social insurance programs should be viewed as one means of building personal financial security (See Exhibit 7–1). They should not be expected to accomplish the entire task, but they form a foundation for personal financial planning. Individual savings, investments, insurance, and other elements of long-term financial planning are still essential.

Four basic types of insurance protection are included under the federal OASDHI program, which is the most important part of the social insurance structure in the United States. These protections include (1) retirement benefits, (2) survivors' benefits, (3) disability benefits, and (4) health insurance for the aged.

EXHIBIT 7–1
Your Personal
House of
Protection

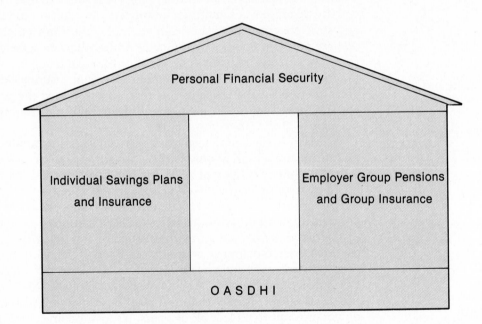

Retirement Benefits _____

The first type of Social Security benefit offers pensions to workers who have been employed in occupations subject to OASDHI taxes and who are "insured" as defined by law. Nearly all occupations are covered, so if you are employed in the United States, you will probably be eligible for a pension under OASDHI. Your pension is based on the average earnings on which OASDHI taxes are levied. These earnings are adjusted for inflation so that when you retire, the average earnings, called **average indexed monthly earnings (AIME)**, will bear some reasonable relationship to the living standards of people currently employed in your occupation. (The method of determining the value of AIME is quite complex, and the details need not be discussed here.) After you retire, your pension is further adjusted, at least annually, for inflation. This protection against inflation is a very significant benefit; without such a safeguard your pension could be seriously eroded in just a few years by a continuous upward price spiral. In addition, your retirement income under OASDHI is not subject to federal or state income tax—another important benefit. Exhibits 7–2 and 7–3 show typical average monthly retirement benefits in 1981, based on different assumed levels of average earnings for different classes of beneficiaries.

EXHIBIT 7–2   Typical Monthly Benefits under Social Security, 1981

Income Level (AIME)	Worker, Age 65 (Retirement or Disability Benefits)	Spouse, Age 65	Maximum Family Benefit	Widow, 60, No Children
Average wage earner (AIME of $1,000)	$442	$221	$801	$316
Maximum wage earner (AIME of $1,400)	$549	$274	$961	$393

Notes: Benefits are based on having an earnings record that will produce the average indexed monthly earnings (AIME) shown. In 1981 average annual earnings were about $13,000; the maximum AIME a worker could have in 1981 was estimated at $1,340 monthly.

OASDHI places a limit on family benefits, which might reach large amounts if a single family had several dependents.

Source: Dale R. Detlefs, *1981 Guide To Social Security* (Louisville, Ky.: Meidinger, Inc., 1981).

In reviewing Exhibit 7–2, note that benefits apply separately to retired workers and their spouses. The wife's benefit is one-half of her husband's benefit if both are age sixty-five, unless the wife has a larger benefit based on her own earnings—in which case a larger amount (up to the maximum family benefit) is payable. One may retire before age sixty-five; widowers and widows may retire and receive benefits at age sixty. For others, retirement can come as early as age sixty-two. Benefits are reduced by five-ninths of 1 percent for each month of retirement before the month in which one reaches

EXHIBIT 7–3
Average Social
Security
Payments to
Different Classes
of Beneficiaries,
1981

Beneficiary Unit	Average Monthly Payment
All retired workers	$374
Couple, both receiving benefits	640
Mother and two children	870
Widow over 60	348
Disabled worker, wife, and children	812
All disabled workers	413

Note: The average payment is based on average taxed earnings levels, which were lower than typical current earnings levels in 1981. Payments reflect 11.2% cost-of-living adjustment made in 1981.

Source: Social Security Administration, Release SFX 4–1.

age sixty-five. In effect, then, the benefit payable at age sixty-two is about 80 percent of the benefit payable at age sixty-five. Retirement benefits are allowed for each unmarried child who is eighteen or younger, subject to a family maximum payment. Exact benefit levels are calculated by the Social Security Administration, a federal government agency, after the employment earnings record of each applicant is verified.

According to Exhibit 7–2, if the average indexed monthly earnings are $1,000, a husband and wife, each aged sixty-five, would receive a total of about $663 ($442 + $221) monthly if the wife had not worked outside the home. However, Exhibit 7–3 shows that actual average payments made to workers in 1981 ($374) was less than the $442 shown in Exhibit 7–2. The discrepancy results from the fact that Social Security taxes in former years were levied on much lower wage levels; therefore, the average wage on which benefits are based was lower. The AIME figure shown in Exhibit 7–2 is a reasonable approximation of what you could expect to receive if you were retiring in 1981 with the average earnings record shown. The amounts shown in Exhibit 7–3 are based on averge earnings lower than that assumed in Exhibit 7–2.

In 1981 the Social Security program was replacing approximately the following proportions of retiring workers' average earnings:

	Worker	Worker & Spouse
Low-income worker (earning the minimum wage)	52%	78%
Average-income worker	41%	62%
High-income worker (earning the maximum taxable wage)	28%	42%

Thus a fairly substantial retirement income, relative to preretirement income levels, was being paid to low-income and average-income workers in 1981. The scheduled earnings on which OASDHI taxes are based for different years, as well as the percentage of these earnings subject to tax, are shown in Exhibit 7–4. As of 1982, for example, all covered earnings up to $32,100 are sub-

EXHIBIT 7–4   Estimated OASDHI Taxes

Calendar Year	Maximum Earnings Subject to SS Taxes	Employees/Employers		Self-Employed Persons	
		Rate	Maximum Tax	Rate	Maximum Tax
1980	$25,900	6.13%	$1,587.67	8.10%	$2,097.90
1981	29,700	6.65	1,975.05	9.30	2,762.10
1982	32,100[a]	6.70	2,150.70	9.35	3,001.35
1983	35,400[a]	6.70	2,371.80	9.35	3,309.90
1984	38,700[a]	6.70	2,592.90	9.35	3,618.45
1985	42,600[a]	7.05	3,003.30	9.90	4,217.40
1986	46,200[a]	7.15	3,303.30	10.00	4,620.00

[a]Based on intermediate economic assumptions used in the 1981 Trustees Report.

Source: Social Security Administration Fact Sheet, September, 1981.

ject to a payroll tax of 6.7 percent, or $2,151.70 for you and $2,151.70 for your employer. If you are self-employed, your tax rate is higher, although not as high as the combined employee-employer rate.

ELIGIBILITY FOR RETIREMENT BENEFITS

To receive retirement benefits, you must meet the OASDHI requirements that determine whether you are "retired." The requirements are based on earnings in covered employment. In 1982, for example, if you were sixty-five or over, still employed, and earning less than $6,000 in covered employment, you were considered "retired" and could draw full OASDHI benefits. (A special earnings test applies in the year in which you retire.) If you earned more than $6,000, you would lose $1 in OASDHI benefits for each $2 earned over the exempt amount. (The $6,000 limitation is subject to increase in later years.) For example, if you earned $10,000 a year, you would lose $2,000 in OASDHI benefits [1/2 ($10,000 – $6,000)]. The earnings limitation is lower for retirement ages below sixty-five. Beginning in January 1983, you could earn any amount in covered employment after reaching age seventy and still draw full retirement benefits. Income received from interest, dividends, employer-sponsored pensions, annuities, unemployment insurance, workers' compensation, gifts or inheritances, and certain other sources is not considered in determination of retirement status.

If you do not retire until after age sixty-five, you receive a larger payment, equal to 1/4 percent a month (3 percent a year) more than your age 65 benefit for each month you delay retirement until you reach seventy; after this age you receive no further increases for delayed retirement.

Spouses may draw OASDHI benefits based on their own earnings or on their spouse's earnings, whichever basis gives them the greater benefit. For

"It's those maximum family benefits that I'm after, Baby."

example, a husband can draw on a wife's earnings if he is 62 or older. Children can draw benefits based on either parent's earnings. Under certain circumstances Social Security also provides benefits to grandchildren, illegitimate children, adopted children, and stepchildren.

Survivors' Benefits

If a worker dies who has been insured by Social Security, certain survivors are eligible for income benefits from OASDHI if given conditions are met. For example, so long as she has dependent children, a widow of any age may draw benefits based on her deceased husband's earnings. After the children no longer qualify as dependents (i.e., when they marry or reach age sixteen), the widow's benefit is halted (except for disability payments) until she reaches age sixty, at which time her benefits resume. The period during which benefits cease is known as the **blackout period**, and individual life insurance is often arranged to provide income during this time.

After age sixty a husband can also draw survivors' benefits based on earnings of a deceased wife; to qualify, the husband need not have been dependent on his wife when she was working. Children are also eligible for benefits as survivors until age eighteen. Maximum amounts payable to any single family are limited; otherwise, very large sums might have to be paid some families.

OASDHI survivors' benefits constitute a rather large life insurance benefit for your survivors. First, a specified survivor receives an allowance of $255 for funeral costs. Second, survivors receive income benefits as long as their period of eligibility lasts. Finally, disability benefits are paid if a survivor becomes disabled. For example, suppose a widow, age forty, is entitled to receive $500 a month for the ten years until her youngest child reaches sixteen. At age sixty she becomes eligible for a retirement benefit of $250 a month for life. Assuming 6 percent interest, the woman would need life insurance totaling $44,000 for the child-raising period and $17,000 for the retirement period, or a total of $61,000, to be as well off as she would be with Social Security benefits. If you were to buy $61,000 of twenty-year decreasing term life insurance at age forty to replace the value of Social Security as a survivors' benefit, it would cost you approximately $300 a year.

ELIGIBILITY FOR SURVIVORS' BENEFITS

You are eligible for survivors' benefits if you are either "currently insured" or "fully insured." To be currently insured, you must have worked in covered employment for at least one and a half years within three years of your death. To be fully insured, you must have a minimum work record, which varies with your age. For example, if you were born after 1929 and you are under twenty-eight, you will be fully insured with only one and a half years of work. This work requirement rises gradually and reaches a period of ten years by age sixty-two.

Disability Benefits

In 1956 Social Security was amended to provide long-term disability payments to insured workers. Benefits were later extended to wives and children of disabled workers. If a disabled worker dies, the widow or widower is entitled to continued benefits if the worker became disabled under OASDHI's definition of disability.

DEFINITION OF DISABILITY

Disability benefits begin after a waiting period of five months. Disability is defined as a condition that prevents you from doing any substantial, gainful work. The condition is expected to last for at least twelve months or to result in death. (Blindness is also cause for being considered disabled.) If you are unable to perform your regular occupation but can perform another job for which you are reasonably equipped by training, experience, or education, you ordinarily are not eligible for disability benefits under the Social Security definition. In deciding whether you are disabled, the Social Security Administration considers not only medical evidence but also age, education, and work experience. For example, if you were too disabled to do anything but sell pencils on the street, you would not be denied benefits because of your ability to perform "another occupation."

ELIGIBILITY FOR DISABILITY BENEFITS

To collect disability benefits, you must have worked in covered employment for at least five of the ten years before you became disabled. If you become disabled between the ages of twenty-four and thirty-one, you can qualify for disability benefits if you have worked one-half of the time between your twenty-first birthday and the date you become disabled. Thus, a person who becomes disabled at age twenty-five need only have worked two years $[(25-21) \times 1/2]$ in covered employment to receive benefits. If you become disabled before age twenty-four, you need a minimum credit of one and a half years' work in covered employment to qualify for benefits. Work before age twenty-one is excluded from disability requirements, except for blind persons who can count such service in meeting minimum work periods.

Disabled widows and widowers or insured workers may also draw benefits. Spouses and children of disabled workers receive benefits based on the amount of benefit being paid to the worker. These benefits may be reduced if the dependents are also working. Spouses under age sixty-two qualify if they are caring for a child under sixteen, a disabled child between sixteen and eighteen, or a child over eighteen who is disabled and requires personal services. Unmarried children under eighteen are eligible if their parents are drawing disability benefits. A wife who becomes disabled may be entitled to disability payments on her own work record, even if her husband is active and working.

If a disability ends, you are able to go back to work, and the disability recurs later, you do not have to wait five months for benefits unless your second disability occurs within five years of the first. Once you have reached age sixty-five, disability payments cease, but you may begin to draw regular old-age allotments of the same amount you received under the disability program.

AMOUNT OF DISABILITY BENEFITS

The amount of the disability payment is equal to the amount you would have drawn as a retirement benefit at sixty-five, based on your average indexed monthly wage. A wife's benefit is 50 percent of her husband's benefit if she is sixty-five and has no children. If she has children, additional benefits are allowed. Total disability benefits are subject to a family maximum allowance (see Exhibit 7–2).

Disability benefits under Social Security may be reduced if you are also drawing workers' compensation payments or other public disability benefits. Total monthly disability payments from these sources may not exceed 80 percent of the average monthly income earned before the disability.

TRIAL WORK PERIOD

If you go back to work while drawing disability payments, you may be considered capable of performing substantial, gainful activity, which would result in loss of your benefits. However, you may be permitted to take a job without a complete loss of benefits to determine if you are "truly, substantially, and continuously disabled." The trial work-period provision gives you an incentive to go back to work if you are able. If you are disabled and are drawing benefits, you should check with your Social Security office before taking a job.

Health Insurance for the Aged: Medicare

In 1965 the government instituted a new program of health insurance, known as "Medicare," for people over sixty-five. In 1973 the program was extended to cover disabled persons under age sixty-five and certain of their dependents. Medicare has two major parts: Part A covers hospitalization expense, and Part B covers doctors' bills.

ELIGIBILITY FOR MEDICARE

The following groups are eligible for Medicare:

1. Persons sixty-five and over who are covered by OASDHI, even if they are not "retired";
2. Persons under age sixty-five who have been entitled to Social Security disability benefits for twenty-four or more consecutive months, including adults who are receiving benefits because they have been disabled since childhood;
3. Insured workers and their dependents who need dialysis treatment or a kidney transplant because of permanent kidney failure.

An individual already receiving Social Security retirement benefits will be automatically enrolled for Medicare at age sixty-five. Application is not necessary. The same is true for individuals receiving disability benefits. Part B, supplementary medical insurance (SMI), is automatic unless declined in writing by the beneficiary.

Individuals who are not receiving Social Security retirement or disability benefits may enroll for health insurance benefits when they are sixty-five, even though they plan to continue working. These individuals are billed quarterly for their Medicare premium payments.

PART A: HOSPITAL EXPENSE COVERAGE

Three kinds of hospitalization expenses are covered by Part A of Medicare: (1) regular hospital expenses, (2) expenses incurred in a skilled nursing facility after a hospital stay, and (3) home health care. The length of each "spell of illness," or benefit period, is limited under each of these three types of care. A spell of illness begins the first time you enter a hospital and ends sixty days after your discharge from the hospital or from a skilled nursing facility. The number of benefit periods is unlimited; each time you start a new benefit period, your hospital insurance protection is renewed.

A doctor must prescribe hospital care for treatment of your illness or injury if you are to be covered by Part A of Medicare. The hospital to which you are assigned must be one approved by the Medicare program. Covered hospital expenses include costs of a semiprivate room (two to four beds in a room), meals, regular nursing service, special care units, drugs furnished in the hospital, lab tests, X-rays, medical supplies, appliances (e.g., wheelchairs), operating room, and rehabilitation services. Hospital expenses not covered by Medicare include charges for personal items, TV rental, radio or telephone, private duty nurses, and the first three pints of blood received during a benefit period.

Your Costs. Medicare requires that you contribute in part to the cost of services through deductibles and other limitations. As of 1981 you are completely covered for all expenses from the first through the sixtieth day after paying a deductible of $204. From the sixty-first through the ninetieth day of each benefit period, Medicare pays for all covered services above a 1981 deductible of $51 a day. If your hospitalization runs longer than ninety days, Medicare provides for an extra sixty days of coverage, known as reserve days. Unlike the ninety hospital days for each spell of illness, reserve days are not renewable. Once used, they are no longer available, regardless of how many spells of illness you may have. The deductible for reserve days is $102 a day. The deductibles charged for Part A of Medicare are changed periodically, depending on inflation and other factors. For low-income persons, welfare programs may pay the cost of deductibles.

Care in a psychiatric hospital is limited to 190 days. Once you have used up these days, you have no further coverage in a psychiatric hospital in your lifetime.

Exhibit 7–5 illustrates Medicare coverage under Part A. The white area shows costs that you must pay personally, and the shaded areas show what Medicare pays. Private, supplemental health insurance is available to cover costs that you would otherwise pay.

EXHIBIT 7–5

Hospital Expense Coverage under Medicare (1981 Rates)

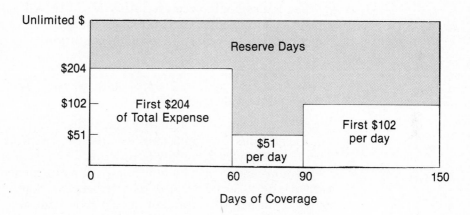

Skilled Nursing Facilities. You may receive coverage for treatment rendered in a skilled nursing facility under the following conditions:

1. You must be in a hospital for at least three consecutive days before you transfer to the skilled nursing facility.
2. You must be transferred to the facility for treatment of the condition for which you were treated in the hospital.
3. You must be admitted to the nursing facility within fourteen days after leaving the hospital.
4. Your doctor must certify that you need care in a skilled nursing facility.

The limit of time allowed in a skilled nursing facility is 100 days for each benefit period. You receive free care for the first 20 days you are in the facility. From day 21 through day 100, you must pay $25.50 a day. Covered expenses include a semiprivate room, all meals, regular nursing services, rehabilitation services, drugs, medical supplies, and use of appliances (e.g., wheelchairs). All hospitals and skilled nursing facilities must be certified as adequate by the Social Security Administration.

Home Health Care. Part A of Medicare reimburses you for the costs of home health care under specified conditions. Home health care is rendered after an illness or injury that prevents you from leaving your home to get needed health services. Home health agencies provide further treatment of a condition that was treated in a hospital or a skilled nursing facility. Treatment may include part-time skilled nursing care or physical or speech therapy. Your doctor must certify that you need more health care and must set up a home health plan for you.

All treatment covered by Medicare requires your doctor's certification that the treatment is reasonable and necessary. For example, you cannot continue to receive Medicare payments if you stay in a skilled nursing facility longer than is absolutely necessary. Also, Medicare will not reimburse you for expenses considered mainly custodial—for example, treatment rendered in long-term life care centers or similar institutions.

PART B: MEDICAL INSURANCE

Part B of Medicare is a voluntary program that covers doctors' bills under specified conditions. Premium rates for this coverage were $11 a month as of July 1981; they vary according to inflation and are changed nearly every year. Premiums are not generally increased at a rate higher than the rate of increase of general Social Security income benefits. Your premium actually meets less than half the total cost of Part B of Medicare.

Once you have satisfied a $60 deductible, Part B pays 80 percent of all reasonable charges for medical services rendered (see Exhibit 7–6). This deductible must be met only once in a calendar year, and it can be met by any combination of covered expenses. Your doctor may make application to the Medicare carrier (an organization that has entered into an agreement with the Social Security Administration to process Medicare claims) for direct payment of expenses, or you may pay your doctor and obtain reimbursement from the Medicare carrier.

Payments for the following kinds of services are covered by Part B of Medicare:

1. Doctors' services rendered in an office, hospital, skilled nursing facility, or other place—even in certain approved Canadian or Mexican hospitals;
2. Radiology and pathology;
3. Outpatient treatment for mental illness, subject to a maximum of $250 in any one year;
4. Certain treatments by a licensed chiropractor;
5. Treatment by a licensed podiatrist;
6. Treatment for dental care if it involves setting fractures or surgery of the jaw or related areas;
7. Doctors' services in connection with X-rays, lab tests, medical supplies, physical therapy, speech pathology, and diagnostic tests;

EXHIBIT 7–6
Doctors' Bills
Covered under
Medicare (1981
Rates)

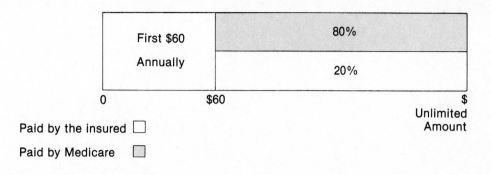

8. Certain prosthetic devices—for example, a substitute internal body organ, a pacemaker, or corrective lenses used after cataract surgery;
9. Blood transfusions after the first three pints.

Under 1981 rules Part B of Medicare will not reimburse you for physical exams, routine foot care, eyeglasses, hearing aids, immunizations, or cosmetic surgery.

FINANCIAL SOUNDNESS OF SOCIAL SECURITY

Social Security is financed by a payroll tax paid by both employers and employees. In recent years great increases in benefits have raised questions about the future financial soundness of the program. If benefits continue to rise, payroll taxes may be inadequate to cover costs because of business recessions, slowdowns in economic growth, and increasing numbers of older people in the system. For example, in 1980 approximately 11 percent of the total population was over sixty-five, compared to about 5 percent in 1920. In 1980 there were approximately three working persons for each recipient of a benefit under Social Security—a ratio expected to drop to only two-to-one by the year 2030 because of slowed population growth. Many people believe that either benefits must be reduced or taxes substantially increased if the system is to remain solvent. Working taxpayers may in the future be neither willing nor able to bear the increased taxes needed to fund the system.

Social Security operates essentially as a "pay-as-you-go" system; current taxes are used to meet current outlays. Only a relatively small fund balance exists in the Social Security account, equal to approximately half of a full year's benefits. Since OASDHI is dependent on tax revenues, large reserves are unnecessary.

The 1977 amendments to the Social Security Act increased scheduled taxes and the wages to which they are to be applied. These amendments went a long way toward overcoming the actuarial solvency problems of the pro-

"SONNY, I SURE HOPE SOME MILK'S LEFT WHEN YOU GET TO THIS END."

By permission of Bill Mauldin and Wil-Jo Associates, Inc.

gram. Unfortunately, the 1977 amendments did not address the problems created by rising costs of medical and hospital insurance for the aged or by anticipated changes in the ratio of active workers to retired workers. In 1981 Congress reduced benefits; in future years further reductions may be necessary.

SOCIAL SECURITY POINTERS

You should understand certain features of Social Security to gain the most from the program. A few important points are listed in the following paragraphs.

1. You should have a Social Security account number and should give it to each of your employers so that you may receive full credit for taxes charged on your wages. You should retain the same number throughout your working life, no matter how many employers you may have.

2. Periodically you should send a postcard (available at the post office) to the Social Security Administration to request a summary of your wage record. This record, which is provided free, will verify whether your employers have sent in their share of OASDHI taxes on your behalf and whether all your earnings have been reported. If an error has occurred, it can be corrected so that you may obtain all the OASDHI benefits to which you are entitled.

3. To collect benefits, you must furnish not only your account number but also proof of age. Acceptable proofs of age include birth or baptismal certificates, school or marriage records, military discharge papers, and employment, union, hospital, or federal census records. Since you also need proof of age to collect in full for life insurance, private pensions, and other benefits, you should assemble adequate proofs and keep them in a safe place (e.g., a safe deposit box). You should also keep proofs of age for your spouse and for all children who might be eligible for benefits.

4. The Social Security Administration administers a welfare program known as **Supplemental Security Income (SSI).** Although this program is not directly related to OASDHI, it may be important to you if your Social Security income is below a specified level. Persons who are blind, disabled, and over sixty-five may qualify for both SSI payments and OASDHI if their income or assets fall below specified amounts.

5. If you are in the military, you are covered by Social Security. You will receive Social Security credit for base pay received while on active duty, and your pay will be reduced by an amount corresponding to the appropriate OASDHI tax.

6. If you are a working wife, you will pay OASDHI taxes, but your benefits will be based on either your own earnings record or that of your husband, whichever will give you the largest return. It may seem inequitable that you

are required to pay OASDHI taxes on wages from which you may never collect benefits. However, social insurance programs are contingent in nature—that is, the system is organized in such a way that total benefits may be larger to those qualified for them than would otherwise be possible. For example, if you were able to collect both as a working person and as a dependent, total OASDHI taxes would have to be higher or benefits lower.

7. If you work at two jobs during the year, both of which are covered by OASDHI, and your total wages exceed the total taxable wages under covered employment, your employers will each deduct OASDHI taxes. Because the deductions will exceed the total taxes due in a given year, you can claim a refund of the excess taxes on your federal income tax return. For example, if in 1981 you earned $20,000 in Job A and $20,000 in Job B, OASDHI taxes of 6.65 percent would have been collected by the two employers on $40,000 of wages, although maximum taxable wages in 1981 were $29,700. On your tax return you could have claimed a tax credit of 6.65 percent of the excess ($10,300), or $685.

8. If you are self-employed, you must pay OASDHI taxes on wages earned in covered work at a higher rate than is applicable to employees. The 1981 rate for self-employed persons, for example, was 9.30 percent, compared with 6.65 percent applicable to employees. OASDHI taxes are not due on income from dividends, interest, royalties, annuities, capital gains, or pensions.

9. As a student aged eighteen to twenty-two and attending post–secondary school or college, you are not eligible for OASDHI benefits after 1985 on the basis of your parents' wage record. However, if you were entitled to a check for August 1981 and were enrolled in college, you can draw benefits until April 1985 or until you finish college, reach age twenty-two, or marry, whichever comes first. These benefits are reduced 25 percent a year starting with your September 1982 check. Summer checks are eliminated, as are cost-of-living increases. You remain eligible if you are disabled.

10. Nearly all occupations, including farm, domestic, and restaurant labor, are now covered by Social Security. Only certain classes of workers are excluded—for example, some employees of state and local governments, civilian employees of the federal government, railroad workers, employees of tax-exempt charitable institutions, and some casual laborers like newspaper delivery workers and college students working in fraternities. Many of the excluded groups may participate in OASDHI on a voluntary basis. Under some conditions certain groups may also terminate Social Security—for example, some school districts have terminated employees' OASDHI participation. However, termination of Social Security coverage eliminates or greatly reduces benefits to which employees would otherwise be entitled.

11. On reaching age sixty-two, all persons eligible for OASDHI should register for benefits at their local Social Security office, even if they do not intend to retire immediately. For example, a sixty-two-year-old husband with a sixty-five-year-old wife may be able to obtain Medicare coverage for his wife

even if he continues to work. Unless you make application promptly, you may incur delays and higher costs when you become eligible for benefits.

COORDINATING SOCIAL SECURITY WITH PRIVATE INSURANCE

For most people Social Security is compulsory and forms a base of coverage on which to build a more complete "house of protection." Although Social Security does not "do the whole job," it forms a good base from which to work. Stated differently, coverages available under Social Security significantly reduce the amount of protection you need to acquire from other financial sources. In particular, you should purchase private life and health insurance coverage with due regard to the Social Security base to which you are entitled. Coordinating private insurance with social insurance to maximize efficiency and economy should be an important objective of your personal financial planning.

Coordination with Private Life Insurance

As noted in Chapter 5, life insurance programming is a process of planning life insurance coverage so that it dovetails with Social Security coverage and other resources. Programming enables you to use life insurance effectively and to economize on its purchase. For example, consider how insurance programming may be used in connection with the "blackout period," the years during which a widow receives no OASDHI survivorship benefits because she no longer has dependent children in the household and has not yet turned sixty. If Mary White's thirty-five-year-old husband, Joseph, were to die when Mary was thirty and had one child, Jimmy, aged six, Mary would receive OASDHI survivorship benefits of $400 a month until Jimmy was sixteen, at which time Mary would be forty. (Jimmy would receive survivors' benefits until he turned eighteen.) At this time Mary's Social Security benefits would cease and would not resume for twenty years, until she turned sixty. Suppose that Joseph White wants to purchase enough life insurance to provide an income of $400 a month ($4,800 a year) to replace Mary's Social Security during the blackout period. How much insurance and what type of insurance should he purchase?

Reference to basic interest tables (see Appendix A–5) reveals that the present value of $4,800 a year for twenty years at 8 percent is $47,127. Thus, Joseph will need to provide about $47,000 of life insurance protection to fill Mary's need for income during the blackout period. Exhibit 7–7 shows the combination of Social Security and life insurance protection needed by Joseph

EXHIBIT 7–7   Life Insurance and Social Security Program for the White Family

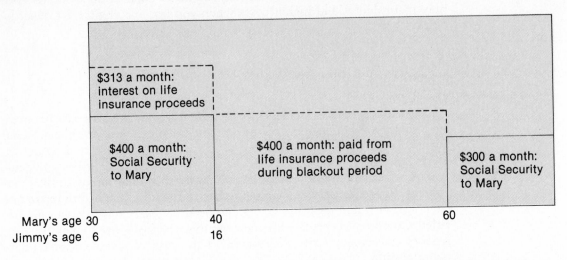

White's survivors if he were to die at age thirty-five. Note that the family's life insurance proceeds will not start to be liquidated until Mary reaches age forty. Joseph may direct the life insurer or a trustee to hold the proceeds at interest from the date of his death until Mary turns forty. If the funds earn 8 percent, Mary will receive $313 a month in interest to supplement Social Security.

Suppose Joseph is still alive and well when Mary reaches age forty-five. For each year that Mary moves closer to age sixty, the amount of life insurance needed to fill the blackout period steadily declines. Therefore, if Joseph dies when Mary is forty-five, the blackout period will consist of only fifteen years, after which her OASDHI benefits become payable. The coverage needed to provide $400 a month for fifteen years amounts to only about $41,000.

For family income needs, the least costly form of life insurance is term insurance, which has no savings element. Joseph could purchase a ten-year level term policy of $47,000 at age thirty-five for approximately $7.40 per $1,000 of face amount, or $348 a year. Alternatively, Joseph could purchase decreasing term insurance when Mary reaches age forty. This type of contract provides no more and no less than the amount of protection really needed. The face amount steadily declines to correspond to the declining period of years during which income must be provided. For example, the cost of $41,000 of decreasing term for a male, aged forty-five, is $10.25 per $1,000, or $420 a year.

Coordination with Private Health Insurance

As noted earlier, many private insurers provide health insurance to supplement Medicare. An insurer may promise to pay expenses excluded under

Medicare—for example, private duty nursing in hospitals and part or all of applicable deductibles. One policy, for example, offered the following protection under contract to supplement Part A coverage:

1. $180 deductible for hospital expenses,
2. $45-a-day deductible from the sixty-first to ninetieth day,
3. $90-a-day deductible for up to sixty reserve days, subject to a $50,000 policy maximum.

The policy offered similar increases in protection under the other parts of Medicare. Issued in 1980 at a monthly premium of $12.95, the policy became outdated in 1981 when the OASDHI deductibles were changed. Since the deductibles change almost every year, you should make sure before you purchase supplementary coverage that the coverage corresponds to the deductible currently being levied by OASDHI.

Coordination with Private Disability Income Insurance

Disability insurance is provided by not only Social Security but also by social insurance programs like workers' compensation, which indemnifies workers for occupational injuries. Private insurance is often used to supplement disability insurance and to "fill gaps" in coverage; one type of social insurance coverage may not always be applicable in a given case. For example, Social Security disability income is not paid until a waiting period of five months has elapsed. Moreover, the disability must be long-term–that is, expected to last at least one year and to prevent the worker from performing "substantially gainful" employment. Privately issued short-term disability income policies offer protection limited to a six-month period. They also define disability as the inability to perform one's regular occupation—a more liberal definition than that used by Social Security.

Disability is defined in workers' compensation policies as related to one's occupation or as incurred in the course of one's work. For example, if you are injured in a car accident on the way home from work, you will not be compensated for lost income under workers' compensation coverage applicable to your job. Furthermore, the amount of workers' compensation protection is often limited under state law to some proportion of your former wage. Also, compensation for disability stemming from illness is very restricted under workers' compensation; the illness must be an occupational disease. Private disability policies are not so restrictive and may be adjusted so that the total income you receive from all sources during disability will replace the disposable income you had before the disability.

Employees are often covered for disability income loss under special group plans provided by their employers or under employer-sponsored retirement plans. These coverages are frequently "integrated" with social insurance through "coordination-of-benefits clauses" under which privately paid benefits can fill whatever gaps exist at the time of disability. For example, the group disability policy may provide that no more than 65 percent of a disabled worker's former income may be received from the combined benefits of Social Security, workers' compensation, the company retirement plan, and the group disability policy. Such a provision allows the private group policy to respond appropriately if the disability is such that other benefits are not payable or are not adequate. To illustrate, assume that before becoming totally disabled, you were earning $2,000 monthly. The combination of disability income benefits, including proceeds from the group disability income policy, would be arranged so as not to exceed $1,300 (65 percent of $2,000). The benefits paid by the group policy would be calculated as follows:

65 percent of predisability income of $2,000	$1,300
Less:	
Workers' compensation allowance	300
OASDHI disability allowance	400
Disability allowance under employer's retirement plan	300
Amount paid by group disability income policy	$ 300

If for some reason the allowances under workers' compensation, OASDHI disability, or the employer retirement plan were changed, the amount paid by the group disability income policy would also be changed to maintain a constant $1,300 a month in disability income. The coordination-of-benefits clause prevents a disabled person from receiving disability income higher than regular earnings and thus provides an incentive for the disabled person to return to work.

Coordination with Other Retirement Income

A major benefit under Social Security is the worker's retirement benefit, which is relatively modest in comparison with a worker's final average income. The retirement benefit is based on average wages earned during your entire career; due to inflation and to career advancement, this average is usually less than your final wage. To supplement the retirement benefit, many employers provide a private pension plan under which eligible workers may qualify for additional retirement benefits. Frequently the benefit formula under these plans is based on the average wages earned in the five years preceding your retirement. For example, the plan may provide for 1 percent of wages (defined as average wages in the last five years) times years of service. A thirty-year employee would thus receive 30 percent of final average wages in addition to Social Security retirement benefits.

You may supplement Social Security and private pension benefits with an individual retirement plan (see Chapter 15). By combining Social Security, an employer-sponsored pension, and private or individual savings, you can build an adequate retirement income.

STATE GOVERNMENT PROGRAMS

State programs provide for the payment of medical expenses and disability income benefits to ill or injured workers. These programs include workers' compensation and temporary disability laws.

Workers' Compensation

A significant type of social insurance, compulsory in every state, provides medical expense and disability income protection for workers who are injured in occupational accidents or disabled from occupational disease. Benefits are determined by state law and are revised frequently to reflect changes in wage levels, inflation, and other factors. In most states workers' compensation coverage is written by private insurers and financed by employer payroll taxes. In six states the workers' compensation funds operate exclusively, and private insurers are not permitted to compete. In most states an employer is also permitted to self-insure, provided certain conditions are met. Although workers' compensation laws cover most occupations, approximately 15 percent of all workers are not covered because of various exclusions that permit some employers—for example, small employers with one or two workers—to remain exempt.

Workers' compensation benefits are of four major types. The first type includes payments to the worker for permanent or temporary disability. In most cases the benefit may be paid for life, but some states limit payments to 400 or 500 weeks. Benefits are calculated so that the average amount paid is about two-thirds of the worker's wage before disability. Most states also permit a lump-sum payment in lieu of monthly payments when, for example, a worker has suffered the loss of a limb in an industrial accident.

The second type of benefit is related to cases of fatal injury. Most workers' compensation laws provide for payments to workers' survivors, including widows, widowers, or children. Survivors may receive both income benefits and funeral allowances. The benefits amount to approximately what would have been paid for permanent, total disability.

The third type of benefit provides virtually complete medical expense coverage for injured workers. Finally, most workers' compensation laws provide benefits for rehabilitation of injured workers after an accident. Both vocational and physical rehabilitation services are provided; the goal is to return workers to their former occupations insofar as possible.

Temporary Disability Laws

Six jurisdictions have passed laws, usually referred to as **temporary disability laws**, that provide nonoccupational income benefits for disabled workers.[2] Under these statutes disabled persons may draw income benefits whether or not they were employed at the time of the accident and whether or not the disability was a result of illness or of accident. To draw benefits, a person must generally demonstrate a physical or mental disability that makes regular or customary work impossible. Benefits are usually limited to twenty-six weeks, and a one-week waiting period is usually required before benefits begin. To qualify, a person must have been attached to the labor force at some time and must have earned a specified amount of wages. Benefits are usually similar to the amounts payable under unemployment insurance laws of the state.

SUMMARY

1. Social Security, which is composed of several types of public insurance programs, provides important income security on which personal financial planning can be based. Social Security generally provides limited protection and does not attempt to "do the whole job." Thus, personal financial planning around Social Security benefits is still essential.
2. Since Social Security programs are generally compulsory, most people pay taxes to support them—a fact that makes efficient utilization of these benefits more important. Several significant differences exist between Social Security and private insurance—for example, Social Security eliminates individual choice regarding the amount of the benefit, sets specific rules for eligibility, and puts conditions on the benefit.
3. The chief types of social insurance are the federal OASDHI program, state workers' compensation programs, and state temporary disability income insurance programs. OASDHI includes retirement benefits for eligible workers, death and disability benefits for workers and their survivors, and payment of hospital and medical expenses (Medicare) for people who have reached sixty-five.

---

2. Rhode Island, New York, New Jersey, California, Hawaii, and Puerto Rico.

"You may be eligible for temporary disability benefits."

The Bettman Archive, Inc.

4. All Social Security programs are financed by payroll taxes on workers. Generally you must have "earned" the right to benefits, which are paid without regard to economic need. Payroll tax rates have been rising in recent years, and in many cases they amount to as much as, or more than, federal and state income taxes combined.

5. A significant part of personal financial planning is the coordination of individual insurance policies with various Social Security programs. You can practice economy in buying private insurance designed to supplement Social Security, because less private insurance is required than would be needed if Social Security did not exist. Private insurance must be carefully arranged so that the benefits will complement, not duplicate, benefits available under Social Security.

REVIEW QUESTIONS

1. Why should social insurance concern you as a financial planner?

2. (a) In what ways is social insurance different from private insurance?
   (b) Why are these differences significant for personal financial planning?

3. (a) What are the four main parts of OASDHI?
   (b) In general, who is eligible for coverage under each of these parts?

4. Do you believe OASDHI is worthwhile in relation to the amount of the tax versus the benefits available?

5. (a) Why are OASDHI retirement benefits stopped or reduced if an eligible worker earns more than a specified amount in covered employment?
   (b) If benefits are an "earned right," is it fair to stop or reduce benefits when a worker earns more than regulations allow?

6. (a) What is the OASDHI definition of disability?
   (b) If you are unable to perform in your regular occupation because of a disability, are you automatically eligible for disability benefits?

7. Should the deductibles under Medicare be eliminated to end the need for private supplemental health insurance? Why, or why not?

8. What, if anything, should be done to improve the financial soundness of OASDHI?

9. (a) What is the "Social Security gap"?
   (b) How does this gap affect the need for private life insurance?

10. (a) Could a disabled worker simultaneously draw income benefits from OASDHI, from workers' compensation, from temporary disability, from auto PIP protection, from an employer's pension plan, from a group disability income plan, and from an individual disability income policy? Why, or why not?
    (b) What problem is created by multiple sources of disability income?

11. During the period from 1970 to 1979, the average annual increase in the Consumer Price Index applicable to wage and clerical workers was 7.1 percent. A table of present values of money at 7 percent reveals that $1,000 to be received ten years from now is worth $508 today.
    (a) What do these figures imply about the future value of retirement income of $1,000 a year?
    (b) Should Social Security income be protected against inflation?

CASE PROBLEMS

I. Life Insurance for the OASDHI Blackout Period

George Jones, aged thirty-five, and his wife, Jane, aged thirty-two, are considering the purchase of life insurance to fill the "blackout period" imposed by OASDHI. The Joneses have one child, Michael, aged three. George wishes to provide $600 monthly for Jane until she reaches age sixty. If George dies, Social Security will provide the family $400 monthly until Michael reaches age sixteen and $300 monthly after Jane turns sixty. Michael receives benefits between ages sixteen and eighteen, but Jane's benefit stops when Michael turns sixteen.

George receives quotations on life insurance as follows: fifteen-year level term, $6 per $1,000; whole life, $14 per $1,000. If George survives fifteen years, he can renew the term coverage on a term-to-65 policy for $15 per $1,000. Whole life, of course, can be retained at the same premium for life.

George consults an interest table and discovers that for each dollar to be paid annually for fifteen years (present value of an annuity), the sum of $10.38 must be available, assuming 5 percent interest; $9.71, assuming 6 percent interest; and $9.11, assuming 7 percent interest.

QUESTIONS

1. When does the blackout period begin for George's family?

2. How much life insurance should George buy to provide $600 a month to Jane until she reaches age sixty? What settlement options should be used? Show your calculations.

3. What type of life insurance should George purchase? What would be the annual premiums?

II. Medicare and Private Health Insurance

The U.S. Department of Health, Education, and Welfare published the guide on page 218 for persons trying to compare coverage available under Medicare with coverage under private health insurance.

The document also stated: (1) One should ask in advance whether the doctor will accept Medicare's reasonable allowance and whether the doctor will accept an assignment so that Medicare can pay the doctor directly. (2) Most private insurance policies also pay claims based on Medicare's reasonable allowance and on Medicare's assessment of whether the service is medically necessary.

Part B, which is optional, costs $11 a month; Part A is "free."

What Medicare Pays	*What Medicare Does Not Pay*
Part A: Hospital Expense Coverage	
• Medically necessary services up to 90 days for each "spell of illness" (plus 60 reserve days). No limit to the number of spells of illness. Reserve days can be used only once. New benefit period begins after you have been out of hospital for at least 60 days.	• Private duty nursing in hospital.
	• First three pints of blood.
	• Dollar deductible amount (amounts in 1981):
	(a) First 60 days, $204.00 total;
	(b) Next 30 days, $51.00 a day;
	(c) 60 reserve days, $102.00 a day;
	(d) 21st to 100th day, $25.50 a day.
• Services in a skilled nursing facility (as certified by Medicare) for up to 100 days.	• Services in a skilled nursing facility or under home care mainly for personal care or assistance.
• Home health care for up to 100 days after hospital stay.	
Part B: Optional Medical Insurance	
• Doctors' services, wherever performed, if medically necessary.	• Routine physical exam.
	• $60 annual deductible.
• Home health visits, up to 100 visits a year (in addition to coverage for visits under Part A).	• 20% of any medical service for which a "reasonable" charge is made.
• Physical therapy and speech pathology services.	• Costs in excess of what is found to be a "reasonable" charge.
• Other services (lab tests, X-rays, ambulance, rental of wheel chairs).	

QUESTIONS

1. Suppose Ethel, who is covered by Parts A and B of Medicare, spends ten days in the hospital after an operation and later receives the following bill:

Hospital room and board	$1,000
Private duty nurse	100
Surgeon's fee (deemed reasonable by Medicare)	500
Physical therapy in the doctor's office	100
Total	$1,700

   How much of the bill would be paid by Medicare, assuming that the bill was Ethel's only medical expense for the year?

2. Do you think Ethel needs supplemental private insurance? If so, what type?

CHAPTER

CHAPTER 8

REAL ESTATE AND HOME OWNERSHIP

LEARNING OBJECTIVES

In studying this chapter you will learn:

The advantages and disadvantages of real estate ownership;

What factors to consider in deciding whether to rent or to purchase a home;

Why real estate may not be as attractive an investment in the future as it has been in the past;

What are the different types of "creative financing";

What are the special characteristics and problems of condominiums;

How to appraise different kinds of real estate as an investment.

Real estate, and specifically home ownership, has received more attention than any other single type of investment. The reasons for investor interest are many. People have traditionally viewed ownership of a home as a foundation of family financial security. Despite high interest rates, the income tax deduction available on the interest expense of home financing has greatly reduced the after-tax cost of ownership. Furthermore, home prices have kept pace with inflation and have given owners an investment that often appreciates in "real dollars." Another reason for investor interest is the fact that many home purchases have been facilitated by government programs. A final inducement is the one-time tax exemption for retired owners on part or all of the gain realized from the sale of a personal residence. These factors, along with property tax deductions to which homeowners are entitled, make home ownership attractive to the consumer.

In addition to being interested in home ownership for purposes of both shelter and investment, many people have also become interested in investing in real estate on a commercial basis. Such investments might include purchasing rental income property and participating in limited partnership ventures on apartment projects or shopping centers.

HOME OWNERSHIP

Real estate can be viewed in three ways: (1) strictly as an investment, (2) strictly as shelter, or (3) as some combination of the two. The potential buyer probably considers the purchase of a home both an investment and a way to obtain needed housing. The qualities you seek in a house will depend on which viewpoint you emphasize. If you look upon a house strictly as a home, the qualities you find desirable are perhaps different from the qualities you would want in a house you viewed mainly as an investment to be resold later at a profit. If you buy a house as an investment, you will give more careful consideration to how easy the house will be to resell. Price, size, and location will be more important than how well the house fits your particular needs as a place to live.

If being close to work is important to you, you may decide not to buy at all, but rather to rent a downtown apartment since single-family houses may not be available or affordable in a downtown location. Thus, the first decision to be made is whether to buy or to rent. Important in that decision are the costs of owning versus renting.

The Own-or-Rent Decision

Often the first decision financial planners must make in the area of real estate investment is whether to own or to rent. This decision is relatively easy for most young people; they usually must rent housing since they lack the finances and income to support the purchase of a house or a condominium. However, after a person becomes relatively established in an occupation, develops a stable source of employment and income, and is able to make a down payment, the question of whether to continue renting or to buy becomes a real choice.

ADVANTAGES OF RENTING

Rental housing has several advantages:

1. Rental housing is usually more available than single-family homes in locations convenient to your work.
2. Rental housing involves less risk of loss in the event of a move necessitated by a job transfer or other circumstances.
3. When you consider all costs, including commuting costs, rental housing often may be less expensive than ownership of a comparable house or condominium.
4. Renting is usually more convenient than owning, because landlords take care of most maintenance and waste disposal and sometimes pay the cost of utilities.
5. Proximity to others may provide the renter a degree of physical security that may not be available to the homeowner, who often lives in a more isolated area (except in the case of condominiums).

CAVEATS FOR RENTERS

If you decide to rent rather than to buy, you should be aware of certain facts regarding leases:

1. You will often be required to sign a lease that binds you to pay rent even if you must leave before the lease expires.
2. The lease may require you to pay any legal fees involved in disputes between you and the landlord.
3. The lease may require you to pay a security or cleaning deposit that may not be returnable when you leave.
4. Some leases give landlords the right to cut off water or heat if you do certain things—for example, organize a renters' union or violate a housing code.
5. Some leases require you to continue paying rent even if your unit is rendered uninhabitable by fire or some other peril.

6. The lease may place restrictions on certain activities—for example, keeping pets, mounting pictures, having specialized furniture like water beds or space heaters, or subleasing your apartment.

You should read a lease very carefully before signing, because courts will generally enforce such an agreement if it was entered into voluntarily. If you object to certain provisions or believe certain provisions to be unlawful, you should register your complaints before you sign the lease, not afterward.

COSTS AND ADVANTAGES OF OWNING

The advantages of owning a home in many cases correspond to the disadvantages of renting, and vice versa. However, you should analyze the costs of home ownership in detail to make valid economic comparisons between buying and renting. All things considered, owning a home is probably cheaper than renting, particularly if you occupy the home for a substantial number of years in a period during which home and land prices are rising. However, for short periods of occupancy, when convenient location is important, and when you are not yet established financially, renting has advantages.

The major differences between the costs of renting and the costs of home ownership stem from (1) tax treatment of some of the costs of home ownership, (2) financial leverage, (3) inflationary pressures on the price of housing, and (4) the expense of ownership transfer.

Tax Treatment. Interest on mortgage loans, property taxes, and other taxes related to home ownership and maintenance are major considerations in the cost of home ownership; all these items are deductible on federal and state income taxes. Renters, on the other hand, may not deduct any portion of a rental payment from their income taxes. To illustrate the tax advantages of home ownership, consider the average single-family home in 1981, which sold for about $70,000. Suppose a home buyer puts $10,000 down and obtains a thirty-year mortgage loan of $60,000 at 12 percent interest on a home with annual property taxes of $1,000. (Taxes vary widely, depending on the locality in which the home is situated.) Under these conditions the buyer will have income tax deductions in the first year of almost $7,200 in interest ($60,000 × .12), because mortgage payments in the early years consist almost entirely of the repayment of interest. In addition, the buyer will have a property tax deduction of $1,000, for a total deduction of $8,200. If the buyer is in the 40 percent combined state and federal tax bracket, the value of the tax deduction will be $3,280 for the first year ($8,200 × .40), or about $273 monthly. The home buyer may view this deduction as a subsidy from the government, because the deduction would not be available had the buyer been paying rent.

Another tax advantage of home ownership is the deferral of income taxes on homes sold at a profit. You owe no income taxes on your profits as long as you invest in another home of equal or greater value within twenty-four months. Furthermore, the tax laws provide that under certain conditions you may exempt up to $125,000 of gain on the sale of a home. To obtain this tax advantage, you must be fifty-five or older, and the home you are selling must be your principal residence. This privilege is available only once in your lifetime. Thus, you could buy and sell a series of homes during your working career and each time accumulate tax-free profits; finally you could exclude all gains up to $125,000 from the sale of your last house.

Financial Leverage. The home buyer controls a substantial investment by making a relatively small down payment and borrowing the rest. In the case just discussed, for example, the home buyer controlled an investment of $70,000 with a down payment of only $10,000. This type of control is known as **financial leverage,** because relatively small changes in the price of the asset produce magnified changes in the amount of the owner's equity. The smaller the down payment, the greater the leverage. For example, if a buyer puts $10,000 down and the price of the house later rises by $10,000, from $70,000 to $80,000 (a gain of 16.6 percent), the owner's equity has increased from $10,000 to $20,000 (a gain of 100 percent). Equity usually increases even more than in this example, since the principal amount of the owner's loan is gradually reduced over the life of the mortgage. Thus, if the house is sold for $80,000 after the $60,000 loan has been reduced to $55,000, the owner's equity increases from $10,000 to $25,000 ($80,000 − $55,000), a gain of 150 percent.

Of course, the market price of a house could also decline, in which case financial leverage would work against the home buyer. (However, in the United States the market value of a house usually rises on account of inflation.) If the price declines, the owner's investment could be wiped out by a relatively small price drop. For example, if the price of the home discussed previously dropped from $70,000 to $60,000 (a decline of 14.3 percent), the owner's equity of $10,000 disappears, a drop of 100 percent.

Inflationary Increases. Home prices in the United States have for many years tended to rise at rates higher than the general rate of inflation. Some areas in the West and in the South have seen especially rapid increases in housing prices. Nationally, the average price of newly built homes insured under conventional mortgages increased from $44,600 to $73,600 between 1975 and 1979, an increase of 64 percent. Prices of previously occupied homes rose on the average from $38,200 to $64,500, an increase of 69 percent. These changes compare to a rise in the Consumer Price Index over the same period from 161 to 209, an increase of 30 percent. Such increases in home prices mean that the cost of carrying mortgages declines in real terms. That is, if incomes continue to increase at approximately the same rate as consumer prices, the burden of carrying a fixed mortgage rate declines correspondingly.

Many forces have influenced the continuous rise in home prices—for example: (1) rising costs of labor and building materials, (2) the increasing scarcity of well-located land on which to construct homes, (3) increased demand for homes by young families formed as a result of the post–World War II "baby boom," (4) rising divorce rates (separated spouses each seek separate homes), (5) the tendency of retired parents to maintain separate homes instead of moving in with grown children, (6) the tendency of young single people to set up separate residences, and (7) the availability of relatively low-cost, fixed-interest mortgages covering periods as long as thirty or forty years.

Fixed-rate mortgages have in the past been encouraged by government programs that guaranteed repayment of the loans and by people's willingness to save in such media as life insurance and savings and loan associations, which paid relatively low and fixed rates of interest. However, fixed-rate mortgages have been difficult to obtain in recent years because lenders have become unwilling to commit their funds for long periods at an unchanging rate.

The widespread availability of low-cost, fixed-rate mortgages was in the past a significant benefit to the homeowner because home prices are directly influenced by the price and availability of mortgage financing. As we will see later in the chapter, in the discussion of real estate financing, interest costs are built into the price of homes. Absence of mortgage credit at affordable interest rates can drastically reduce the market price of homes and may prevent their transfer entirely for extended periods of time.

No one can predict how much longer the forces that have made home buying advantageous will continue to cause real estate, particularly the price of homes, to rise as fast as, or faster than, prices in general. Inflation is a worldwide phenomenon of long duration and probably will not subside for extended periods. Inflation will most likely continue to propel home prices upward, although perhaps not at as fast a rate as existed in the 1970s. Thus, owning real estate as opposed to renting may be viewed as a continuing advantage.

Transfer Costs. One factor that reduces the price advantage of owning real estate is the relatively high cost of ownership transfer. Real estate sales commissions (about 6 percent of the value of the transaction), issuance of a new mortgage, legal fees, taxes, bank charges, appraisals, and other closing costs of a mortgage loan (averaging, in total, perhaps 3 to 4 percent of the value of the transaction) can substantially erode the homeowner's profit. To some extent transfer costs are paid twice—once when you buy and again when you sell. Transfer costs are high enough to make home ownership relatively unprofitable unless you intend to occupy your home for at least three or four years.

The Buy-or-Build Decision

Assuming that you have decided to be a homeowner rather than a renter, should you buy an existing home or build a new one? Several factors enter into this decision. Advantages of buying an existing home are as follows:

1. You can see what you are buying and more confidently decide whether the house will be suitable. Building a house from plans frequently involves unavoidable uncertainties.
2. Existing homes are usually part of established neighborhoods where you can judge the suitability of the surroundings, meet your potential neighbors, and determine the availability of community services and the distance to schools and shopping centers. A new home may be constructed in an undeveloped area, and you may have many unresolved questions about the neighborhood.
3. Since building takes time, you can usually gain access more quickly to an already existing home.
4. Older homes are usually located "close in"; thus, transportation costs for work, shopping, and school may be lower.
5. By buying an existing home, you may obtain "free" many features that you would have had to purchase had you built. Examples include landscaping, fences, driveways, antennas, and indoor furnishings like draperies, carpets and appliances.

Building a new home has the following advantages:

1. Since the house is to be built, it can be tailored to your particular needs and desires, frequently without extra cost. For example, you can select the colors of wall coverings, carpets, drapes, and fixtures to blend with the furnishings you already own.
2. New homes can incorporate without extra cost the latest advances in construction, safety, and other features. For example, adequate insulation, which has become important because of rising energy costs, will automatically be installed in a new home; older homes frequently have less insulation because they were often built without great attention to energy conservation.
3. With a new home you can often obtain better financing—that is, a larger loan at lower interest rates for a longer pay-out period. Lenders usually regard a new house as greater loan security than an older home.
4. New homes can be built in areas just emerging as established neighborhoods, while older homes are often found in deteriorating areas that are frequently subject to higher crime rates and to other urban problems. A choice location may mean a better investment and may make the home easier to resell.

"Existing homes are usually in established neighborhoods, allowing you to judge
the suitability of your neighbors..."

The Bettman Archive, Inc.

Whether to buy an existing home or to build a new home frequently depends on your individual needs and circumstances. Buying a new home probably costs more initially in most cases, but in the long run it may be the less expensive alternative because of energy savings and resale values.

Condominiums

Most locations offer another option in home ownership: the choice between a separate home or a condominium. Each gives the homeowner equity ownership in a residence, and in each case the interest payments on a mortgage loan are tax-deductible. Important differences exist, however, with regard to owner responsibilities and costs.

In purchasing a condominium, you are buying a living space as well as a share in common areas such as recreational facilities, halls, grounds, and out-buildings. You are assessed a monthly fee for such items as ground maintenance, repairs and maintenance of the outside walls and the building equipment, and insurance and taxes on the building and grounds. Occupants of the complex become members of a homeowners' association that elects officers to manage the property and makes decisions regarding the common interests of the owners.

ADVANTAGES OF CONDOMINIUM OWNERSHIP

Condominiums offer the tax advantages of ownership, relative freedom from ground and exterior maintenance, and the right to enjoy common facilities such as clubhouses, tennis courts, and swimming pools. Since condominiums usually have less living space than do single family homes, condominium prices tend to be correspondingly lower. Often condominiums are located closer to a person's place of work since the more costly land close to urban, industrial centers is more affordable when the cost is shared by a number of owners.

DISADVANTAGES OF CONDOMINIUM OWNERSHIP

Disadvantages and risks of condominium ownership include the following:

1. Since the owners' association makes decisions affecting the quality and cost of your living experience, you do not have complete control over these matters. Thus, you may have to devote some time to the affairs of the association to prevent arbitrary increases in monthly maintenance fee assessments.
2. Many condominiums are converted from former apartment complexes that may not have been well built nor built for energy efficiency. The result may be excessive energy and maintenance costs.

3. The original developers of a condominium complex frequently retain control over facilities such as swimming pools and tennis courts through ground leases of management contracts. The owners' association may thus be subject to excessive charges for these facilities.

4. To entice buyers, some condominium developers underestimate monthly association assessments. Once the complex is sold out, these fees may have to be raised to a level you did not anticipate when you bought your unit.

5. Like apartment living, condominium ownership may be subject to annoyances such as noisy neighbors, late-night parties, and other owners' lack of consideration in sharing common facilities.

6. The bylaws of your association may place restrictions on the use of your unit—for example, many bylaws restrict an owner's right to rent a unit to other people.

7. A condominium may be more difficult to resell than a detached house because of the uncertainties mentioned above.

Services of Real Estate Brokers

In buying or selling a home, you must decide whether to use the services of a real estate broker or to sell the home yourself. Brokers' services are expensive; they frequently amount to 6 percent or more of the amount of the transaction. However, real estate commissions are sometimes negotiable, and you can perhaps obtain brokerage services at a commission lower than the "standard" charge in your community.

Many people believe that if you can sell a house without having to pay a commission, you can obtain a higher net price than would be the case if you sold through a broker. Obviously, if you can obtain on your own the same price you would obtain through a broker, you are financially better off if you sell the home yourself. However, the potential buyer of a home being sold by the owner knows the owner is not paying a commission, and the buyer will thus be more inclined to offer less money. Therefore, it is not necessarily financially advantageous to attempt to sell your house personally. A qualified broker offers certain services that both buyers and sellers ought to consider carefully.

BROKERAGE SERVICES TO THE SELLER

The following services offered by competent brokers frequently cannot be duplicated by individuals attempting to deal directly with each other:

1. Brokers deal continuously with real estate market prices and can more readily arrange a mutually agreeable price than can buyers and sellers dealing "at arm's length."

2. Brokers frequently know of prospective buyers and can arrange a sale more quickly than can a seller who must advertise in the newspapers.

3. Because brokers do not have emotional attachments to a particular house, they can more objectively explain its advantages to a prospective buyer. Brokers can also discover and try to overcome objections that a buyer may be hesitant to reveal to the seller.

4. Brokers can suggest ways to make a house more salable.

5. Brokers bear the cost of advertising, respond to inquiries, and show the property.

6. Brokers can screen unqualified prospects—people who are not financially qualified to purchase a home or who are merely curious.

7. Brokers can frequently assist in arranging financing on terms favorable enough to "swing the sale."

BROKERAGE SERVICES TO THE BUYER

By using a broker, a prospective buyer obtains without direct cost the following services:

1. Brokers know most of the available property that would satisfy the needs of the buyer; therefore, the buyer saves time in looking for a home.

2. Brokers are a source of information about quality of the neighborhood, the schools, the churches, taxes, transportation, zoning, and other matters of importance to the buyer.

3. Brokers are frequently more effective than buyers at conveying offers to the seller. For example, a broker may demonstrate to a seller that the price is unrealistically high by showing how several prospects have viewed the property.

4. Brokers can arrange escrow accounts to hold funds until details of the purchase are finalized.

SELECTING A BROKER

You should exercise care in selecting a broker, since all brokers are not equally qualified or equally effective for selling all types of property. The first consideration is whether the broker is scrupulously honest. A dishonest broker might not be above doing something illegal—for example, the broker might list a house at a relatively low price, obtain a customer at a higher price, purchase the house for the broker's own account, and then resell it immediately at the higher price.

Brokers should be informed about the particular neighborhoods or types of property they list; some brokers specialize in given neighborhoods or in certain types of homes. Some brokers also have formal arrangements with associates in other cities and are helpful when the buyer is moving to a distant area. Ideally, brokers should be associated with a **multiple listing serv-**

ice (MLS), a pool of real estate listings in a given area that enables all broker members to know what properties are available, whether or not a broker member has obtained a listing personally. By using a broker who is affiliated with a multiple listing service, you have a much wider selection of homes from which to choose if you are buying, and a potentially larger number of buyers if you are selling. Finally, if as a buyer or as a seller you will need appraisals, financing, or other services, you should inquire whether a particular broker can supply the needed contracts and services.

Factors That Affect Value

1. *Location and quality of the neighborhood.* Quality includes such factors as convenience to public transportation, absence of undue noise, nearness to parks and recreational facilities, availability of police and fire protection, accessibility to shopping and schools, and general worth and appearance of other homes in the area. It is generally better to avoid property that is more expensive than other properties nearby, because property values often tend to sink to the value of the least expensive house in a given neighborhood, not the other way around.

2. *Landscaping and characteristics of the lot.* Lot value is enhanced if the lot is large enough for the house, for driveways, for children's playing space, and for out-buildings such as garages. Lots should have good drainage, adequate landscaping that includes trees, and satisfactory views.

3. *Exterior condition and appearance.* Value is enhanced if the house has straight roof lines, sound gutters, sashes, screens, weather stripping, a porch, and a deck. Chimney siding and brick facing should be in good repair, as should shingles, paint, and steps. Peeling paint suggests water damage or vapor buildup inside the walls.

4. *Interior condition and appearance.* Value is significantly reduced by sagging or crooked floors and walls, squeaking steps, doors that do not close properly, broken locks, the absence of dampers in a fireplace, and sticking windows. Rooms should be large enough to accommodate furniture, and the accesses to bathrooms should not require one to pass through other rooms. Storage space should be adequate, and each bedroom should have adequate closet space. There should also be easy access from the garage to the kitchen. Electrical outlets should be placed on each wall, and light should be controlled by switches. Plumbing and heating fixtures should be adequate and in good working condition. Garages and basements should be dry, even in wet weather. Insulation should be adequate in both ceilings and walls.

An integral part of most home evaluations is inspection for damage due to termites, water leakage, cracking foundations, and failing structural supports in floors and roofs. Damage due to these conditions can be extremely expensive to repair. Water pressure should also be checked; poor pressure may

"And the backyard is so big, you can raise rabbits."

mean that water pipes are corroded and must be replaced. If you are buying a house, particularly an older house, you would do well to hire the inspection services of an expert. You can then consider the estimated cost of necessary repairs before making an offer.

THE RENOVATION DECISION

Some conditions are serious enough to warrant outright rejection of a property by a buyer who is considering the house for possible renovation. These conditions include foundation supports that are not repairable or a frame that is out of square or infested with termites. A house that requires replacement of numerous components—for example, roof, plumbing fixtures, and electrical wiring—may also be a poor investment. Furthermore, if a house is not located in a desirable area, major renovations will probably not be worthwhile from an economic standpoint.

Appraisals

Any of several methods of property appraisals can help you obtain an unbiased estimate of the value of a home. In general, estimates are means of determining current market value. Market value may be estimated in the following ways: (1) by reviewing recent selling prices of similar properties in the same neighborhood or in an equivalent neighborhood, (2) by studying current replacement costs of similar property, (3) by reviewing assessed value for property taxes in the community, (4) by obtaining estimates of loan value from potential lenders, and (5) by trying different price levels in advertising media and elsewhere to determine what the market will accept at a given point in time.

Brokers can frequently be of considerable service to both buyers and sellers in the appraisal of property. Because of their familiarity with real estate prices and market conditions, brokers can frequently make fairly accurate estimates of what a house will bring. However, an owner should use the more formal methods of appraisal rather than rely on a broker's quick estimate of value. For example, a review of recent selling prices of similar property is very helpful to an owner who wants to obtain a realistic estimate of what a particular house may bring.

Knowing what a given house would cost to replace is also important, although such an estimate is of greater value for insurance purposes than for judging current market value. Exhibit 8–1 is an illustration of construction classes used to determine replacement values. If an owner is asking $70,000 for a house that can be replaced for $50,000, you can conclude that the land in that location is being valued at $20,000. Assessed values for property tax purposes are usually much lower than market values. However, you can use assessment figures to estimate market value in a given community. For example, if houses in a community are assessed at 40 percent of "market value" and a given house is assessed at $50,000, tax assessors have estimated that the market value of the property is $125,000 ($50,000/.40 = $125,000).

In the case of a particularly valuable home, you probably should not rely solely on the appraisal methods so far discussed. Whether you are buying or selling a very valuable property, you should consider using the services of a qualified real estate appraiser.

EXHIBIT 8–1   Basic Construction Classes of Homes

BASIC CLASSES

CLASS I

- Usually plain box-shaped design
- Low cost is primary consideration; just meets building codes
- Mass-produced; built for speculation
- Few or no features; little or no ornamentation
- Usually no special-purpose rooms; dining area part of living room or kitchen
- Specifications include softwood trim, flush doors, minimal cabinetry, inexpensive floor finishes

CLASS II

- Simple design; usually slight shape and roofline changes
- Average-quality materials and workmanship
- Built for speculation or contracted
- Some features and ornamentation to attract buyers
- Usually has dining room; frequently has den or family room; may have foyer
- Specifications include panel doors; ample cabinetry; hardwood or carpet, vinyl asbestos and ceramic tile floors

CLASS III

- Customized floor plan but not necessarily one-of-a-kind
- Average to above-average-quality materials and workmanship
- Contracted by a specific buyer
- Some individual features and ornamentation
- Usually has dining room, den or family room, and foyer
- Specifications include hardwood trim; panel doors; ample cabinetry; hardwood or carpet, vinyl asbestos and ceramic tile, and slate floors

CLASS IV

- One-of-a-kind floor plan custom-designed and specified by an architect for a specific client
- Very-good-quality materials and workmanship
- Contracted by a specific buyer
- Many individual features and much ornamentation
- Large rooms with dining room, den or family room, foyer, and other special-purpose rooms
- Specifications include ornate hardwood trim; panel doors; ample cabinetry; hardwood or carpet, vinyl asbestos and ceramic tile, and slate floors

PRE-1940 SPECIAL CLASSES

SPECIAL CLASS 2B

- Usually constructed prior to 1940
- Most similar to Basic Class II
- Simple design; usually slight shape and roofline changes
- Average-quality materials and workmanship
- Built for speculation or contracted
- Some features and ornamentation
- Dining room and porches common
- Specifications include ornate hardwood trim; adequate kitchen cabinetry; hardwood, linoleum, and ceramic tile floors

SPECIAL CLASS 2C

- Usually constructed prior to 1940
- Most similar to Basic Class III
- Individual design but not necessarily one-of-a-kind
- Average to above-average-quality materials and craftsmanship
- Contracted by a specific buyer
- Some special features and ornamentation
- Large dining room and foyer common
- Specifications include ornate woodwork, molded plaster cornices, ample kitchen cabinetry; hardwood, vinyl and ceramic tile, and slate floors

Source: Amica Insurance Company.

Warranties

Real estate appraisal is frequently quite technical and demands attention to hidden defects, breakdown of appliances, and other losses that affect value and price. Builders of new homes must warrant that the property is free from hidden defects and must stand ready to make needed repairs or replacement within a given time (usually one year) after the new house is delivered. The sale of used property is usually contingent on all integral parts of the house (e.g., air conditioning, heating, and builtin appliances) being in good working order. Sometimes the buyer holds part of the purchase price in an escrow account until convinced that all is well with a recently purchased house.

Since 1974 a new program, called a **homeowners warranty program (HOW)**, has been available. Started by the National Association of Home Builders, the program provides the buyer of a new home a ten-year guarantee against major defects in construction, a one-year guarantee against faulty workmanship or materials, and a two-year guarantee against defects in heating, electrical, air conditioning, and plumbing systems. The warranty becomes effective when the owner takes title to the house, and the same protection automatically passes to subsequent buyers. The cost of this protection is modest—$2 per $100 of selling price—and is paid by local building groups.

In some areas buyers of used homes may purchase a home warranty contract from private insurers. One such insurer charges between $175 and $250 for an eighteen-month contract covering the parts of a home found to be in good condition after an inspection. The policy covers whatever defects may later appear, including structural defects in the basement and the foundation.

Financing Home Ownership

For most people, owning a home would be impossible without credit. Most people have or are able to save only a modest down payment—for example, 10 or 20 percent of the selling price; they must usually borrow the rest on terms that will keep the monthly payments on the loan affordable.

Before selecting any method of borrowing for a home, you should determine how large a monthly payment you can afford. In the past most homeowners selected financing that would keep total monthly mortgage payments from exceeding between 25 and 35 percent of their gross monthly salary. That is, the price of the house could not be more than two to two and a half times the annual income of the buyer. Because of higher mortgage interest rates, however, the old standards no longer apply. For example, in 1980 mortgage interest rates on new home loans varied from 12 to 14 percent. The average price of a new home was $75,000; therefore, after a down payment of 10 percent, the loan amount was approximately $67,500. Paying off a loan of $67,500 over thirty years at 12 percent requires a monthly payment of $694, a figure that does not include property taxes or insurance. If you were to pay off such a loan and adhere to the 25 percent of gross salary standard, you would need a gross monthly income of $2,776 ($694 × 4), or more than $33,300 a year—an amount much higher than the 1980 estimated average family income of slightly over $18,000.[1] Adhering to the 25 percent standard would thus mean that the average family could not afford a house with an average sale price (see Exhibit 8–2).

Even if you adopted a 35 percent standard, ownership of an average-priced house in 1980 would have been difficult unless you had an above-average salary. In the above example a 35 percent standard would mean that you would need about $2,000 a month in gross income to make a monthly payment of $694 "affordable" ($2,000 × .35 = $700). A gross monthly income of $2,000, or $24,000 a year, was still considerably higher than the average family income in 1980.

Thus, high interest rates and shortages of money have greatly complicated the financing process, and many innovative and complex methods of financing have been developed—for example, graduated payments, second mortgages, higher down payments, and other types of "creative financing." Some of the traditional methods and terms of financing home ownership, and a few of the more innovative methods, are described in the following subsections.

CONVENTIONAL MORTGAGES

Conventional mortgages are mortgages given on homes for long periods (e.g., twenty-five or thirty years) at fixed interest rates, which in 1981 tended to range from 14 to 17 percent. Under the terms of a conventional mortgage, the buyer makes a down payment, which usually does not exceed 20 percent of the purchase price, and borrows the rest. The loan creates an obligation for 360 equal monthly payments if the loan is for thirty years. Initially, each monthly payment is composed mostly of interest, and the amount allocated to principal is quite small. Over the life of the loan, the proportion allocated to principal repayment increases, and the proportion allocated to interest declines. With the final payment, the loan is paid off, and the mortgage on the home, which has been pledged as collateral, is lifted. Loans of this type are known as amortized, fixed-payment loans. An **amortized loan** requires you to make payments for many years before the monthly payments consist mainly of principal repayment rather than of interest. If you accept a twenty-five-year mortgage rather than a thirty-year mortgage, you will save a great deal of interest at only a small increase in monthly payments (which must, of course, be higher for a twenty-five-year mortgage). For example, to pay off a $60,000 loan at 13 percent over thirty years, you must make monthly payments of $663.72. To pay off the same loan over twenty-five years, you must make monthly payments of $676.70—only about $13.00 more a month. The amount of interest contained in the $663.72 payment is $650.00 at first;

1. U.S. Department of Commerce, *Consumer Income*, P–60 No. 122 (Washington, D.C.: U.S. Government Printing Office, March, 1980).

EXHIBIT 8-2
Median Prices of
New Homes and
Percentage of
Families Able to
Afford Them

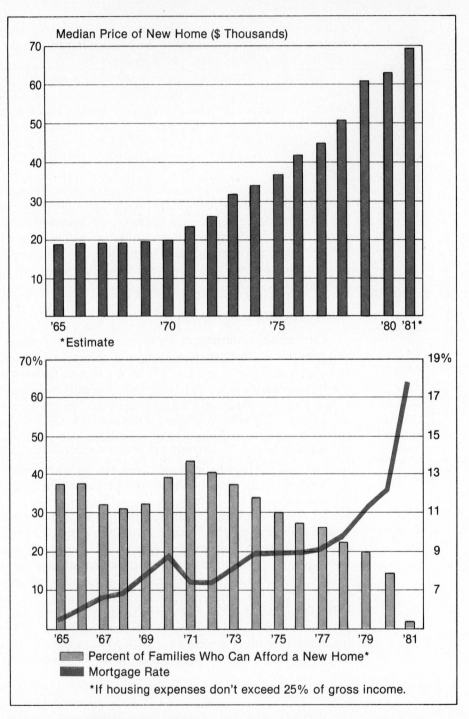

Source: *Forbes* (September 14, 1981), p. 151.

only $13.72 goes toward reducing the loan principal. Hence, most of the payments for the initial years are composed of interest. In fact, it takes nearly twenty-five years of payments on a $60,000, thirty-year, 13 percent mortgage before the proportion of your monthly payment devoted to repaying principal is equal to one-half of the total payment. If you can afford the higher monthly payment, you will pay out fewer dollars by selecting a shorter amortization schedule.

In times of inflation, conventional mortgages have proven very favorable for the borrower, because ability to repay tends to increase along with inflation, while the number of dollars to be repaid remains fixed. Hence, the relative proportion of income devoted to mortgage repayment declines. For example, if you must pay $700 a month on a mortgage when your gross monthly income is $2,100, your mortgage is consuming one-third of your income. However, if inflation runs at 10 percent annually and your wages keep pace, your monthly income will rise to $3,382 within five years. The $700 monthly payment will then comprise only 20.7 percent of your wages. Thus, homeowners with conventional mortgages benefit from inflation. However, in periods of rapid inflation, lenders become increasingly dissatisfied with fixed-payment mortgages. In recent years they have sought alternative arrangements more favorable to them.

VARIABLE-RATE MORTGAGES

Because inflation and soaring interest rates have made long-term, fixed-rate mortgages less attractive to lenders, a new instrument known as a **variable-rate mortgage,** or **flexible-rate mortgage,** has been introduced. These mortgages allow the lender to raise or lower interest rates during the life of the loan to correspond to changes in the market rates of interest. Usually the amounts of the adjustments are restricted so that the rate of interest cannot be raised by more than, say, one percentage point per year or five percentage points over the life of the loan, depending on changes in the cost-of-money index published by the Federal Home Loan Bank Board (FHLB). Thus, a 13 percent mortgage could rise to a maximum of 18 percent or drop to as low as 8 percent. Increases are optional, but reductions are mandatory if the interest rate index declines.

The limitations on rate adjustments offer the borrower some protection against unusual or rapid escalations in interest charges and at the same time offer the benefit of an automatic reduction in interest charges if interest rates decline. The initial lending rate can be lower than that charged for a fixed-rate mortgage, since the lender knows that the rate is subject to adjustment and that the lending institution will not be "stuck" with a long-term mortgage at a fixed rate that may prove to be unprofitable.

For the borrower, the obvious disadvantage of variable-rate mortgages is the possibility that payments will rise beyond available income and may result in the borrower's losing the home. To overcome this possibility, some contracts allow the adjustment in interest rates to be made in the form of a lengthened payment period rather than an increased monthly payment. Some combination of these two methods is also possible. Even though variable-rate mortgages may contain some new risks, the borrower may be better off having such a mortgage than not being able to obtain a housing loan at all.

The Depository Institutions Deregulation and Monetary Control Act of 1980 contained, among other things, new rules designed to increase the availability of mortgage loans. For example, state usury laws on mortgages above $25,000 were eliminated; thus, barriers that in some states had prevented lenders from charging more than a state-mandated maximum rate were removed. The new act also permitted second mortgages and eliminated lending territory restrictions; it thus increased competition in the lending business.

A variation of the variable-rate mortgage is the **rollover mortgage,** in which the interest rate and the mortgage payment are renegotiated every three to five years. Another variation is a type of mortgage in which the loan payments cover only interest (with no reduction in principal) for the first five years. At the end of five years, the loan payments must be arranged so as to be fully amortizing the principal and interest over a definite time period.

GRADUATED PAYMENT MORTGAGES (GPMs)

Another new form of mortgage loan is the **graduated payment mortgage,** in which monthly payments are low at first but rise in stages until, after a given period (e.g., five years), the payments level off at a point higher than they would have been with a conventional, amortized mortgage loan. In 1981, for example, a $50,000 loan insured by the Federal Housing Administration (FHA) for thirty years at 14 percent would carry initial monthly payments (principal, interest, and FHA insurance premium) of $482.78. This payment would rise by seven and one half percent a year for five years, at which time it would reach $685.07 and remain at that level for twenty-five additional years. This loan payment compares to the conventional FHA 13-1/2 percent mortgage loan rate of $593.80. The borrower ends up paying about 42 per-cent more on the GPM after five years than was paid at the beginning. The payments after the fifth year are about 16 percent higher on the GPM than they would have been under a conventional loan (see Exhibit 8–3).

The lower initial payment on a GPM makes it easier for the first-time buyer to qualify for a loan. However, the reduced initial payment must be made up in later years—presumably when the borrower has an increased in-come and can afford the higher payments. The lower initial payments are possible because these payments do not cover the true interest being charged. An initial loan of $50,000 builds up to about $55,000 at the end of five years, at which time the loan is, in effect, converted to a conventional amortized loan of $55,000 for twenty-five years. GPMs can take various forms; the size

EXHIBIT 8–3
Conventional
versus
Graduated-
Payment
Mortgage
($50,000 for 30
years at 14%)

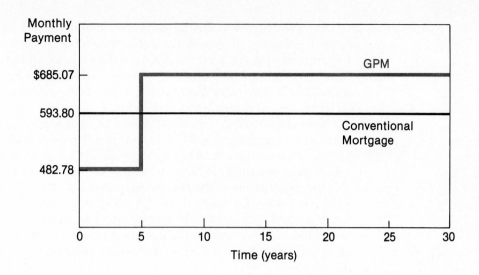

of the initial payment may be raised or lowered. The higher the initial payment, the lower the ultimate payment after five years.

GPMs were started by the FHA in 1977 as a way to enable a new borrower to purchase a first house. The loans were insured by the FHA, and at first the interest rates were the same as the rates for other FHA-insured mortgages. However, in 1980 a higher rate was allowed on GPMs because of their increased complexities and uncertainties and the consequent reluctance of lenders to make the loans. Before the higher rate was allowed, lenders were requiring an extra payment known as **discount points** as a condition of making GPM loans. The seller usually had to pay the points, which in effect were extra dollars added to the price of the house and payable in cash at the time of sale. One point amounted to 1 percent of the loan amount and served to increase the effective yield of the loan to the lender. Any time that maximum FHA interest rates fail to meet market rates, lenders may charge discount points, a practice that increases the cost of borrowing and hence the cost of home ownership.

SHARED-APPRECIATION MORTGAGES (SAMs)

Shared-appreciation mortgages (SAMs) are mortgages in which the lender shares in the appreciation in value of a home on which a mortgage loan is made. Usually the mortgage loan is made at an interest rate below that of conventional mortgages or of graduated-payment loans. After the mortgage has been in force for a few years, and if the home is sold, the borrower and the lender share any increase in value on some predetermined basis. Sometimes the loan provides that the house must be refinanced after a given period—say, ten years. The home is then appraised, and whether or not the house is sold, the increased value (if any) is divided between the borrower and the lender. In 1981, for example, a lender offered a SAM on the following basis: The interest rate was 9.9 percent, compared to about 14 percent for conventional mortgages. After seven years the borrower would have to pay the lender up to 40 percent of the home's increased value. For example, if the home appreciated at an average of 8 percent annually, a $66,666 house would have appreciated by $47,588 after seven years, and the borrower would pay the lender 40 percent of $47,588, or $19,035. Furthermore, the borrower would have to renegotiate with the lender the remaining loan balance of $56,500, presumably at the then current interest rates. The terms offered by SAM lenders are favorable to the borrower only insofar as they reduce the initial monthly payments. But if the owner has improved the home and done part of the work personally, the increased value that results from the owner's labor will benefit the lender to the extent agreed upon under the terms of the mortgage.

EQUITY SHARING

A variation of SAM loans is known as **equity sharing.** Under this arrangement an outside investor contributes part of the down payment or contributes to the monthly payments of the homeowner in return for a share of the profit when the home is sold. Under some equity-sharing arrangements the owner has an option to buy out the investor's "equity" in the home. In one example of equity sharing, Stanford University contributed to the down payments of new faculty members the school was trying to attract. When the homes of these faculty members were later sold, the university and the faculty members shared any gains in proportion to the amount that each had contributed to the original cost.

As another example of equity sharing, a real estate investor might contribute part of the down payment—say, $10,000—in exchange for a 20 percent share of any increase in the value of the property after five years. At that time the house is appraised and the homeowner pays off the investor, either through new borrowing or through refinancing the amount due the investor—perhaps by means of a new equity-sharing contract. Since the homeowner is not paying interest on the investor's $10,000 for five years, total monthly payments are reduced considerably. The investor's incentive to enter into the arrangement arises from the fact that no income taxes will be due until the gain is realized at the end of the five-year period.

SECOND MORTGAGES

An increasingly popular way to finance a home is through a **second mortgage,** or **second deed of trust,** under which two mortgage loans are placed on the property. The first and second mortgages have first and second priority, respectively, for repayment, in case the home is sold or in case of foreclosure in bankruptcy. The first mortgage is usually the larger of the two and is issued by a traditional lender—for example, a bank or a savings and loan association. A second mortgage is usually taken by a homeowner who wishes to sell a house; in this case the second mortgage is part of the down payment that otherwise would be required. For example, suppose you wish to sell your house for $100,000. It has an assumable first mortgage of $50,000 at a favorable interest rate—say, 10 percent. You find a potential buyer, but this person has only $20,000 for a down payment. To make the sale, you agree to accept the $20,000 and issue a second mortgage to the buyer for the $30,000 difference. The buyer repays you over a period of years and also assumes your obligations on the $50,000 first mortgage.

A second mortgage issued to a buyer in this manner is sometimes called a **purchase money mortgage** since in effect it constitutes part of the purchase price. If the buyer fails to make payments on the second mortgage but continues payments on the first mortgage, the seller may institute foreclosure proceedings and ultimately get the house back. However, the legal proceedings are long, costly, and potentially disadvantageous to the seller who issues a second mortgage. Furthermore, before taking a second mortgage the seller must usually obtain permission of the original lender, the holder of the first mortgage, who might have the right to charge a higher interest rate to the second buyer than it charged to the first. In other cases the original lender will insist on being paid back in full if the house is sold by the first buyer; in such an event a second mortgage may not prove feasible. The right of the first mortgagee to insist on full repayment when the house is sold is known as a **due-on-sale** clause. A recent decision by the U.S. Supreme Court has upheld the legality of such clauses.

WRAPAROUNDS

The **wraparound,** another example of "creative financing" used when normal financing is difficult to obtain, is an arrangement in which different types of loans are "packaged" together into an all-inclusive financing instrument. For example, suppose you own a $100,000 house with a first mortgage of $40,000 at 10 percent. Current market interest rates are 15 percent for first mortgages. A potential buyer has a $20,000 down payment. You issue a second mortgage to the buyer for $80,000 at 12 percent, and you agree to continue paying on the first mortgage. In effect, the $80,000 note "wraps around" the first mortgage. Both parties profit from this arrangement because the buyer obtains financing at a rate lower than the going market rate, and the seller not only sells the house but makes a profit on the first mortgage. The profit stems from the fact that the buyer is paying the seller 12 percent, but the seller has to pay only 10 percent on the first mortgage and thus collects a bonus of two percentage points on the $40,000 first mortgage. Some first-mortgage lenders do not allow wraparounds; their terms require payment of the outstanding mortgage balance on the sale of the house.

LEASE-OPTIONS

Under a **lease-option** a potential buyer leases a home with a legal option to purchase within some time period, usually twelve to eighteen months. The buyer pays a certain amount for the option, which is applied to the purchase price if the option is exercised. If the option is not exercised, it expires, and the potential buyer's monthly payments are considered as rent for the use of the premises. In some cases part of the monthly rent can also be applied to the purchase price. For the buyer, the advantage of the lease-option is that a relatively small down payment, the **option price,** is needed, and yet the buyer accumulates some "equity" in the house if the decision is made to exercise the option. In the meantime the seller continues to enjoy the tax benefits of home ownership; the seller is able to deduct interest and other expenses until such time as the option is exercised.

COMMERCIAL AND INCOME PROPERTIES

Many people are interested in investing in other types of real estate besides their own homes. They view real estate as a hedge against inflation and as a means of reducing their income taxes. The main types of real estate available for investment purposes include (1) rental income properties such as duplexes, apartment houses, or single-family homes; (2) commercial rental property such as retail stores and warehouses; (3) farms and farm property; and (4) land, both improved and unimproved. Ownership of these types of real estate can be effected through direct purchase by individuals, through limited partnerships (syndicates), and through ownership in mutual fund shares, known as real estate investment trusts (RIETS), which represent various real estate properties. Investment in real estate may also be accomplished indirectly through ownership of shares of corporations whose assets are heavily invested in real estate and land—for example, railroads, public utilities, and real estate investment companies.

Advantages of Real Estate Investments

Commercial real estate shares in many of the advantages of home ownership—for example, tax shelter, financial leverage, and inflation protection. Tax shelter in real estate investments stems not only from the deductibility of interest and property taxes, as is true of home ownership, but also from the deductibility of expenses such as maintenance and depreciation. Depreciation is often available on an accelerated basis—that is, you may receive a cash flow from rentals that is offset by depreciation; thus, you obtain a tax-free income. In fact, depreciation and other deductions may be great enough to produce a "tax loss" that shelters your other income, which would otherwise be subject to income tax. "Tax loss" is particularly advantageous for investors who are in high tax brackets. For example, consider the following hypothetical case:

Price of commercial building	$250,000
Net rental income after cash expenses	20,000
Available depreciation allowance (not requiring cash outflow)	(30,000)
"Tax loss"	($10,000)

The owner has $20,000 of cash income on which no income tax is due and has another $10,000 offset against other taxable income. If the owner is in a 50 percent income tax bracket, the "tax write-off" is worth $5,000 currently. The owner may consider spendable income from the investment to be $25,000 ($20,000 excess of cash inflow over cash outflow, plus $5,000 tax savings), even though a loss of $10,000 is recorded for tax purposes.

Another tax benefit of real estate stems from what is called the **tax-free exchange.** You may be able to trade your equity in one type of real estate for equity in another, similar property without paying income tax. For tax purposes, such an exchange does not involve your realizing a gain. For example, suppose you own a duplex that has appreciated in value over a period of years. If you sell the duplex, you have to pay an income tax; but if you exchange it for another duplex or apartment house of equal or greater value, no gain is recognized.

In investment-type real estate, the advantages of financial leverage in periods of inflation are especially significant; a relatively small investment can control a large amount of assets in areas where space is likely to be in short supply—for example, downtown locations. Good locations are relatively scarce, so well-chosen real estate can appreciate much faster than other investments. For example, a retail store in a major shopping center gains from traffic generated by other stores and has a specific location value that is unique.

For some people, an additional advantage of real estate as an investment is its tangible nature. They can see their property, walk on it, and touch it, in contrast to intangible investments. They might view a share of common stock as merely a piece of paper and might not derive any pride of ownership from the unseen corporate property it represents.

Disadvantages of Real Estate Investment

As a financial planner, you should be aware of several important disadvantages of investment in real estate: high transaction costs, illiquidity, the extra care and expense involved in investigating real estate and analyzing its investment qualities, and the financial and market risk from factors beyond your knowledge or control.

TRANSACTION COSTS

Because real estate investment is complex, it requires the services of many different parties—for example, salespersons, attorneys, accountants, financial institutions, and professional managers. Therefore, the costs of real estate transfers and real estate management are high. Brokerage commissions alone may absorb 6 to 10 percent of the sales price of real estate; attorneys must be hired to handle closing statements and title searches; various legal fees are involved in payment of taxes and in registration of title. In addition, financial institutions may charge substantial fees for arranging mortgages, making appraisals, and handling the collection of mortgage payments. Accountants' fees for preparing income tax statements and other necessary financial analyses may also be substantial. If you invest in rental housing, you may pay 6 or 7 percent of the gross rental income of an apartment house to employ a real estate firm or a property manager to collect rents, advertise for tenants, and arrange for repairs and maintenance. You may be able to perform some of these tasks yourself, but you should consider the value of your own time and the worry these added responsibilities may cause as negative factors not usually present in other types of investments.

ILLIQUIDITY

Unlike stocks and bonds, for which a ready market usually exists, real estate may not always be easy to sell and convert into cash. It may take weeks or months to dispose of real estate on satisfactory terms since each type of property is somewhat unique and requires individual consideration and investigation by potential buyers. Illiquidity particularly affects real estate designed to serve specialized needs—for example, warehouses or retail stores—and real estate syndicates. If you need cash quickly, you may have to sell at a greatly reduced price and thus erase many of real estate's investment advantages.

ANALYSIS AND INVESTIGATION EXPENSES

Purchasing real estate wisely is usually not possible without extensive investigation and market analysis. Location is of great importance to real estate value, and understanding future trends in the growth of a community may take sophisticated analysis. For example, buying into a shopping center in a part of a city that is losing population would probably not be wise unless other circumstances overcame this disadvantage. But learning how and where a city is growing could involve considerable time and study. In some cases you must pay for engineering inspections to establish that given areas have soil stability, water availability, and other necessary physical characteristics.

Other factors must also be investigated. For example, if you are planning to purchase an apartment house, you must know who will make up the tenant population from which you will draw. What are the characteristics of this group? Do they have stable incomes sufficient to cover their rents? Is this group composed largely of students who leave town for the summer and leave your apartments unoccupied? Only study and investigation may enable you to answer such questions accurately, and study involves skill, time, and expense.

FINANCIAL AND MARKET RISK

Real estate is subject to random, unanticipated events that can cause losses, many of which are beyond your control as an investor. This fact introduces a potentially serious risk, especially when you consider the illiquidity that characterizes much real estate. Examples of unanticipated events would be neighborhood deterioration stemming from the sudden exodus of a supporting industry, an adverse zoning regulation, institution of local rent control laws, or downgrading of police and fire protection. Moreover, entire geographic areas may suffer losses—for example, during the seventies Florida suffered petroleum shortages that cut down on large numbers of tourists. The shortages stemmed from embargoes on foreign oil from the Middle East, which in turn stemmed from political events. During the shortages investors in Florida real estate suffered declining real estate values and were unable to sell newly constructed properties.

Another factor that may upset the financing of real estate and make it difficult to buy or sell properties is rapidly fluctuating interest rates. Such fluctuations may stem from an influx or an exodus of sources of investment capital from foreign investors, which in turn stems from changes in financial conditions in foreign countries. Interest fluctuation may also be a result of national monetary policy designed to restrain or to stimulate the economy. Unfortunately, real estate may suffer unduly from monetary restraint, which not only increases the cost of financing but may reduce or eliminate sources of funds for real estate purchase.

Appraising

A significant problem in buying real estate for investment purposes is deciding on a suitable purchase price. The methods of appraising properties to be used as private homes are to some extent applicable to commercial or income properties. Traditional appraisal methods include assessing replacement values, comparing the asking price with prices of similar properties recently sold, and reviewing values assessed for tax purposes and values used by potential lenders. Three important methods of determining commercial value are a comparison of price to available income to arrive at what is called the gross income multiplier, the capitalization of income approach, and the discounted cash flow method.

GROSS INCOME MULTIPLIER (GM)

The **gross income multiplier (GM)** is the ratio of the total price of the property to the gross rental income. For example, if the price of an apartment house is $480,000 and the gross rental income is $80,000, the GM is 6. Real estate publications show average GMs for different types of properties in a community, so you can determine whether a particular property is reasonably priced. Generally, any property priced at a GM higher than 7 or 8 is probably yielding too low an income to justify the asking price. Unless the rentals have been set unrealistically low and can be raised, you should probably look elsewhere for investment property.

CAPITALIZATION RATE

The **capitalization rate,** or **cap rate,** is the ratio of anticipated income to the asking price of the property. The definition of income used in calculating the cap rate may vary. Generally income is defined as gross income less expenses, including allowances for vacancies and not considering mortgage repayments or depreciation. For example, if income (as defined above) is $100,000 and the asking price is $500,000, the cap rate is 20 percent. Cap rates in real estate investments are generally higher than long-term mortgages or bond interest because of the risk element and the expenses and illiquidity associated with real estate. The higher the cap rate, the lower the perceived risk to the investor and the lower the price paid for a given stream of earnings. Informed real estate personnel can tell you the going rates for both GMs and cap rates for typical properties in a given community. Typical capitalization rates in 1980 are shown in Exhibit 8–4.

Most real estate investors also consider the potential tax benefits when considering a real estate purchase. If you can obtain such a large depreciation allowance that you can show a "tax loss," you might appraise a particular property at a higher rate.

You can decide whether the capitalization rate for a particular property is satisfactory by comparing returns available on similar real estate investments and on other types of investments. For example, is a 15 percent return on a short-term basis in a money market fund (see Chapter 3) preferable to a ten-year investment return of 12 percent in real estate? You must decide.

DISCOUNTED CASH FLOW METHOD

A more sophisticated way of determining the value of real estate investment is known as the **discounted cash flow method.** You must first determine the after-tax cash flow on a given investment for a certain number of years. To each year's anticipated after-tax cash flow, you apply a discount

EXHIBIT 8–4
Typical
Capitalization
Rates, Third
Quarter, 1981

Property	Cap Rate
Apartment houses	12.95
Commercial retail properties	13.39
Office buildings	14.17
Commercial service properties	13.64
Industrial properties	14.54
Hotels and motels	15.00
Total	14.33

Note: Capitalization rates are defined as the ratio of "net stabilized earnings" to the purchase price of the property. Net stabilized earnings are defined as gross earnings less vacancy allowance, operating expenses, and property taxes, but before depreciation and mortgage repayments.

Source: "Mortgage Commitments on Multifamily and Non-residential Properties Reported by 20 Life Insurance Companies," *Investment Bulletin* (Washington, D.C.: American Council of Life Insurance, January 6, 1982).

factor at a rate of return satisfactory to you. If you intend to sell your investment at the end of the predetermined period, you assume that a certain level of profit will be realized after taxes. You then apply the appropriate discount factor to the assumed amount and sum the discounted cash flows. This figure represents the maximum price you should pay for the property.

As a very simplified example, assume that you expect to realize $1,000 a year from an investment and to sell it at the end of five years for $50,000 after selling costs and taxes. Your required rate of return is 12 percent. Exhibit 8–5 shows that you should not pay more than $31,976.28 for the property.

Real Estate Investment Alternatives

DUPLEXES AND SINGLE-FAMILY HOMES

Many beginning investors see the purchase of single-family homes or duplexes as an opportunity to make money. Because inflation has driven up the price of such housing in the past, these investors assume that similar price hikes will occur in the future. When they consider the rising value of these properties, along with financial leverage and the tax shelter available in real estate, investors may conclude that they are acquiring an attractive, tax-free cash flow.

However, because of the risk factors associated with real estate—for example, declining neighborhoods or high vacancy rates—you cannot assume that a particular property will always increase in price. For example, you may easily be able to rent out a new duplex, but as it gets older and perhaps more

EXHIBIT 8-5
Appraising
through the
Discounted Cash
Flow Method

Number of Years	Cash Flow after Taxes	Present Value of $1 at 12%	Present Value of Cash Flow
1	$ 1,000	.89286	$ 892.86
2	1,000	.79719	797.19
3	1,000	.71178	711.78
4	1,000	.63552	635.52
5	1,000	.56743	567.43
5	50,000	.56743	28,371.50
Present Value of the Property			$31,976.28

Note: See Appendix A–4 for calculations of present value.

run down, rents may decline greatly. The prices of duplexes and single-family homes are frequently so high that the gross income multiplier is also high (often 8, 10, or more)—too high for you to make a profit unless unusual circumstances exist. High mortgage rates, repairs, and other expenses often mean that your investment produces a negative cash flow that you must make up out of other income. In addition, your investment is usually too small to warrant your employing a professional manager to collect rents, arrange for repairs, advertise for new tenants, and perform other chores in connection with real estate ownership. Therefore, you may find that a great deal of personal time is involved in supervising your investment and in performing manual or skilled labor in connection with it. In addition, you may be bothered by renters' telephone calls regarding small problems such as lost keys or broken windows.

In spite of the difficulties and disadvantages, many people like the relative simplicity of investing in single-family homes or duplexes. If the property is well located and easily rented, and if favorable financing can be arranged, the return on investment can be satisfactory. Before making such an investment, however, you must consider *all* of the costs you are likely to incur and make a systematic analysis of all other factors that enter into the buying decision.

LAND

Some investors believe unimproved farm land or urban lots improved with streets and sewers make good investments. Such properties have the disadvantage of producing no current income. Instead they require current expenditures for taxes, and they frequently require repayment of mortgage principal and interest incurred as part of their purchase price. The holding costs of unimproved property may be substantial; to be profitable, such investments must ultimately be sold for profits sufficient to offset the holding costs. Unless the property is well located, the prospect of final gain is relatively small. Investing in land is thus risky and probably should be avoided by people who are not experts.

REAL ESTATE INVESTMENT TRUSTS (REITs)

Real estate investment trusts (REITs) are another way to invest in real estate. Investing in a REIT is similar to buying a common stock that represents a share of real estate in which the funds of the organizer are invested. A REIT is an incorporated association that originated with the Real Estate Investment Trust Act of 1960, designed to allow small investors to buy real estate more easily. REITs pay no corporate income tax if certain rules are obeyed—for example, at least 90 percent of the income must be paid out to shareholders, at least 75 of the funds must be invested in assets related to real estate, and direct management of any property owned must be avoided. Thus, as an investor in a REIT you avoid "double taxation." That is, any income is taxed only to you rather than being taxed to the corporation when earned and then again to you when you receive the corporate income in the form of dividends.

A REIT may be used to do one of three things: (1) invest mainly in short-term loans to construction companies, (2) invest mainly in long-term mortgages on real estate, and (3) own real estate property directly. REITs of the first type are considered riskiest, although in the past their dividend returns have been the greatest since interest charged to construction companies during the construction period is usually high. However, in 1974–75 many REITs of this type failed and caused losses to their owners when interest rates began to escalate. High interest rates not only caused failures among borrowers by preventing them from repaying loans, but greatly increased the cost to the REITs of supplying funds. Dividends were suspended, and many REITs were unable to sell properties, some uncompleted, on which they foreclosed.

REITs emphasizing long-term loans have fared much better, but many have had trouble making profits because borrowers have often been unable to attract enough tenants to repay the loans. REITs in which properties are owned directly (called **equity trusts**) are considered the least risky; however, their total returns are the lowest of the three types of REITs.

The investment history of REITs suggests that these investments are more suitable for experienced and sophisticated investors than for first-time investors with limited capital. The experience of REIT investors demonstrates the high risk associated with many types of real estate investments.

LIMITED PARTNERSHIPS (SYNDICATES)

A **limited partnership (syndicate)** is a form of organization that enables investors to buy into real estate projects too large for a single investor. For example, a group of investors form a partnership, each putting up a stated amount of funds—say, $5,000 or multiples thereof—to purchase a large project such as a shopping center or an apartment complex. Syndicates have both general and limited partners. The **general partner** usually originates and manages the project, while the **limited partners** invest funds and have their liability limited to the amount they have invested. The general partner receives a fee for originating and managing the project. Some syndicates are formed for buying a specific piece of property, and others are formed for general investment in several yet-to-be-determined projects. The latter type of syndicate is known as a **blind pool** since the limited partners rely on the general partner to select particular properties in which to invest after the funds are assembled. Frequently, large investment and brokerage firms distribute shares of various syndicates and receive a sales commission for this service.

The main advantages of syndicates are as follows:

1. Syndicates enable you to invest in a project of substantial size in which professional management can be used, whereas small real estate investments often produce too little a return to enable you to afford a professional manager.
2. Syndicates offer you the hope of price appreciation on your investment.
3. Syndicates make it possible for you to obtain a tax-sheltered cash flow from the project, together with a substantial capital gain when the project is sold—usually within five or ten years, after the available depreciation has been taken and the tax shelter has become minimal.

The disadvantages, or risks, of syndicates are the ones most common to real estate generally and are as follows:

1. Syndicates suffer from illiquidity; shares of the syndicate usually cannot be sold easily on the open market.
2. Syndicates carry the risk that the project will not be successful and hence that the price will not rise as expected.
3. Adverse tax rulings can destroy the expected tax benefits.
4. High management expenses, fees, and sales commissions are associated with syndicate investment.
5. Unsophisticated investors may not understand the complex risks and rewards usually associatd with syndicates. Frequently the "full story" is reported only in a lengthy prospectus, or informational document, approved by the Securities and Exchange Commission, and only the most determined investor can study such a document sufficiently to understand fully the proposed investment and the previous record of the organizers.

In conclusion, limited partnerships are recommended only to the most experienced real estate investors.

SUMMARY

1. A significant element of personal finance is the ownership of a home or of other types of real estate. Decisions about real estate frequently depend on whether you view a house as a consumer durable good, as an investment, or as both. The buy-or-build and the own-or-rent decisions may also depend at least in part on how you view real estate. In any case, you must give careful consideration to the advantages and disadvantages of buying or building, as well as of owning or renting, before you decide to invest in real estate.

2. The income tax advantages of home ownership in periods of inflation are a significant influence on most people's decisions to buy property. Financial leverage is also a significant factor that may tip the scales in favor of buying rather than renting. Disadvantages of home ownership include high transfer costs of homes, illiquidity of the investment, and the costs and difficulties of arranging favorable financing.

3. Real estate brokers offer several valuable services to buyers and sellers of real property. Brokers bring buyer and seller together, help arrange financing, assist in appraisals, and provide needed information about the property to both parties. Because real estate is complex, brokers should be selected with care to ensure they are qualified to handle the particular property you wish to buy or sell.

4. Major factors affecting the value of real estate properties include location, quality of neighborhood, landscaping and physical aspects of the lot, and physical condition of the property. Market prices reflect these factors as well as recent prices of other similar properties, financing terms, extent and quality of selling effort, and other factors. Homes can be purchased with warranties against loss due to hidden defects in the property—losses not normally covered by commercial insurance.

5. In recent years home financing has been complicated by high interest rates on long-term mortgages, the need for relatively high down payments, and shortages of funds. Fixed-payment, long-term mortgages at relatively low interest rates may no longer be readily available to potential home buyers.

6. New types of home financing include variable-rate mortgages, shared-appreciation mortgages, graduated-payment loans, equity-sharing arrangements, second mortgages, and wraparounds. Another alternative is the lease-option, which gives the buyer an opportunity to rent a home for a set period and then to apply the rental payments to the purchase of the home.

7. Investments in real estate other than homes offer both advantages and disadvantages. Potential advantages include several types of tax benefits, financial leverage, and inflation protection. Disadvantages include high transaction costs, illiquidity, expense of investigation and research, and high financial and market risk.

8. Methods of appraising real estate as an investment include the use of gross income multipliers, capitalization rates, and discounted cash flows.

9. Types of direct real estate investment include purchase of properties such as single-family homes, land, lots, apartment houses, and commercial buildings. Indirect methods of investment include purchase of REITs and investment in limited partnerships or syndicates.

REVIEW QUESTIONS

1. Discuss what difference it makes whether you view a house as one of the following:
   (a) An investment.
   (b) A consumer durable.
   (c) Both an investment and a consumer durable.

2. (a) From a financial planner's viewpoint, what are the most important advantages of renting your living quarters as opposed to owning your living quarters?
   (b) What advantages are most important to you personally?

3. A government publication advised that when you are thinking about renting a house, you should make a list of all damages that exist and get the landlord to acknowledge these damages and indicate whether and when they will be repaired. What other possible value might there be to having such a list of damages?

4. (a) What is meant by financial leverage?
   (b) Give an example of a situation in which leverage works against you and an example of a situation in which it works for you.

5. Explain why inflation helps the homeowner more than the renter.

6. (a) What are the advantages of building a new home instead of purchasing a used home?
   (b) What are the advantages of purchasing a used home?

7. In purchasing a condominium, you do not own the building, only the living space.
   (a) Who owns the building?
   (b) What are the advantages of owning a condominium rather than a separate home?
   (c) What are the disadvantages of owning a condominium?

8. Do you think real estate brokers earn their commissions? Why, or why not?

9. (a) What are the major factors affecting the value of a house?
   (b) Which factors do you feel are most important?

10. (a) Why does a difference usually exist between the replacement cost and the market value of a house?
    (b) What purposes do each of these concepts serve?

11. As higher interest rates make mortgage financing more expensive, home buyers are challenging builders to devise ways to keep down the cost of new homes. One result is the "no frills" house, built without fireplaces, patio slabs, tiled bathtubs,

and other options. Suggest possible advantages and disadvantages of buying a "stripped-down" house.

12. In *The Wall Street Journal* (February 12, 1981) a writer stated: "The fixed-rate, thirty-year mortgage isn't dying in California. It is just about dead and buried. In the past couple of months, several of the giant, state-chartered savings and loan associations . . . decided quietly and independently to stop offering long-term, fixed-rate mortgages except to fulfill existing commitments. An officer stated, 'the long-term, fixed-rate home loan is no longer a practical and viable instrument in today's inflationary environment.' "
    (a) Explain the reluctance of lenders to offer long-term, fixed-rate home loans.
    (b) Presumably, what types of loans will be substituted for conventional mortgages? Why?

13. A financial writer stated: "GPMs have proven popular with borrowers, but insurance companies, pension funds, and other mortgage investors are so delighted with GPMs, irreverently called 'gyp 'ems.' . . . Consumers lured by GPMs' seductively low initial payments are getting less of a good deal than they might have hoped." Explain why GPMs might be misleading to the borrower.

14. A financial writer stated: "Soaring mortgage rates, home prices, and land costs have made real estate developers an endangered species these days, but they are not giving up without a fight. The latest weapon: land leasing. Instead of owning the house and land it sits on, home buyers purchase only the house, lease the land, and save about 25 percent on the down payments. Monthly payments, at least for the first few years, also can be lower . . . usually the buyer has the option of buying the land later on, subject to an annual surcharge of, say, 10 percent, with the right to apply the lease payments to the purchase price." What might be some of the advantages and disadvantages of land leasing?

15. A financial writer stated: "Most people want to own their own homes. But few can afford to buy that first one. The first-time home buyer is the real loser today. With interest rates so high and houses so expensive, these kids are really getting squeezed. How can they save as much as they need?" What solutions are possible for the first-time buyer?

16. In which of the following types of mortgages are monthly payments fixed?
    (a) Conventional mortgages.
    (b) Graduated-payment mortgages.
    (c) Variable-rate mortgages.
    (d) Shared-appreciation mortgages.

17. Which type of mortgage, the second mortgage or the wraparound, gives the seller the greater possibility of profit?

18. Do you believe the disadvantages of real estate outweigh the possible rewards of real estate as an investment? Why, or why not?

19. Jorge is considering buying a duplex as an investment. The gross rentals are $5,000 a year without allowance for vacancies. The gross income, less allowances for vacancies and expenses (except mortgage repayments and depreciation) is $4,000 a year.

The asking price is $50,000.
(a) What is the gross income multiplier?
(b) What is the capitalization rate?
(c) Do you think the project is competitive with other investments? Why, or why not?

20. A business newspaper reported: "When Gerald Lamberti bought his four-bedroom, three-bath home in Pleasanton, California, in 1974, the seller threw in as a bonus a warranty contract guaranteeing free repair of any major component of the house for one year. The rambling redwood house was just nine years old. . . . Within months after moving in . . . the furnace stopped working, then the oven broiler went out, and then the dishwasher broke, and it was unrepairable. Fortunately, all were repaired or replaced under the warranty contract."
(a) Do you believe the typical buyer of a used home should be willing to pay, say, $200 extra for a warranty similar to the one described?
(b) How could an insurer protect itself against issuing contracts on homes most likely to suffer losses and thus keep premiums low?

21. In 1980 a financial writer stated: "Triton, a REIT formerly known as Chase Manhattan Mortgage and Realty, had nearly $1 billion in assets, but ran up $300 million in debts and went into bankruptcy. Triton now has about $2 million in net assets."
(a) What major factors caused difficulties for REITs, particularly in the business recession of 1974–75?
(b) Do these factors introduce significant risk for small investors?

CASE PROBLEMS

I. Determining Affordable Monthly Payments

The following table shows how much income a family requires to qualify for mortgages of different amounts and at different interest rates, assuming that 25 percent of salary can be devoted to mortgage payments.

| House Price | 8% Interest | | 10% Interest | | 12% Interest | | 14% Interest | |
	Monthly Payment	Needed Annual Salary	Monthly Payment	Needed Annual Salary	Monthly Payment	Needed Annual Salary	Monthly Payment	Needed Annual Salary
$45,000	$297	$14,256	$356	$17,088	$417	$20,016	$480	$23,040
55,000	363	17,424	435	20,880	509	24,432	587	28,176
65,000	429	20,592	514	24,672	602	28,896	693	33,264
75,000	495	23,760	593	28,464	695	33,360	800	38,400
85,000	562	26,976	672	32,356	787	37,776	907	43,536

Note: Assumes 10% downpayment, 30-year mortgage term, with 25% of gross monthly salary for mortgage payment (principal and interest only). Source: MGIC Investment Corporation.

QUESTIONS

1. Assume that you are a potential buyer. You and your spouse together earn $24,000 annually. Interest rates are 12 percent. What price can you afford to pay for a house if you base your calculations on the 25 percent standard?

2. What price could you afford to pay based on a 35 percent standard?

II. Creative Financing

The Wall Street Journal (May 1, 1980) contained the following report:

For real-estate people, creative financing is the most promising game in town. John W. Steffey, a Baltimore Realtor, says 80% of his home sales are creatively financed, and he adds, "You won't stay in business unless you're doing it."

Edward and Suzette Blanke found that out when they began seeking a home loan in the St. Louis area. A banker, Mrs. Blanke recalls, "laughed in my face" and "said that if I was a depositor, I could come back later and he might talk about a 30% down payment." But Mr. Blanke, a 31-year-old civil engineer transferred to St. Louis from Dubuque, his wife and three-year-old daughter couldn't afford to wait. During their two-month search, Mrs. Blanke says, "Every day interest rates went up," and the houses that they looked at got smaller.

The Solution

While the Blankes were searching fruitlessly for financing and a home, another family was trying fruitlessly to sell a four-bedroom house in Kirkwood, Mo., an affluent St. Louis suburb. "We had a tremendous number of people look at our place, but they just couldn't come up with the financing," says Stuart Purvines, a retired executive who, with his wife, Norma, already had refurbished a retirement home. Asked by real-estate people whether he would carry part of the financing, Mr. Purvines at first rejected the idea. "But later," he says, "it occurred to me: I'm going to reinvest the money anyway. Why not?"

An enterprising agent brought the two families together and meshed their individual needs in a typical example of creative financing.

The Purvines still had a $14,600 balance on their mortgage, which, at 5¼%, the Blankes assumed. The buyers made a $20,000 down payment patched together from several sources, including savings and family help. The rest of the $64,200 purchase price came from a $29,600 second deed of trust on the house at 12.8%.

Mr. Purvines, who could afford to grant the loan because he already had his retirement home, calls the 12.8% "an adequate yield." Mr. Blanke says flatly, "The financing sold the house." And Mrs. Blanke, recalling that they once braced for conventional-loan payments of $800 a month, says "we're lucky" with the $528-a-month payments at an effective overall interest rate of about 10¼%. "More and more people are going to have to do creative financing," she adds.

QUESTION

1. What are the advantages and disadvantages for both the Blankes and the Purvines in the type of "creative financing" described in the article?

III. A Real Estate Investment

Smith is considering a real estate investment—a 50-unit apartment house, well located, for which the asking price is $1,600,000. Rentals average $400 monthly for a "gross income" of $240,000. There is an assumable first mortgage of $1,000,000 for twenty-five years at 14 percent. The buyer is asked to pay $600,000 down. Estimated annual net income is as follows:

Gross Income		$240,000
Less:		
Vacancy allowance (5%)	$12,000	
Management expense (7%)	16,800	
Repairs, maintenance, taxes, utilities, insurance (5%)	12,000	40,800
Gross Cash Flow to Owner		$199,200
Less: Mortgage payments (see Appendix A–6)		145,498
Net Cash Flow		$ 53,702

$$\text{Gross Income Multiplier:} \quad \frac{1,600,000}{240,000} = 6.66$$

$$\text{Capitalization Rate:} \quad \frac{199,200}{1,600,000} = 12.45\%$$

Smith realizes that part of the mortgage payments represents loan repayment and produces "equity buildup" (the value of the property less indebtedness). This equity is realized when the property is finally sold. In this case, equity buildup initially is about $5,500, the difference between total mortgage payment and the interest element [($145,498 − .14($1,000,000) = $5,498)]. He realizes, too, that depreciation allowances may produce a "tax loss" that reduces his other taxable income.

Smith assumes that depreciation of 6.1 percent of the building price may be deducted for income taxes and that he will be in the 50 percent tax bracket. He calculates taxable income as follows:

Gross Cash Flow		$199,200
Less: Interest (.14 × 1,000,000)	$140,000	
Depreciation (6.1% × 1,400,000*)	94,000	234,000

Tax Loss	($34,800)
Tax Benefit (34,800 × .50)	$17,400
Equity Buildup (initial)	5,498
Cash Flow (not taxable)	53,702
Total Current Return	76,600

Cash-on-cash Return on Investment (tax free):

$$\frac{\$76,600}{\$600,000} = 12.77\%$$

*Assumes land value of $200,000, a nondepreciable item.

QUESTIONS

1. What advantages and disadvantages should Smith consider in making the commercial real estate investment described above?

2. Evaluate the methods of calculating the gross income multiplier, the capitalization rate, and the cash-on-cash return. Interpret these numbers as indications of the attractiveness of real estate investments. Would any of them be changed when the property is sold?

3. Considering the 1980–81 average capitalization rates (see Exhibit 8–4), average returns on negotiable bonds (14 percent or higher), and average returns on tax-exempt bonds (10 to 12 percent for rated bonds), are the returns available on the above investment attractive for Smith?

4. Using the discounted cash flow method of analysis, decide whether Smith should purchase the property. Assume 14 percent is the minimum desired return, six years the holding period, $1,000,000 the net gain after all costs and income taxes, and $71,102 the annual cash flow ($53,702 + $17,400 annual tax benefit).

CHAPTER 9

TAX PLANNING AND INVESTMENTS

LEARNING OBJECTIVES

In studying this chapter you will learn:

The amount and significance of different kinds of taxes as they affect personal finance;

The difference between tax avoidance and tax evasion;

How tax credits differ from tax deductions;

What kinds of income are exempt from taxes;

Why it is advantageous to convert investment income to capital gains rather than to ordinary income, and how to do so;

How to delay the recognition of taxable income to future periods;

How to reduce taxes through income averaging;

The advantages of life insurance from a tax standpoint;

The importance of tax records;

How to reduce your chance of being audited.

Tax considerations are an important part of investment and financial-planning decisions. During 1979–80, approximately 40 percent of our national output was paid as taxes to federal, state, and local governments. Stated another way, taxpayers as a group must work "for nothing" for about 4.7 months of each year to support the various costs incurred by governments.

Of course, taxpayers obtain government services in return for their payments, and many citizens receive **transfer payments** from the government in the form of subsidies, retirement income, and welfare. Nevertheless, money taken as taxes from you as an individual and spent by government represents funds placed beyond your direct control—funds that you might otherwise have used to advance personal goals. To minimize the taxes you pay, you must do some advance planning. This chapter presents a coordinated discussion of the interacting effects of many different types of taxes.

SOURCES OF GOVERNMENT REVENUE

Exhibit 9–1 summarizes the major sources of government revenue during 1979–80. In that year the federal government received about 60 percent of the revenue collected; the states, about 23 percent; and local governments, about 17 percent. A major source of federal government revenue is corporate and individual income taxes, while state and local governments depend on sales taxes for 17.7 percent of their revenues; on property taxes for 15.2 percent; and on federal government revenue sharing for 18.4 percent. Most states also levy state income taxes. Since the federal revenue-sharing program also depends on income tax collections, the income tax is obviously a major source of government revenue.

Exhibit 9–1 also shows that revenues from various insurance trust funds account for a significant portion of the income of both federal and state governments. Dominant among these programs are the Social Security trust funds at the federal government level.

During 1978–79 total taxes per capita amounted to $4,115 and represented about 40 percent of the gross national product. Thus, governments use up a sizable portion of our total income and account for a large percentage of our gross expenditures.

EXHIBIT 9–1
Total Revenue
by Major
Financial Sectors
for the Federal
Government and
for State and
Local
Governments,
1979–80

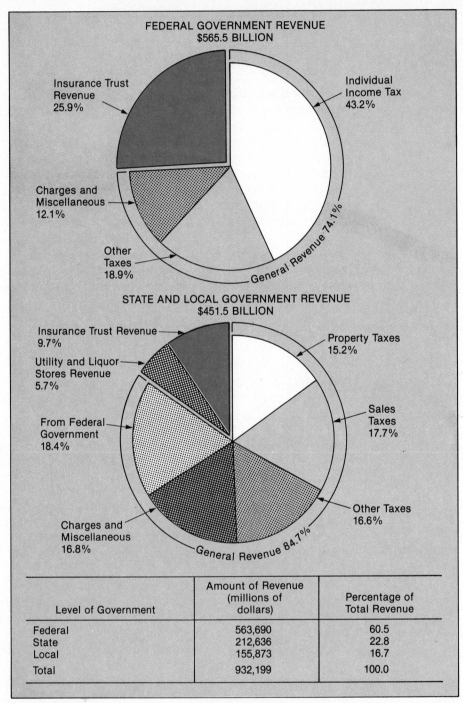

FEDERAL GOVERNMENT REVENUE
$565.5 BILLION

Insurance Trust Revenue 25.9%

Charges and Miscellaneous 12.1%

Other Taxes 18.9%

Individual Income Tax 43.2%

General Revenue 74.1%

STATE AND LOCAL GOVERNMENT REVENUE
$451.5 BILLION

Insurance Trust Revenue 9.7%

Utility and Liquor Stores Revenue 5.7%

From Federal Government 18.4%

Charges and Miscellaneous 16.8%

Property Taxes 15.2%

Sales Taxes 17.7%

Other Taxes 16.6%

General Revenue 84.7%

Level of Government	Amount of Revenue (millions of dollars)	Percentage of Total Revenue
Federal	563,690	60.5
State	212,636	22.8
Local	155,873	16.7
Total	932,199	100.0

Source: U.S. Department of Commerce, *Governmental Finances in 1979–80* (Washington, D.C.: U.S. Government Printing Office, 1981), p. 2.

TAXES THAT AFFECT PERSONAL FINANCES

Hundreds of different types of taxes affect our finances and investments, but a full description of all types of taxes is beyond the scope of this book. The following subsections deal with those taxes that generate the greatest amount of government revenue and have the greatest effect on personal finances.

Income Taxes

Taxes on personal income are levied by both federal and state governments. Some large cities also impose income taxes. These taxes are usually progressive—that is, the percentage of your income paid in taxes increases as your income increases. The purpose of progressive taxation is to place the tax burden more heavily on persons who can better afford to carry it and less heavily on persons who cannot.

Exhibit 9–2 gives the federal income tax rates on surviving spouses and married people filing jointly for various years. For 1982 federal income tax purposes, income in the band $11,900–$16,000 was taxed at 19 percent, while income in the next highest band, $16,000–$20,200, was taxed at 22 percent. The exhibit shows that these rates are scheduled to decline to 16 percent and 18 percent, respectively, by 1984. Note that only the marginal income is taxed at the rate given for a particular bracket. For example, only the taxable income between $11,900 and $16,000 is taxed at the 19 percent rate. The $1,234 of tax appearing in the rate schedule represents the tax on the first $11,900 of income, which was computed at the lower rates of 12 percent, 14 percent, and 16 percent that precede 19 percent in the rate schedule.

In 1981 federal income tax rates went as high as 70 percent on some types of income. As shown in Exhibit 9–2, rates are scheduled to drop in stages through 1984, with a maximum rate of 50 percent. Most state income taxes do not rise beyond 11 percent on the top bracket, although rates on top brackets are higher in Delaware (19.8 percent), New York (15 percent), Iowa (13 percent), and Minnesota (17 percent). The combined effect of federal and state income taxes is very great, since persons earning even modest salaries bear a heavy burden. For example, in Georgia in 1982, a single person with a taxable income of $15,000 was in the 23 percent federal tax bracket and the 6 percent state tax bracket. Thus, every additional dollar of income for such a person was taxed at 29 percent—a rate that is a considerable incentive to find ways of reducing taxes. A few states (e.g., Florida, Nevada, South Dakota, Texas, Washington, and Wyoming) have no income tax but compensate by relying more heavily on other forms of taxes.

EXHIBIT 9-2   Tax Rate Schedules for Surviving Spouses and Married Individuals Filing Joint Returns

Taxable Income	1981 Pay +	1981 % on Excess	1982 Pay +	1982 % on Excess	1983 Pay +	1983 % on Excess	1984 Pay +	1984 % on Excess
0– $3,400	0	0	0	0	0	0	0	0
$ 3,400– 5,500	0	14	0	12	0	11	0	11
5,500– 7,600	$ 194	16	$ 252	14	$ 231	13	$ 231	12
7,600– 11,900	630	18	546	16	504	15	483	14
11,900– 16,000	1,404	21	1,234	19	1,149	17	1,085	16
16,000– 20,200	2,265	24	2,013	22	1,846	19	1,741	18
20,200– 24,600	3,273	28	2,937	25	2,644	23	2,497	22
24,600– 29,900	4,505	32	4,037	29	3,656	26	3,465	25
29,900– 35,200	6,201	37	5,574	33	5,034	30	4,790	28
35,200– 45,800	8,162	43	7,323	39	6,624	35	6,274	33
45,800– 60,000	12,720	49	11,457	44	10,334	40	9,772	38
60,000– 85,600	19,678	54	17,705	49	16,014	44	15,168	42
85,600–109,400	33,502	59	30,249	50	27,278	48	25,920	45
109,400–162,400	47,544	64	42,149	50	38,702	50	36,630	49
162,400–215,400	81,464	68	68,649	50	65,202	50	62,600	50
215,400–......	117,504	70	95,149	50	91,702	50	89,100	50

Notes: Rates for 1981 are unadjusted for a reduction of 5 percent, effective 1 October 1981. An approximation of the actual tax due can be made by reducing the tax shown by 1.25 percent.

Percentage paid on excess is applied to the difference between taxable income and the lower base of the tax bracket.

Sales Taxes

Most states and some cities have sales taxes, which are collected each time you buy goods or services.[1] Unlike income taxes, sales tax rates are a flat percentage, usually ranging between 3 and 6 percent of the value of the item. Sales taxes are not levied against all types of sales; the sale of real estate and of stocks and bonds, personal transactions, and, in some states, food and drugs, are exempted. The sales tax is known as a **regressive tax** since the rate is the same for everyone, regardless of ability to pay. Thus, a larger percentage of income is paid as sales tax by low-income families, who, unlike upper-income families, spend most of their income on taxable items.

---

1. As of 1979–80, sales taxes were not levied in Delaware, Montana, New Hampshire, and Oregon.

Estate and Gift Taxes

Property in your estate is taxed to the estate under progressive federal estate tax brackets, which, before 1982, ranged from 18 percent on estates of $10,000 to 70 percent on estates over $5,000,000. Under the Economic Recovery Act of 1981, the top bracket will be reduced in stages to 50 percent by 1985. If you give away your property to remove it from your estate, you must pay a gift tax, subject to exemptions of up to $10,000 a year per donee ($20,000 if you are filing jointly with your spouse). State inheritance tax is also levied on recipients of property under a will. The combined effect of federal estate and gift taxes and state inheritance taxes is explored more fully in Chapter 16. Suffice to say here that these taxes are great enough to require advance planning to minimize their effects, particularly in the case of large estates worth more than $2,500,000.

Social Security Taxes

Nearly everyone is subject to Social Security taxes on earned income. On your payroll statement these taxes are called FICA (Federal Insurance Contributions Act) deductions. They amounted to 6.70 percent on all earned income up to $32,400 in 1982. The employer matches your contribution. Social Security taxes are scheduled to rise gradually to 7.15 percent on earned income up to $39,600 by 1987. These taxes may be viewed as contributions to a compulsory retirement plan from which you may draw at retirement. For some people Social Security may reduce the need for personal savings and financial planning (see Chapter 7).

If you are self-employed, you are required to report your earnings and to pay Social Security taxes on them if they amount to $400 or more annually. The self-employment tax is one and a half times the tax paid by employees of companies subject to Social Security taxes. The higher rate is necessary because no one matches the contributions of self-employed persons.

Property Taxes

The property tax on real estate is significant for homeowners. It is also significant for renters, because landlords "pass along" the tax in the form of higher rents. Homeowners can deduct property taxes when determining their income tax. The property tax supports local schools and local government programs. The rates vary widely; they tend to be lowest in the "sun belt" states. Rates vary according to a number of factors—for example, the local industrial base and the public willingness to support education. In 1977, as a percentage of estimated market value of property, residential real estate taxes ranged from 7.5 percent in Boston to 0.8 percent in Honolulu; the average was about 2.0 percent.[2]

Insurance Premium Taxes

All states levy a tax, usually about 2 percent, on premiums paid to insurance companies. Since life insurance is often considered a form of savings, this tax represents a penalty on life insurance savings as opposed to other forms of savings. A few states also tax annuity premiums, which may discourage potential buyers of annuities for retirement income.

IMPLICATIONS OF INCOME TAXES FOR FINANCIAL PLANNING

The complexity of income tax law makes it difficult for you to manage your affairs so as to reduce the negative impact of taxation on your income and wealth. The following discussion suggests many ways to avoid paying unnecessary taxes and thus to obtain greater control over your financial future. Most of the principles and guides relate to federal income taxes, which are the largest taxes you pay. Since most state income tax laws are similar (but not identical) to federal tax laws, the principles are usually also applicable at the state level.

Avoidance versus Evasion

There is a difference between avoiding taxes and evading them. **Tax avoidance** is entirely legitimate and enables you to keep from overpaying taxes in accordance with laws and regulations laid down by Congress. The key to minimizing your taxes is effective planning of your personal and business affairs, planning based on knowledge of the tax consequences of your actions. **Tax evasion** is the deliberate failure to pay the taxes you owe; it includes failing to report taxable income and claiming deductions to which you are not entitled. Tax evasion is a criminal act and is punishable by fine and/or imprisonment.

Most citizens are honest about paying their taxes. In fact, individuals typically "lean over backward" to pay taxes they need not pay. In many cases people fail to take legitimate deductions, often because of ignorance, failure

---

2. *Statistical Abstract of the United States, 1980,* p. 317.

to keep adequate records, or fear of being audited by the Internal Revenue Service.

Exemptions and Deductions

In filing income tax returns, you are permitted several types of deductions or exemptions that reduce your taxable income. Personal exemptions are permitted for the taxpayer and for each qualified dependent, such as a spouse or a child. In 1982 each personal exemption was $1,000.

In addition, the law permits several expenses, known as **itemized deductions,** to be subtracted. Typical deductions (all subject to various limitations) are medical and dental expenses, interest expense, various taxes, contributions to charities, casualty and theft losses, employees' educational expenses, and certain expenses in connection with your job, such as union dues, special uniforms, and professional books.

Because not everyone incurs all types of allowable expenses—or, if they do incur them, they have inadequate proofs—the law permits what is known as the **standard deduction,** or **zero bracket amount,** an estimate of all deductions that may be taken by a taxpayer. Even when you have relatively few deductions, you can still deduct the zero bracket amount. All taxpayers filing federal income tax returns must decide whether to "itemize" their deductions or to use the zero bracket amount method. In making your decision, you should total all your known deductions, compare this total to the zero bracket amount, and deduct whichever amount is larger.

The zero bracket amount, as an estimate of permitted deductions, was as follows in 1982: married persons filing jointly, $3,400; single person, $2,300; married person filing separately, $1,700. Thus, if you are filing a joint return and have itemized deductions that total more than $3,400, it will benefit you to keep the necessary supporting records and to take the itemized deduction on your tax return. Any homeowner with a new mortgage of over $30,000 at 12 percent interest, for example, will be paying mortgage loan interest in an amount that alone will exceed the 1982 zero bracket amount of $3,400. Since most married wage earners are in state and federal tax brackets exceeding 30 percent, any additional deduction you can take is the equivalent of obtaining a "rebate" of thirty cents in taxes for each dollar paid out in expenses.

Tax Credits versus Deductions

Many types of expenses are deductible against income in determining the taxable income on which the amount of the tax is computed. Other types of expenses can be subtracted from the tax after it has been computed. The former expenses are termed **tax deductions,** and the latter, **tax credits.** A tax

"Sorry, you don't qualify as a dependent."

credit is more valuable than a tax deduction because the credit reduces the amount of the tax, whereas the deduction merely reduces the income subject to the tax. For example, if you were in the 40 percent tax bracket, a $100 deduction would save you only $40 in taxes, whereas a $100 credit would be offset against the tax itself and would thus save you $100.

Credits against your tax include income tax withheld from your paycheck, advance payments of estimated additional taxes, foreign taxes already paid on foreign earnings, energy credits (certain expenses incurred for defined types of energy conservation in your home), investment credits, earned-income credits, child care credits, credits for the elderly, and credits for political contributions. Some of these credits are illustrated in the following examples.

Assume that you have spent $10,000 on an automobile used entirely for business. Under the tax rules of the Economic Recovery Tax Act of 1981, you may depreciate this automobile over three years for tax purposes. You are entitled to depreciate the car 25 percent the first year, 38 percent the second year, and 37 percent the third year. In addition, you are entitled to an investment credit of $600 (6 percent credit on property depreciated over three to five years, 10 percent credit on property depreciated over five years or more) against the tax you would otherwise have to pay in the first year of ownership. Many taxpayers do not realize they may take both a depreciation allowance and a tax credit in such cases.

You may be entitled to what is called an **earned-income credit** if your earned income and your adjusted gross income are each less than $10,000.[3] Even if you owe no tax at all, up to $500 may be refunded to you as a sort of "negative income tax."

If you pay someone to care for a child or a disabled dependent while you are working or looking for work, you may be entitled to a child care credit that, depending on your income level, ranges from 20 percent to 30 percent of the first $2,400 you paid ($4,800, if you have more than one qualified dependent). If you are working and your spouse is a full-time student, your spouse is considered to be working; therefore, payments made for the care of your child will qualify for the credit.

A frequently overlooked credit is the credit available when you have worked for more than one employer in a given year, each of whom has deducted Social Security taxes from your wages. The maximum earnings on which these taxes must be paid in 1982 were $32,400. Suppose you worked during 1982 for two employers, each of whom paid you $20,000 and deducted the full Social Security tax of 6.7 percent that year. Because taxes were due only on $32,400, you would receive a tax credit of 6.7 percent on the excess of $7,600 ($40,000 – $32,400), or $509.

Another significant tax credit is known as the **tax credit for the elderly** For persons over sixty-five who earn less than a specified amount (for example, married persons, each over sixty-five, with an adjusted gross income of less than $17,500 in 1982), a tax credit of 15 percent of earned income (reduced by certain other nontaxable income such as Social Security) is available.

Joint versus Individual Returns

If you are married at any time during the year, you are entitled to file a joint tax return instead of an individual return. Exhibit 9–3 gives the tax rate schedules for single persons in various years. Comparing these rates with

---

3. Adjusted gross income is your gross income (wages, dividends, interest, and so on) less expenses such as business-related costs, capital losses, contributions to individual retirement plans, alimony, and certain disability income payments.

EXHIBIT 9-3   Tax Rate Schedules for Single Individuals

Taxable Income	1981 Pay +	1981 % on Excess	1982 Pay +	1982 % on Excess	1983 Pay +	1983 % on Excess	1984 Pay +	1984 % on Excess
0– $2,300	0	0	0	0	0	0	0	0
$ 2,300– 3,400	0	14	0	12	0	11	0	11
3,400– 4,400	$ 154	16	$ 132	14	$ 121	13	$ 121	12
4,400– 6,500	314	18	272	16	251	15	241	14
6,500– 8,500	692	19	608	17	566	15	535	15
8,500– 10,800	1,072	21	948	19	866	17	835	16
10,800– 12,900	1,555	24	1,385	22	1,257	19	1,203	18
12,900– 15,000	2,059	26	1,847	23	1,656	21	1,581	20
15,000– 18,200	2,605	30	2,330	27	2,097	24	2,001	23
18,200– 23,500	3,565	34	3,194	31	2,865	28	2,737	26
23,500– 28,800	5,367	39	4,837	35	4,349	32	4,115	30
28,800– 34,100	7,434	44	6,692	40	6,045	36	5,705	34
34,100– 41,500	9,766	49	8,812	44	7,953	40	7,507	38
41,500– 55,300	13,392	55	12,068	50	10,913	45	10,319	42
55,300– 81,800	20,982	63	18,968	50	17,123	50	16,115	48
81,800–108,300	37,677	68	32,218	50	30,373	50	28,835	50
108,300–......	55,697	70	45,468	50	43,623	50	42,085	50

Notes: Rates for 1981 are unadjusted for a reduction of 5 percent, effective 1 October 1981. An approximation of the actual tax due can be made by reducing the tax shown in the 1981 column.

Percentage paid on excess is applied to the difference between taxable income and the lower base of the tax bracket.

the rates for married persons filing jointly (see Exhibit 9–2) shows that it pays to file a joint return if you were the main producer of income during the year and your spouse had little or no income. For example, suppose George, who had a taxable income of $28,800 in 1981, married Janet on December 31. She earned nothing during 1981 and therefore owed no income taxes. Exhibit 9–3 shows that George's tax would be $7,434 if he filed as a single individual; Exhibit 9–2 shows that his tax would be only $5,849—that is, $4,505 + 32 percent of $4,200 (the difference between taxable income and the lower base of his tax bracket)—if he filed a joint return with his wife. By filing jointly, George would save $1,585.

The situation would be different if Janet had also been working and had taxable income in 1982. Assume that Janet also had taxable income of $28,800. If they filed a joint return, their combined taxable income would be $57,600, and the resulting tax (computed from Exhibit 9–2) would be $16,649, $3,265 more than the $13,384 (see Exhibit 9–3) total they both would have paid as single individuals. This penalty, $3,265, termed the **marriage**

tax, was reduced by Congress in 1981. Starting in 1983, a two-earner family filing a joint return may deduct 10 percent of the first $30,000 of the lower-paid spouse's earned income, for a maximum deduction of $3,000. The change reduces but does not eliminate the "marriage tax." For example, using 1983 scheduled tax rates, George and Janet would receive a deduction of $2,880 (10 percent of $28,800), which would reduce their income taxes by about $1,150—an amount that doesn't come close to making up the "marriage tax" of $3,265, calculated above.

Income Exempt from Taxes

Several types of income are exempt from federal and state taxation. Income exempt from federal taxes includes the following:

1. Interest from tax-exempt municipal bonds;
2. Dividends from life insurance policies (such dividends are considered a return of premium, not "true" income);[4]
3. Dividends from a corporation (such dividends are considered as paid from the corporation's invested capital, not from its earnings);
4. Social Security retirement income;
5. Disability income up to $100 weekly (but "sick pay" is fully taxable);
6. The value of most employee benefits—for example, employer pension contributions, health insurance, and life insurance;
7. Allowances for business expense reimbursements;
8. Gifts;
9. Income used for tax-deferred retirement plans—for example, individual retirement annuities or self-employed retirement plans (see Chapter 15);
10. Dividends received in stock (not considered "true" income since they only divide your present ownership share of a corporation into smaller fractions);
11. Certain types of interest income (see the following subsection);
12. Accident insurance proceeds—for example, the $100 you might receive from an insurance claim if your car was wrecked;
13. Life insurance proceeds (considered as compensation for loss; if the deceased's spouse takes life insurance proceeds in installments instead of in a lump sum, he or she does not have to report the first $1,000 of interest income attributable to the proceeds);

---

4. Interest credited to your life insurance policy is not currently reportable; such interest is not exempt, only deferred until the policy is surrendered for its cash value.

14. Annuities (the portion of annuity income considered as part of the original investment is not taxable);
15. Health loss reimbursements (payments for accident, injury, or illness are not taxable as income, nor are workers' compensation benefits or veterans' disability compensation benefits);
16. Unemployment insurance benefits.

In addition, various other types of income not taxable as income include inheritances, car pool receipts of the car owner, federal income tax refunds, scholarship and fellowship grants, and certain veterans' allowances.

To be sure you are not reporting exempt income on your return, consult a current, comprehensive list of various types of exempt income. Such a list appears in a free booklet available from the Internal Revenue Service (Publication 17, *Your Federal Income Tax*).

INTEREST AND DIVIDEND INCOME EXEMPT FROM TAXES

In 1981 Congress took three actions regarding interest and dividend exemptions. The first action dealt with corporate dividends. Effective in 1982, you need not pay taxes on the first $100 ($200 on a joint return) of corporate dividends. The exemption is available on joint returns regardless of which spouse receives the dividend.

Congress also authorized an **All Savers Certificate** that allows you to exempt up to $1,000 ($2,000 on a joint return) in interest income on specified savings in savings and loan associations and in commercial banks. Authorized initially on 1 October 1981, the certificates are available in denominations of $500 and carry a yield of 70 percent of the average yield of the most recently issued one-year U.S. Treasury bill. These bills were yielding over 17 percent in the month in which the certificates were first offered, so you would have received more than a 12 percent return on a tax-free basis if you had purchased them at that time. All Savers Certificates contain certain limitations. First, the $1,000 ($2,000 on a joint return) interest exemption is a lifetime limit, not an annual limit. Second, if you redeem the certificate or pledge it as collateral prior to maturity, you lose the tax exemption. Third, if you borrow funds to purchase these certificates, interest paid on such loans is not tax-deductible.

The third action of Congress was to set up, beginning in 1985, a new "net interest" exemption. Qualified interest income is reduced by all qualified interest expense, and 15 percent of the remainder—but not over $450 ($900 on a joint return)—is exempt from income taxes. You do not have to count home mortgage interest or interest incurred on a business loan as "qualified interest expense." For example, if during the year you have $2,000 of interest income and $1,000 of interest expense, you could exempt $150 (.15 × $2,000 − $1,000) from income taxes.

Ordinary Income versus Capital Gains

Some types of income are taxed at higher rates than other types. If you sell at a profit an asset you have held for longer than one year, the profit is termed a **long-term capital gain,** and only 40 percent of it is subject to tax. Thus, you receive 60 percent of the gain tax-free. If you are in the 30 percent tax bracket for ordinary income tax purposes and have a long-term capital gain, the gain will be taxed at only 12 percent (.30 × .40 = .12). Thus, you benefit by obtaining as much of your income as possible in the form of long-term capital gains.

One method of taking advantage of the tax difference between capital gains and ordinary income is to invest in stocks that are expected to show a substantial increase in market price because of reinvestment of profits in the enterprise. Such stocks, usually termed **growth stocks** (see Chapter 10), normally pay little or nothing in dividends because earnings are "plowed back" into the enterprise in the form of reinvestment in plant and equipment and in research and development; the investor expects to realize a profit by later selling the stock at a gain. Stocks that are growing more slowly typically pay out most of their profits in dividends and are termed **income stocks** These dividends are taxable as ordinary income.

The higher the tax bracket of the investor, the more advantageous it is to invest in growth stocks rather than in income stocks (see Chapter 11). For example suppose that you are in the 50 percent tax bracket and are considering investment in two stocks—G, a growth stock paying no dividends, and I, an income stock paying $1 of dividends per share. Each stock is selling for $5 a share. Assume that in one year you expect G to double in price to $10, and I to increase only to $9 because it is a slower-growing stock. In each case your total gain is expected to be $5. How much would your after-tax gain be in each stock? The answers are shown in Exhibit 9-4. Note that in stock G the investor may keep 80.0 percent of the $5 gross gain, as opposed to only 75.4 percent for stock I.

If you hold an asset in which you have a loss instead of a gain, it is advantageous to consider the difference in the ways losses are handled for tax purposes. If the loss is a **short-term capital loss**—that is, if it results from assets held for one year or less, you can deduct the loss in full—to a limit of $3,000 in any one year—and thus reduce taxes on other income. If you hold the asset for longer than one year and then sell it at a loss, the amount of the loss deductible against other income is only 50 percent—that is, for each $1.00 of long-term loss, only $.50 can be deducted. Thus, if you are go-

EXHIBIT 9–4
After-Tax Gain
on Growth and
Income Stocks

Type of Gain	Gross Gain		Tax		Net Gain after Tax	
	G	I	G	I	G	I
Ordinary income (dividend)	—	$1.00	—	$ .50	—	$ .50
Capital gain[a]	$5.00	$4.00	$1.00[b]	$ .80[c]	$4.00	$3.20
Total	$5.00	$5.00	$1.00	$1.30	$4.00	$3.70
Percentage of gross gain retained after taxes					80.0%	75.4%

[a]Assumes 40% of long-term gain is subject to tax. Note that the effect of taxation is to favor growth stocks, which increase in value through investment.
[b]$5.00 × 50% × 40%.
[c]$4.00 × 50% × 40%.

ing to have to accept a loss, it may be best to sell the asset and qualify for a short-term loss rather than hold the asset for longer than a year; it would then take $2.00 of long-term loss to offset $1.00 of ordinary income.

When Gains Must Be Reported

U.S. income tax law governs when and what types of income or gains must be reported. For tax purposes some gains may be deferred until the money is received—for example, interest income on life insurance policies or certain government savings bonds. Other income or gains must be reported in the year the gains are earned—for example, interest on bank savings accounts—whether or not the cash is withdrawn. One case in which you are not required to recognize a gain currently is the trading of similar real estate properties. For example, if you purchase an apartment house for $25,000 and trade it for another apartment house valued at $50,000, you do not have to recognize, for tax purposes, the $25,000 profit until after the second apartment house has been sold.

Another common case in which gains or losses do not have to be recognized for tax purposes lies in the area of **installment sales.** If a property is sold at a gain, but the owner is paid in installments over a period of years, the law views a portion of each installment as profit and the other portion as the return of the owner's original cost. Only the first portion is subject to income tax. For example, suppose you sold a building for $20,000, to be received in portions of $4,000 a year for five years, and your cost basis was $15,000. You have made a $5,000 profit, 25 percent of the sale price. In each of the five years you would report $1,000 (25 percent of $4,000) as profit.

Without this allowance you would have to report the entire $5,000 profit in the year of the sale, even though most of this profit had not yet been received.

Nonrecognition of gains also applies to the sale of your main residence at a profit and the reinvestment in a new residence within twenty-four months. In this case you must report any gain on the sale of your residence only if you fail to reinvest the proceeds in another house. The new house takes the cost basis of your old house in computing any subsequent gain on the outright sale of the home. However, if you sell your main residence after you reach age fifty-five, you can exempt all gains under $125,000 from income tax. This lifetime exemption is available only once.

Still another example of the restrictions governing recognition of gains and losses is the case of **wash sales,** in which the investor sells securities to realize a loss and then within thirty days purchases substantially identical securities. The government views such a sale as an improper way to avoid taxes and thus disallows deduction of the loss. For example, suppose you sell 100 shares of stock Y, originally purchased at $1,000, for $500. You then repurchase 100 shares of Y twenty-five days later for $400. The capital loss deduction of $500 will not be allowed on your tax return. The required cost basis of the new stock will be $400 plus the unrecognized loss of $500.

Tax Shelters

Because a higher income will place you in a higher income tax bracket, you should consider ways to receive income without having it taxed in successively higher brackets or ways to reduce the bracket in which you are taxed currently. One way to avoid higher taxes is to take advantage of various **tax shelters**—for example, retirement plans that permit you to deduct contributions in computing your taxes. Such a plan enables you to postpone income taxes until you remove funds from the plan—presumably at retirement, when you are in a lower tax bracket.

Another method of avoiding higher tax brackets is to make investments that provide substantial deductions. Examples of such deductions are real estate depreciation, mortgage loan interest, and depletion allowances permitted on investments such as oil and gas properties.

To illustrate the substantial savings possible from sheltering income from current taxation, consider two savings plans: Plan A and Plan B. Under Plan A you can avoid taxes on $100 monthly by investing in a tax-free savings account to supplement your retirement income. The savings account may be expected to earn a return of 10 percent a year, which would also be sheltered from current income taxes. If you save $100 a month at 10 percent for twenty years, you will have a total savings fund of $75,936.

Plan B involves savings in an account that is not a tax-sheltered retirement fund. Under Plan B you must pay current income taxes both on the

$100 of earnings before investing in the account and on the 10 percent interest income per year. Assuming that you are in the 35 percent combined state and federal income tax bracket, you will have only $65 to invest after paying these taxes. Since the 10 percent interest income is also taxable, your net return is only 6.5 percent after taxes. Net monthly savings of $65 at 6.5 percent for 20 years under Plan B produces a savings fund of $31,877, only 42 percent of the amount you would have at your command had you saved under Plan A.

Under Plan A you must, of course, pay taxes on the $75,936 fund as you withdraw from it. The amount of taxes depends on the tax bracket you are in at retirement. For various reasons, this bracket is likely to be lower than the 35 percent bracket you were in as a wage earner. Your total taxable income is likely to be less at retirement because you are entitled to additional exemptions after age sixty-five. Moreover, you may be able to use a device called income averaging, which is explained later in this chapter. Also, some income—Social Security, for example—is not subject to federal income taxation.

Even if your fund were taxable at 35 percent, the same rate as before retirement, you would be better off by using the tax shelter contained in Plan A. The fund would be reduced by taxes to $49,358 ($75,936 × .65). Even if you withdrew the entire fund in one year, you would still have a cash sum much larger than the $31,877 you would have had under Plan B, because you enjoyed a "tax-free loan" of the taxes otherwise due and accumulated these savings at compound interest at a higher net rate.

Tax shelters have become more important in recent years because of inflation, which has tended to cause taxable incomes to rise with increases in living costs. Higher income is taxable in higher brackets, so after you pay the higher taxes, your disposable income is reduced substantially below the level needed to offset inflation. This phenomenon, termed **bracket creep,** means that individuals are "creeping" into higher tax brackets, not because "real" income has increased, but because of inflation. The greater the attempt to offset inflation through increased wages, the greater is the resulting tax burden. If taxpayers are to maintain a given living standard, they must find ways to reduce taxable income. Thus, tax shelters have become very popular.

In 1981 Congress agreed to index individual tax brackets, the zero bracket amount, and personal exemptions in accordance with changes in the Consumer Price Index. **Indexing** means that only increases in income that exceed the inflation rate will be taxed in higher brackets. This much-needed reform, scheduled to begin after 31 December 1984, will probably reduce the attractiveness of some tax-sheltered investments.

CONSUMER CAVEAT

In the process of discovering new tax shelters, some financial planners have made unsound investments or investments in which the supposed tax shelter is later disallowed by the government. Many so-called tax shelters are, in fact, thinly disguised attempts at self-enrichment by certain promoters whose dubious schemes not only produce losses but do not even contain tax advantages. Before committing any funds, you should thoroughly investigate all potential investments advertised as tax shelters. It does little good to save in taxes 50 percent of each investment dollar if you lose the dollar itself.

Taxed versus Nontaxed Equivalent Yields

Exhibit 9–5 shows what return you would have to obtain in a taxable investment to yield the same return in a nontaxable investment. For example, if you are in a 45 percent combined federal and state income tax bracket, divide a tax-exempt return by (1.00 − 0.45) to obtain the corresponding taxable return. A tax-exempt return of 6 percent would thus be divided by .55 (1.00 − 0.45) to obtain 10.9 percent, the corresponding taxable return. That is, you would have to earn 10.9 percent on a taxable investment to net 6 percent after taxes. Since you usually accept less risk in a lower-yielding investment, tax-sheltered returns are especially attractive to many investors. The All Savers Certificates, for example, carry little or no risk; yet in 1981–82 they yielded tax-free returns between 10 and 12 percent, equivalent to returns of between 14 and 17 percent for a person in the 30 percent tax bracket and to returns of between 20 and 24 percent for a person in the 50 percent tax bracket.

Deductibility of Interest

Since interest expense is tax-deductible, its true cost is much less than most investors realize. If you borrow money at 12 percent and are in the 50 percent tax bracket, the true cost to you is only 6 percent. If the asset you are purchasing with a 12 percent loan is rising in value at a rate faster than

EXHIBIT 9–5
Taxed versus
Nontaxed
Equivalent Yields

	Equivalent Taxable Yield in Various Income Tax Brackets					
Tax-Free Yield	25%	30%	35%	40%	45%	50%
6%	8.0%	8.6%	9.2%	10.0%	10.9%	12.0%
8	10.7	11.4	12.3	13.3	14.5	16.0
10	13.3	14.3	15.4	16.7	18.2	20.0
12	16.0	17.1	18.5	20.0	21.8	24.0
14	18.7	20.0	21.5	23.3	25.5	28.0
16	21.3	22.9	24.6	26.7	29.1	32.0

6 percent, you will make a profit (see Chapter 8 for a discussion of interest deductibility as it relates to real estate investment).

You should be aware that not all types of interest are deductible. For example, if you borrow money to invest in securities that offer a tax-exempt return (e.g., municipal bonds), the interest is not deductible to the extent that you received a tax-exempt return on the investment. Before borrowing money with the idea of investing in such securities, you should check the consequences with a competent tax adviser.

Another illustration of limitations on the deductibility of interest is interest on funds borrowed to buy investment property. You cannot deduct more interest than $10,000 a year (or $5,000, if you are filing a single return) plus the net income of the property. To illustrate, suppose you borrow $100,000 at 12 percent to purchase a "growth stock" paying no dividends. Although the interest expense is $12,000 annually, you will not be allowed to deduct more than $10,000. This limitation prevents the taxpayer from incurring a large debt, the interest on which reduces other income that would normally be fully taxable.

Income Averaging

You might be able to save a substantial amount of income taxes—especially if, in a given year, your taxable income has greatly increased and put you into a higher tax bracket—if you take advantage of a provision known as **income averaging.** Income averaging reduces your taxes if your income during a given year was more than 20 percent higher than the average of your income in the preceding four years, plus $3,000. Thus, the higher earnings are taxed as if they had been earned over a five-year period. The effect of income averaging is to narrow the tax differences between people who earn stable incomes and people subject to widely fluctuating earnings—for example, athletes and entertainers.

How Life Insurance Is Taxed

Several facts about the taxation of life insurance are important in personal financial planning. Some of these facts have already been mentioned; they and other important points are summarized in the following paragraphs.

1. Life insurance death proceeds pass free of income tax to the beneficiaries. Death proceeds are considered as reimbursements for a loss, not as "earned income."

2. Dividends received on life insurance are not taxable income; they are considered as a return of a portion of the premium already paid.

3. Interest credited to a cash value life insurance policy escapes current taxation but must be accounted for when the policy is surrendered for its

cash value. If you "cash in" your life insurance, you must pay the ordinary income tax rate on any gain over and above what you paid for the policy. For example, suppose you have paid in $200 a year for twenty years (a total of $4,000), and at the end of twenty years you surrender your policy and receive $4,500. You must report $500 as ordinary income in the year of surrender. Normally, the cash value of life insurance will not exceed the total amounts paid, which include a charge for pure protection. Thus, the interest that has accumulated on the policy will in most cases escape taxation altogether. Losses, however, are not deductible.

4. If you elect to leave the cash value of a life insurance policy with the insurer and draw only interest earnings, these payments are taxable as ordinary income. However, a surviving spouse is entitled to exclude up to $1,000 annually from reportable income when the interest income stems from death proceeds.

5. If, instead of receiving a lump sum, you receive life insurance cash values under one or more of the various income options available, you will be taxed on the interest element of these payments only. You may exclude the portion of the payment that represents a return of your original cost.

6. The value of any group life insurance policy up to $50,000 paid on your behalf by your employer is not subject to current income taxation. If your employer provides more than $50,000 of life insurance on you, you are required to report the excess premiums as ordinary income at rates (called P.S. 58 rates) contained in a table provided by the IRS.

7. The cost of life insurance is not deductible, whether you pay personally for an individual contract or whether you contribute to a group life insurance plan sponsored by your employer. However, an employer may deduct as a business expense the cost of employee life insurance provided under group life policies.

8. If you are divorced and, as a part of the divorce settlement, agree to continue the premiums on life insurance with your former spouse as beneficiary, such premiums are a deductible expense for you and are reportable as income for your spouse.

9. Interest on a loan used to purchase a life insurance policy as part of a systematic plan to borrow the cash surrender value of the contract is not deductible. However, the restriction is relaxed in some cases—for example, when no part of any four of the first seven annual premiums are paid with funds borrowed under the plan. If you have a policy that has been in force for seven years and have not borrowed any of the cash value, you are not subject to this restriction; you may deduct the interest cost of any loan you obtain on the cash value of the policy. However, such interest must actually be paid each year; you may not add the interest cost to the indebtedness to make it deductible (see Chapter 15).

10. Several income tax benefits are available in the field of insured annuities; they are explored fully in Chapter 15.

Some Additional Principles of Income Tax Planning

Several techniques are available for meeting income tax obligations. The techniques described in the following subsections may help save you time and money.

EXTENSIONS

You may obtain extra time to file your return (usually due on 15 April) by filing a formal request with the IRS. Permission is granted automatically for a two-month extension, and with an adequate reason you can obtain a six-month extension. Even if you obtain an extension, you must pay any estimated tax due on time and pay interest on any additional amount that is subsequently determined due when the return is eventually filed. Thus, the extension applies to filing the return, not to making the tax payments.

CLAIMING EXEMPTIONS

You are required to file with your employer a Form W-2, which states the number of exemptions to which you are entitled. By law your employer must withhold from your paycheck an estimated tax based on the number of exemptions you have claimed. Some people deliberately understate the number of exemptions to which they are entitled; thus, the amount withheld increases, and they are eligible for a tax refund shortly after the first of the year in which their returns are filed. This tactic amounts to a sort of enforced saving program, but it makes very little financial sense because the government pays no interest on overpayments. Allowing the government free use of your money deprives you of interest you could otherwise be earning.

For example, suppose you are in the 30 percent tax bracket and are permitted four exemptions of $1,000 each but claim no exemptions through your employer. Your tax withholding is approximately $100 a month more than it would be if you claimed your exemptions. If you save $100 a month at 10 percent interest, your savings fund in one year will amount to $1,256 as opposed to the $1,200 you would obtain in a tax refund. Furthermore, if you had an emergency need for funds before the end of the tax year, your savings would be available to you; you would have to wait until after 1 January of the following year to apply for and finally receive your tax refund.

ESTIMATED TAX

If you earn income not subject to withholding, you must file an estimate of your income and pay an estimated tax quarterly (every three months) during the year. Failure to do so means that you must pay an additional charge (20 percent as of 1 February 1982) for underestimates or for unpaid installments of the estimated income taxes. Effective in 1983, estimated tax forms must be filed by anyone expecting to earn enough income to pay more

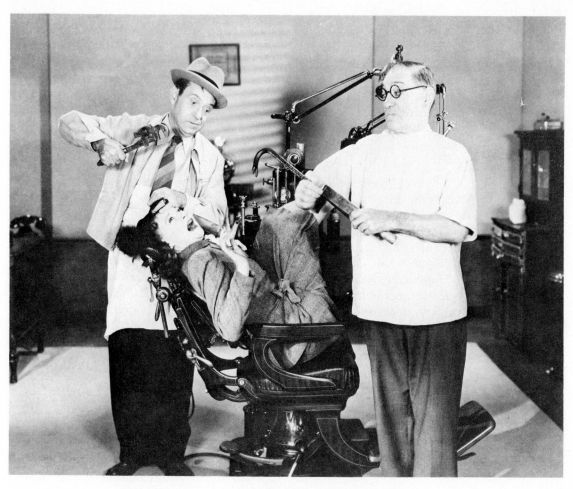

"Withholding is a relatively painless way to pay taxes."

The Bettman Archive, Inc.

than $300 in income tax. This limit becomes $400 in 1984, and $500 in 1985 and beyond. Penalties are not charged unless the amount paid in through withholding and estimated tax payments is less than 80 percent of the final tax liability determined when the return is filed.

ASSISTANCE VERSUS DO-IT-YOURSELF

In preparing tax returns, you can obtain assistance from accountants, from attorneys, or from the IRS. The fees charged for this service are deductible as an expense. Professional help may save you money by making you aware of deductions you might not otherwise have claimed. Good tax preparers know enough tax law to guide you in claiming deductions that may or may not be allowed by the government. Tax preparers also guide you in keeping pertinent tax information and records to be used in filling out your tax forms. However, you may decide that the most difficult part of preparing your tax return is the assembly and preparation of the necessary data, not the filling in of the form itself. If you prepare your own return, you become knowledgeable about tax methods, deductions, and rules, and this knowledge will help you maintain better records for tax forms in the future.

GIFTS

You can save on taxes by making gifts to your children so that the investment income will be taxed in a bracket lower than yours or will escape taxes altogether. For example, you can register a savings certificate in the name of your minor child and name yourself as custodian. The child thus becomes the legal owner of the certificate, which can be set aside for, say, a college fund. The savings certificate interest is now taxable to the child, who probably will pay no income tax on it because of lack of other earnings. Subtracting the interest from your income will not only reduce your taxable income in accordance with the tax bracket you are in, but it may actually place you in a lower tax bracket and thus permit tax savings on other income.

AMENDED RETURNS

If you make an error in preparing your tax return—for example, suppose you pay more tax than you owe—you may file an amended return and claim a refund of the overpayment. Amended returns can be filed within three years of the time you filed your original return.

Tax Records

Most tax experts believe that individuals overpay their income taxes because of failure to take the deductions and credits permitted by law. You must maintain adequate records if you wish to claim the deductions and credits to which you are entitled. The time to establish the proper records is at the beginning of the tax year. You will then find it far easier to prepare your tax returns and to avoid overpayment. You should retain most tax records for at least three years, and in some cases for longer periods. For example, you may need records for five years to take advantage of income averaging.

Knowing which records to keep may require some special study of tax regulations governing the deductions and credits to which you are entitled. In general, the following records will probably be necessary for most taxpayers: check registers and returned checks showing proof of payment of bills; receipts for all deductible purchases—for example, business travel and meals; and automobile expense record booklets. If your tax returns are audited (i.e., examined by tax agents), you must be able to produce records supporting all your deductions and credits; otherwise they will be disallowed, and you will have to pay additional tax plus any applicable interest charges and tax penalties for maintaining inadequate records.

Tax Audits

If the IRS discovers an error on your return, or if it disagrees with your claiming some deduction or your failing to report income, your tax return may be audited. An **audit** is usually a routine examination of specific deductions and credits rather than an examination of your entire return. In the course of an audit, you will be required to produce records supporting the items in question.

Chances are greater that your return will be audited if your income is high, if you claim unusually large deductions, or if your return is complicated because of tax-sheltered investments or sales of assets. To avoid an audit, you should double-check your return for mathematical accuracy. Be sure to sign the return and, if necessary, to attach some supplemental information explaining deductions or other items. Note, however, that while some extra explanation may be helpful in avoiding an audit, too much extra information may give tax auditors additional items about which to raise questions.

If you have a dispute with the IRS, you may appeal to other tax division personnel on an informal basis, or you may appeal formally to the IRS appellate division. If your case involves less than $500, it probably can be heard by a small claims tax court.

SUMMARY

1. Because taxes consume approximately 40 percent of the gross national product, and because most financial planners are in high tax brackets, finding ways to minimize or to avoid income taxes is an important part of successful financial and investment planning.

2. The major types of taxes affecting personal finance are income taxes, sales taxes, estate and gift taxes, property taxes, and Social Security taxes. Personal income tax accounts for about 30 percent of all taxes; however, taxpayers have opportunities legally to avoid or reduce the burden imposed by personal income taxes.

3. Understanding certain important principles of income tax helps you to minimize the burden of income taxes. These principles include recognizing available deductions and tax credits, splitting income so that it is taxed in lower brackets, earning income exempt from taxation, taking advantage of the difference between ordinary income and

capital gains, deferring taxes to a future time through the use of tax shelters, using the deductibility of interest in making investments, and using income averaging.

4. In the field of life insurance and annuities, several important tax advantages are significant to the personal financial planner. These include tax-deferred interest earnings, deductibility of interest paid on life insurance loans, and exemptions of dividends from current taxation.

5. The keeping of adequate tax records is vital if you are to take advantage of the principles of tax management and avoid the expenses, difficulties, and uncertainties of tax audits.

REVIEW QUESTIONS

1. In considering the burden of taxes, Peter states that sales taxes affect him more significantly than income taxes, and that he is not worried about estate taxes at all.
   (a) Suggest possible reasons for Peter's position.
   (b) What other type of tax is likely to be very significant to a person like Peter?

2. June and Mary each get a raise of $1,000. June's current taxable income is $15,000, while Mary's current taxable income is $12,900.
   (a) Based on 1981 rates, how much of their $1,000 raises are taxed away from each woman? (Refer to Exhibit 9–3.)
   (b) What do your answers imply about the nature of the federal income tax?

3. When "Proposition 13," a measure that reduced property taxes, was passed in California, the total reduction in property taxes was partly offset automatically by an increase in other taxes. Explain what other taxes might have been increased and why.

4. For purposes of financial planning, why is it important to distinguish between the following:
   (a) Ordinary income and capital gains.
   (b) Short-term gains or losses and long-term gains or losses.

5. (a) What is a "tax shelter"?
   (b) Do tax shelters eliminate taxes or merely defer taxes?
   (c) Why is the difference between eliminating and deferring important?

6. Why do many persons use the zero bracket amount rather than itemize deductions, even when they could profit by itemization in calculating their federal income taxes?

7. Why does interest expense "cost less" than it appears to cost?

8. (a) What is the difference between a tax deduction and a tax credit?
   (b) Give some examples of both credits and deductions.
   (c) Why is the difference between credits and deductions important?

9. (a) Give examples of some income that is exempt from income taxes.
   (b) Suggest reasons why some types of income are exempt.

10. Explain the difference between tax avoidance and tax evasion.

11. (a) Why are tax records important?
    (b) Discuss the importance of a check register as a tax record.

12. One Christmas Eve two couples decided to get married within the next month. Mary Brown had not earned taxable income during the year, while her husband-to-be had been regularly employed. Mary White had been employed during the year and had earned as much as her husband-to-be. A financial adviser suggested that each couple "tie the knot" before the end of the year to save on income taxes. Explain why you agree or disagree with this advice for:
    (a) Mary Brown and her husband to be.
    (b) Mary White and her husband-to-be.

13. A financial writer stated: "Commonly overlooked deductions are sales taxes on autos, boats, and home-building material, which may greatly exceed allowances suggested in tax booklets. Other items frequently overlooked are one-half of the cost of hospitalization insurance up to $150 and medical transportation expenses when you go see the doctor."
    (a) Why might sales taxes on items mentioned above exceed commonly suggested allowances?
    (b) Suggest reasons why some taxpayers might overlook the cost of hospitalization insurance and medical transportation as tax deductions.

14. A tax consultant advised: "Finding a good tax consultant is an imprecise art. Certified public accountants, tax attorneys, and enrolled agents are the best bets. But avoid storefront preparers, for they won't venture into the gray area where the loopholes lie." Do you agree with this advice?

15. A financial writer stated: "The IRS gets suspicious of people in high income brackets who file their returns themselves. In fact, if you have a complex return involving stock purchases and sales, pension plan contributions, rental property income, and the like, and file yourself, it is very likely you will be audited. Even if you do hire someone to do your return, you might unwillingly invite an audit because he or she is on the 'problem preparers' list. The agency keeps tabs on preparers who do slipshod work or who have poor track records on audits."
    (a) Suggest reasons why audits are more likely on the type of return described above.
    (b) How would you avoid going for tax help to persons on the "problem preparers" list?

16. In 1978 some 69 million income tax returns, representing 77 percent of the taxpayers, claimed refunds that averaged $495. In other words, the government received a temporary interest-free loan of $34 billion from taxpayers.
    (a) Suggest probable reasons for these refunds.
    (b) How can you avoid making what amounts to an interest-free loan to the government?

17. Gifts to charities are deductible, including gifts of property. Gifts of property up to 30 percent of adjusted gross income may be allowed, but such gifts must be carefully substantiated with receipts and explanations. An item you possess may be worth more as a tax deduction than it would be if you sold it on the market.
    (a) Explain how the donation of an item could, for tax purposes, benefit you more than its sale.
    (b) Is the donor's tax bracket a significant matter in this case?

18. Donald sells his house for $80,000. He had purchased it originally for $40,000. He immediately reinvests in a new house costing $100,000.
    (a) Must the $40,000 gain be reported in the year of the sale?
    (b) What tax principle governs your answer?

19. (a) What income tax advantages are associated with life insurance?
    (b) Are there any tax disadvantages connected with life insurance?

CASE PROBLEMS

I. Economics of Taxation

A financial writer stated: "The personal income tax is a prodigious generator of revenue for the federal government. As incomes rise, individuals move into higher brackets and the government gets an even larger share of national income. And when there is rapid inflation of the current sort, revenue grows with alarming speed . . . everyone agrees that . . . personal tax rates should be cut. The only question is how."

QUESTIONS

1. From the viewpoint of financial planning, why is it desirable to limit government tax revenues?

2. Which type of tax provision would best encourage saving: (a) an exemption of the first $200 of interest from taxable income or (b) an exemption of 50 percent of all interest earned?

3. Suggest other types of tax incentives that might encourage savings.

II. Tax-Sheltered Savings

A comparison of the savings available under tax shelters shows the dramatic effect of compounding interest (assumed to be 9 percent) on funds that otherwise would be paid to the government. In the following table, taxes are assumed to be 32 percent at the federal level and 5 percent at the state level. For example, after twenty years you are ahead by $1,443, even after paying all taxes, if you use a tax-sheltered plan ($3,239 − $1,796 = $1,443).

Number of Years	Value of $1,000 in Savings		
	After Taxes Paid Currently	No Taxes Paid Currently	Tax Shelter: Taxes Paid after Savings Withdrawn
1[a]	$ 630	$ 1,000	$ 630
5	786	1,412	889
10	1,035	2,172	1,318
20	1,796	5,142	3,239
30	3,118	12,172	7,668

[a]Investment is assumed to have been made at the end of year 1.

Source: Abstracted from *Tax Guide for College Teachers, 1982* (Washington, D.C.: Academic Information Service, Inc., 1982), p. 191.

QUESTIONS

1. Explain why you end up ahead by using a tax-sheltered plan, even after paying all taxes due upon withdrawal.

2. By referring to interest tables or by using a hand calculator, demonstrate how the above numbers were obtained.

III. Which Returns Are Audited?

"Commerce Clearing House Inc. used newly released IRS data to compute (for 1973) average deductions by income class. The IRS criteria for selecting returns for audit are sophisticated, and whatever the averages, a taxpayer is entitled only to deductions he can substantiate. In the $20,000 + brackets, total deductions consistently averaged 18 percent or 19 percent of adjusted gross income. That percentage was much higher in lower brackets, where more taxpayers chose the zero bracket amount."

Adjusted Gross Income (thousands of dollars)	Average Deductions		Average Taxes Paid
	Contributions	Interest	
$10–15	$ 347	$1,090	$1,025
15–20	421	1,308	1,400
20–25	530	1,538	1,764
25–30	663	1,736	2,169
30–50	964	2,221	2,965
50–100	2,121	3,919	5,142

QUESTIONS

1. If your actual deductions substantially exceed the averages shown in the table, do you think your chances of having your return audited would increase? Why, or why not?

2. Suggest reasons why deductions were larger as a percentage of adjusted gross income for persons in lower tax brackets than for persons in higher tax brackets.

3. In general, what features probably describe the taxpayer whose itemized deductions exceed the zero bracket amount deduction?

CHAPTER 10

AN INTRODUCTION TO STOCKS AND BONDS

LEARNING OBJECTIVES

In studying this chapter you will learn:

    What stocks and bonds are;

    The main features of corporate and government bonds;

    What you should know about stocks and bonds before making investments;

    How to understand stock market indexes;

    Why bond prices go down when interest rates rise, and vice versa;

    What short selling is;

    The effects of stock splits and stock dividends on stock prices;

    How to interpret a price/earnings ratio;

    The differences between cyclical and growth stocks;

    What a discount broker is;

    Some of the language of investments: odd lots, bull and bear markets, stop orders;

    The nature of the marketplace in which stocks and bonds are traded.

Judicious investment of surplus monies is important to sound financial management. This chapter provides you with information about the types of stocks and bonds available.

Securities referred to as stocks and bonds are issued by both private corporations and government bodies. Corporations and governments amass capital from diverse individuals and organizations by issuing claims against themselves in the form of stocks and/or bonds. **Stocks** are certificates of ownership giving the stockholder equity in the corporation. **Bonds** are contracts under which a corporate or a governmental debt is assumed by the bondholders.

BONDS

A **bond** is an evidence of debt, issued to the general public by either a corporation or a government. When issuing corporate bonds, instead of negotiating with one lender (a bank, for example), a corporation arranges with an **underwriter** (a securities firm, for example) to sell an issue of debt. The issue is divided into many small denominations of $1,000 and up for easier sale to the public.

A bond is a contract between the lender and the borrower. The contract states that a given sum of money has been borrowed and will be repaid by a certain date—usually twenty to thirty years from the date of issue, in the case of corporate bonds. The contract also states that the bondholder will receive a given sum of interest—usually paid semiannually, in the case of corporate bonds—as long as the bond is outstanding. A bond issued by Georgia Power Company is illustrated in Exhibit 10–1.

A supplemental contract, called the **indenture contract,** offers protection to the bondholder by naming a **trustee,** a person who acts for the bondholder in the case of corporate difficulties. The indenture contract also contains the details of how the bond will be retired—that is, through repayment in installments or through the redemption of the entire issue at one time.

In addition to corporations, the other major issuer of bonds to the investing public is government. You can buy the public issues of the federal agencies as well as the debt of the various state and local governments and authorities.

EXHIBIT 10-1   A Bond Issued by the Georgia Power Company

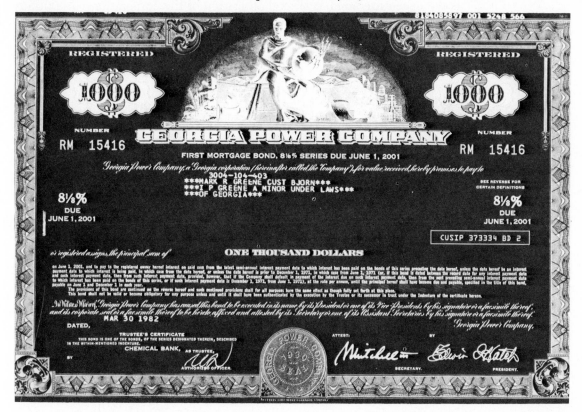

Corporate Bonds

Corporate bonds can be differentiated in several ways. Two important features are the collateral (if any) backing the bonds and the convertibility of bonds into other securities.

SECURED VERSUS UNSECURED BONDS

Some bonds are issued with special collateral pledged to the benefit of the bondholder. These bonds are called **secured bonds,** or **mortgage bonds,** because some corporate asset is pledged to the bondholder as security for the loan. If the corporation encounters difficulty in repaying either the principal or the interest on the bond issued, the bondholder may foreclose on the collateral.

The most important form of corporate bond in terms of total dollars issued is the **debenture bond,** a general obligation of the corporation without any specific asset pledged as collateral. Some debenture bonds are called **subordinated debentures,** which means that all other forms of debt have a prior claim against earnings and assets in any determination of which creditors are to be paid first.

CONVERTIBLE BONDS

A **convertible bond** is a special sort of hybrid—a common form of corporate security that is "half bond and half stock." Convertible bonds are bonds in every practical and legal sense—they pay interest at specific intervals and repay the principal at maturity. However, a convertible bondholder is given an option to convert the bond to common stock at a predetermined price. This option gives the bondholder several important advantages. For example, the convertible bondholder has the same basic protections as other bondholders, but if corporate earnings rise and the stock price also rises, the convertible feature of the bond becomes more valuable. The bond price will rise relative to the convertibility ratio.

A simple illustration may make the advantages of convertible bonds easier to understand. A convertible bond of the XYZ Company sells for $1,000 and pays 10 percent interest ($100 a year). It is due in the year 2010. The XYZ stock sells for $40 a share and pays a $2 annual dividend from corporate profits. The convertible option permits the conversion of the bond at any time into 22 shares of common stock.[1] The conversion value ($1,000/22) is $45.45, as compared to the share price of $40. Suppose the stock price rises to $60, a gain of $20 a share. The bond can be converted into 22 shares worth $60 a share. The bond price will rise to about $1,320 (22 × $60), its worth in XYZ stock.

If you purchased $1,000 worth of stock when the price per share was $40 a share (25 shares at $40 a share), you would earn $50 ($2 × 25) a year in dividends and have the potential of making $500 if the stock price rose by $20 a share (25 × $20 = $500). In comparison, the holder of the convertible bond would receive $100 in interest (10 percent of $1,000) and have the potential of making $320 ($1,320 − $1,000). Thus, you as a stockholder have earned more than the convertible bondholder, who has less chance of making a large profit on the appreciation in market value. However, the bondholder usually has a higher and surer cash income in the form of interest than you as a shareholder have in the form of dividends.[2]

---

1. The conversion option on many convertible bonds is variable—in the example, 22 shares for 10 years, 20 shares for the next 10 years, and 15 shares for the last 10 years. The concept of convertibility is designed to force bondholders to convert their bonds as soon as possible.

2. Convertible bonds usually sell for a small premium over their straight bond value. In other words, their speculative value always attracts some extra buyers.

An investor buying a convertible bond, then, takes less risk, and usually gets less return, than does a stockholder. The major advantage of the convertible bond to the corporation is that it enables the corporation to issue bonds that might be converted to stock. Thus, the corporation need not necessarily repay the bond with cash at its maturity.

Zero-Coupon Bonds

One financial innovation developed during the period of high interest rates is the **zero-coupon bond.** Unlike standard corporate or government bonds, a zero-coupon bond offers repayment only through its stated maturity value. Unlike other bonds, no interim interest payments are made to the bondholder. Thus, a twenty-year, zero-coupon bond with a face value of $1,000 and selling for a 14 percent yield is priced at $72.76 (see Appendix A–4). The present value of $1.00 due in twenty years at 14 percent is $.072761 ($1,000 × .072761 = $72.76). A corporation selling $50 million of bonds due in twenty years would receive $3,638,000 today ($50,000,000 × .072761).

Zero-coupon bonds are issued for a variety of reasons, not the least of which is the tax benefit available to the issuing corporation, which is allowed to write off a portion of the bond interest, even though no cash is paid currently to the saver. However, the key question is: Why should an intelligent investor buy these bonds when no current interest is received and taxes must still be paid on this accrued interest? A forty-five-year-old physician in the highest tax bracket might be an ideal customer if she purchased the bonds for either an IRA account or a Keogh account that is not taxed currently. For a $7,270 cash layout now, the physician owns $100,000 face value of bonds. If she holds the bonds until maturity, she owes no income tax on them until the bonds mature. When she retires, the income tax owed on the bond interest probably will be computed at lower rates because her total taxable income should be less. The total return is "locked in" and known in advance; if interest rates fall, she is not subject to lower return, as would be the case with most other savings media. Thus, zero-coupon bonds may offer important advantages to investors who are in high tax brackets.

Government Bonds

The two major types of government securities are (1) federal debt instruments and (2) state and local debt instruments. Securities of the U.S. government and of its various debt-issuing agencies are considered free of the risk of default. Investors are willing to accept less return, in the form of lower interest, in exchange for a minimal risk of default. A major characteristic of state and local government securities is that the income from such bonds is exempt from federal taxation.

As of May 1981, $236 billion in treasury bills was outstanding in the hands of the public. In addition, $96 billion in marketable notes and bonds and $72 billion in U.S. savings bonds were outstanding. Approximately $234 billion in securities was owned by the government itself. The total debt was $963 billion, and it has been growing at an annual compounded rate of more than 8 percent. The government currently must raise $98 billion a year to pay the interest on this debt—an annual cost equal to about 10.2 percent of all government expenditures. Approximately $135 billion worth of U.S. agency debt and other debt is not included in these statistics.

SAVINGS BONDS

One way to categorize U.S. debt is its quality of negotiability. Some debt instruments may be traded between investors, and others may not. A **savings bond** cannot be sold (or transferred) to another person, nor can it be used as collateral for a loan. The only way to cash in the bond is to hold it to maturity or to redeem it under specific conditions permitted by the U.S. Treasury.

U.S. savings bonds either pay interest periodically or allow interest to accumulate and be paid at maturity or upon redemption.[3] The interest rate does not change after issuance and is usually less than that paid on bank or thrift institution certificates.

One of the most interesting features of U.S. savings bonds is their tax status. An investor holding a U.S. savings bond (series EE) need not pay taxes on the earned interest until the bond matures or is redeemed. But more importantly, the Series EE bond can be converted to a Series HH bond, which pays cash interest periodically. The conversion can be accomplished without the payment of any income tax on the accrued interest. Interest paid by the Series HH bonds after conversion is subject to income tax.

NEGOTIABLE SECURITIES

The vast majority of U.S. securities are fully negotiable—that is, they can be sold to another person. These securities' dates of maturity vary from thirty days to thirty years. The three major types are treasury bills, treasury notes, and treasury bonds.

A **treasury bill (TB)** is an evidence of government debt sold with a maturity of less than one year—most often 90 to 180 days. The minimum denomination is $10,000. A TB's most distinguishing characteristic is that it is sold at discount. For example, a 180-day TB issued to yield 10 percent will sell for $9,500 [$10,000 − ($10,000 × 10% × 180/360)]. Such bills have a large

---

3. Accrual bonds (Series EE) do not accrue interest in the way a passbook savings account, for example, accrues interest. If a passbook pays 5.5%, it pays this rate from the first day of deposit. A Series EE bond pays something less than the guaranteed rate in the early years of the bond, and more than the guaranteed rate in the later years. This averages out to the guaranteed rate over the whole period, but it penalizes the holder of the bond during the early period.

market and are easily bought from banks and brokers for a small commission. The small investor may write to the nearest Federal Reserve Bank for specific instructions on how to buy bills and bonds directly from the Federal Reserve and thus avoid paying a commission.

Negotiable debts issued by the U.S. government in maturities greater than one year are either **treasury notes** or **treasury bonds.** The main distinction between them is that notes are issued for less than ten years; bonds, for more than ten years. Both are usually issued in minimum denominations that vary from as little as $1,000 to as much as $10,000. U.S. government bonds and notes, like corporate bonds, are issued with coupons to be clipped and deposited in a bank account. They can also be registered in the name of the owner, and an interest check may then be mailed semiannually.

STATE AND LOCAL BONDS

All governments issue debt when their expenditures are greater than their receipts. Debt is issued to cover budgetary deficits (where the law permits), and special-purpose bonds known as **revenue bonds** are issued for specific capital projects such as jails, bridges, schools, or roads. The project's receipts provide the funds for paying the interest and principal on the bonds.

Where the debt is issued for general purposes, the debt becomes a general obligation for the issuing body, and thus the "full faith and credit" of the issuer is involved. That is, all government receipts are in effect pledged for the payment of these outstanding bonds, called **general obligation bonds.** They invariably have a higher credit rating—that is, they are considered safer—than do special authority or revenue bonds issued by the same borrower, which are only backed by the revenue from the special project that was financed.

The most important characteristic of state and local bonds is that they are exempt from federal income tax.[4] This feature is the basis of the heavy demand for such bonds and explains why they can be sold at a markedly lower rate of interest than competing forms of debt.

Features of Bonds

Several features of bonds are not generally known. For example, corporate bonds are repaid through a "sinking fund," and state and local bonds are issued with differing maturities. Determining the yield of a bond is tricky; it must be done with special tables (see Appendix A) or with a business calculator. Interest rate risk is a special risk that affects bond values only if the bond

---

4. The legal principle on which this exemption is based has been tested repeatedly in the courts and could probably be changed only by a constitutional amendment.

is sold before maturity. These features are discussed in greater detail in the following subsections.

REPAYMENT PROVISIONS

Almost all corporate debt and some U.S. Treasury bonds are subject to a unique method of repayment, a device called a **sinking fund.** That is, the borrowing company agrees to repurchase a given amount of its debt each year and to turn over these bonds to the trustee (the legal representative of the bondholders) for cancellation. The bonds can be purchased by the corporation in the open market as long as the price does not exceed some designated figure. If the market price exceeds the designated price, the debtor corporation can call in by lot number and repay the correct number of bonds to satisfy the sinking fund requirement.[5]

Unless otherwise specified, corporate bonds and some few government bonds are subject to "call provisions" during the life of the issue. A **call provision** means that the corporation has the option of redeeming the outstanding bonds prior to maturity. If the corporation "calls" the bonds prior to maturity, it must pay a penalty in the form of a premium (bonus amount) over the face value of the bonds. This premium is a function of the interest rate at which the bonds were issued and of the remaining years to maturity. Thus, if twenty-five-year bonds were called in five years after issuance, the premium would be quite high. However, if the bonds were called in at the end of twenty years, the amount of the premium would be negligible.[6]

YIELD

Bonds are sold with a guaranteed annual income called the **coupon.** A $1,000 bond of the XYZ Corporation, paying 12 percent and due in the year 2010, contains two financial contracts: (1) the promise to repay the $1,000 face amount in the year 2010 and (2) the promise to pay $120 in interest a year ($1,000 × 12%), usually paid in two $60 semiannual installments until 2010. The combination of these two contracts makes the calculation of the yield somewhat difficult.

Exhibit 10–2 gives some dimension to changing investment yields through time. Notice that the yield on high-quality bonds was consistently higher than the dividend yield on stocks for the period depicted (1973–1981).

---

5. Many accounting textbooks discuss sinking funds in a different manner. The procedures discussed here correspond to modern corporate practice.

6. The premium is a nuisance charge paid by the corporation to the bondholder to compensate for the annoyance of having to reinvest the money. Although most people think that the faster someone pays off, the better, reinvesting is a nuisance to giant insurance companies with millions of dollars flowing in every day. In periods of high interest rates, some corporations are able to offer noncallable bonds at slightly less than the going rate because the lender is willing to concede a small amount of current income in return for a guarantee that it will receive a higher income over the life of the issue.

EXHIBIT 10-2

Stock and Bond
Yields,
1973-1981

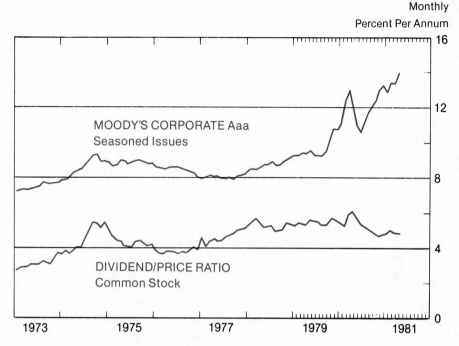

Monthly
Percent Per Annum

Source: Standard & Poor's Corporation.

If we had shown a similar chart for the 1960s, the relationship would have been reversed. The most surprising line in the chart is the behavior of the bond yield curve from 1979 to 1981. The high yields of bonds meant extremely low bond prices.

Another way to calculate the bond yield is to use a set of standard present-value tables. Assume that a 10 percent coupon bond, due in twenty-five years, is selling in a 12 percent market. The $1,000 face value of the bond is worth $1,000 × .05882, or $58.82. (From Appendix A-4 the present value of $1 payable in twenty-five years if money earns 12 percent annually is $.05882.) The present value of $100 in interest a year for twenty-five years at 12 percent is $100 × 7.8431, or $784.31 (from Appendix A-5). Thus, in a 12 percent market the $1,000 bond is worth $784.31 + $58.82, or $843.13.

Before sophisticated hand calculators were readily available, another method of approximating bond yields was widely used. This method, the **average yield basis,** uses simple arithmetic. Suppose, for example, you have a $1,000 bond due in twenty-five years, paying $100 a year and selling for $843. What is the approximate yield? First add the annual interest income ($100) and the face value minus the market price ($1,000 – $843) divided by the number of years to maturity (25). This value, the numerator, is then divided by the average value of the bond during its life ($1,000 + 843)/(2):

$$\text{Approximate yield} = \frac{100 + \dfrac{(1000 - 843)}{25}}{\dfrac{1000 + 843}{2}}$$

$$= \frac{106.28}{921.50}$$

$$= 11.53\%.$$

We know from using the discount table that the correct answer is 12 percent, so 11.53 percent is only an approximation.

INTEREST RATE RISK

Suppose that market interest rates on the bonds in the previous example rise to 14 percent five years later. The coupons are now worth only $662 in the higher interest market, and the present value of the principal has dropped to approximately $73. The bond is now worth only $662 + $73, or $735, even though the bond is five years closer to maturity. As interest rates have risen sharply with inflationary pressures, the value of corporate bonds has fallen correspondingly. Bonds that were sold as safe investments have not proven quite so safe if the bond has had to be liquidated before maturity, when the entire amount of principal would have been repaid. The general fall of bond prices has not been caused by any credit deterioration of bond quality, but by the mathematics of finance working on bond values as interest rates have risen to unprecedented levels. The phenomenon of **interest rate risk** means that as interest rates rise, bond prices fall; as interest rates fall, bond prices rise.

CORPORATE STOCKS

A **stock** is a share of ownership in a corporate business enterprise. As a part owner of the business, a shareholder accepts all business risk and shares in all profits earned. The portion of corporate profits paid out to shareholders after a vote of the corporation's board of directors is called a **dividend.** Dividends may be increased, decreased, or eliminated as business conditions warrant. Stockholders have a right to vote in corporate elections and to elect representatives to the board of directors. They are entitled to receive quarterly reports on the corporation's financial condition, as well as an annual report. These financial statements must conform to certain minimal government requirements regarding disclosure of all pertinent information. Nonfinancial corporations that have more than 500 shareholders and more than $1 million in assets and do business in interstate commerce must comply with federal laws and regulations administered by the Securities and Exchange Commission.

Features of Stock

Some of the important features of corporate stock include returns on stock, par value and book value, stock splits (or dividends), and preferred stock.

RETURNS ON STOCK

The shareholder may receive a return or profit in two ways—through dividends and through gains in the price per share for which the stock is traded in the stock market. The corporation is under no obligation to pay a dividend, although all stocks listed on the New York Stock Exchange are supposed to pay quarterly dividends if they are financially able. The exchange considers it best for a company to establish a dividend per share that it can maintain even in times of economic hardship. If the company makes larger and perhaps unexpected profits, it may pay an "extra" dividend. Suppose, for example, that the XYZ Company is paying a quarterly dividend of $.50 a share and a year-end extra dividend of $.40. The total dividend for the year would be $2.40, and if the stock is selling for $40 a share, the current yield (return) would be:

$$\text{Dividend yield} = \frac{\text{Dividend per share}}{\text{Market price per share}} = \frac{\$2.40}{\$40} = 6\%.$$

Most investors expect to receive more than a dividend when they buy stock. They most often buy shares with expectations of an increase in the market price per share. In the XYZ example, the investor who bought at $40 a share might have expected the stock to rise to $50 a share. If the investor held the stock for a year, the investor's annual return would be $2.40 plus $10 profit, for a total return of $12.40 (ignoring stockbrokers' commissions), or a return of 31 percent a year on the original investment of $40:[7]

$$\text{Total return} = \frac{\text{Dividend per share} \pm \text{Gain (Loss) per share}}{\text{Market price per share}}$$

$$= \frac{\$2.40 + \$10}{\$40} = 31\%.$$

7. The dividend is taxed as ordinary income, and the appreciation in market price is taxed at a lower capital gains rate. Current returns are always calculated ignoring the tax effect, since each investor has a different tax position.

PAR VALUE AND BOOK VALUE

When stock is originally issued by a corporation, the stock must have a value for accounting purposes. One such measure is **par value,** the monetary value assigned to each share of stock at the time of issue. The par value printed on the stock certificate seldom agrees with the market price of the stock. Par value is significant only because it represents the permanent invested capital that may not be paid out in dividends. It thus provides some minimum level of protection for creditors. Exhibit 10–3 shows a stock certificate issued by Eagle Corporation with a par value of $10.

The **book value** of a corporation—also termed its **net worth**—is defined as assets minus liabilities. When this amount is divided by the number of shares of outstanding stock, the result is the **book value per share.** Thus, if net worth is $100 million and there are 1 million shares outstanding, the book value per share is $100. Sometimes book value is considered as the value of each share of stock if the corporation were to be dissolved or liquidated. Generally, however, book value has little effect on the market price of shares.[8]

STOCK SPLITS OR DIVIDENDS

A corporation may wish to change the number of its outstanding shares of stock. One way to do so is to sell more stock to the investing public. Another way is to issue more stock to the present owners, through either a stock dividend or a stock split.

A **stock dividend** is an increase in the number of shares outstanding without a change in the par value per share. For example, suppose you own 100 shares of the ABC Corporation (which pays a $1 a share cash dividend), and the company also issues a 5 percent stock dividend. You now have 105 shares, and instead of receiving $100 in cash dividends a year, you will now receive $105 a year.[9] To the extent that you receive a greater cash dividend, you are better off; but because you still own the same proportion of total shares of the corporation, your actual wealth has not changed. Corporations generally issue stock dividends as a signal that corporate earnings are rising and that the future of the company is considered healthy. Stock dividends may also be issued in lieu of cash dividends by companies that wish to "plow back" all their earnings into capital investment.

---

8. However, certain types of investors are always on the lookout for hidden values—situations where the liquidating value of a business is greater than book value and/or market value. For example, in the mid-1960s the government forced the breakup of Loew's/MGM into two different companies. MGM had a huge inventory of films that could be sold to television, and Loew's had theaters in downtown areas in every major city in the United States. Both the theaters and the films were carried on the books for almost nothing but actually were worth fortunes. The book values in both cases were misleading as indicators of subsequent market values.

9. The company could just as easily have increased the dividend by $.05 a share to get the same cash effect.

EXHIBIT 10-3   Stock Certificate Issued by Eagle Corporation

Stock splits are similar to stock dividends in effect but are technically different; the par value per share is adjusted to offset the increased number of outstanding shares. For example, suppose the corporation declares a one-for-one split. There will now be two shares outstanding for each one that was outstanding prior to the split. If the par value was $100 prior to the split, it will be adjusted to $50 after the split. If the market price per share was $200 prior to the split, it should drop to approximately $100 after the split. One reason corporations split stock is to adjust the market price into some range where, in their opinion, they will capture the largest number of shareholders and a wider trading in the stock.

Another technique, the **reverse stock split,** is used more rarely than the stock split. The reverse stock reduces the number of shares outstanding with the purpose of raising the stock price into the desired trading range. A process somewhat similar to the reverse split is repurchase of the stock on the open market by the corporation when the stock is selling below book value. All splits, reverse splits, and market repurchase plans are in the nature of recapitalization plans and must be approved by a vote of the shareholders.

PREFERRED STOCK

If a corporation has only one class of stock outstanding, it is called **common stock.** To appeal to a broader base of investors, the corporation may issue additional classes of stock known as **preferred stock,** which gives stockholders certain preferential rights over holders of common stock. These rights usually involve priority rights over common stockholders in regard to receipt of dividends and receipt of assets in the event of liquidation of the corporation.

Preferred stock pays a dividend almost always stated as a fixed percentage of the original par value or as a fixed dollar amount per share.[10] For example, a $50 par value, $3.75 pfd. (preferred) stock means that the company is obligated to pay $3.75 a year on the par value of $50 as long as the company has sufficient earnings to cover the dividend. Dividends not paid accumulate as a debt of the corporation, and the corporation has to pay the accumulated dividend on the preferred stock before it can pay any dividend to the common stockholders. This feature is called **cumulative preferred.**

As an investment, a preferred stock is a hybrid that has features of both a stock and a bond. Like a bond, it has a preferred position over common stock in relation to corporate income (if earned) and corporate assets. Like a stock, it bears certain risks to which bonds are not exposed. For example, if the company earns no money, the company is not obligated to pay a dividend to the preferred stockholder, even though it still is obligated to pay interest on its bonded indebtedness.

These "hybrid" qualities of preferred stocks make them an unpopular type of investment for most investors. Investors owning preferred shares receive limited payments, as with bonds. Increased earnings do not normally increase preferred dividends. Decreased earnings often endanger the payment of the preferred dividend. Worst of all from the issuing corporation's viewpoint, the preferred dividend, unlike bond interest, is not deductible for corporate income taxes.

Regulation of Stock

All corporations that deal in interstate commerce are under the jurisdiction of the **Securities and Exchange Commission (SEC).** Because the number of corporations is so large, the SEC, as a practical matter, only involves itself in the affairs of corporations that have more than 500 shareholders and more than $1 million in assets. The commission's responsibility is to ensure that when new stock is sold to the public, the corporation in question discloses all significant facts to its stockholders and to the investing public. The com-

---

10. Some very rare preferred stocks are called **participating preferred shares.** In addition to the fixed preferred dividend, the holder of these shares participates in earnings in some designated manner over and above the stipulated preferred dividend.

pany must disclose everything, good and bad. For example, the occurrence of an oil strike must be disclosed before corporate insiders are allowed to trade in the stock of the oil company involved. If the company president is paid $1 million a year, that must also be disclosed. Companies are not permitted to distort or conceal facts that might affect a potential investor's judgment about the value of a stock.

Corporations must publish financial data that conform to generally accepted accounting principles and must use certified public accountants (CPAs) in the preparation of their financial statements. (The SEC insists on full disclosure of the facts, not on perfect, or even ethical, performance.) Company financial reports must conform to SEC standards. Companies must file with the SEC more detailed financial reports than they provide to their stockholders. Form 10-K, the report filed with the SEC, becomes a matter of public record. You may request a copy of a company's Form 10-K as well as its annual report.

In the annual election of the board of directors, the company solicits votes using what is called a **proxy statement,** which must contain information about how the chief executive officers of the corporation are compensated. Another piece of information filed with the SEC is material dealing with **insider trading** of stock—that is, trading by corporate officers, directors, and large stockholders.

THE LANGUAGE OF INVESTMENTS

The language of investments is widely known within the investment community but is unfamiliar to the uninitiated. The following sections discuss some of the commonly used terms.

Earnings per Share

Earnings per share (EPS) is the basic number used for stock market valuation purposes. How much did the company earn per share? Are the earnings increasing or decreasing? The pattern of EPS very often is the major factor in explaining the movement of stock prices. Rising corporate earnings are not as important to the investor as rising EPS. Increased earnings may not translate into increased EPS—and it is increased EPS that usually makes stock prices rise. Often corporations issue or sell new stock to corporate officers and stockholders, or even to the general public. If the number of shares outstanding increases faster than corporate earnings, EPS will not rise. For example, assume a corporation's earnings rose from $1 million to $1.5 million. When earnings were $1 million, 100,000 shares were outstanding, resulting in EPS of $10. During the period when earnings were rising to $1.5 million, the number of new shares issued or sold was 50,000. EPS after earnings rose to $1.5 million was still $10 ($1,500,000/150,000 shares). The stock price probably did not rise, even though earnings in dollars increased by 50 percent.

Price/Earnings Ratio

A concept universally used in the stock market is the derivative of the EPS—namely, the **price/earnings multiplier,** or **P/E ratio.** The P/E ratio is easily derived by dividing the current market price of the stock by its current earnings per share. This earnings multiplier shows the investor how many dollars must be paid for each dollar of corporate earnings. Investors compare ratios of stocks to past averages or to other competitive stock ratios in making investment decisions.

Exhibit 10–4 is a typical stock financial sheet, issued by Standard & Poor's Corporation, which analyzed the financial condition of International Business Machines (see Chapter 12 for more detailed analysis of financial information). The exhibit shows two aspects of earnings per share. First, we can read that earnings per share are as follows:

	1981	1980	1979	1978	1977
Earnings per share	$6.60 (est.)	$6.10	$5.16	$5.32	$4.58
P/E ratio (range)	10	12–8	16–12	15–11	16–13

Thus, earnings have increased at a 7.6 percent average annual rate.

Whether the price/earnings ratio of IBM indicates whether the stock is cheap or expensive is very difficult to say. Certainly the P/E ratio has been dropping since 1977; but this has been true for the market as a whole. By March 1981 the P/E ratio was 10, which means that the market was willing to pay $10 for each dollar of IBM earnings:

$$\frac{\text{Market price per share}}{\text{Earnings per share}} = \frac{63.25}{6.60} = 9.6, \text{ or 10 approximate.}$$

At that point in time, the market averages for all stocks were at about eight times earnings. That is, IBM sold for about a 25 percent premium per dollar of earnings as compared to the market as a whole.

Looking at the variation in the price/earnings ratio since 1977, we can see that as the stock price went up and down relative to the slowly growing earning per share, the P/E ratio varied an average of 36 percent—much greater than the average change in EPS, which was only 10 percent. Obviously, investors held many different opinions about the stock during the period from

"Your mission, if you decide to accept, is to find stocks with low P/E ratios."

The Bettman Archive, Inc.

1977 to 1981.[11] A more detailed discussion of the averages and their construction is contained in Chapter 12; see Exhibit 10–5 for a picture of a typical average and some statistics on different measures.

Stock Indexes

When we say that stocks are rising or falling, we must have some measure of stock market performance. These performance measures of market levels are called **stock indexes.** The three most widely used in the United States

---

11. John Maynard Keynes, the great English economist, was an avid speculator and investor who left a sizable personal fortune when he died. He once wrote that picking stocks successfully was like a newspaper contest where you had to pick the prettiest girl from the photos. The astute investor is not the one who picks what appears to be the prettiest girl; rather, the astute investor is the one who picks the girl whom the majority will pick as the prettiest girl. If you can pick the one the experts will pick as the one the general public will pick, you can make a fortune.

EXHIBIT 10-4

Typical Stock Financial Sheet

Int'l Business Machines

NYSE Symbol IBM Put & Call Options on CBOE

Price	Range	P-E Ratio	Dividend	Yield	S&P Ranking
Mar. 13'81 63¼	1981 71½-60¼	10	3.44	5.4%	A+

Summary

IBM is the world's largest manufacturer of computers and information processing equipment and systems. Earnings increased in 1980, following a rare decline in 1979, although unusual tax adjustments exaggerated the degree of improvement. Further gains are anticipated in 1981. Projected strong demand for improved productivity is expected to fuel long-term growth.

Current Outlook

Earnings for 1981 are estimated at $6.60 a share, versus 1980's $6.10 (which included gains of $0.38 from tax adjustments).

Dividends at $0.86 quarterly are the minimum expectation.

Although economic uncertainties in some geographic areas could be reflected in softenings of some order patterns, high backlogs and generally strong new order activity should lead to a good gain in revenues in 1981. Margins are likely to remain under pressure, partly due to continued major investments for future growth, but cost control and productivity programs may provide some relief. With demand for information processing and handling products expected to rise steadily, IBM's leading position in the industry, together with its ongoing commitment to technological innovation to meet the need for improved productivity, should enable it to maintain strong growth rates over the longer term.

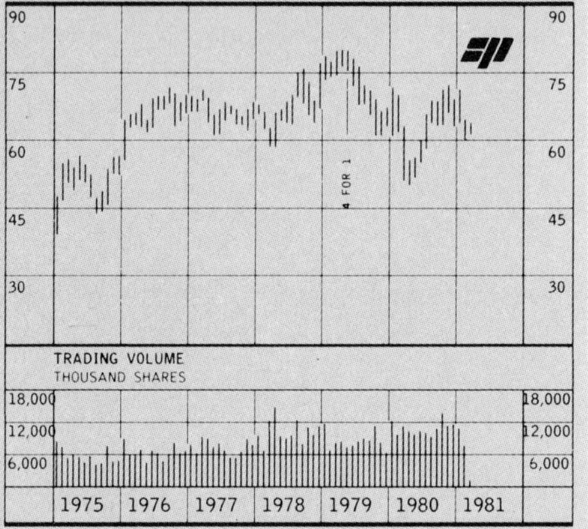

Gross Income (Billion $)

Quarter:	1980	1979	1978	1977
Mar.	5.75	5.30	4.43	4.09
Jun.	6.18	5.35	4.92	4.42
Sep.	6.48	5.38	5.28	4.59
Dec.	7.81	6.83	6.44	5.04
	26.21	22.86	21.07	18.14

Revenues for 1980 advanced 15%, year to year, aided by an improved purchase/lease mix for data processing equipment, and much higher service revenues. Larger cost increases limited the gain in pretax earnings to 6.2%, but tax adjustments reduced the effective tax rate, and net income rose 18%.

Capital Share Earnings ($)

Quarter:	1980	1979	1978	1977
Mar.	1.17	1.14	1.00	0.96
Jun.	1.31	1.15	1.19	1.11
Sep.	1.51	1.14	1.39	1.17
Dec.	2.11	1.73	1.74	1.35
	6.10	5.16	5.32	4.59

Important Developments

Nov. '80—IBM introduced its largest computer, the 3081. IBM said that the 3081 offered twice the internal performance of the 3033, its previous largest processor, with significantly reduced space, cooling and power requirements. The 3081 was priced at $3.7 million for purchase, and initial shipments were scheduled for the fourth quarter of 1981.

Next earnings report due in mid-April.

Per Share Data ($)

Yr. End Dec. 31	1980	1979	1978	1977	1976	1975	1974	1973	1972	1971
Book Value	**NA**	25.64	23.14	21.39	21.15	19.05	17.05	15.02	13.00	11.50
Earnings	**6.10**	5.16	5.32	[1]4.58	[1]3.99	3.34	[1]3.12	[1]2.70	[1]2.21	[1]1.88
Dividends	**3.44**	3.44	2.88	2.50	2.00	1.62½	1.39	1.12	1.08	1.04
Payout Ratio	**56%**	67%	54%	54%	50%	49%	45%	42%	49%	56%
Prices—High	**72¾**	80½	77½	71½	72⅛	56⅞	63½	91⅜	85⅜	73¼
Low	**50⅜**	61⅛	58¾	61⅛	55⅞	39⅜	37⅝	58⅞	66⅜	56¾
P/E Ratio—	**12-8**	16-12	15-11	16-13	18-14	17-12	20-12	34-22	39-30	39-30

Data as orig. reptd. Adj. for stk. div(s). of 300% Jun. 1979, 25% May 1973. **1.** Ful. dil.: 4.57 in 1977, 3.98 in 1976, 3.12 in 1974, 2.69 in 1973, 2.21 in 1972, 1.88 in 1971. NA-Not Available.

Income Data (Million $)

Year Ended Dec. 31	Revs.	Oper. Inc.	% Oper. Inc. of Revs.	Cap. Exp.	Depr.	Int. Exp.	Net Bef. Taxes	Eff. Tax Rate	Net Inc.	% Net Inc. of Revs.
1979	22,863	7,215	31.6%	5,991	1,970	140	5,553	45.8%	3,011	13.2%
1978	21,076	7,265	34.5%	4,046	1,824	55	5,798	46.3%	3,111	14.8%
1977	18,133	6,657	36.7%	3,395	1,999	40	5,092	46.6%	2,719	15.0%
1976	16,304	5,928	36.4%	2,518	1,858	45	4,519	46.9%	2,398	14.7%
1975	14,437	5,245	36.3%	2,439	1,822	63	3,721	46.5%	1,990	13.8%
1974	12,675	4,871	38.4%	2,913	1,708	69	3,435	46.5%	1,838	14.5%
1973	10,993	4,363	39.7%	2,186	1,589	97	2,946	46.5%	1,575	14.3%
1972	9,533	3,731	39.1%	1,728	1,419	78	2,425	47.3%	1,279	13.4%
1971	8,274	3,228	39.0%	1,882	1,254	70	2,056	47.5%	1,079	13.0%
1970	7,504	3,051	40.7%	2,160	1,169	50	2,012	49.4%	1,018	13.6%

Balance Sheet Data (Million $)

Dec. 31	Cash	Current Assets	Current Liab.	Ratio	Total Assets	Ret. on Assets	Long Term Debt	Common Equity	Total Cap.	% LT Debt of Cap.	Ret. on Equity
1979	3,771	10,851	6,445	1.7	24,530	13.3%	1,589	14,961	16,690	9.5%	21.2%
1978	4,031	10,321	5,810	1.8	20,771	15.7%	286	13,494	13,889	2.1%	24.0%
1977	5,407	10,073	5,209	1.9	18,978	15.0%	256	12,618	12,962	2.0%	21.7%
1976	6,156	9,920	4,082	2.4	17,723	14.4%	275	12,749	13,088	2.1%	19.8%
1975	4,768	8,115	3,363	2.4	15,531	13.4%	295	11,416	11,756	2.5%	18.4%
1974	3,805	7,010	3,210	2.2	14,027	13.9%	336	10,110	10,482	3.2%	19.3%
1973	3,322	5,830	2,555	2.3	12,290	13.6%	652	8,812	9,496	6.9%	19.2%
1972	2,577	4,822	2,259	2.1	10,792	12.5%	773	7,566	8,367	9.2%	17.9%
1971	1,875	3,949	2,088	1.9	9,576	11.9%	676	6,642	7,358	9.2%	17.1%
1970	1,339	3,389	1,877	1.8	8,539	12.7%	573	5,947	6,570	8.7%	18.1%

Data as orig. reptd.

Business Summary

IBM is primarily involved in information-handling systems, equipment and services.

1980	Gross Inc.	Op. Income
Data processing	82%	91%
Office products	16%	8%
Federal systems	2%	1%

Outright sales provided 42% of revenues in 1980, rentals 41%, and services 17%. Operations outside of the U.S. contributed 53% of both revenues and earnings.

In the data processing segment, IBM provides a wide range of computer products, systems and software, as well as systems engineering, education and related services and supplies.

Office products include electric and electronic typewriters, magnetic media typewriters and systems, information processors, printers, copiers and related supplies and services.

The Federal systems business supplies specialized information handling products and services, primarily for U.S. government space, defense and other agencies.

IBM also offers educational, training and testing materials and services for school, home and industrial use.

Dividend Data

Dividends have been paid since 1916. A dividend reinvestment plan is available.

Amt. of Divd. $	Date Decl.	Ex-divd. Date	Stock of Record	Payment Date
0.86	Apr. 28	May 8	May 14	Jun. 10'80
0.86	Jul. 29	Aug. 7	Aug. 13	Sep. 10'80
0.86	Oct. 28	Nov. 5	Nov. 12	Dec. 10'80
0.86	Jan. 27	Feb. 5	Feb. 11	Mar. 10'81

Next dividend meeting: late Apr. '81.

Finances

Tax adjustments applicable to reductions of tax liabilities in prior periods added $224 million ($0.38 a share) to net income in 1980.

Capitalization

Long Term Debt: $2,099,000,000.

Capital Stock: 583,806,832 shs. ($1.25 par). Institutions hold approximately 49%. Shareholders: 737,230.

Office—Armonk, New York 10504. Tel—(914) 765-1900. Stockholder Relations Dept—717 Fifth Ave., NYC 10022. Tel—(212) 223-4400. Chrmn—F. T. Cary. Pres & CEO—J. R. Opel. Secy—J. H. Grady. Treas—C. A. Northrop. Investor Contact—D. Otis. Dirs—S. D. Bechtel, Jr., G. B. Beitzel, J. E. Burke, F. T. Cary, W. T. Coleman, Jr., J. M. Fox, G. K. Funston, C. A. Hills, A. Houghton, Jr., J. N. Irwin II, N. deB. Katzenbach, T. V. Learson, R. W. Lyman, D. R. McKay, M. McK. Moller, W. H. Moore, J. R. Munro, J. R. Opel, P. J. Rizzo, W. W. Scranton, I. S. Shapiro, C. R. Vance, T. J. Watson, Jr., A. L. Williams. Transfer Agents—Company's NYC & Chicago offices. Registrars—Morgan Guaranty Trust Co., NYC; First National Bank, Chicago. Incorporated in New York in 1911.

EXHIBIT 10-5
Common Stock Prices and Yields

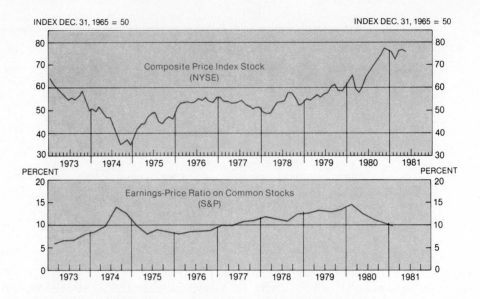

	Common stock prices[1]						Common stock yields percent[5]	
	New York Stock Exchanges index (Dec. 31, 1965 = 50)[2]					Dow-Jones industrial average[3]	Standard & Poor's composite index (1941-43 = 10)[4]	Dividend/ price ratio	Earnings/ price ratio
Period	Composite	Industrial	Transpor- tation	Utility	Finance				
1975	45.73	50.52	31.10	31.50	47.14	802.49	86.16	4.31	9.15
1976	54.46	60.44	39.57	36.97	52.94	974.92	102.01	3.77	8.90
1977	53.69	57.86	41.09	40.92	55.25	894.63	98.20	4.62	10.79
1978	53.70	58.23	43.50	39.22	56.65	820.23	96.02	5.28	12.03
1979	58.32	64.76	47.34	38.21	61.42	844.40	103.01	5.47	13.46
1980	68.10	78.70	60.61	37.35	64.25	891.41	118.78	5.26	12.65
1980: May	61.38	69.39	51.07	37.31	61.47	828.19	107.69	5.77	
June	65.43	74.47	54.04	38.53	65.16	869.86	114.55	5.39	13.08
July	68.56	78.67	59.14	38.77	66.76	909.79	119.83	5.20	
Aug	70.87	82.15	62.48	38.18	67.22	947.33	123.50	5.06	
Sept	73.12	84.92	65.89	38.77	69.33	946.67	126.51	4.90	11.67
Oct	75.17	88.00	70.76	38.44	68.29	949.17	130.22	4.80	
Nov	78.15	92.32	77.23	38.35	67.21	971.08	135.65	4.63	
Dec	76.69	90.37	75.74	37.84	67.46	945.96	133.48	4.74	10.88
1981: Jan	76.24	89.23	74.43	38.53	70.04	962.13	132.97	4.80	
Feb	73.52	85.74	72.76	37.59	68.48	945.50	128.40	5.00	
Mar	76.46	89.39	77.09	37.82	72.82	987.18	133.19	4.88	
Apr	77.60	90.57	80.63	38.34	74.59	1,004.86	134.43	4.86	
May	76.28	88.78	76.78	38.27	74.65	979.52	131.73	4.98	
Week ended:									
1981: Apr 25	77.69	90.59	80.67	38.46	75.25	1,011.90	134.58	4.87	
May 2	77.24	90.11	78.54	38.14	75.30	1,007.73	133.68	4.92	
9	75.73	88.47	75.72	37.44	73.10	975.94	131.02	5.02	
16	75.75	88.08	75.89	38.45	73.62	972.21	130.89	5.01	
23	76.49	88.86	77.22	38.60	75.47	978.19	131.94	4.97	
30	77.27	89.75	78.46	38.80	76.86	990.78	133.15	4.92	

1. Average of daily closing prices.
2. Includes all the stocks (more than 1,500) listed on the NYSE.
3. Includes 30 stocks.   4. Includes 500 stocks.
5. Standard & Poor's series. Dividend/price ratios based on Wednesday closing prices.
Earnings/price ratios based on prices at end of quarter.
Note: All data relate to stocks listed on the New York Stock Exchange (NYSE).

Source: *Economic Indicators* (Washington, D.C.: U.S. Government Printing Office, 1982).

are the Dow Jones Industrial Average (DJIA), the Standard and Poor's 500 (S&P), and the New York Stock Exchange Index. (Indexes are described in more detail in Chapter 12.)

Cyclical and Growth Stocks

Many different ways of classifying and describing stocks exist. Two major classes are cyclical stocks and growth stocks.

CYCLICAL STOCKS

The typical industrial stock fluctuates with the market and with general economic conditions—hence it is called **cyclical stock.** If the market drops, cyclical stock will drop proportionally with the market; if the market rises, the stock will also rise proportionally. However, if companies are heavily **leveraged,** their stock will drop even more than proportionally with the market—that is, they carry more market risk.[12] Similarly, when the market rises, their stock will tend to rise more than proportionally.

GROWTH STOCKS

A **growth stock** frequently sells for very high earnings multiples (i.e., has a high P/E ratio), typically pays little or no dividend, and involves a product that is usually something on the frontier of science.[13] But beyond these characteristics, growth stocks possess a glamorous mystique that makes the investing public very much aware of the doings of the typically small companies that issue the stocks.

Finding growth stocks is not easy. The best thing to look for is a growth in earnings per share at a rate faster than the real growth of the economy plus the inflation rate. Generally speaking, 15 to 20 percent growth in earnings per share each year for five years qualifies a company as a growth company.

What makes a growth stock desirable is its accelerated growth of earnings per share. In a typical company, earnings might grow at an average rate of 8 percent compounded annually. In this case earnings will double every

---

12. Leverage refers to the proportion of debt in the capital structure of the corporation. The greater the proportion of debt to equity, the greater will be the change in earnings per share relative to a given change in earnings.

13. Sometimes a growth stock is identified with producing an old product in a new manner—for example, McDonald's and Howard Johnson's were once identified as strong growth stocks. Sometimes the growth stock consists only of an illusion—National Student Marketing is perhaps the most famous example of illusionary growth. Teledyne grew by choosing an electronic-sounding name and maintained growth through clever merger tactics.

9 years.[14] If the company consistently sells for eight times earnings, it is worth $8 for every dollar of current earnings and will be worth $16 in 9 years. But suppose the stock was a growth stock growing at 16 percent a year; the stock should double in price in 4.5 years. Stock that doubles in half the time is very valuable, and the investor will typically pay a premium for this faster growth.

The magic of growth can be demonstrated by an example. Suppose we have three stocks: A, B, and C. All stocks initially earn $1 a year and sell for $6 a share. Suppose earnings grow at 8 percent annually for A, 16 percent for B, and 24 percent for C. Earnings at the end of five years, based on the annual growth rate, will be shown in Exhibit 10–6. But the "magic" is that investors are willing to pay more for growth. For example, they might pay 50 percent more for B's earnings (P/E ratio of 9 vs. 6) and 200 percent more for C's (P/E ratio of 18 vs. 6). The exhibit shows that you can do much better if you can find C's stocks as compared to A's stocks. Earnings in the fifth year are almost double for C as compared to A ($2.93 vs. $1.47), but the stock is worth almost six times as much ($52.74 vs. $8.82). Investors are willing to pay for expected future earnings as well as current earnings.

Growth Curves. One important fact to remember about growth stocks is that companies are no different from any other observable social, physical, or economic phenomenon. When companies or organizations "take off," growth occurs first at an accelerating rate and then at a decreasing rate; finally growth ceases entirely. For example, the physical growth of an infant first occurs at an accelerating rate (from birth to age four or five), then at a decreasing rate (ages five to twenty), and then not at all. So it is with growth companies; not many people can recall when Xerox was still a small office-machinery company. Likewise, punch cards were used as far back as 1890, but before 1950 it would have been difficult to identify IBM for the growth company it was. Often, by the time the outside investor recognizes a growth company, the growth rate has slowed.

Primary and Secondary Markets

Corporate securities are sold in two distinctive markets, generally called primary and secondary. A **primary market** refers to the original-issue market, where securities are sold by the corporation directly to the investor. (Insofar as corporations issue stock to their own executives, families, and friends, no organized market is required. But in the case of giant corporations like Exxon

---

14. These calculations are based on the rule of 72. Divide the growth rate into 72 and you will find how long it will take the sum to double. The rule of thumb is quite accurate. For example, the actual doubling period is 9.01 years for 8%, and 4.67 years for 16%.

EXHIBIT 10-6

Investment Results under Different Growth Assumptions

	Stock A	Stock B	Stock C
Annual growth rate	8%	16%	24%
Past year			
Price	$6.00	$6.00	$6.00
Earnings	$1.00	$1.00	$1.00
P/E ratio	6×	6×	6×
Year 5			
Price	$8.82	$18.90	$52.74
Earnings	$1.47	$2.10	$2.93
P/E ratio	6×	9×	18×

or Xerox, their capital needs are so immense that an organized procedure is needed to market their original issues.)

Almost all stockbrokers are also investment bankers. An **investment banking firm** or **underwriter** purchases securities at the time of issue from a corporation and then sells them at slightly higher prices to the general public. This process is called underwriting and is a part of the primary security market. The **secondary markets** refers to the vast stock and bond markets where securities are traded by investors after having been issued by corporations.

PRIMARY MARKETS

A full description of all the underwriting functions of investment bankers is beyond the scope of this book. One basic underwriting function has to do with primary markets. The typical process involves the XYZ Corporation arranging through an investment banker—for example, the Morgan Stanley Company of New York—to sell to the general public 1 million shares of XYZ stock at $50 a share. The actual price at which the stock will be sold is determined at the last minute by the underwriting firm. If the company were well known and financially sound, Morgan Stanley would agree to underwrite the issue and might pay as much as $47.50 for the stock and sell it to the public for $50. The difference between the price per share paid to the company and the price paid by the investing public is known as the **spread** on the transaction.

SECONDARY MARKETS

Another basic underwriting function involves secondary markets. Once the stocks and bonds have been issued and sold, they enter the secondary market, the world of the organized securities markets such as the New York Stock Exchange, the American Stock Exchange, various regional exchanges, and the huge over-the-counter market (OTC).

A **stock exchange** is essentially a national marketplace where securities buyers and sellers are brought together. Securities are bought and sold in a constantly active auction market. Without such an exchange a seller of stock in Portland, Oregon, for example, would need to find another person in Portland wanting to buy that particular stock. But the Portland seller can sell a particular stock much more easily and rapidly if the stock is offered for sale in New York, where buyers from all areas are concentrated through the stock market mechanism.

For the market to work effectively, **stockbrokers** must act as "middlemen." The broker receives the order to sell in Portland. The broker wires the offer to sell, either at the market price or at some designated price, to a representative at the New York Stock Exchange. The floor broker representing the firm then goes to the post on the floor of the exchange where that stock is sold and offers it at the highest price bid by other brokers with buy orders for the stock. When the deal is made, both brokers file slips confirming the same sale. The price is flashed to the central reporting station, which notifies the markets all over the world, through the stock ticker, of the completed transaction. Within four days after the transaction, the buyer pays for the stock and pays the broker's commission and fees, and the seller's account is credited in the amount of the sale less broker's commission and fees. The process is efficient and rapid.

The **stock ticker** (tape) is the record of each transaction occurring on the floor of the exchange. While the process is now totally automated, on very busy days (days on which the share volume is greater than 50 million shares) the tape may fall behind actual trades. This slowdown can cause fifteen-minute to half-hour delays in reporting of prices.

Before the stock can be sold to the public, it must be registered with the Securities and Exchange Commission (SEC). Details of the issue and of the corporation are contained in a document called the **prospectus.** Theoretically, every buyer of the new securities must receive a prospectus before purchase. This prospectus must be totally correct and totally revealing. Under the SEC policy of full disclosure, all information must be provided, even if some of it is negative. After the prospectus is prepared, the major underwriter forms a syndicate of selling firms. These firms share partially in the spread and sell the securities directly to the investing public. In case they cannot sell the securities, the underwriters are obligated to purchase the stock for their own accounts. In case of a change in securities prices, an international crisis, or any random event that affects security prices, the underwriting firms, once committed, must bear the risk.

Commissions

The business of stockbrokering involves earning commissions from both buyer and seller. Generally speaking, the larger the purchase, the proportionally smaller the commission. Assuming that the client buys or sells a **round lot** (100 shares), the typical broker will earn a commission that approximates 2 percent of the market value of the securities traded. Brokers no longer charge on a fixed-commission scale; large retail brokerage firms will typically be a few dollars apart on their commissions.

In recent years a new type of broker has developed: the **discount broker.** A typical discount broker might advertise in the *Wall Street Journal* and offer to buy 500 shares of a $20 stock for a commission of $80, compared to a typical $205 charge for the same service from a large brokerage house. If investors do not need investment aid, financial information, advice, brokerage letters, and the like, they are well advised to use a discount broker. The discount broker will provide market quotes, a monthly statement, and little else. Beginning investors should probably not use a discount broker, since beginners usually need market advice and some "hand holding."

Odd Lots

Many small investors do not buy in round lots. If an investor buys only 50 shares of a stock, for example, the broker turns to an **odd lot broker** who sells (or buys) the odd lot from inventory and typically charges one-quarter of a point ($.25) on stocks priced more than $55 a share and one-eighth of a point ($.125) for stocks priced lower than $55. The broker, in turn, adds the odd lot broker's commission to the price.

Over-the-Counter Market (OTC)

The **over-the-counter market (OTC)** is the largest security market in terms of dollar volume and number of issues traded. This market trades everything from U.S. government negotiable securities to the stocks of small, publicly traded companies. It is a market for the thousands of smaller, regional, less well known stocks. It is the market, for example, for the majority of banks that are publicly traded. Roughly one out of four shares traded in the United States are bought and sold in the OTC.

The method of trading on the OTC market is quite different from the regular exchanges, which are auction markets. The OTC is a **dealer market.** When the investor places an order to buy or to sell in the OTC, the investor is dealing with a broker/dealer who sells or buys the stock. (Note the difference between the OTC and the stock exchange, where the broker brings buyer and seller together and makes a commission.) The broker/dealer in the OTC, for example, makes a market in the XYZ stock. The dealer offers to buy XYZ stock at $29 a share (the **bid price**) or offers to sell the stock at $30 per share (the **ask price**). The dealer makes a profit (rather than a commission) from the spread between the bid price and the ask price.

Bulls and Bears

The terminology of the market is full of special jargon, the most familiar of which are the terms "bulls" and "bears." A **bull** is an investor who buys in anticipation of a rising market. This optimistic view surely applies to most people. A **bear,** a much rarer animal, is one who anticipates falling markets and therefore **sells short** or waits for lower prices to enter the market.[15]

A **bull market** is a rising market characterized by rising prices, rising stock volume, increasing new issues, and a general feeling of investor euphoria. Because of the laws of supply and demand in the marketplace, investor euphoria is always reinforced by rising prices, which bring the happy expectations of rising prices to fulfillment. That is, expectations of rising prices increase the demand for stocks, which increases the prices, which increase the demand. The long bull market of the 1960s, for example, was a self-fulfilling prophecy.

A **bear market** is one in which prices are falling. The outlook is bleak, and buyers stand on the sideline, many with funds committed to **short positions.** A short position is when a trader has "sold short" a number of stocks in the belief their prices will fall. Literally, the trader has bet money on this belief. Bears are pessimists and suffer from melancholia, the opposite of euphoria.

The pattern of bull and bear markets is such that rising markets typically take a long time to develop before they reach their peak. Bear markets are usually short and savage. The average bull market is often three to four times as long as a bear market. In other periods (1978–1981, for example), no discernible trends exist and the market drifts back and forth in a narrow trading range.

Stop Orders

Most investors do not have the time or the inclination to be totally involved with their investments. They go away on vacations, become preoccupied with career and families, and don't supervise investments very closely. Certainly they are not **tape watchers,** investors who haunt brokers' of-

---

15. Selling short refers to borrowing a security, selling it, putting up the cash proceeds as collateral for the loan on the stock and then hoping that the security will fall in price. If the stock does fall in price, the short seller buys the stock in the market, replaces it in the loan, and gets back the cash collateral. If the speculator sells short at $100 and the stock then falls to $50, the short seller makes $50 a share profit, less commissions. If instead the stock goes up to $150, the investor takes a loss of $50 a share. Short selling has a few rules that make it even riskier and more expensive. While the investor waits for the fall in the stock, the lender of the shares has the use of the money. Every dividend or other distribution while the investor is short the security becomes an obligation. Further, it is almost impossible by stock exchange rules to short the stock in a falling market. Short selling is pure speculation and is not covered further in this book.

"There are bulls and then there are bears, but dinosaurs?"

The Bettman Archive, Inc.

fices, their eyes glued to the minute-by-minute quotations of stock prices as they are flashed on the tape (really an electronic display board). Tape watchers believe that monitoring prices gives them important clues as to what prices will do in the near future.

One way to guard against disaster arising out of inattention is to use market techniques called stop orders and limit orders. A **stop order** is always associated with a stock sale at a price lower than the present market price. Suppose your stock is selling for $50, that you are going to Europe for a two-week vacation, and that you do not want to be exposed to any loss greater than 20 percent. You leave a stop order with your broker, good for two weeks, to sell the stock if the price drops to $40. If the stock reaches $40, the specialist broker with whom the stop order has been left will sell the stock.

In the same way you can leave a **limit order** to sell a stock in a rising market. In the above example $60 seems like a reasonable profit, so you leave an order to sell the stock if it rises to $60. Limit orders to buy at a designated price—invariably below the market—can also be left and executed by the specialist broker. As securities prices fluctuate, buy or sell orders are activated, and the specialist broker completes the transaction. Limit orders must be placed for specific prices and are usually placed for specific periods like one day, one week, or one month.

Institutional Buying

Increasingly, financial and other institutions (as opposed to individuals) are among the most important buyers of securities. The fastest-growing class of investors in the United States is composed of managers of pension funds. Pension funds are usually very conservatively managed; the preponderance of such funds are in corporate bonds.[16] Smaller percentages—typically 10 to 20 percent of the total—are in stocks, and rarely more than 10 percent are usually found in mortgages. With interest rates at record-high levels and becoming more volatile, pension funds have tended to shift away from traditional, long-term investments and more toward liquid, short-term debt securities such as commercial paper and treasury bills.

Institutional buying on the part of pension funds, trust companies, insurance companies, and other corporations has had an important impact on the securities markets. Many analysts watch buying patterns of institutions for guidance as to which securities to buy or sell. Institutions tend to copy one another and can cause some security prices to fluctuate widely.

Regional Markets

Among the many forces that influence the stock market is the impact of regional forces on certain companies. In recent years resources and population have shifted to the "sun belt." Houston, Tampa, Phoenix, San Diego, and Fort Lauderdale are the rapid-growth metropolitan areas of the 1980s. Chicago, New York, Boston, Pittsburgh, Akron, and Saint Louis are examples of metropolitan areas whose rates of growth have slowed or ceased. Businesses that primarily service growth areas have a natural advantage; their sales and profits increase more rapidly.

---

16. Almost all pension funds make self-limiting rules as to what investments they can or cannot make. For example, they typically do not buy bonds that are not in the first three investment grades. They also limit the amount of funds they will put in a particular industry or in a particular company in the industry.

All these factors should be reflected in a better market for selected stocks. Examples might be a bank in Phoenix, a department store in the San Francisco Bay area, or a restaurant chain based in South Florida.

INVESTING IN STOCKS AND BONDS

This chapter has discussed the "what-is-it" aspect of stocks and bonds. The next chapter discusses the "how-to-do-it" aspect. First, however, a comment is in order on the major advantages and risks of both kinds of securities.

Stocks are usually the investment vehicle of the far-seeing optimist. The investor hopes for financial growth through purchases of stock in profitable companies with proven success records or in new companies with great potential. The successful investor usually secures a return on the investment in the form of dividends as well as a gain due to the appreciation in market value of the stock.

As opposed to "the good news," what is the potential "bad news" about stocks? Any stock buyer must share in the company's fortunes, both good and bad. Profits may not materialize as expected. Earnings projected to rise may in fact fall. The economy as a whole or the specific industry may fall on hard times. All these factors may have an adverse impact on the company, on its earnings, and on stock prices. Moreover, the stock market is like a leaf in a hurricane of changing investor expectations; the market goes up with the expectation of good news and may just as quickly fall when the good news is not good enough. Optimism may change to pessimism overnight, and stocks may slide rapidly.

Bonds, on the other hand, do not fluctuate for the same reasons as stocks. Most bonds are immune to rumors about earnings and markets. Even if bad times come, the interest payment has to be paid. As long as the corporation survives, it must pay the interest coupon on its bonds and the face value of the bonds at maturity. Assuming that the bond investor stays away from speculative risks, the risks are considerably less than the risks of owning stocks. Exhibit 10–7 presents a comparison of the differences between stocks and bonds.

As interest rates have risen to unprecedented levels and inflation has eroded the value of promises to pay in the future, bonds are no longer risk-free. As inflation rises, the promise to pay a set amount of money in the future has less value at the present moment. As inflation rises to the double-digit level, interest rates must rise to keep pace. Rising interest rates make fixed-payment securities less valuable. The price of older bonds with lower interest coupons falls badly on high-interest-rate markets. The promise to pay has not been threatened—only the value of that promise.

EXHIBIT 10-7   Differences between Stocks and Bonds

	Voting Rights	Income	Priority of Claim	Unit of Purchase	Price Stability
Stocks	Common: 1 vote 1 share.	Common: tends to vary with corporate income; not fixed.	Common: residual (left over) after all prior claims paid.	Stocks are usually sold in units of 100 shares. Value can be anything from pennies to thousands of dollars.	Market varies according to number of shares out-standing relative to corporate income. Changing investor perception of future causes prices to vary.
	Preferred: non-voting unless dividend not paid.	Preferred: fixed as long as corporate income suf-ficient. If not paid, accumu-lates as claim against corporate income.	Preferred: same as common except prior to common.		
Bonds	Nonvoting.	Interest income paid by check or coupon.	Prior claim against cor-porate income and assets before any form of stockholder claim. Bonds represent debt. Some bonds are mortgage bonds, and some specific asset is pledged as collateral.	Bonds are usually sold in multiples of $1,000.	Bond values vary relative to changes in interest rates. Sometimes bond prices change according to condition of firm.

SUMMARY

1. Stocks are the evidence of ownership in private corporations. Investors in stocks expect to receive dividends and to realize an increase in the market value of their shares. Preferred stocks are a cross between stocks and bonds; they are preferred with reference to payment of the dividend and to the receipt of assets in the event of corporate liquidation, but they do not share in any increased profits made by the corporation issuing them.

2. Bonds carry a pledge to pay a given sum of money (interest) over the life of the bond plus the face value of the bond at maturity. Because they are a prior claim against the income and assets of the corporation, corporate bonds have less financial risk than stocks. Convertible bonds are a cross between stocks and bonds in that they give the protection of bonds and a possible increase in market value if the stock goes up in price.

3. Government securities are of two major types. U.S. government securities are totally free from financial risk but are subject to changing interest rates. Bonds issued by state and local governments do have some financial risk, but enjoy total exemption from federal taxes. Thus, they are very attractive to institutional and high-tax-bracket investors.

4. Yield can be calculated in three different ways. Essentially, the problem is how to estimate the present values of monies to be paid in the future.

5. Stock splits and stock dividends are means of giving the stockholders something at a minimum cost to the corporation. Generally speaking, receiving a stock dividend or stock split does not increase the wealth of the stockholder.

6. The Securities and Exchange Commission is the federal government agency charged with overseeing corporate financial reporting and securities markets. Its major objective is to see that everything of financial significance is reported to investors and to the public.

7. Earnings per share and how it changes is the key financial variable looked at by professional investors. Most skilled investors compare values by determining the relative price and trends of how much must be paid for a share per dollar of earnings.

8. Stocks are of two basic types. The ordinary industrial, or cyclical, stock moves with the market. Growth stocks are those of a company that either is producing a new product or is producing an old product in a new way and is thus creating an above-average rate of growth of earnings. Such companies are usually very difficult to identify early enough for the investor to make a huge profit.

9. Primary markets refer to the new-issues markets where corporations sell their securities directly to investors via the underwriting services of investment bankers. Secondary security markets refer to the stock exchanges and the huge over-the-counter markets where securities already issued are sold by investors to other investors.

10. "Bulls" and "bears" refer to the psychology of investors. Bulls, the typical investors, expect stock to rise. Bears are the pessimists who either sell short or stay out of the market while looking for bargains.

11. When buying securities, investors should be aware of several factors—namely, policies of institutional investors, government actions, and regional considerations. All these pressures are difficult to track and interpret.

12. Risk is always present in investment. The markets for stocks are subject to changes in the company and changes in investor sentiment. Bonds are less subject to changes in corporate fortunes and investor sentiment, but bond prices are very sensitive to changes in interest rates. Interest rates, in turn, are affected severely by investor estimates of future inflation.

QUESTIONS

1. Ownership of corporate stock entitles the investor to certain rights. What are the major rights?

2. (a) What is a bond?
   (b) What are the rights that a bondholder has as compared to a stockholder?

3. Contrast debenture bonds with mortgage bonds.

4. You buy IBM for $56 when it is paying a dividend of $3.44 a year, and you sell it for $60 one year later.
   (a) What is the current yield?
   (b) What is the holding period yield?

5. Contrast a stock split with a stock dividend.

6. Stock splits increase the number of shares outstanding.
   (a) How does this affect stock price?
   (b) How does it affect par value?

7. Why are preferred stocks considered the "worst of both worlds"?

8. What is the basic function of the Securities and Exchange Commission?

9. What are the major signs the investor should look for in earnings per share?

10. What major factors must be present for a company to be identified as a "growth company"?

11. In underwriting, why do you suppose that stock is never issued at a price greater than the market price of the current outstanding stock?

12. What major function does the stock market perform?

13. What is the fundamental difference between the way the over-the-counter-market works as opposed to stock exchange transactions?

14. Explain the difference between "bulls" and "bears."

15. What is a stop order?

16. Why must the investor pay attention not only to economic news but also to the general news in attempting to make wise investment decisions?

17. Why are government actions so difficult to assess relative to the stock market?

18. (a) Define risk.
    (b) Why is risk so important to investing?

19. What are the risks associated with investing in bonds?

20. What is the major advantage of U.S. Savings Bonds?

21. (a) How does the lower yield of a tax-exempt security translate into a higher effective rate for some high-income investors?
    (b) How much would you need to earn to make tax-exempt securities worthwhile for you?

22. Why do bond prices fall as interest rates rise? Give a numerical example.

CASE PROBLEMS

I. Convertible Bonds

The XYZ Company stock sells for $50 a share and pays a $2-a-share dividend. At the same time the company sells a new convertible bond for $1,000, yielding $120 a year. The bond is convertible into fifteen shares of common stock. Debts of similar-quality companies at the same maturity are selling to yield 13 percent.

QUESTIONS

1. What is the bond worth as a bond?

2. If you were told that earnings and dividends would double in four years and that continued growth at the same rate was predicted for another four years, what would be the best course of action with regard to buying the convertible bond?

II. Identifying Growth Companies _____

The Electronic Chicken Company has experienced marvelous growth. Because of the tremendous market acceptance of its product, sales have doubled over the last five years. Corporate profits are increasing at a rate that doubles every 10 years. The product has achieved market acceptance by a great marketing program, but, except for the copyrighted name, there is nothing really different about the product.

QUESTION

1. Do you think Electronic Chicken is a growth company?

III. Effect of Stock Splits _____

Mrs. Patricia Curry owns 100 shares of the Blue Bell Telephone Company. The stock has a par value of $20.00, a book value of $30.00, earnings per share of $4.00, a dividend of $2.00, and a price of $40.00. Blue Bell announces a 2/1 split and a new dividend of $1.25 per share.

QUESTION

1. Explain what you think will happen to each of the numbers given in the case.

CHAPTER 11

INVESTMENT GOALS AND STRATEGIES

LEARNING OBJECTIVES

In studying this chapter you will learn:

How to set investment goals;

What are the types of investment risk;

How to align investment goals with appropriate investments;

What are the major types of investment theory;

How to control for investment risk.

This chapter discusses the two foundations of a successful investment program. First, through consideration of your future goals, you must determine the purpose for which you are undertaking an investment program. Second, once your goals are set, you must devise investment strategies to achieve these goals.

SETTING INVESTMENT GOALS

The first step in successful investing is to decide which investment goals have priority and to determine the time frame within which the goals can be met. These decisions depend substantially on what stage of the financial life cycle you are in. A typical set of goals is shown in Exhibit 11–1.

Risk

Risk is the possibility of incurring an outcome different from the one planned. **Speculative risk** involves buying a given asset in the hope that its price will rise; of course, prices fall as well as rise. Fundamental to successful investing is deciding how much speculative risk you wish or can afford to take. Young people with good future prospects can perhaps accept more risks than older people nearing retirement; young people have time to recoup losses, whereas older people may not be able to make certain investments that pose greater risk than others.

Normally, higher rewards and less liquidity tend to accompany higher risks. In deciding how much risk you can take, ask yourself the following questions:

1. If I should lose my investment entirely, would it seriously disrupt my normal living standard?
2. Would I worry unduly if the value of my investment fluctuated upward and downward over some period of time?
3. How much return am I seeking within the investment planning period? (By what percentage am I trying to increase my fund during the investment planning period?)
4. If I should require funds for an emergency, would I be able to liquidate my investment without undue loss?
5. Do I have the time and ability to supervise my investments on a continuous basis?

EXHIBIT 11–1   Life Cycle Goals and Conditions

Stage of Life Cycle	Typical Goals	Conditions
1. Young, single working person	To start a business; to purchase a car	Emphasis on capital growth rather than on current income No need for immediate liquidity Investment time-planning horizon of 3–5 years Willing to take moderate to substantial risk
2. Young married couple, no children	To purchase a home	Similar to Stage 1
3. Young married couple, two children	To build an education fund for the children	Investment time-planning horizon of 3–5 years Unwilling to take quite as much risk as in Stages 1 and 2 Other conditions similar to Stage 1
4. Middle-aged married couple, children grown	To build a retirement fund	Willing to take moderate risk Other conditions similar to Stage 1
5. Married couple in retirement	To supplement retirement income	Emphasis on preservation of capital Need for current income and liquidity Low risks preferred

Deciding how much risk you wish to accept is not easy. The main factors to consider are the need for investment return, the length of the investment planning period, and the need for liquidity. If you will need your investment fund by next summer to finance a vacation trip, you obviously cannot afford significant risk and must accept investments with relatively low return and high liquidity—for example, a savings account. If you will need your money in fifteen years to pay for your child's education, you obviously do not need high liquidity, and you can afford to take more risk and to seek investments with greater returns—for example, common stocks.

Some investors believe they can accept no risk at all and hence seek what they perceive to be very "safe" investments. However, no investment is "fail-safe"; every investment contains some risk. Merely holding cash exposes your funds to loss through the declining purchasing power of the dollar during periods of inflation. Also, cash investments are easy to liquidate and tempt savers to spend for short-term goods or services that preclude the possibility of satisfying longer-term needs. The decision about risk, therefore, is not whether you will accept it, but rather how much of it you are willing to accept.

RISK AND RETURN

A fundamental concept of finance is that risk and return are directly related. If you want to double your money, you stand a good chance of losing your money. Investment safety means that you are giving up income in order not to have an uncertain outcome. Reaching for higher yields invariably involves a bigger chance of not achieving the anticipated result. Life and investments are full of surprises. The greater the return sought, the more likely you will be surprised. All of finance boils down to this axiom: You cannot earn more without taking a chance of earning less.

TYPES OF INVESTMENT RISK

Investment risk can be categorized as follows:

1. Short-term versus long-term risk,
2. Market risk versus company or industry risk,
3. Inflation and interest rate risk,
4. Political risk.

Short-term versus Long-term Risk. Normally, short-term risk is less than long-term risk since the near term can usually be analyzed more easily than the distant future. An investment that offers little short-term risk—cash, for example—can offer considerable risk in the long run because of inflation. On the other hand, many investments with considerable short-term risk might offer low long-term risk—for example, a well-located apartment house might not be saleable immediately except at a loss, but would probably appreciate greatly in market value over a five-to-ten-year period.

Market Risk versus Company Risk. Market risk (sometimes called **systematic risk**) is a risk that affects several types of investments simultaneously. It is caused by such factors as a decline in business conditions, a change in investor psychology, a sudden and unexpected event (e.g., an oil embargo) or a change in interest rates. Market risks are unpredictable, but they usually last less than a year.

Company risk, or **industry risk**, is produced by events that mainly affect one company or industry. This risk is caused by such factors as diminished profitability due to poor management, loss of customers due to competition from other sources (e.g., the U.S. auto industry's loss of market share to foreign auto manufacturers), and adverse financial or credit conditions in a given area—caused, for example, by excessive debt. (Company risk can usually be minimized through adequate diversification of investments, which is discussed later in this chapter.) If the stock market as a whole is going down (a bear market), individual stocks are likely to decline too, even though their profit expectations are excellent. Obviously, if the stock market is in rapid decline, new investment commitments should probably be delayed until the bear market is over; however, you should keep in mind that a bear market produces some of the best buying opportunities.

Inflation and Interest Rate Risk. High inflation adversely affects all types of investments since rising prices tend to reduce present and future profits, and profits are perhaps the single most important influence on stock market prices. Rising interest rates also cause the price of bonds to decline; old bonds that carry low-interest coupons will be less valuable if higher interest rates are being paid on new bond issues of the same general quality. The steps in the economic process that contribute to inflation and interest rate risk are shown in Exhibit 11–2 (see Chapter 1 for a detailed discussion of inflation).

Political Risk. **Political risk** stems from government actions that adversely affect business profits. Government can affect both market and company risk. For example, reducing the oil depletion allowance granted as a tax deduction or imposing a windfall profits tax on oil may directly reduce profit prospects in the oil industry and cause a decline in oil-related stocks. Government regulations mandating environmental controls on automobiles may directly affect the profits of auto manufacturers. A general increase in consumer taxes may depress retail industry stocks and indirectly affect many other types of industry sales.

RISK SCALES

Most investors consider risk subjectively and make little attempt to measure it formally. Assigning **risk scales** to investments might be beneficial—for example, you might measure each prospective investment on a scale of one to five, according to its perceived risk. On such a risk scale the numbers would be interpreted as shown in Exhibit 11–3.

The potential return can be compared to the risk taken. For example, suppose you were considering a certain mutual fund investing mainly in "natural resource" stocks. Such stocks generally have a low dividend return and, because of the scarcity of mineral reserves, are considered to be good "inflation hedges" in the long run. Assume that you have an investment time horizon of five years and that you are less concerned with current income than with appreciation in the market price of the stock. Because your time horizon is five years, market risk may be considered quite low. Also, five years allows you to consider an energy stock mutual fund that invests in a number of different energy companies as carrying relatively low levels of short-term risk. Because of the diversification inherent in a mutual fund, company (industry) risk is also low. However, political risk could be substantial since government actions (e.g., the windfall oil profits tax) frequently affect natural resource pricing and markets. The absence of a substantial dividend income

EXHIBIT 11–2
Factors That
Contribute to
Inflation and
Interest Rate
Risk

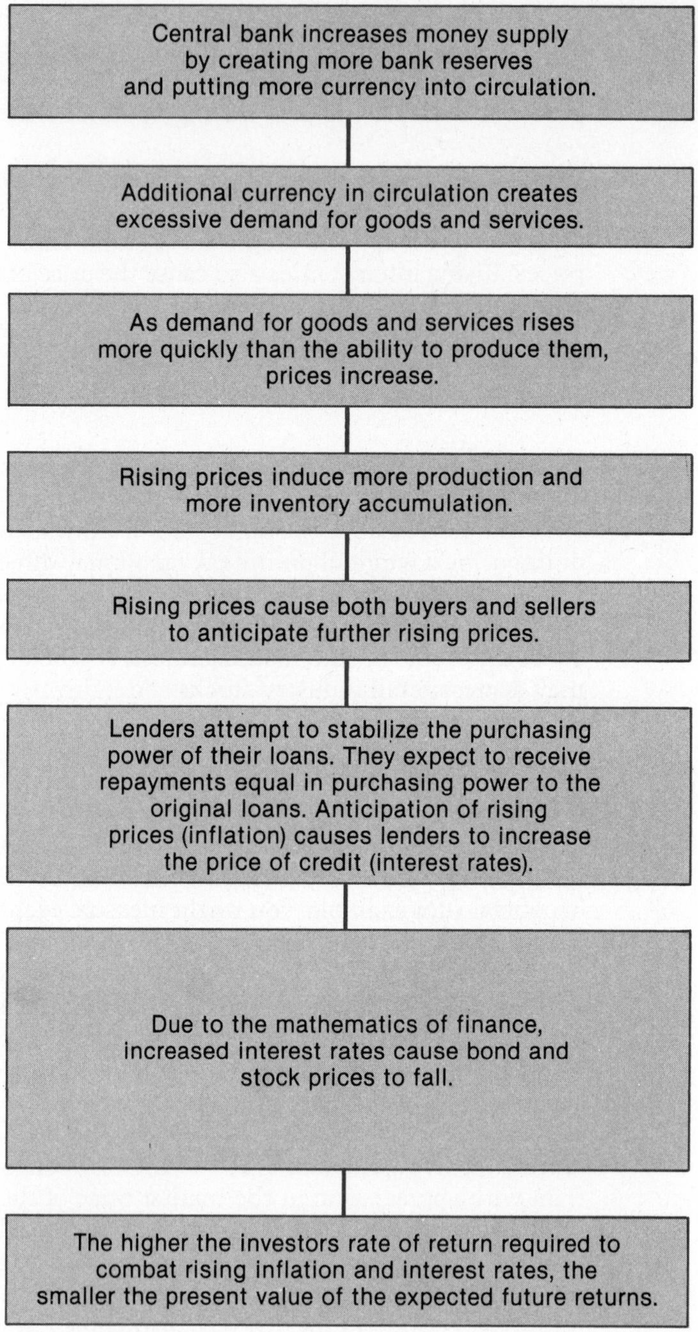

Central bank increases money supply
by creating more bank reserves
and putting more currency into circulation.

Additional currency in circulation creates
excessive demand for goods and services.

As demand for goods and services rises
more quickly than the ability to produce them,
prices increase.

Rising prices induce more production and
more inventory accumulation.

Rising prices cause both buyers and sellers
to anticipate further rising prices.

Lenders attempt to stabilize the purchasing
power of their loans. They expect to receive
repayments equal in purchasing power to the
original loans. Anticipation of rising
prices (inflation) causes lenders to increase
the price of credit (interest rates).

Due to the mathematics of finance,
increased interest rates cause bond and
stock prices to fall.

The higher the investors rate of return required to
combat rising inflation and interest rates, the
smaller the present value of the expected future returns.

EXHIBIT 11-3   Interpretation of Risk

Risk Level	Meaning
1. Lowest risk	Little chance of price changes over your investment time horizon. Liquidity is very high if you should have to convert investment to cash. Returns considered ''low'' but very reliable.
2. Below-average risk	Similar to Level 1 but with less certainty as to price stability, return, and liquidity.
3. Moderate risk	Past experience shows the possibility of fluctuations in price, so that at the end of the time horizon, a loss could result. Interim liquidity is only average, so that if a sale must be made, a loss is very possible. Income is reasonably secure, but reductions are possible. Potential for price increase is higher than at Level 2.
4. Above-average risk	Similar to Level 3, but the potential for a greater degree of price fluctuations and/or dividend return exists.
5. Highest risk	Very uncertain in terms of price change, dividend, and liquidity. The possibility of substantial losses as well as gains exists.

is an important negative factor because some investors, particularly institutions, require a given income level. Inflation risk is low because natural resources tend to keep pace with changing price levels.

After considering these factors, you may decide to place this potential investment at Level 3, moderate risk. You then observe price changes in the mutual fund over the past five and the past ten years and discover that the average annual return, assuming all dividends were reinvested, was only 12 percent. In the end you decide that other available investments offer the same rate of return and involve substantially less risk. For example, government bonds may be yielding more than 12 percent with no uncertainty about the stability of the income.

An important investment principle is to choose any investment in a given risk class that offers a higher expected return than other investments in the same class. For example, if ten stocks carry what you perceive to be moderate risk, rank the stocks according to the level of return you can reasonably expect and allocate your investment funds accordingly. Alternatively, among all potential investments that offer the same total return (dividends plus average market-price appreciation), select the investment with the least perceived risk.

Aligning Goals with the Appropriate Investments

Once you have determined investment goals and risk levels, you must decide what types of investments will be consistent with them.

LEVEL 1: SMALL RISK

If your main goal is income and you wish to preserve capital and accept small risk levels, your investments should include **fixed-income securities** such as money market funds, short-term bonds, and short-term savings certificates, all of which offer currently available interest returns with very low risk levels. You can cash them in within stated time periods with little risk of loss of principal.

LEVEL 2: INCOME PLUS MARKET GROWTH

If your goal is to emphasize current income that will tend to rise with inflation over time, and if you are willing to accept more risk, you might seek "quality" common stocks with a history of paying consistent and rising dividends. Securities meeting these criteria would normally include public utility stocks and stocks of large corporations in noncyclical industries producing consumer-oriented goods and services.

In selecting such stocks, you might use the following typical investment criteria:

1. The stock must offer a current dividend sufficient to yield at least 6 percent of the purchase price.
2. The stock must show a record of rising dividends by some minimum amount for several years.
3. The dividend must have been supported by rising earnings adequate to cover the dividend by a substantial margin.
4. The industry of which the company is a part must be considered stable and must offer necessary services to the public (e.g., electric power, food production or distribution, transportation, or freight service).

A representative list of stocks that meet these criteria appears in Exhibit 11–4.

At Level 2 you can expect to receive a dividend return that tends to keep pace with inflation and to enjoy modest appreciation in the market price of the stock because of steadily rising earnings or dividends. Stocks at Level 2 would be appropriate for investors who are in the retirement stage of the life cycle, because these stocks offer protection against loss of principal and steady, rising dividends that tend to keep up with inflation.

LEVELS 3 AND 4: MORE AGGRESSIVE GROWTH

If you wish to emphasize aggressive, long-term (eight to ten years') growth in the value of a stock, and if you care less about interim price fluctuations or current dividend payments, you should select stocks that correspond to risk levels 3 or 4. The stock should have enjoyed a continuous increase in earnings per share for several years, with no more than one or two years of declining earnings during the period (*no* years of declining earnings would be best). This growth must have been accompanied by rising corporate sales

EXHIBIT 11-4   Level 2 Stocks: Basic Stocks

These issues are basic building blocks for the portfolio. They offer the prospect of long-term appreciation, along with moderate but growing income. The investor seeking to build an estate should start with stocks from this list, augmenting them with issues from other groups according to one's objectives and temperament.

| | Earnings Per Share ($) | | | Indi-cated Div. $ | 1980-82 Price Range | Recent Price | P/E Ratio | Yield % | Annual Growth Rates — for Latest 5 Years — | | | Price Action vs. Mkt. 3-6-78 to 11-28-80 ▼ | Since 11-28-80 ■ | Listed Options Traded |
	1980	1981	E1982						Sales	Earn.	Div.			
Citicorp	4.08	4.40	5.80	1.72	38-3/8 - 17	28	4.8	6.1	8%	7%	10%	0.65	1.57	C
CPC Int'l	4.14	4.57	5.30	2.10	38-3/4 - 27-3/8	37	7.0	5.7	11	13	11	0.87	1.39	:
Dow Chemical	4.42	3.00	2.75	1.80	39-1/4 - 20	24	8.7	7.5	17	3	13	0.92	0.85	C
Eastman Kodak	7.15	7.66	▼8.25	3.50	85-3/8 - 42-7/8	73	8.8	4.8	15	16	12	0.99	1.29	C
Heinz (H.J.)(Apr.*)	3.62	E4.10	4.65	1.44	33-3/4 - 17-1/2	32	6.9	4.5	11	16	19	0.71	1.77	:
Int'l Business Machines	6.10	5.63	▲6.75	3.44	72-3/4 - 48-3/4	64	9.5	5.4	12	8	12	0.67	1.15	C
Int'l Paper	5.97	5.74	▼3.50	2.40	51-1/2 - 30-1/2	38	10.9	6.3	8	3	5	0.75	1.03	C
Mobil Corp.	6.62	5.72	▼4.50	2.00	44-7/8 - 20-1/8	25	5.6	8.0	20	21	18	1.75	1.39	C
Procter & Gamble (June)	7.78	8.08	▲9.40	4.20	89-3/4 - 62-3/4	85	9.0	4.9	13	11	13	0.55	1.47	A
Sonat Inc.	3.43	4.24	5.00	1.10	37-1/4 - 20-1/8	27	5.4	4.1	30	17	19	1.35	0.96	:

Earnings are for calendar years or for fiscal years ending as indicated after names. Unless otherwise noted, they are based on common and common share equivalents, excluding nonrecurring items and including restatements. A—Actual. E—Estimated. ▲Estimate revised upward since last publication of the Master List; ▼estimate revised downward. *Of the following year.

Listed options traded: C—Chicago Board Options Exchange; A—American Stock Exchange; Ph—Philadelphia Stock Exchange; Pac—Pacific Stock Exchange.

Indicated Dividends include actual or possible extras. Dividend increased; dividend decreased. Price/earnings ratios are based on latest shown estimated or actual earnings. Growth rates for sales and earnings are through latest completed years reported; for dividends, through 1981.

All stocks currently in the Supervised Master List are listed on the New York Stock Exchange.

▼A figure above 1.0 indicates that the stock outperformed the S&P industrial stock price index in this period. It is computed by taking the ratio of the stock's price at the end of the period vs. the beginning of the period and dividing it by the corresponding ratio of the index. The time periods covered are updated periodically to conform to the latest major market cycle.

■This column compares share earnings of the latest six months with those of the corresponding year-earlier period.

Source: Standard & Poor's, *The Outlook* (May 19, 1980).

that have roughly paralleled the growth in earnings per share. If earnings per share have doubled over the last five years, the company's earnings are increasing at a compound rate of about 15 percent annually.[1] The company should pay dividends equal to a relatively small part of total earnings (e.g., 25 percent) to permit the reinvestment of a major portion of the earnings to ensure continuous growth. Such companies are likely to exist in industries experiencing above-average expansion—for example, electronics, petroleum exploration, and pharmaceuticals.

Stocks included in Exhibit 11–5 have been growing at rates generally considered above average, as reflected in the growth of earnings per share over the period from 1977 to 1981. The relatively low dividend yield characteristic of these stocks, compared to yields of stocks as a whole, indicates a considerable "plow-back" of earnings into the company. Yet, because the firms have reasonable histories of stability and continuity of dividends, dividend growth is expected to keep pace with earnings growth and to give investors some protection against inflation. The stocks reveal a considerable range in price/earnings ratios. Generally (though not always) the higher the price/earnings ratio, the higher the growth rate in earnings per share. Risk of price variability over short periods (less than a year) in stocks shown in Exhibit 11–5 is considered fairly high.

Potential investors in stocks at this risk level should examine the stock's price range over the preceding few years and attempt to make purchases near the low end of the price range. Many investors who purchase without a general plan tend to buy at the high end of the price range because they have been attracted by recent price increases in the stock and hope to "cash in" on the rise. Unfortunately, many investors become aware of the stock only after most of the price increase has already been realized, when it is too late to make large short-term gains. Since stocks in this group are rather price-volatile, you should minimize risk by purchasing them at price/earnings ratios low in relation to past performances.

LEVEL 5: TRADING FOR PROFIT

Suppose your goal is not current income, inflation-protected income, or long-term growth, but rather profitable "trading" of securities. You expect to hold your investments for relatively short periods and to reinvest your profits from their sale in other similar securities. You are likely to care little for current dividends, long-term prospects of the company, or other traditional selection criteria. Your central goal is to "buy cheap and sell dear." Trading securities with these goals in mind is usually termed **speculation,** a risky process that requires continuous study of the stock market, considerable skill in the timing of purchases, and considerable patience.

---

1. According to Appendix A–1, $1.00 will increase to $2.01 in five years at 15%.

EXHIBIT 11–5   Level 3 and Level 4 Stocks: Growth Stocks

These stocks promise to enjoy well above average growth rates in earnings per share for the foreseeable future. Stocks in the second category carry a higher degree of risk, but by the same token offer greater reward potential. Income is not a consideration here.

Established Growth

	Earnings Per Share ($)			Indicated Div. $	1980-82 Price Range	Recent Price	P/E Ratio	Yield %	Latest 5-Year Growth Rates		No. of Earn. Gains '77-'81	Interim ■Earn. Trend	▼ Price Action vs. Mkt.		Listed Options Traded
	1980	1981	E1982						Sales	Earn.			3-6-78 to 11-28-80	Since 11-28-80	
Abbott Laboratories	1.73	2.01	2.40	0.72	32-1/4 - 17-1/8	31	12.9	2.3	17%	20%	5	+16%	1.20	1.41	Ph
Big Three Industries	2.05	2.57	2.95	0.60	38 - 18-3/4	23	7.8	2.6	24	22	5	+12	1.37	0.84	C
Bristol-Myers	4.08	5.58	5.25	1.84	59-3/8 - 30-1/2	57	10.9	3.2	12	14	5	+14	0.95	1.52	C
PepsiCo, Inc.	3.20	3.61	▼4.15	▲1.62	39-3/8 - 20	39	9.4	4.2	20	14	5	+14	0.61	1.88	C
Philip Morris	4.63	5.41	6.35	2.40	55-1/8 - 29-1/8	52	8.2	4.6	27	19	5	+17	0.80	1.55	A
Schlumberger Ltd.	3.23	4.37	5.25	▲0.96	87-1/8 - 27-1/2	49	9.3	2.0	29	34	5	+20	1.80	1.04	C
Upjohn Co.	5.75	6.04	6.00	2.28	69 - 41-1/2	47	7.8	4.9	14	19	5	- 4	1.16	0.88	C

More Speculative Growth

	Earnings Per Share ($)			Mill. Shs. Outst.	1980-82 Price Range	Recent Price	P/E Ratio	Yield %	Latest 5-Year Growth Rates		No. of Earn. Gains '77-'81	Interim ■Earn. Trend	▼ Price Action vs. Mkt.		Listed Options Traded
	1980	1981	E1982						Sales	Earn.			3-6-78 to 11-28-80	Since Nov. 28, '80	
Digital Equipment (June)	5.45	6.70	▼7.60	54.7	113-1/4 - 56-3/4	78	10.3	...	33	27	5	+12	1.38	1.04	A, C
Harris Corp. (June)	2.63	2.97	▼2.40	31.3	60-1/4 - 26-3/4	30	12.5	2.9	25	21	5	-20	1.41	0.70	C
Nat'l Med. Enter. (May)	0.91	1.24	1.75	46.4	28-3/4 - 4-1/4	15	8.6	2.7	53	32	5	+38	3.20	0.99	A

Earnings are for calendar years or for fiscal years ending as indicated after names. Unless otherwise noted, they are based on common and common share equivalents, excluding nonrecurring items and including restatements. A—Actual. E—Estimated. ▲ Estimate revised upward since last publication of the Master List; ▼ estimate revised downward. *Of the following year.

Listed options traded: C—Chicago Board Options Exchange; A—American Stock Exchange; Ph—Philadelphia Stock Exchange; Pac—Pacific Stock Exchange.

Indicated Dividends include actual or possible extras.   Dividend increased; dividend decreased. Price/earnings ratios are based on latest shown estimated or actual earnings. Growth rates for sales and earnings are through latest completed years reported; for dividends, through 1981.

All stocks currently in the Supervised Master List are listed on the New York Stock Exchange.

▼A figure above 1.0 indicates that the stock outperformed the S&P industrial stock price index in this period. It is computed by taking the ratio of the stock's price at the end of the period vs. the beginning of the period and dividing it by the corresponding ratio of the index. The time periods covered are updated periodically to conform to the latest major market cycle.

■This column compares share earnings of the latest six months with those of the corresponding year-earlier period.

Source: Standard & Poor's, *The Outlook* (May 19, 1980).

You should consider speculation in securities only if you are willing to accept the highest levels of risk and use funds you are able to lose. Furthermore, you must be able to concentrate on your objectives; you cannot be a successful "part-time" speculator, because the job is time consuming. Securities most likely to be candidates for speculation include young companies in relatively new industries, cyclical stocks currently in a depressed phase of their cycle, stocks depressed because of impending bankruptcy or reorganization, or stocks that are candidates for mergers with a corporate "suitor" willing to pay considerably more than the current market price.

Investment characteristics of speculative securities are likely to include the following: a past record of very small earnings or deficits, no consistent growth record in earnings per share, absence of dividends or unstable history of dividends (if any are paid at all), and above-average price/earnings ratios. Companies are likely to have only regional operations, not national operations. Frequently the stock available is a new issue representing stock not previously traded. Often the stock will not be traded on a major exchange, but rather will be traded "over the counter" under the sponsorship of a regional stock brokerage firm that "makes the market" in the stock by owning large blocks of stock it offers to the public. Exhibit 11–6 shows stocks that, as of late 1982, had certain speculative characteristics. Generally, you cannot characterize these kinds of securities, since the conditions for making them worthwhile speculations vary greatly. Speculative stocks generally are characterized by unstable earnings and dividends, unusual asset characteristics, and changing market structure.

SELECTING INVESTMENTS: THEORIES TO CONSIDER

To make intelligent investment selections after setting your goals, you must choose among a multitude of possibilities. Several schools of thought on how best to make your choice—among the most prominent, fundamental analysis and technical analysis—are discussed in the following subsections.

Fundamental Analysis

Fundamental analysis rests on a very simple concept: Certain stocks have hidden financial values that are only revealed through financial analysis. These **hidden values** mean that certain stocks are worth more than their current market prices would indicate. The value of fundamental analysis depends on the skill of the security analyst in recognizing certain values that are not known by, revealed to, or understood by the typical investor. When properly recognized, these hidden values become the basis for the reappraisal of the

EXHIBIT 11-6 Level 5 Stocks: Volatile Stocks

This group comprises stocks selected for high reward potentials stemming from a variety of considerations—including emerging opportunities, turnaround situations, stocks to benefit from cyclical upswings, and the like. Readers can expect to see more frequent changes in this list than in the others. The risk factor in some of the issues in this group may be high and the stocks recommended may not be suitable for those concerned with income or with investment grade securities.

Earnings Per Share ($)			Indicated Div. $	1980-82 Price Range	Recent Price	P/E Ratio	Yield %	Listed Options Traded		Remarks
1980	1981	E1982								
6.54	3.97	2.00	1.80	38-1/4 - 21-7/8	26	13.0	6.9	C	Aluminum Co. of Amer.	Cyclical upturn in aluminum demand to develop before long.
5.68	4.07	2.00	2.20	43-3/4 - 22-3/8	27	13.5	8.1		American Standard	Modestly valued on long-term profit prospects.
5.18	5.13	5.60	1.60	38 - 25-5/8	37	6.6	4.3	Pac.	Amer. Broadcasting	TV network benefiting from strong ad background.
4.73	4.97	▼3.00	1.80	41-3/4 - 18-1/2	19	6.3	9.5		Armco Inc.	Diversification and steel recovery benefit outlook.
1.88	2.47	▲3.05	1.00	37-3/8 - 12-1/4	34	11.1	2.9	A	Browning-Ferris (Sept.)	Regulation of waste disposal methods aids growth prospects.
7.55	7.02	7.75	1.52	77 - 25-3/4	50	6.5	3.0	C	Burlington Northern	Superior rail and natural resource potentials.
2.43	2.65	2.80	0.56	30-3/4 - 17-1/4	23	8.2	2.4		Engelhard Corp.	Favorable prospects for catalytic products.
2.85	3.36	3.75	1.40	24-1/8 - 10-3/4	23	6.1	6.1	A	Goodyear Tire & Rub.	Best-situated in industry experiencing a profit resurgence.
3.40	3.86	4.10	1.40	55-5/8 - 28-1/4	36	8.8	3.9	C	Raytheon	Strong growth likely in missile & defense electronic systems.
2.47	1.67	▼1.50	1.30	40-3/4 - 24-1/4	28	18.7	4.6	C	Weyerhaeuser Co.	Timber self-sufficiency enhances long-term prospects.
4.31	4.78	▼5.10	1.80	65-7/8 - 27-1/2	34	6.7	5.3		Wheelabrator-Frye	Engineering/construction projects expanding.

Earnings are for calendar years or for fiscal years ending as indicated after names. Unless otherwise noted, they are based on common and common share equivalents, excluding nonrecurring items and including restatements. A—Actual. E—Estimated. ▲ Estimate revised upward since last publication of the Master List; ▼ estimate revised downward. *Of the following year.

Listed options traded: C—Chicago Board Options Exchange; A—American Stock Exchange; Ph—Philadelphia Stock Exchange; Pac—Pacific Stock Exchange.

Indicated Dividends include actual or possible extras. Dividend increased; dividend decreased. Price/earnings ratios are based on latest shown estimated or actual earnings. Growth rates for sales and earnings are through latest completed years reported; for dividends, through 1981.

All stocks currently in the Supervised Master List are listed on the New York Stock Exchange.

▼ A figure above 1.0 indicates that the stock outperformed the S&P industrial stock price index in this period. It is computed by taking the ratio of the stock's price at the end of the period vs. the beginning of the period and dividing it by the corresponding ratio of the index. The time periods covered are updated periodically to conform to the latest major market cycle.

■This column compares share earnings of the latest six months with those of the corresponding year-earlier period.

Source: Standard & Poor's, The Outlook (May 19, 1980).

stock at some value above its current market price. If the appraisal value is significantly higher than the market price, the security should be purchased.[2]

The first technique of fundamental analysis is to reappraise a company's assets or its special position in the industry. For example, the wave of mergers between oil companies and other corporations in the early 1980s can be traced to the revaluation of the oil companies' domestic oil reserves. With domestic oil decontrolled, the value of a barrel of proven oil reserve in the ground was worth approximately the world price of oil ($34.00 a barrel) in 1981. Thus, analysis of Conoco's financial statements showed that the book value of their oil in the ground was perhaps $8.50.[3] This "hidden value" made the company quite valuable. Du Pont was the successful bidder over several other companies, which also had discovered the undervalued domestic oil reserves on Conoco's financial statements.

Many "hidden values" exist—for example, many paper and lumber companies have huge holdings of timber acreage, both owned and leased. For some companies the average **book cost (book value)** per acre—that is, what the company originally paid per acre—may be as low as $10 when similar forest land may be selling for as high as $300 an acre.[4] Strangely, the market does not recognize this discrepancy as a hidden value—but let this land find an alternative use, and stock values may skyrocket. For example, the same forest acreage near an interstate highway interchange may be worth $10,000 an acre—a fact that may be recognized by the market.

Another example of hidden value would be copper-mining companies. Every ton of copper processed produces silver as a byproduct. At $40 an ounce for silver, this may have a significant effect on earnings. At $10 an ounce, the effect is small.

Typical students may not consider themselves competent to find hidden values. But surprisingly, a student may be in a position to discover special factors. For example, a student stopping for lunch in 1959 at a place where a semiautomated approach to making the hamburgers was used might have recognized McDonald's as a "real comer." An alert person can find special

---

2. The concept of fundamental analysis can be traced to Benjamin Graham, who wrote *Security Analysis* and *The Intelligent Investor*. Both books are sadly out of date but are so well written and clear that they are still worth reading. In 1926 Benjamin Graham as a young man organized the Graham-Newman Fund with about $600,000. When the fund was liquidated in the mid-1950s, it was reputed to be worth $26 million. Most of the profits apparently were made by buying stocks and bonds of corporations Graham found to be undervalued.

3. The fact that foreign oil sells for $34.00 a barrel does not make domestic oil reserves equal to the foreign-oil price. The oil is in the ground, and only a small portion can be pumped out in any year. The reserves in the ground to be retrieved later are worth less now in present-value terms. For example, at a return of 15%, $8.50 a barrel *now* is justified, at a $34.00-a-barrel price, if you pump that oil out ten years in the future (see present-value tables in Appendix A–4).

4. Book cost, or book value, is what a company originally paid for an asset, less any accumulated depreciation taken to date. (Of course, depreciation would not be appropriate in the case of land.) This amount appears in the financial statements according to generally accepted accounting principles.

"The whole concept of fundamental analysis rests on the premise of hidden values."

The Bettman Archive, Inc.

situations and "hidden values" everywhere. Unfortunately, most of us ignore special situations.

Fundamental analysis involves looking at the earnings per share (EPS) and their quality. It may require recalculating EPS if some peculiar accounting methods have been used by a particular company. For example, companies sometimes use unusual depreciation or depletion accounting methods, which in effect understate earnings to minimize taxes.[5] If earnings are restated in a manner similar to other companies' accounting methods, the stock may be worth more.

---

5. Depreciation refers to allocating the cost of fixed assets to expenses over their estimated usual life; depletion is based on the same idea but refers to natural resources. Depletion also refers to a tax credit given to producers of certain mineral products like oil and coal.

Suppose a special situation exists that is not known to the average investor. For example, suppose you work in an automobile agency and discover that the company that makes many of the parts for your line of automobiles is about to be acquired by a larger corporation. Buying stock in the company before the news becomes generally known might prove to be a good speculation.

Fundamental analysis may also be performed through strict financial analysis. Finding on the balance sheet values not recognized by the market is the essence of fundamental analysis. For example, security analysts always look for companies with large cash or cash-equivalent holdings that, when valued on a per-share basis, are large in relation to the price of the company's stock. In terms of earning power, however, a very large cash position is synonymous with a stagnant company—that is, a company whose earnings are low relative to its assets. Companies that have low earnings sometimes sell at relatively poor price/earnings multiples. Exhibit 11–7 lists a sample of "cash-heavy" companies.

Merger-minded companies often are looking for cash-rich "cows" that they hope to milk. The merger-minded company seeks to buy control of cash-heavy companies to acquire their cash and other assets. Buying into companies such as those listed in Exhibit 11–7 may prove very profitable if the company is later acquired by a merger-minded raider, since acquisition will invariably drive up the price of stock in the acquired company.

TESTING FUNDAMENTAL ANALYSIS

Fundamental analysis rests on the idea that there are "hidden" values to be found and that the market is not always right. This theory is in direct contradiction to modern investment theory, which holds that it is impossible to beat the market, since the market already takes into account all the special features of a stock in determining the stock price.

An enterprising finance scholar, Henry Oppenheimer, has derived a method to test some of Graham's ideas as applied to portfolios of randomly selected stocks.[6] We will not review Oppenheimer's elaborate statistical and computer procedures; we only will provide the basic strategies and the results of the simulation, assuming an investing period was from 1955 to 1975.

The defensive investor, according to Oppenheimer, will use the following rules:[7]

1. A stock will be bought only if a dividend has been paid each year for ten years.

---

6. Henry R. Oppenheimer, *Common Stock Selection: An Analysis of Benjamin Graham's Intelligent Investor's Approach* (Ann Arbor, Mich.: UMI Press, 1981).

7. These rules were devised by Oppenheimer to follow Graham's rules, set in the 1950s. Rule 2 would have to be changed to at least $100 million to conform to values in the 1980s.

EXHIBIT 11-7 Cash-Heavy Companies, October 1981

Company	Cash (in Millions)	Cash as a % of Assets	Cash per Share	Price	P/E Ratio
American Home Products	$ 589.5	25%	$ 3.85	$30.13	10
Boeing	1,660.2	25	17.22	24.00	4
Kaiser Steel	430.8	33	60.34	43.25	19
Loral	75.4	32	7.41	31.00	14
Maytag	71.1	29	8.07	26.25	9
Redman Industries	25.9	25	2.66	11.13	10
Skyline	81.3	60	7.25	15.13	22
Western Pacific	118.4	52	51.06	52.50	5

Source: *Fortune* (October 5, 1981); *Wall Street Journal* (September 30, 1981).

2. A firm must have at least $50 million in assets or sales to be eligible. The firm must be in the upper third of its industry in size.
3. The price of the stock cannot exceed twenty times the average earnings of the last five years, or fifteen times the current earnings at the time or purchase.
4. Equity (book value) is to be no less than 50 percent of total capital.

According to Oppenheimer, Graham suggested further restrictions: Not only must a stock meet rational tests of underlying soundness; it also must be a stock ignored by other investors.

An aggressive policy requires looking for **special situations**—that is, companies whose market value (current market price times the number of shares outstanding) is two-thirds or less of their net current asset value. Graham defines **net current asset value** as total current assets (cash and equivalents plus accounts receivable plus inventory) minus total liabilities, including preferred stock. Such companies, according to Graham, are real bargains because the liquidating values of the net current assets are greater than the market price. (The fixed assets, such as plant, equipment, and so on, have no economic value in special situations.)

Of course, you should keep in mind that there are reasons why companies in special situations are severely undervalued by the market. These companies typically manufacture buggy whips in an electronic world. But Graham's theories rest on the idea that someone will later buy the company, find an alternative use for the assets, or dissolve the company for a big profit.[8]

---

8. An example of alternative use was Loew's MGM. This company was broken into two parts by government court order in 1965. The MGM part was particularly valuable because of the huge inventory of films that had been written down to minimal values and could be leased to theaters in major American cities. These theater sites were later redeveloped as hotels and office buildings.

Oppenheimer's tests of investment performance show that during the period from 1955 to 1975, a defensive investor would have received an average total return of 10.41 percent, as compared to a 7.35 percent return for the market as a whole. Both results ignore taxes and commissions. According to Oppenheimer, if Graham's further restrictions had been followed, returns could have been increased an additional 90 percent.

Present-Value Analysis

Another approach to security evaluation is through some variant of **present-value analysis.** Theoretically, any security is at a given moment worth the present value of all expected future payments discounted back to the present at the investor's required rate of return. This theory is difficult to put into practice because the investor is operating with future payments that are at best uncertain. Also, the uncertain payments are discounted by a rate of return that can vary with the investor's estimate of risk.

Assume that you pay $50.00 for a stock that pays a $5.00 dividend and grows at the rate of 5 percent a year for five years. At the end of five years, you expect to sell the stock for $64.00. If you expect to earn 10 percent on the investment, the net present value would be computed as follows:

Year	Payment	10% Present Value	Present Value
1980	$(50.00)	1.00	$(50.00)
1981	$ 5.00	.909	$ 4.55
1982	$ 5.25	.826	$ 4.34
1983	$ 5.51	.751	$ 4.14
1984	$ 5.79	.683	$ 3.96
1985	$6.08 + 64	.621	$ 43.51

Net Present Value of Returns @ 10% = $ 10.50.

For an investment of $50.00, you receive a gross return over five years of $60.50. At a 10 percent required rate of return, the investment returns a positive net present value of $10.50. Under these assumptions the investment is worth making.

All of the calculations in the above example look quite simple, precise, and accurate, but they are based on a set of assumptions that may or may not be accurate. However, this type of analysis does provide a numerical answer that can be easily compared to present market prices. Different present values can be determined by changing numerical assumptions.

Technical Analysis

One of the most important and controversial methods of investment is **technical analysis,** a theory that proposes that value can be determined without financial analysis. That is, you need not know dividends, earnings per share, financial data, industry data, product information, or the quality of the firm's management. According to technical analysts, or **chartists,** all this information is captured in the price of the stock relative to past prices.

The technical analyst looks for patterns that tell where the market is going. Analysis and interpretation of these price patterns seem to require some mystical knowledge; chartists, tracking the same stock, often do not agree on the proper time to buy or sell. Technical analysis usually requires simultaneous inspection of both price and volume data. Rising prices on rising volume usually indicate a further rise in stock prices. Similarly, falling prices with a falling volume of stock trading imply a bear market and indicate that it is time to sell.

The simplest chart, and the one probably most widely used by technical analysts, is the **bar chart.** A good example of one form of bar chart is shown in Chapter 12, Case 2. Note that the Value Line Investment Service plots a high and a low price as well as a trend line. Movements of stock prices relative to trend and volume are usually considered important signals.

More advanced chartists develop something called a **point-and-figure chart** (see Exhibit 11–8), which has no time dimension. Only significant price changes are plotted. An *X* refers to a significant price increase, and an *O* to a decrease. A column of *X*s reflects an upward drive in prices and a column of *O*s shows a downward drift.

Looking at Exhibit 11–8 we can see how the system works. Suppose we plot only price rises of $1 or more (usually closing prices only). We begin at Point A at $36. The stock closes at $37½. We mark an *X* right about Point A. As long as the price stays between $37 and $38 no new mark is made. The stock continues to move upward, but not above $39 (Point B). When the stock price falls, *O* is entered on each $1 move downward. When the stock rises again, a new column is begun. From analyzing the *X*s and *O*s, skilled chartists claim they can calculate future movements of the stock price.

Almost all modern financial economists reject technical analysis. However, rejection of the procedure does not justify ignoring the predictions of the more influential chartists. The advice of such prominent technical analysts as Joseph Granville is closely followed by many people, even if they do not believe in the value of his pronouncements, because if many investors follow a certain piece of advice, the effect on the stock market will be direct and far-reaching. Indeed, the effect is often self-fulfilling. Dire warnings about breakthroughs and new "bottoms" can cause a selling wave that results in a severe decline in market prices.

EXHIBIT 11-8   A Point-and-Figure Chart

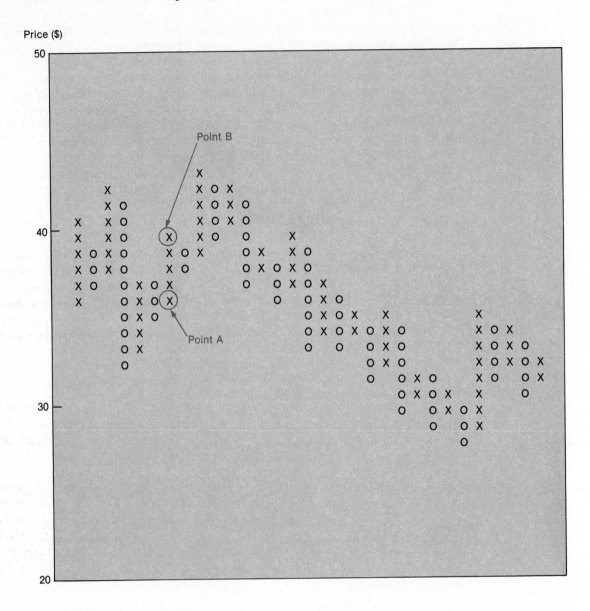

Perhaps the real distinction between technical analysis and fundamental analysis is that fundamental analysis is a technique for choosing investments; technical analysis is a method of timing purchases and sales once the security has been chosen. Technical analysis is too specialized a topic to be within the scope of this book; the interested reader is advised to read a more advanced text.[9]

Contrarianism

The famous presidential adviser Bernard Baruch was once quoted as saying, "First, I find out what the crowd is doing, and then I do the opposite." The principles of **contrarianism** may be summarized as follows:

1. Stock prices in general, or some groups of stocks, are sometimes pushed to the extreme by mass psychology.
2. Profits in the stock market cannot be made by the majority of participants. In the end only a small minority will profit.
3. Once an idea or a fact is known and widely pursued by the general public, its usefulness is usually at an end.
4. The best investment strategy is to act according to the contrary of what the general public firmly believes—that is, if the public believes that the future direction of the stock market or stock groups is upward, the wise investor will act on the assumption that the true direction is downward.

Based on an analysis of various principles of investor psychology, contrarianism essentially says to "buy low and sell high," using price/earnings ratios as a guide to when a stock is "low" and when it is "high." In other words, this school of investment thought holds that the time to purchase a stock is when most investors do not want it and have allowed its price/earnings ratio to decline relative to other stocks. Contrarianism seems to "fly in the face" of general investment advice, since one of the reasons for a low P/E ratio is investor judgment that something is wrong with the company in question and that a dollar's earnings from the company is not worth a dollar earned by another, more favorably situated company.

Among the rules of contrarianism advanced by Dreman are the following:[10]

1. Buy stocks with low P/E ratios only if they meet other favorable tests—for example, financial strength, a high dividend yield consistently and adequately supported by earnings, and near-term earnings forecasts, conservatively stated, that are positive.
2. Buy at least fifteen to twenty stocks, diversified among ten to twelve industries, to reduce company risk.

---

9. A fairly comprehensive and even-handed treatment can be found in Stanley Huang, *Investment Analysis and Management* (Englewood Cliffs, N.J.: Winthrop, 1981), ch. 16.

10. David Dreman, *Contrarianism Investment Strategy* (New York: Random House, 1979).

"When Corporal Contrarianism talks, people listen."

3. Buy only medium- or large-sized stocks, such as those listed on the New York Stock Exchange, or stocks of large firms listed on the American Stock Exchange or traded over the counter.

Dreman advises that stock should be sold when the price increases to the point where the P/E ratio approaches or exceeds that of the overall market, regardless of how favorable the prospects appear for the individual stock. Stocks thus sold should be replaced by other stocks that meet the buying criteria outlined above. Dreman also advises that if a stock has not gone up within a two-year period, it should be sold and replaced by another stock.

Contrarianism holds that the investor should be wary of unusual deviation from past norms in a stock's performance. Unusual increases in earnings, for example, are likely to be followed by subsequent declines; yet many investors eagerly purchase a stock upon the publication of a large jump in earnings, only to be subsequently disappointed. Such investors reason that if recent earnings have risen, the trend will more likely continue than be reversed. Unfortunately, the opposite is often true. On the other hand, a sudden decline in earnings of an otherwise sound company may offer the investor a buying opportunity, because such a decline probably will not be permanent.

How well has contrarianism worked in practice? Dreman cites many studies to demonstrate statistically that properly selected, low P/E stocks (i.e., those meeting Dreman's criteria) have consistently outperformed high P/E stock portfolios and have also outperformed general stock market averages—for example, Standard and Poor's 400 or the Dow Jones Industrial Average.

Efficient-Market Hypothesis

Modern financial theory is based on a set of statistical findings that often run counter to established market wisdom. The major premise of modern theory, the **efficient-market hypothesis,** is that the stock market conforms to a random process, and stock price movements conform to a **random walk.**[11] Clever, informed, careful, and technical analysis is therefore just so much wasted effort. Like technical analysts, modern theorists believe that the current price represents all there is to know about a stock. But current price represents nothing else; it contains no forecast of the future.

The efficient-market theorists say to financial analysts: "Why bother—increased returns only mean increased risks." That is, if you can beat the market by correctly analyzing the financial factors of some corporations, you can only do so within some framework of probability (chance). When you bet that a given investment can do 50 percent better than the market, you are also saying that the probability is equal that it can do 50 percent worse than the market. If you want to take a smaller risk of losing, you must take a smaller risk of gaining.

The efficient-market theorists hold that stock prices reflect all publicly available information; only a few insiders with really secret information can earn a profit greater than could be achieved by a naive investor with a buy-and-hold strategy.

The efficient-market hypothesis leads in two directions. First, you can scientifically construct a portfolio of securities by selecting companies whose returns are unrelated to one another. Thus, no one business risk will affect all companies in the same way (see the discussion of beta in the following section). On the other hand, you can do as well as the market by putting the

---

11. A random walk refers to a statistical process in which the next observation is related to the last observation, but in a random manner. Starting with a price, the next observed price could be higher or lower, but at least related to the last price. The term *random walk* was coined to describe the erratic walk of observations that resembles the behavior of a drunken person hanging on to a lamp pole; no one can tell in which the direction he will go next, but he is sure to keep on hanging to the lamp pole.

"Care to join me for a random walk, little girl?"

financial pages on the wall, throwing darts, and selecting the stocks the darts hit. Fifteen selections chosen at random will resemble the market as a whole 95 times out of 100.

Diversification and Beta

Diversification, the fundamental way to cope with investment risk, is a simple concept by which you can remove some, but not all, risk. As the old adage says: "Don't carry all your eggs in one basket." Carrying two baskets removes the risk that you will lose all your eggs if you brush up against the cow. But if you trip over the hay rake, you will probably drop both baskets. Diversification thus protects the investor against the risk associated with one company or one industry. But not even the most complete diversification can protect the investor against the market itself. If the market falls, almost all stocks will also fall. Market risk cannot be diversified away.

Beta is a market measure of risk. It involves the statistical relationship between the returns from an individual stock and the returns from the market as a whole. The market return is by definition 1.0; all other individual betas are relative to this value. Most betas are positive and fall in a range of values between 0.2 and 2.0. Generally speaking, the higher the value of beta, the greater the risk of the stock relative to the market as a whole.

Solving for beta values, suppose that we derive a beta of 1.50 for one stock and 0.50 for another. The first number means that, for any given change in total market returns, the first stock will change 1.50 times as much. For example, if total returns on the market index rise 100 points, the stock with a beta of 1.50 will tend to rise, on the average, 150 points. If the beta is 0.50 and the market falls 100 points, the stock in question will fall, on the average, only 50 points. In Chapter 10 we used the Value Line investment survey on International Business Machines (see Exhibit 10–3). Value Line calculates IBM's beta to be 0.95—that is, IBM stock should rise and fall almost exactly as the market does.

If you are generally bullish, high beta stocks are what you want. If the market rises, these stocks will rise farther and faster. If you are bearish, low beta stocks are desirable. As the market falls, low beta stocks will fall less than the market as a whole.[12]

When you build a portfolio, you must measure the beta of the whole portfolio as well as the beta of the individual securities. The combination of different betas from individual stocks will produce a new beta for the portfolio as a whole. The greater the diversification in the portfolio, the more closely the portfolio beta will match the market as a whole. Thus, you diversify individual risk and possess a portfolio that does as well as the market average.

But doing as well as the market average may not be good enough. If you can do only as well as the market average, why bother picking individual stocks? The same effect can be secured by buying an investment fund that mirrors the market average. The careful investor ought to be able to do better than the market average. The average implies a normally distributed population with as many stocks below the average as above the average. Elimination of the potentially worst performers will raise your portfolio's performance above the market average.

For example, suppose you are considering ten different stocks, all of which are equal in cost. These stocks have an expected annual return varying from $1.00 to $10.00 (i.e., $1.00, $2.00, $3.00, $4.00, $5.00, $6.00, $7.00, $8.00, $9.00, and $10.00). The books on security analysis tell us all about picking the $9.00 and $10.00 winners. But it is much easier to eliminate the $1.00

---

12. The reader should be aware that "beta" is calculated from past values. They do not always accurately predict future values.

and $2.00 performers than to pick the big winners. The average return on the series $1.00 to $10.00 is $5.50 [($1.00 + $10.00)/2]. Elimination of the two worst possibilities increases the average return to $6.50 [($3.00 + $10.00)/2], an increase of 18 percent. Perhaps the real secret of portfolio construction is not picking winners but eliminating big losers.

CONTROLLING FOR RISK

Risk has many dimensions in finance. In general, risk can be defined and measured as all the causes that would keep possible returns different from the average expected return. The greater the spread of possible returns, the greater the risk. Whenever you say, "If I invest in such and so, I can make a fortune," it is the same as saying, "I can also lose my shirt." Most of us are more scared of losing our shirts than we are eager to make a fortune.

The risks associated with investments have already been mentioned. But it is worthwhile to note again that risk is everywhere. Yet all of us go about our business, ignoring or coping with the risks of everyday life. The same can be said in relation to investment—you can either ignore risk or cope with it. Advising an investor to ignore risk is foolhardy, but certain risks are unavoidable once funds are committed. The alternative is to live the life of a recluse, safely away from life's problems. However, only the very, very rich can be totally safeguarded from all problems; the rest of us can't afford to be so well protected. If the risks of investment seem too much to bear, the option is to spend all your money and hope that you will not outlive your resources and become a burden on society.

Dollar Cost Averaging

The most widely used technique of reducing price risk is **dollar cost averaging (DCA).** The principle is simple: A constant dollar amount of stock is purchased periodically. If the stock price drops, the purchase of the constant dollar amount increases the number of shares purchased. As stock prices rise, fewer shares will be purchased. Supposedly, if you follow the DCA program long enough (five years, at least), the overall results will be superior to the results of a simple buy-all-at-one-time-and-hold strategy.

To obtain the best results from a DCA program, you should observe the following simple rules:

1. Maintain periodic buying as the market falls. Buying when prices are low is the key to overall profits.
2. Continue investing through an entire cycle—usually three to five years.

3. Invest frequently—usually once a month. Bear markets are usually of short duration, and unless you buy frequently, you will miss the down market.

4. Do not use a DCA fund as an emergency fund; you might have to sell in a down market when you should be buying.

Unfortunately, DCA is not always a panacea for successful investing. First, if the price at which you buy continues downward indefinitely, you will lose money, even though you purchased fewer shares at higher prices than you purchase when prices are low. DCA produces investment gains only if the average price of your securities rises at some point. Second, since stock market declines typically last for shorter periods than do market increases, you have a shorter time to buy when prices are low than when they are high. A successful DCA program involves buying a stock with a volatile price pattern, since volatility assures the purchase of more shares at lower prices.

Mathematically, DCA rests on the fact that the average cost of the program (total sum invested divided by the number of shares acquired) will always be less than the average price. But knowledge of this fact does not ensure success. A successful DCA program involves discipline in purchasing, a volatile stock, and a downward price pattern with a return near the initial price. If prices rise and then fall, or fall and never recoup, the DCA program will be unsuccessful.

Exhibit 11–9 shows the price pattern of a stock with low volatility. Compare this pattern to the price pattern of a stock with high volatility, as shown in Exhibit 11–10. The stock shown in Exhibit 11–10 yields 10 percent more than that shown in Exhibit 11–9.[13] Finally, in Exhibit 11–11 we see a pattern that is perverse in the sense that the stock rises and then falls, producing a poor result—a negative 10 percent return.[14]

The average investor should adopt DCA as an ideal vehicle for building an estate. First, regular payments fit the typical budget. Second, the market is not easy to predict, and regular payments will tend to eliminate the need for a market forecast. Finally, DCA fits the way most of us accumulate pension funds and various types of tax-deferred annuities.

Formula Plans

The term **formula plans,** of which dollar cost averaging is one, refers to predetermined plans for buying and/or selling securities. The objective of such plans is to buy stocks when they are low and sell them when they are high relative to some norm. The plans, simple or complex, all are based on a com-

---

13. $6,870/$6,243 equals 110%.

14. $5,409/$6,000 equals 90%.

Exhibit 11–9   Numerical Example of Dollar Cost Averaging with $1,000 Invested per Period
                in Low-Volatility Stock

Period	Price	No. Shares per $1,000	Total Shares	Total Invested	Weighted Average Cost per Share	Average Price (Total Market Prices/Number of Periods)
1	$100.00	10.00	10.00	$1,000	$100.00	$100.00
2	95.00	10.53	20.53	2,000	97.42	97.50
3	90.00	11.11	31.64	3,000	94.81	95.00
4	95.00	10.53	42.17	4,000	94.85	95.00
5	97.50	10.26	52.43	5,000	95.37	95.50
6	100.00	10.00	62.43	6,000	96.11	96.25

Ending value = $6,243 [ending price ($100) × ending shares ($62.43)].
Cost = $6,000.
Gain = $243 ($6,243 – $6,000).

Exhibit 11–10   Numerical Example of Dollar Cost Averaging with $1,000 Invested per Period
                in High-Volatility Stock

Period	Price	No. of Shares Purchased	Total Shares	Total Invested	Average Cost per Share	Average Price (Total Market Prices/Number of Periods)
1	$100.00	10.00	10.00	$1,000	$100.00	$100.00
2	90.00	11.11	21.11	2,000	94.74	95.00
3	80.00	12.50	33.61	3,000	89.26	90.00
4	75.00	13.33	46.94	4,000	85.22	86.25
5	85.00	11.76	58.70	5,000	85.18	86.00
6	100.00	10.00	68.70	6,000	87.34	88.33

Ending value = $6,870 [ending price ($100) × ending shares ($68.70)].
Cost = $6,000.
Gain = $870 ($6,870 – $6,000).

mon assumption: There are times when stocks are attractive—typically, when prices are low and the market is bearish. Of course, this is the time when most investors are hesitant to buy. The formula plan exploits the psychology of the market by going against the trend; it operates mechanistically, regardless of the attitudes of the market. Formula plans and contrarianism go together very well.

EXHIBIT 11–11   Numerical Example of Dollar Cost Averaging with $1,000 Invested per Period in Stock with a Perverse Price Pattern

Period	Price	No. of Shares Purchased	Total Shares	Total Invested	Average Cost per Share	Average Price (Total Market Price/Number of Periods)
1	$100.00	10.00	10.00	$1,000	$100.00	$100.00
2	110.00	9.09	19.09	2,000	104.77	105.00
3	120.00	8.33	27.39	3,000	109.53	110.00
4	125.00	8.00	35.39	4,000	113.03	113.75
5	115.00	8.70	44.09	5,000	113.40	114.00
6	100.00	10.00	54.09	6,000	110.93	111.67

Ending value = $5,409 [ending price ($100) × ending shares (54.09)].
Cost = $6,000.
Loss = $591 ($6,000 – $5,409).

Of the many different types of formula plans, one of the simplest is the **constant-ratio plan.**[15] You maintain a portfolio that contains a constant ratio (say, 60 percent) of stocks to bonds. The plan calls for some arbitrary switching period, which usually occurs twice a year on predesignated dates. As a further formula plan restriction, no buying or selling will occur except in amounts of at least $1,000.

Exhibit 11–12 is an example of a constant-ratio plan. Each time stock prices fall, the plan forces you to buy more stocks. Buying more stock maintains a stocks-to-bonds ratio of 60 percent. For example, when stocks fall to $8, the value of the portfolio becomes $44,000. To maintain 60 percent in stock, you must buy $2,400 worth of stock at $8 and sell $2,400 worth of bonds. The new portfolio values equal $26,400 in stock and $17,600 in bonds. The constant-ratio plan assumes that prices first fall and then finally return to the point at which they started. The final result of the plan shown in Exhibit 11–12 is that, not counting dividends, interest income, or commissions, the plan ends with a profit of 3.4 percent [($51,751 – $50,000)/$50,000], as compared to a profit of zero from a simple buy-and-hold strategy.[16]

Plans can be as complicated as the mind of the investor doing the designing. But complicated plans mean making complicated forecasts. If you can make a complicated forecast that really works, you probably do not need a formula plan.

---

15. For a discussion of various types of formula plans, see R.R. Dince, *Handbook of Wealth Management*, ed. L. Barnes and S. Feldman (New York: McGraw-Hill, 1977), Sec. 9, pp. 1–30.

16. The assumption of no commission is not as unrealistic as it may seem. If the plan was being run through a no-load mutual fund, switches between funds of various types at no cost would be possible (see Chapter 12).

EXHIBIT 11-12 Constant-Ratio Plan

Stock Price		Value of Stock	Value of Bonds	Units of Stock	Total Value
$10.00		$30,000	$20,000	3,000	$50,000
8.00	(B)	24,000	20,000	3,000	44,000
	(A)	26,400	17,600	3,300	44,000
6.40	(B)	21,120	17,600	3,300	38,720
	(A)	23,232	15,488	3,630	38,720
5.10	(B)	18,513	15,488	3,630	34,001
	(A)	20,400	13,601	4,000	34,001
6.40	(B)	25,600	13,601	4,000	39,201
	(A)	23,200	16,001	3,625	39,201
8.00	(B)	29,000	16,001	3,625	45,001
	(A)	27,000	18,001	3,375	45,001
10.00	(B)	33,750	18,001	3,375	51,751
	(A)	31,050	20,701	3,105	51,751

Note: (B) denotes values before buying/selling has taken place; (A) denotes values after buying/selling.

"Riskless" Plans

One way to avoid risk is to invest money only in short-term "riskless" assets—for example, money market funds or six-month money market certificates. But inflation, as well as the public expectation of future inflation, has made even "riskless" investments very risky. As of September 1981, you could receive as much as 17 percent without risk, as compared to a stock market dividend yield of only 5.4 percent. But if you depend on 17 percent to maintain a standard of living, you must take into account the extreme volatility of "riskless" yields. During May 1981, for example, yields fluctuated from 10 percent to almost 15 percent. A retired person living on a pension and on investment income might attempt to avoid the risks inherent in the stock and bond market by turning to six-month money market certificates or to money funds. At certain times this strategy may appear to be the smart thing to do, but yields from these investments are notoriously volatile. As inflation recedes, short-term interest rates will fall accordingly.

We have already discussed the various types of risk that have an impact on the investment decision. You can find ways to avoid a given risk, but in so doing, another risk is almost invariably created. Risk can be lowered but never eliminated.

Leverage

Leverage in finance means using borrowed funds to increase the amount of assets under your control. When you use credit to buy a piece of property for income or for speculation, you are using leverage. Buying a stock of any financial asset and then using the stock as collateral to borrow more funds is also leverage.

Leverage has another dimension. Not only does it involve using borrowed funds to increase the amount invested, but true leverage also exists when an investment (speculation) is made where the expected gain is greater than the after-tax cost of the borrowed money. As long as you expect to make a return greater than the cost of the money, it is worthwhile to borrow. The use of borrowed funds, in this manner leverages potential profits upward.

Leveraging has some drawbacks; whenever borrowed funds are used, the potential for large losses also exists. Leverage works both ways. Greater-than-proportional profits can be made, but greater-than-proportional losses can also be suffered.

For example, suppose you buy XYZ stock at $50 a share and expect the price to rise to $100 within a year. You expect to double your money. You are so sure of this potential gain that you increase your investment to $100, using your own $50 and borrowing $50 from your stockbroker or from the bank.[17] If the stock doubles, you have $200 and have made a profit of $100 instead of the original $50. But when you borrowed the $50, you had to pay interest. Suppose the interest was 20 percent, or $10 a year. Since the 100 percent gain in price is greater than the 20 percent cost of money, positive leveraging occurred. But if the stock had risen only 5 percent, you would have made $5 and paid $10 in interest, for a $5 net loss. By using leverage, you would have converted a small gain into a loss.

Using borrowed funds and the tax deductions on interest can increase the possibilities of positive leverage without increasing your risk. Suppose a stock pays 5 percent and the interest rate on borrowed funds is 15 percent. If you are in the 40 percent tax bracket, your interest owed, dividend paid, and personal tax rate can be balanced in such a way as to increase the investment and pay the interest with the dividend. For example, suppose you buy $150.00 worth of stock with $100.00 of equity and $50.00 borrowed funds. The total dividend is $7.50 less taxes at 40 percent, or a net yield of $4.50. The interest cost on $50.00 of borrowed funds is $7.50 ($50.00 × .15) less the tax deduction of $3.00 ($7.50 × .40), for a net cost of $4.50. The cost equals the yield.

---

17. Buying a stock with credit is regulated by the Federal Reserve System, which determines how much the investor can borrow on "margin"—that is, the percentage of borrowed funds. If the permitted margin is 50 percent, you can borrow $50 for every $100 of stock held.

OPTIONS AS A FORM OF LEVERAGE

Options on stocks are like options on land. Suppose you think that a certain parcel of land will rise in value shortly. You negotiate with the landowner a contract that gives you the privilege of buying the land at any time during the next six months at a given price of $100,000. The landowner will charge you, say, $3,000 for this option. If the land value rises to $120,000 before the deadline for exercising the option, you could exercise your option to buy at $100,000 and could then resell at $120,000. Alternatively, you could sell the option to someone else. If the land is worth $120,000, a prospective buyer could buy it outright for $100,000 plus the option contract; hence prospective buyers would bid up the price of your option contract to somewhere near $20,000 ($120,000 − $100,000).

If you had bought the land outright in the first place, you would have had $100,000 invested and would have made $20,000 (a 20 percent gain) if the price rose to $120,000. By buying the option, you invested $3,000, and you might later sell the option at $20,000 (a gain of $17,000 on a $3,000 investment, or a 467 percent profit). The chances for huge percentage gains always exist in buying options. On the other hand, the underlying assets might just as easily fall in value, in which case you lose the amount invested in the option and have nothing to show for it. The important fact about options is that you can't lose more than the option cost. In our example, you would lose only the $3,000 you had spent for the option, even if the land declined in value; if you had bought the land outright, your loss might have been much greater.

In sum, options present the opportunity for good gain, but the loss can be no greater than the option price. Because of the lopsided advantage options carry, they generally sell at a premium over their immediate exercise value. Owning an option, however, gives only a limited time in which to make the profit (see Chapter 12 for a discussion of the option market).

Just as land options are attractive investments, there is a large and active market for options to buy or sell certain stocks. Using options to enter the stock market is cheaper and more speculative than purchasing stock outright. A **call option** gives the buyer the right to purchase a given security for a given period of time at a stated price. For example, assume that an investor thinks XYZ stock now selling at $30 will rise to $35 within three months. One obvious way to speculate is to buy, say, 100 shares of the stock and sell it if the price reaches the hoped-for $35. But suppose you could buy a call option for $200 (without commission). If the stock rises to $35 a share before the option expires, you can exercise the option and sell the shares or the option in the open market for a profit of $300 [$35 − ($30 + $2) × 100]. Thus, you have made a profit of 50 percent on the option, as opposed to the profit of 16.7 percent you would have made by investing directly in the stock. If the stock price does not increase as expected, you have invested only $200 plus commission, instead of $3,000 plus commission.

Looked at another way, you could buy the option for $200 and put $2,800 in a money fund. Thus, you would earn a possible 16 percent on your money and still control the amount of stock you would have controlled had you invested your entire $3,000 in the market. By buying the option, you take the risk of total loss of the option price, but you minimize your total risk. However, it is important to note that the option price (**strike price**) is usually so high relative to the market price that most option buyers do not make any money on their options. Options are a cheap way to speculate in the market without risking too much capital. Options to sell stock at given prices can also be purchased. For example, if the stock falls from $50 to, say, $20, the option buyer can deliver the stock for the guaranteed price of $50. This tactic is the same as selling short and is called a **put option**.

SUMMARY

1. The first step in developing an investment program is setting investment goals. These goals are a function of many different factors, but the most important is the stage of the investor's life cycle.
2. Risk is the basic factor affecting all investment decisions. You must select the level and type of risk you can accept. Risk and return are related. Investors seeking higher returns invariably have to accept higher risk.
3. Risk takes various forms. Long-term investments are usually exposed to more risk than are short-term investments. Market (systematic) risk refers to the risk of the whole market rising or falling. Market risk is usually compared to the risk faced by an individual company as reflected in the changing price of that company's stock. Inflation and interest rate risk go hand in hand because, as inflation rates rise, interest rates must also rise to keep the real rate of interest (market rate minus the inflation rate) stable. Political risk refers to the effect of changing political policies on investment values.
4. Risks can be categorized—for example, investments may be divided into five classes according to risk level. Class 1 would include the lowest risks, and Class 5 the highest, most speculative ones. Once you have set your investment goals, you must decide what level of risk is consistent with them.
5. Securities can be selected through use of various techniques. One important technique is fundamental analysis, which involves the appraisal of stocks through financial analysis to discover hidden values significantly different from market values. You can obtain superior results from fundamental analysis by following a simple set of rules.
6. Another technique for choosing securities, present-value analysis, uses discount tables to estimate the present value of a stock.

7. Technical analysis, or charting, refers to buying and selling securities according to the pattern of stock prices.

8. Contrarianism is a method of selecting securities that is based on doing the opposite of the market consensus. Because the market tends to overreact, it depresses some securities unduly. Contrarianism holds that among these depressed stocks great bargains may lie.

9. The efficient-market hypothesis is a concept of modern financial theory, according to which all financial information is reflected in the market price of the stock. Analyzing any individual stock is therefore irrelevant, since everything that can be known about the stock is already revealed in its price.

10. Beta is the modern statistical method of measuring the risk of individual stocks relative to the market as a whole. The risk of holding individual stocks can be eliminated by diversification of the portfolio.

11. Risk can be handled by ignoring price movements and using dollar cost averaging—that is, periodically buying a constant dollar amount of stock at various market prices. This technique will yield excellent results over time.

12. Another way to control for risk is the formula plan, a mechanistic device that forces you to buy stocks when they are cheap and sell them when they are dear.

13. Leverage is a method of using borrowed funds to increase resources under your control with the hope of more than proportionally increasing profit relative to cost. While leverage can be used effectively, its use increases risk.

14. Options are another means of increasing the resources under your control. Instead of trading in a stock directly, you purchase a contract to buy or sell the stock within a given period of time.

REVIEW QUESTIONS

1. (a) Define your own investment goals.
   (b) What major problem do you foresee that may limit your ability to achieve these goals?

2. What do you think your goals will be five years from now?

3. (a) Make a list of recent economic and political events that affected stock and bond prices.
   (b) Distinguish between events that affected individual stocks and events that affected the market as a whole.

4. (a) What is your estimate of the U.S. inflation rate for the next year?
   (b) How will inflation affect your investment goals?

5. (a) Find two stocks for each risk level from 2 to 5.
   (b) Explain why you assigned each stock to a particular category.

6. (a) Can you find a company whose assets are worth much more than the price of its stock?
   (b) Why do you think its assets are worth so much?

7. Do you think past prices predict future prices? Why, or why not?

8. Give an example of contrarianism.

9. Do you believe in the efficient-market hypothesis? Why, or why not?

10. Using any of the stock portfolios exhibited in this chapter, show how the portfolio result would be improved by the elimination of the worst stock in the portfolio.

11. Choose any stock on which you can find the price for the last five years. Suppose you had bought $100 worth of stock every month for three years. What would your results be?

12. Examine a month-old issue of the *Wall Street Journal*. Would you have made or lost money by buying a 90-day option on the last stock option listed?

13. Suppose you could buy a stock with a beta of 1.5.
    (a) What does the beta tell you if the market is expected to rise?
    (b) What does beta tell you if the market is going to fall?

14. A formula plan forces an investor to sell when prices are rising and to buy when prices are falling. Why is such a plan desirable?

15. Technical analysis holds that price movements describe certain formations that will repeat themselves. Does this assumption fit with the random-walk theory?

16. Recently Coca-Cola bought Columbia Pictures. The price paid was slightly in excess of book value. Why do you think Coca Cola bought Columbia?

17. Suppose you are twenty-six, married, working, and renting an apartment. You and your spouse are together entitled to put as much as $4,000 into an IRA. Would you consider this investment wise? Consider the "financial life cycle" in your answer.

CASE PROBLEMS

I. Investing an Inheritance

Mary and Hal are a young married couple with two children, age two and four. They live comfortably on Hal's salary. He has $50,000 of group life insurance and is covered by adequate health insurance. They own a modest home in a good school district. Mary has just received a $35,000 inheritance from her uncle.

QUESTION

1. What advice would you give Mary and Hal for investing the inheritance?

II. Effect of Job Dissatisfaction on Financial Planning

Joe and Muriel, both aged thirty-two, have been married for several years; they have one child, age five. Both work, and their combined income approaches $50,000. They are both covered by life and health insurance plans, and both are in company pension plans. Muriel's job requires constant traveling, and Joe is not sure whether he wants to stay in his present employment. At the present time they do not save much, preferring to use their money for expensive vacations and personal expenditures. They do not own a home.

QUESTION

1. What advice concerning their finances would you give Joe and Muriel?

III. Investment Alternatives

Jack and Mary Livingstone own a home whose value has tripled since they bought it. They have three children aged nine, fourteen, and seventeen, whom they expect to attend the local state college. Jack owns and runs a prosperous hardware store. The store provides him with health and life insurance. He feels that he now can provide $4,000 to $5,000 a year for investments.

QUESTION

1. What investment advice would you give to the Livingstones?

CHAPTER 12

HOW TO FIND AND INTERPRET INVESTMENT INFORMATION

LEARNING OBJECTIVES

In studying this chapter you will learn:

Where to find investment information;

How to read the financial pages;

What stock market indexes mean;

Why organized stock exchanges are important to investors;

The uses and limitations of options;

How to judge the safety and profitability of companies in which you might invest;

How to understand and use various financial ratios in investment analysis.

SOURCES OF FINANCIAL INFORMATION

There seems no end to investment information. Wall Street security analysts spend approximately 60 percent of their time reading technical material. The sources of financial information may be grouped as follows: (1) newspapers (metropolitan and financial), (2) financial services, (3) stockbrokers, and (4) annual reports of corporations.

Newspapers

The daily newspaper generally includes a financial section. Although metropolitan newspapers may be excellent sources of financial information about current stocks, the *Wall Street Journal* provides much more detail and extended coverage. While the *Journal* is published daily, some of the best financial newspapers are published weekly. For example, the *Wall Street Transcript* reproduces company and industry analyses, investment letters, and roundtable discussions about investments. The *Financial Media General* specializes in chart presentations of stock price histories along with a mass of other relevant information. This publication also includes many charts of interest to technical analysts (see Chapter 11 for a discussion of technical analysis). *Barron's* is a weekly in tabular form that can be useful to the fundamental investor as well as to the technical analyst.

Financial Services

The main sources of "raw" financial statement data are Moody's and Standard & Poor's services. These companies' publications are found in many public libraries and brokerage offices. They carry precise historical summaries of financial income and balance sheets as well as detailed summaries of capital structure (type and term of debts, and so on). They also have detailed summaries of bond terms (contractual agreements) and are especially noted for the quality rating they assign to stocks and bonds. For example, a triple-A bond rating (AAA) is the highest rating given; it signifies that the bond involves little or no risk of default (failure to pay on time). The ratings CCC,

---

Professor Mark Hanna, University of Georgia, took primary responsibility for preparation of this chapter.

CC, and C indicate speculative bonds. The B rating indicates bonds that fall between the riskless and the speculative. Stocks are given similar ratings. A widely used source for one-line summaries of stocks and bonds are S&P *Stock Guides* and *Bond Guides*, published monthly.

Many investors subscribe to investment services that mail weekly investment letters; for an extra charge some services will telephone their clients. Some libraries subscribe to investment letters, and many letters are reproduced in the *Wall Street Transcript*. The most widely known investment services in the United States are Value Line and Standard & Poor's, which publishes *Stock Reports*, found in most good libraries.

Stockbrokers

Stockbrokers are an important source of investment information. They are usually happy to supply customers with their own firm's analysis of a stock or with duplications of pages from Standard & Poor's or Moody's publications. However, factual information is one thing, and an opinion is quite another. You should not expect your broker to pick winners for you, and you should beware of brokers who claim to be able to do so. What you want is expertise without bias; you should consider your broker's advice carefully, but the final investment decision should be your own, after careful review of all available sources of information.

Annual Reports

The annual report of a corporation provides much of the information you need to evaluate that corporation as an investment. The annual report usually gives a financial history of the company, comparisons of financial data for the last five or ten years (including the range of stock prices), a description of the company's products and services, an assessment of the company's future prospects, news of lawsuits against the company, information about competitive products, and other information that can be obtained nowhere else in as much detail. Reporting requirements mandated by the Securities and Exchange Commission as well as by the Financial Accounting Standards Board help ensure that the bad news as well as the good is reported.

You can obtain a copy of the annual reports of most large companies in good libraries. You may also obtain a free personal copy by writing to the treasurer of the company at the home office, the address of which may be found in your local library.

"Are you Dalrymple, the discount broker?"

UNDERSTANDING THE FINANCIAL PAGES

Since the financial pages of newspapers are the most commonly available source of financial and stock market information, you should learn how to read and understand the data they report on a daily basis. Reading these pages daily will help you keep track of what is going on in the financial markets and obtain the specific information you need to make investment decisions.

Stock Market Indexes

Perhaps the first questions investors ask are: "What happened to the market? Did it go up or go down, and by how much?" The quickest way to answer these questions is to note the price movements of the stock market as a whole, as revealed by various stock market price indexes. One of the most widely followed indexes is the **Dow Jones Industrial Index (DJI)**, often called the Dow, an index of price movements of thirty major industrial corporate stocks listed on the New York Stock Exchange (see Exhibit 12–1). For example, the DJI stood at about 860 on 2 October 1981. This number represents what would be the average price of the thirty stocks if no splits had occurred in the stocks in this century. This adjustment allows the index to be compared over the years without fluctuations stemming from stock splits. Separate Dow indexes are maintained for transportation and public utility stocks. Financial newspapers and other sources frequently report other stock market indexes—for example, the **S&P 500 Stock Index** shown in Exhibit 12–2.

These indexes help you to judge where the stock market is today in comparison with past years. If you are considering making an investment today, you can tell from the indexes whether you are buying near the historical high, near the low, or somewhere in between. As shown in Exhibit 12–2, the S&P 500 stood at about 120 at the end of 1972; it stood as low as 60 near the end of 1974. If you had purchased stock in 1976, you would have been buying at the "somewhere-in-between" range.

The right-hand column of Exhibit 12–2 shows the ratio of average prices to average earnings. Note that the S&P 500 has tended to sell at lower and lower price/earnings ratios over the period from 1964 to 1981. The boxes of various lengths represent the annual range of the price/earnings ratio. By matching the boxes with the figures in the column labeled "P/E Ratio," you can see that investors could purchase $1 of earnings in 1981 for between $8 and $9, compared with a cost of over $18 in 1971. This information is helpful as an indicator of what is a reasonable price for a stock with earnings of a given amount. You would know from the chart, for example, that if your stock had earned $5 a share over the previous twelve months, a price of $45 ($5 in earnings times a P/E ratio of 9) would be fairly typical in September 1981.

Exhibit 12–3 shows numerical values for several stock market indexes, including the **New York Stock Exchange (NYSE) Index,** which includes every stock traded on the New York Stock Exchange. The New York Stock Exchange Index is perhaps a more accurate index of stock prices than either the DJI or the S&P 500, although it is not as well known.

Indexes such as the DJI, the S&P 500, and the NYSE Index tend to move together, because they mainly reflect price movements of the large company stocks. The thirty Dow stocks, for instance, have a total value equal to about 35 percent of all the 1,300 or so stocks listed on the New York Stock Exchange. In general, the DJI moves about ten times the amount that the S&P moves. Thus, if the S&P index is up $1, the DJI is generally up about $10, or ten points. A dollar is one point in the stock market; to say a stock is up two points is to say it is up $2.

EXHIBIT 12–1
The Dow Jones
Averages, July–
October 1981

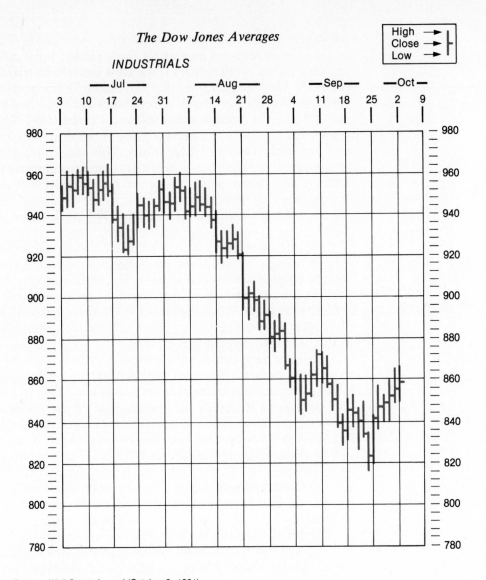

The Dow Jones Averages

INDUSTRIALS

High ⟶
Close ⟶
Low ⟶

Source: *Wall Street Journal* (October 2, 1981).

The DJI shows not only the closing price and the change from the previous day's closing price, but also the open, high, and low prices. The open price is the first price at which a stock trades during the day. The **high price** is the highest trade price during the day, and the **low price** is the day's lowest trade. The **close** is the price of the last trade of the day. The difference between the high and the low price during the day is called the **price range,** or **spread.** Some investors check carefully to see if stocks close in the upper half

EXHIBIT 12-2   S&P 500 Stock Index

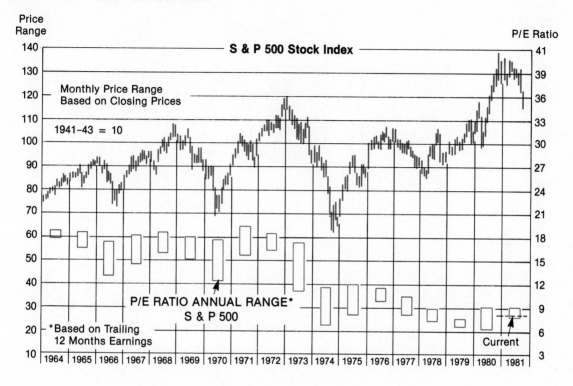

Source: Standard & Poor, *The Outlook* (September 16, 1981).

of the daily range; they think the market's direction the following day is likely to be upward if the DJI closed in the upper half of the range, and down if it closed in the lower half of the range.

Most Active Stocks

A highlighted feature in the daily paper's financial page is a list of the fifteen most active stocks of the day. Activity is measured by the number of shares traded. For example, Exhibit 12–4 shows that the most active stock, Sony Corporation, traded 617,500 shares on 29 March 1982, closing at 13-3/8, or $13.375, down 1/8, or $.125, from the previous day's closing price. The fifteenth most active stock was Penn Central, which traded about 44 percent as much as Sony but closed up that day. The companies listed, their volume and trading, and their price changes give an idea of which companies and industries are receiving the most investor attention.

EXHIBIT 12–3
Values of Stock
Market Indexes

| | Common stock prices[1] | | | | | | | Common stock yields percent[5] | |
| | New York Stock Exchanges index (Dec. 31. 1965 = 50)[2] | | | | | | Standard & Poor's composite index (1941–43 = 10)[4] | Dividend/ price ratio | Earnings/ price ratio |
Period	Composite	Industrial	Transpor- tation	Utility	Finance	Dow- Jones industrial average[3]			
1975	45.73	50.52	31.10	31.50	47.14	802.49	86.16	4.31	9.15
1976	54.46	60.44	39.57	36.97	52.94	974.92	102.01	3.77	8.90
1977	53.69	57.86	41.09	40.92	55.25	894.63	98.20	4.62	10.79
1978	53.70	58.23	43.50	39.22	56.65	820.23	96.02	5.28	12.03
1979	58.32	64.76	47.34	38.21	61.42	844.40	103.01	5.47	13.46
1980	68.10	78.70	60.61	37.35	64.25	891.41	118.78	5.26	12.65
1980: May	61.38	69.39	51.07	37.31	61.47	828.19	107.69	5.77	
June	65.43	74.47	54.04	38.53	65.16	869.86	114.55	5.39	13.08
July	68.56	78.67	59.14	38.77	66.76	909.79	119.83	5.20	
Aug	70.87	82.15	62.48	38.18	67.22	947.33	123.50	5.06	
Sept	73.12	84.92	65.89	38.77	69.33	946.67	126.51	4.90	11.67
Oct	75.17	88.00	70.76	38.44	68.29	949.17	130.22	4.80	
Nov	78.15	92.32	77.23	38.35	67.21	971.08	135.65	4.63	
Dec	76.69	90.37	75.74	37.84	67.46	945.96	133.48	4.74	10.88
1981: Jan	76.24	89.23	74.43	38.53	70.04	962.13	132.97	4.80	
Feb	73.52	85.74	72.76	37.59	68.48	945.50	128.40	5.00	
Mar	76.46	89.39	77.09	37.82	72.82	987.18	133.19	4.88	
Apr	77.60	90.57	80.63	38.34	74.59	1,004.86	134.43	4.86	
May	76.28	88.78	76.78	38.27	74.65	979.52	131.73	4.98	
Week ended:									
1981: Apr 25	77.69	90.59	80.67	38.46	75.25	1,011.90	134.58	4.87	
May 2	77.24	90.11	78.54	38.14	75.30	1,007.73	133.68	4.92	
9	75.73	88.47	75.72	37.44	73.10	975.94	131.02	5.02	
16	75.75	88.08	75.89	38.45	73.62	972.21	130.89	5.01	
23	76.49	88.86	77.22	38.60	75.47	978.19	131.94	4.97	
30	77.27	89.75	78.46	38.80	76.86	990.78	133.15	4.92	

1. Average of daily closing prices.
2. Includes all the stocks (more than 1,500) listed on the NYSE.
3. Includes 30 stocks.   4. Includes 500 stocks.
5. Standard & Poor's series. Dividend/price ratios based on Wednesday closing prices.
Earnings/price ratios based on prices at end of quarter.
Note: All data relate to stocks listed on the New York Stock Exchange (NYSE).
Sources: New York Stock Exchange, Dow-Jones & Company, Inc., and Standard & Poor's
Corporation.

Source: Council of Economic Advisers, *Economic Indicators* (May, 1982).

Individual Stock Quotes

With respect to individual stock quotes, the numbers are explained by the heading of each column (see Exhibit 12–5). Under the heading "52 Weeks" are two columns labeled "High" and "Low." American Can's high price for the previous fifty-two weeks was 45-1/2, and its low, 27.

Under the heading "Dividend," $2.90 is the annual dividend per share. The *x* that appears before the dividend means that the stock is selling on that date **ex-dividend.** That is, the current buyer is not entitled to a dividend that has already been declared by the corporation but not yet paid. If you buy a stock before the ex-date—usually several days before actual payment—you will be paid the dividend. If you buy after the ex-date, the previous owner receives the dividend. For example, suppose a stock goes ex-dividend on 2 October, and the amount of the dividend is $1. Since the owner of the stock

EXHIBIT 12–4   Two of the Fifteen Most Active Stocks, Monday, 29 March 1982

Stock	Open	High	Low	Close	Change	Volume
Sony Corporation	13-3/8	13-3/8	13-1/8	13-3/8	– 1/8	617,500
Penn Central	27-3/8	28-1/8	27	28-1/8	+ 1/2	272,400

Source: *Wall Street Journal* (March 30, 1982).

EXHIBIT 12–5   Daily Quotations for a Typical Stock, 6 October 1981

52 Weeks High	Low	Stock	Div.	Yield %	P/E Ratio	Sales 100s	High	Low	Close	Net Change
45-1/2	27	Amer. Can	x 2.90	6.8	10	9728	u 45-1/4	42	42-3/4	+ 5/8

as of 1 October will receive the dividend, and the new owner as of 2 October will not, the price of the stock will generally fall by $1 on 2 October to reflect this fact. However, it is not advisable to buy on 1 October to get the dividend, because you will have to pay income tax on the dividend, which is really a return of part of your purchase price.

The yield (6.8 percent) is determined by dividing the closing market price (42-3/4) into the dividend ($2.90). The P/E ratio of 10 is the current price divided by the earnings per share (EPS) over the previous twelve months.

American Can had a trading volume on 6 October 1981 of 972,800 shares. It is reported as 9,728 because a unit of trading of stocks is a 100-share lot, or a **round lot.** The exhibit also shows that the price of the stock reached a high for the day of 45-1/4 and a low of 42. The price had been much higher during the day than it was at its close of 42-3/4. The *u* in front of the 45-1/4 indicates a new fifty-two-week high for the stock (*d* identifies a new low). For American Can the difference in value for 100 shares between the high and low points on 6 October was 325 [(45-1/4 – 42) × 100]. The net change of + 5/8 indicates that the closing price was $.625 higher than the previous day's closing price.

Where Stocks Are Traded

Stocks and bonds are traded in national marketplaces called **exchanges.** The two major exchanges are in New York City. The oldest and largest is called the **New York Stock Exchange (NYSE),** and the other is the **American**

Stock Exchange (AMEX). Regional exchanges operate in other cities. Stocks are also traded over the counter, where the trade is negotiated by brokerage firms operating as principals.

One advantage of an organized exchange is that it offers a central place where all offers to buy and sell from traders all over the nation may be considered at a given moment. Without such a mechanism, a person living in an isolated place might not be able to find a buyer locally for a stock—certainly not at a price considered reasonable in view of the total supply or demand for the stock. Likewise, a buyer for a given stock might not be able to find someone who owns the stock and is willing to sell it. (However, if you know of someone who owns a stock you wish to buy, you can buy it directly, without paying commissions. You can arrange such a trade by writing to an office designated by the corporation's **transfer agent,** whose address is on the stock certificate.)

The NYSE has the most stringent requirements and usually lists the largest companies. The AMEX requirements are much more lenient; it is not nearly so sought-after a place to be listed. Generally, medium- to small-sized companies are traded on the American Exchange.

Another group of stocks shown on the financial pages of most large city newspapers is the **over-the-counter (OTC)** group. These stocks generally comprise companies of local interest that are not listed on any exchange. OTC trades are made over the telephone between brokers. Often a particular brokerage house specializes in **making a market** in a particular stock. Other dealers contact that brokerage house to make transactions for their customers in that stock.

The quotations of over-the-counter stocks are generally shown under the heading "Bid-Ask." The **bid price** is the highest price a dealer is willing to pay for another dealer's stock, and the **ask price** is the lowest price for which a dealer is willing to sell a stock to another dealer.

Specialist Brokers

If a seller wants to sell a stock at a price different from the going market price, the broker leaves the order with a **specialist broker.** These brokers operate on the floor of the stock exchange and specialize in the trading of a relatively limited group of stocks—typically, between seven and fifteen. For example, suppose General Motors is selling at $40 a share, and a buyer in Portland wants to purchase the stock at a price not over $36. The seller's broker leaves the order to buy with the specialist broker, who makes an entry that an order to buy at $36 is open for some designated period—say, a day or a week—or until canceled. If the price reaches $36, the specialist either sells the Portland buyer the stock from inventory or matches the buy order with a sell order from the floor of the exchange.

The specialist's major function is to make an orderly market for the stocks in which the specialist deals. If the market temporarily attracts more buyers than sellers, the specialist is supposed to sell stock out of personal inventory to make the market less "jumpy" and to smooth out price fluctuations. Exchange rules require the specialist to **trade against the wind**—that is, to sell stocks out of personal inventory only if the previous trade was higher—and to buy only if the previous trade was lower—than the trade immediately before. This requirement helps keep stock prices stable.

Because only the specialist broker knows how many shares are available for buying or selling at prices other than the current market prices, the exchange expects the broker to intervene when necessary to smooth out abrupt price changes. Because of the special knowledge these brokers possess, their role is under close scrutiny by both the exchange and the SEC.

A TYPICAL TRADE OF A LISTED SECURITY

The following scenario recounts the progress of a typical order. Mr. Jones tells his broker to buy 100 shares of IBM "at the market"—that is, at the best price for which it can be bought—and to hurry. The broker wires the New York office of the firm, which, in turn, telephones the order to the floor of the exchange. Order takers signal their floor broker that an order is in. The floor broker collects the orders for IBM and goes to the area (post) where IBM is traded.

"How's IBM?" the broker asks the specialist who handles the trades in that stock.

"60–61-1/2."

"How about the size?"

"400 bid and 600 offered."

"Take 100 at 61-1/8."

There is no response from the crowd of brokers around the post—no one is willing to sell at 61-1/8. Someone from the crowd then chimes in, "Sell 100 at 61-3/8."

Silence. Stalemate. The specialist might then offer 100 at 61-1/4, and Mr. Jones's broker might accept. Mr. Jones is then informed that he has bought 100 shares of IBM at $61.25 a share.

The specialist is involved in approximately one in eight trades and helps narrow the distance between bid price and ask price. The role of the specialist increases the marketability of stocks because if there are no orders to buy, specialists must use their own capital to make purchases.

Listed Options

Most financial newspapers contain a section showing the trading activity of listed options. A typical option listing is contained in Exhibit 12–6. To

EXHIBIT 12-6   A Typical Option Listing, Chicago Board

Option & N.Y. Close	Strike Price	Calls—Last			Puts—Last		
		Dec.	Mar.	June	Dec.	Mar.	June
Apache							
19-1/8	15	r[a]	8-1/4	6	r[a]	3/8	r[a]
19-1/8	20	1/16	1-5/8	2-3/4	1-1/8	1-1/2	2-1/8
19-1/8	25	r[a]	1-1/16	1-1/4	3-1/2	r[a]	5-1/8

[a]r = not traded.

Source: *Wall Street Journal* (December 16, 1981).

read option listings, you must understand the terms and symbols employed. In Chapter 11 we discussed options and what you can accomplish with them as an investment medium. Recall that when you buy an option, you are not buying or selling a stock, but only the right to buy or sell it. The right to buy a stock is termed a **call,** and the right to sell is termed a **put.** The price at which you have the right to buy or sell is called the **strike price.** The time in which you must exercise the option is identified by month. Conventionally, the option expires on the twenty-second day of a given month. In Exhibit 12–6, for instance, in December 1981 the $20 March call option for Apache Corporation was priced at 1-5/8. That is, on 16 December 1981 you could have purchased the right to buy Apache stock, selling for 19-1/8 in December, at a price of $20 any time before 22 March 1982. The cost of purchasing this right was $1.62 (1-5/8) per share in 100-share lots. Thus, you would have had to invest $162 plus commissions to engage in this type of trade. The prices of put options have a pattern similar to the prices quoted for call options. Thus for $150 (1-1/2 × 100 shares) plus commissions, you could have purchased the right to sell Apache at $20 any time before 22 March 1982.

Why would you want to buy or sell the right to purchase a security rather than purchasing the security itself? First, the amount of funds needed is much smaller. In the example given in Exhibit 12–6, you could have purchased the right to buy 100 shares of Apache stock at any time before 22 June, a six-month period, for only $275 plus commissions. If you were to buy the stock itself, you would have had to invest $1,912 plus commissions. Second, if the stock rises in price, you will make a larger relative gain on your investment by owning the option rather than owning the stock. For example, if Apache were to rise to $25 at the expiration of the option period, the option to buy at $20 would be worth $5. You would have made $225 ($500 − $275) on the option transaction, a gain of 81 percent on the $275 investment. If you had purchased the stock directly, you would have had a profit of $588 ($2,500 − $1,912), a gain of 31 percent on the $1,912 investment. (This comparison ignores brokers' commissions, which would reduce the profit percentages.)

"Don't feel bad, Pops, everybody eventually gets 'put' on 'options' if the 'strike price' is right."

The Bettman Archive, Inc.

Thus, a small dollar outlay enables you to control a relatively large investment and to earn a magnified return.

Note that if the stock were to remain at or below the strike price, you would realize no gain by exercising the option. For example, a June call option on Apache at a strike price of $20 a share would have no value unless Apache stock rose above $20. If it did not, the June call option would expire on 22 June 1982 without value, and you would have lost your entire investment of $275 plus commissions. Thus, investing in options is considered risky; if the stock does not rise in price during the period covered by a call option, you lose everything. Investors take this risk in the hope of making a large relative profit if the stock rises. In the case of puts, investors take the risk that the price of the stock will fall.

Because option trading is risky, it is appropriate only for experienced investors. Some investors, however, engage in option trading as a way to increase their returns from stock they already own. For example, if you already own Apache stock, you can sell a $20 March call option on your stock and receive $162 (less commissions). This practice is called **writing options.** You continue to receive any dividends paid on your stock. If the stock price rises above the strike price, you must sell the stock at the strike price and thus forfeit any increase you otherwise would have made. In effect, you have traded your potential investment gains above the strike price in return for the premium you received when you sold the call option.

The Bond Section

The term *bond* includes, for the most part, different types of fixed-income securities—namely, corporate bonds, government bonds, and municipal bonds. Generally a bond pays a fixed amount of interest every six months and carries a promise of redemption by the issuer at some specific future date. For example, suppose that for Corporation X, "6s of '91 (i.e. 6 percent bonds due in 1991)" is listed in the corporate bond section. The "6s" refers to the coupon rate on this bond—namely, 6 percent interest a year. Bonds are usually issued in $1,000 denominations; thus $60 of interest (6 percent of $1,000) is promised per year and is usually paid in two semiannual installments of $30 each. These payments are promised to continue until the bond is paid off (redeemed) by the issuing corporation in '91 (i.e., 1991). Suppose that the price of the bond is shown as 40-3/4. The 40-3/4 refers to the percentage of face value for which the bond is now selling: .4075 × 1,000 = $407.50 per $1,000 bond. The current yield on the bond is the ratio of the interest payment ($60.00) to the market price ($407.50). The following is a typical bond listing in the newspaper:

Corporation	Coupon	Maturity	Yield	Volume	High	Low	Last	Change
Mid Bank	8-7/8	84	11%	3	81	81	81	−3

First is the bond description: Midland Bank 8-7/8's of '84 signifies that interest payments of 8-7/8 percent of the face value will be made each year until the bond matures in 1984. The 11 is the current yield: 11 percent ($8.87/81). Under "Volume," the 3 refers to the number of $1,000 bonds traded that day ($3,000 worth of bonds, in this case). The 81 is the percentage of face value at which the bond sold (the high, low, and last prices were all at 81, or $810, on this day). The − 3 means that the bond fell three points from the previous day's close. Each point with respect to a $1,000 bond equals $10—thus, the bond fell $30 (probably in a single trade involving three bonds). Such a price change is considered relatively large. The volume (3) partly explains why the price fell so much: The bond was very inactive; only three bonds were traded all day. The fewer bonds traded per day, the less marketable the security. The lower the marketability of a security, the more a seller has to sacrifice in price to find a buyer. You should not buy bonds of low marketability unless you plan to hold them until maturity. At that time the company will pay you the full face value of the bonds.

Bond Averages

The Dow Jones bond averages are published in the *Wall Street Journal*. Exhibit 12–7 shows that on 19 May 1981, the 20-bond index stood at 59.13, down .13 from the day before. A comparison of each year's high (or lows) shows that the highs fell from 86.10 in 1979 to 76.61 in 1980 and to 65.78 in May 1981. Bonds fell from a high of 86.10 in 1979 to a low of 58.37 in 1981. Thus, there has been great volatility in the bond market and a large decline in bond prices. Bonds would have to rise about 50 percent to reach 1979 highs. Bond prices fell during most of the 1970s, for as inflation increased, interest rates tended to rise commensurately. Bond prices move in the opposite direction from interest rates; as interest rates rise, old bonds with lower coupon rates can only be sold at substantial discounts from their face amounts. The rise in interest rates in the 1980–81 period caused an enormous deterioration in bond prices.

EXHIBIT 12–7   Dow Jones Bond Averages

—1979— High	Low	—1980— High	Low	—1981— High	Low		— — TUESDAY — — —1981—		—1980—		—1979—	
86.10	73.35	76.61	60.96	65.78	58.37	20 Bonds	59.13	–.13	72.01	....	83.55	–.24
88.60	72.40	78.63	59.40	66.18	56.48	10 Utilities	58.58	–.09	74.11	+.09	85.40	–.23
84.28	74.25	74.92	61.55	66.15	59.68	10 Industrial	59.68	–.17	69.91	–.09	82.61	–.24

Source: *Wall Street Journal* (May 20, 1981).

INTERPRETING FINANCIAL INFORMATION

You need to know something about the financial condition of companies in which you are considering an investment. You would not normally buy the stock of a company about to go bankrupt, nor would you favor companies with declining earnings. If you are to invest successfully, you should be familiar with certain guidelines for interpreting available financial information.

Although interpreting financial information is a complex subject, you can obtain valuable insights merely by knowing how to formulate certain ratios and how to interpret other financial information regularly reported about corporations whose stock is widely traded. Two general classes of ratios are useful: (1) ratios that measure financial safety and (2) ratios that measure profitability. These ratios are based on information found in the firm's balance sheet and income statement, available quarterly (every three months).

Ratios for Judging Safety

Three basic ratios are used for judging the financial safety of an enterprise—that is, the firm's ability to pay its debts and to avoid bankruptcy (a condition that would spell losses for both creditors and stockholders). These ratios are as follows:

1. **Current ratio** (the ratio of current assets to current liabilities;
2. **Debt-to-equity ratio** (the ratio of total debt of the enterprise to the stockholders' equity);
3. **Interest coverage ratio** (the ratio of earnings before tax available to cover payment of fixed interest to the amount of interest expense).

To understand these ratios, you need to understand the concepts on which they are based. **Current assets** include the firm's cash, inventory, accounts receivable, and other assets normally converted into cash within a twelve-month period. **Current liabilities** include all debts due within twelve months—that is, short-term debt. If the current ratio is at least 2:1, most analysts agree that the firm is reasonably "liquid"—that is, under most circumstances the firm will have enough cash available within the year to repay any debts coming due within the year. As long as a firm can pay its current debts on time, it is considered solvent.

Total debt comprises both short-term and long-term debt; the latter is usually represented by bonds, mortgages, and bank loans coming due in a period longer than one year. **Stockholders' equity,** or **net worth** of the firm, is represented by the portion of the company's assets contributed by the stockholders plus the amount of company earnings retained in the company. Stockholders' equity is determined by subtracting total debt from total assets. For example, if assets are $1,000 and debt is $500, the stockholders' equity is the difference between these amounts ($500). The ratio of total debt to equity is a measure of the firm's long-term ability to discharge all debts, both short term and long term, in a satisfactory manner. When the proportion of debt is too high, financial difficulty may lie ahead because the "cushion" against financial adversity provided by the stockholders' equity may be too thin to tide the firm over in lean years. A ratio of debt to equity of at least 1:1 is considered normal for most financially solvent enterprises.

EXHIBIT 12–8   Ajax Company Balance Sheet, 31 December 19—

Assets			Liabilities		
Cash	$ 10,000		Accounts payable	$ 15,000	
Accounts receivable	20,000		Notes payable (90 days)	15,000	
Inventory	30,000				
			Current liabilities		$ 30,000
Current assets		$ 60,000	Mortgage payable		$ 45,000
Building	60,000				
Equipment	30,000		Total liabilities		$ 75,000
Fixed assets		$ 90,000	Common stock (1,000 shares, par $40)	40,000	
			Retained earnings	35,000	
Total assets		$150,000	Stockholders' equity		$ 75,000
			Total liabilities and stockholders' equity		$150,000

To illustrate safety ratios, let us consider the balance sheet of Ajax Company, a hypothetical hardware retailer, as shown in Exhibit 12–8. Assume that you are considering making an investment in Ajax Company and wish to know how safe the company is. Will it be able to pay its debts on time? You calculate two of the ratios for judging safety as follows:

$$1.\ \text{Current Ratio} = \frac{\text{Current Assets}}{\text{Current Liabilities}} = \frac{\$60,000}{\$30,000} = 2{:}1.$$

$$2.\ \text{Debt/Equity} = \frac{\text{Total Debt}}{\text{Stockholders' Equity}} = \frac{\$75,000}{\$75,000} = 1{:}1.$$

Since Ajax Company's current ratio is 2:1, it has $2 of current assets for each $1 of current liabilities. If the company's current assets had to be sold to cover its current debts, there would probably be enough cash to discharge its obligations with "room to spare." You would probably also wish to observe the current ratio for prior years to see whether any noticeable trend exists, and particularly to see whether the ratio is getting progressively smaller. Such a condition would be a warning sign that the firm's debt-paying ability may be declining. Lastly, you would want to compare the current ratio to the current ratios of other firms in the same industry to determine how Ajax Company stacks up against the industry as a whole.

The debt/equity ratio of 1:1 means that Ajax Company's stockholders and creditors have each contributed an equal share of the total capital employed by the company. Stated differently, for each $1 of capital contributed by stockholders, $1 has been contributed by creditors. The higher the ratio of debt to equity, the smaller the cushion for the protection of creditors. A "normal" level for the debt/equity ratio depends on the type of industry and on other factors. Some industries—for example, transportation enterprises and public utilities—commonly have greater debt/equity ratios than other industries. However, a trend of rising debt/equity could spell financial difficulty in the future. Firms with large ratios of debt to equity are said to be using financial leverage (see Chapter 11). Excessive financial leverage tends to produce wide fluctuations in stockholder earnings as business conditions change.

The third measurement of financial safety, interest coverage, is the ratio of earnings available for the payment of interest on bonds or mortgages to the amount of interest expense. This ratio is also called **times interest earned (TIE).** To calculate this ratio, you must compare Ajax Company's earnings with its interest obligations. Assume that Ajax's income statement for the preceding year appeared as follows:

Sales	$200,000
Cost of goods sold	130,000
Gross margin	$ 70,000
Expenses, except interest	40,000
Income before interest expense	$ 30,000
Interest expense	6,000
Income before taxes	$ 24,000

$$\text{Times interest earned (TIE)} = \frac{\text{Income before interest expense}}{\text{Interest expense}} = \frac{\$30,000}{\$6,000} = 5:1$$

In this year Ajax company earned $5 for each $1 of interest owed—a coverage of 5:1, which would be considered acceptable by most financial analysts.

To summarize, most analysts would interpret the three ratios for Ajax Company as indicating a satisfactory level of financial safety. In the absence of any other unfavorable factors or trends that might jeopardize the financial safety of the company, the investor's judgment that the company is "safe" would be justified.

Ratios for Judging Profitability

In judging the profitability of a company, the following measures are commonly employed:

1. **Rate of return on equity** (the ratio of available stockholder profits to the amount of stockholder investment);
2. **Rate of return on total capital** (the ratio of net income—that is, income after financial charges—to total assets employed by the business);
3. **Net profit margin** (the ratio of net income to sales, expressed as that portion of sales available to stockholders, either for dividends or for reinvestment in the enterprise);
4. **Growth in earnings and sales** (the compound growth of earnings per share for five or ten years—typically related to the number of shares of common stock outstanding).

We can calculate the first three ratios by reference to the data given for the hypothetical Ajax Company as follows:

$$\text{Rate of return on equity} = \frac{\text{Income before taxes}}{\text{Stockholders' equity}} = \frac{\$\ 24,000}{\$\ 75,000} = 32\%.$$

$$\text{Rate of return on total assets} = \frac{\text{Income before taxes}}{\text{Total assets}} = \frac{\$\ 24,000}{\$150,000} = 16\%.$$

$$\text{Net profit margin} = \frac{\text{Income before taxes}}{\text{Sales}} = \frac{\$\ 24,000}{\$200,000} = 12\%.$$

How should these ratios be interpreted? Note that the rate of return on stockholders' equity (32 percent) is greater than the return on total assets (16 percent) because creditors are being paid a fixed rate of return that is relatively small when compared to the return on total assets. Note that mortgage interest of $6,000, expressed as a percentage of mortgage debt, $45,000, is only 13.3 percent, whereas the company is earning 16 percent on all the funds it has available. The result is a greater return to stockholders, a reflection of the use of financial leverage. When a firm prudently employs debt capital, a larger return is available to stockholders as long as the company remains profitable. But financial leverage also introduces risk insofar as excessive use of debt may endanger the financial solvency of the enterprise. However, in the case of Ajax Company the debt-to-equity and the times interest earned ratios are both satisfactory, so the use of financial leverage is both profitable and safe.

Without the use of mortgage debt, the rate of return to the stockholders would have been reduced, since the $45,000 furnished by creditors presumably would have been furnished by stockholders and would have increased the required net worth by that amount. Instead of the current 32 percent, the rate of return would have been:

$$\frac{\text{Income without interest payments}}{\text{Total stockholders' equity}} = \frac{\$30,000}{\$75,000 + \$45,000} = 25\%.$$

Net profit margins, growth rates of sales and earnings, and other ratios may best be interpreted by comparing the firm in question with similar firms in a given industry and by comparing trends in profit margins and earnings per share over a period of years. Various studies, published on a more or less continuous basis by reliable sources, are available to help you make such comparisons. For example, an annual survey published by *Forbes* compares the management performance (profitability) of over a thousand major corporations in the United States. In the 1981 survey records of eight ethical drug manufacturers were shown; Smith Kline ranked first and Squibb ranked eighth on measures of profitability and growth over the previous five years (see Exhibit 12–9). The differences were large; the leader, Smith Kline, enjoyed a five-year average rate of growth in earnings per share of 24.7 percent, compared to only 7.4 percent for eighth-place Squibb. These figures may be compared with the eight company medians, also shown in the exhibit.

If you were considering buying the stock of a drug manufacturer for investment, the comparisons shown in the exhibit would be valuable. Certainly, other things being equal, you would prefer Smith Kline stock over Squibb. You would expect Smith Kline to be selling for a higher price per share relative to earnings, and, at the time of the survey, Smith Kline was selling for a price/earnings ratio of 18, compared with price/earnings ratio of 10 for Squibb. Investors obviously valued Smith Kline stock more highly because of its faster growth, even though Squibb paid a higher dividend rate—4.5 percent, compared with 2.5 percent for Smith Kline.

Locating Information on a Specific Stock

Before purchasing a given stock, you should look up the stock in one of the financial services or guides, where much of the information you will need to judge safety, profitability, and market position is contained in useful and convenient summaries. Frequently, using similar years and data reporting bases, you can compare the stock you are interested in with others in the same industry. An example is Standard & Poor's report for RCA Corporation, shown in Exhibit 12–10. This report includes the most recent stock price (22-7/8), the price range for the preceding ten years, the nature of RCA's business operations, a chart showing recent price fluctuations, past data on sales, earnings, operating margins, and ratios on safety and profitability similar (but not identical) to the ratios discussed earlier in the chapter. For example, RCA's current ratio, 1.5 in 1980, has declined gradually over the years from a 1.8 level in the years 1971–1973. However, its ratio of long-term debt to

EXHIBIT 12–9

Excerpts from a
Profitability
Survey of Drug
Manufacturers,
1981

Company	Five-Year Coverage Annual Growth Rate in EPS	Net Profit Margin	Returns on Equity (previous 12 months)
Smith Kline	24.7%	17.3%	38.1%
Merck	12.9	15.7	25.1
Schering Plough	14.3	14.5	23.5
Eli Lilly	12.0	14.0	21.3
Upjohn	16.0	9.8	22.4
Pfizer	10.7	8.4	17.6
A. H. Robins	8.5	11.6	18.4
Squibb	7.4	7.7	13.1
Industry median	12.5%	12.8%	21.9%

Source: *Forbes* (January 5, 1981), p. 244.

capital has declined from 52.3 percent in 1971 to its 1980 level of 42.3 percent, a favorable trend. RCA's safety level seems satisfactory.

The exhibit shows that RCA's profitability has tended to fluctuate considerably. Note, for example, that the column headed "Return on Equity" shows that the stockholders' return has varied from a low of 10.2 percent in 1975 to a high of 19.8 percent in 1977 and 1978. RCA's net profit margins (found in the column headed "% Net Income of Revenues") have been fairly steady (in the range of 3–4 percent in recent years), although they fell as low as 2.3 percent in 1975. Current earnings per share are expected to be down in 1981 from the 1980 level by a substantial amount—$2.50 a share in 1981, compared with $3.35 a share in 1980.

The Standard & Poor's report does not calculate compound average increases in sales, earnings per share, or other net earnings for prior periods. You can determine these data, however, by inspecting the original numbers and consulting the equivalent rates of increase from compound interest tables shown in Appendix A–1. For example, RCA's earnings per share have increased from $1.66 in 1971 to $3.35 in 1980—approximately a twofold increase over a nine-year period. Appendix A–1 shows that $1 doubles in nine years if it increases at an annual compound rate of 8 percent. Thus, RCA's compound growth rate of earnings per share is about 8 percent. The exhibit shows that RCA's price has actually declined over the period from 1971 to 1980. The high price in 1971 was $40.75, compared with a high of $33.00 in 1980. Investors in 1971 paid a high of 25 times earnings for RCA stock, compared with a high of only 10 times earnings in 1980. (The P/E ratio range in 1971 is given in the report as 25–16, compared to a range of 10–6 in 1980.) You may conclude from this comparison that RCA's stock is relatively inexpensive by historical standards. Yet RCA's safety seems adequate, and its growth of sales and earnings is fairly steady.

EXHIBIT 12–10
Standard &
Poor's Stock
Report on RCA
Corporation

RCA Corp.

NYSE Symbol RCA   Call Options on CBOE

Price	Range	P-E Ratio	Dividend	Yield	S&P Ranking
Jun. 25'81	1981				
22⁷/₈	32¹/₄–22³/₈	8	1.80	7.9%	A

Summary

RCA is a leader in the color television industry, broadcasting (NBC), vehicle renting (Hertz) and defense electronics. It is also an important factor in commercial electronics and international communications. In January, 1980 RCA acquired C.I.T. Financial Corp., a leading financial services company. Excluding nonrecurring gains, earnings should continue to be soft in 1981.

Current Outlook

Earnings for 1981 (excluding nonrecurring gains) are estimated around $2.50 a share, down from 1980's $3.35.
Dividends are expected to continue at $0.45 quarterly.

Earnings improvement is expected in the consumer products group in 1981 (excluding substantial start-up costs associated with RCA's videodisc system which was introduced in March). Reflecting the absence of the Moscow Olympics write-off and costly political coverage, NBC's earnings should show a recovery. However, earnings from the Hertz Corp. and the commercial electronics group are not likely to recover this year, and C.I.T.'s earnings are expected to remain flat. Further progress is expected for the communications and Government electronics group. Heavy introductory costs for the videodisc system and higher interest expenses will restrict earnings in 1981. Nonrecurring gains may result from several relatively small divestitures (to be reported at one time) and the possible sale of C.I.T.'s headquarters building in NYC.

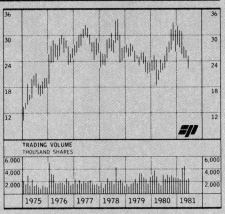

TRADING VOLUME
THOUSAND SHARES

Sales & Other Rev. (Million $)

Quarter:	1981	1980	1979	1978
Mar.	1,990	2,065	1,795	1,504
Jun.		2,031	1,895	1,612
Sep.		2,053	1,839	1,680
Dec.		2,160	2,016	1,849
		8,309	7,545	6,645

First quarter 1981 sales declined 1.1%, year to year. Pretax income fell 53%. After taxes at 37.1% against 44.3%, net income was down 47%.

Common Share Earnings ($)

Quarter:	1981	1980	1979	1978
Mar.	0.33	0.89	0.81	0.72
Jun.		0.80	1.13	1.02
Sep.		0.84	0.86	0.92
Dec.		0.82	0.92	0.99
		3.35	3.72	3.65

Important Developments

Apr. '81—Earnings comparisons for the first quarter of 1981 were penalized by lower operating profits from NBC and Hertz Corp., lower equity earnings from C.I.T. Financial, heavy costs associated with the introduction of RCA's videodisc system, higher interest expenses, and the inclusion of a nonrecurring insurance gain of $18.1 million in the first quarter of 1980.

Per Share Data ($)

Yr. End Dec. 31	1980	1979	1978	1977	1976	1975	¹1974	1973	1972	1971
Book Value	21.23	21.71	19.59	17.34	15.30	14.01	13.63	13.19	11.22	10.15
Earnings²	³3.35	³3.72	³3.65	³3.23	³2.30	1.40	1.45	³2.39	³2.05	1.66
Dividends	1.80	1.60	1.40	1.20	1.00	1.00	1.00	1.00	1.00	1.00
Payout Ratio	54%	43%	38%	37%	43%	71%	69%	42%	49%	60%
Prices—High	33	28¹/₄	33⁷/₈	32¹/₂	30¹/₈	21³/₈	21¹/₂	39¹/₈	45	40³/₄
Low	18¹/₂	21¹/₈	22⁵/₈	24³/₈	18⁷/₈	10³/₈	9¹/₄	16¹/₂	32¹/₈	26
P/E Ratio—	10–6	8–6	9–6	10–8	13–8	15–7	15–6	16–7	22–16	25–16

Data as orig. reptd. 1. Reflects merger or acquisition. 2. Bef. results of disc. opers. of −0.46 in 1971, and spec. item(s) of −3.36 in 1971. 3. Ful. dil.: 3.19 in 1980, 3.57 in 1979, 3.50 in 1978, 3.11 in 1977, 2.24 in 1976, 2.33 in 1973, 2.01 in 1972.

Income Data (Million $)

Year Ended Dec. 31	Revs.	Oper. Inc.	% Oper. Inc. of Revs.	Cap. Exp.	Depr.	Int. Exp.	Net Bef. Taxes	Eff. Tax Rate	[4]Net Inc.	% Net Inc. of Revs.
1980	8,011	972	12.1%	986	494	279	[3]507	37.8%	315	3.9%
1979	7,455	976	13.1%	865	438	[5]163	[3]472	39.8%	284	3.8%
1978	6,601	942	14.3%	700	364	113	[3]515	45.9%	278	4.2%
1977	5,881	848	14.4%	869	332	97	[3]470	47.5%	247	4.2%
1976	5,329	689	12.9%	780	300	94	[3]343	48.3%	177	3.3%
1975	4,790	518	10.8%	681	272	98	[3]189	41.7%	110	2.3%
[1]1974	4,594	525	11.4%	749	260	96	202	43.8%	113	2.5%
1973	4,247	602	14.2%	621	232	69	335	45.2%	184	4.3%
1972	3,838	532	13.9%	464	230	58	269	41.3%	158	4.1%
[2]1971	3,530	463	13.1%	490	202	61	215	40.2%	129	3.6%

Balance Sheet Data (Million $)

Dec. 31	Cash	Current Assets	Current Liab.	Ratio	Total Assets	Ret. on Assets	Long Term Debt	Common Equity	Total Cap.	% LT Debt of Cap.	Ret. on Equity
1980	175	3,403	2,277	1.5	7,148	4.8%	1,771	1,597	4,183	42.3%	15.6%
1979	206	3,230	2,136	1.5	5,990	5.2%	1,474	1,625	3,234	45.6%	18.0%
1978	241	2,758	1,612	1.7	4,873	6.0%	1,118	1,464	2,717	41.1%	19.8%
1977	264	2,376	1,400	1.7	4,352	6.0%	1,076	1,295	2,507	42.9%	19.8%
1976	178	2,038	1,261	1.6	3,838	4.7%	944	1,142	2,222	42.5%	15.7%
1975	280	2,047	1,287	1.6	3,728	3.0%	958	1,044	2,137	44.8%	10.2%
1974	318	1,898	1,162	1.6	3,647	3.3%	1,054	1,015	2,204	47.8%	10.8%
1973	287	1,835	1,043	1.8	3,301	5.7%	908	982	2,024	44.8%	19.6%
1972	394	1,807	1,026	1.8	3,137	5.1%	909	836	1,885	48.2%	19.2%
1971	236	1,678	923	1.8	3,022	4.1%	983	755	1,879	52.3%	13.8%

Data as orig. reptd. **1.** Reflects merger or acquisition. **2.** Excludes discontinued operations. **3.** Incl. equity in earns. of nonconsol. subs. **4.** Bef. results of disc. opers in 1971, and spec. item(s) in 1971. **5.** Reflects acctg. change.

Business Summary

RCA is a broadly diversified company. Business segment contributions in 1980 were:

	Sales	Profits
Consumer electronics............	16%	19%
Commercial electronics.........	16%	12%
Broadcasting	19%	9%
Vehicle renting	16%	16%
Communications	3%	11%
Government systems.............	10%	6%
Financial services	---	22%
Other business......................	20%	5%

Foreign businesses accounted for 17% of sales and 22% of pretax income in 1980.

Consumer electronics products consist of color and black-and-white TV sets and video cassette recorders. In electronic components, products include color TV picture tubes, semiconductors and broadcasting equipment.

Hertz is a leading vehicle renting and leasing organization. The Global Communications division is an international communications common carrier.

NBC furnishes network TV and radio services and owns TV and radio stations. Electronic equipment is made for the U. S. Government.

C.I.T. Financial is engaged in consumer and industrial financing and life and health insurance.

Dividend Data

Amt. of Divd. $	Date Decl.	Ex-divd. Date	Stock of Record	Payment Date
0.45	Sep. 3	Sep. 9	Sep. 15	Nov. 1'80
0.45	Dec. 3	Dec. 9	Dec. 15	Feb. 2'81
0.45	Mar. 4	Mar. 10	Mar. 16	May 1'81
0.45	Jun. 3	Jun. 9	Jun. 15	Aug. 1'81

Next dividend meeting: early Sep. '81.

Capitalization

Long Term Debt: $1,872,900,000.

$4 Conv. Pfd. Stock: 1,023,200 shs. (no par); conv. into 2.22 com.

$3.65 Cum. Pref. Stk.: 10,647,778 shs. (no par).

$2.125 Conv. Pref. Stk.: 10,647,191 shs. (no par); conv. into 0.7143 com.

Common Stock: 75,294,717 shs. (no par). Institutions hold some 40%. Shareholders: 225,000.

Office—30 Rockefeller Plaza, NYC 10020. **Tel**—(212) 621-6000. **Chrmn & CEO**—T. F. Bradshaw. **Secy**—W. P. Alexander. **VP-Treas**—M. Cornfield. **Investor Contact**—J. Reynolds. **Dirs**—T. F. Bradshaw, R. Cizik, G. H. Fuchs, I. O. Funderburg, E. H. Griffiths, W. C. Hittinger, W. S. Holmes, Jr., J. Koppelman, F. A. Olson, P. G. Peterson, J. R. Petty, R. H. Pollack, C. C. Selby, A. C. Sigler, D. B. Smiley. **Transfer Agents**—Company's Office, NYC; First National Bank of Chicago. **Registrars**—Continental Illinois National Bank & Trust Co., Chicago; Chemical Bank, NYC. **Incorporated** in Delaware in 1919.

Standard & Poor's Corporation (July 2, 1981).

RCA's dividends have not quite kept pace with its earnings, having increased from $1.00 per share in 1971 to $1.80 in 1980 (an increase of 80 percent in nine years). This feature is also reflected in the stock's **payout ratio,** which has declined from 60 percent in 1971 to 54 percent in 1980—that is, RCA is paying out only slightly more than one-half of its earnings and is reinvesting the remainder. Some investors would interpret this statistic as a favorable trend, since reinvested earnings tend to assure steady growth of the company and reduce the need for debt. In RCA's case, the company is indeed relying less on debt, having reduced the percentage of long-term debt from 52.8 percent in 1971 to 42.3 percent in 1980. On its price of 22-7/8, RCA was yielding about 7.9 percent to the investor ($1.80/22-7/8 = 7.9%), a fairly generous return at the time for well-rated stocks (S&P rated this stock "A," above average in quality). You can determine from the report that RCA pays dividends quarterly and that you must be a stockholder of record as of 15 June to receive on 1 August the dividend declared on 3 June.

SUMMARY

1. General sources of financial information include newspapers (especially their financial sections), stock guides, statistical sources, stockbrokers, and annual reports of companies. Two newspapers that provide the most complete investment information are the *Wall Street Journal* (published daily) and *Barron's* (published weekly). Among stock guides, Standard & Poor's *Stock Guide* (published monthly) is perhaps the most frequently consulted source for short information summaries. Value Line also offers complete one-page summaries of financial information about stocks. A rich but frequently overlooked source of information about investment opportunities is the corporate annual report, available without charge from issuing companies.

2. You can learn how to interpret financial information if you understand the various stock market indexes that tell you "what the market is doing." The most widely known indexes are the Dow Jones Industrial indexes of industrial, transportation, and utility stocks. More complete indexes include the Standard & Poor's 500 stock composite index and the New York Stock Exchange's index of price movements of all stocks listed on the New York Stock Exchange.

3. Knowing how to read individual stock quotes in the financial pages of newspapers is a first step in understanding investments. A large amount of valuable information about any given stock is summarized daily in one short line.

4. Organized markets exist for trading securities; these markets permit free-market forces to determine prices. The auction process and other

parts of the market system ensure that you can always find a buyer or a seller for your securities at some price level and give your investment portfolio marketability when you so desire. The New York Stock Exchange is perhaps the best known of the organized markets.

5. Trading in options, while mainly for the experienced investor, offers some opportunities that enlarge the number of available investment alternatives in the stock market. You should be aware of the substantial risks involved in trading in options.

6. In considering investments in bonds, you must be aware of the inverse relationship between bond prices and interest rates. Even small changes in long-term interest rates cause large contrary changes in bond prices. A convenient way to keep track of changes in bond prices and in interest rates is to observe the movement of bond price indexes, quoted daily in the financial sections of most newspapers.

7. In judging the appropriateness of stock investments, you can use several guidelines available in the form of financial ratios. Ratios for judging the financial safety of the enterprise in which you are investing include the current ratio, the debt-to-equity ratio, and the interest coverage ratio. Ratios for judging profitability of the company include the rate of return on stockholders' equity, the rate of return on total assets, the net profit margin, and growth rates of earnings and sales. In interpreting these ratios, you should observe trends from year to year and make comparisons with similar firms in the same industry.

REVIEW QUESTIONS

1. Consult the stock market section in your daily newspaper for two stocks in an industry in which you are interested.
   (a) For each stock, determine the high, the low, the closing price, yearly price range, dividend rate, P/E ratio, and volume of shares traded.
   (b) Based on the information obtained, compare the two stocks and indicate which you would prefer to buy.

2. For the two stocks selected in Question 1, look up further information in Standard & Poor's *Stock Guide* (available from your stockbroker), *Barron's,* Value Line publications, or other sources. Based on the new information, have you changed your opinion about which stock you prefer? Why, or why not?

3. Consult a local broker for an opinion on the two stocks you have selected.
   (a) Evaluate the broker's advice.
   (b) Has it changed your opinion? Why, or why not?

4. Write for the annual reports of the two stocks you have selected.
   (a) Evaluate the information contained in these reports.
   (b) What information was not available to you elsewhere?

5. (a) Find the current level of the DJI index. By what percentage has the market moved up or down from the previous day? The previous week? The previous year?
   (b) Discuss how this information may be valuable to you in making investment decisions.

6. (a) Compare the most active stocks in the financial section of today's newspaper with the most active stocks listed one week ago. Are any stocks on both lists?
   (b) Of what value is such a comparison in making investment decisions?

7. Should you buy stock just before it goes ex-dividend so that you will be entitled to receive the dividend? Why, or why not?

8. Does the fact that a stock is trading on the New York Stock Exchange rather than some other exchange mean anything to the investor?

9. Why does the auction process that is part of organized stock exchanges tend to improve the liquidity of your investment?

10. (a) Explain the meaning of the statement that specialists on the stock exchange must trade "against the wind."
    (b) What protection, if any, does this regulation give the investor?

11. Consulting Exhibit 12–6, explain why the Apache Oil Company's June $25 call option is trading at 1-1/4, while the June $25 put option is trading at 5-1/8. (Hint: Compare the strike price with the current price of the stock in December.)

12. Why is trading in options considered risky? Use an example to illustrate your answer.

13. In the discussion of bonds, the text states that the Midland Bank bonds of 1984, with a coupon of 8-7/8, are yielding 11 percent currently.
    (a) Show how the 11 percent was calculated.
    (b) Is 11 percent the "true" yield?

14. (a) Referring to Exhibit 12–8, the balance sheet of Ajax Company, explain how the current ratio would be affected if the mortgage became due within one year.
    (b) Explain the value of the current ratio to the investor who wants to judge corporate liquidity.

15. (a) If the rate of return on stockholders' equity and the rate of return on total assets are the same, is the company using financial leverage effectively? Why, or why not?
    (b) Why is reasonable financial leverage "good" for the stockholders?

16. (a) If a firm shows a high compound five-year rate of growth in sales but shows "flat" earnings per share over the same period, what is the implication for the potential investor?
    (b) Discuss the possible causes of such a phenomenon.

17. Look up the latest *Forbes* survey of management performance (published in January each year), or consult a similar source such as Value Line or Standard and Poor's, and report on an industry in which you are interested. Tell which companies in the industry you prefer as potential investments and defend your selections.

CASE PROBLEMS

I. Financial Statement Analysis
of Schering-Plough Corporation and Subsidiaries

Schering-Plough Corporation and Subsidiaries

Consolidated Balance Sheets

At December 31	1980	1979	1978
(Dollars in millions, except per share figures)			
ASSETS			
Current Assets			
Cash	$ 17.8	$ 23.8	$ 7.2
Time Deposits	317.3	171.6	192.0
Marketable securities, at cost which			
approximates market	87.9	94.0	49.5
Accounts receivable, less allowances—			
1980, $28.6; 1979, $20.8; 1978, $12.3	290.3	258.0	209.9
Inventories:			
Finished products	172.0	153.8	71.6
Goods in process	86.7	87.2	56.0
Raw materials and supplies	141.3	106.3	88.1
Total	400.0	347.3	215.7
Prepaid expenses, future income tax benefits			
and other current assets	110.8	90.4	72.0
Total current assets	1,224.1	985.1	746.3
Marketable Securities and Time Deposits, Non-Current,			
at cost which approximates market	110.7	92.8	118.1
Property, at cost			
Land	26.6	24.4	15.4
Buildings and improvements	319.9	289.5	250.3
Equipment	268.4	221.9	178.0
Construction in progress	116.6	58.1	29.4
Total	731.5	593.9	473.1
Less accumulated depreciation	206.7	178.5	153.5
Property, net	524.8	415.4	319.6
Goodwill, net	58.1	58.4	3.7
Other Assets	66.2	41.0	9.0
	$1,983.9	$1,592.7	$1,196.7

	1980	1979	1978

LIABILITIES AND SHAREHOLDERS' EQUITY

Current Liabilities

	1980	1979	1978
Accounts payable	$ 107.5	$ 90.7	$ 70.2
Short-term borrowings and current portion of long-term debt	359.6	182.7	29.0
United States, foreign and state income taxes	54.4	71.1	76.6
Accrued compensation	57.6	53.1	36.2
Other accrued liabilities	65.5	57.9	40.4
Total current liabilities	644.6	455.5	252.4

Other Liabilities

	1980	1979	1978
Long-term debt	41.2	7.6	1.6
Deferred income taxes	33.7	24.6	18.3
Other long-term liabilities	12.5	9.2	3.9
Total other liabilities	87.4	41.4	23.8

Redeemable Preferred Shares—Authorized, 7,000,000 shares of $1 par value each; issued—1980 and 1979, 656,944 shares of Series B, $5.07 cumulative; stated at redemption value of $60 per share

	1980	1979	1978
	39.4	39.4	—

Common Shareholders' Equity

	1980	1979	1978
Common shares—Authorized, 70,000,000 shares of $1 par value each; issued—1980, 55,042,029 shares; 1979, 55,030,495 shares; 1978, 54,084,567 shares	55.0	55.0	54.1
Paid-in capital	38.7	37.9	11.7
Retained earnings	1,176.8	1,023.6	878.1
Total	1,270.5	1,116.5	943.9
Less treasury shares, at cost—1980, 1,919,971 shares; 1979, 1,991,326 shares; 1978, 792,500 shares	58.0	60.1	23.4
Total common shareholders' equity	1,212.5	1,056.4	920.5
	$1,983.9	$1,592.7	$1,196.7

Statements of Consolidated Income

For the Years Ended December 31	1980	1979	1978
(Dollars in millions, except per share figures)			
Sales	**$1,740.4**	$1,434.0	$1,082.5
Operating Costs and Expenses:			
Cost of sales	612.4	466.2	318.1
Selling, general and administrative	732.6	606.2	447.5
Research and development	90.0	74.8	65.7
	1,435.0	1,147.2	831.3
Operating Income	305.4	286.8	251.2
Non-Operating Income (Expense):			
Interest income	42.6	26.2	23.5
Interest expense	(26.6)	(9.3)	(8.1)
Foreign exchange losses	(3.9)	(7.3)	(1.4)
Other, net	10.3	12.3	7.5
	22.4	21.9	21.5
Income Before Income Taxes	327.8	308.7	272.7
Income taxes	88.5	86.4	79.1
Net Income	$ 239.3	$ 222.3	$ 193.6
Net Income Per Common Share	$ 4.45	$ 4.12	$ 3.62

Statements of Consolidated Retained Earnings

For the Years Ended December 31	1980	1979	1978
(Dollars in millions, except per share figures)			
Retained Earnings, Beginning of Year	**$1,023.6**	$ 878.1	$ 749.3
Net income	239.3	222.3	193.6
Cash dividends on common shares (per share— 1980, $1.56; 1979, $1.39; 1978, $1.21)	(82.8)	(74.3)	(64.8)
Cash dividends on preferred shares (per share— 1980, $5.07; 1979, $3.81; none in 1978)	(3.3)	(2.5)	—
Retained Earnings, End of Year	**$1,176.8**	$1,023.6	$ 878.1

Source: Schering-Plough Corporation, *Annual Report,* 1981.

QUESTIONS

1. For each of the three years (1978, 1979, 1980) calculate the following ratios and interpret the information they provide about company safety and profitability:

   (a) Current ratio;
   (b) Total debt-to-equity ratio (include preferred stock as part of stockholders' equity);
   (c) Times interest earned (add back interest expense to income before taxes);
   (d) Rate of return on total assets (use net income);
   (e) Rate of return on total equity (use net income; count preferred stock as part of stockholders' equity);
   (f) Net profit margin (use net income).

2. Are any adverse trends present over the three-year period?

II. A Value Line Report on Flow General

(See Flow General report on opposite page.)

QUESTIONS

1. Using what you have learned about finding and interpreting financial information, prepare a report on Flow General summarizing (a) the company's safety and (b) its profitability.

2. Do you agree with Value Line's summary rating of "4" (below average) for safety? Why, or why not?

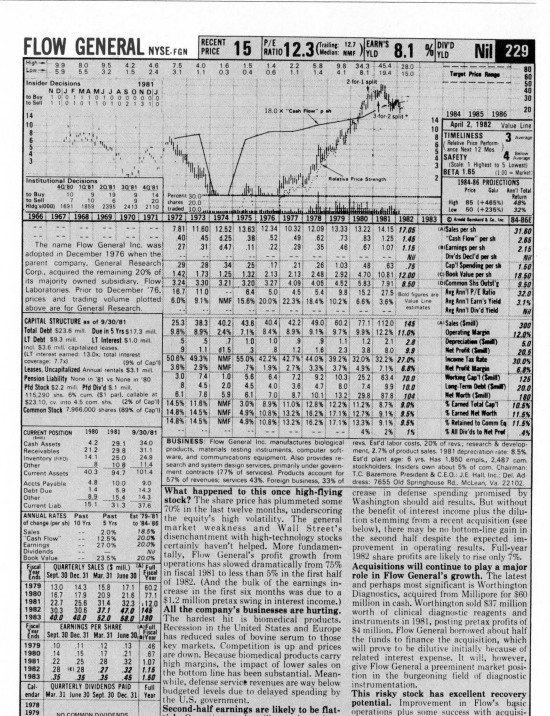

FLOW GENERAL NYSE-FGN

| RECENT PRICE | 15 | P/E RATIO | 12.3 (Trailing: 12.7 Median: NMF) | EARN'S YLD | 8.1 % | DIV'D YLD | Nil | 229 |

	9.9	8.0	9.5	4.2	4.6	7.5	4.0	1.6	1.5	1.4	2.2	5.8	9.8	34.3	45.4	28.0
High–	5.9	5.5	3.2	1.5	2.4	3.1	1.1	0.3	0.4	0.6	1.1	1.4	4.1	8.1	19.4	15.0
Low–																

Target Price Range 1984 1985 1986

Insider Decisions 1981
N D J F M A M J J A S O N D J
to Buy 1 0 0 1 1 1 0 1 0 0 0 0 0 0
to Sell 1 1 0 1 0 1 1 1 0 1 0 2 1 3 1 0

2-for-1 split
18.0 × "Cash Flow" p sh
3-for-2 split

April 2, 1982 Value Line

TIMELINESS **3** Average
Relative Price Performance Next 12 Mos.
SAFETY **4** Below Average
(Scale: 1 Highest to 5 Lowest)
BETA 1.65 (1.00 = Market)

Relative Price Strength

Institutional Decisions
	4Q'80	1Q'81	2Q'81	3Q'81	4Q'81
to Buy	10	9	19	9	14
to Sell	7	10	6	9	20
Hldg's(000)	1691	1859	2395	2413	2110

Percent shares traded 30.0 20.0 10.0

1984-86 PROJECTIONS
	Price	Gain	Ann'l Total Return
High	85	(+465%)	48%
Low	50	(+235%)	32%

© Arnold Bernhard & Co., Inc.

1966	1967	1968	1969	1970	1971	1972	1973	1974	1975	1976	1977	1978	1979	1980	1981	1982	1983		84-86E
--	--	--	--	--	--	7.81	11.60	12.52	13.63	12.34	10.32	12.59	13.33	13.22	14.15	17.05		(A)Sales per sh	31.60
--	--	--	--	--	--	.40	.45	d.25	.38	.52	.49	.62	.73	.83	1.25	1.45		"Cash Flow" per sh	2.65
--	--	--	--	--	--	.27	.31	d.47	.11	.22	.29	.35	.46	.67	1.07	1.15		(B)Earnings per sh	2.15
						--	--	--	--	--	--	--	--	--	--	Nil		Div'ds Decl'd per sh	Nil
						.29	.28	.34	.25	.17	.21	.35	1.03	.48	.63	.75		Cap'l Spending per sh	1.50
						1.42	1.73	1.25	1.32	2.13	2.13	2.48	2.92	4.70	10.81	12.00		(C)Book Value per sh	18.50
						3.24	3.30	3.21	3.20	3.27	4.09	4.05	4.52	5.83	7.91	8.50		(D)Common Shs Outst'g	9.50
						16.7	11.0	--	6.4	5.0	4.5	5.4	9.8	15.2	27.5	Bold figures are Value Line estimates		Avg Ann'l P/E Ratio	32.0
						6.0%	9.1%	NMF	15.6%	20.0%	22.3%	18.4%	10.2%	6.6%	3.6%			Avg Ann'l Earn's Yield	3.1%
						--	--	--	--	--	--	--	--	--	--			Avg Ann'l Div'd Yield	Nil
						25.3	38.3	40.2	43.6	40.4	42.2	49.0	60.2	77.1	112.0	145		(A)Sales ($mill)	300
						9.8%	8.9%	2.4%	7.1%	8.4%	8.9%	9.1%	9.7%	9.9%	12.2%	11.0%		Operating Margin	12.0%
						.5	.5	.7	1.0	1.0	.9	.9	1.1	1.2	2.1	2.8		Depreciation ($mill)	5.0
						.9	1.1	d1.5	.3	.8	1.2	1.6	2.3	3.8	8.0	9.9		Net Profit ($mill)	20.5
						50.6%	49.3%	NMF	55.0%	42.2%	42.7%	44.0%	39.2%	32.0%	32.2%	27.0%		Income Tax Rate	30.0%
						3.6%	2.9%	NMF	7%	1.9%	2.7%	3.3%	3.7%	4.9%	7.1%	6.8%		Net Profit Margin	6.8%
						3.0	7.4	1.0	5.6	6.4	7.2	9.2	10.3	25.2	63.4	70.0		Working Cap'l ($mill)	125
						.8	4.5	2.0	4.5	4.0	3.6	4.7	8.0	7.4	9.9	10.0		Long-Term Debt ($mill)	20.0
						6.1	7.6	5.9	6.1	7.0	8.7	10.1	13.2	29.8	87.8	104		Net Worth ($mill)	180
						14.5%	11.6%	NMF	3.0%	8.9%	11.0%	12.8%	12.2%	11.2%	8.7%	9.0%		% Earned Total Cap'l	10.5%
						14.8%	14.5%	NMF	4.9%	10.8%	13.2%	16.2%	17.1%	17.1%	9.1%	9.5%		% Earned Net Worth	11.5%
						14.8%	14.5%	NMF	4.9%	10.8%	13.2%	16.2%	17.1%	13.3%	9.1%	9.5%		% Retained to Comm Eq	11.5%
						--	--	--	--	--	--	--	--	4%	2%	1%		% All Div'ds to Net Prof	.4%

The name Flow General Inc. was adopted in December 1976 when the parent company, General Research Corp., acquired the remaining 20% of its majority owned subsidiary, Flow Laboratories. Prior to December '76, prices and trading volume plotted above are for General Research.

CAPITAL STRUCTURE as of 9/30/81
Total Debt $23.6 mill. Due in 5 Yrs $17.3 mill.
LT Debt $9.3 mill. LT Interest $1.0 mill.
Incl. $3.6 mill. capitalized leases.
(LT interest earned: 13.0x; total interest coverage: 7.7x) (9% of Cap'l)
Leases, Uncapitalized Annual rentals $3.1 mill.
Pension Liability None in '81 vs None in '80
Pfd Stock $2.2 mill. Pfd Div'd $.1 mill.
115,290 shs. 6% cum. ($1 par), callable at $23.10, cv. into 4.5 com. shs. (2% of Cap'l)
Common Stock 7,966,000 shares (89% of Cap'l)

CURRENT POSITION
	1980	1981	9/30/81
($mil.)			
Cash Assets	4.2	29.1	34.0
Receivables	21.2	29.8	31.1
Inventory (FIFO)	14.1	25.0	24.9
Other	.8	10.8	11.4
Current Assets	40.3	94.7	101.4
Accts Payable	4.8	10.0	9.0
Debt Due	1.4	5.9	14.3
Other	8.9	15.4	14.3
Current Liab.	15.1	31.3	37.6

ANNUAL RATES
of change (per sh)	Past 10 Yrs	Past 5 Yrs	Est '79-'81 to '84-'86
Sales	--	2.0%	18.5%
"Cash Flow"	--	12.5%	20.0%
Earnings	--	27.0%	20.0%
Dividends	--	--	Nil
Book Value	--	23.5%	20.0%

QUARTERLY SALES ($ mill.)
Fiscal Year Ends	Sept. 30	Dec. 31	Mar. 31	June 30	(A)Full Fiscal Year
1979	13.0	14.3	15.8	17.1	60.2
1980	16.7	17.9	20.9	21.6	77.1
1981	22.7	25.6	31.4	32.3	112.0
1982	30.3	30.6	37.1	47.0	145
1983	40.0	40.0	52.0	58.0	190

EARNINGS PER SHARE
Fiscal Year Ends	Sept. 30	Dec. 31	Mar. 31	June 30	(A)Full Fiscal Year
1979	.10	.11	.12	.13	.46
1980	.14	.15	.17	.21	.67
1981	.22	.25	.28	.32	1.07
1982	.28	(E).28	.27	.32	1.15
1983	.35	.35	.45	.45	1.60

QUARTERLY DIVIDENDS PAID
Cal- endar	Mar. 31	June 30	Sept. 30	Dec. 31	Full Year
1978					
1979		NO COMMON DIVIDENDS BEING PAID			
1980					
1981					
1982					

BUSINESS:
Flow General Inc. manufactures biological products, materials testing instruments, computer software, and communications equipment. Also provides research and system design services, primarily under government contracts (77% of revenues). Products account for 57% of revenues; services 43%. Foreign business, 33% of revs. Est'd labor costs, 20% of revs.; research & development, 2.7% of product sales. 1981 depreciation rate: 8.5%. Est'd plant age: 6 yrs. Has 1,850 empls., 2,487 com. stockholders. Insiders own about 5% of com. Chairman: T.C. Bazemore. President & C.E.O.: J.E. Hall, Inc. Del. Address: 7655 Old Springhouse Rd., McLean, Va. 22102.

What happened to this once high-flying stock? The share price has plummeted some 70% in the last twelve months, underscoring the equity's high volatility. The general market weakness and Wall Street's disenchantment with high-technology stocks certainly haven't helped. More fundamentally, Flow General's profit growth from operations has slowed dramatically from 75% in fiscal 1981 to less than 5% in the first half of 1982. (And the bulk of the earnings increase in the first six months was due to a $1.2 million pretax swing in interest income.) **All the company's businesses are hurting.** The hardest hit is biomedical products. Recession in the United States and Europe has reduced sales of bovine serum to those key markets. Competition is up and prices are down. Because biomedical products carry high margins, the impact of lower sales on the bottom line has been substantial. Meanwhile, defense service revenues are way below budgeted levels due to delayed spending by the U.S. government.

Second-half earnings are likely to be flattish. Operating results will get a boost from new biomedical products, which ought to do well as the economy improves. Too, an increase in defense spending promised by Washington should aid results. But without the benefit of interest income plus the dilution stemming from a recent acquisition (see below), there may be no bottom-line gain in the second half despite the expected improvement in operating results. Full-year 1982 share profits are likely to rise only 7%.

Acquisitions will continue to play a major role in Flow General's growth. The latest and perhaps most significant is Worthington Diagnostics, acquired from Millipore for $60 million in cash. Worthington sold $37 million worth of clinical diagnostic reagents and instruments in 1981, posting pretax profits of $4 million. Flow General borrowed about half the funds to finance the acquisition, which will prove to be dilutive initially because of related interest expense. It will, however, give Flow General a preeminent market position in the burgeoning field of diagnostic instrumentation.

This risky stock has excellent recovery potential. Improvement in Flow's basic operations plus some success with acquisitions might push the company's earnings—and the stock price—sharply higher by 1984-86.

R.C.C./M.S.

CHAPTER 13

INVESTMENT COMPANIES

LEARNING OBJECTIVES

In studying this chapter you will learn:

What investment companies and mutual funds are and what they have to offer the investor;

The advantages and disadvantages of different kinds of funds;

The differences between closed-end and open-end funds and their relative investment merits;

Why diversification, the major advantage of mutual funds, can also be a disadvantage;

Whether professional management of investment always produces superior investment results;

How you can select mutual funds with investment objectives similar to your own;

How to measure the investment performance of an investment company and of mutual funds;

How mutual fund investments are made and how a periodic purchase plan may be especially advantageous;

The costs of mutual fund services and management.

An **investment company** is a corporation that sells shares of common stock so that it may accumulate capital to invest for the benefit of its shareholders. By combining the investment funds of many shareholders, a company may buy different securities, which are referred to as the company's **portfolio.** The investor in such a company owns a proportionate share of a diversified portfolio of securities.

The current underlying market value of each investor's share in an investment company is called the **net asset value (NAV)** per share. As illustrated for the XYZ Investment Company in Exhibit 13–1, the NAV is determined by adding all the company's assets, including the portfolio of securities at their current market values, and subtracting all accrued liabilities to arrive at the net assets, or shareholders' equity (equal to $501 million in this example). The net assets are then divided by the total number of currently outstanding shares of the investment company (in this illustration, 50 million shares). The NAV per share of the XYZ Company on 31 December 1983 was $10.02. Investment companies try to maintain or increase the market value of their securities portfolios to maintain or increase the NAV of the shares owned by the company's shareholders.

To carry out their investment objectives and policies, companies employ professional portfolio managers who continuously supervise the portfolios by buying and selling securities as investment considerations warrant. The operating expenses of the company, including the portfolio management advisory fee, are paid by the company out of the investment income earned by the portfolio. In the example of the XYZ Company in Exhibit 13–2, the gross investment income in 1983 amounted to $19.76 million from stocks and bonds in the portfolio. The total operating expenses (including an investment advisory fee of one-half of 1 percent of the average net assets) amounted to $2.76 million, leaving a net investment income of $17 million, or a dividend income rate of $.34 per company share. The operating expenses of $2.76 million amounted to one-half of 1 percent of the total net assets ($501 million, see Exhibit 13–1) of XYZ Corporation. This percentage is called the **operating expense ratio.** Other things being equal, the shareholders prefer as high a gross investment income and as low an operating expense ratio as possible. Results count; low operating expenses and mediocre results are not a high recommendation.

Investment companies are a popular medium, particularly among small investors who have an opportunity to pool their funds, obtain diversification among many different securities, delegate portfolio management responsi-

---

Professor Scott Bauman, Northern Illinois University, took primary responsibility for the preparation of this chapter.

EXHIBIT 13–1
XYZ Investment Company: Statement of Assets and Liabilities as of 31 December 1983

Assets		
Cash	$	190,000
Receivables		2,800,000
Securities portfolio		500,000,000
Miscellaneous assets		10,000
Total		$503,000,000
Accrued liabilities		2,000,000
Net assets applicable to outstanding shares		$501,000,000
Outstanding shares		50,000,000
Net asset value per share		$10.02

EXHIBIT 13–2
XYZ Investment Company: Income Statement for 1983

Gross investment income (from portfolio dividends and interest)		$19,760,000
Operating expenses		
Investment advisory fee (0.5% of average net assets)	$2,505,000	
Custodian and transfer agent fees	110,000	
Legal and auditing fees	20,000	
Registration fees and expenses	30,000	
Printing and postage	40,000	
Stockholders' reports	35,000	
Miscellaneous	$ 20,000	
Total		$2,760,000
Net investment income		$17,000,000
Total dividends paid		$17,000,000
Dividends per share (50 million shares)		$.34
Operating expense as a percentage of net assets (operating expense ratio)		0.551%

bilities to a full-time professional staff, and derive financial benefits in direct proportion to the growth in NAV and dividend income.

Investment companies are of two major types—**closed-end companies**, which have a fixed number of shares outstanding, and **open-end companies** (also called **mutual funds**), which continuously offer to sell new shares and to redeem or retire outstanding shares.

CLOSED-END SECURITIES

The closed-end company, the oldest form of investment company, dates back to nineteenth-century Britain and New England. The legal structure of closed-end companies resembles that of regular corporations. When the company is formed, a fixed number of shares of common stock are issued and sold to investors. The proceeds from the sale of these shares are used to purchase a portfolio of securities.

How Shares Are Traded

After a closed-end company is established, the shares of the company are bought and sold on a stock exchange or on the over-the-counter market. An investor who wishes to buy or sell shares of a closed-end company places a securities order with a stockbroker.

Prospective investors may obtain information about closed-end companies in the same way that they gather information about other publicly traded stocks. Investment reports are available from stockbrokers and are also found in the business reference section of many libraries. Investment company industry surveys and individual company research analyses are available in the following publications:

Standard & Poor's *Stock Reports* (on individual companies);
Standard & Poor's *Industry Survey* ("Investment Companies" section);
Wiesenberger Investment Companies Service: *Investment Companies* (annual manual);
Wiesenberger Investment Companies Service: *Current Performance & Dividend Record* (monthly);
Wiesenberger Investment Companies Service: *Management Results* (quarterly);
Value Line Investment Survey: ("Investment Company Industry" section);
Moody's *Bank and Finance.*

A book on closed-end companies is also available: Thomas J. Herzfeld, *The Investor's Guide to Closed-End Funds: The Herzfeld Hedge* (New York: McGraw-Hill, 1980).

Investment Objectives and Policies

Although closed-end companies pursue a variety of investment objectives and policies, the number of companies from which the investor may choose is not as great as in the case of mutual funds. Some companies whose shares are readily available for purchase are listed in Exhibit 13–3. **Diversified com·**

EXHIBIT 13–3   Examples of Publicly Traded Closed-End Funds, 17 July 1981

	Net Asset Value	Market Price	Percentage that Net Asset Value Is below Market Price
Stock Funds			
Adams Express	$18.04	$14-1/8	21.7%
General American Investment	21.00	19	9.5
Lehman	16.42	14-5/8	10.9
Madison	26.89	20-1/4	24.7
Tri-Continental	28.38	21-5/8	23.8
Bond Funds			
American General BD	$16.30	$16	1.8
CNA Incorporated	9.26	9-1/8	1.5
Drexel Bond	14.21	15-5/8	10.0
John Hancock Investment	16.58	14-7/8	10.3
Pacific American Income	11.61	10	13.9
Transamerica	16.03	15-5/8	2.5

Source: *Barron's* (July 21, 1981).

mon stock funds hold portfolios invested predominantly in common stocks of a number of different industries; specialized funds, as their name suggests, hold portfolios that concentrate in a particular category of securities (e.g., the Japan Fund invests in Japanese stocks).

Closed-end bond funds invest predominantly in long-term marketable bonds. Some of these funds invest in only high-quality bond issues (e.g., Excelsior Income Shares and Fort Dearborn Income Securities have been investing most of their portfolios in bonds with a rating of A or higher). Other funds invest predominantly in bonds of medium quality (e.g., American General Bond has had about 60 percent of its portfolio in bonds with ratings below A). Investment information about most closed-end investment companies is available from a number of sources, including those already cited.

A question for the investor is which type of fund—open-end or closed-end—has had the best performance. Exhibit 13–4 contains NAV data gathered by Wiesenberger, a large investment company reporting service, that show that during the seventies selected groups of closed-end funds did not perform as well as average open-end funds or as well as the "market average" of all stocks (the S&P 500). However, since closed-end funds usually sell at a discount, the buyer's average return is greater than the change in NAV, so closed-end funds may be a better investment than the exhibit suggests. The writer

EXHIBIT 13-4   Management Results, Closed-End Diversified versus Open-End Growth Funds,
1971–1980: Percentage Change in Net Assets per Share and Standard & Poor's
500 Stock Index

	S&P 500	Average % Change of 12 Closed-End Funds	Average % Change of 80 Open-End Growth Funds	Average % Change of 114 Open-End Funds (Long-Term Growth, Income Secondary)
1971	14.1%	18.3%	27.6%	20.8%
1972	18.8	19.7	11.8	13.8
1973	− 14.5	− 12.5	− 29.2	− 22.9
1974	− 26.0	− 25.6	− 27.6	− 26.7
1975	36.9	− 33.1	39.3	32.7
1976	23.7	27.1	29.9	23.4
1977	− 7.2	− 1.6	8.2	.4
1978	6.4	13.4	15.7	12.5
1979	7.0	32.5	40.0	28.9
1980	31.6	32.0	41.7	35.1
10-year average results	9.17%	7.0%	15.7%	11.8%
Ending value of portfolio, % of 1971	201%	153%	323%	250%
Annual compounded rate of return	8.1%	4.8%	13.9%	10.7%

Note: Average percentage change refers to the net assets per share, with capital gains
and dividends reinvested. There is a difference between the way closed- and open-end
funds handle reinvestment. For purposes of this comparison, it was assumed that capital
gains and dividends could be reinvested without cost. This would not be true for most
closed-end funds and for some mutual funds.

Source: Reprinted by permission from the Wiesenberger Investment Companies Service, 1981 Edition, Copyright
© 1981, Warren, Gorham and Lamont Inc., 210 South Street, Boston, Mass. All Rights Reserved.

and scholar Dean Burton G. Malkiel of Yale University has concluded: "I consider them [closed-end funds] unusually attractive vehicles for investment
in stocks during the early 1980s, even for large investors."[1]

---

1. Burton G. Malkiel, *A Random Walk Down Wall Street*, 2d ed. (New York: W.W. Norton, 1981), p. 327.

How to Evaluate and Select Closed-End Companies _____

How should you go about deciding whether to invest in the shares of closed-end companies? If you decide to do so, in which companies should you invest? Closed-end companies can be analyzed by the same methods used to analyze regular stocks and bonds (see Chapters 10 through 12). Similar methodology is also used for evaluating mutual funds. However, because a closed-end company has a fixed or permanent capitalization (amount of investment), the principal funds invested in its portfolio remain there permanently and are not subject to principal additions or withdrawals by the shareholders, as is the case with a mutual fund, which is an open-ended company. Permanency of capital can be an investment advantage in the case of some types of portfolio policies. For example, investment managers do not have to contend with the occasional pressures of purchasing or liquidating portfolio security holdings at inopportune price levels; closed-end shareholders, unlike mutual fund shareholders, are not allowed to have their shares redeemed on demand from the investment company. The manager of a closed-end company can time the purchases and sales of securities solely on the basis of investment policy considerations.

In closed-end companies the market price of the shares is usually traded at a discount in relation to the NAV, and only occasionally at a premium above the NAV. In comparison, the shares of mutual funds never trade at a discount, and many of them are purchased at a premium. This discount phenomenon is readily observable in any comparison of a closed-end company's NAV with the market price prevailing on the same date. (These data are reported weekly in *Barron's*; the *Wall Street Journal* reports every Monday on closed-end companies with equity portfolios and every Wednesday on closed-end companies with bond portfolios.)

Referring back to Exhibit 13–3, we can examine the NAV and either the market closing price or the asking (offering) price for a group of widely traded closed-end companies. Except for one company, the market prices of the shares were selling at discounts ranging from 1.5 percent to 24.7 percent below NAV on the dates indicated. For example, on 17 July 1981 Tri-Continental, a diversified common stock fund, had a NAV per share of $28.38 and a closing (last sale) price of $21-5/8 per share ($21.625), which represents a discount of 23.8 percent below its NAV. That is, on that date you were able to acquire an interest in a portfolio of securities with a market value of $28.38 (per share) at a price or cost to you of only $21.625 (plus brokerage commissions)—a discount of 23.8 percent.

Several studies have attempted, with only limited success, to explain the reasons for these bargain prices. One theory is that investors believe they can invest at least as successfully as can closed-end managers and can thereby avoid management expenses charged against the gross portfolio return. A second explanation is that new (incoming) shareholders assume a tax liability; they will be required to pay capital gains taxes after the sale of portfolio securities that have unrealized gains earned prior to the shareholders' purchase of the closed-end shares. For example, if the fund holds ABC stock, currently valued at $1,000, that it purchased originally for $500, it has an unrealized gain of $500. An investor who purchases the fund's shares also purchases, in part, the shares of ABC at the $1,000 price. If ABC shares are later sold, the fund must report the $500 gain and pay income tax. In effect, the investor has purchased ABC shares at their current price—shares subject to tax liability. Therefore, investors as a group will not pay full reported NAV for the fund shares. The discount represents, in part, the assumed tax liability. A third explanation for the bargain prices is that an investor does indeed get shares at a bargain purchase price, but the savings may be more than offset if the price falls to a deeper discount at the time the investor decides to sell the shares. While all these reasons may appear plausible, they do not fully account for the substantial discounts at which shares of closed-end companies are traded. For example, discounts exist for companies with successful portfolio performance records as well as for companies whose portfolios exhibit very modest, unrealized capital gains. Furthermore, a long-term investor would be able to enjoy a higher return on the portfolio over a number of years, which could more than offset any moderate widening in the discount.

The most plausible reason for the discount is market inefficiency. Closed-end shares are not actively promoted or marketed to investors. Therefore, investors are not generally aware of them and not generally able to choose with confidence a well-managed company that is pursuing investment objectives compatible with personal investment objectives. In simpler terms, more shares than willing buyers are available. Supply exceeds demand, and the price falls. In addition, portfolio managers of large institutional investors tend to avoid these issues because some closed-end funds have only a small floating supply of stock available at discount price levels, and clients may object to a double management fee—one charged by the closed-end management and the other charged by the institution's portfolio managers.

Discounts in the stock-oriented closed-end company industry tend to narrow when the stock market falls and to widen when the market rises. Conversely, the discounts in the bond-oriented closed-end company industry tend to widen when interest rates rise (i.e., when bond prices fall) and to narrow when interest rates fall (i.e., when bond prices rise). Given these market tendencies, some investors track the percentage size of the discounts over time; they buy shares when the discounts are relatively wide and consider selling when the discounts become narrow or go to an occasional premium.

MUTUAL FUNDS

In comparison to closed-end funds, mutual funds are much more widely known and more popular among investors. In 1940 shareholders owned less than $500 million in 300,000 accounts invested in approximately 70 mutual funds. In 1981, due mainly to the growth in popularity of mutual funds, investors had $180 billion in 12,000,000 accounts invested in more than 800 mutual funds.

How Shares Are Traded

The most important difference between a closed-end company and a mutual fund is that the capital structure (the equity side of the balance sheet) of a mutual fund is open-ended. A mutual fund offers and issues new shares for sale on each business day. The purchase price for each share is equal to its current net asset value (plus a sales commission, if it is the policy of the particular fund to charge one). The NAV portion of the purchase price is added to the portfolio for investment in new assets. Each business day the mutual fund also offers to redeem, or buy back (usually at no cost), shares from its existing shareholders at the redemption price, which is equal to the current NAV. The mutual fund uses money from the portfolio to buy back the shares.

Shares are sold in one of three ways. Some funds sell their shares through salespersons associated with brokerage firms, who charge the investor a sales commission. Some funds employ their own salespersons to sell shares directly to investors, who pay a sales commission. Other funds, called **no-load funds,** sell their shares (with no sales charge) directly to investors by mail and through advertisements in financial periodicals.

Advantages of Mutual Funds

The small investor can enjoy several advantages by investing in mutual funds. First, risk is reduced through ownership of an interest in a broadly diversified portfolio of securities. Second, the investor receives the benefits of professional investment management at an economical cost. Third, mutual funds offer several convenient services in the areas of bookkeeping, administration, and purchase and disbursement of funds.

DIVERSIFICATION

As we saw in Chapters 10 and 11, investment in any industry or company involves unique uncertainties and risks of possible loss. One easy way to minimize the possibility of losses is to refrain from placing "all your eggs in a single basket" and, instead, to spread your capital over many different industries and companies. Thus the loss on any one investment will be limited and may be more than offset by the gains on other investments. A mutual fund portfolio with $50 million or more typically owns more than fifty different securities and thus provides safety through broad diversification. The transaction costs (brokers' fees) for building and maintaining a personal portfolio with such broad diversification would be substantial for a small or moderate investor. In addition, keeping track of all the separate assets would be time consuming.

PROFESSIONAL MANAGEMENT

Many investors do not have the time, interest, or abilities to manage their own investments. Professional portfolio managers and securities research analysts study economic, political, business, and security market conditions and keep abreast of industrial and corporate developments. Intelligent and conscientious investment managers can take advantage of profitable investment opportunities and avoid unattractive risk situations. The total costs for such management are considerable, but the expense incurred by individual investors is small when the funds of many investors are pooled. Indeed, the expenses pay for themselves if management is successful in obtaining an above-average portfolio rate of return—that is, a net rate of return greater than what individual investors could obtain by investing on their own in assets of comparable risk.

Performance of Mutual Funds. Mutual fund portfolios have, on the whole, performed favorably over the years as compared with the securities markets generally and as compared with other professionally managed portfolios. The simplest and most straightforward method of measuring the performance of an investment over a period of time is to add the change in market value over a calendar quarter to the receipt of income and then divide by the market value at the beginning of the quarter. For example, the performance (rate of return) during the second quarter of 1983 for an investment that had a market price of $20.00 on 31 March, paid a dividend of $.20 per share on 30 June, and had a market price of $20.50 on 30 June would be 3.5 percent. The rate of return is calculated as follows:

Assumptions:

P_0 = the market price at the end of the preceding calendar quarter ($20.00 on 31 March);

P_1 = the market price at the end of the calendar quarter to be measured ($20.50 on 30 June);

D_1 = the dividend paid per share during the quarter to be measured ($.20).

$$\frac{P_1 - P_0 + D_1}{P_0} = r_1$$

$$\frac{\$20.50 - \$20.00 + \$.20}{\$20.00} = 0.035, \text{ or } 3.5\%.$$

"An advantage of professionally managed mutual funds is that you have the benefit of more than one opinion."

The return, r_1, can be measured and compared with any investment or portfolio. Depending on the type of investment being measured, P is the market value of a share of stock, the NAV of a mutual fund, or the market value of a stock index. In like manner, D is the quarterly dividend paid per share on an individual stock, a mutual fund, or a stock index.

For comparison purposes, when performance is measured over several quarters (e.g., for one year), the quarterly rates of return are normally compounded by assuming that dividends received are reinvested in the investment each quarter. In our example, if the quarterly rates of returns on our investment during 1983 amounted to 0.040, 0.035, −0.020, and 0.050, the total rate of return for 1983 would be 10.76 percent, where

r_n = rate of return in quarter n;
$r = (1 + r_1)(1 + r_2)(1 + r_3)(1 + r_4) - 1$;
$r = (1 + 0.040)(1 + 0.035)(1 - 0.020)(1 + 0.050) - 1$;
$r = 1.1076 - 1$;
$r = 0.1076$, or 10.76%.

With this understanding of performance calculations, we are able to measure the past performance of individual investments, portfolios including mutual funds, and the stock market (i.e., stock market indexes).

The Wiesenberger Investment Companies Service, the Lipper Analytical Distributors, Inc., and other services measure the performance of over 500 mutual funds. Their analyses are reported from time to time in financial periodicals such as the *Wall Street Journal* and *Barron's.* Exhibit 13–5 is a page from the Lipper Mutual Fund performance analysis, special second quarter 1981 report. The report shows the cumulative performance of mutual funds through 30 June 1981. The columns from left to right cover the periods for the last twenty years, ten years, five years, six months, and three months, respectively. Notice that in each period the equity funds as a group and the all funds average (after deducting operating expenses and assuming in each instance that dividends were reinvested) outperformed Standard & Poor's Index of 500 stocks. At least half of the 508 funds analyzed outperformed the S&P Index in all periods, except in the twenty-year period, when the median figure for all funds (the measure against which half of the funds did better and the other half did worse) was only 277.4 percent, while the S&P Index was 333.8 percent.

Considering that the portfolio objectives of some of the bond funds and special-purpose funds do not necessarily include keeping up with the stock market indexes, a clear majority of the equity-oriented fund managers were successful in outperforming the market after the deduction of all operating expenses. In comparison with other classes of professional equity portfolios, such as those of bank-pooled pension funds, insurance companies, and investment counselors, the performance of mutual funds as a group has also been favorable.

Quality of Investment Clients. Another way to gauge the reputation of professional investment managers is to investigate the quality of the investment clients being served. The proportion of mutual fund shares, excluding money market funds, owned by institutional investors has increased steadily over the years. Institutional investors in mutual funds include trusts and estates, pension funds, nonprofit organizations, schools, and other agencies. Compared with small, individual investors, institutional investors are thought of as more deliberate. Also, because of the size of their accounts, they have a wider number and variety of professional investment managers from which to choose. Based on a survey conducted by the Investment Company Institute, institutional investors in 1980 held $17.7 billion of mutual fund shares in 1.4 million accounts, which represented 37.7 percent of the total assets of the funds surveyed.[2]

---

2. *1981 Mutual Fund Fact Book* (New York: Investment Company Institute, 1981), p. 45.

EXHIBIT 13–5   Report on Mutual Fund Performance, 30 June 1981

No. of Current Funds	Type of Fund	Total Reinvestment Cumulative Performance				
		6/30/61 to 6/30/81	6/30/71 to 6/30/81	6/30/76 to 6/30/81	12/31/80 to 6/30/81	3/31/81 to 6/30/81
65	Capital Appreciation Funds	+432.10%	+184.67%	+170.91%	+ 5.28%	+ 1.76%
163	Growth Funds	+389.06%	+126.55%	+126.62%	+ 2.73%	− 0.22%
79	Growth and Income Funds	+400.84%	+134.47%	+ 86.81%	+ 3.09%	− 0.35%
22	Equity Income Funds	+435.98%	+155.22%	+ 83.22	+ 8.82%	+ 2.71%
329	Equity Funds Average	+399.42%	+140.13%	+121.88%	+ 3.74%	+ 0.34%
23	Balanced Funds	+232.07%	+ 85.58%	+ 53.47%	+ 1.44%	− 0.57%
29	Income Funds	+279.55%	+ 78.87%	+ 46.05%	+ 2.87%	+ 1.24%
3	Insurance Stock Funds	+231.41%	+131.56%	+116.31%	+ 16.46%	+ 3.14%
7	Specialty Funds	N/A	+ 65.85%	+150.22%	− 0.02%	− 0.86%
6	Gold Oriented Funds	+663.31%	+216.72%	+303.38%	− 27.84%	− 17.88%
9	International Funds	+226.02%	+138.57%	+ 92.95%	+ 6.85%	+ 3.29%
12	Option Funds	+241.43%	+ 39.94%	+ 41.71%	+ 5.77%	+ 1.95%
90	Fixed Income Funds	+181.30%	+ 62.52	+ 25.33%	+ 2.38%	+ 0.77%
508	All Funds Average	+356.41%	+127.50%	+102.36%	+ 3.08%	+ 0.30%
508	All Funds—Median	+277.41%	+103.82%	+ 82.02%	+ 2.71%	+ 0.45%
	No. of Funds in Universe with a % Change	165	349	413	501	505

	Value	Unmanaged Indices Without Dividends Cumulative Performance				
Dow Jones Ind. Aver.	976.88	+ 42.83%	+ 9.62%	− 2.58%	+ 1.34%	− 2.69%
Standard & Poor's 500	131.25	+103.05%	+ 31.65%	+ 25.86%	− 3.32%	− 3.49%
Standard & Poor's 400	147.58	+115.76%	+ 34.23%	+ 25.73%	− 4.45%	− 4.29%
N.Y.S.E. Composite	76.14	+121.08	+ 38.21%	+ 36.67%	− 2.21%	− 2.72%
A.S.E. Index	374.63	N/A	+227.19%	+255.47%	+ 7.35%	+ 3.89%

	6/30/81	Estimated Reinvested Unmanaged Indices Cumulative Performance				
		6/30/61 to 6/30/81	6/30/71 to 6/30/81	6/30/76 to 6/30/81	12/31/80 to 6/30/81	3/31/81 to 6/30/81
S&P 500 Reinvested	131.25	+333.82%	+103.05%	+ 61.78%	− 0.97%	− 2.27%
Dow Jones Ind. Reinvested	976.88	+234.59%	+ 79.26%	+ 29.40%	+ 4.27%	− 1.29%

Note: The method of calculating total return data on indices utilizes actual dividends on x-dates accumulated for the quarter and reinvested at quarter end. This calculation is at variance with SEC Release 327 of August 8, 1972, which utilizes latest 12 month dividends. The latter method is the one used by Standard & Poor's.

Source: Lipper Analytical Distributors, Inc., 74 Trinity Place, New York, N.Y. 10006.

OTHER SERVICES

A major reason for the attractiveness of mutual funds is the many convenient services offered to shareholders. Eight examples of mutual fund services or features are described in the following numbered paragraphs and are summarized in Exhibit 13–6.

1. A mutual fund performs some of the bookkeeping and administrative chores that shareholders would have to do themselves if they owned a portfolio of individual securities. The mutual fund handles cash as well as the receipt, delivery, and custody of portfolio security certificates bought, sold, and held. It collects the income received on security investments. It maintains the records for all these transactions as well as the tax records for ordinary income resulting from dividends and interest and for long-term and short-term capital gains arising from the sale of securities. The shareholders receive account statements that show this tax information, which they use for preparing their income tax returns.[3] An example of a quarterly report to an investor is shown in Exhibit 13–7.

2. After mutual funds collect the income and capital gains (if any) on their portfolios and deduct their operating expenses, they provide their shareholders with several disbursement options. Shareholders may (a) have both the dividend income and the capital gains distributions paid in cash, (b) have the capital gains distribution automatically reinvested through the purchase of additional shares in the fund and the dividend income paid in cash, or (c) have both the dividend income and the capital gains distributions automatically reinvested in additional shares, including **fractional shares,** which are less than whole shares. About three-fourths of all shareholders use these reinvestment plans.

3. Mutual funds offer the shareholder the convenience of periodic investing—that is, investing additional money in mutual fund shares (including fractional shares) for as little as $25 or $50 at regular or irregular intervals. If a constant dollar amount is invested at regular intervals, investors gain the advantages of **dollar cost averaging** (see Chapter 11).

4. Under periodic investment plans and automatic reinvestment plans, you may arrange without charge to have the mutual fund's bank custodian hold your certificates for safekeeping. You periodically receive account statements that show how many shares have been purchased, at what price, and how many total shares are credited to your account.

5. Some mutual fund management organizations manage a "family," or group, of different mutual funds, each of which has a particular investment objective (see, for example, the Fidelity Group or the Vanguard Group in Ex-

---

3. Mutual funds pass all dividends and capital gains directly through to the individual investor, who is then responsible for the income taxes. Some closed-end companies pay some or all of the taxes. The proportional share of taxes paid by these companies can be reported as a personal tax credit by the investor.

EXHIBIT 13-6   Eight Convenient Features of Mutual Funds

1. Shareholders receive portfolio bookkeeping and administrative services; the fund handles cash income and receipt, delivery, and custody of securities bought and sold; the fund maintains tax records.

2. Shareholders may elect to have dividends and capital gains paid in cash, have gains automatically reinvested, or have both gains and dividends reinvested each quarter.

3. Shareholders may purchase small amounts of additional shares at periodic intervals.

4. Shareholders may arrange for the fund's bank custodian to hold their certificates for safekeeping.

5. Shareholders may have exchange privileges among a group of mutual funds, so that shares in one fund may be exchanged for shares in another fund.

6. Shareholders may purchase shares as a gift to a minor and have them registered in the name of a family custodian until the child becomes an adult.

7. Shareholders can take advantage of mutual funds' tax-sheltered retirement plans, including Keogh, IRA, and IRA rollover accounts.

8. Retired shareholders may establish a withdrawal plan that will redeem shares and automatically send them monthly checks.

hibit 13–8). Many of these fund groups offer **exchange privileges**—that is, if market conditions change or if a shareholder's objectives change, the investor is permitted to exchange shares in one fund for shares in another fund at little or no expense. The exchange can be effected by mail or telephone (a toll free number is frequently available).

6. When parents and grandparents give mutual fund shares to children under the Uniform Gift to Minors Act, the account is usually held in the name of one of the parents as custodian for the minor. If the child is in a sufficiently low tax bracket, the annual mutual fund distributions may be automatically reinvested without a tax liability. The child gains control of the account upon legally becoming an adult (usually at eighteen or twenty-one, depending on state laws). A donor can give up to $10,000 ($20,000 with the spouse's consent) each year to each deserving child, and the donation is free of federal and estate taxes.

7. High personal income tax rates have caused tax-sheltered retirement savings programs to become increasingly popular. Mutual funds provide a variety of services to help you capitalize on these tax advantages and at the same time to plan for your retirement needs. Approximately 2 percent of all corporate pension plans are invested in mutual funds. In addition, in 1980 $3.8 billion was held by mutual funds in Keogh accounts (retirement accounts for the self-employed), $761 million in individual retirement accounts (IRAs),

EXHIBIT 13-7   Quarterly Report of a Mutual Fund to an Investor

Financial Investments, Inc.

Post Office Box 204
New York, N.Y. 10013

This portion of the form may be used
to add to your investment account
or to change or correct an address.

Make Checks Payable To:
FINANCIAL INVESTMENTS, INC.

Account Number	Investments by Mail
F036882	MINIMUM 25

Account Number
F036882

Tax ID Number
534-12-7983

Julio J. Gonsalves
882 Beacon St.
Boston, MA 02215

Amount Enclosed $

☐ Address Change—Check Box And
Make Change on Reverse Side of Stub

Fund

FINANCIAL INDUSTRIAL INCOME FUND, INC.

Date	Transaction	Dollar Amount of Transaction	Price Per Share	Shares for This Transaction	Total Shares Owned
07/10/81	SHARES PURCHASED	600.00	6.8541	87.54	4,985.12
08/17/81	SHARES PURCHASED	600.00	6.9118	86.81	5,071.93
09/08/81	SHARES PURCHASED	600.00	6.5113	92.15	5,164.08
09/30/81	INCOME DIV REINV .1100	568.04	6.4315	88.32	5,252.40

IF YOUR ACCOUNT IS A FEDERAL INCOME TAX-SHELTERED PLAN, THE EARNINGS
APPEARING IN THE 1099 INFORMATION BELOW ARE NON-TAXABLE. THESE EARN-
INGS COMPOUND TAX-DEFERRED UNTIL DISTRIBUTED FROM THE PLAN.

1981 FEDERAL INCOME TAX INFORMATION (FORM-1099)

Qualifying Dividends	Non-Qualifying Dividends	Total Dividends	Long-Term Capital Gain	Tax-Exempt Dividends	Total Dividends and Other Distributions	Shares Held in Certificated Form
2,279.03	94.71	2,373.74	3,902.74	0.00	6,276.48	

RETAIN THIS FORM FOR YOUR RECORDS. A CHARGE WILL BE MADE FOR DUPLICATE COPIES.

and $219 million in IRA rollover accounts.[4] Frequently you are able to
transfer ownership from one fund to another in the same retirement account
when exchange privileges are available. (Tax-sheltered retirement plans are
described in greater detail in Chapter 15.)

8. Many mutual funds offer a withdrawal plan service. Shareholders with
a minimum account, such as $5,000 or $10,000, may instruct their fund to
send them a monthly check for a fixed dollar amount—say, $200—or to
redeem a fixed number of shares monthly. Periodic payments are financed

---

4. *1981 Mutual Fund Fact Book* (New York, N.Y.: Investment Company Institute, 1981).

EXHIBIT 13-8
Families of
Mutual Funds

Vanguard Funds	
Explorer	Municipal Long Term
Index Trust	Qualified Div. Portfolio, I
GNMA Portfolio	Qualified Div. Portfolio, II
Quest	Wellesley Income
W.L. Morgan Growth	Wellington
Municipal High Yield	High Yield Bond
Money Market Trust	Investment Grade Bond
Municipal Money Market	Trustees
Municipal Short Term	Windsor
Municipal Intermediate Term	

Note: Vanguard funds are no-load funds—that is, investors may exchange funds at asset value for shares of other funds in the group at no charge.

Source: Reprinted by permission from the Wiesenberger Investment Companies Service, 1981 Edition, Copyright © 1981, Warren, Gorham and Lamont Inc., 210 South Street, Boston, Mass. All Rights Reserved.

in part by dividend and capital gain distributions; however, the withdrawals usually systematically reduce the principal in the account. These payments are used by shareholders as retirement income or as a supplement to income from other sources.

Disadvantages of Mutual Funds

Mutual funds offer disadvantages as well as advantages to investors. A feature one investor may consider an advantage may be a disadvantage to another investor. For example, the benefits of professional management may more than offset costs of management fees for one investor, but not for another investor who has superior investment selection skills. The cost-benefit equation in respect to a particular feature will differ from fund to fund. Therefore, the factors identified as advantages and disadvantages should not necessarily be attributed to all investors nor to all mutual funds.

DIVERSIFICATION AND SIZE

Many people presume that a large, broadly diversified portfolio is advantageous. For one thing, the management fees paid by a large fund will be a lower percentage of assets, because economies of scale come into play—that is, lower unit costs are achieved due to spreading fixed costs over a larger volume. The absolute amount of fees can thus support a larger and more thorough investment management and research effort. In addition, broad diversification generally reduces the magnitude of adverse investment performance attributable to the risks incurred in one security or one industry group.

However, diversification also reduces possible favorable performance; a portfolio that is too diversified not only reduces downside risk but also limits upside gains. For example, if a management invests in 200 different companies in thirty different industries, the portfolio's performance will quite likely resemble the performance of the stock market as a whole. If the objective of the investor is to select professional management to outperform the market, the investor will likely be disappointed when a portfolio employs very broad diversification. What the investor often is looking for is concentration in a small number of high-performance stocks.

The investment organization, which manages half a billion dollars or more, faces problems not present in smaller companies. A large investor frequently cannot easily and quickly trade a representative portfolio position in the market—say, a transaction of $10 million or $20 million in a typical stock—without running the risk of adversely disrupting the market price of the stock. Giant mutual funds cannot move quickly or easily in or out of the market.

In contrast to closed-end funds, all mutual funds are to some degree exposed to a portfolio marketability problem because they are open-ended. Because a mutual fund stands ready each business day to issue new shares and to redeem old shares, a fund can be subjected to unexpectedly large cash inflows or outflows. If, for example, mutual fund shareholders suddenly decide to buy bank money market certificates, liquidation of their mutual fund shares on demand can cause the fund management serious problems. Selling large blocks of shares is never easy. Large sales are usually associated with falling share prices, which may trigger further fund redemptions. The need to guard against the possibility of large redemptions can adversely affect the planned investment policy of the mutual fund.

UNSATISFACTORY PROFESSIONAL MANAGEMENT

In the minds of most shareholders, the most important feature of a mutual fund is active professional portfolio management. While the record of portfolio performance of mutual funds has been, on the whole, quite satisfactory, an unmanaged benchmark portfolio (such as the S&P Index) does occasionally outperform the group average of relevant mutual fund portfolios. Even in those instances when the fund's median modestly outperforms a market index, a significant number of funds underperform it. Exhibits 13–4 and 13–5 show the variation in performance of different types of funds.

This shortfall in the performance of mutual funds as compared with an unmanaged index such as the S&P 500 can be explained by several variables: management and operating expenses; transaction costs from portfolio turnover of securities; poor investment selections or timing; and differences in portfolio policy characteristics—for example, qualities of investment risks and security group orientation (i.e., growth stocks, income stocks, and small companies). Regardless of the reasons, a mutual fund shareholder will be inclined to believe that professional management is a disadvantage if the fund's portfolio is not able to outperform an unmanaged market index on a risk-adjusted basis after the deduction of management expenses. Likewise, the management expenses will be a net disadvantage to investors who are willing and able to manage their own funds successfully.

Although mutual fund investors are relieved of the responsibility of making ongoing portfolio decisions, they still must decide when to buy and sell shares in mutual funds and which of over 500 funds to choose. Because of the wide selection of available funds, some investors prefer to diversify against the risk of concentrating on only one management or on one particular portfolio policy. Therefore, they own shares in two or more mutual funds. Ownership of shares in more than one fund is possible because the minimum initial purchase required in a fund is usually only a few hundred dollars.

How to Select a Mutual Fund

Once you have become familiar with mutual funds and want to choose one or more from a universe of over 500, you must analyze and evaluate the funds to make intelligent investment choices.

REQUIRED DISCLOSURE TO INVESTORS

Through extensive regulation of the investment company industry, investors are furnished with a great deal of information. The industry is regulated by the Securities and Exchange Commission under several major federal laws—the Securities Act of 1933, the Securities Exchange Act of 1934, the Investment Company Act of 1940, and the Investment Advisers Act of 1940. The objective of these regulations, insofar as mutual funds are concerned, is to protect investors by requiring mutual funds to provide full and truthful disclosure of relevant information so that investors can make reasonably informed investment selections. The standards of disclosure for the sale of mutual funds and other investment securities are much more rigorous than the standards involved in the sale of most other goods and services. Some of the information disclosed is difficult for the average investor to understand because it is stated in technical and legal language.

PORTFOLIO OBJECTIVES AND POLICIES OF VARIOUS TYPES OF FUNDS

Before choosing a mutual fund, you should analyze your personal financial circumstances and determine your investment objectives. You must determine how much risk and what types of risks you are willing to assume—for example, the risks associated with market price volatility, inflation, and interest rates. You must also determine your planning time horizon—for example, are your funds to be used for retirement in forty years, or are they to be used for a child's college education in five years? Once you have determined your investment goals and requirements, you should consider funds with portfolio objectives and policies that best match your own. If you have more than one objective, or an objective with several facets, you may wish to use two or more funds with different portfolio objectives. (Mutual funds' past investment performance based on their objectives was shown in Exhibit 13–5.) In the following subsections we consider funds with different objectives (see Exhibit 13–9). Information about each fund's objectives and policies is available in the sources cited earlier and in the literature provided by the funds. No uniformity exists in classifying funds according to objectives; however, the classification given in the exhibit is typical.

Money Market Funds. Because relatively high short-term interest rates have been available in the money market in recent years, **money market funds** have been especially popular among investors. Their portfolio objective is to obtain the maximum current interest income yield consistent with preserving the amount of principal invested. These portfolios are composed of very high quality, short-term, marketable, interest-bearing debt securities—primarily bank certificates of deposit, commercial paper, and U.S. Treasury bills. Many investors use these funds as emergency, contingency, or liquid reserves and as a means of earning a yield higher than that available from accounts at thrift institutions.

Bond Funds. **Bond funds** invest predominantly in intermediate-term and long-term corporate bonds. (Intermediate-term bonds mature in three to eight years; corporate bonds, in eight to thirty years.) Depending on the portfolio policy, the fund may own high-quality (high credit-rated) bonds or lower-quality bonds. The objective, based on interest rate fluctuations, is to earn a generous yield and possibly some appreciation in the market price of the bond.

Tax-Free (Municipal) Bond Funds. **Municipal bond funds** invest in bonds issued by state and local governments. Because the interest earned on these bonds is exempt from federal income taxes, investors in high tax brackets are able to earn a higher yield from a municipal bond portfolio than from a corporate bond portfolio after taxes. If your top tax bracket was 40 percent, for example, you would earn a higher net yield from a municipal bond fund that yielded 10 percent than from a corporate bond fund that yielded 14-1/2 percent; on the corporate bond fund you would have a net yield of only 8.7 percent (versus 10 percent for the municipal bonds) after you had paid a tax of 40 percent on the 14-1/2 percent taxable yield:

Taxable yield $(1 - \text{tax rate}) = \text{after-tax yield}$.
Therefore, $.145\ (1 - .40) = .087$.

EXHIBIT 13–9   Investment Objectives of Various Mutual Funds

INVESTMENT OBJECTIVES
AGGRESSIVE   CONSERVATIVE   TAX-FREE

DIRECTORS FUND	SPECIAL FUND	TIME FUND	A.I.M. FUND	OPPEN-HEIMER FUND	INCOME FUND	OPTION INCOME FUND	HIGH YIELD FUND	MONEY MARKET FUND	TAX-FREE BOND FUND
Aggressive Capital Growth	Aggressive Capital Growth	Above Average Capital Growth	Capital Growth	Capital Growth and Possible Income Growth	Current Income and Possible Capital Growth	High Current Income (Equity Portfolio)	High Current Income (Bond Portfolio)	Current Income and Principal Stability	Tax-Free Current Income

Source: Oppenheimer Investment Services, New York, N.Y. 10004.

The attractiveness of a municipal bond fund thus depends on your tax bracket and on the prevailing difference in the marketplace between taxable bond yields and tax-exempt bond yields.

Tax-Exempt Money Market Funds. Tax-exempt money market funds invest in short-term, good-quality municipal bonds. These funds are similar to money market funds, but their interest income is exempt from federal income taxes. Because these funds invest in tax-exempt securities with maturities of less than a year, they are subject to little interest rate risk. Thus, the fund can supply investors excellent liquidity with little danger of price fluctuation. Bond funds, regardless of their tax-exempt status, are always exposed to price fluctuations because of interest rate risk.

Capital Growth Funds. The most popular equity-oriented funds are those whose objective is seeking growth in principal. **Growth funds** invest in quality common stocks of companies that the investment managers believe will grow at a rate above the average for the economy as a whole. Growth companies typically experience an above-average demand for their products, retain and reinvest a large portion of their earnings to finance expansion in their production and distribution systems, or spend heavily on research and development of new products.

Growth funds are suitable for investors who have little or no need for current investment income and who have long-term planning time horizons—that is, investors who will need funds at some time in the distant future, such as at retirement. Growth funds are also suitable for investors in middle and high tax brackets, because a larger portion of the total investment return is expected from long-term capital gains, taxed at approximately half the rate at which dividends are taxed.

Capital Appreciation (Aggressive Growth) Funds. Aggressive growth funds have portfolio objectives that emphasize price appreciation in common stocks. The specific investment strategy varies among the funds. One strategy is to

"Next time you get a hot tip on the eighth at Churchill Downs, how about putting the cash in a conservative bond fund instead?"

The Bettman Archive, Inc.

own small, rapidly growing companies. Another is to trade in speculative, quality stocks with volatile market prices—that is, to buy them when their prices are expected to rise rapidly and to sell them when they appear overvalued. These funds assume a higher risk of loss to pursue the opportunity of getting a substantially higher rate of return.

Because aggressive growth funds involve more risk, and because successful performance requires good investment management skills, it is important for an investor to determine whether a fund uses a portfolio strategy with a probability of success and employs a strongly qualified investment management. A capital appreciation fund might be suitable for a portion of the funds of an investor who has a long planning time horizon, a strong personal financial position, or an aggressive risk/return temperament.

Growth and Income Funds. Funds whose investment objective is growth and income typically invest in good-quality common stocks of companies that pay out a moderate amount of their earnings in dividends and reinvest the balance for steady future growth. These types of funds are suitable for an investor who wants some current income, some future growth, and only a moderate amount of risk (e.g., the Oppenheimer Fund and the income fund described in Exhibit 13–9).

High Current Income Funds. As the name implies the investment objective of **high current income funds** is to produce generous current dividend yields on common stocks. Typically, these companies are in stable, mature industries and pay out a large proportion of their earnings in current dividends. The expectation is that the current dividend yield will be a large part of the investment's total long-term rate of return and that the growth rate in future dividend payments will be moderate. These types of funds may be suitable for investors who need a current and steady investment income and some modest future growth in dividends to offset inflationary increases in the cost of living.

Balanced Funds. **Balanced funds** have portfolios that invest about 20 to 40 percent in bonds and the remainder in stocks. Consequently, these funds diversify against the total risks in the stock market cycle and against the risks of inflation and interest rate fluctuations in the bond market. (None of the funds shown in Exhibit 13–9 are balanced funds.)

These funds may be suitable for the conservative investor who wants to place a large proportion of money in one fund that has a total or comprehensive investment program. Many investors, however, prefer to separate their funds and place the portion of their assets earmarked for fixed-dollar investment directly in thrift accounts, money market funds, life insurance policies, and so on; they place the equity portion of their assets in all-equity investments. The advantage of this separation is that the market values and fluctuations of both components are not tied together in a single net asset value when the investor makes a transaction, and the investor can decide independently the asset mix proportions between fixed-dollar assets and equity investments.

Specialty Funds. **Specialty funds** provide investors the opportunity to concentrate funds in one industry or one investment concept instead of experiencing the averaging effect from broad portfolio diversification. If you believe, for example, that unusually attractive investment opportunities exist in stocks in a specific area—for example, insurance companies, banks, energy, natural resources, gold mining, international economy, or stock options— you can invest in a mutual fund with a portfolio that concentrates in that area. By concentrating, you have the opportunity of doing very well or very poorly. Note that in Exhibit 13–5 the six gold-oriented funds had a total return of 663.31 percent over a twenty-year period, the best return of any fund type, while the nine international funds had a mediocre return of only 226.02 percent. (However, past performance is no guarantee of future performance.)

The portfolio policies, investment objectives, and other relevant information about individual mutual funds are available in several financial reference sources. Exhibit 13–10 is a description of the Windsor Fund that appeared in *Investment Companies*, an annual reference work on funds and their performance.

MANAGEMENT CAPABILITIES

Once you have narrowed the list of mutual funds to those with portfolio objectives and policies that fit yours, the next step is to select the fund or funds that have the management capabilities for successfully carrying out these policies and achieving these objectives. Because of a lack of useful information available on appraising management capabilities, this step is not always easy to complete.

Evaluating Past Performance. One of the most popular approaches used in evaluating investment capability is to measure and compare the past performance of portfolios. Many periodicals and financial services, including the references already cited, report the past performance of many mutual funds over a variety of time intervals. Exhibit 13–11 shows an excerpt from *Management Results*, a monthly analysis of funds published by the Wiesenberger Investment Companies Service. Note that the mutual fund performances are grouped according to the type of investment objectives. Portfolio performance of most mutual funds should be measured over at least a three-to-ten-year period to reflect the different phases of the stock market and of business cycles and to reveal how the management coped with the various cycles. The performance of the portfolio should be compared with a suitable benchmark securities market index; past performance could also be compared with the average of other mutual funds that had similar portfolio policies. For example, a growth fund could be compared with the growth fund group average.

If a fund displays an above-average return, you should try to determine whether it is accounted for by superior management skill, by assumption of excessive risks, or by luck. Some managers are able to show above-average performance over a period of a year or two, but fewer managers are able to show superior performance consistently over a five-to-ten-year period. Also try to determine whether the mutual fund that produced superior performance over the last three to five years plans to use the same management and policies in the future. If the fund has grown considerably, it may not have the market maneuverability to perform the same way it did in the past.

EXHIBIT 13–10
Investment
Service Report on
a Mutual Fund

WINDSOR FUND, INC.

Organized in October 1958, Windsor Fund is one of several funds in the $2.4 billion Vanguard Group of Investment Companies. The 14 funds in the group jointly own a subsidiary, The Vanguard Group, Inc., which provides at cost all but investment management services to the members of the group.

Long-term growth of capital and income, through investment in equity securities, is the primary objective. However, the fund may invest, without restriction, in high-grade bonds and preferred stocks. Emphasis is on industries and companies believed to have particularly favorable long-term prospects for appreciation, based on increasing earnings and dividends.

At the 1979 year-end, the fund had 99.7% of its assets in common stocks, diversified among four broad categories: cyclical (37.6% of assets), lesser-recognized (30.3%), moderate growth (28%), and highly-recognized (3.8%). The five largest individual investments were in Exxon (4.9% of assets), General Motors (4.7%), Kaiser Aluminum & Chemical and Western Bancorp. (each 4.1%) and Interco (4%). The rate of portfolio turnover during the latest fiscal year was 53% of average assets. Unrealized appreciation was 4.6% of calendar year-end assets.

Special Services: An open account arrangement serves for accumulation and provides for automatic dividend reinvestment. Minimum initial investment is $500; subsequent purchases may be $50 or more. Accumulation payments may be made by way of pre-authorized checks drawn against the investor's checking account. A monthly or quarterly withdrawal plan is available without charge to holders of shares valued at $10,000; withdrawal payments may be of any designated amount. Shares may be exchanged at no charge for those of other funds in the group. Keogh Plans (which may be split-funded); prototype corporate profit-sharing, thrift and pension plans, and Individual Retirement Accounts are offered.

Statistical History

| | AT YEAR-ENDS | | | | | — % of Assets in — | | | ANNUAL DATA | | | | |
Year	Total Net Assets ($)	Number of Share-holders	Net Asset Value Per Share ($)	Offer-ing Price ($)	Yield (%)	Cash & Equiv-alent	Bonds & Pre-ferreds	Com-mon Stocks	Income Div-idends ($)	Capital Gains Distribu-tion ($)	Expense Ratio (%)	Offering Price ($) High	Low
1979	704,306,325	66,220	9.72	—	5.0	—	—	100	0.53	0.85†	0.66	11.57	9.06
1978	598,756,910	67,567	9.12	—	4.7	2	—	98	0.48	1.01†	0.67	11.98	8.77
1977	528,009,704	59,298	9.77	††	4.1	—	1*	99	0.42	0.54	0.67	10.70	9.14
1976	573,405,573	62,548	10.68	11.67	3.2	5	2*	93	0.38	0.22	0.65	11.67	8.56
1975	438,040,874	68,033	7.77	8.49	3.8	—	2*	98	0.32	—	0.72	8.97	5.90
1974	302,663,750	70,467	5.25	5.74	5.4	1	2	97	0.31	—	0.75	8.23	5.40
1973	390,081,898	73,789	6.64	7.26	4.3	—	1	99	0.32	0.14	0.57	10.39	6.73
1972	553,651,335	77,900	9.39	10.26	2.7	5	—	95	0.29	0.57†	0.61	10.74	9.77
1971	537,356,681	82,287	9.34	10.21	2.7	5	1*	94	0.29	0.50	0.64	11.43	9.08
1970	443,005,412	72,712	9.48	10.36	2.3	15	1*	84	0.24	0.02	0.79	10.50	7.76
1969	306,699,125	50,800	9.19	10.04	2.0	2	—	98	0.21	0.52	0.76	11.49	9.67

Note: Figures adjusted for 2-for-1 stock split, effective 4/29/69.
* Includes substantial proportion in convertible issues.

†Includes $0.03 short-term gains in 1972; $0.01 in 1978; $0.02 in 1979.
††On no-load basis, effective 2/9/77.

Directors: John C. Bogle, Chmn. and Pres.; Paul B. Firstenberg; Barbara B. Hauptfuhrer; John T. Jackson; John Jeppson III; Burton G. Malkiel; James S. Riepe; Charles D. Root, Jr.; James O. Welch, Jr.

Investment Advisor: Wellington Management Company. Compensation to the Adviser is at an annual rate of 0.35% on the first $200 million of net assets, scaling down to 0.15% on net assets in excess of $750 million. This base fee may be increased or decreased by specifically stated percentages depending on the fund's performance relative to that of the Standard & Poor's 500 Stock Index.

Custodian: State Street Bank and Trust Company, Boston, MA 02105.

Transfer Agent: The Vanguard Group, Valley Forge, PA 19482.

Distributor: Vanguard Marketing Corp., Valley Forge, PA 19482.

Sales Charge: None; shares are offered at net asset value.

Dividends: Income dividends are paid semi-annually in the months of May and November. Capital gains, if any, are paid in November.

Shareholder Reports: Issued quarterly. Fiscal year ends October 31. The 1979 prospectus was effective in March.

Qualified for Sale: In all states and DC.

Address: P.O. Box 1100, Valley Forge, PA 19482.

Telephone: (215) 293-1100. Toll Free: (800) 523-7910.

An assumed investment of $10,000 in this fund, with capital gains accepted in shares and income dividends reinvested, is illustrated below. The explanation on Page 153 must be read in conjunction with this illustration.

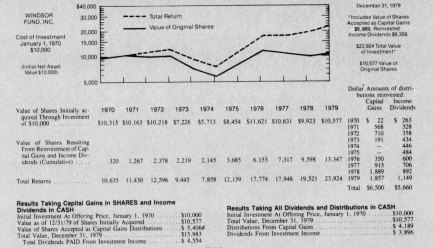

WINDSOR FUND, INC.
Cost of Investment January 1, 1970 $10,000
(Initial Net Asset Value $10,000)

Total Return
Value of Original Shares

December 31, 1979
*Includes Value of Shares Accepted as Capital Gains $6,989; Reinvested Income Dividends $6,358.
$23,924 Total Value of Investment*
$10,577 Value of Original Shares

	1970	1971	1972	1973	1974	1975	1976	1977	1978	1979		Capital Gains	Income Dividends
Value of Shares Initially acquired Through Investment of $10,000	$10,315	$10,163	$10,218	$7,226	$5,713	$8,454	$11,621	$10,631	$9,923	$10,577	1970	$ 22	$ 263
											1971	568	328
											1972	710	358
											1973	191	434
											1974	—	446
Value of Shares Resulting From Reinvestment of Capital Gains and Income Dividends (Cumulative)	320	1,267	2,378	2,219	2,145	3,685	6,153	7,317	9,598	13,347	1975	—	484
											1976	350	600
											1977	913	706
											1978	1,889	892
Total Returns	10,635	11,430	12,596	9,445	7,858	12,139	17,774	17,948	19,521	23,924	1979	1,857	1,149
											Total	$6,500	$5,660

Results Taking Capital Gains in SHARES and Income Dividends in CASH
Initial Investment At Offering Price, January 1, 1970 .... $10,000
Value as of 12/31/79 of Shares Initially Acquired $10,577
Value of Shares Accepted as Capital Gains Distributions...... $ 5,406#
Total Value, December 31, 1979 .... $15,983
   Total Dividends PAID From Investment Income .... $ 4,554

#Dollar Amount of these distributions at the time shares were acquired: $5,013

Results Taking All Dividends and Distributions in CASH
Initial Investment At Offering Price, January 1, 1970 .... $10,000
Total Value, December 31, 1979 .... $10,577
Distributions From Capital Gains .... $ 4,189
Dividends From Investment Income .... $ 3,896

Examining Fund Literature and the Management Team. The literature furnished by a mutual fund sometimes offers clues about the reputation and qualifications of the management. The literature may reveal the background of the officers and directors—for example, their age, years of investment experience, important current and past business affiliations, college degrees, and professional designations such as chartered financial analyst (CFA). The literature may also show whether a significant number of the mutual fund shares are owned by discrete, large institutional investors such as corporate pension funds, foundations, and college endowment funds.

The reputation of the management may also be reflected by the organization or by the parent organization responsible for the management of the mutual fund. Some mutual fund management organizations are owned and operated by prominent investment advisory firms, insurance companies, or brokerage firm affiliates. Finally, acquaintances in the investment industry whose judgment you respect may provide useful assessments of capable mutual fund managers.

Methods of Fund Purchases and Sales

In an earlier section we discussed some of the ways in which shares of funds are purchased and the types of mutual fund accounts that shareholders can open. The following subsections describe the procedures used to open new accounts once you have completed the selection process.

REGULAR ACCOUNTS

To make a new or initial purchase of shares in a mutual fund, you must establish a regular account in your name (in your name and in the name of the co-owner, in the case of a joint account) and make an initial minimum payment, usually amounting to several hundred dollars. The channels used to process the initial purchase order depend on whether the mutual fund is a load fund or a no-load fund.

A **load fund** is one in which a load, or sales commission, is charged to the investor. The charge usually amounts to about 8-1/2 percent of the purchase price. The commission is paid to the fund distributor, dealer, and salesperson to compensate for the time and expense incurred in effecting the sale and in processing the order. The salesperson may either be employed by an independent brokerage firm that sells shares of mutual funds and individual securities or may be a member of a "captive" sales force that sells only the mutual funds managed by the employer organization. The sales commission is a justifiable expense if the sales staff provides information and advice to prospective investors who need to learn which mutual funds would be most suitable for their particular financial objectives and circumstances.

EXHIBIT 13-11   Investment Service Report on Past Performance of Mutual Funds

| | Total Net Assets 6/30/81 ($ Million) | 6 Months 1981 | Year 1980 | 5½ Years 1976 to 6/30/81 | 10½ Years 1971 to 6/30/81 | Classification of Assets (Percent) 6/30/81 | | | Percent Yield Last 12 Months |
						Cash & Gov't	Bonds & Prfd.	Common Stock	
I. Growth Funds									
B. Long Term Growth Income Secondary									
New Perspective Fund	474.6	3.7	25.6	140.7		31	3	66	3.0
Newton Growth Fund	17.7	4.9	45.3	151.9	109.4	2	3*	95	2.0
**One Hundred Fund (1974)	13.2	7.2	35.2	158.9	40.6	0	11*	89	1.1
Oppenheimer Directors Fund	43.4	7.0	48.1			19	0	81	1.0
Over-the-Counter Securities	51.3	8.0	22.9	347.9	471.8	22	0	78	3.1
Paramount Mutual Fund	10.1	2.8	11.4	134.0	166.1	8	8*	84	2.5
Penn Square Mutual Fund	160.6	9.0	25.6	117.6	178.0	5	0	95	4.8
Pilgrim Fund	50.8	8.2	22.5	213.2	164.2	11	2*	87	3.2
**Pligrowth Fund (1967)	20.9	3.6	34.0	111.0	123.5	1	8*	91	2.9
T. Rowe Price Growth Stock	1,028.4	-4.2	30.1	62.6	68.1	4	1*	95	3.6
T. Rowe Price New Era Fund	492.1	-7.9	52.0	192.0	241.2	12	1*	87	3.1
**Pro Fund (1976)	43.1	3.1	15.8	116.7	31.2	0	2*	98	3.9
Progress Fund	5.4	6.2	36.5	149.0	103.9	26	0	74	0.8
Putnam Growth Fund	679.0	-2.6	37.2	128.0	180.6	31	5	64	4.0
Putnam Investors Fund	667.7	-2.1	44.3	125.6	197.7	2	0	98	2.2
Safeco Growth Fund	46.5	5.3	30.6	308.7	225.3	6	0	94	3.0
St. Paul Growth Fund	36.3	4.1	63.1	311.4	343.8	30	0	70	0.9
St. Paul Special Fund	10.0	1.3	63.7	209.2	252.9	25	0	75	0.8
Scudder Common Stock Fund	157.3	-8.2	34.4	107.7	114.9	5	0	95	3.6
Security Equity Fund	159.9	-7.4	48.7	177.5	208.6	4	1	95	2.1
Sentinal Growth Fund	27.4	3.0	42.5	112.2	164.0	12	0	88	1.9
Sentry Fund	27.1	8.4	41.8	171.3	192.2	12	0	88	2.4
Sierra Growth Fund	4.1	-9.0	37.4	140.2	102.5	1	0	99	1.9
Sigma Special Fund	9.6	5.1	27.1	176.3	213.3	2	0	98	2.1
Sigma Venture Shares	23.8	11.9	41.1	350.3	363.7	14	0	86	1.1
Smith, Barney Equity Fund	58.1	-2.7	43.4	135.9	166.2	12	2*	86	2.5
Sogen International Fund	25.4	3.9	31.7	113.2	128.1	24	25	51	5.9
State Farm Growth Fund	230.5	4.5	25.4	203.8	231.0	2	0	98	2.8
**Stein Roe & Farnham Cap Opp (1969)	126.1	-12.2	78.7	270.6	272.5	11	0	89	0.9
Stein Roe & Farnham Stock	201.7	-11.7	63.1	111.5	133.0	8	0	92	1.8
Sun Growth Fund	11.3	-11.0	31.8	64.7		14	0	86	3.3
Surveyor Fund	103.0	-1.9	46.6	151.8	95.5	14	0	86	1.5
Templeton World Fund Inc.	559.4	10.5	20.8			9	4*	87	2.0
Transamerica Capital Fund	41.8	-0.7	35.1	73.6	96.6	9	1	90	3.2
Travelers Equities Fund	42.1	-4.5	47.3	157.9	183.0	20	0	80	4.0
United Accumulative Fund	400.4	1.1	34.6	102.4	102.2	12	3	85	3.9
United Contl Growth Fund	57.4	9.0	31.6	109.4	77.3	44	2	54	3.9
United Science & Energy Fund	170.1	-6.7	39.9	97.5	75.2	26	1	73	3.1
USAA Mutual, Growth Fund	63.9	-4.1	43.9	80.3		7	0	93	2.6
Value Line Fund	74.4	7.6	41.6	308.8	300.4	20	0	80	1.7
**Vance Sanders Common Stk Fd (1968)	58.9	5.9	32.6	163.1	189.2	4	0	96	1.9
Variable Stock Fund	5.8	6.0	25.7	110.7	109.0	2	4*	94	3.1
Windsor Fund	976.8	18.1	22.9	186.2	227.0	8	0	92	5.0
Total	$18,058.7								
Averages		2.3	35.1	152.7	153.9				2.7

No-load funds have no sales commission; the purchase price is equal to the NAV of the fund. With the possible exception of money market mutual funds, no-load mutual funds employ no sales force. Consequently, the investor must take the initiative in learning about and evaluating no-load funds. Because investors have become more knowledgeable about mutual funds in recent years, no-load funds have become more popular, and their assets have grown more rapidly than the assets of load funds. No-load funds advertise in financial periodicals such as the *Wall Street Journal* and *Barron's* and in the business section of major daily newspapers. Both no-load funds and load funds are described in the reference sources cited in the earlier discussion of closed-end companies, and their prices or NAVs are reported in leading financial periodicals and major newspapers. The referenced sources and advertisements furnish addresses, and sometimes toll-free telephone numbers, that investors can use to request literature and to place purchase orders. Once you have established a regular account, you can elect to have dividends and capital gains reinvested and to make additional purchases by mail.

PERIODIC PURCHASE PLANS

Dollar cost averaging (see Chapter 11), an investment strategy whereby an investor purchases an investment at fixed time intervals with a payment of a constant number of dollars, can produce financial benefits in which mutual fund investors can also share. Mutual fund shareholders are able to purchase additional shares—say, each month or quarter—for as little as $25 or $50. The plans are of two types—voluntary and contractual. Under a **voluntary plan** the investor pays a commission (if the fund is a load fund) on each purchase only at the time of purchase; no penalty charges are incurred if a payment is skipped or if the plan is terminated.

Under a **contractual plan** the investor agrees to make periodic purchases over a stipulated time period (e.g., ten years), during which a substantial portion of the sales commissions calculated for the total period is deducted from the payments made by the investors during the first few years. The investor thus incurs a much higher sales commission under a contractual plan that is terminated prematurely than under a voluntary plan. However, some investors might choose a contractual plan over a voluntary plan because the former constitutes a type of forced savings.

RETIREMENT PLANS

As was previously mentioned, individuals and employers can establish tax-exempt retirement plans in which shares of mutual funds are purchased. Mutual funds can be helpful to prospective investors in retirement plans, because they provide literature, advice, and account application forms that make it easy for investors to comply with Internal Revenue regulations for various tax-exempt retirement programs (Keogh, IRA, simplified pension plans, and section 403(b) plans). Retirement plans are described in greater detail in Chapter 16.

EXCHANGE PRIVILEGES

Shares may be purchased by exchanging the shares in one fund for shares in another fund managed by the same mutual fund organization. The exchange usually involves little or no cost and can be effected by writing a letter of request or by placing a toll-free telephone call if a prior written agreement is on file at the fund.

SALES

When a shareholder wishes to sell shares, the mutual fund redeems them at the NAV on the day the order is processed. If the stock certificates are not on deposit at the custodian bank, they must be delivered.

Costs of Mutual Fund Services

Some of the costs incurred by investors in mutual funds are quite visible—for example, the front-end load, or sales commission. Other costs are not so visible—for example, operating expenses and possible poor portfolio performance. You should compare various mutual fund costs with the costs of alternative strategies—for example, making your investments directly. If you decide to invest in mutual funds, you should compare the costs of the different funds as a basis for your selection.

One might suppose that the best mutual fund managements, or those with the best performance, have relatively high management expenses. However, some of the most well managed funds charge only moderate expenses—for example, the Windsor Fund shown in Exhibit 13–10 has a low expense rate of about .66 percent of assets per year.

COSTS OF LOAD FUNDS

At the time of purchase, some funds have no loads; others have sales commissions ranging from 1 percent to 9-1/4 percent, depending on each fund's policy and on the dollar size of the purchase order. If an investor pays an 8-1/2 percent load, for example, for every $100.00 invested, $8.50 goes for the sale commission and only $91.50 is actually invested. In recent years sales of new shares of no-load funds have been growing more rapidly than sales of load fund shares. Likewise, the rate of redemption of no-load shares has been less than the rate of load fund redemptions. The growth in assets of no-load funds may be explained by an increased investor awareness of the existence of no-load funds. The lower rate of redemption may be due to no-load shareholders being more deliberate in the initial purchase, whereas shareholders of load funds are "sold" on a purchase through the efforts of a sales force. Salespersons are occasionally influenced by the size of the sales commission they can earn rather than by the fund that has the best investment management and the most suitable portfolio objectives for a particular investor. In contrast, a no-load fund has no sales staff and therefore must promote the fund more on the basis of its reputation and investment performance record.

OPERATING COSTS

Annual operating expenses contribute to the cost of the mutual fund. These expenses pay the investment management fee and general administrative fees of the organization—for example, the costs of shareholder reports, postage, office maintenance, accounting, and legal services. These expenses are not readily visible to investors because they are paid out of the investment income of the portfolio. Operating expenses tend to be positively correlated to the amount of the fund's assets. Therefore, one way to judge the reasonableness of a fund's operating expenses is to examine the ratio of annual expenses to average annual net assets, which are reported in a fund's prospectus and in the publications of reporting services—for example, Wiesenberger's *Investment Companies*. The expense ratio for the Windsor Fund was shown in Exhibit 13–10. The ratio can be computed with a fund's aggregate accounts, as was illustrated for the XYZ Investment Company in Exhibits 13–1 and 13–2. The largest component of annual expenses is normally the investment management fee, usually between 0.3 percent for large funds and 0.6 percent for smaller ones. The management fee covers the research costs for portfolio strategy, industry and security analysis, and market analysis.

TRANSACTION COSTS

One important, if not immediately obvious, cost is portfolio transaction costs, incurred when portfolio securities are traded in the market. One way to gauge these costs is to analyze the annual portfolio turnover rate, which is disclosed in the prospectus. If a $500 million portfolio, for example, had a portfolio turnover rate of 25 percent in a given year, 25 percent of the portfolio, or $125 million of securities, was sold and replaced with new securities. The turnover rate varies widely from fund to fund, as well as for a given fund from year to year. The rate can range from 5 percent to 200 percent, or even 300 percent, per year. Excessive trading, called **churning,** is usually a negative sign; however, investment performance is what counts.

Shareholders may also be charged for special services—for example, establishing and maintaining a Keogh or IRA account or furnishing duplicate account records to replace those a shareholder may have lost. However, many special services provided by funds are free.

As a potential investor, you should compare the costs of each fund, because costs vary from fund to fund. You should then relate the costs to the benefits offered. In the cost-benefit equation, the most important consideration is usually the portfolio performance benefit. The rate of return is calculated after the deduction of operating expenses and portfolio transaction costs. Consequently, if the fund management has been able to achieve your objectives and to produce a superior rate of return, management expenses, regardless of amount, have been well worth the cost. Conversely, if portfolio performance objectives have not been achieved, the expenses, no matter how small, have not been worthwhile.

SUMMARY

1. An investment company is a company that receives funds from investors and reinvests the funds in securities of other firms. All investment companies feature professional management that attempts to conform to a predetermined set of goals and policies in managing the company's portfolio.
2. Investment companies, regardless of their portfolios, are of two basic types: (a) closed-end funds with a fixed number of shares outstanding and (b) open-end funds that continuously offer new shares to the public and redeem outstanding shares at their net asset value.
3. Closed-end companies traded on the major exchanges and on the OTC often sell at market prices, which are at a discount from their net asset value. Having more assets working for the dollar often yields important advantages. Dividend yields are higher than the yields of underlying stocks purchased separately. If stocks in general rise, the discount tends to narrow, and vice versa.
4. Mutual (open-end) funds are available in many different forms and with varying objectives. They can be purchased from salespersons (in which case they include a sales charge, called a load) or direct from the company (in which case they are called no-load funds). All mutual funds state in their prospectus what their investment objectives are and how they will attempt to achieve these objectives.
5. A skilled professional investment adviser attempts to maximize the investor's wealth within the stated policies of the funds. Professional investment managers charge for their services; charges vary widely from fund to fund. A key factor in choosing a fund is not the amount of the charges but the results achieved by the fund in managing the securities it owns.
6. Mutual funds cater to the small investor by selling shares in convenient installments. They also provide record-keeping and tax information. Mutual funds are in many respects ideal vehicles for accumulating an estate through regular savings at less risk than is involved in purchasing shares individually.

7. Disadvantages of mutual funds include (a) the fact that their management fees may not be "worth it" to some investors, (b) their broad diversification, which tends to reduce the size of potential capital gains that might otherwise be possible, (c) the relatively poor investment performance by some fund managements, and (d) the need for investors to analyze which fund is best for their specific investment goals.

8. Major types of mutual funds include money market funds, bond funds, free bond funds, tax-exempt money market funds, capital appreciation (growth) funds, growth and income funds, high current income funds, balanced funds, and specialty funds. Each of these types tends to serve different investment objectives.

9. A significant factor in selecting investment companies is the operating expenses of management. Annual expenses may range from .5 percent to 1 percent or more of average assets, in addition to sales charges applicable to load funds.

REVIEW QUESTIONS

1. From the standpoint of the investor, what are the advantages and disadvantages of investing in shares of investment companies as compared with investing directly in individual stocks and bonds?

2. From the standpoint of the investor, what are the advantages and disadvantages of investing in shares of closed-end funds as compared with investing in shares of mutual funds?

3. (a) What steps should you take in deciding which closed-end fund to buy and when to buy it?
   (b) Explain why these steps are not required when you invest in mutual funds.

4. (a) What is NAV and how is it calculated?
   (b) What is NAV used for?

5. Why do closed-end funds usually trade at a discount from their NAV?

6. Have the investment managements of mutual funds been successful?

7. Describe five convenient services mutual funds provide to shareholders.

8. "An investor should never purchase shares of a load fund, especially through a contractual periodic purchase plan." Explain why you agree or disagree.

9. "Mutual funds are subject to extensive federal laws and regulations designed to protect investors from losses." Explain why you agree or disagree.

10. Explain why, in selecting a mutual fund, you should evaluate the funds on the basis of the following factors:
    (a) Portfolio objectives and policies;
    (b) Investment management capabilities;
    (c) Costs of services.

11. (a) What was the trend in the expense ratio for the Windsor Fund during the 1969–1979 period as shown in Exhibit 13–10?
    (b) What apparently accounts for this trend?

12. (a) In Exhibit 13–5, which type of fund provided the best performance over the five-, ten-, and twenty-year periods?
    (b) Was high fund performance due primarily to a specific portfolio policy objective or to management skill in making good individual security selections?

CASE PROBLEMS

Consult the publications of the Wiesenberger Investment Companies Service, Moody's *Bank and Finance,* the *Value Line Investment Survey,* or *Forbes* to solve the following problems.

I. Selecting Mutual Funds

Compare the performance of individual mutual funds and of groups of mutual funds for varying time periods. Do the portfolio performance rankings remain the same from period to period, or do they change? What do these observations tell us about trying to pick a fund on the basis of its past ranking?

II. Comparing Mutual Fund Performance to Market Indexes

Compare the performance of mutual funds with a market index such as the Standard & Poor's Composite Stock Index or the Dow Jones Industrial Average. Notice that some funds underperformed the market index. Can you identify funds that probably underperformed because of particular investment objectives and portfolio policies rather than because the managers lacked investment skill?

III. Mutual Fund Risk

Identify some funds that had exceptionally high returns, and some that had large losses, because they assumed large risks. What kind of risks did the funds assume?

CHAPTER 14

SOME PRACTICAL ADVICE ON INVESTMENTS

LEARNING OBJECTIVES

In studying this chapter you will learn:

Various ways, including borrowing, to obtain funds for investment;

How to determine the proper time to buy or sell securities;

How to react to a stranger's "hot tips" and to over-the-telephone requests to buy securities;

How to admit investment mistakes and correct them promptly;

The importance of avoiding too frequent trading of securities;

How tax selling can save you money;

How to set up records to keep track of your investments;

The uses of special orders;

Some pointers about investing in common stocks;

Why mutual funds warrant consideration as investment media;

The role of bonds and preferred stocks in investment planning;

Why collectibles, gold, and vacation homes may not be good investment media for beginners.

Each year publishers release many books that tell potential investors "how to do it." The authors are seldom held to account for bad advice, but they are often quick to take credit for advice that turns out to have been good. Valid generalizations about how to invest successfully on a continuous basis are hard to make. As one investment counselor has stated: "All generalizations made about investing are most likely false, including this one."[1] Nevertheless, some points about investing are time tested and generally accepted. Much of the advice included in this chapter is based on facts discussed in the preceding chapters.

OBTAINING INVESTMENT FUNDS

The first step in investing is obtaining funds to invest. Many people never take this first step because they lack the will to form a plan for obtaining investment money. Perhaps the best initial advice is that you decide you want to invest for some future goal and to develop a plan to save or borrow the necessary money. Generally your plan should involve systematic saving over a period of time. No matter how small your income, you can save a portion of it if you have enough will and desire to do so.

Saving to Invest

Before beginning to save money for investment, you must decide how much to set aside. You should not attempt to set aside more than your consumption requirements will permit (see Chapter 1 for an analysis of consumption needs).

One method of accumulating cash for investment is to "pay yourself first"—that is, when you receive your paycheck, make your savings deposit before other expenses crowd out the funds you intended to save. Employee payroll savings plans or bank savings plans in which your checking account is automatically charged each month for a savings deposit are two means of "paying yourself first."

---

1. Sam Shulsky, *Sam Shulsky on Investing* (New York: New York Institute of Finance, 1980), p. 76.

Borrowing to Invest

Income taxes and inflation sometimes make it advantageous to borrow for investment (see Chapter 3). For example, if you can borrow at 15 percent, your after-tax cost is only 9 percent if you are in the combined federal and state income tax bracket of 40 percent: [15% − 40%(15%) = 9%]. If the investment will average an after-tax return greater than 9 percent, you will gain by borrowing. Since the rate of inflation in recent years has been greater than the after-tax cost of borrowing, many investments that have kept up with inflation (e.g., real estate and some growth stocks) return an after-tax amount greater than the after-tax cost of borrowing.

LIFE INSURANCE LOANS

Owners of life insurance policies often find it advantageous to borrow cash and loan values (at rates between 5 and 8 percent) to reinvest elsewhere at a greater return. The loan interest on life insurance is tax-deductible if you have paid any four of the first seven annual premiums in cash. Furthermore, although you are paying the life insurer interest, the life insurer is simultaneously crediting your policy with some minimum guaranteed interest rate, as well as with any dividends you may have earned. This return is not currently taxable. The net cost of borrowing is the difference between what you are paying the insurer and what the insurer is paying you. You may be paying 8 percent on the loan, but in the policy you are being credited with 6 percent; thus, the cost of borrowing is only 2 percent before tax considerations. Since in most instances the loan interest is tax-deductible, the net after-tax cost of borrowing may be zero or even negative. (Loan interest is not deductible when the funds are used to purchase tax-exempt securities such as municipal bonds.)

The advantages of borrowing on life insurance are illustrated in Exhibit 14–1. Borrowing $1,000 from your life insurer at 8 percent may produce a net borrowing cost of only 2 percent, as shown in Case 1. If you reinvest the $1,000 at an after-tax rate of 12 percent, your net return, after loan costs, accumulates at 10 percent and produces a savings fund of $2,593 in ten years, compared with only $1,868 produced by funds left to accumulate at 5 percent in the life insurance policy. If you can also deduct the insurance loan interest, the true net cost of borrowing may be zero, depending on your marginal income tax bracket. In Case 2 the net cost of borrowing from the life insurer after taxes is assumed to be zero. In this event the entire 12 percent return assumed to be available will accumulate to your account, and the initial $1,000 will grow to $3,106 within ten years; you would have accumulated only $1,868 had you left the funds in the insurance policy.

The success of any life insurance borrowing program depends on the low-interest loans available from your policy compared with the returns you can earn elsewhere on investments similar to life insurance. In making com-

EXHIBIT 14–1
Borrowing on
Life Insurance
and Reinvesting
Proceeds

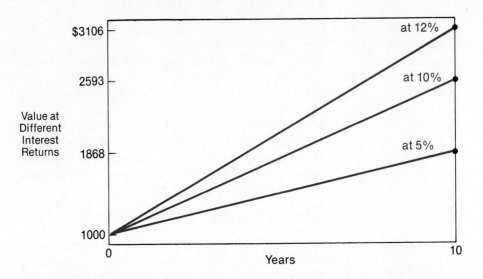

Hypothetical Conditions	Case 1[a]	Case 2[b]
You pay life insurer (net % of tax)	8%	6%
You earn on policy	6%	6%
Net borrowing cost	2%	0
% at which you reinvest	12%	12%
Net gain	10%	12%
Value of $1,000 in 10 years	$2,593	$3,106

[a]Case 1—You do not deduct loan interest.
[b]Case 2—You deduct loan interest and you are in the 25% marginal tax bracket,
       reducing the net amount paid to the insurer from 8% to 6% [.08 −
       .25(.08)].

parisons, remember that life insurance funds carry tax deferral on interest earned and offer high liquidity and great safety.

SECURITY LOANS

You can borrow from your broker or banker by pledging as collateral the securities you are buying. This procedure is known as **margin trading.** Government rules limit the amount that may be borrowed—currently, 50 percent of the market value of the securities.

Margin trading increases your leverage. For example, suppose you put up $1,000 to purchase $2,000 worth of stock, and the stock rises to $3,000. You have made $1,000 on your investment of $1,000—a 100 percent increase, less borrowing costs. If you had bought the stock outright, paying the full $2,000, your gain would have been only 50 percent ($1,000/$2,000).

Beginning investors usually avoid margin buying because of the considerable risk involved: If the value of the stock declines, you must maintain the required margin by paying in more funds to restore the borrowing percentage to 50 percent. If you cannot maintain the margin percentage, you will have to sell the securities at an inopportune time (i.e., when stock prices are declining) to repay the loan.

Some investors borrow only amounts that can be supported by interest or dividends being paid on the selected stock. Thus, their holding costs are reduced. For example, if a stock pays an annual dividend of $200 and you are paying $200 interest annually to borrow $1,000, the loan interest is offset by the return on your stock.

TIMING YOUR INVESTMENTS

The question of when to purchase or sell securities has a significant bearing on your investment goals. Obviously, it is desirable to "buy low and sell high." Unfortunately, no one knows in advance when the price of a security will be high or low. Although many investment advisers are not hesitant to make judgments about the securities they are recommending, the record of most stock market forecasters is not encouraging. In short, you must make the final decision. Timing is affected by three major influences: general market factors, motives of sellers, and your plan for trading.

General Market Factors

Stock prices are affected by general business conditions and, in fact, are thought to be a leading indicator or forecaster of things to come. For example, if the market declines, it may be anticipating a business recession; if the market rises, it may be anticipating better business conditions. The period of lead time generally ranges between six and twelve months (see Exhibit 14–2). Current information on leading business indicators may be found in publications such as the *Business Conditions Digest.*

Investors who have good market timing do not make purchases simply because they have money available and "now is as good a time as any." The safest time to enter the stock market is when prices appear to be fairly stable and have not recently risen or fallen rapidly. For example, purchasing a specific stock when the market has been in a state of rapid decline subjects you to the risk that the price of your stock will be swept downward along with the general market. You have little to lose and much to gain by waiting until the market settles down.

EXHIBIT 14-2
Stock Prices as a
Leading Indicator

Market Peak	Recession Onset	Months of Lead Time
June 1948	November 1948	+5
January 1953	July 1953	+6
July 1956	August 1957	+13
July 1959	April 1960	+9
December 1968	December 1969	+12
January 1973	November 1973	+10
February 1980	January 1980	−1
April 1981	September 1981	+5

Source: *Business Conditions Digest*, various issues.

Frequently the price of one or more stocks in a given industry may vary from the price of the general market for all stocks. In other words, some stocks may be "hot" or "cold," even though the market as a whole is moving sideways. For example, oil stocks rose considerably in the period from 1974 to 1980, even though the market as a whole stayed about even. If your analysis of specific stocks is sound, the fact that the stock market generally is flat is not a reason for delaying purchase.

One aid in achieving good timing is observing what the price range of the stock has been for the preceding years. This information is quoted daily in most financial papers. You should know whether you are purchasing the stock at its year's high, at its year's low, or somewhere between. Obviously, more risk is present if you are buying at the high end of the price range rather than at the low end.

Motives of Sellers

When you are buying, you are doing so because another stock owner has decided to sell; thus, someone has to be wrong. You may ask, "What does the seller know that I do not?" (A story is told of two brokers on Wall Street who, while looking out the window, observed a body hurtling downward to the street below. The first broker said, "Say, that looks like Smedly—I wonder what he knows that we don't?") In buying speculative securities, in particular, you should bear in mind that someone may recommend a stock because the seller has an inventory of the issue and wishes to unload it. To encourage you to buy, the seller may have been "making a market"[2] in the stock so

---

2. "Making a market" refers to the practice of making stock purchases solely to maintain trading activity and to prevent significant price fluctuations in that stock.

that the price would go up. After the inventory has been sold, the support purchases will also cease; without these purchases the stock usually declines.

It is not unknown for the management of a company to issue favorable publicity about the company's prospects to lay groundwork for a new stock issue or simply to enable the "insiders" to unload positions they may wish to dispose of. Therefore, you should not purchase an investment when good news is first published, but rather wait to see what happens to the stock's price. Usually, if the news about the future of a stock is truly good, some insiders will know beforehand and will make their purchases well before the news is available to the investing public. Thus, the price of a stock often falls before publication of a report showing an increase in the latest quarterly earnings of the stock.

A frequent motive for selling stocks is to take income tax losses or gains. If the price of the stock you are considering has gone up or down markedly within the preceding year, the current owners may have decided to sell solely to recognize tax gains or losses. This phenomenon occurs particularly near the end of the calendar year, because investors must register gains or losses for income tax purposes before 31 December. **Tax swaps,** as such transactions are called, may start as early as October or November. Tax swaps usually have nothing to do with the intrinsic value of the stock but are an element to recognize if you are planning to purchase stock. Since stock prices tend to be artificially depressed by tax selling near the end of the calendar year, these months may be a good time in which to concentrate your stock purchases. Your chances for gains are increased because stock prices frequently rise early in the calendar year; most of the tax selling has been completed, and stocks are again traded more on their own merit than for tax reasons.

A Plan for Trading

You should have a plan to use as a guide for timing the sale of stock. For example, if a stock has advanced in price to a level you anticipated when you originally purchased it, you should probably sell the stock unless new developments have given you reason to be optimistic about further advances. Similarly, if you have purchased a stock that, within a reasonable time, has failed to live up to the market performance you expected, you should seriously contemplate selling. Some investors clean out their holdings once a year by replacing losers with other stocks.

Some guidelines for selling an investment include the following:

1. Sell if you believe another available stock of equal quality offers a better chance of gain and a smaller chance of loss.
2. Sell if adverse changes in management, profitability, financial structure, or competitive environment become evident.
3. Sell if the company's main products or services are in decline.

4. Sell if a general depression is threatening and your securities are particularly vulnerable—for example, if they are cyclical.
5. Sell if the conditions you anticipated when you first bought the security have not developed as expected. For example, if you expected sales and earnings to increase 15 percent within the year, and instead they were flat and offered little hope of improvement in the coming year, you should seek replacement securities.

The Perkin Elmer Corporation offers an illustration of a good time to sell. In 1981 the company, a manufacturer of scientific instruments, sold as high as 33 with earnings per share of $1.82—a price/earnings ratio of 18. Earnings per share were estimated at $2.40 for 1982. In 1982 a competitor announced major improvements in its product line, and per-share estimates for 1982 earnings for Perkin Elmer dropped to $1.80. Because of the relatively high P/E ratio and the downward revision in earnings, the stock was a good "sell" candidate. By February 1982 it had declined to just over 21.

Patience and study are necessary for successful investing. Stocks should not be sold solely because the following conditions may exist:

1. The stock is judged to be of good quality, but its price has not changed or is below what you paid for it.
2. Some temporary bad news has developed. If a good-quality stock declines on the strength of some temporary bad news, it may present a new buying opportunity rather than a reason for selling.
3. Although the stock price is down, the original conditions leading to your purchase of the stock have not changed, and better opportunities for investment are not present.

MAKING YOUR INVESTMENTS

Handling "Hot Tips"

The best advice on market tips is to ignore them. Most tips concern stocks supposedly about to be bought out at a much greater price by another company or stocks in companies about to announce a new, revolutionary product or process that, supposedly, will generate great profits. You should study the stock carefully before you act on any tip, no matter how urgent you believe prompt action to be. By the time you get the tip, others have generally heard about it and acted on it; therefore, any remaining price rise is unlikely. The average investor cannot easily judge whether a tip is accurate, how many other investors know about the tip, what the price of the stock was before other investors acted, or how much more the stock might go up if the tip turns out to be true.

Using Special Knowledge

In selecting securities for purchase, do not be afraid to use any special knowledge you may have about a company or industry. Specialized knowledge may give you a considerable advantage over other investors by enabling you to act on favorable developments that only a few people normally possess. For example, students of insurance may understand better than the average investor the phenomenon of the underwriting cycle, which represents the underwriting profit of property-liability insurers. Normally the stocks of insurance companies respond to profit changes that can be anticipated by changes in the underwriting cycle. Likewise, students of pharmacy might be in a position to predict the effect of the development of new drugs on the stock prices of certain drug-manufacturing companies.

Avoiding Swindles

Investors occasionally lose money in investment swindles. A good way to minimize this possibility is to deal only with reputable brokers and advisers and to refuse to buy or sell investments in a telephone transaction with someone you do not know. You should never make a purchase without prior investigation. Agents often try to sell land in Florida, Colorado, or other places "sight unseen." The telephone sales pitch includes the promise that the investor may cancel the purchase at any time within some stated period. An investor who wishes to cancel, however, may find it impossible to locate the sales agent or to recover the down payment.

Considering Special Orders

In purchasing or selling stocks, you can place orders with "strings attached." For example, you can use a **limit order**—that is, you can order your broker to purchase a stock at a price no greater than a specified amount. If you place a **market order,** the broker will execute your instructions at whatever price the trade demands on a particular day. Thus, if the stock you are buying is not actively traded, you may end up paying a high price for it. You can also place a **stop loss order**—that is, you can order your broker to sell your stock if the price drops to a predetermined level. For example, assume that you paid $20 for a stock with a current market value of $30. You believe the price will rise further, but to protect your current profit, you instruct your broker to sell if the stock drops as low as $28. Thus, you "lock in" an $8-per-share gain.

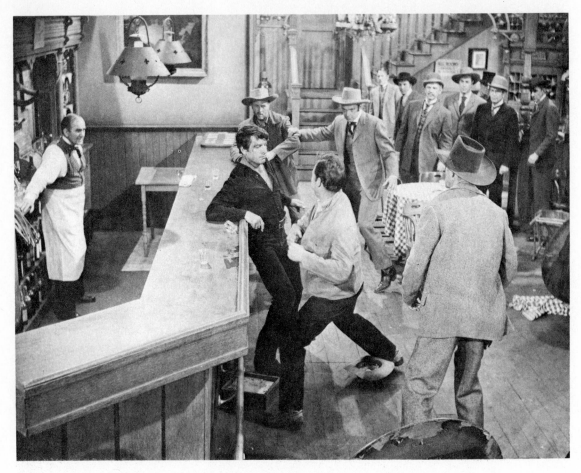

"All right, so the 'greater fool' theory doesn't always work."

The Bettman Archive, Inc.

Admitting Mistakes

If you have made an investment on the basis of an objective that later appears unattainable, you should generally sell the stock promptly and accept any loss without delay. If you hang on in the belief that your original judgment will be verified, your stock will very likely decline further and your loss will be greater—particularly if you are trading for profit, since the securities appropriate for this purpose are likely to be volatile. Thus, you might buy a stock at $30 with the idea of selling at $40. If the stock declines to $25, it should probably be sold; it will probably be available later at a still lower price.

Minimizing Transaction Costs

Too frequent trading of securities results in brokerage commissions that can absorb a large proportion of your gains. To minimize transaction costs, you should reduce the necessity of frequent trading by selecting investments only after careful study and deliberation. You can also minimize transaction costs through the use of discount brokers and through **dividend reinvestment plans** whereby the corporation permits you to accept dividends in the form of new stock issued without brokerage commissions.

Another method of minimizing transaction costs is to invest in a family of no-load mutual funds that permits you to switch from one fund to another without charge. Two of the largest such families are the Fidelity Group and the Vanguard Group, each of which includes more than ten funds with varying investment objectives. Thus, if your investment objectives were to change from "aggressive growth" to "income," you could telephone order the fund management to switch your investment without charge from one fund to another.

Reevaluating Your Investments

At one time financial advisers counseled clients to invest in high-quality stocks or bonds and to leave investments undisturbed indefinitely. This advice was based on the belief that high-quality corporations would remain sound and productive over long periods; thus, it would be unnecessary for clients to change their investment portfolios. If this advice was ever sound, it is certainly less valid today. Investment conditions change rapidly, and investments that were appropriate yesterday may be quite inappropriate today. For example, during the 1980–1981 period bond prices fluctuated drastically because of rising and falling interest rates. Investors who held bond portfolios, formerly thought to be stable investments with little risk of loss of capital, found their portfolios falling 30 percent or more over this relatively short period.

Thus, it is important for you to monitor your investments continuously to see if they remain appropriate for your current investment goals. Never put your investments away in a safe deposit box and forget about them.

Using Tax Shelters

Sheltering investment income from income taxes is increasingly important if you hope to maximize investment gains. Ways of using tax shelters are discussed in detail in Chapters 9 and 15.

Tax Selling

You should review your investments near the end of the tax year to determine whether you can profit by selling some securities to establish a tax loss or a tax gain. For example, assume you made a long-term gain of $1,000 from the sale of stock *G* in July. Reviewing your portfolio in November, you notice that the price of stock *L* is down. If the outlook for *L* is poor and you see no compelling reason to keep the stock, it could be sold and part of the accompanying loss offset by a reduction in income taxes due. If you sell *L*, you might establish a loss of $1,000, which would just offset the gain you made in *G*. Thus, you would avoid paying a capital gains tax on *G*, and the funds from the sale could be invested in securities with more promise.

Even if you believe that *L* is a good prospect and should be retained, you can sell it, establish the tax loss, and repurchase the stock after thirty days. The wait is mandated by income tax regulations governing **wash sales** (see Chapter 9).

You can sell securities to establish a tax loss, $3,000 of which may currently be deducted against other ordinary income in each tax year. You can replace these securities with comparable securities to keep your funds fully invested. Recall from Chapter 9 that you can deduct against ordinary income 100 percent of all short-term losses (losses involving less than a one-year holding period) and 50 percent of all long-term losses (losses involving a holding period of one year or more), up to a limit of $3,000. Any excess losses can be carried forward indefinitely to future periods until they have been exhausted.

Setting Up a Record-Keeping System

It is important that you establish a record-keeping system to monitor your investments. Income tax regulations require you to report on your tax returns gains and losses on sales of securities as well as dividends and interest. To provide this information, you should include in your record book the following information: name of security, date purchased, date sold, number of shares, original purchase cost, and total receipts upon sale (see Exhibit 14–3).

So that you will know whether you received proper dividend or interest payments, your records should include a space for the receipt of these items. The record should show the amount and date of receipts (see Exhibit 14–4). Although many investors rely on information sent after the close of the year by the corporations issuing the securities, these returns are not always prompt or reliable sources of information. It is better to have your own records confirming actual payments.

Proper records can keep you abreast of how well your investments are performing. Some investors maintain records showing monthly changes in

EXHIBIT 14-3   Record of Investment Transactions in Stocks

Name of Stock	Number of Shares	Date of Purchase	Purchase Price	Total Cost	Date of Sale	Price When Sold	Total Received on Sale	Gain (Loss)	Comments
General Motors	100	12/10/74	$33	$3,392	5/18/82	$44	$4,350	$958	Other stocks looked better
Raytheon	100	6/5/79	$50	$5,085					
Procter & Gamble	100	1/10/80	$66-1/4	$6,705					

EXHIBIT 14-4   Dividends Received on Stocks, 1981

Name of Stock	Quarter	Date of Receipt	Dividend Rate	Total Amount Received
General Motors	January	1/10/81	$.60	$60.00
	April	4/10/81	.60	60.00
	July	7/10/81	.60	60.00
	October	10/10/81	.60	60.00

the value of their portfolios (see Exhibit 14–5). In this way you can identify and possibly eliminate from the portfolio stocks and bonds that are performing poorly. It is helpful to write comments about what motivated the purchase of each security; later the facts can be compared with expectations. Investor learning is thus enhanced, and guidelines for future investment behavior are established.

CHOOSING AMONG INVESTMENT ALTERNATIVES

In earlier chapters we discussed several different types of investment opportunities. The following discussion focuses on some factors you should consider concerning the investment alternatives available to you.

Common Stocks

Purchasing common stocks is perhaps the main way for you as an investor to participate in the success (or failure) of the free enterprise system. Although common stocks have varying degrees of risk, they are also an important means of obtaining returns that help offset inflation (see Exhibit 14–6). Studies show a superiority of returns on common stocks versus alternatives such as bonds and mortgages over long periods of time. For example, a well-

EXHIBIT 14–5   *Price Changes of Stocks Owned, 1981*

Name of Stock	Number of Shares	Date of Purchase	Price at Purchase	1981 End-of-Month Prices					
				Jan.	Feb.	Mar.	Apr.	May	June
Stock 1 General Motors	100	12/10/74	$33	46	50-1/8	52-7/8	55	55-5/8	53
Comments: Outlook weak.									
Stock 2 Raytheon	100	6/5/79	$50	94-1/2	95	104-3/4	104	104-7/8	45
Comments: 2-for-1 stock split in June. Adjusted cost price is $25 per share.									
Stock 3 Procter & Gamble	100	1/10/80	$66-1/4	67	71-3/8	70-1/2	70	70-1/2	75-3/4
Comments: Company is introducing new products.									

known study of the fifty-year period 1926–1976 revealed that the average rate of return on common stocks was 9.2 percent annually in price appreciation and dividends—approximately twice the average annual return on bonds and mortgages.[3]

RISK

Unfortunately the favorable performance of the stock market over long periods is not steady from year to year. During some relatively long periods (e.g., 1970–1979) the market did quite poorly compared with other investments. On the other hand, the market may rise spectacularly over short periods (e.g., the S&P Industrials Index rose from 11 to 16, an increase of 45 percent, from April to November 1980). The investor in common stocks must be willing to assume risk, particularly in the short term, in return for the possibility of larger-than-average gains in the longer term.

Over the 1926–1976 period stocks lost 10 percent or more in value in the following years: 1930, 1931, 1937, 1941, 1956, 1966, 1973, and 1974. On the other hand, stocks gained 40 percent or more in 1928, 1933, 1935, 1954, and 1958.[4] By careful attention to stock selection, you can reduce the risk of losses in common stocks purchased as medium-to-long-term investments.

---

3. Roger G. Ibbotson and Rex A. Sinquefield, *Stocks, Bonds, Bills, and Inflation: The Past (1926–1976) and the Future (1977–2000)* (Charlottesville, Va.: Financial Analysis Research Foundation, 1977).

4. Ibid.

EXHIBIT 14-6　　Stocks as a Means of Offsetting Inflation

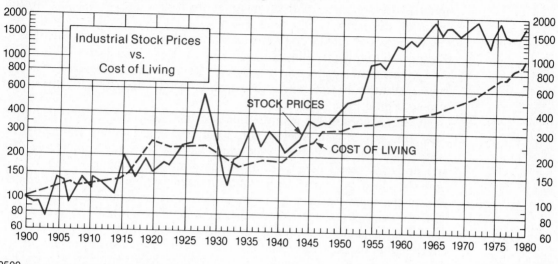

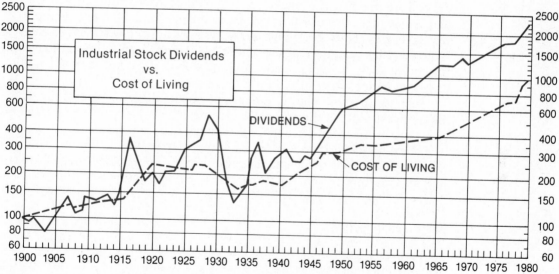

DIVIDENDS

Many investors refuse to purchase a common stock unless it pays dividends, which they believe to be a symbol of a high-quality stock. These investors view a company that pays no dividends (or pays only a small dividend when earnings permit a larger one) as financially unsuccessful. They believe that the only way an investor can be rewarded financially is to receive dividends; the only alternative way for an investor to receive any cash would be to sell the stock.

Most "good" stocks do pay at least some share of corporate earnings in the form of dividends. However, plowing earnings back into the company for reinvestment is also important; reinvestment can increase future earnings capabilities. In fact, reinvested earnings may be the most efficient source of new capital for a company.

If reinvested earnings result in increased business operations, they should cause the price of your stock to rise. Recall that the total return on your investment is made up of these price gains plus the dividends you receive. The dividends you receive are taxed as ordinary income, while the capital gains from the sale of your stock at a profit are taxed at a lower rate. (Only 40 percent of the capital gain must be reported if you have held the stock for at least one year.) If you purchase securities in which your total expected return is made up partially of capital gains, your after-tax returns will be increased. On the other hand, if you are in the retirement stage of the financial life cycle and are in a low tax bracket, you should probably purchase stocks that emphasize high dividend payouts. Exhibits 14–7 and 14–8 list examples of stocks that, as of late 1981, appeared to satisfy various investment objectives. Note that high-yielding stocks (Exhibit 14–7) tend to sell at lower price/earnings ratios than do high-growth stocks (Exhibit 14–8). Investors are willing to pay more for growth than for current yield.

Suppose that you plan to emphasize stocks that pay modest dividends and reinvest most of the corporate earnings in the company. How can you tell whether the stock price will rise enough to compensate for the relatively modest dividends you will be receiving? One way is to observe whether the company's book value and rate of return on stockholders' equity are rising (see Chapters 11 and 12). If they are not rising, reinvested dividends are not producing the rising capital base needed to achieve increased earnings.

PRICE APPRECIATION

Investors tend to bid for stocks in accordance with some perceived acceptable price/earnings ratio. For example, a common ratio for high-quality stocks in 1981 was about 8 or 9. Thus, Procter and Gamble, the largest soap manufacturer, was selling for about $78.00 a share in November 1981; it paid a dividend of $4.20 for a yield of 5.4 percent on the $78.00 selling price. Dividends were rising 10 percent annually. The P/E ratio was 9.6 and earnings were $8.08 a share, growing at an average of 11.5 percent annually. Using this information and assuming that investors do not change their ideas about Procter and Gamble's P/E ratio, we can calculate the expected gain to the investor in 1982:

1. 1981 stock price (November) $78.00
2. Assumed earnings per share in 1982
   (increased 11½% over 1981) 9.00

EXHIBIT 14–7   High-Yielding Stocks in 1981

Stock	Recent Price	P/E Ratio	Estimated Dividend Yield	Industry Group
Sierra Pacific Power	$11	6.3	14.5%	Electric utility (west)
Cascade Natural Gas	8-3/4	4.7	13.6	Natural gas
Ohio Edison	13	6.3	13.5	Electric utility (central)
Hackensack Water	17	13.1	13.2	Water utilities
PNB Mortgage	9-1/2	7.1	13.2	R.E.I.T.
Mesabi Trust	12	8.3	13.0	Iron ore
Manville Corporation	15	32.6	12.8	Building
Otter Tail Power	18	9.8	12.7	Electric utilities (central)
Kentucky Utilities	17	8.7	12.5	Electric utilities (central)
Wicor, Inc.	18	5.5	12.3	Natural gas
Alagasco, Inc.	14	4.9	12.1	Natural gas
Middle South Utilities	14	5.8	12.1	Electric utilities (central)

Source: *Value Line Investment Survey*, current stock reports (November 27, 1981), p. 28.

3. Estimated price in 1982: P/E ratio of 9.6
   (same as 1981) times 1982 earnings 86.40
4. Stockholders' gain from price appreciation
   (Line 3 – Line 1) $8.40
5. Dividend in 1982 (1981 dividend increased by 10%) 4.62
6. Total return $13.02
7. Ratio of total return to 1981 stock price
   (Line 6 ÷ Line 1) 16.7%

In this example we can see that, even though the current dividend yield is only 5.4 percent, the total expected return—dividends plus growth in the value of the shares—is over 16 percent. Most investors consider an average return of 16 percent very satisfactory. A well-known investment scholar, using a similar method of analysis, concluded: "While there may be leaks in the house of capitalism, the roof does not appear to be caving in. . . . Over the long pull, common stocks have protected investors against inflation, and I believe they will continue to do so in the future."[5]

CROWD PSYCHOLOGY

If you recognize that the stock market is subject to crowd psychology, which is often unreasonable, you can avoid many losses. Investor overreac-

---

5. Burton G. Malkiel, *A Random Walk Down Wall Street*, 2d ed. (New York: W.W. Norton, 1981), p. 302.

EXHIBIT 14-8   High-Growth Stocks in 1981

Stock	Recent Price	Growth (Past 10 Years)	Estimated Growth (3–5 Years)	P/E Ratio	Estimated Dividend Yield (12 Months)	Industry Group
Amarex, Inc.	$20	27%	19%	57.1	N/L	Petroleum producing
Baker Int'l. Corporation	37	24	26	9.7	1.9%	Oil field services
Dover Corporation	29	18	19	10.4	2.4	Machinery
Great Lakes Chemical	43	27	22	15.6	1.1	Chemical (specialty)
Hughes Tool	39	27	23	8.1	2.1	Oil field services
Jerrico, Inc.	21	37	21	10.2	0.6	Fast-food service
Mark Controls	13	21	19	8.8	2.5	Electrical equipment
Marriot Corporation	34	19	19	10.0	0.9	Hotel/gaming
Payless Cashways	17	22	20	11.3	1.2	Building
Raychem Corporation	52	27	20	11.9	1.0	Electronics
Schlumberger, Ltd.	53	25	26	11.5	2.0	Oil field services
Wal-Mart Stores	42	39	27	16.9	0.7	Retail store

Source: *Value Line Investment Survey,* current stock reports (November 27, 1981), p. 35.

tion to both good and bad news sends stocks up or down far in excess of what the news may justify. Crowd psychology was recognized as a significant market influence by John Maynard Keynes, the English economist, who devoted a chapter to the stock market in his book *The General Theory of Employment, Interest, and Money.* Keynes, a successful investor himself, likened the stock market to a beauty contest in which the judges select a winner not on the basis of their own judgment but on the basis of whom they think other people would select as the most beautiful.

A recent example of Keynes's point occurred in the 1960s. Stocks of fifty leading companies (termed "the nifty fifty") were bid up to very high price/earnings multiples by institutional investors, while more reasonably priced stocks of equally good companies languished. For example, in 1961 one stock, Control Data, sold for over 200 times its previous year's earnings. Later the stock fell dramatically. When a stock is very highly priced in relation to earnings, investors are probably purchasing the stock on "the greater fool theory," which states that any price for a stock is justified if you can later sell it at a higher price to someone else—that is, to a person who is a greater fool than you were when you bought it.

SELECTING SPECIFIC STOCKS

If you invest in individual stocks on your own, Malkiel offers the following practical rules:[6]

6. Ibid., pp. 309–311.

1. Confine stock purchases to companies that appear able to sustain above-average earnings growth for at least five years.
2. Never pay more for a stock than can reasonably be justified by a "firm foundation of value."
3. Buy stocks associated with stories of anticipated growth on which investors can build "castles in the air."
4. Trade as little as possible.

Rules 1 and 2 reflect Malkiel's acceptance of fundamental analysis, as described in Chapter 11. You can follow rule 1 by observing a stock's statistical history as outlined in stock guides such as *Value Line*, where average annual past growth rates for varying numbers of years are calculated. You can follow rule 2 by refusing to pay above-average prices as measured by the stock's P/E ratio. In other words, you can refuse to purchase stocks selling for a P/E ratio of 20 when the average P/E ratio for other good-quality stocks is only 10.

If you observe these two rules, you will probably be rewarded not only by increases in stock prices but also by a rising P/E ratio accorded the stock by other investors. Spectacular gains are possible when the investing public increases the price it is willing to pay for a given dollar of earnings—that is, increases the P/E ratio. Consider the following example:

Stock A: 1982 P/E ratio, 10. Earnings, $5. Price, $50.
Stock A: 1983 P/E ratio, 12. Earnings, $6. Price, $72.
Gain in earnings ($1/$5): 20%.
Gain in stock price ($22/$50): 44%.

In this example, when earnings rise 20 percent, the public has more confidence in the stock's future and is willing to pay 12 times earnings rather than 10. Although this "vote of confidence" would not appear unusual, the stock price is bid up 44 percent. Remember, however, that an equally precipitous decline occurs when the investing public accords a lower price/earnings ratio to earnings. This sort of decline occurred to most of the "nifty fifty" stocks during the 1970s, when earnings either declined or failed to increase as much as investors expected.

Malkiel's third rule recognizes the element of crowd psychology in investors' decisions regarding common stocks. The stock market is "emotional" and does not follow statistical rules consistently, particularly in the short run. (If it did so, we would not have to study investments but could invest according to set formulas.) The stock market is subject to fads and fashions that change constantly and unexpectedly. Thus, in some years any new stock issue with a name suggesting computers or electronics is quickly bid up. In other years the favored issues may be in petroleum, pollution control, or bank stocks. For example, the newly issued stock of Apple Computer, a manufacturer and distributor of computers for home and small-business use, came out in 1981 at $22 a share and rose to about $29 the same day. The stock subsequently rose to a high of $36 before falling to a low of about $14 within a few months. About a year later (February 1982) the stock was selling for $19. During these gyrations in price, little basic change occurred in the company itself or in its investment outlook.

Malkiel's fourth rule takes into account the fact that frequent trading of securities is expensive in terms of the brokerage commissions that must be paid each time a stock is bought or sold. Too frequent trading can quickly consume profits. (Earlier in the chapter we discussed a selling plan that will help you avoid unnecessary transactions or rash decisions.)

Mutual Funds

Hundreds of different mutual funds are available to serve different investment objectives. Exhibit 14–9 shows the different rates of change in the value of funds with different investment objectives. For example, balanced funds, which contain both bonds and common stocks, have had the least growth over the period 1959–1981, and growth funds, the most. Future periods may or may not display similar patterns. Most investors should give serious consideration to mutual funds, not only for the diversification the funds offer but also because of their professional management services (see Chapter 13). Mutual fund performance tends to be unspectacular; violent price fluctuations are uncommon. Investors should not expect to "get rich overnight." However, neither will they lose everything quickly if the market goes sour.

Various studies have demonstrated that no load funds (funds sold without sales commissions) have enjoyed investment performance roughly equal to load funds. Since the load, or sales charge, may be 8 or 9 percent of the acquisition price, no-load funds are preferable, other things being equal, because more of your funds work for you.

Mutual funds are particularly appropriate for investment programs in which you are investing regular amounts over fairly long periods. They are thus appropriate for meeting retirement income objectives and for various tax-deferred savings programs.

Some individual fund managements have exhibited performance records far superior to others. Statistical services such as *Wiesenberger's Investment Companies*, published annually (see Chapter 13), provide an easy-to-understand table that compares investment performances over varying periods for hundreds of mutual funds classified according to their investment objectives. For example, the Templeton Growth Fund and the Twentieth Century Growth Fund have both had outstanding records among funds specializing in growth stocks.

Closed-end mutual funds (also listed and compared by Wiesenberger) offer all the advantages of a mutual fund's diversification and safety at prices that are frequently at a discount from the value of their underlying secur-

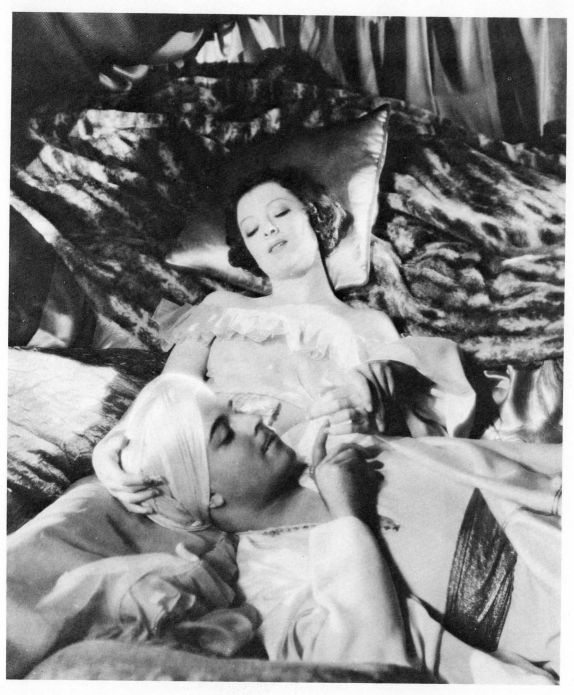

"What can you tell me about Apple Computer—will it really double next week?"

The Bettman Archive, Inc.

EXHIBIT 14–9   Wiesenberger Mutual Fund Indexes

	Growth Funds Index	Growth/Income Funds Index	Income Funds Index	Balanced Funds Index
December 31, 1958	100.00	100.00	100.00	100.00
December 31, 1959	120.82	110.21	108.56	107.53
December 31, 1960	129.21	111.00	110.01	113.07
December 31, 1961	171.13	139.50	128.09	135.42
December 31, 1962	144.56	127.97	127.82	128.90
December 31, 1963	171.72	151.80	146.50	142.83
December 31, 1964	196.36	176.27	166.47	161.74
December 31, 1965	243.87	200.30	189.15	174.47
December 30, 1966	247.21	184.90	177.99	161.37
December 29, 1967	360.08	227.42	213.67	183.16
December 29, 1968	412.31	259.91	250.12	202.84
December 31, 1969	347.43	229.70	215.21	186.72
December 31, 1970	316.54	234.58	230.24	194.15
December 31, 1971	381.70	265.38	263.83	220.07
December 29, 1972	431.77	299.57	287.29	251.62
December 31, 1973	333.54	257.80	265.18	224.22
December 31, 1974	244.40	202.85	235.41	181.01
December 31, 1975	320.71	269.81	300.36	225.19
December 31, 1976	389.31	341.30	386.30	277.42
December 30, 1977	381.29	324.62	394.32	270.33
December 29, 1978	424.65	347.17	405.94	284.11
December 31, 1979	527.36	422.12	456.35	318.20
January 31, 1980	561.27	449.68	467.42	325.36
February 29, 1980	554.56	443.69	453.85	317.19
March 31, 1980	495.27	399.28	425.89	298.25
April 30, 1980	515.89	414.19	452.96	316.05
May 30, 1980	544.97	436.59	482.49	333.44
June 30, 1980	565.88	447.69	493.83	342.37
July 31, 1980	616.25	479.44	507.52	354.63
August 29, 1980	632.63	483.15	505.83	353.57
September 30, 1980	653.27	496.54	508.98	356.92
October 31, 1980	665.17	504.32	511.26	359.06
November 28, 1980	733.14	551.18	531.60	380.49
December 31, 1980	711.50	539.73	526.48	379.57
January 30, 1981	677.33	521.91	524.23	370.64
February 27, 1981	688.55	534.17	529.00	373.39
March 31, 1981	724.66	557.12	552.97	386.26

ities. Purchasing at a discount increases your yield proportionately. For example, if the securities held by a given closed-end fund are paying $8 for dividends for each $100 of market value (an 8 percent yield), and you can purchase the same securities through the closed-end fund for $80, your yield is 10 percent ($8/80). It is not unusual for a closed-end fund to be selling at a discount of as much as 20 percent.

When you sell the closed-end fund, you will probably have to sell at a discount—just as you bought at a discount when you purchased the fund. Assuming the market value of the underlying stocks is unchanged, if the discount narrows, you will earn an additional profit when you sell; you will lose money if the discount widens. If you own a closed-end fund and the discount narrows, you should consider selling and accepting your profit, since the discount may possibly return later to its normal level.

Preferred Stocks

On the receipt of dividends, preferred stocks offer investors a priority over that accorded to holders of common stock. Preferred stock is presumably safer than common stock. Unfortunately, the safety feature also tends to limit the potential for price appreciation, since the dividend will not normally be raised even if earnings permit it. Investors tend to treat preferred stock more as a bonded debt of the enterprise than as an equity. Yet the position of preferred stock is below that of debt in the event that the company should fail and have to enter bankruptcy or reorganization. Thus, preferred stock tends to have the worst features of both stocks and bonds; the investor has limited possibilities for price appreciation and a low rank as a claimant on assets in case of financial difficulty. However, the preferred stock of corporations with stable earnings serves as a good investment for people who need current income.

Bonds

Bonds tend to emphasize current return as a trade-off for reduced risk. Bonds are supposed to reward the investor with generous interest income currently and with safety of principal when the bonds mature. The disadvantage of bonds is that, due to fluctuations in current interest rates, the price of the bonds often fluctuates greatly. Thus, if you must sell them prior to maturity, you may have to take a loss. Some bonds are not traded widely and may tend to be either difficult to sell or salable only at a loss, until they mature.

Long-term bonds (bonds that mature in twenty or thirty years) present the most risk, and short-term bonds the least. An obvious disadvantage of investing in bonds, especially in long-term bonds, is that they offer no change in interest return and hence no protection against inflation. The interest coupon is fixed for the life of the bond and is not altered. Although the yield on the bond is initially often higher than yields on alternative investments, inflation may soon render the income increasingly less valuable. Inflation thus depresses the value of the bond, which may produce capital losses if it must be sold. Bonds are therefore usually not suitable for investors seeking capital growth; they are more appropriate for investors seeking to enhance income needed for current living expenses.

Bonds are assigned ratings according to their general quality. For example, S&P ratings range from AAA (the highest) to CCC (the lowest). The higher the ratings, the lower the risk—and generally, also, the lower the yield. The top four ratings (AAA, AA, A, and BBB) are assigned to bonds that are considered to be **investment-grade bonds**—that is, eligible for purchase by most institutional investors. The top grades tend to be more marketable, and hence they carry less risk. Unrated bonds, or bonds whose rankings are lower than the first four grades, should be purchased only after considerable investigation and with due regard to the higher risk they carry.

A substantial spread in yield is usually apparent among various grades of bonds (see Exhibit 14–10). Occasionally this spread narrows to the point where the investor can obtain a top-rated bond at almost the same yield as a lower-quality bond. For example, in 1981 U.S. government bonds maturing in 1990 were yielding about 13.5 percent, within two percentage points of similar top-grade corporate bonds. Many investors would prefer the practically riskless government bonds at a modestly lower yield rather than corporate bonds of high quality.

As we saw earlier, when interest rates rise, the price of existing bonds with lower coupon rates declines because the new bonds being issued have a higher stated (coupon) rate of interest. When bonds are selling for less than their par or maturity value, they are said to be selling at a discount. If the coupon rate is very low compared with current investment rates, the bond may be available in the market for, say, 60 percent of its ultimate redemption value. Such a bond is called a **deep discount bond;** if you hold it to maturity you will not only receive the periodic interest payments but also will have a capital gain when the bond is redeemed for its $1,000 face value. Your total return will be made up of two elements: interest payments and capital gains upon redemption. Since capital gains are taxed at a lower rate than interest, these bonds offer you an advantage, provided they are otherwise satisfactory (i.e., have a good quality rating).

TAX-EXEMPT BONDS

Bonds issued by government entities such as states or cities pay interest exempt from federal income taxes (and also from state income taxes within the state of origin). Known as **municipal bonds,** these investments appeal

EXHIBIT 14–10

Comparative Yields on High-, Medium-, and Low-Rated Bonds, 1980

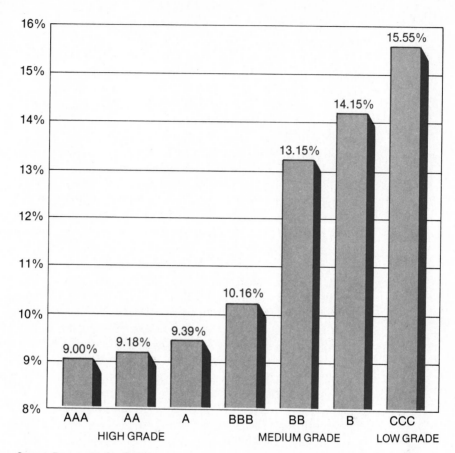

Source: Bureau of Labor Statistics.

mainly to investors who are in high tax brackets. Certain institutions also purchase them with the intention of holding them until maturity. Although municipals have the same limitations as other bonds, they enjoy a good overall safety record. In 1981–82 they produced a tax-free yield of 12 percent or greater, compared with rates of 14 or 15 percent for fully taxable bonds. For investors who are in the 50 percent tax bracket or in higher brackets, municipals may offer a return equivalent to 24 percent (.12/.50) or higher on taxable investments.

Collectibles

It has become popular in recent years to invest in stamps, coins, paintings, photographs, antique cars, and other items called **collectibles.** Some investors believe these items will appreciate at a rate faster than the rate of inflation and thus will prove to be good investments as well as objects of personal enjoyment.

Collectibles provide no regular dividend income, nor are they particularly liquid. To dispose of collectibles, you must often submit them to auction houses, where they are placed on the block and sold for whatever they will bring. You then receive the proceeds, less a commission (usually 15 or 20 percent) charged by the auction house. The fact that collectibles must be stored and insured adds to their holding costs. When you buy a collectible, you must generally pay the retail price plus a sales tax, but you sell either at the wholesale price or at an auction.

Prices of collectibles are irregular; they vary over time as fashions come and go. For example, a 1981 report stated: "With inflation waning and the dollar looking strong, hard assets have gone strikingly soft. . . . Suffering are such items as precious stones, antique Persian rugs, fine photography, French furniture, coins, and Art Nouveau *objets* such as Tiffany lamps. . . . Prices of Ansel Adams prints . . . are off 50%."[7]

Unless you are an expert in a given type of collectible, you must depend on the honesty of the seller to avoid collecting some of the many fake items on the market. If you purchase a collectible, be sure you do so from a reputable source willing to guarantee in writing the authenticity of the item.

In spite of the substantial risks involved, collectibles may be appropriate for some—generally for wealthy—investors. Profits are taxed at favorable long-term capital gains rates, and average prices of collectibles have tended to keep pace with inflation over a fairly long period.

For most investors, however, collectibles should be viewed not as investments but as personal objects to be enjoyed for their intrinsic value. Remember that the most valuable aspect of any collectible is its scarcity. If it can be reproduced at will, or if similar items are readily available, the investment value of the collectible vanishes.

If you are considering a collectible for its investment value, ask the following question: After sales commissions, taxes, and holding costs, will I double my money in ten years? If the answer is yes, you are doing no better than an after-tax return of about 7 percent, an amount you can easily obtain from liquid savings certificates without any risk. Unless the item has substantial personal value, you are generally well advised to avoid collectibles as an investment.

Gold

Many analysts advise holding gold in one form or another in an amount equal to a modest proportion of your investment portfolio. Investor interest in gold, and hence its price, tends to vary in direct proportion to interest rates,

---

7. *Business Week* (June 15, 1981), pp. 106–7.

inflation, and declining faith in the value of national currencies. Gold increased in price from $35 an ounce in 1945 to about $400 an ounce in late 1981; it went higher than $850 an ounce in 1980. However, the price of gold tends to be quite unstable and subject to the vagaries of international tension and speculation.

Like collectibles, gold must be stored and insured, and it pays no dividends or interest. Unlike collectibles, however, gold may be disposed of easily and converted to cash without delay. Its value tends to rise when other investments fall, and vice versa. Gold has great worldwide psychological value among investors; to many, gold represents "hard" currency that is better than paper money.

Gold may be held in various ways. Direct investments include coins, medallions, jewelry, and bullion. You may also hold gold indirectly by investing in gold-mining stocks or in mutual fund shares specializing in these stocks. Some advantages of holding gold through common stocks or mutual funds are the professional management offered and the availability of generous dividend income.

A disadvantage of holding gold directly derives from the tendency of governments to seize gold during "national emergencies" and to require you to accept paper money in its place. Direct investments in gold might best be held in unnumbered Swiss bank accounts. At least one Swiss bank, the Ueberseebank AG of Zurich, offers a gold investment plan under which investors can systematically purchase gold by making regular monthly deposits in Swiss francs, which are used to purchase the metal. Thus, acquisition prices are averaged out. The bank also permits investors to write checks against the value of their gold once they have made a stated minimum investment.

Vacation Homes

Second homes are frequently purchased as investments as well as for personal use. Owners seek inflation protection as well as tax shelters. Because of the various tax advantages involved in real estate (e.g., deductibility of interest and of property taxes), its investment value depends to a significant degree on the tax laws.

If you meet certain conditions, you can sometimes deduct not only mortgage interest and property taxes but also depreciation and other maintenance expenses. You may thus be able to create a substantial tax loss that can be deducted against other ordinary income. Consequently, you can substantially reduce the costs of owning a vacation home. The inflationary increases in the value of the home may eventually produce an after-tax capital gain when the house is sold.

Unlike your regular residence, a vacation house does not qualify for the once-in-a-lifetime $125,000 exclusion of profit on the sale for homeowners older than fifty-five. Neither does the vacation house qualify for exemption from any gain that is reinvested in another house. If you sell a vacation house at a profit, the gain must be treated like any other gain; the amount of tax owed will depend on whether the gain is short-term or long-term. (If the home has been held for more than twelve months, the gain is long-term.)

A vacation home may not be a good investment unless you consider it strictly as a business enterprise and use it yourself only minimally. You must usually be in at least the 50 percent tax bracket to make the investment profitable, assuming that you can obtain enough rental income to offset direct expenses. If you purchase a vacation house under any other conditions, consider it a fairly expensive luxury. Remember, too, that you are losing potential income from the money tied up in the down payment or in the house's furnishings.

SUMMARY

1. The first step in a practical investment plan is to obtain funds for investment. Acquiring funds involves planning, setting goals, budgeting, and, under some circumstances, borrowing.
2. Before making purchases or sales of securities, you should consider the question of proper timing. Even though buying or selling a stock may seem appropriate, a particular moment might be the wrong time to buy or sell. You should consider general market trends and the motives of those with whom you are trading. You should also have a plan for future trading and should review your investments periodically in accordance with your plan.
3. The following pieces of advice are recommended to investors: avoid "hot tips," use your special knowledge of an industry, be on the lookout for investment swindles, use limit orders where appropriate, be willing to admit mistakes, expect to have some losses. Consider using discount brokers, keep continuous watch on your investments, use tax shelters where appropriate, take advantage of income tax rules in maximizing returns, and establish a good record-keeping system.
4. Investors have a large number of alternatives from which to choose. Potential investments include common and preferred stocks, bonds, real estate, mutual funds, and collectibles. Each type of investment has advantages and disadvantages for meeting specific investment goals.
5. When buying or selling securities, you should take into account the phenomenon of crowd psychology, which exaggerates price movements. Recognizing the effects of crowd psychology allows you to avoid errors in trading.
6. In choosing common stocks, you should consider a company's dividend policy, P/E ratios, and growth in earnings—all of which are fundamental factors in stock selection. Some basic rules of common stock investing are (a) select companies that have exhibited above-average

growth and offer hope for good future growth, (b) favor stocks with relatively low P/E ratios and good fundamental characteristics, and (c) avoid too frequent trading.

7. Among various investment alternatives, purchasing through mutual funds seems the best procedure for a great majority of investors. Both stocks and bonds, including tax-exempt bonds, can be purchased through mutual funds. Mutual funds offer diversification and professional management at modest fees. Gold, collectibles, and vacation homes are among the investment opportunities that are usually not suitable for most investors unless special circumstances exist. Individual bonds and preferred stocks usually offer the long-term investor a relatively high current income. Because these securities fluctuate in price as interest rates change, the investor is often subject to capital gains or losses, just as is the case in owning common stocks.

REVIEW QUESTIONS

1. It has been stated: "Financial markets, with varying success, try always to look ahead. Hence it is not confusing that stocks and the economy may be going in opposite directions on a given day."
   (a) Do you agree with this statement?
   (b) What does this statement imply about timing your own purchases or sales of common stocks?

2. (a) Under what conditions is it advisable to borrow on life insurance and reinvest the funds elsewhere?
   (b) What are the advantages and disadvantages of borrowing on life insurance?

3. Maria Sanchez is considering purchasing a stock whose price has ranged from $20 to $45 in the preceding twelve months. The price is now $44. How can Maria benefit by considering the price range of a stock before making a purchase?

4. Explain why it is common for stock prices to *fall* at the publication of a quarterly earnings report showing that earnings have *risen* for that stock.

5. Explain why, when an investor purchases a given stock on the advice of a broker, the stock frequently declines shortly thereafter.

6. Why do the prices of common stocks frequently fall near the end of the year and rise again after the first of the next year, especially if these stocks have had a substantial change in price during the year?

7. (a) List some acceptable reasons for selling a stock.
   (b) What are some unacceptable reasons for selling?

8. Why is it good advice to ignore a "hot tip"?

9. "It is difficult for a fish to swim against the current." What is the significance of this quotation to a person making investments?

10. A news report stated: "A computerized 'beat-the-market' investment scheme has ensnarled an attorney and a small group of his business associates, who together invested a total of $26 million in an alleged fraud. . . . A computer expert enticed investors to simultaneously purchase a security at a lower price on one exchange and sell it at a higher price on another, reaping huge profits in a matter of seconds and rewarding investors with annual rates of return as high as 85 percent. . . . While the computer did exist, its programming was fake. Everyone thought he had found the goose that laid the golden egg. People were falling over one another trying to borrow money to invest in the program." Describe what steps should be taken by anyone considering investing in programs similar to the one described.

11. Too rapid a turnover of one's portfolio will produce very high transactions costs; depending on the size of the portfolio and the average price of the shares traded, transactions costs (brokers' commissions) may run 1.5 percent annually if stocks are traded, on the average, once each year. A buy-and-hold strategy minimizes these costs.
    (a) Do you believe the transactions costs described above are excessive?
    (b) How do they compare with other transactions costs—for example, real estate transactions costs?
    (c) Should you favor a buy-and-hold strategy because of the high cost of buying and selling securities?

12. In 1981 a stock market analyst recommended stock in a company called Biomedical Reference Labs, a clinical laboratory, selling at 22-1/8. Earnings per share in the previous five years had been $0.20, $0.46, $0.61, $0.76, and $0.99 (latest year). The P/E ratio was about 22. No dividends were paid. Total sales were relatively small ($25 million), and the stock was traded over the counter. The price range in 1980 was 24-3/4 to 9-1/2. The analyst stated: "We expect that it will more than double its current sales and earnings over the next 2-1/2 years primarily through internal expansion and without the need for outside capital." Which of Malkiel's four investment rules appears to be violated by this advice? (For current information, look up the stock in Standard and Poor's *Stock Guide*.)

13. A financial writer stated: "Here are some of the techniques for leverage in speculating in bonds. You can borrow for about 75% of the market value . . . assume that the bank interest charge is 20% per annum . . . the current yield on Treasury 10s of 2010 is 13% . . . you pay $780 for the bond, which yields $100 a year, and pay $117 on the $585 you borrowed. So you are out of pocket $17 a year on each $1,000 bond. But if interest rates drop, say, to 12% from the 12.9% currently, the price of the 10s would rise to 84 from the current 78, a price improvement of 8% or $80 per bond—a 41% profit on your cash investment of $195 per bond."
    (a) Explain why the $1,000 U.S. Treasury bond due in 2010 would be selling for only $780 in the market.
    (b) What risk would you be taking by following the writer's advice? Is the risk worth the potential reward of a 41 percent profit?

14. A financial writer stated: "The flood of undiscriminating investment capital that flows toward art these days may yet produce a crisis analogous to the one that nearly sank the Bordeaux wine industry in the early 1970s. A surge of investment in Bordeaux vintages . . . shoved prices so high that traditional consumers of claret switched to Italian and other wines, thus tearing the bottom out of the market. . . . In any case, whom does the art boom benefit? Only collectors and middlemen. Few artists get to share in it." In your opinion, who takes the greater risk in collectible investing, collectors or "middlemen"?

15. In discussing crowd psychology and the stock market, a financial writer stated: "It's like betting on a marathon race where a prize is given to all who finish. . . . Forgetting that most will finish, they (the crowd) concentrate only on those ahead at the moment, betting heavily on them and heavily against the marathoners doing poorly at the time . . . the evidence strongly favors betting against the crowd." In what sense is it true that in the stock market most contestants (companies) manage to "finish the race" and thus warrant purchase of their shares, even though they are out of favor with most investors at the time?

16. An article on electric utility stocks in *Business Week* (June 22, 1981) stated: "Because buyers are still few, the potential opportunity is great. The inflation-wracked electric utility stocks are selling at an average of 6.1 times earnings, a 15-year low. Dividends yields, meanwhile, have climbed to an all-time high of 12.5%, . . . even if the stocks do not pick up in value, investors can still lock in a yield that is outstripping inflation." Assess the value of this for a person in the retirement stage of the financial life cycle.

17. A consultant on financial management stated: "Because of the tremendous markup in diamonds, they have to be held for an inordinately long period of time to ever realize any kind of profit. . . . The interesting thing about the Persian carpet is that it is now easily duplicated by machine. . . . Silver, china, and crystal can add a lovely touch to any home, but how would you feel if your spouse announced that your silver was being put on the market tomorrow? An investment is something we acquire in hopes of getting rid of it at a profit." Discuss the investment principles illustrated in the above quotation.

18. Assume that a given stock is selling for $100 a share, earns $10, sells at a P/E ratio of 10, and has a $5 dividend that has been growing at a rate of 10 percent annually.
    (a) Calculate the total return to the investor in the next year if the stock continues to sell at the same P/E ratio, and earnings and dividends are increased 10 percent.
    (b) Why is the total return greater than 5 percent, the current dividend rate?

19. Look up the record of a mutual fund in *Wiesenberger's Investment Company Service.* Compare the management results, as reported for the past ten years, with the investment objectives. Try to account for any differences you observe.

20. A news report stated: "A federal judge sentenced a former top broker in the Century City, Calif., office of Shearson/American Express, Inc. to 1,000 hours of com-

munity service for failing to disclose to customers that she had accepted money for promoting a stock. She had convinced Shearson customers in 1976 to buy 2,300 shares of West America Automotive Corp. without disclosing she had received a substantial amount of money from an official of West America (now defunct). Do you believe such practices to be extensive among the brokerage community?

CASE PROBLEMS

I. A Broker's Advice

Uncommon Values in Stocks, January 1981

	Price 12/31/80	Price 6/18/81	% Change	P/E	E/P/S 1980
Amerada Hess	43-3/8	27-1/8	− 37	6.7	6.40
Boeing	44-1/8	31-3/4	− 30	6.9	6.40
Houston Natural Gas	54	43-5/8	− 20	10.8	5.06
Lennar Corp.	22-1/8	19-3/8	− 14	8.3	2.65
Northwest Airlines	23-3/4	34-1/4	+ 48	46.0	.50
Sea Containers	19-1/4	25-5/8	+ 32	4.2	4.50
Syntex	72-1/4	59-7/8	− 17	16.8	4.28
Tidewater, Inc.	50-3/4	34-1/4	− 32	16.6	3.00
Towle Mfg.	17-1/8	18-7/8	+ 10	7.7	2.20
Average	38.5	32.7	− 15	9.9	3.88
Dow Jones Average	964	990	+ 2.7		
S&P 500	136	131	− 3.0		

Note: E/P/S based on 12/31/80 price and on previous 12 months' earnings.

In January 1981 a large brokerage firm published a list of common stocks that it regarded as ten uncommon values. Nine of these issues are shown in the accompanying table, together with their prices six months later. (The tenth was merged with another corporation.) The firm stated that these stocks had substantially outperformed the market over the previous six months, appreciating 43.8 percent in comparison to a gain of only 11 percent in the Dow Jones Industrial Average, and 18.8 percent in comparison to the S&P 500. The prices of these stocks were, on the average, 15 percent lower as of 18 June 1981, although the general market was about the same as it had been on 31 December 1980. Only two stocks increased during these six and a half months.

QUESTIONS

1. Consult a financial newspaper or Standard and Poor's monthly *Stock Guide* and record the current price and twelve-month earnings per share of these issues. How would an investor have fared who had followed the firm's recommendation to purchase these securities at December 1980 prices?

2. Select any five stocks you believe are good values and chart their prices for three months. Calculate your total return. In making your chocies, follow Malkiel's four investment rules.

II. Investment Performance

	10 Years	5 Years	1 Year
Oil	30.8%	20.9%	14.3%
Gold	28	30.7	− 13.9
Oriental Carpets	127.3	20.9	− 0.2
U.S. Coins	27.1	29.7	− 8
U.S. Stamps	23.5	32.9	18
China, Ceramics	22.9	30.7	36.5
Silver	21.5	20.1	− 26.6
Rare Books	16.8	13.8	18
Old Masters	15.4	16.8	22.9
Farmland	14.6	14.8	9.7
Diamonds	14.5	16.9	0
Housing	10.3	11.6	8.1
Consumer Price Index	8.3	9.7	10
Stocks	5.8	9.8	25.3
For. Exchange	5.3	3.1	− 17.3
Bonds	3.8	1.1	− 9.6

Source: *Wall Street Journal* (June 19, 1981), p. 45.

The accompanying table reproduces results of a study by Robert S. Salomon, Jr., showing changes in average annual returns on fifteen investments, both tangible and financial, over past years. Mr. Salomon concluded: "Present interest rates should ultimately provide stiff competition for stocks in a similar fashion to the impact that high rates are already having on tangibles. In sum, we believe we've entered a period of speculative excesses in the stock market that may be sustained for a while."

Another analyst, however, argued that the poor performance of the stock market during the 1970s was due to the failure of investors adequately to account for the effects of inflation on liabilities of corporations as well as upon assets. Investors recognize that inflation tends to create illusory inventory profits and underdepreciation of plant and equipment, both of which adversely affect the longer-term outlook for profits. But inflation also tends to reduce the real cost of corporate debt, which may be repaid in inflation-cheapened dollars. If this adjustment were considered, the effects of inflation on corporate earnings should be roughly neutral.

QUESTIONS

1. Why would high interest rates adversely affect the price of tangibles and provide stiff competition for stocks?

2. In your opinion, does inflation increase asset values more than it decreases liabilities or profits?

CHAPTER

CHAPTER 15

PLANNING FOR RETIREMENT

LEARNING OBJECTIVES

In studying this chapter you will learn:

Why planning for retirement is necessary;

The economic problems of the aged;

How to go about setting up a financial plan for retirement, including how to estimate spending and savings needs;

How to recognize the effects of inflation and how to help offset inflation;

How to understand employer pension plans and their benefits;

The ways in which pension plan benefits are taxed;

The different types of tax-sheltered individual retirement plans—for example, IRAs and Keoghs;

How annuities can be used for retirement income planning.

Your retirement years will not be "golden years" unless you have sufficient income to enable you to live comfortably. Careful long-range planning will help you reach the security you desire for those years. In this chapter we examine ways to maximize your resources and to minimize the effects of taxes and inflation during retirement.

THE ECONOMIC PROBLEMS OF THE AGED

The economic and social problems of old age have been increasing in recent years, and more effort is being spent to solve these problems. When the German leader Bismarck established a social insurance program in the 1880s, sixty-five was the age established as the normal time for retirement. (At that time few people lived to be sixty-five; therefore, a generous program of social benefits could be set up without a significant cost burden. Few people would live to collect their pensions.)

Nowadays, due to improvements in health care, economic conditions, and medical science, most people live to age sixty-five and beyond. In fact, nearly one-fourth of the adult population of the United States is over sixty-five, and the proportion is growing. Of the approximately 25 million people over sixty-five, about one-third are over seventy-five. Furthermore, the number of people retiring before age sixty-five is adding to the number of nonworkers in the economy.

Compounding the problem of support is the fact that many young workers do not start working until their mid-twenties because longer periods of education and training are needed for careers in our complex industrial society. In 1981 there were about three active workers for each one dependent person drawing Social Security; within twenty-five years the proportion will drop to two to one. Thus, fewer and fewer active workers are available to support nonworkers. The working population, being proportionately fewer in number, must become more productive. But productivity in the United States has been falling—a factor that has contributed to inflation, increased foreign competition, and increased unemployment. Not surprisingly, economists and social scientists, worried about these conditions, have been devoting much time to solving the economic problems of the aged.

Statistics on income for people over sixty-five reveal a somewhat grim picture. Data collected by the U.S. Department of Commerce for 1977 showed that the median income of persons sixty-five or older was only about 54 percent of the median income of all families. Only a little over 1 percent of families whose heads were sixty-five or older relied solely on personal earnings, and nearly half (47 percent) relied on earnings supplemented by other sources. The data showed that people with private pensions in addition to Social Security were in the most favorable position. However, less than one-fourth of the aged had supplementary pensions.

The current situation, therefore, indicates a poor economic outlook for most people beyond age sixty-five. Many will be poor in old age, and because life expectancy has increased, they will live in poverty for longer periods than their predecessors. Through adequate retirement planning you can avoid the situation that appears to be in store for many people, particularly for those who do not plan ahead for a better life after retirement.

Government Remedies

Government has taken several steps to help solve some of the problems of old age. To protect the purchasing power of retirement benefits, Congress has indexed Social Security for inflation. Government has also tried to discourage early retirement by reducing the amount of Social Security benefits people can collect if they decide to retire early. In addition, employers have been prohibited from mandating retirement before age seventy. Income tax deductions have been granted for certain types of savings to encourage more people to save individually for retirement. Congress has also strengthened the private-employer pension system to prevent abuses and to increase the likelihood that more people will be covered by employer-sponsored pensions and will collect them during retirement. Finally, national economic policy has been aimed at reducing the level of inflation, which has worsened the economic plight of retired people.

Nevertheless, it is still your responsibility to plan for your own retirement. You must decide what your needs and goals are and when you wish to retire, take advantage of various opportunities made possible by federal tax legislation, and pursue other steps to assure yourself a financially secure old age.

ESTABLISHING RETIREMENT NEEDS

Establishing your retirement needs is the first step in retirement planning. Although our focus is mainly on economic needs, you should also consider other factors—for example, what hobbies or recreational activity you intend to pursue, where you will live (sunny Florida?), and how much traveling you expect to do. These goals also have economic implications and therefore should not be ignored. The following list contains the steps you must take in handling what will be some of your major economic needs at retirement:

"How about at least giving me the same opportunity to age gracefully?"

The Bettman Archive, Inc.

1. Set the age at which you plan to retire.
2. Determine the amount of income you will require to maintain your lifestyle (take inflationary pressures into account).
3. Determine financial needs for special purposes—for example, a round-the-world trip, relocation to a warmer climate, or new living quarters more suitable for retirement living.
4. Determine financial responsibilities that will attend your death—for example, a continuing income for your dependents, tax payments, and bequests to children.
5. Make contingency plans in the event of disability.
6. Plan how your financial and income needs will be met—from private savings, pensions, Social Security, continued employment, life and health insurance, annuities, or other sources.

Needs and goals usually change throughout your life, and retirement goals are no exception. Early in the financial life cycle, when retirement is a long way off, planning for retirement usually gets scant attention. In the middle of the cycle, at age forty or forty-five, retirement is barely twenty years away. At this point you give more time and consideration to the topic of retirement, because you know more about your financial status and future income over the remainder of your career. You also know more about your family obligations, your health maintenance needs, how large your pension income might be, and what other ambitions you want to satisfy. The closer you get to retirement, the more frequently your long-range retirement plan will be amended and adjusted to fit existing and expected circumstances.

Setting Retirement Age

You should determine what retirement age is best for you and base your planning on that age. If you are thirty when you begin to plan and your expected retirement age is sixty-five, you have thirty-five years in which to save funds and arrange other financial resources to meet your retirement goals. If you do not begin to plan until you are forty, you only have twenty-five years to accomplish your goals. Obviously, the later you begin, the more you must save. If you need $10,000 for some purpose at retirement, and you have thirty-five years to accumulate it, you need to save $37 annually at 10 percent compound interest; if you have only twenty-five years, you must save $101 (an additional $64) annually. (Consult Appendix A–1 to solve similar problems based on different interest rates and savings periods.)

Analyzing Spending Needs

If, as recommended in Chapter 1, you have adopted budgeting as a part of your family financial planning, setting expenditure needs for retirement will be relatively easy. You will need to make adjustments only for the expected changes in living patterns during your retirement. During retirement you will discover that some of your expenditures are lower and others higher. For example, housing costs may be lower if you have paid off your mortgage. Other expenses, such as income taxes and health insurance, may also be reduced considerably. Go-to-work costs (transportation, lunches, clothing, and so on) will be eliminated, as will deductions for Social Security, retirement plans, and union dues. On the other hand, expenditures for hobbies, travel, leisure activities, entertaining, and medical care may be higher after retirement. Therefore, you must make an estimate of what your regular retirement expenditures will be. Your estimate should be based on what your lifestyle will be, on your intended geographical location, and on other factors. If you are planning to move from a northern climate to the Sun Belt, for example, costs of heating and of winter clothing will be less, but costs of air conditioning will be much higher.

A HYPOTHETICAL RETIREMENT BUDGET

One approach to planning specific retirement expenditures is to summarize your current major expenditures, make adjustments for expected retirement needs, and develop a spending budget for the years following retirement. Consider a hypothetical case, that of John and Susan Marker, who are both fifty-five, in good health, and looking forward to retirement within ten years. John has been with his current employer for ten years, so he will have twenty years of service at age sixty-five to apply toward his employer's retirement plan. John earns $20,000 annually as an auto mechanic, and Susan does not work outside the home. The Markers do not plan to leave their present home, since they want to be near their children, who live and work in the same state.

The Markers still have ten years left to pay off their mortgage, which costs $2,400 annually, so this debt will be eliminated by the time they retire. Besides a retirement plan, John's employer maintains a health insurance program (covering hospital and doctor expense) that will terminate when John retires; to supplement Medicare benefits, the Markers expect to take out a health insurance policy at a cost of $100 a year. John has a modest life insurance program: a $10,000 whole life policy with a $200 annual premium and a cash value of $5,000, in addition to employer-paid group term coverage of $40,000. The group term will be reduced to $10,000 after retirement and will require the Markers to contribute $100 a year to maintain it. They are saving $200 a year in 10 percent savings certificates, a program they wish to continue after retirement. Total savings have accumulated to $10,000 in addition to the $5,000 cash value of the whole-life insurance policy.

In developing specific spending estimates after retirement, the Markers are making the following assumptions: Mortgage payments of $2,400 a year will be eliminated. Clothing and transportation costs will be reduced modestly, because John will no longer have to drive to work each day or purchase work clothes. Medical and personal care expenses will be somewhat higher because of normal increases in these costs during old age. More money will be needed for leisure-time activities, including some traveling to visit children and grandchildren. John expects to stop payments on the whole-life policy after retirement and to convert it to a paid-up policy in a reduced amount. The largest reductions in outlay will stem from the reduction of income and elimination of Social Security taxes. The Markers' budget, as revised for annual living expenditures during retirement, is shown in Exhibit 15–1.

EXHIBIT 15-1

Marker Family
Preliminary
Retirement
Budget

Item	Current Expenditure	Expenditure after Retirement (in today's dollars)
Food	$ 4,000	$ 4,000
Housing (including $2,400 in mortgage payments)	5,000	2,600
Transportation	2,500	2,000
Clothing	1,200	1,000
Personal care	300	500
Medical care	1,000	1,500
Leisure activities	300	1,000
Miscellaneous	1,000	1,000
Savings	200	200
Life insurance	200	100
Health insurance	0	100
Social Security taxes	1,300	0
Income taxes*	3,000	0
Total	$20,000	$14,000

*For simplicity in this illustration, income taxes in retirement are assumed to be zero. In practice, some retirement income is taxable, but at much lower rates. Social Security income is currently exempt entirely.

Effects of Inflation. The Markers realize that, because of inflation, $14,000 will not be enough to purchase in ten years the same package of goods and services it purchases today. The amount needed will depend, of course, on the inflation rate as it affects the various goods and services they purchase. Therefore, the Markers estimate future living costs by using the average expected increase in the Consumer Price Index for the relevant period. From a compound interest table (see Appendix A-1) the Markers determine that if inflation averages 8 percent annually for ten years, their $14,000 budget will have to be multiplied by a factor of 2.16—that is, $30,240—to maintain present living standards at the beginning of retirement.

Of course, inflation will continue during retirement as well. Thus, the Markers' income will rapidly become insufficient unless it comes from a source like Social Security, which is indexed for inflation. If only part of their income is indexed, an additional amount will have to be provided initially and put into savings to be held for the later stages of retirement. For example, if the Markers have fifteen years of retirement, inflation will require that the following amounts be available:

Year	Retirement Expenses (Assuming 8% Annual Growth Rate)	
1	$30,240	
2	32,659	
3	35,272	
4	38,094	
5	41,141	
6	44,432	
7	47,987	
8	51,826	
9	55,972	
10	60,450	
11	65,286	
12	70,509	
13	76,149	
14	82,241	
15	88,820	
Total		$821,078
Less total amount needed if inflation were zero ($30,240 × 15)		453,600
Extra income needed because of inflation		$367,478
Fifteen-year inflation adjustment ($821,078/$453,600)		1.8

Therefore, due to expected inflation, the total amount of dollars needed during the retirement period is 1.8 times the amount that would be required if inflation were not a factor. For the Markers the amount required is $367,478.

EXTRA RETIREMENT NEEDS

Advance planning is necessary for other financial needs in addition to living expenses—for example, relocation or the purchase of new living quarters. If you know in advance, for example, that you will be moving to Florida or some other location in the Sun Belt, you can often make plans to purchase a home or some land well ahead of time and thus obtain a better price or a preferred location. Your existing home can be refinanced to supply part of the cost. You may even decide to sell your present home prior to retirement, rent temporary quarters, and be able to move to your new location without delay or loss of time and money.

Another goal might be the big trip you have always wanted to take. If your trip will cost $10,000, you can begin to set aside funds well in advance. Without a plan you will probably never realize such a goal.

If funds must be available upon your death for such things as estate taxes, an income for your spouse, or bequests to your children or to your church, advance preparations are usually necessary. Such needs can typically be met through life insurance, which should be purchased when it is most affordable—that is, well in advance of retirement age. Again, long-term planning is needed for realization of such goals.

CONTINGENCY PLANS

A contingency plan answers the questions "What will I do if . . ." and "How will I do it and where will the money come from?" For example, if you become disabled after you retire, you may have to enter a long-term nursing-care facility, which is very costly. Insurance is not generally available for this contingency, except for short periods. Therefore, advance planning is necessary. Perhaps an emergency fund could be planned to meet such needs. Also, a retirement residence should be selected with due regard for the ease with which it could be sold to meet emergency needs. Entry into a **life care center,** a home complex catering to the needs of the aged, could also be investigated.

TOTAL RETIREMENT NEEDS

To estimate the amount necessary for extra needs during retirement, let us assume that in today's purchasing power $10,000 will be required for a round-the-world trip and $40,000 (roughly two years' salary) for an emergency fund. Adjusted for 8 percent inflation, these two needs translate to a lump sum of $108,000 ($50,000 × 2.16) that must be accumulated within ten years for extras. Applying this amount to the hypothetical budget described earlier, the Markers' needs for retirement income will be as follows:

Annual income needs (assuming zero inflation during retirement)	$30,240
Lump sum needs (adjusted for inflation)	$108,000

The annual income is the amount needed at the beginning of retirement. However, if inflation continues, plans must be made to supplement this income. As shown earlier, if inflation continues at 8 percent, an additional $367,478 must be provided over a fifteen-year retirement period. This amount appears extremely large because most people fail to appreciate how much even a modest inflation rate will cost when the annual rate is compounded over a fairly long period.

SOURCES OF RETIREMENT INCOME

Planning and developing the means with which to fund your retirement goals and financial requirements is the final step in retirement planning. Not only must you develop the means to provide the required funds, you must also ensure that your money is invested and distributed in the most advantageous manner. Sources of retirement income include Social Security, employer pension plans, individual retirement plans made under a tax shelter, personal savings and investments, and employment (see Exhibit 15–2). Our focus here is on tax-sheltered individual retirement plans, including IRAs, SEP-IRAs, Keogh plans, and section 403(b) plans. Because Social Security and private savings and investments have been discussed earlier, they are not analyzed here in detail. However, you should not forget their importance in any financial plan for retirement.

Social Security

Social Security retirement income is significant for three reasons: First, nearly everyone is covered by Social Security. Second, Social Security income is protected against inflation, which makes it especially important in an era characterized by increasing levels of inflation. Third, Social Security restores a larger portion of the wages of low-income workers than of high-income workers; therefore, high-income workers must usually develop supplemental sources to have a retirement income that will support their standard of living.

Employer Pension Plans

About half of all workers in the United States are covered by private pension plans sponsored by their employers. In most cases the worker does not contribute to the plan personally; it is paid for by the employer as an employee benefit. The employer may deduct the cost of the pension for income tax purposes, but the employee is not required to report the value of the pension for tax purposes. The pension is ultimately subject to income tax when the employee receives it. Employer pension plans are subject to requirements of the federal Employee Retirement Income Security Act of 1974 (ERISA) and of the Internal Revenue Service (IRS).

BENEFIT FORMULAS

The first question that most of us ask about a pension plan is: How much do I get out of it at retirement? The answer depends on a benefit formula

EXHIBIT 15–2
Sources of
Retirement
Income

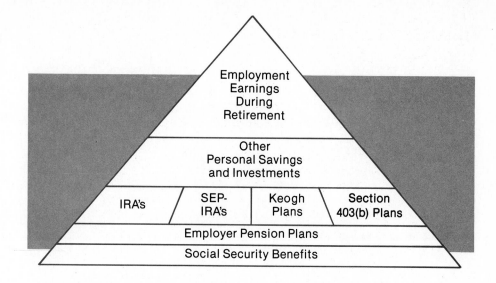

spelled out in the plan. Most plans contain a **defined benefit formula**, which you can use to estimate your ultimate pension. A typical formula states that the eligible employee will receive for each year of service some percentage (usually between 1/2 and 2 percent) of the average salary in the last five years of employment. For example, under a 1 percent benefit formula, if your salary for the five years preceding retirement averaged $2,000 a month and you had thirty years of service, you would receive $600 a month (30 × 10% × $2,000) at retirement.

Usually a worker covered by a pension plan also receives Social Security, so the total retirement benefit might amount to between 50 or 60 percent of the final average salary. Some benefit formulas define "pension" in terms of some flat amount—for example, $200 annually for each year of credited service. A thirty-year employee would thus receive $6,000 a year (30 × $200) under such a formula.

Another type of benefit formula is a **defined contribution formula**, under which the amount paid at retirement depends on the total contributions made by the employer and the employee over the years. Under typical mortality assumptions made in 1981, a male beginning retirement at sixty-five would receive about $100 a month for life for each $12,000 in the fund. The contribution to the pension fund each year is usually fixed as some percentage (e.g., 10 percent) of the worker's salary. For example, assume that a worker earns a career average annual salary of $20,000 and makes a $2,000 annual contribution to the fund. The $2,000 annual contribution would accumulate, at 8 percent interest, to a fund of about $226,566 after thirty years. Based on typical annuity rates, such a fund would be enough to provide a pension of about $1,888 a month for life. Exhibit 15–3 illustrates the structure of both types of benefit formulas.

EXHIBIT 15–3
Benefit Formula

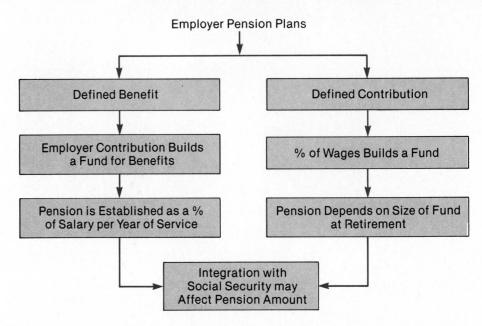

Some private pension plans are integrated with Social Security so that an adjustment is made automatically for the fact that the worker will receive Social Security benefits as well as private pension benefits. A common arrangement is to offset (reduce) the private pension by half of what is received from Social Security benefits. In a sense this arrangement is a protection to both the employee and the employer: If Social Security benefits are reduced, the reduction's impact on the worker is partially offset by the private pension plan; if Social Security benefits are increased, the cost is borne not only by the employer but also by the worker through a reduction in the amount of the private pension plan. For example, if a retiree is entitled to $1,500 a month from an integrated employer pension plan and to $700 a month from Social Security, the private pension would be reduced by $350 a month (one-half of $700)—that is, to $1,150—under a 50 percent offset-type integrated plan. Total benefits would then be $1,150 a month from the private pension and $700 a month from Social Security, or $1,850 a month for life.

VESTING

Vesting refers to the ultimate right of the worker to pension benefits paid for by the employer. The shorter the time you must work to be entitled to vested benefits, the better; the usual period is ten years. Once you have worked for ten years (or for the stated period), all the benefits that have been promised by the employer are yours, collectible when you reach retirement age or meet other requirements of the plan. If you terminate your employment in less than ten years, you will receive no pension benefits from the employer's contributions to the plan. Therefore, over the course of your career you could work for three or four employers, each of whom has a pension plan, and never collect a private pension at retirement because you failed to meet the vesting requirements of any of the plans. For example, you might work nine years each for several employers whose plans had ten-year vesting provisions.

You should pay close attention to the vesting provisions of any pension plan under which you are covered; otherwise you might fail to receive a pension (or equivalent cash settlement) from the service you have rendered. For example, if you are thinking of changing jobs but discover that you have only one year to go before obtaining full vesting of pension rights in your present job, it may pay to postpone the job change for a year. To leave immediately would mean the loss of nine years of accumulated pension rights. Under a 1 percent annual benefit formula, this loss might translate to 9 percent (9 years × 1%) of your present salary, payable at retirement.

If you are considering two jobs, the first offering full vesting after ten years and another offering partial vesting after only five years, the second job is clearly preferable, other things being equal. Under the second job you will not lose pension rights if you change jobs after five years, whereas under the first job you would carry no pension rights unless you stayed at least ten years.

ELIGIBILITY

All private pension plans have stated requirements that must be met before you are eligible for benefits. Usually you must have had some minimum period of service or have reached some minimum age. If you are twenty-five or older, an employer cannot delay your joining the plan beyond one year. Sometimes not every class of worker is covered, so you should obtain clarification of the plan that applies to you.

CONTRIBUTORY PLANS

Some employers require the employee to contribute some percentage of salary—often 5 percent—to the pension plan. Such contributions are usually not deductible for income tax purposes. However, if you should terminate your employment, you are entitled to receive in cash both your contributions and interest accrued. If you should leave after meeting the vesting-period requirement, you may withdraw your funds and still be entitled to the benefits that have been purchased by your employer.

FUNDING AND INSURANCE

The **Employee Retirement Income Security Act of 1974 (ERISA)** requires an employer with a tax-qualified plan to make advance payments into a separate fund under the management of an independent trustee to guarantee the ultimate payments of the pension when it is due. The employer must also purchase **termination insurance** from a federal agency, the **Pension Benefits Guaranty Corporation (PBGC),** as additional protection for covered workers in case the employer goes bankrupt or otherwise terminates the plan with assets inadequate to pay the promised benefits. If your employer goes out of business and terminates your job and your pension plan, you should contact the PBGC to determine whether you have some benefits due.

SURVIVING SPOUSE BENEFITS

ERISA requires an employer with a tax-qualified plan to offer to the worker an option that would permit the surviving spouse to receive a pension if the worker dies. This option must offer the surviving spouse at least 50 percent of what both husband and wife received during their lifetimes. The worker may reject the option; however, it provides retirement protection for both the worker and the spouse at a modest cost. The cost of the option is borne through a reduction of the total amount of the pension. The amount of the reduction depends on the ages of both spouses at retirement.

DISABILITY BENEFITS

Some private pension plans allow payment of the pension when and if the covered worker becomes permanently and totally disabled. The amount of the disability allowance depends on the benefit formula used; the formula usually requires the worker to be vested in the plan at the time of the disability.

DEATH BENEFITS

If the worker dies before retirement, the death benefit is paid in addition to any accumulated employee contributions. In some cases, if the pension is vested, the surviving spouse receives income from a supplemental group life insurance plan. If the death benefit is part of the pension plan itself, these benefits, in order to be nontaxable, may not exceed 100 times the expected monthly pension benefit at retirement. Thus, a $500 monthly pension plan benefit could not provide death benefits in excess of $50,000. Death benefits after retirement depend on the type of annuity the worker has selected upon retirement (annuity options are discussed later in the chapter).

EARLY RETIREMENT

Many pension plans permit you to retire before some customary retirement age, usually sixty-five. If you accept early retirement, your pension may be reduced to compensate for the fact that you may be drawing a pension for a longer time than will people who wait until the customary retirement age. Also, the employer will have had less time to accumulate the funds needed to pay your pension. The amount of the reduction for early retirement is approximately 7 percent for each year prior to the customary retirement age.

"Early retirement might not be such a bad idea, but couldn't you at least make it voluntary?"

The Bettman Archive, Inc.

TAXABILITY

Most private pension plans are subject to federal and state income tax insofar as they are paid for by funds not previously subject to tax. If your plan is noncontributory (i.e., if the employer paid the entire cost), it will normally be fully taxable during retirement. If you contribute to the plan yourself, the amounts you pay toward the plan are not currently deductible for income tax purposes, and your pension income will be subject to taxation under two special rules—the three-year recovery rule and the annuity rule.

Under the **three-year recovery rule,** if your pension will allow you to recover your entire contribution within a three-year period, none of the pension will be subject to income tax until you have recovered all the funds you originally paid in. Thereafter the entire amount of the pension will be subject to ordinary income tax. To illustrate, suppose you are entitled to a pension of $1,500 a month and have paid in a total of $30,000 over the years. The $1,500 a month will amount to $30,000 within twenty months—a span of time within the three-year limit for recovery of your own contribution. Thus, you will pay no income tax on your pension during the first year; during the second year you will pay tax on only $6,000. The three-year recovery rule is illustrated in Exhibit 15–4.

The **annuity rule** is employed if you will not recover all your contributions to an employer pension program within three years. Under this rule an additional number is needed—the number of years of life expectancy at retirement, as indicated by IRS longevity tables. The amount excluded from your pension, and hence not taxable, is calculated by the following formula:

$$\text{Proportion excluded} = \frac{\text{Your total contributions}}{\text{Years of life expectancy} \times \text{pension amount}}.$$

For example, assume that your contributions had totaled $67,500. Based on the facts in the preceding example, you would not be receiving all of this amount within three years, and therefore you would be taxed according to the annuity rate. If your life expectancy at age sixty-five is fifteen years, the amounts excluded for tax purposes from the $18,000 annual pension would be as follows:

$$\frac{\$67,500}{15 \times \$18,000} = \frac{67,500}{270,000} = \frac{1}{4}.$$

Thus, one-quarter of your pension, or $4,500 a year, would be excluded from taxation because it constitutes a return of your own contributions. The remainder of your pension, $13,500, would be fully taxable.

Under the annuity rule the exclusion from taxable income exists no matter how long you live, even if you live many years beyond your life expectancy and have received more than the amount of your original contributions. If you die, your beneficiary receives installments on the same tax basis that applied to you.

Estate Taxes. Federal estate taxes can frequently consume a substantial share of your total property at the time of your death. Fortunately, the value of the employer-paid pension plan is not considered "property" for estate tax purposes under most circumstances. For example, the value of future installments being paid to your beneficiary after your death will not be subject to estate taxes in either your estate or that of your beneficiary.

Taxes on Lump Sum Payments. Sometimes an employer-sponsored pension plan is not settled by installment payments but is paid out in a lump sum at retirement—or before that time if the employer's plan is terminated for some reason. If you receive a lump sum payment at retirement or earlier and

EXHIBIT 15-4   Three-Year Recovery Rule

Year	Amount Considered Return of Your Contribution (Not Taxed)	Amount Considered a Result of Employer's Contribution (Fully Taxed)	Total Pension
1	$18,000	0	$18,000
2	12,000	$ 6,000	18,000
3 and thereafter	0	18,000	18,000

meet certain conditions (e.g., if you have been a participant in the plan for at least five years and are receiving all the money within one taxable year), you may receive favorable income tax treatment. First, all the funds you have personally contributed will be exempt from taxation. Second, the funds attributable to your employer will be taxed according to a **ten-year averaging rule** that greatly reduces the amount of income tax due. (Consult tax regulations, IRC Code, Para. 402, for details of this rule.) Under this rule, for example, a distribution of $50,000 would be subject to $7,680 in income taxes—a total tax rate of only 15.36 percent.

Taxes on Life Insurance and Disability Insurance. An employee need not report for tax purposes the premiums on term life insurance paid by an employer if the amount of the life insurance policy is $50,000 or less. If the amount is higher, the income tax assessed is low since the government evaluates the excess according to special tables whose values are quite low in comparison to commercial rates. Death proceeds from life insurance are not subject to income tax because they are considered indemnity for a loss, not income.

Many pension plans provide income benefits if the employee becomes disabled after reaching age fifty or fifty-five or after completing some minimum period of service, often ten years. The disability payments are taxed according to the formula of the annuity rule. In addition, disability payments may be subject to a further exclusion from taxable income because of the **disability income exclusion,** under which payments of up to $100 a week are not subject to tax under certain conditions.

Coordination of Sources

If you are entitled to an employer pension, it can be a major factor in providing financial security during retirement. To illustrate, let us return to the hypothetical budget of the Marker family. Suppose John Marker currently has a gross salary of $20,000 without inflation adjustment. If his employer pension plan has a 1 percent-per-year-of-service benefit, John will be entitled to an annual retirement income benefit of 20 percent of his income of $20,000 (twenty years of service times 1 percent per year), or $4,000. John's Social Security receipts, based on current price levels, will amount of $8,400. Total retirement benefits will therefore be $12,400.

If we assume that John's salary will increase proportionately to inflation, his employer pension will also increase correspondingly, as will Social Security benefits. If the inflation factor for 8 percent for ten years is 2.16, John's annual retirement income (now calculated at $12,400) should be $26,784 ($12,400 × 2.16) when he reaches sixty-five. Let us compare the Markers' income needs as described earlier with the combined resources available from Social Security and the pension plan.

Income needs		
Total income needs at retirement		$ 30,240
Less income provided by Social Security and the employer pension		26,784
Additional income needed		$ 3,456
Lump Sum Needs		
Total lump sum needs		$108,000
Less:		
Current savings account, increased 10 percent a year for 10 years (see Appendix A–1)	$25,937	
Expected cash value of whole life ($5,000 increased by 5 percent for 10 years*)	8,144	
Amount to which $200 a year annual savings for 10 years will accumulate at 10 percent (see Appendix A–3)	3,187	
Subtotal		37,268
Additional lump sump amount needed		$70,732

Based on this analysis of their needs, the Markers can calculate how much additional annual savings they must put aside to meet their stated goals. The alternative to additional saving is to scale down expected spending levels. Before cutting back on goals, however, they should examine ways to supplement retirement income.

---

*5 percent is the estimated return paid under typical whole life policies in 1981.

Tax-Sheltered Individual Retirement Plans

Not everyone is covered by an employer pension plan. In fact, only about half of the workers in the United States are currently covered, and many of them will not actually draw pensions because of failure to satisfy vesting requirements. If you are not covered by an employer pension plan, you can nevertheless supplement your retirement income on an individual basis. In a major liberalization of tax rules after 1981, Congress authorized several types of individual retirement plans that offer varying degrees of tax shelter. Current rules are outlined in Exhibit 15–5. Depending on your work status, you probably are entitled to at least one of the individual retirement plans.

GENERAL ADVANTAGES

Perhaps the main advantage of a tax-sheltered individual retirement plan is that the amounts you contribute to the plan are deductible for current federal and state income taxes. You pay no income tax on the funds contributed, or on the investment earnings from these funds, until you receive them at retirement. Since you will probably be in a lower tax bracket at retirement, the tax burden will be much lower than if you paid taxes currently on the amounts contributed. For example, if you are in the 40 percent combined tax bracket and are planning to save $2,000 annually in an individual retirement account (IRA), the entire $2,000 "goes to work" for you. Without tax shelter, only $1,200 would be available for investment after you had paid the $800 combined federal and state income taxes ($.40 \times \$2,000 = \$800$).

Even if you are not in a lower tax bracket after retirement, you will still be ahead by using a tax-deferred plan; you will have had the advantage of what amounts to an interest-free loan of the amounts otherwise payable in current taxes. Not only is the $2,000 exempt from current taxes, but all investment earnings on the $2,000 are also tax-exempt until your retirement.

Other advantages of tax-deferred retirement plans include the following: (1) You enjoy complete ownership of the account from the moment you set it up—that is, you are 100 percent vested in your own plan from the beginning. (2) You may exercise some control over the way in which your retirement funds are invested. For example, you can invest in money market funds that currently pay a higher interest rate than is available in most other types of liquid savings, or you can choose to invest in other mutual funds, whose investment objectives match your own. (3) You may use tax-deferred plans to receive **rollovers,** distributions from an employer-sponsored, tax-qualified plan terminated with lump-sum payments. You can receive such distributions without current taxation if you meet certain conditions. Thus, if you change employers and receive lump sums from your employer pension plan, you can use a tax-deferred plan to help preserve your ultimate goal: maintaining your standard of living after retirement.

EXHIBIT 15–5   Rules Governing Tax-Sheltered Individual Retirement Plans

Worker Status	Type of Plan	General Annual Limit of Contributions Eligible for Tax Deferral
Any employee, including those eligible for an employer tax-qualified plan	Individual retirement account (IRA)	$2,000 annually ($2,250 if you have a nonworking spouse)
Employee who may or may not be eligible for another employer tax-qualified plan	SEP-IRA	$15,000 annually or 15% of income, whichever is less
Self-employed worker	Keogh (H.R. 10) plan	$15,000 or 15% of self-employment income, whichever is less
Worker employed by a nonprofit institution	Section 403(b) (TSA) plan	20% of "includible income"

REQUIREMENTS AND LIMITATIONS

Certain conditions and limitations are attached to individual retirement plans. Only the major ones are described in the following subsections. You should obtain specific information about these plans before you set one up; the limitations and conditions change constantly along with changes in the tax law. The following discussion is based on 1981 conditions.

Individual Retirement Account (IRA). Under the **individual retirement account (IRA)** plan you are limited to savings of $2,000 (for 1982 and beyond) unless you have a nonworking spouse, in which case you can set up an IRA for the spouse, too, and contribute a total of $2,250 for you and your spouse. If you and your spouse work, you can claim up to a $4,000 deduction on a joint return. You may also make tax-deductible contributions (if they are voluntary) to a tax-qualified pension plan sponsored by your employer. The total annual limit of tax deductions, however, is $2,000 ($2,250 if your have a nonworking spouse or $4,000 if both spouses work), which can be divided between an IRA and an employer plan. You can begin receiving payments from your IRA no earlier than age 59-1/2 or no later than age 70-1/2. IRA funds may not be invested in life insurance or endowment policies; they may be invested in the following three ways:

1. An IRA account set up by a bank or trust whose custodian invests the money, according to your wishes, in savings accounts, certificates

of deposit, savings and loan accounts, mutual fund shares, real estate limited partnerships, or bank-pooled funds;

2. An individual retirement annuity from a life insurance company;
3. A U.S. retirement bond, which may be purchased from any branch of the Federal Reserve Bank (in 1981 these bonds paid 6-1/2 percent).

You may incur penalties for violating the legal restrictions governing IRAs. For example, if money is withdrawn from your IRA before you reach age 59-1/2 (unless you die or become disabled), the money is subject to a 10 percent penalty tax. Regular income tax payments must also be made on these amounts in the year in which they are withdrawn. Congress imposed the penalty to encourage tax-paying workers to use IRA funds strictly as a supplement to retirement income.

Simplified Employee Pension (SEP-IRA) Plans. Simplified employee pension (SEP-IRA) plans were authorized by Congress in 1979 to encourage smaller employers to establish employee pension plans with IRAs as a funding method. For the employer no fixed annual contribution is required; therefore, SEP-IRA plans offer employers an advantage over regular tax-qualified pension plans. Employers may increase, decrease, or omit contributions to the plan from year-to-year as economic conditions vary. Furthermore, SEP-IRAs eliminate much of the paperwork and other restrictions of regular tax-qualified pension plans.

A SEP-IRA is similar to an IRA as far as the employee is concerned, with two major differences: (1) The employee may contribute to a SEP-IRA even if covered by another employer tax-qualified pension plan. (2) The allowable amount invested in the plan—$15,000 a year or 15 percent of earnings, whichever is less—is higher than the limit imposed on IRAs; the contribution allowed to the employee alone is the same as is allowed under an IRA ($2,000 a year) but the employer can make contributions up to the $15,000 limit. For example, assume you are earning a salary of $20,000 a year, and your employer contributes $1,000 a year to a SEP-IRA. You will be permitted to contribute an additional $1,000 to your plan to bring the total contribution up to the $2,000 limit applicable to employees. On the other hand, assume your employer is contributing $2,500 to your plan. In this case you could make no tax-deductible contribution, since the total amount going into the plan exceeds the $2,000 limit for employees. As long as your salary stays at $20,000, the most your employer can contribute to the SEP-IRA is $3,000 (15% × $20,000).

The employer using the SEP-IRA must cover all employees who have been employed for at least three of the five preceding years and have reached age twenty-five or above. The employer may not discriminate in favor of more highly paid workers—that is, the same percentage of earnings must be contributed for all eligible workers. Also, the employee must have nonforfeitable rights in the plan from the beginning—that is, 100 percent immediate vesting. The employer may not restrict the employee's rights to funds, even if the employee quits or is discharged for any reason. The plan can be integrated with Social Security so that, in making contributions on behalf of workers, the employer may take credit for amounts paid for Social Security contributions.

Keogh (H.R. 10) Plans. Under a **Keogh plan** for the self-employed, available since 1962, you may invest more than is allowed in an IRA ($15,000 rather than $2,000), but you must also include in the plan any employees you may have. These employees must be covered in a nondiscriminatory manner— that is, in general you must contribute to the plan the same proportion of a low-paid worker's earnings as the proportion of earnings you contribute to your own account or to the accounts of more highly paid workers. Thus, if you contribute 15 percent of your own earnings to the plan, you must contribute 15 percent of an employee's salary as well. The amounts you contribute are fully deductible and also serve as an attractive, low-cost benefit that helps you retain valuable employees.

As with the IRA plan, all contributions to your employees must be nonforfeitable. Distributions from the plan are limited to people between the ages of 59-1/2 and 70-1/2; a 10 percent, nondeductible tax penalty and a five-year suspension from participation in the plan are imposed for early withdrawal. You are also prohibited from obtaining a loan against assets in the plan and from assigning any of its benefits to others before age 59-1/2; such actions are considered as early withdrawals and are subject to the 10 percent penalty.

Keogh contributions are restricted to $15,000 or 15 percent of **earned income** in any one year. Income such as interest, rents, and other investment revenues do not count as earned; earned income is your net income after business expenses, including pension contributions for employees. If you exceed the allowable contributions, the excess contributed is subject to a 6 percent, nondeductible excise tax penalty for each year the excess is allowed to exist. If you have contributed more than the amount allowed, you should reduce your contributions in the following year by the amount of the excess in the previous year to prevent the 6 percent tax from accumulating year after year.

Considerable flexibility is permitted in the investment of Keogh contributions. You can set up a trusteed custodial account at a bank for the purchase of stocks, bonds, mutual funds, savings certificates, and other types of investments. You may also purchase a fixed or variable annuity or retirement income contract from a life insurer. Finally, you may fund your plan with U.S. retirement bonds in denominations ranging from $50 to $1,000, with 6.5 percent interest payable upon redemption.

Section 403(b) (TSA) Plans. Employees of certain nonprofit institutions may save extra funds in specified ways under tax shelter in accordance with the requirements set forth by Section 403(b) of the U.S. Internal Revenue Code. These plans have been called simply **403(b) plans** or **tax-sheltered annuities (TSAs)** because originally the law permitted only insured annuities to be purchased by employees who were qualified under this section of the tax code. In 1974 the law was amended to permit investments in mutual funds.

To be eligible for a TSA plan, you must be employed by an organization described in the tax code in Section 501(c)(3) as nonprofit or by a public school system. The employer must purchase the contract, usually (but not necessarily) under terms of a side agreement with the employee to "reduce the salary" of the employee by the amount to be contributed. The employee's rights to the contract must be nonforfeitable.

A limitation exists on the amount of the contribution, generally expressed as 20 percent of the employee's *includible income*—that is, the income left after the contribution has been made. For example, if you are a public school teacher earning $18,000 a year and you elect to contribute $3,000 a year to a 403(b) plan, the $3,000 contributed is exempt from income tax in that year because it does not exceed 20 percent of your includible income of $15,000 ($18,000 − 3,000). Under some circumstances you might be able to contribute more than $3,000 a year; the laws allows catch-up provisions for years in which you may have contributed less than the full amount permitted.

In case of death, disability, or "financial hardship," 403(b) funds are withdrawable prior to retirement. Unlike IRA or Keogh plans, 403(b) plans do not include 10 percent penalties for early withdrawal.

Section 403(b) plans may be invested in fixed or variable annuities from life insurers, in mutual funds, and in retirement income or endowment policies in which the life insurance (death protection) element is incidental. The protection element is incidental if protection amounts to less than 100 times the monthly pension expected at retirement. Thus, a TSA providing $500 a month in expected retirement benefits could also include a $50,000 life insurance element, the premiums on which would be included in the taxable income of the employee each year. If you contribute more than is permitted under the regulations governing TSAs, you will be subject to income tax on the excess contributions. However, no additional penalties, such as exist with Keogh plans, are imposed.

When you receive benefits from your TSA, all the income is subject to ordinary income tax rates if the income stems from contributions previously untaxed to you. If part of the funds have been previously subject to income tax because you contributed too much in a particular year, they may be recovered tax-free or in accordance with the three-year recovery rule or the annuity rule.

Multiple Plans. You can simultaneously enjoy the benefits of tax deferral from more than one type of individual retirement plan. For example, a public school teacher may set up a TSA plan to supplement a regular teachers' retirement plan offered by the school district. In addition the teacher may establish an IRA or a Keogh plan for self-employment income earned from sources such as royalties, consulting, and public speaking. The teacher may simultaneously be covered by Social Security and by veterans' or military allowances.

How Much to Save

You should consider how much to lay aside in tax shelters or other savings after you have completed the budgeting and planning steps. In the Marker family example, an additional annual lifetime income of $3,456 is required for meeting stated spending goals. Also, an additional lump sum of $70,732 is required. How much the Markers need to save may be determined by answers to the following questions:

1. How much must be saved annually for ten years at some assumed interest rate (say, 10 percent) to accumulate enough funds for a lifetime income of $3,456?
2. How much must be saved annually for ten years at, say, 10 percent to accumulate $70,732?

To answer the first question, we must know the price of an annuity sufficient to provide the desired income. (Annuities and their prices are discussed in the following subsection.) To answer the second question, we must refer to an interest table that gives sinking fund numbers similar to house mortgages (see Appendix A–2). Equal annual installments of $4,438 at 10 percent for ten years will be sufficient to provide the required sum of $70,732.

Adjustments in calculations must be made for other factors—for example, the possibility of having to pay income taxes on some parts of the retirement income or the need for inflation protection. For example, if the Marker family must pay $500 a year in income taxes on John's pension, this amount must be added to their income needs. If inflation is 8 percent annually, the Markers' income must be increased by 8 percent each year if they wish to avoid reductions in living standards during retirement.

ANNUITIES

In planning for retirement, your goal is to receive pension income in a way that guarantees a lifetime of payments without the possibility that you will outlive your income. You also want to protect your dependents in the event of your early death during retirement; you want to ensure that they have at least some of your pension income. Meeting these goals requires an understanding of annuities and of annuity options.

What Is an Annuity?

An **annuity** is a contract that provides for a series of payments to a person known as the **annuitant.** Most life insurance policies may be settled on an installment basis, and annuity contracts are issued to accomplish such a settlement. The series of payments is often termed simply an annuity, but more accurately it is **annuity rent.** The issuer is almost always a life insurer or a pension trustee. Annuity rent can be guaranteed for the life of the annuitant, with no refund to anyone at death, in which case it is called a **straight life annuity.** If the rent is paid over the lives of two persons and stops at the death of the second person, it is called a **joint and last survivorship annuity. Fixed annuities** are paid in dollars of a fixed number, while **variable annuities** are paid in varying numbers of dollars; the amount of the variation depends on fluctuations of the stock market.

A significant characteristic of annuities is that the issuer employs both interest or investment income and part of the principal amount to pay the rent. In other words, under an annuity you are drawing down your principal funds as well as your interest. In the case of life annuities, the rent is also affected by mortality factors. The longer people are expected to live, the lower the rent. Annuitants who die early make some contribution to the income of those who live longer. Women receive lower annuity rents than men because, on the average, women live seven or eight years longer. Charges for annuities are also affected by the amount of interest return the issuer expects to receive and by the issuer's cost of doing business, usually called **loading.** Because most people are interested in receiving annuity rent for life, the following discussion is confined to forms of life annuities.

Classification of Life Annuities

Life annuities may be classified according to several basic characteristics (see Exhibit 15–6): (1) the number of payments guaranteed, (2) when the rent begins, (3) the method of purchase (e.g., a single sum or annual premium payments), (4) the number of lives covered, (5) whether the rent is fixed in dollars or is variable, and (6) whether the annuity is insured or noninsured.

GUARANTEES OF RENTS

Three common arrangements exist for paying annuity rents: (1) It may be paid for the life of the annuitant with no refund to others at death (called the **nonrefund,** or **straight life annuity**). (2) It may be paid for life but with a period of years (say, five or ten) guaranteed for a named beneficiary (called a **minimum period guaranty annuity**). (3) It may be paid for life but with some minimum refund to the named beneficiary of unpaid amounts (called **cash refund,** or **installment refund, annuity**).

EXHIBIT 15–6
Types of Life
Annuities

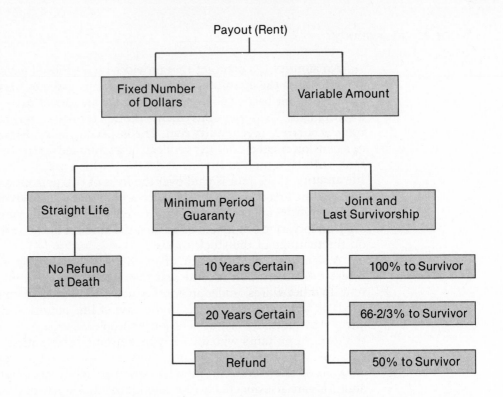

A straight life annuity offers the largest rent (lowest price) because the insurer is not obliged to pay any part of the purchase price of the annuity to any beneficiary of the insured, even if the insured were to die the day after purchasing the contract. Under a minimum period guaranty annuity the insured's beneficiary will be guaranteed any remaining installments if the insured dies before the named period has expired. For example, if an annuitant is receiving $100 monthly under a ten-year guaranteed period option and dies after seven years, the beneficiary will receive the $100 monthly for the remaining three years. Under the cash refund annuity, if the sum of the installments that has actually been paid to the annuitant at the time of death does not yet equal the original purchase price of the annuity, the balance is refunded to a named beneficiary either in installments or in cash, depending on the contract.

WHEN RENT BEGINS

If the rent of an annuity is to begin as soon as the annuity has been purchased, it is termed an **immediate annuity.** If the rent is to begin after some period of years, the annuity is termed a **deferred annuity.** Often group annuities purchased by employers on behalf of their employees are deferred, since the rent is intended to begin at retirement.

METHOD OF PURCHASE

Annuities purchased in a single cash payment are called **single-premium annuities.** If the annuitant purchases the annuity over a period of years in annual installments (which is usually the case), it is called an **annual-premium annuity.** A common type of annuity in connection with employee benefit plans is the **single-premium deferred annuity,** in which an employer purchases each year a deferred annuity sufficient to fund an employee's future retirement income as determined by that year's salary.

NUMBER OF LIVES COVERED

An annuity may be based on one life or on more than one. The most common example of an annuity based on multiple lives is the joint and last survivorship annuity, under which a person can arrange for payments to continue as long as either the person or the spouse lives. Under these terms neither spouse can outlive the income provided. This type of annuity can be arranged to continue full payment, two-thirds of the full payment, or one-half of the full payment.

FIXED OR VARIABLE RENT

Annuities may be arranged to pay a rent that is either fixed or variable. Fixed annuities are paid in dollars, the number of which are fixed at the beginning and do not change. Variable annuities are also paid in dollars, the number of which varies according to fluctuations in the value of common stocks in which the insurer has invested the funds paid for the annuity (see the following discussion of variable annuities).

INSURED OR NONINSURED

Most annuities are issued by life insurance companies; hence they are insured and possess guarantees of safety of principal and a minimum interest return. Many annuities paid under employer pension plans are issued by trustees and are uninsured. Such annuities are considered safe, although perhaps not as safe as insured plans. Other annuities are private—that is, they are issued by private parties and are noninsured. Private annuities are the least secure type of annuity.

Variable Annuities

The variable annuity was designed to overcome a major weakness of a regular, or fixed, annuity—namely, that while the dollars representing the rent of the annuity are guaranteed for life, inflation may cause the purchasing power of these dollars to fall. The variable annuity's funds are invested in common stocks, so the annuitant has a chance to receive more dollars if the stock market rises. On the other hand, the variable annuitant takes the financial risk that if the stock market falls, the number of dollars received will also fall. By 1979 about 2 million people in the United States were covered by variable annuities.

LIMITATIONS OF VARIABLE ANNUITIES

For several reasons the variable annuity has not been an unqualified success in achieving its goals. In the United States, particularly since 1970, the stock market has remained relatively flat, although consumer prices have risen steadily and at a much greater rate than existed prior to 1970. Thus, the basic assumption of the variable annuity—that a fairly close correspondence would exist between stock prices and the cost of living—has not held up. In several periods consumer prices and stock market prices have gone in opposite directions and have thus defeated the purpose of the variable annuity.

Another limitation of the variable annuity is that it requires a long-term planning perspective. However, many investors do not persist in a consistent savings program over time. The variable annuity is based on the assumption that the long-term saver will accumulate some units at low prices and some at higher prices. If savers put away regular, fixed amounts, they will accumulate more units when the stock market is depressed and fewer when the stock market is high. But when the stock market falls, savers tend to become discouraged; they often drop out of the variable annuity plan and switch to fixed-dollar savings. When the stock market recovers, they may reenter the variable annuity plan because they do not want to miss out on the rising trend in the market. In practice, then, some participants may purchase more variable annuity units at high prices and fewer at low prices.

A third problem with variable annuities is the relatively high costs of selling and managing them. One study has shown that the total cost of insurer management over a ten-year period approximates 18.25 percent of the initial investment.[1] These costs may reduce the merit of variable annuities in comparison to alternative investments. Another factor that has discouraged the use of variable annuities is that rising interest rates in fixed annuities and other debt obligations have attracted savers away from the stock market.

ADVANTAGES OF VARIABLE ANNUITIES

In spite of its weaknesses, the variable annuity has some advantages as a long-term savings vehicle. For one thing, it offers the long-term saver some opportunity for offsetting erosion in the purchasing power of the dollar, albeit

---

1. Mark R. Greene and J. Paul Copeland, "Factors in Selecting Tax-Sheltered Annuities," *CLU Journal* 24, no. 4 (October, 1975), p. 44

at some risk. It also offers the saver some guarantee that the applicable annuity rate will be at some minimum value when the savings fund is converted into an annuity. The insurer offers the annuitant the opportunity to switch from a variable annuity to a fixed annuity as investment conditions and the needs of the saver change. The switch is usually made without charge, although some limitation on the frequency of change (e.g., no more than once or twice a year) may be imposed. The savings fund in the variable annuity is also protected from the claims of creditors of the insured or of the beneficiary. In addition, most insurers offer a guarantee that in the event of the saver's death prior to retirement (i.e., during the accumulation period), the beneficiary will never receive less than the amount invested, even if the stock market has declined so that the values of the stocks are less than the invested sum. Finally, through the use of the joint and last survivorship options, the insured may protect a beneficiary, such as a spouse, against outliving the annuity income if the principal annuitant dies first.

Annuity Prices

Annuity prices are usually quoted on the basis of the number of dollars you must pay to be entitled to a specified monthly lifetime rent under different options with different numbers of payments guaranteed (see Appendix A–7). Exhibit 15–7 shows the various prices an insurer might quote for a life annuity paying $10 a month. Note that the price of a no-refund annuity is less than the price of one in which a number of guaranteed payments are made. Thus, a sixty-five-year-old male pays $1,112 if the annuity carries no refund, and $1,196 (7.5 percent more) if the annuity provides for ten years of guaranteed payments. For a no-refund annuity a sixty-five-year-old woman must pay $1,241 (11.6 percent more than the $1,112 payable by a man of the same age). This discrepancy is due to the fact that women have greater longevity than men.

Sometimes annuity prices are quoted in terms of the amount of rent offered for each $1,000 of proceeds available at the age the annuity begins. If you want to convert from one basis to the other, divide the $1,000 by the price quoted in Exhibit 15–7. For example, an insurer whose price is $1,112 per $10 of monthly rent would quote $1,000/$1,112, or $8.99 a month [$1,000/$1,112) × $10] for each $1,000 of proceeds. Frequently funds accumulated in pension accounts or in life insurance policies are converted to life annuities. A good rule of thumb for determining the monthly lifetime income available on an annuity basis is to divide the accumulated funds by $1,000 and multiply the result by $9 (for a male) or $8 (for a female).

In times of high interest rates, the price of annuities may seem too high because many annuity contracts guarantee a very low minimum rate of interest. For example, in 1981 a typical annuity guaranteed only 5.0 or 5.5 per-

EXHIBIT 15-7   Costs of a Life Annuity Paying $10 a Month

Option	Male		Female	
	Age 60	Age 65	Age 60	Age 65
1. No refund at death (straight life annuity)	$1,272	$1,112	$1,393	$1,241
2. Ten years of payments guaranteed to a beneficiary regardless of when annuitant dies	1,323	1,196	1,427	1,297
3. Refund at death, paid in installments to named beneficiary until original purchase price has been paid back	1,346	1,211	1,449	1,319

cent interest, whereas long-term government bonds paid over 13 percent. Suppose you had $10,000 to invest at retirement and were considering the annuity whose price was quoted in Exhibit 15–7 for a sixty-five-year-old female. You could have purchased for $10,000 a no-refund annuity that paid about $80 a month [($10,000/$1,000) × $8] for life. The $80 rent would employ both interest and principal and would cease upon your death. Alternatively, you could have invested the $10,000 in a long-term government bond earning $1,300 a year ($108.33 a month) for as long as you kept the bond. The $108.33 would not use up principal, and the value of the government bond could be willed to your heirs. Both investments had roughly equal safety levels. In 1981 the price of the annuity was clearly noncompetitive, unless the issuer was also paying sufficient dividends to compensate for the relatively low rent offered in comparison to the interest earnings on the government bond.

It pays to shop for annuities because insurers quote large variations in the prices of these products. In a 1975 study[2] annuity rates quoted among forty-two life insurers varied from a low of $7.87 a month for each $1,000 of proceeds to a high of $9.64—a difference of $1.77. If you had had $10,000 to invest, you could have obtained $17.70 a month more from the insurer with the highest rent than from the insurer with the lowest. If you are saving money in annuities, you should be aware that wide variations exist in investment performance. The same study found, for example, that if you had saved $100 a month for twenty years, you would have had an account valued at $54,403 with the insurer earning the most, and only at $36,743 with the insurer earning the least. Annual data are available allowing you to make price comparisons among annuities in such sources as *Best's Flitcraft Compend.*

---

2. Mark R. Greene, Lester I. Tenney, and John Neter, "Annuity Rents and Rates—Guaranteed vs. Current," *Journal of Risk and Insurance*, Vol. 44, no. 3 (September, 1977), pp. 383–401.

THE MARKER FAMILY PLAN FOR RETIREMENT

Let us review the financial-planning program of the Marker family to determine whether there is a role for annuities, fixed or variable. Earlier we saw that the couple must supplement their retirement income in the amount of $3,456 a year to meet planned spending needs. Since they will need inflation protection for this income, they may well consider a variable annuity. Although the variable annuity is not perfect protection, it is better than forgoing all protection against inflation. The Markers can also realize other advantages in using annuities—for example, John can arrange a joint and last survivorship option for the variable annuity. He should also make sure that he has selected a joint and last survivorship annuity available under his employer's pension plan.

Susan Marker will have survivors' income from Social Security. Through this income and the income from the annuities, her financial future will be assured in the event that John's death occurs before hers.

Furthermore, the Markers should consider any available tax-sheltered individual retirement plan as a means of accumulating funds to meet their supplemental retirement income needs. If they use one of the tax-sheltered plans, they will need to save a lesser amount. For example, if John is in the 25 percent income tax bracket, $75 of gross salary devoted to retirement saving in a tax-sheltered plan is equivalent to $100 saved in a taxable plan; after paying income taxes, John would have only $75 left for savings.

How much must the Markers have on hand at age sixty-five to provide the additional $3,456 they will need annually? Since they will require about $280 a month, they will need twenty-eight annuity units of $10 each. If the price of a joint and last survivorship annuity paying 50 percent to the survivor is $1,200, then at John's and Susan's ages, for each $10 a month initial rent, the sum of $33,600 (28 × $1,200) must be accumulated. To accumulate $33,600 in ten years at 10 percent interest, they must save $2,108 a year (see Appendix A–2). This amount could probably be saved under a tax-sheltered IRA plan that used a savings and loan account.

As noted before, the Markers also will need a lump sum of $70,732. Accumulating this amount in ten years at 10 percent interest requires annual savings of $4,438. Thus, additional annual savings for income ($2,108) and lump sum needs ($4,438) total $6,546—more than $500 a month. Unless the Markers scale down their retirement budget, they must find ways to increase their current annual savings level of $2,400 to about $6,546.

The Marker family retirement plan is shown in Exhibit 15–8. They should ask why they really need such a large supplemental fund ($108,000). Their life and health insurance is adequate for meeting emergency health care costs or last expenses if one of them should die. Through the use of joint and last survivorship options and Social Security, Susan's retirement income is assured. They will also have the value of their home, whose mortgage will

EXHIBIT 15-8   The Marker Family Financial Plan for Retirement

	Current Prices		Inflation-Adjusted Prices	
Income Needs				
Spending needs		$14,000		$ 30,240
Resources				
Social Security	$8,400		$18,144	
Employer pension	4,000	12,400	8,640	26,784
Balance needed		$ 1,600		$ 3,456
Amount provided by a 10-year annuity for amount of $33,600, costing $2,108 annually				3,456
Balance				0
Lump-Sum Needs				
Round-the-world trip		$10,000		$ 21,600
Emergency fund		40,000		86,400
Total lump-sum needs		$50,000		$108,000
Resources				
Current savings account ($10,000) increased at 10% a year for 10 years			$25,937	
Whole life insurance ($5,000 cash value) increased at 5% a year for 10 years			8,144	
Value of additional savings, $200 a year			3,187	$ 37,268
Balance needed				$ 70,732
Additional annual savings required				$ 4,438
Summary				
Additional annual savings required for income needs				$ 2,108
Additional annual savings required for lump-sum needs				4,438
Total annual savings required for all needs				$ 6,546

be fully paid at retirement. The home could be borrowed against in case of an emergency. If they gave up plans for the round-the-world trip, they would be freed from having to save an additional $500 a month. However, only the individuals involved can decide whether to sacrifice future spending in favor of current spending.

SUMMARY

1. Financial planning for retirement involves a careful analysis of present and future income and spending needs. The process involves setting retirement goals, determining retirement needs, cataloging financial resources to meet these needs, and making sometimes difficult decisions about how to overcome deficits between anticipated spending needs and resources.

2. Important factors to consider in retirement planning include allowances for inflation and income taxes. Both employer-sponsored retirement plans and individual retirement plans offer income tax advantages and some inflation protection. They are essential elements in adequate financial planning, and they should be coordinated with benefits available from Social Security. In selecting funding media for retirement plans, you should consider media that offer some inflation protection—for example, common stocks, mutual funds, and variable annuities.

3. Employer pension plans constitute an important source of retirement income for about half the working population. You can estimate the amount of your pension by studying the type of benefit formula it uses, if any (for defined benefit plans), or by estimating the size of a future retirement account in your name (for defined contribution plans). Your eligibility for benefits depends on the vesting provisions, which usually require ten years of service with the employer. Most pension plans will allow benefits to a spouse, and some offer disability and death benefits, as well.

4. Retirement benefits under private employer pensions are insured by the Pension Benefits Guaranty Corporation up to stated limits. Most pension plans are supported by employer contributions, which are not taxable to you during your employment but are subject to taxation when benefits are paid during retirement. If you have contributed to the cost of your pension, you may recover these contributions tax free during retirement under one of two applicable annuity rules set forth by the Internal Revenue Service. The value of an employer-supported pension is not subject to estate taxes in your estate. Lump sum distributions of the value of pension plans are subject to favorable tax rules to reduce the income taxes that might otherwise be applicable.

5. Four major types of tax-sheltered individual retirement plans exist under which you may supplement retirement income from other sources. These are (a) individual retirement accounts (IRAs) for all employed workers, (b) Simplified Employee Pension plans (SEP-IRAs) established by employers, (c) Keogh plans for the self-employed, and (d) Section 403(b) plans (tax-sheltered annuities) for employees of nonprofit institutions. Each of these plans is subject to different sets of tax rules and limitations on contributions.

6. The major advantages of using tax-sheltered retirement plans is that you can deduct their costs for income taxes and pay no tax on interest

earnings. They provided much larger benefits than would be possible without tax shelter. These plans also provide fully vested benefits since they are the property of and are controlled by the employee. You must pay income taxes on the full amount when you start receiving benefits.

7. The annuity offers an arrangement under which you can receive benefits from retirement saving in the form of an income you cannot outlive. Benefits can be paid as a fixed number of dollars (fixed annuities) or as a fixed number of "units" (similar to shares of mutual funds) whose value varies with the stock market (variable annuities). Annuities can be arranged to cover two lives, so that you can guarantee an income to a spouse for as long as either spouse lives. You can arrange to have life insurance cash values and other individual savings plans converted to annuities; frequently an employer pension plan is set up to make payments in the form of an annuity. Normally, annuities issued by life insurers are preferred to noninsured annuities.

8. The variable annuity is designed to offer a retirement income that roughly keeps pace with inflation and with changing standards of living in the economy. Past experience suggests that the rents paid under variable annuities only roughly correspond to cost-of-living changes because the stock market does not conform to changes in the consumer price index, especially in the short run. However, this form of annuity offers some degree of protection against inflation.

REVIEW QUESTIONS

1. (a) Explain the economic problem that confronts the aged.
   (b) What forces have produced this problem?
   (c) How is the problem related to the need for retirement planning?

2. Explain how you would estimate your financial needs for retirement.

3. Harold, age thirty-five and self-employed, estimates that, in addition to the amounts he has planned, he will require $4,800 a year at retirement to satisfy his spending needs. An annuity to provide the additional income would cost $50,000.
   (a) Assuming that Harold retires at age sixty-five and that he can earn 10 percent annually on funds saved under a tax shelter (consult Appendix A for appropriate interest tables), how much must he save annually to achieve his goal if he started immediately (age 35)?
   (b) How much must he save if he starts at age forty-five?

4. Given the other facts in Question 3, assume that Harold can earn only 8 percent on his savings. How large a difference will this percentage make in your answers to Question 3?

5. Carol is covered by her employer's tax-qualified pension plan, whose benefit formula provides for each year of service 1.25 percent of average salary during the five years immediately prior to retirement. Carol's current income is $10,000 a year and is expected to increase with inflation until her retirement twenty years from now. If Carol has ten years of service already, and inflation averages 8 percent annually, how much can she expect to receive in benefits from her employer's pension plan? Show your calculations (consult interest tables in Appendix A).

6. (a) Explain the word *integration* as it is used in connection with pension plans.
   (b) Does the use of integrated pension formulas mainly benefit the employer or the employee? Why?

7. Why is the joint and last survivorship option in annuities an important tool of retirement planning?

8. Homer, age sixty-five, has a life expectancy of fifteen years according to IRS tax tables. He has contributed $10,000 to his employer's retirement plan, under which he will receive $15,000 a year in pension. The employer has contributed the rest of the cost.
   (a) Which of the tax rules discussed in this chapter—the three-year-recovery rule or the annuity rule—govern how Homer should report the pension for tax purposes?
   (b) Determine how much of Homer's income will be subject to income tax in the first year.

9. What would be the answer to Question 8 if Homer had contributed $50,000 to the plan?

10. Distinguish between a fixed and a variable annuity.

11. Discuss the major strengths and major weaknesses of variable annuities.

12. Why might you expect single-premium annuities to be increasingly important tools of retirement planning?

13. What status must a person have to be eligible for the following plans:
    (a) an IRA plan,
    (b) a Keogh plan,
    (c) a SEP-IRA plan,
    (d) a TSA Section 403(b) plan.

14. What limits of annual retirement saving exist for each of the plans mentioned in Question 13?

15. Why did Congress require that people begin to draw out funds from IRA and Keogh plans only between the ages of 59-1/2 and 70-1/2 or be subject to special penalties.

16. (a) Why have vesting provisions tended to deprive many workers of benefits from employer-sponsored retirement plans?
    (b) Should employer-sponsored plans be required to offer full and immediate vesting?

17. (a) What is meant by funding?
    (b) In what ways does the problem of inflation influence funding?

18. One function of the Pension Benefits Guaranty Corporation is to insure minimum pensions for eligible persons whose employers have terminated their pension plans. Why is such a guarantee desirable?

19. (a) Why is saving for retirement under tax shelter advantageous?
    (b) Do tax shelters merely delay payment of the inevitable tax until a time when the employee can least afford it?

20. A report from an executive placement firm indicated that managers aged fifty to fifty-four averaged three employers during their careers, or one every ten years. For managers aged forty to forty-four, the job changing jumped to an average frequency of once every seven years. What implications do these findings have for the ability of an average executive to collect on the typical employer pension plan?

21. A financial analyst stated: "Since a relatively modest pension of perhaps $1,600 per month at current prices requires about $170,000 contributed over thirty years, and an average investment return is about 8 percent a year, an IRA just about makes it."
    (a) From interest tables in the Appendix, verify the truth (or falsity) of the above statement. Use the $1,500-a-year- IRA limit (which existed before 1981) in your calculations.
    (b) What annuity price (per $10-a-month rent) did the analyst apparently use?

CASE PROBLEMS

I. Retirement Income Planning

The Finch family, composed of Mr. and Mrs. Finch and two college-age children, has developed a retirement budget totaling $35,000 a year. Mr. and Mrs. Finch are both fifty-five. Mr. Finch expects to retire at sixty-five. He is covered by an employer tax-qualified pension plan and by Social Security. By age sixty-five Mr. Finch will have twenty-five years of service. The employer's pension has a defined benefit formula that will provide 1.5 percent of Mr. Finch's average final salary in five of the preceding ten years for each year of service. Mr. Finch expects his salary to average $50,000 for purposes of the employer pension. He expects Social Security income to be $800 monthly. His current salary is $40,000 annually. Mrs. Finch earns $5,000 annually as a freelance writer, and they spend most of her earnings on home improvement projects. They are saving $1,000 a year in savings certificates that are currently earning 14 percent annually. Their savings fund amounts to $20,000 at present. They believe Medicare will provide sufficient health insurance protection following retirement; they also believe their life insurance protection is sufficient—it is composed of $50,000 of group term coverage with the employer and a $20,000 ordinary life policy that carries a premium of $400 annually. The policy currently has a cash value of $7,000.

QUESTIONS

1. Will the Finchs have sufficient retirement income for their needs? If not, how much additional annual savings must they accumulate to meet their goal? Show all calculations and assumptions.

2. Offer some criticisms and suggestions for improvement in the family's current financial program.

II. Variable Annuities and Inflation

The accompanying table gives variable annuity unit values for the College Retirement Equities Fund (CREF) for 1952–1981 and values of the Consumer Price Index (CPI) for various years. CREF has the longest variable annuity record of any life insurance company plan in the United States.

CREF Annuity Unit Values since 1952 (Annuity Year: May through April)			
1952	$10.00	1967	$31.92
1953	9.46	1968	29.90
1954	10.74	1969	32.50
1955	14.11	1970	28.91
1956	18.51	1971	30.64
1957	16.88	1972	35.74
1958	16.71	1973	31.58
1959	22.03	1974	26.21
1960	22.18	1975	21.84
1961	26.25	1976	26.24
1962	26.13	1977	24.80
1963	22.68	1978	39.44
1964	26.48	1979	43.19
1965	28.21	1980	51.77
1966	30.43	1981	48.33
Source: TIAA-CREF Annual Report, 1980.			
CPI Values for Various Years			
1955	80.2	1975	161.2
1960	88.7	1977	181.0
1965	94.5	1982 (July)	292.2
1970	116.3		

QUESTIONS

1. To what extent did CREF units correspond to changes in the CPI?

2. What conclusions, if any, can you draw about the value of a variable annuity in offsetting inflation?

CHAPTER 16

ESTATE PLANNING

LEARNING OBJECTIVES

In studying this chapter you will learn:

The meaning and objectives of estate planning;

How recent changes in tax law have affected estate planning;

How to reduce estate transfer costs;

The advantages and disadvantages of various ways to transfer property at death;

Why you should have a will, and what provisions to include in it;

How trusts can accomplish estate-planning objectives;

The role of life insurance in estate planning.

The following story demonstrates the necessity of careful estate planning. A man with $200,000 of property wished to benefit one of his sisters, who was poor, with most of his estate when he died. He also wished to make a small bequest to each of two children of another sister, who was financially well off. In his will the man left $10,000 each to the children and the remainder to the first sister. However, the man had a long series of expensive medical treatments for the disease that ultimately took his life. When he died, his estate had been reduced through probate costs, lawyers' fees, and medical expenses to $25,000. The children's bequest consumed $20,000 of the estate, and the sister received the remaining $5,000. This unexpected result could easily have been avoided if the man had made his bequests in terms of percentages. For example, he could have willed 10 percent of his estate to the children and 90 percent to his sister; she would then have received $22,500, and the children, $1,250 each.

ESTATE PLANNING DEFINED

In a broad sense **estate planning** encompasses the activities involved in the accumulation and management of property during one's lifetime and the disposition of one's property at death. In a narrower sense estate planning refers to the process by which you can ensure that your wishes will be carried out after your demise and that taxes and other types of estate shrinkage will be minimized. Recent changes in estate and gift tax laws in the United States have reduced estate tax burdens. These changes have made estate planning even more important, since most people will be able to leave more property to their heirs. In a sense the whole subject of personal financial management culminates in estate planning. If you have pursued good financial management, you will likely have some property to be distributed at your death. The main tools involved in estate planning are wills, trusts, gifts, and life insurance policies. The planning process can be complex and may require not only careful thought but also the help of specialists who keep up with legal and financial changes in the field. Estate-planning specialists include attorneys, trust officers, certified public accountants, life insurance agents, and financial planners.

OBJECTIVES OF ESTATE PLANNING

The objectives of estate planning are (1) to create an estate, (2) to develop adequate and efficient methods by which property can be distributed after your death, (3) to minimize the costs (particularly the taxes) involved in transferring property at death, and (4) to provide liquidity (cash or near-cash assets) sufficient to pay the costs of estate transfer without sacrificing estate values through the forced sale of property for payment of current debts.

Creating an Estate

Before you need be concerned about the ultimate disposition of your assets, you must first build an estate. Estates are created and protected through the programs of saving, investment, and insurance described in earlier chapters. Just as success in creating an estate requires careful financial planning and tax management, so does success in disposing of your property.

Distributing an Estate

With an estate plan of your own design, disposition of all the property you own and all rights to income you have accumulated—for example, savings, pensions, annuities, and life insurance settlement options—is in your control rather than in someone else's. If you do not have a will, state law controls how your property is distributed, and the terms may not be appropriate for your family or other heirs. It is said that President Abraham Lincoln died without a will, and one-third of his estate went to one son, Tad Lincoln. Was this the settlement Mr. Lincoln would have preferred, or would he have wished his widow to benefit from all of his estate while she was living and the children to benefit after her death? To put the issue in more immediate terms, do you want your father's gold watch to pass to someone to whom you have promised it? Without a will, chances are small that this wish will be granted after your death. For example, suppose John and Mary, a married couple with no children, are involved in an automobile accident. John is killed immediately, but Mary survives for three months. If John had no will, Mary will have received all the jointly held property, and at her death her family members will inherit what is left. John's family members will receive nothing, although he perhaps would have wished to will something to his own family. The laws of inheritance govern how property is distributed in the event that no will exists.

"Estate planning should start at an early age."

Minimizing Estate Transfer Costs

The following expenses, incurred in settling estates, commonly absorb a substantial portion of estate assets:

1. Court costs,
2. Attorneys' fees,
3. Bond premiums,
4. Accounting fees,
5. Income taxes and other debts of the deceased,
6. Estate and inheritance taxes.

The amount of these expenses varies according to the size and complexity of the estate. The expenses must usually be paid in cash. If sufficient cash is not available, other assets must be sold to raise the necessary funds. Frequently, the sale of assets is a forced, or distress, sale that results in losses that could have been avoided had the estate possessed sufficient liquidity. Knowing how much liquidity is needed requires advance planning that includes careful estimates of what your assets and liabilities are likely to be.

Providing Liquidity

In an estate without sufficient liquidity, property may have to be sacrificed at a forced sale to pay the taxes. Particularly in the case of a business enterprise, a quick sale on favorable terms may be impossible. Take, for example, the case of a small manufacturing plant that makes parts for a larger customer, as is common in an industry such as auto manufacturing. If the enterprise must be sold immediately, perhaps the only available buyer is the major customer, who will have a superior bargaining position. With more time, however, the small plant's manufacturing operations might be converted to the manufacture of other products, which might enlarge the number of potential buyers and boost the purchase price of the business. (The laws generally contain special rules under which payment of estate taxes may be stretched out over a period of years at low interest rates.)

Liquidity in an estate can be provided through life insurance, which has several advantages, or through possession of assets that can be disposed of easily and without difficulty or delay—for example, listed securities, savings accounts, or cash. Life insurance offers two major advantages in providing liquidity to an estate: (1) Life insurance is secure; you can assume that the cash will be paid promptly by the insurer at the time it is needed most. (2) You can purchase life insurance under a convenient installment plan during your lifetime, and it is unlikely that the sum of all the premiums you pay will exceed the death proceeds of the policy. Therefore, you can meet estate transfer costs in *fractional dollars.* For example, if you have determined that $100,000 will be necessary to meet the liquidity needs of your estate, you can purchase a $100,000 ordinary life policy at rates varying from 2 to 5 percent of the face value of the policy, depending on your age at the time of purchase. Thus, life insurance is both an economical and an efficient means of meeting last expenses.

ESTATE TAXES

A major expense charged to your estate after your death requiring special prior attention is the federal estate tax. Recent reductions in taxes and in the amount of estate subject to tax significantly affect estate planning.

Under 1981 tax legislation the amount of an estate that may pass to others free of estate tax increases in stages through 1987 from $175,625 to $600,000. Congress effected the increase by raising the **unified gift and estate tax credit** in amounts shown in Exhibit 16–1. This credit is applied once the tax is calculated according to the rate schedule shown in Exhibit 16–2. For example, suppose your estate in 1983 was valued at $275,000—an amount chosen by the authors so that no estate tax would be due. The federal estate tax would be calculated as follows:

Gross estate	$275,000
Tax (from Exhibit 16–2, $70,800 + 34% of $25,000)	79,300
Less: unified estate and gift tax credit	
(from Exhibit 16–1)	79,300
Tax due	0

Besides reducing tax rates and raising the unified tax credit, the Economic Recovery Tax Act of 1981 made other important changes. First, the act removed limits on the **marital deduction,** the amount that could be given to your spouse free of estate tax. Formerly this deduction was limited to one-half of the estate; now you can give your entire estate to your spouse and delay any estate tax until your spouse dies. For example, suppose you have an estate of $300,000 and will it all to your spouse. No estate tax would be due at the time of your death. The estate tax due upon your spouse's death, if your spouse died in 1983 and the estate value had not changed, would be calculated as follows:

Gross estate	$300,000
Tax (from Exhibit 16–2, $70,800 + 34% of $50,000)	87,800
Less: unified estate and gift tax credit	
(from Exhibit 16–1)	79,300
Tax due	$ 8,500

As we will see later in the chapter, it may not be advantageous to leave all of your estate to your spouse if your goal is to minimize federal estate taxes. Taxes due upon your spouse's death can be minimized by proper planning.

The Economic Recovery Tax Act of 1981 also repealed the law that presumed that gifts a person had made in the three years prior to death were made "in contemplation of death" and therefore were subject to estate taxes. Now such gifts are not generally considered when the estate tax is computed; one exception is gifts of life insurance made within three years of death.

In another reform, the act stated that if you and your spouse hold property in joint ownership, only half of the value of the property is counted in your estate for tax purposes; the other half is considered entirely in your

EXHIBIT 16–1
Amounts That
May Pass Free of
Estate Tax

Year	Unified Gift and Estate Tax Credit	Exemption Equivalent
1981	$ 47,000	$175,625
1982	62,800	225,000
1983	79,300	275,000
1984	96,300	325,000
1985	121,800	400,000
1986	155,800	500,000
1987	192,800	600,000

spouse's estate, regardless of who furnished the funds to acquire the property. The act also raised gift tax exclusions and reduced in stages from 70 to 50 percent estate tax rates on estates valued over $2,500,000 (see Exhibit 16–2). Exhibit 16–3 shows how estate taxes will be lowered by 1987 as a result of tax reductions and increased credits. For example, a taxable estate of $10 million will have estate taxes reduced from about $6 million in 1981 to about $4.6 million in 1987, approximately a one-quarter reduction. A taxable estate of $500,000 was subject to $108,800 of estate taxes in 1981; the same estate will escape taxation entirely by 1987. Approximately 99-1/2 percent of all estates will escape federal estate taxes entirely if estate planners take full advantage of the new law through proper financial planning.

GIFTS AND GIFT TAXES

Many people believe that one way to eliminate estate taxes is to give their property away before death. To some extent taxes can be eliminated in this fashion, but the law imposes a gift tax on all gifts whose value exceeds given levels. The gift tax rate is the same as the estate tax rate. Gifts in excess of stated limits are taxed at the rates shown for estates in Exhibit 16–2.

The gift tax law taxes gifts "of a present interest"—that is, at the current (reasonable) market value of the property. Gifts of a "future interest"—for example, life insurance without a current cash value—are not subject to current gift taxation. Many employed persons make their spouse the irrevocable owner of all rights to the proceeds of life insurance. If the insurance has a cash value, it can be borrowed on, and thus the potential gift tax can be avoided. At the donor's death the spouse owns the insurance, and the proceeds of the policy are not included in the donor's estate for estate tax purposes. It is better in many cases to make a gift of your life insurance to your spouse rather than to make the spouse a beneficiary under the policy.

EXHIBIT 16-2   Federal Estate Taxes

Amount on Which Tax Is to Be Computed	Tentative Tax
Not over $10,000	18% of such amount
Over $10,000 but not over $20,000	$1,800 plus 20% of the excess of such amount over $10,000
Over $20,000 but not over $40,000	$3,800 plus 22% of the excess of such amount over $20,000
Over $40,000 but not over $60,000	$8,200 plus 24% of the excess of such amount over $40,000
Over $60,000 but not over $80,000	$13,000 plus 26% of the excess of such amount over $60,000
Over $80,000 but not over $100,000	$18,200 plus 28% of the excess of such amount over $80,000
Over $100,000 but not over $150,000	$23,800 plus 30% of the excess of such amount over $100,000
Over $150,000 but not over $250,000	$38,800 plus 32% of the excess of such amount over $150,000
Over $250,000 but not over $500,000	$70,800 plus 34% of the excess of such amount over $250,000
Over $500,000 but not over $750,000	$155,800 plus 37% of the excess of such amount over $500,000
Over $750,000 but not over $1,000,000	$248,300 plus 39% of the excess of such amount over $750,000
Over $1,000,000 but not over $1,250,000	$345,800 plus 41% of the excess of such amount over $1,000,000
Over $1,250,000 but not over $1,500,000	$448,300 plus 43% of the excess of such amount over $1,250,000
Over $1,500,000 but not over $2,000,000	$555,800 plus 45% of the excess of such amount over $1,500,000
Over $2,000,000 but not over $2,500,000	$780,800 plus 49% of the excess of such amount over $2,000,000
Over $2,500,000[a]	After 1985, $1,025,800 plus 50% of excess over $2,500,000

Note: Taxes are applicable to estate values after adjustment for settlement costs, administrative expenses, and the unified estate and gift tax credit.
[a]Before 1981, estates over $2,500,000 were taxed at rates up to 70%. This maximum rate has been reduced in stages as follows: 1982, 65%; 1983, 60%; 1984, 55%; 1985 and thereafter, 50%.

In 1982 a significant change was made in the exemptions allowed under the federal gift tax. You are permitted to give away annually up to $10,000 each ($20,000, if the gift comes jointly from husband and wife) to as many individuals as you wish without owing any federal gift tax. Formerly the limit was $3,000 a year ($6,000 in the case of a married couple). In addition, the law provides that any amounts paid to any individual for tuition or for medical care do not count as part of the $10,000 or $20,000 limitation. By making

EXHIBIT 16–3
Comparison of
Estate Tax After
Full Rate
Reduction and
Credit Increase

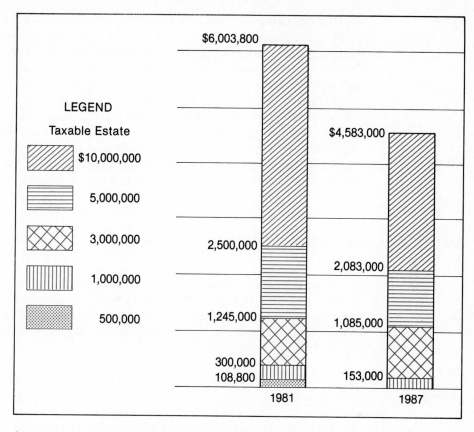

Source: *Economic Recovery Tax Act of 1981* (Chicago: Arthur Andersen & Co., 1981), p. 13.

substantial annual gifts, even wealthy people can significantly reduce the amount of property subject to federal estate taxes.

You can reduce estate taxes greatly, or eliminate them altogether, by making gifts before you die and by using the **unlimited marital deduction** for both gifts and bequests to your spouse. In this way the property is not subject to federal estate taxes in your estate. Property not in your estate is also free of expenses such as attorney's fees and probate charges, so additional savings are generated.

STATE INHERITANCE TAXES

Like estate and gift taxes, state inheritance taxes can reduce the value of your estate unless you have done prior planning. An inheritance tax is levied in all states except Nevada and is paid by the inheritors of the property rather than by the estate of the property owner. Inheritance taxes are progressive—that is, the percentage of the tax increases as the size of the estate increases. Most states provide for reduced tax rates or exemptions (e.g., $10,000) for certain eligible heirs. The closer the relationship between the deceased and the heir, the less the inheritance tax and the greater the exemptions. Through proper planning you can reduce the full burden of inheritance taxes. For example, you can bequeath cash to a favorite heir so that inherited property will not have to be sold to pay inheritance taxes; forced sale of the property would defeat the purpose of the bequest. The federal estate tax is reduced, up to stated limits, by amounts paid in state inheritance taxes.

WAYS OF TRANSFERRING PROPERTY AT DEATH

After the owner's death, property may be distributed in one of five ways. First, if a person dies without leaving a will, the property is distributed according to the laws of the state. Property may also be distributed through wills, through joint ownership of property, through beneficiary designations in life insurance, and through trusts.

Intestacy

Unfortunately, many people die without leaving a will—that is, they die **intestate.** In this case their property is distributed according to the laws of the state in which they resided. In other words, if you don't make a will, the state makes one for you. State laws vary; in the absence of a will and without some research into the laws of the state in which you live and in which your property is located, you can have little knowledge of, or control over, how your property will be divided at your death.

For several reasons you should not die intestate. First, you cannot take into consideration special situations in which you may need to give greater protection to some of your beneficiaries. For example, you may have a handicapped child who will need special care, or you may want to give more to a child who is attending college than to another child who is working and is well established financially. The law cannot take special needs into consideration.

Second, without a will you will not be able to name an executor to administer the distribution of your estate. If you have not done so, the court will appoint an administrator, but perhaps not the same person you would have chosen and perhaps even a stranger to your particular situation.

Third, although the laws of the state in which you live determine how personal property is distributed, the laws of states in which you own real estate govern how the property is distributed. Because the laws of several states may be involved, settlement of your estate may be more costly and complicated.

Finally, if you have minor children, they will inherit a share of any real estate, and this real estate cannot be sold or leased except through a legally appointed guardian. Disposition of real estate and other property of minors can be simplified by means of a will in which you specify a guardian.

Wills

A **will** is a formal, written document that specifies your wishes regarding the disposition of your estate after your death. It also names a guardian for any minor children. A will is the ideal vehicle for ensuring that your wishes in regard to the handling of your estate will be followed. A person who makes a will is called a **testator** because the will, a public document, is said to be a **testament,** or evidence, of the person's last wishes.

VALIDITY

To be valid, a will must meet certain requirements set forth by state law. Most importantly, it must be the product of a person of sound mind who is not under the undue influence of others and who is free of fraud. The testator must possess the legal capacity to make a will or the capacity to know that a will is being made. The testator must understand what property is being willed and must recognize the rights of those expecting to benefit from the will by referring to these persons in the will, even if nothing is given to them.

In most cases wills must be written and signed by the testator. Except in unusual cases, oral wills are not valid, nor are wills not properly witnessed; a will must usually have at least two witnesses. In most cases a beneficiary who is also a witness cannot receive bequests in excess of what would be forthcoming in the absence of a valid will. Thus, third parties who are not members of your family or otherwise beneficiaries should witness your will.

Most states set a minimum age requirement for making a valid will. An attorney should be employed to draw up your will so that you are sure it is valid in your state. If you move to another state, you should have your will checked for validity under that state's laws.

You should keep your will in a safe place—for example, in your safe deposit box or in the office of the attorney who drew it up—but be sure to make its location known to family members. Do not keep an original will lying around the house; it is possible to tamper with a will.

A will can be changed, rewritten, or revoked at any time. Minor alterations are usually made by means of amendments called **codicils.** Divorce revokes a will automatically, as does the subsequent marriage of the testator.

PROBATE COSTS

The word *probate* stems from the Latin verb *probare,* meaning "to prove." **Probate costs** are court costs involved in proving the validity of a will. Probate costs include filing fees, estate appraisers' fees, publication fees (notification to creditors to make their claims known), compensation for the attorneys and executors who administer the estate until it can be distributed to the heirs, and inheritance and estate taxes. For example, executors' and attorneys' fees may run between 2 and 4 percent of the value of the estate. Typically a will takes seven or eight months to probate, mainly because of the time required to notify all parties—creditors, for example—to make their claims.

PROVISIONS

Wills can be of varying degrees of complexity. Very simple wills may contain only a few sentences in which one spouse simply leaves everything to the other. Commonly both spouses make out similar documents and leave their respective property to each other. If they have children, however, special needs for the children may be mentioned. For example, a guardian of the estate will be named for minor children. An automobile and a home may be willed to one child, while a business interest may be willed to another.

Wills usually direct that all debts of the testator be paid—an unnecessary provision, since the court will order these debts paid in any event. The will normally appoints an executor or executrix to supervise settlement of the will and to carry out its provisions. The will can excuse the executor from providing surety for a court bond ordered to ensure honest and faithful performance. The will can empower the executor to perform certain functions—for example, operating a business until it can be disposed of.

A will sometimes attempts to impose limitations upon bequests. For example, the will may direct that an heir be disinherited if he or she marries a certain person, or that a child not inherit anything until the child reaches a certain age. Sometimes a will attempts to disinherit beneficiaries who would normally be expected to receive property—for example, children or next of kin. If the court holds that the testator understood the significance of such action, the disinheritance will usually stand. Courts will normally not enforce provisions deemed to be against public policy. For example, Joseph Pulitzer put his newspaper the *New York World* into a trust and decreed that the paper should never be sold. The beneficiaries were able to break the trust and merge the paper with another firm after convincing the court that otherwise the paper would go bankrupt.[1]

If you leave your spouse less than he or she would have been able to obtain had no will be drawn, the spouse may renounce the will. The court will probably allow the minimum legal benefit—for example, a half-interest in the real estate and a share of the personal property.

A will should recognize everyone who might be expected to benefit from it, whether or not each person is to inherit. For example, if you have three children and fail to mention a fourth child born after your will was made, the court will usually treat the situation as though no will had existed and will provide the fourth child a legal share equal to the shares of the other children.

Wills should contain some provision covering the possibility of simultaneous, or nearly simultaneous, death of both husband and wife. A simple statement can be used—for example, "I leave my estate to my wife if she survives me and does not die within six months of my death." Without such a provision, if a husband dies and his wife also dies a short time afterward, two sets of probate costs will be incurred. When the husband dies, the property enters the wife's estate; when she dies, the property passes to her heirs and thus sets off another round of probate costs. However, a provision dealing with the possibility of simultaneous death ensures that the estate will pass directly to other heirs with only one set of courts costs.

The following example demonstrates why it is wise for both husband and wife to make wills at the same time. A husband and wife were killed in the same accident; the husband had a will, but the wife did not. The husband had left everything to the wife. The wife's relatives brought suit, arguing that the husband had died first and the wife had inherited everything; therefore they, the wife's relatives, should get the estate. The husband's relatives brought a similar suit, arguing that the wife had died first. No one gained except the attorneys who represented the various parties. Had both husband and wife drawn wills, no such problem would have arisen.

Your attorney should keep an original copy of your will to facilitate probate. You should also maintain and keep available an inventory of your assets to facilitate the settlement of your estate and to ease the burden that would otherwise fall on your spouse. You should leave your spouse instructions concerning significant financial and real estate matters (see Exhibit 16–4). These instructions should include your wishes in regard to a funeral; names and locations of insurance policies, securities, real estate deeds, notes, debts, and wills; and names and addresses of your attorney, life insurance agent, bank trustee, accountant, and employers. Your instructions should contain special

---

1. *Money* (August, 1981), p. 98.

EXHIBIT 16–4
What to Include
in a Letter of
Instruction

GET IT DONE THIS YEAR: YOUR LETTER OF INSTRUCTION

Here's the organized way to give your family all the facts about your finances—and have a basic tool for your own money management.

A "Letter of Instruction" tells someone else everything he or she needs to know in order to handle your personal affairs efficiently, if anything happens to you.

Everybody who has (or needs) a will should write a Letter of Instruction. But it's not only useful to others when you die: It can also be vital to *you* if you should be incapacitated by serious illness or injury. And it simplifies your own continuing money management now.

The Letter isn't a will or a substitute. A will tells an executor *how* to dispose of property and personal effects, and has the force of law behind it. The Letter helps that person do the best possible job.

People put off writing the Letter. It is—frankly—a *big* job of organizing and detail gathering. So here's a set of worksheets to help.

Don't try to write the Letter all at once. You won't complete it. Tackle one section at a time. Allow a month if needed. If you get stopped because of indecision or an emotional block, put that section aside and move on. The object is to keep going, to get as much on paper as possible.

It's best when a husband and wife do the Letter together. If your spouse won't or can't collaborate, go it alone.

Though personal and intimate, addressed to your spouse, grown child, lawyer or other executor, the Letter should be clear to any person who may have to find and work with your papers. Be specific about locations—"in safe deposit box" or "in bottom-left drawer of my study desk" or "in red file in attic."

This is the time to go into personal desires too intimate for a will: your thoughts about a child's education, desire that a person be given a specific piece of jewelry or other personal effect or small treasure, any preferences for your own funeral.

Once it's done, send one copy to your lawyer or executor, clip another to your copy of your will, keep the original in the desk drawer your family will turn to first. Update annually—that's much easier than the first Letter—and get on to the business of living with a clear, and organized, conscience.

OVERVIEW: YOU CAN EXPECT 1

From my employer:_____

(person to contact, dept., phone)

_____

(life insurance)   (profit sharing)

_____

(accident insurance)   (pension plan)

_____

(other benefits)

From insurance companies:_____

_____

(total amount)

From social security:_____

(lump sum plus monthly benefits)

From the Veterans' Administration:_____

(you must inform the VA)

From other sources:_____

UPDATED:_____(date)

FIRST THINGS TO DO 2

1. Call _____to help.

(relative or friend)
2. Notify my employer:_____

(phone)
3. Make arrangements with funeral home. See page_____
4. Request at least 10 copies of the death certificate. (Usually, the funeral director will get them.)
5. Call our lawyer: _____

(name, phone)
6. Contact local social security office.
7. Get and process my insurance policies.
8. Notify bank that holds our home mortgage.

SOCIAL SECURITY 3

Name:_____Card number:_____
Location of cards: _____
File a claim immediately to avoid possibility of losing any benefit checks.
Call local social security office for appointment. They tell you what to bring. _____

(phone)

Expect a lump sum of about $_____, plus continuing benefits for children under 18, or until 22 for full-time students.

A spouse may receive benefits until children reach 18, between ages 50–60 if disabled, or if over 60.

SAFE DEPOSIT BOX* 4

Bank:_____
Address: _____
In whose name: _____Number:_____
Location of key:_____
List of contents:_____

*In the event of death the bank must by law seal the owner's box as soon as notified, even if jointly owned.

LOCATION OF PERSONAL PAPERS 5

Last will and testament: _____

Birth and baptismal certificates: _____

Communion, confirmation certificates:_____

School diplomas:_____

Marriage certificate: _____

Military records:_____

Naturalization papers:_____

Other (adoption, etc.):_____

CHECKING ACCOUNTS* 6

Bank: _____
Address: _____
Name(s) on account: _____
Account number:_____
Kind of account:_____

Repeat to cover all accounts of husband and wife. Canceled checks and statements are in:

_____

(location)

*The bank must by law freeze the owner's account as soon as notified of death, even if jointly owned, and will probably open a new account in your name.

SAVINGS ACCOUNTS AND CERTIFICATES* 7

Bank:_____
Address: _____
Name(s) on account: _____
Account number:_____Type:_____
Location of passbook (or certificate receipt):_____
Any special instructions:_____
Repeat for each account.

*The bank must by law freeze the owner's account as soon as notified of death, even if jointly owned.

DOCTORS' NAMES/ADDRESSES 8

Doctors:_____

(name, address, phone, whose doctor)

Dentists: _____
Pediatrician: _____
Children's dentist: _____

CREDIT CARDS   9

All credit cards in my name should be canceled or converted to your name.
Company: _____ Phone:_____
Address: _____
Name on card: _____ Number:_____
Location of card: _____
Repeat for each card.

LOANS OUTSTANDING
(OTHER THAN MORTGAGES)   10

Bank: _____
Address: _____
Name on loan: _____
Account number: _____
Monthly payment: _____
Location of papers: _____
_____(and payment book, if any)
Collateral, if any: _____
Life insurance on loan? ☐ (yes) ☐ (no)
Repeat for all loans.

CAR   11

Year, make and model: _____
Body type:_____
Cylinders: _____
Color:_____
Identification number: _____
Location of papers: _____
_____(title, registration)
Repeat for each car.

INCOME TAX RETURNS   12

Location of all previous returns — federal, state, local:
_____
_____
Our tax preparer:_____
_____(name, address, phone)
Check: Are estimated quarterly taxes due?

SPECIAL WISHES   13

1. _____
2. _____

PERSONAL EFFECTS   14

I would like certain people to be given these personal effects.
                                    Person
My white jade pendant _____
My camera _____
My photography books_____
All my other books_____
Other items_____

INVESTMENTS   15

Repeat for each investment
Stocks
Company: _____
Name on certificate(s): _____
Number of shares:_____
Certificate number(s):_____
Purchase price and date:_____
Location of certificate(s): _____
Bonds/Notes/Bills
Issuer: _____
Issued to: _____
                    (owner)
Face amount: _____ Bond number:_____
Purchase price and date:_____
Maturity date: _____
Location of certificate:_____
Mutual Funds
Company: _____
Name on account:_____
No. of shares or units: _____
Location of statements, certificates:_____
Other investments (US Savings Bonds, etc.)
For each list amount invested; to whom issued; issuer; maturity date and other applicable data; location of certificates and other vital papers.

CEMETERY AND FUNERAL   16

Cemetery Plot
Location: _____
When purchased: _____
Deed number: _____
Location of deed:_____
Other information: _____
_____(perpetual care, etc.)
Facts for Funeral Director (Bring this with you, and bring cemetery deed if possible)
My Full Name: _____
Residence: _____ Phone:_____
Marital status:_____ Spouse:_____
Date of Birth: _____ Birthplace:_____
Father's name and birthplace:_____
Mother's maiden name:_____
Length of residence in state:____ In USA:_____
Military service: ☐ (yes) ☐ (no) When:_____
(Bring veteran's discharge papers if possible.)
Social security number:__ Occupation: ____
Life insurance: (Bring policy if proceeds will be used for funeral expenses)
_____
        (company names and policy numbers)

FUNERAL PREFERENCES   17

My choice of funeral home (if any): _____
Type of funeral preferred: _____
Other personal preferences or desires:_____

RELATIVES, FRIENDS TO INFORM   18

List names, addresses, phone numbers: _____

LIFE INSURANCE   19

Location of all policies: _____
To collect benefits, a copy of the death certificate must be sent to each company.

Policy: _____
                              (amount)
Whose life is insured: _____

Insurance company: _____

Company address: _____

Kind of policy: _____Policy number:_____

Beneficiaries: _____

Issue date: _____ Maturity date:_____

How paid out:_____

Your other options on payout:_____

Other special facts:_____

Repeat information above for each policy.

For _____in veterans' insurance
         (amount)
call local Veterans' Administration office: _____
                                            (phone)

OTHER INSURANCE   20

Accident
Company:_____
Address: _____
Policy number:_____
Beneficiary:_____
Coverage:_____
Location of policy: _____
Agent, if any: _____

Car, Home and Household
Give information below for each policy.
Coverage:_____
Company:_____
Address: _____
Policy number:_____
Location of policy:_____
Term (when to renew):_____
Agent, if any: _____

Medical
Coverage:_____
Company:_____
Address: _____
Policy number:_____
Location of policy:_____
Through employer or other group: _____
Agent, if any: _____
Repeat for all medical insurance policies.
Mortgage insurance: See page_____ .

HOUSE, CONDO OR CO-OP   21

In whose name: _____
Address: _____
Lot:_____Block:_____On map called:_____
Other discriptions needed:_____
Our lawyer at closing:_____
                        (name)   (address)
Location of statement of closing, policy of title insurance, deed, land survey, etc.:

_____

Mortgage
Held by:_____
                      (bank)
Amount of original mortgage: _____
Date taken out: _____
Amount owed now: _____
Method of payment: _____
Location of payment book, if any (or payment statements):_____
Life insurance on mortgage?   □ (yes)   □ (no)
If yes, policy number: _____
Location of policy: _____
Notify bank of my death; the unpaid amount will be paid automatically by the insurance, and the house is owned free and clear.

Veteran's exemption claim, if any
Location of documentation papers: _____
Annual Amount:_____
Contact local tax assessor for documentation needed or more information.

House Taxes
Amount:_____
Location of receipts: _____

Cost of House
Initial buying price: _____
Purchase closing fee: _____
Other costs to buy: (real estate agent, legal, taxes, etc.):_____
Improvements as of_____come to:_____
                      (date)   (total so far)
Itemized House Improvements
Improvement: _____Cost:_____Date:_____
Location of bills:_____
If Renting: Lease?   □ (yes)   □.(no)
Lease location: _____Expires:_____
                                          date

IMPORTANT WARRANTIES, RECEIPTS   22

Item:_____

(warranty location)   (receipt location)

Source: Reprinted by courtesy of *Consumer Views,* published by Citibank, Vol. XI, No. 3 (Citicorp.), March 1980.

wishes regarding the disposition of matters not covered in your will—for example, special counsel on problems in your business or investment plans could be included. You should also include a description of all benefits in connection with your employment—for example, survivors' benefits, annuities, health insurance, and life insurance—and the name and address of a contact person at your job.

Joint Ownership

A third method of passing property after the owner's death is through registering title to the property in the **joint tenancy** of two or more persons (usually husband and wife), who each then own an undivided interest in the property. If one owner dies, the surviving owner automatically becomes the sole owner of the property; no legal action is necessary to transfer title. The formal name for this arrangement is **joint tenancy with right of survivorship**.[2] This form of ownership is commonly used for land, automobiles, residences, bank accounts, and securities. Joint tenancy is a convenient and automatic way to pass property; it is perhaps the most widely used arrangement for property ownership.

DISADVANTAGES OF JOINT OWNERSHIP

Although joint tenancy transfers property with a minimum of expense or delay, the system has some disadvantages. Perhaps the main danger of registering property jointly is that nothing may remain to be transferred by will. In this case the purposes of your will may be defeated, since most of your goods pass to the joint owner directly. Other people whom you may have wanted to benefit from the will may be left out.

Another disadvantage of joint ownership of property is that it may cause a surviving owner to owe a larger income tax upon subsequent sale of the property. Since 1982 the estate of the first to die has included half of any jointly held property; the other half has been considered the property of the survivor. The half received by the survivor is valued at the original cost to the joint owners, and the other half is valued at its current market value. Upon resale of the property, the capital gains income tax owed by the survivor will be higher than if the property had been registered solely in the name of the deceased spouse. If the property had been so registered, the cost basis (current market value) of the property would normally have been higher than the original cost, which must be used as the basis if the property is jointly held. If the property is registered in the name of the husband, usually the

---

2. Joint tenancy should be differentiated from **tenancy in common**, a form of joint ownership in which each owner possesses a divisible interest that may be sold or given to third parties.

first to die, the wife will inherit at the higher cost basis and thus pay a lower income tax upon resale (see Exhibit 16–5).

Another income tax disadvantage of joint tenancy is that all of the income stemming from jointly owned property will be taxed to the surviving owner, who may already be in a high tax bracket. If the property is not held in joint tenancy, it may be distributed to several beneficiaries (e.g., children) who may be in lower tax brackets. Property may be distributed through trusts set up to split the income into several low tax brackets.

Beneficiary Designation

Beneficiary designation is a method of property transfer that applies only to one type of property—life insurance. Through a beneficiary designation the person named as beneficiary will receive the policy's funds or income directly from the life insurer without any legal action being required. Such benefits are not subject to probate costs.

You may name a primary beneficiary to receive the policy proceeds and may also name contingent beneficiaries in case the primary beneficiary is no longer living at the time of distribution. A beneficiary designation is subject to change during the life of the owner of the policy. The owner may change beneficiaries at any time unless the existing beneficiary has been named irrevocably.

Proceeds of life insurance are exempt from the claims of creditors. You can also protect the proceeds of life insurance from claims of your beneficiary's creditors by including a **spendthrift trust clause** in your insurance. Moreover, you can direct that the life insurance proceeds be paid in installments rather than in a lump sum. Thus you provide the beneficiary with an income, but no one, not even the beneficiary, can reach the principal, borrow on it, or sell his or her interest in the principal. The clause protects the improvident beneficiary from actions that might cause loss of the inheritance.

The person named as beneficiary will receive the life insurance proceeds even if the owner of the policy might later have preferred that some other person receive them. For example, if you are divorced and remarried and you fail to name your new spouse as beneficiary of your life insurance, your first spouse, not your second, will benefit.

Trusts

The final way of transferring property is through a legal instrument known as a **trust**, which allows property to be owned by one party for the benefit of another. Under the trust the legal owner of the property is the **trustee**, often a bank or a trust company. The **equitable owner** of the property is the person

EXHIBIT 16-5
How Should
Family Property
Be Owned?

WHOSE CAR?
If a family car is jointly owned and insured, both owners in some states can be sued for an accident, and the property of each is then subject to court judgment.

SAVINGS AND CHECKING
It's usually practical to have a joint checking account large enough to handle running household needs, and permit each spouse to get some cash in an emergency and make payments when one is absent.

But in many states banks must stop access to joint accounts as soon as notified of the death of a joint depositor, which can create serious problems for a surviving spouse.

So experts often advise separate checking and savings accounts as well—especially if you keep really large cash balances. In a two-income family that also can avoid having to trace who put in and took out how much in case of a possible gift or estate tax.

STOCKS AND BONDS
Because of recent changes in the tax law there are now few, if any, income-tax advantages to joint ownership of stocks, bonds (including U.S. Savings Bonds), certificates of deposit and other such investments.

Divided or separate ownership removes the sometimes trouble-some need for both signatures to sell an investment. It also avoids most, if not all, the legal and tax problems of joint ownership—which we'll come to.

THE SAFE-DEPOSIT BOX
Many spouses hold safe-deposit boxes jointly. Note that joint registration of the box doesn't create joint ownership of the property inside—whether jewelry or intangible property—stocks, bonds, insurance policies, etc.

And be aware that in many states, banks must seal the box on the death of a joint owner as soon as notified—until local tax authorities inventory the contents.

CREDITORS' RIGHTS
Whether you own property jointly or separately can limit or expand the rights of your creditors—while you are alive and in case of either spouse's death. The legalities and impact are intricate and vary from state to state. Get expert advice about your state's rules.

YOUR HOME
A family home usually is the biggest and is the most common joint asset of husband and wife. Most advisers, for psychological reasons and perceptions of equity, agree with joint ownership of a marital home if it isn't of extraordinary value.

Source: Reprinted by courtesy of *Consumer Views,* published by Citibank, Vol. XI, No. 10, October 1980.

named to receive the benefits—that is, the beneficiary. The trust has certain terms or instructions to guide the trustee in the management of the property. A **living trust** is one set up during your life to manage property for your benefit. A **testamentary trust** becomes activated only at your death and benefits the persons you have named. (You may also set up a trust and become its major beneficiary.) A testamentary trust is a substitute for a will as far as the property put into the trust is concerned.

The usual purpose of a trust is to relieve beneficiaries—for example, the surviving spouse and the children—of the burden of managing property. In the case of children, a common arrangement is for the trustee to hold and invest funds until the child reaches the age of twenty-one. Occasionally a trustee is instructed to provide support payments until the child is twenty-one and then to transfer some proportion (say, one-half) of the principal to the child. The remainder would be transferred when the child reached age twenty-five or thirty. Property placed in trust for a spouse can be very beneficial to a person who is inexperienced in making investments or in managing property. The trust can be set up to make income distributions to enable the beneficiary to maintain a "customary living standard." Thus, if inflation or other circumstances increase the beneficiary's need for funds, the trustee can accommodate this need.

The protection a trust can offer a beneficiary is illustrated by the following case. A mother had left an estate in trust for a daughter. The trustee had instructions to make discretionary extra distributions "as needed." The daughter came to the trustee and asked for $45,000 to help her new husband purchase an automobile dealership. The trustee checked into the husband's background and refused to grant the daughter's request. The daughter was quite bitter, but in a few weeks she came back to thank the trustee. The husband had proved to be irresponsible and the marriage had broken up.

A frequently used provision, the **spendthrift trust clause,** protects the beneficiary from creditors' claims against the property held in the trust. If this clause is included in a trust, a creditor may not bring a legal action for debts of the beneficiary that could be satisfied with trust property. (Creditors can attack income received from the trust once the income has been paid to the beneficiary and is no longer identified as part of the trust.) Thus, actions taken by a beneficiary will not endanger the financial security the trust creator intended the beneficiary to have, because a spendthrift beneficiary is protected from the consequences of imprudent financial actions. The spendthrift trust clause is often employed in life insurance trusts.

People often use trusts during their lifetimes to make a gift of property and thus eliminate property for estate tax purposes and to reduce current income taxes. For example, you may place income-producing property (stocks, bonds, or real estate) into an **irrevocable trust** for the benefit of your children. Income from the property is then taxed to the children, who are in a tax bracket lower than yours. To escape taxes, you must set up the trust on an irrevocable basis—that is, the legal rights to the income or to the property

"Would your answer be different if I set up a trust for you first?"

The Bettman Archive, Inc.

will no longer belong to you. Certain types of trusts, sometimes called **Clifford trusts,** transfer property irrevocably for a minimum period of ten years, after which the property reverts to the original donor.

The use of trusts to settle estates can minimize estate and inheritance taxes as well as probate costs. Trusts can relieve the heirs of considerable responsibility for managing property; they are particularly valuable if the heirs are inexperienced in matters of investment and financial management. At the same time the trust agreement can be flexible enough to cover contingencies like an heir's unexpected need for additional funds because of inflation, medical expenses, or changed marital status.

LIMITATIONS OF TRUSTS

One limitation or disadvantage of a trust is that the trustee does not guarantee the absolute safety of your principal; nor does the trustee promise some minimum income, as does the life insurer. An insured annuity, for example, guarantees payments for the life of the beneficiary, no matter how long the beneficiary lives. The insurer guarantees safety of the principal amount of the proceeds left with it. All the trustee promises is to use "due diligence" in making investments and to perform duties honestly and faithfully. The beneficiary obtains the advantages of any investment gains but also runs the risk of investment losses.

Another disadvantage is that the trustee charges a predetermined fee for services. Fees might average one-half of 1 percent per year of the average assets in the trust. The life insurer makes no additional charge for management of life insurance proceeds under the settlement options.

LIFE INSURANCE TRUSTS

A special type of trust, a **life insurance trust,** may be set up to receive the proceeds of life insurance and to distribute them to beneficiaries in a more flexible and beneficial manner than is possible through the life insurer. Settlement options in life insurance tend to be rigid; the amount paid through them remains fixed according to the particular option selected (see Chapter 5). Life insurers traditionally guarantee only a small rate of return (3.0 to 4.5 percent), far below levels obtainable elsewhere at comparable safety and liquidity. The trustee can be given considerable flexibility in making payments to beneficiaries—for example, the trustee can adjust amounts to take account of inflation. Life insurers are unwilling to accept such a responsibility.

To set up a life insurance trust, you need only sign a trust agreement saying that after your death your life insurance policies are to be paid to the trustee, who shall invest them prudently and disperse the income and principal "as follows"—that is, according to your specifications. The trustee then is made the beneficiary of the policies. You can retain the rights to revoke or to amend the trust, to borrow on the policies, and to continue to collect any other benefits from the policies. If you do not want to give the trustee sole authority over how the funds will be used, you can have the trustee guided by recommendations from an outside consultant, whom you can name as a part of the trust agreement.

SPLIT ESTATE (MARITAL DEDUCTION) TRUSTS

A common use of trusts is to manage estates in such a way as to minimize the effect of estate taxes. The 1981 changes in estate taxes eliminated most people's need to consider estate taxes in their financial planning; the $600,000 exemption (available after 1987) is high enough so that most persons will no longer be subject to estate taxes. Nevertheless, **split estate trusts,** sometimes called **marital deduction trusts,** remain relevant for many financial planners. If a person leaves an estate worth more than $600,000—that is, an estate large enough to make a spouse's property subject to estate taxes after the spouse's death—the amount of assets available to children or other heirs will thus be reduced. In such a case a split estate trust can be employed to reduce or avoid the subsequent tax. As many as three trusts can be set up—one under the total control of the spouse, one under limited control of the spouse, and a third, called the **family trust interest,** that controls sufficient property to qualify for the full tax credit available to the decedent under the 1981 Economic Recovery Tax Act (see Exhibit 16–1). The beneficiaries of the family trust interest are usually children or heirs other than the surviving spouse.

The surviving spouse receives property under two trusts. The first, called the **standard marital trust,** gives the spouse complete rights to all income and the right to use up the principal. The second, called the **terminable marital interest trust,** only gives the spouse the right to the trust income; the spouse may not use up any of the principal. The person setting up the trust may decide who will ultimately inherit the principal after the death of the spouse. If these and other conditions are met, no estate taxes are due and no probate expenses are incurred on assets in the second trust when the surviving spouse dies; yet the arrangement allows the surviving spouse to enjoy a lifetime income from the trust.

LIFE INSURANCE AND ESTATE PLANNING

Life insurance and life insurance options have many important uses in connection with retirement and estate planning. First, life insurance can provide liquidity in an estate and thus facilitate payments that must be met with cash. Life insurance offers a secure way to provide needed cash; the cost—that is, the premiums—normally represents only a fraction of the total policy proceeds. Thus, the estate settlement expenses can be met with *fractional dollars.* For example, if you will need $100,000 to meet the cash expenses, you can purchase an ordinary life policy at age forty for approximately $2,130 annually on a nondividend basis. Your cost represents only 2.13 percent of the face amount payable at death. Sufficient liquidity in your estate helps preserve the value of your other assets because it eliminates the need for the forced sale of assets to pay expenses.

Gifts of life insurance made during your lifetime minimize federal estate and inheritance taxes. Moreover, life insurance beneficiaries receive all proceeds free of probate costs since life insurance proceeds pass outside the will. Proceeds payable to named beneficiaries also escape state inheritance taxes, though they are subject to federal estate taxes.

Through settlement options you can make proceeds of life insurance fill an income need of your beneficiaries. For example, by instructing the insurer to hold all proceeds under the interest option until a given time and then to pay your child the accumulated balance in equal installments over a four-year period, you can guarantee that the child will be paid a given sum each year for college expenses. You can achieve similar results by making life insurance payable under a trust arrangement. In either case you can be assured that the stated amount of funds will be on hand in cash at the time it is needed.

The income tax advantages of life insurance should not be forgotten in estate planning. Dividends paid under life insurance policies are considered not as taxable income but as a return of a portion of the premium paid. Death proceeds escape income taxes; life insurance settled under an annuity option is taxed under the relatively favorable annuity rule discussed in Chapter 15.

If you cash in your life insurance and receive more than the sum of total premiums paid in, you must recognize any gain as ordinary income in the year that you cash it in. However, the cost basis of the policy is the sum of the gross premiums that you paid, which include a charge for life insurance death protection. In effect, you receive a deduction for the cost of life insurance protection when you surrender the policy for its cash value. For example, assume that you purchase a $100,000 ordinary life insurance policy for $2,100 a year. After twenty years you have paid in $42,000 (20 × $2,100), an amount approximately equal to the cash value in the policy. If you cash in your policy, you will have no taxable gain. Therefore, the cost of the life insurance protection included in the $2,100 premium has been "tax-free."

Another advantage of life insurance in estate planning is that cash values are exempt from the claims of your creditors. Moreover, these proceeds can also be made exempt from the claims of your beneficiary's creditors through use of the spendthrift trust clause.

Life insurance can be used to add to the value of your estate. You can borrow the cash value of life insurance at relatively favorable interest rates (currently between 6 and 8 percent) and reinvest elsewhere at higher rates of return (see Chapter 14). You can also use dividends under participating policies to purchase additional life insurance coverage—an economical and effective means of enlarging your estate, since you pay no sales commissions on new coverage. Dividends on life insurance may amount to 20 percent of the premiums and can increase your estate substantially over a period of time. If you need to do so, you can borrow the cash values of the paid-up coverage.

TIPS ON ESTATE PLANNING

1. You and your spouse should make your wills simultaneously and coordinate the two. The disadvantages of dying without a will are too great and defeat many of the gains that result from effective estate planning. Have your wills drawn by a qualified attorney and reviewed periodically as your circumstances change—particularly after a move to another state. In addition

to your will, you should draw up a letter of instruction dealing with significant financial, real estate, and personal matters not covered by your will.

2. Coordinate provisions of your will with an overall financial and estate plan. Be certain that joint ownership of property does not defeat the purpose of your will be allowing most of your property to pass outside the will.

3. Consider the financial effects of estate and gift taxes on the property available to your heirs. Take advantage of the unlimited marital deduction and of annual gift tax exemptions.

4. Consider the merits of trusts as a means of transferring property at your death. Trusts allow your estate to be free of a second set of probate and estate taxes when your spouse dies; thus, your children ultimately inherit a larger proportion of your estate. Income tax can be reduced by spreading your assets among several beneficiaries in tax brackets lower than yours. Trusts do not guarantee against investment losses nor guarantee to pay a minimum return to beneficiaries; trustees also make a charge for their services.

5. Maintain an inventory of your assets to facilitate the settlement of your estate and ease the burden that would otherwise fall on your spouse to perform this task. Keep such records handy. Let your attorney keep an original copy of your wills to facilitate their probate.

6. Consider the advantages of using life insurance to increase the liquidity of your estate and to minimize taxes. You can employ the settlement and dividend options of life insurance to fill an income need of your beneficiaries. You can also add to the value of your estate by borrowing the cash values of your life insurance and reinvesting the funds elsewhere at higher rates of return.

7. Leave instructions to your spouse on significant financial and estate matters (see Exhibit 16–5). These instructions should include concern for funeral wishes, names and locations of insurance policies, securities, real estate deeds, notes and debts, and wills. The names and addresses of your attorney, life insurance agent, bank trustee, accountant, employers, and others should be listed. Special wishes regarding the disposition matters not covered in the will should be made known. For example, special counsel on problems in your business or investment plans could be included.

8. A description of all benefits in connection with your employment should be summarized. These will include survivor benefits, annuities, health insurance, life insurance, and other benefits. The name and address of a contact person at your job should be listed.

SUMMARY

1. The objectives of estate planning include providing for: (a) the accumulation and distribution of property, (b) the minimization of transfer costs and taxes, and (c) sufficient liquidity to meet all reasonable needs of beneficiaries including the payment of taxes and other obligations.

2. The changes in estate tax law included in the Economic Recovery Act of 1981 were extensive. A much larger estate than previously may pass free of estate taxes. Larger tax-free gifts became possible, enabling estate planners to distribute more property during their lifetime. The tax rates on estates and gifts were also reduced and will not exceed 50 percent after 1985.

3. Five major methods exist for transferring property at death: intestacy, through wills, by joint ownership, by beneficiary designation in life insurance, and through trusts. Each method has its advantages and limitations. A careful analysis of each method is required for optimum estate planning.

4. A major pitfall in estate planning is the failure to create a valid will. Without a will, property passes to others in accordance with the laws of each state, and these laws may not be in accordance with the wishes of the estate planner.

5. The trust device, including split estate trusts, has many uses, particularly for planning larger estates. Often used in conjunction with life insurance, the trust offers great flexibility in meeting various needs of the estate planner.

6. There are still important uses for and advantages of life insurance in estate planning, even though the 1981 tax law changes may reduce the amount of life insurance needed.

REVIEW QUESTIONS

1. List and explain the main advantages of estate planning.

2. A trust officer stated: "We often run into homemade wills that are defective. We tell everyone with whom we talk to have their wills drawn by an attorney. One well-educated woman, a doctor, made a will in her own handwriting and had it witnessed by two witnesses, as she should have done. Her ideas were pretty well set forth in it, but she neglected to take care of one provision that the law required. The result was that the will had to be brought before the court for judicial interpretation. The cost was about $450, and I expect that the will would have cost her about $25 to have it drawn in the first place."
   (a) Give some examples of errors that invalidate a will.
   (b) Do you believe that an attorney should draw up your will?

3. In his will a certain man reportedly disinherited his two sisters because they had voted for Franklin D. Roosevelt twenty-five years earlier. In another will a man provided for a fund to educate deserving young persons in the art of bank robbery. A woman willed money to her daughter on the condition that the daughter never marry. In another case a man insulted a beneficiary by including in his will the following provision: "To my dishonest nephew, John, I leave five dollars to squander at his favorite gambling den."
   (a) Which of the above provisions might be held invalid? Why? Which provisions are probably valid?
   (b) What advantages of having a will do the above provisions illustrate?

4. Sometimes individuals keep cash or negotiable securities in safe deposit boxes because they assume that such assets will escape taxation upon the owner's death, since only the intended beneficiary will have the keys to the box. Criticize this procedure.

5. In a letter to a family counselor, a woman stated that her mother-in-law, in bidding her good-bye at an airport when she and her husband were leaving on vacation, asked: "Did you make a will in case something happens to both of you at the same time?" The woman had been upset at this remark and asked the counselor for advice. How would you have replied?

6. An estate planner stated: "Many state laws provide that the estate of a childless person who dies intestate must be split between the surviving spouse and the relatives of the deceased—parents, brothers, or sisters. Many husbands and wives have been shocked to learn that they had to divide with their former spouse's relatives money that the relatives themselves had given them."
   (a) Discuss the implications of this statement as it applies to sound financial planning.
   (b) Name some of the disadvantages of dying intestate.

7. A financial writer stated: "The trust that coordinates an executive's company benefits with his or her will is especially important, since only an executive's house, bank accounts, and investments normally go to the heirs under will. The will misses benefits. Furthermore, benefits will not become a part of the property of any trust set up under the will. The solution is a "fringe benefits trust" to receive all company benefits. This trust can be instructed to "pour over" all assets, at the employee's death, into another trust set up under the will." Why should the value of employee benefits be placed in a trust rather than paid outright to the employee's family?

8. (a) Why might it be advantageous to borrow on your life insurance policies as a means of increasing your estate?
   (b) What assumptions underlie a successful borrowing program?

9. (a) Why is estate liquidity important?
   (b) What problems does sufficient liquidity overcome?

10. How does life insurance reduce estate settlement costs?

11. Explain which method you would choose as a means of providing your child with funds for education: a trust fund or the settlement options of a life insurance policy.

12. Why should you always specify that the spendthrift trust clause be included in a life insurance contract that employs installment options?

CASE PROBLEMS

I. Effect of the New Estate Tax Law on the Need for Life Insurance

A financial writer stated that under the 1981 estate tax changes, many people will plan to lower their life insurance coverage and invest the money elsewhere. "Some policyholders may reduce their existing coverage . . . others will buy less than they had planned. And those with modest estates may forgo policies altogether. . . . This will definitely affect the need for insurance, particularly with small estates. . . . In 1986, when the law would fully take effect, some 6,500 estates would then be taxed annually, compared to 56,000 in 1981." Life insurers are said now to be developing a new type of joint life policy that would be payable at the death of the second named policyholder rather than at the death of the first.

QUESTIONS

1. Why should the demand for life insurance be lessened under the new estate tax schedules? Can you think of any reasons why the demand may not be reduced as much as the writer quoted believes?

2. Why would a joint life policy be more appropriate than a regular life insurance policy in light of the new estate tax laws?

II. Using Gifts to Reduce Estate Taxes

One way to reduce estate taxes is to make gifts during your lifetime that reduce the estate subject to tax at your death. A university made the following appeal: "Consider making gifts in appreciated securities rather than cash. You benefit and the donee benefits more. For example, suppose that you are considering a gift of $1,000. If you donate stock now valued at $1,000 for which you originally paid $100, you can deduct $1,000 as a charitable gift against your income tax. If you wish to retain the stock, take the cash that you otherwise might have given to the university and repurchase the stock for $1,000. The repurchased stock is valued at $1,000 (not $100) as a basis from which to compute future gains if it is ultimately sold. Thus, you reduce your future income tax liability. If you are in the 50 percent tax bracket, you will save $500 in income taxes when you make the gift. The true cost of your gift is thus $600, made up of the original $100 cost plus the tax savings.

QUESTIONS

1. Evaluate the university's appeal. Can you make a tax-deductible gift and still receive investment income, until your death, on the property being donated?

2. Evaluate the following alternative to the university's plan: Sell the stock for its $1,000 current value, pay the tax, take out a paid-up life insurance policy with the remaining sum, and donate the policy to the university.

III. Preparing a Will

Regarding specific provisions of a will, a financial writer recommended the following steps: (1) Include a clause revoking all previous wills. (2) Consider owning U.S. Treasury bonds to pay estate taxes, since these bonds will be valued at par for tax payments, regardless of their current market value. (3) Make a specific disposition of your tangible personal property; otherwise your executor may have to pay a professional appraiser to value items in your estate and then have them sold at a nominal price. (4) Have married women witness to your will, since they are less likely to change their names than are single women. (5) Don't list assets in your will; you might dispose of them during your lifetime. (6) Give fractions or percentages of your estate to your beneficiaries.

QUESTIONS

1. Evaluate the writer's advice on a point-by-point basis.

2. Do you disagree with any of the writer's instructions?

IV. Executor's Fees

In 1975 a statement of executor fees for the state of Georgia appeared as follows:

EXECUTOR'S OR ADMINISTRATOR'S FEE—Statutory rates are as follows: 2½% of cash received; 2½% of cash disbursed; and reasonable fee not exceeding 3% of property delivered in kind. Additional compensation may be allowed for extraordinary services.

Example follows of customary rates under agreement with testator: 2½% of cash received; 2½% of cash disbursed; 2½% of property delivered in kind. Distribution fee: 2½% on value of assets distributed.

QUESTIONS

1. Estimate potential executor's fees, including both initial fees and distribution fees, for an estate made up as follows: cash, $10,000; listed securities, $10,000; farm, $500,000; apartment house, $150,000; personal property, $100,000; life insurance, $5000.

2. What problems might exist in settlement of the above estate? Discuss potential solutions.

APPENDIX

HOW TO USE INTEREST TABLES

Problems in financial planning may be solved by using small computers or calculators, which may be set for any interest rate, including fractional interest rates, and for any period of months or years. For convenience, interest tables are included in this book to facilitate the solving of problems requiring the use of frequently quoted rates of interest and periods of time. Examples given below show how to use these tables.

Compound Interest (Appendix A-1)

If $1,000 in the bank earns 10% interest compounded annually, what will the account's value be in five years? In ten years?

Referring to the 10% column in Appendix A-1 on page 533, we see that $1 will accumulate to $1.610510 in five years and to $2.593742 in ten years. Thus, $1,000 will accumulate to $1,615.10 (1.61510 × $1,000) in five years and to $2,593.74 (2.593742 × $1,000) in ten years.

Sinking Fund (Appendix A-2)

If you wish to save $1,000, how much must you deposit each period at 12% interest compounded annually to reach your goal at the end of five years? At the end of ten years?

Referring to the 12% column in Appendix A-2 on page 534, we discover that the appropriate factors are .157409 for each period if the savings period is five years, and .056984 if the savings period is ten years. Multiplying these factors by $1,000, we obtain the answer: $157.41 annually for five years, or $56.98 annually for ten years.

Periodic Savings Accumulation (Annuities) (Appendix A-3)

If you save $1,000 annually and earn 14% interest compounded annually, how much will your savings fund amount to after five years? After ten years?

Referring to the 14% column of Appendix A-3 on page 535, we discover that $1 saved annually will accumulate to $6.610104 in five years, and to

$19.337295 in ten years. Thus, $1,000 will accumulate to $6,610.10 in five years, and to $19,337.30 in ten years.

Present Value of a Sum (Appendix A–4)

If a debtor promises to pay you $1,000 one year from today, and money is worth 10%, what is the value of this promise now? To find the answer, look at the 10% column of Appendix A–4 on page 536, and discover that the present value of $1 to be paid one year from now is $.909090. That is, if you had $.909090 today and deposited it in the bank at 10%, the account would accumulate in value to $1 after one year. We can check the result by looking at the compound interest table in Appendix A–1 and multiplying the $.909090 by the factor 1.10 shown in the 10% column. The answer: $1.

Similarly, the amount you must have on hand now to accumulate to $1,000 in five years at 10% interest compounded annually is $620.92 ($1,000 × the 5-year factor of .620921 = $620.92).

Present Value of an Annuity (Appendix A–5)

Suppose you wish to fund a promise to pay someone a sum of money for varying periods of time. To know the value of the promise, you must find the present value of an annuity. For example, how much must you pay an insurance company now for the insurer to guarantee payments to you of $1,000 a year for five years, or ten years, if money earns 12% interest compounded annually? Referring to the 12% column of Appendix A–5 on page 537, we see that $3.604776 must be on hand now for the insurer to be able to pay out $1 a year for five years. The last payment will just exhaust the account, reducing its balance to zero. Accordingly, you must deposit $3,604.78 now ($1,000 × 3.604776) to be able to receive $1,000 a year for five years.

The 10-year factor is 5.650223. Thus, you must deposit $5,650.22 now for the insurer to pay you $1,000 a year for ten years.

Amortization of a Loan (Appendix A–6)

If you wish to find how much the periodic payment must be to pay off a loan and its interest over some fixed period at a given interest rate, refer to the numbers shown in Appendix A–6 on page 538. In this table it is assumed that payments occur at the end of each period. For example, if a home mortgage loan is 14%, refer to the 14% column. If the mortgage loan of $40,000 is to be paid off over twenty-five years, an annual payment of $40,000 ×

.145498, or $5,819.92, will be required; the first payment will be due at the end of the first year.

If the problem is to find the payment to amortize a 14% loan in twenty years, multiply the 20-year factor of .150986 times $40,000 to obtain $6,039.44. Note that you must increase your annual payment by only $219.52 ($6,039.44 − $5,819.92) to reduce the payment period from twenty-five to twenty years, because most of the early payment in amortized loans is composed of interest.

Loan amortization tables can also be used to solve the following type of problem: "How much can I receive from an insurer over a ten-year period if the cash value of the policy is $10,000, assuming the insurer is paying 10% interest?" Look up the 10-year factor under the 10% interest column to obtain .162745. Multiply $10,000 times .162745 to obtain the answer of $1,627.45 a year for ten years, with the first annual payment due at the end of the first year.

Monthly Life Income (Life Annuities) (Appendix A–7)

Appendix A–7 contains typical rates offered by life insurers in 1981 under insurance proceeds. These numbers approximate the cost of purchasing a life annuity. For example, suppose a sixty-five-year-old man wishes to know how much income can be guaranteed for life, on varying bases, for a payment of $20,000. Assume that his wife is the same age. Referring to Appendix A–7 on page 539, we see that for each $1,000, the following monthly life incomes can be obtained:

No refund at death (straight life annuity)	$8.79
Ten years certain and life	7.21
Installment refund	8.18
Joint life income, 2/3 to the survivor and ten years certain, female age 65	5.59

Multiply these amounts by 20, and the subsequent totals by 12, to obtain the expected amounts of monthly and annual income, respectively.

			Monthly Income			Annual Income
No refund at death	20 × $8.79 =		$175.80	× 12 =		$2,109.60
Ten years certain and life	20 × 7.21 =		144.20	× 12 =		1,730.40
Installment refund	20 × 8.18 =		163.60	× 12 =		1,963.20
Joint life income	20 × 5.59 =		111.80	× 12 =		1,341.60

Some insurers quote annuity prices as so much for each $10 of monthly life income. Monthly life incomes (MLI) per $1,000 (shown in Appendix A–7) may be converted to the basis "price of $10 monthly life income" by the following procedure:

$$\frac{\$1,000}{\text{MLI}} \times 10 = \text{price of each } \$10 \text{ of MLI}.$$

For example, assume that the insurer offers $8.79 per month for life for each $1,000. Then

$$\frac{\$1,000}{\$8.79} \times 10 = \$1,138, \text{ the price of each } \$10 \text{ of monthly life income}.$$

APPENDIX A–1   Compound Interest: Amount to Which $1 Will Compound if Left at Interest for Different Periods

Periods	5.00%	8.00%	10.00%	11.00%	12.00%	13.00%	14.00%	15.00%	Periods
1	1.050 000	1.080 000	1.100 000	1.110 000	1.120 000	1.130 000	1.140 000	1.150 000	1
2	1.102 500	1.166 400	1.210 000	1.232 100	1.254 400	1.276 900	1.299 600	1.322 500	2
3	1.157 625	1.259 712	1.331 000	1.367 631	1.404 928	1.442 897	1.481 544	1.520 875	3
4	1.215 506	1.360 488	1.464 100	1.518 070	1.573 519	1.630 473	1.688 960	1.749 006	4
5	1.276 281	1.469 328	1.610 510	1.685 058	1.762 341	1.842 435	1.925 414	2.011 357	5
6	1.340 095	1.586 874	1.771 561	1.870 414	1.973 822	2.081 951	2.194 972	2.313 060	6
7	1.407 100	1.713 824	1.948 717	2.076 160	2.210 681	2.352 605	2.502 268	2.660 019	7
8	1.477 455	1.850 930	2.143 588	2.304 537	2.475 963	2.658 444	2.852 586	3.059 022	8
9	1.551 328	1.999 004	2.357 947	2.558 036	2.773 078	3.004 041	3.251 948	3.517 876	9
10	1.628 894	2.158 924	2.593 742	2.839 420	3.105 848	3.394 567	3.707 221	4.045 557	10
11	1.710 339	2.331 638	2.853 116	3.151 757	3.478 549	3.835 861	4.226 232	4.652 391	11
12	1.795 856	2.518 170	3.138 428	3.498 450	3.895 975	4.334 523	4.817 904	5.350 250	12
13	1.885 649	2.719 623	3.452 271	3.883 280	4.363 493	4.898 011	5.492 411	6.152 787	13
14	1.979 931	2.937 193	3.797 498	4.310 440	4.887 112	5.534 752	6.261 349	7.075 705	14
15	2.078 928	3.172 169	4.177 248	4.784 589	5.473 565	6.254 270	7.137 937	8.137 061	15
16	2.182 874	3.425 942	4.594 972	5.310 894	6.130 393	7.067 325	8.137 249	9.357 620	16
17	2.292 018	3.700 018	5.054 470	5.895 092	6.866 040	7.986 077	9.276 464	10.761 263	17
18	2.406 619	3.996 019	5.559 917	6.543 552	7.689 965	9.024 267	10.575 169	12.375 453	18
19	2.526 950	4.315 701	6.115 909	7.263 343	8.612 761	10.197 422	12.055 692	14.231 771	19
20	2.653 297	4.660 957	6.727 499	8.062 311	9.646 293	11.523 087	13.743 489	16.366 537	20
21	2.785 962	5.033 833	7.400 249	8.949 165	10.803 848	13.021 089	15.667 578	18.821 517	21
22	2.925 260	5.436 540	8.140 274	9.933 574	12.100 310	14.713 830	17.861 039	21.644 745	22
23	3.071 523	5.871 463	8.954 302	11.026 267	13.552 347	16.626 628	20.361 584	24.891 457	23
24	3.225 099	6.341 180	9.849 732	12.239 156	15.178 628	18.788 090	23.212 206	28.625 176	24
25	3.386 354	6.848 475	10.834 705	13.585 463	17.000 064	21.230 542	26.461 915	32.918 952	25
26	3.555 672	7.396 353	11.918 176	15.079 864	19.040 072	23.990 512	30.166 583	37.856 795	26
27	3.733 456	7.988 061	13.109 994	16.738 649	21.324 880	27.109 279	34.389 905	43.535 314	27
28	3.920 129	8.627 106	14.420 993	18.579 901	23.883 866	30.633 485	39.204 492	50.065 611	28
29	4.116 135	9.317 274	15.863 092	20.623 690	26.749 930	34.615 838	44.693 121	57.575 453	29
30	4.321 942	10.062 656	17.449 402	22.892 296	29.959 922	39.115 897	50.950 158	66.211 771	30

APPENDIX A–2   Sinking Fund: Amount That Must Be Saved Each Period to Accumulate to $1

Periods	5.00%	8.00%	10.00%	11.00%	12.00%	13.00%	14.00%	15.00%	Periods
1	1.000 000	1.000 000	1.000 000	1.000 000	1.000 000	1.000 000	1.000 000	1.000 000	1
2	0.487 804	0.480 769	0.476 190	0.473 933	0.471 698	0.469 483	0.467 289	0.465 116	2
3	0.317 208	0.308 033	0.302 114	0.299 213	0.296 348	0.293 521	0.290 731	0.287 976	3
4	0.232 011	0.221 920	0.215 470	0.212 326	0.209 234	0.206 194	0.203 204	0.200 265	4
5	0.180 974	0.170 456	0.163 797	0.160 570	0.157 409	0.154 314	0.151 283	0.148 315	5
6	0.147 017	0.136 315	0.129 607	0.126 376	0.123 225	0.120 153	0.117 157	0.114 236	6
7	0.122 819	0.112 072	0.105 405	0.102 215	0.099 117	0.096 110	0.093 192	0.090 360	7
8	0.104 721	0.094 014	0.087 444	0.084 321	0.081 302	0.078 386	0.075 570	0.072 850	8
9	0.090 690	0.080 079	0.073 640	0.070 601	0.067 678	0.064 868	0.062 168	0.059 574	9
10	0.079 504	0.069 029	0.062 745	0.059 801	0.056 984	0.054 289	0.051 713	0.049 252	10
11	0.070 388	0.060 076	0.053 963	0.051 121	0.048 415	0.045 841	0.043 394	0.041 068	11
12	0.062 825	0.052 695	0.046 763	0.044 027	0.041 436	0.038 986	0.036 669	0.034 480	12
13	0.056 455	0.046 521	0.040 778	0.038 150	0.035 677	0.033 350	0.031 163	0.029 110	13
14	0.051 023	0.041 296	0.035 746	0.033 228	0.030 871	0.028 667	0.026 609	0.024 688	14
15	0.046 342	0.036 829	0.031 473	0.029 065	0.026 824	0.024 741	0.022 808	0.021 017	15
16	0.042 269	0.032 976	0.027 816	0.025 516	0.023 390	0.021 426	0.019 615	0.017 947	16
17	0.038 699	0.029 629	0.024 664	0.022 471	0.020 456	0.018 608	0.016 915	0.015 366	17
18	0.035 546	0.026 702	0.021 930	0.019 842	0.017 937	0.016 200	0.014 621	0.013 186	18
19	0.032 745	0.024 127	0.019 546	0.017 562	0.015 763	0.014 134	0.012 663	0.011 336	19
20	0.030 242	0.021 852	0.017 459	0.015 575	0.013 878	0.012 353	0.010 986	0.009 761	20
21	0.027 996	0.019 832	0.015 624	0.013 837	0.012 240	0.010 814	0.009 544	0.008 416	21
22	0.025 970	0.018 032	0.014 005	0.012 313	0.010 810	0.009 479	0.008 303	0.007 265	22
23	0.024 136	0.016 422	0.012 571	0.010 971	0.009 559	0.008 319	0.007 230	0.006 278	23
24	0.022 470	0.014 977	0.011 299	0.009 787	0.008 463	0.007 308	0.006 302	0.005 429	24
25	0.020 952	0.013 678	0.010 168	0.008 740	0.007 499	0.006 425	0.005 498	0.004 699	25
26	0.019 564	0.012 507	0.009 159	0.007 812	0.006 651	0.005 654	0.004 800	0.004 069	26
27	0.018 291	0.011 448	0.008 257	0.006 989	0.005 904	0.004 979	0.004 192	0.003 526	27
28	0.017 122	0.010 488	0.007 451	0.006 257	0.005 243	0.004 386	0.003 664	0.003 057	28
29	0.016 045	0.009 618	0.006 728	0.005 605	0.004 660	0.003 867	0.003 204	0.002 651	29
30	0.015 051	0.008 827	0.006 079	0.005 024	0.004 143	0.003 410	0.002 802	0.002 300	30

APPENDIX A–3   Periodic Savings Accumulation (Annuities): Amount to Which $1 per year Will Accumulate if Saved for Different Periods

Periods	5.00%	8.00%	10.00%	11.00%	12.00%	13.00%	14.00%	15.00%	Periods
1	1.000 000	1.000 000	1.000 000	1.000 000	1.000 000	1.000 000	1.000 000	1.000 000	1
2	2.050 000	2.080 000	2.100 000	2.110 000	2.120 000	2.130 000	2.140 000	2.150 000	2
3	3.152 500	3.246 400	3.310 000	3.342 100	3.374 400	3.406 900	3.439 600	3.472 500	3
4	4.310 125	4.506 112	4.641 000	4.709 731	4.779 328	4.849 797	4.921 144	4.993 375	4
5	5.525 631	5.866 600	6.105 100	6.227 801	6.352 847	6.480 270	6.610 104	6.742 381	5
6	6.801 912	7.335 929	7.715 610	7.912 859	8.115 189	8.322 705	8.535 518	8.753 738	6
7	8.142 008	8.922 803	9.487 171	9.783 274	10.089 011	10.404 657	10.730 491	11.066 799	7
8	9.549 108	10.636 627	11.435 888	11.859 434	12.299 693	12.757 263	13.232 760	13.726 819	8
9	11.026 564	12.487 557	13.579 476	14.163 972	14.775 656	15.415 707	16.085 346	16.785 841	9
10	12.577 892	14.486 562	15.937 424	16.722 008	17.548 735	18.419 749	19.337 295	20.303 718	10
11	14.206 787	16.645 487	18.531 167	19.561 429	20.654 583	21.814 316	23.044 516	24.349 275	11
12	15.917 126	18.977 126	21.384 283	22.713 187	24.133 133	25.650 177	27.270 748	29.001 667	12
13	17.712 982	21.495 296	24.522 712	26.211 637	28.029 109	29.984 700	32.088 653	34.351 917	13
14	19.598 631	24.214 920	27.974 983	30.094 917	32.392 602	34.882 711	37.581 064	40.504 705	14
15	21.578 563	27.152 113	31.772 481	34.405 358	37.279 714	40.417 464	43.842 414	47.580 410	15
16	23.657 491	30.324 282	35.949 729	39.189 948	42.753 280	46.671 734	50.980 352	55.717 472	16
17	25.840 366	33.750 225	40.544 702	44.500 842	48.883 673	53.739 060	59.117 601	65.075 093	17
18	28.132 384	37.450 243	45.599 173	50.395 935	55.749 714	61.725 138	68.394 065	75.836 357	18
19	30.539 003	41.446 263	51.159 090	56.939 488	63.439 680	70.749 406	78.969 234	88.211 810	19
20	33.065 953	45.761 964	57.274 999	64.202 832	72.052 442	80.946 828	91.024 927	102.443 582	20
21	35.719 251	50.422 921	64.002 499	72.265 143	81.698 735	92.469 916	104.768 417	118.810 119	21
22	38.505 214	55.456 754	71.402 749	81.214 309	92.502 583	105.491 005	120.435 995	137.631 637	22
23	41.430 474	60.893 295	79.543 024	91.147 883	104.602 893	120.204 836	138.297 035	159.276 383	23
24	44.501 998	66.764 758	88.497 326	102.174 150	118.155 240	136.831 465	158.658 620	184.167 840	24
25	47.727 098	73.105 939	98.347 059	114.413 307	133.333 869	155.619 555	181.870 826	212.793 017	25
26	51.113 453	79.954 414	109.181 765	127.998 770	150.333 934	176.850 097	208.332 742	245.711 969	26
27	54.669 126	87.350 767	121.099 941	143.078 635	169.374 006	200.840 610	238.499 326	283.568 765	27
28	58.402 582	95.338 829	134.209 935	159.817 285	190.698 886	227.949 889	272.889 232	327.104 079	28
29	62.322 711	103.965 935	148.630 929	178.397 186	214.582 753	258.583 575	312.093 724	377.169 691	29
30	66.438 847	113.283 210	164.494 022	199.020 877	241.332 683	293.199 214	356.786 846	434.745 145	30

APPENDIX A–4 Present Value of a Sum: Amount That Must Be on Hand Now to Accumulate to $1 at the End of Different Periods

Periods	5.00%	8.00%	10.00%	11.00%	12.00%	13.00%	14.00%	15.00%	Periods
1	0.952 380	0.925 925	0.909 090	0.900 900	0.892 857	0.884 955	0.877 192	0.869 565	1
2	0.907 029	0.857 338	0.826 446	0.811 622	0.797 193	0.783 146	0.769 467	0.756 143	2
3	0.863 837	0.793 832	0.751 314	0.731 191	0.711 780	0.693 050	0.674 971	0.657 516	3
4	0.822 702	0.735 029	0.683 013	0.658 730	0.635 518	0.613 318	0.592 080	0.571 753	4
5	0.783 526	0.680 583	0.620 921	0.593 451	0.567 426	0.542 759	0.519 368	0.497 176	5
6	0.746 215	0.630 169	0.564 473	0.534 640	0.506 631	0.480 318	0.455 586	0.432 327	6
7	0.710 681	0.583 490	0.513 158	0.481 658	0.452 349	0.425 060	0.399 637	0.375 937	7
8	0.676 839	0.540 268	0.466 507	0.433 926	0.403 883	0.376 159	0.350 559	0.326 901	8
9	0.644 608	0.500 248	0.424 097	0.390 924	0.360 610	0.332 884	0.307 507	0.284 262	9
10	0.613 913	0.463 193	0.385 543	0.352 184	0.321 973	0.294 588	0.269 743	0.247 184	10
11	0.584 679	0.428 882	0.350 493	0.317 283	0.287 476	0.260 697	0.236 617	0.214 943	11
12	0.556 837	0.397 113	0.318 630	0.285 840	0.256 675	0.230 705	0.207 559	0.186 907	12
13	0.530 321	0.367 697	0.289 664	0.257 514	0.229 174	0.204 164	0.182 069	0.162 527	13
14	0.505 067	0.340 461	0.263 331	0.231 994	0.204 619	0.180 676	0.159 709	0.141 328	14
15	0.481 017	0.315 241	0.239 392	0.209 004	0.182 696	0.159 890	0.140 096	0.122 894	15
16	0.458 111	0.291 890	0.217 629	0.188 292	0.163 121	0.141 496	0.122 891	0.106 864	16
17	0.436 296	0.270 268	0.197 844	0.169 632	0.145 644	0.125 217	0.107 799	0.092 925	17
18	0.415 520	0.250 249	0.179 858	0.152 822	0.130 039	0.110 812	0.094 561	0.080 805	18
19	0.395 733	0.231 712	0.163 507	0.137 677	0.116 106	0.098 063	0.082 948	0.070 265	19
20	0.376 889	0.214 548	0.148 643	0.124 033	0.103 666	0.086 782	0.072 761	0.061 100	20
21	0.358 942	0.198 655	0.135 130	0.111 742	0.092 559	0.076 798	0.063 826	0.053 130	21
22	0.341 849	0.183 940	0.122 845	0.100 668	0.082 642	0.067 963	0.055 987	0.046 200	22
23	0.325 571	0.170 315	0.111 678	0.090 692	0.073 787	0.060 144	0.049 112	0.040 174	23
24	0.310 067	0.157 699	0.101 525	0.081 704	0.065 882	0.053 225	0.043 080	0.034 934	24
25	0.295 302	0.146 017	0.092 295	0.073 608	0.058 823	0.047 101	0.037 790	0.030 377	25
26	0.281 240	0.135 201	0.083 905	0.066 313	0.052 520	0.041 683	0.033 149	0.026 415	26
27	0.267 848	0.125 186	0.076 277	0.059 741	0.046 893	0.036 887	0.029 078	0.022 969	27
28	0.255 093	0.115 913	0.069 343	0.053 821	0.041 869	0.032 644	0.025 507	0.019 973	28
29	0.242 946	0.107 327	0.063 039	0.048 487	0.037 383	0.028 888	0.022 374	0.017 368	29
30	0.231 377	0.099 377	0.057 308	0.043 682	0.033 377	0.025 565	0.019 627	0.015 103	30

APPENDIX A–5 Present Value of an Annuity: Present Value of a Promise to Pay $1 a Year for Different Periods

Periods	5.00%	8.00%	10.00%	11.00%	12.00%	13.00%	14.00%	15.00%	Periods
1	0.952 381	0.925 926	0.909 091	0.900 901	0.892 857	0.884 956	0.877 193	0.869 565	1
2	1.859 410	1.783 265	1.735 537	1.712 523	1.690 051	1.668 102	1.646 661	1.625 709	2
3	2.723 248	2.577 097	2.486 852	2.443 715	2.401 831	2.361 153	2.321 632	2.283 225	3
4	3.545 951	3.312 127	3.169 865	3.102 446	3.037 349	2.974 471	2.913 712	2.854 978	4
5	4.329 477	3.992 710	3.790 787	3.695 897	3.604 776	3.517 231	3.433 081	3.352 155	5
6	5.075 692	4.622 880	4.355 261	4.230 538	4.111 407	3.997 550	3.888 668	3.784 483	6
7	5.786 373	5.206 370	4.868 419	4.712 196	4.563 757	4.422 610	4.288 305	4.160 420	7
8	6.463 213	5.746 639	5.334 926	5.146 123	4.967 640	4.798 770	4.638 864	4.487 322	8
9	7.107 822	6.246 888	5.759 024	5.537 048	5.328 250	5.131 655	4.946 372	4.771 584	9
10	7.721 735	6.710 081	6.144 567	5.889 232	5.650 223	5.426 243	5.216 116	5.018 769	10
11	8.306 414	7.138 964	6.495 061	6.206 515	5.937 699	5.686 941	5.452 733	5.233 712	11
12	8.863 252	7.536 078	6.813 692	6.492 356	6.194 374	5.917 647	5.660 292	5.420 619	12
13	9.393 573	7.903 776	7.103 356	6.749 870	6.423 548	6.121 812	5.842 362	5.583 147	13
14	9.898 641	8.244 237	7.366 687	6.981 865	6.628 168	6.302 488	6.002 072	5.724 476	14
15	10.379 658	8.559 479	7.606 080	7.190 870	6.810 864	6.462 379	6.142 168	5.847 370	15
16	10.837 770	8.851 369	7.823 709	7.379 162	6.973 986	6.603 875	6.265 060	5.954 235	16
17	11.274 066	9.121 638	8.021 553	7.548 794	7.119 630	6.729 093	6.372 859	6.047 161	17
18	11.689 587	9.371 887	8.201 412	7.701 617	7.249 670	6.839 905	6.467 420	6.127 966	18
19	12.085 321	9.603 599	8.364 920	7.839 294	7.365 777	6.937 969	6.550 369	6.198 231	19
20	12.462 210	9.818 147	8.513 564	7.963 328	7.469 444	7.024 752	6.623 131	6.259 331	20
21	12.821 153	10.016 803	8.648 694	8.075 070	7.562 003	7.101 550	6.686 957	6.312 462	21
22	13.163 003	10.200 744	8.771 540	8.175 739	7.644 646	7.169 513	6.742 944	6.358 663	22
23	13.488 574	10.371 059	8.883 218	8.266 432	7.718 434	7.229 658	6.792 057	6.398 837	23
24	13.798 642	10.528 758	8.984 744	8.348 137	7.784 316	7.282 883	6.835 137	6.433 771	24
25	14.093 945	10.674 776	9.077 040	8.421 745	7.843 139	7.329 985	6.872 927	6.464 149	25
26	14.375 185	10.809 978	9.160 945	8.488 058	7.895 660	7.371 668	6.906 077	6.490 564	26
27	14.643 034	10.935 165	9.237 223	8.547 800	7.942 554	7.408 556	6.935 155	6.513 534	27
28	14.898 127	11.051 078	9.306 567	8.601 622	7.984 423	7.441 200	6.960 662	6.533 508	28
29	15.141 074	11.158 406	9.369 606	8.650 110	8.021 806	7.470 088	6.983 037	6.550 877	29
30	15.372 451	11.257 783	9.426 914	8.693 793	8.055 184	7.495 653	7.002 664	6.565 980	30

APPENDIX A-6 Amortization of a Loan: Amount Needed to Pay Off Principal and Interest of Loans over Different Periods

Periods	5.00%	8.00%	10.00%	11.00%	12.00%	13.00%	14.00%	15.00%	Periods
1	1.050 000	1.080 000	1.100 000	1.110 000	1.120 000	1.130 000	1.140 000	1.150 000	1
2	0.537 805	0.560 769	0.576 190	0.583 934	0.591 698	0.599 484	0.607 290	0.615 116	2
3	0.367 209	0.388 034	0.402 115	0.409 213	0.416 349	0.423 522	0.430 731	0.437 977	3
4	0.282 012	0.301 921	0.315 471	0.322 326	0.329 234	0.336 194	0.343 205	0.350 265	4
5	0.230 975	0.250 456	0.263 797	0.270 570	0.277 410	0.284 315	0.291 284	0.298 316	5
6	0.197 017	0.216 315	0.229 607	0.236 377	0.243 226	0.250 153	0.257 157	0.264 237	6
7	0.172 820	0.192 072	0.205 405	0.212 215	0.219 118	0.226 111	0.233 192	0.240 360	7
8	0.154 722	0.174 015	0.187 444	0.194 321	0.201 303	0.208 387	0.215 570	0.222 850	8
9	0.140 690	0.160 080	0.173 641	0.180 602	0.187 679	0.194 869	0.202 168	0.209 574	9
10	0.129 505	0.149 029	0.162 745	0.169 801	0.176 984	0.184 290	0.191 714	0.199 252	10
11	0.120 389	0.140 076	0.153 963	0.161 121	0.168 415	0.175 841	0.183 394	0.191 069	11
12	0.112 825	0.132 695	0.146 763	0.154 027	0.161 437	0.168 986	0.176 669	0.184 481	12
13	0.106 456	0.126 522	0.140 779	0.148 151	0.155 677	0.163 350	0.171 164	0.179 110	13
14	0.101 024	0.121 297	0.135 746	0.143 228	0.150 871	0.158 667	0.166 609	0.174 688	14
15	0.096 342	0.116 830	0.131 474	0.139 065	0.146 824	0.154 742	0.162 809	0.171 017	15
16	0.092 270	0.112 977	0.127 817	0.135 517	0.143 390	0.151 426	0.159 615	0.167 948	16
17	0.088 699	0.109 629	0.124 664	0.132 471	0.140 457	0.148 608	0.156 915	0.165 367	17
18	0.085 546	0.106 702	0.121 930	0.129 843	0.137 937	0.146 201	0.154 621	0.163 186	18
19	0.082 745	0.104 128	0.119 547	0.127 563	0.135 763	0.144 134	0.152 663	0.161 336	19
20	0.080 243	0.101 852	0.117 460	0.125 576	0.133 879	0.142 354	0.150 986	0.159 761	20
21	0.077 996	0.099 832	0.115 624	0.123 838	0.132 240	0.140 814	0.149 545	0.158 417	21
22	0.075 971	0.098 032	0.114 005	0.122 313	0.130 811	0.139 479	0.148 303	0.157 266	22
23	0.074 137	0.096 422	0.112 572	0.120 971	0.129 560	0.138 319	0.147 231	0.156 278	23
24	0.072 471	0.094 978	0.111 300	0.119 787	0.128 463	0.137 308	0.146 303	0.155 430	24
25	0.070 952	0.093 679	0.110 168	0.118 740	0.127 500	0.136 426	0.145 498	0.154 699	25
26	0.069 564	0.092 507	0.109 159	0.117 813	0.126 652	0.135 655	0.144 800	0.154 070	26
27	0.068 292	0.091 448	0.108 258	0.116 989	0.125 904	0.134 979	0.144 193	0.153 526	27
28	0.067 123	0.090 489	0.107 451	0.116 257	0.125 244	0.134 387	0.143 664	0.153 057	28
29	0.066 046	0.089 619	0.106 728	0.115 605	0.124 660	0.133 867	0.143 204	0.152 651	29
30	0.065 051	0.088 827	0.106 079	0.115 025	0.124 144	0.133 411	0.142 803	0.152 300	30

APPENDIX A-7   Monthly Life Income for Males per $1,000 Proceeds (5.75% Interest Assumption)

Age	Without Refund	Ten Years Certain and Life	Installment Refund	Joint Life Income, ⅔ to Survivor, 120 Months Certain	
				Female Age	Amount Paid if Male Is Age 65 at Death
45	$ 6.03	$5.81	$ 5.90	—	—
46	6.12	5.87	5.98	—	—
47	6.22	5.94	6.06	—	—
48	6.32	6.01	6.15	—	—
49	6.42	6.08	6.24	—	—
50	6.53	6.15	6.33	50	$4.59
51	6.64	6.23	6.42	51	4.65
52	6.76	6.30	6.52	52	4.71
53	6.88	6.38	6.62	53	4.77
54	7.00	6.45	6.73	54	4.83
55	7.14	6.53	6.84	55	4.90
56	7.27	6.61	6.96	56	4.96
57	7.42	6.69	7.08	57	5.02
58	7.57	6.77	7.21	58	5.08
59	7.73	6.85	7.35	59	5.15
60	7.90	6.93	7.49	60	5.22
61	8.06	6.99	7.61	61	5.29
62	8.22	7.05	7.74	62	5.36
63	8.40	7.10	7.88	63	5.43
64	8.59	7.16	8.03	64	5.51
65	8.79	7.21	8.18	65	5.59
66	8.99	7.25	8.33	66	5.67
67	9.20	7.28	8.48	67	5.75
68	9.42	7.31	8.64	68	5.83
69	9.66	7.34	8.81	69	5.91
70	9.92	7.37	8.99	70	5.99
71	10.20	7.39	9.19	71	6.07
72	10.50	7.41	9.39	72	6.14
73	10.82	7.42	9.61	73	6.22
74	11.16	7.44	9.83	74	6.29
75	11.52	7.45	10.07	75	6.37
76	11.91	7.46	10.33	—	—
77	12.32	7.46	10.60	—	—
78	12.76	7.46	10.89	—	—
79	13.23	7.47	11.19	—	—
80	13.72	7.47	11.51	—	—

Note: Monthly life income for a female is approximately equal to that shown for a male five years younger.

GLOSSARY

A

Accidental death and dismemberment insurance (AD&D). A health insurance policy reimbursing an insured up to specified amounts for accidental death or dismemberment.

Accidental means clause. A clause in health insurance policies specifying that a loss must have occurred by accidental methods in order to be covered. The clause requires that in the act that immediately preceded the loss, something unusual, unexpected, and abnormal happened.

Add-on interest. A method of calculating interest charged for the use of credit in which the charges are related to the total amount borrowed. Unlike annual percentage rate (APR), add-on rates do not reflect the declining credit in use over the life of the loan. Under Regulation 2, add-on interest is no longer permitted.

Aggressive growth fund. A type of fund that emphasizes price appreciation in common stocks as a portfolio objective.

All-risk coverage. A feature of HO-3 and HO-5 Homeowners Insurance whereby a loss is a covered loss unless specifically excluded by the policy.

All-savers certificate. A savings certificate, available from September 30, 1981, to January 1, 1983, on which interest is exempt from federal income taxation, subject to lifetime limit of $1,000 ($2,000 if filing jointly). The yield is set at 70 percent of the U.S. Treasury bill rate.

American agency system. Distribution system for property-liability insurance utilizing independent middlemen, usually called local agents.

American Stock Exchange (AMEX). Major national marketplace for trading securities of firms which are usually smaller than firms whose shares are traded on the larger and better known New York Stock Exchange.

Amortized loan. Any loan that is paid off in periodic installments and includes varying portions of principal and interest.

Annual percentage rate (APR). The finance charge over a full year expressed as a percentage that reflects all costs of the credit transaction as required by the Truth-in-Lending Act.

Annual-premium annuity. An annuity in which the annuity right is established by the payment of an annual premium for a given period.

Annuitant. The person receiving the rent (payments) of an annuity.

Annuity. A contract providing for a series of payments (rent) to a person known as an annuitant.

Annuity rate. The price of an annuity; usually expressed as the sum required to purchase an income of some amount such as $100 or $1,000 a month for life.

Annuity rent. The term applied to payments under an annuity.

Annuity rule. An income tax rule governing the way in which a pension benefit is taxed.

Ask price. The price at which an owner offers to sell securities.

Assigned risk plan. Plan under which one can obtain insurance after having been rejected for coverage by individual insurers. In "assigned risk" all insurers operating in a given state usually share proportionately in premiums and losses.

Audit. Review of financial statements or income tax returns to determine accuracy and validity.

Automatic premium loan clause. A clause in life insurance providing that an insurer may automatically borrow from whatever accumulated cash values the policy may have to pay a premium when due. The interest rate is usually specified in the insurance contract.

Average indexed monthly earnings (AIME). A concept used in Social Security to determine the size of retirement and other Social Security benefits. AIME is an inflation-adjusted measure of career-average monthly wages.

B

Balanced fund. An investment company whose investment objective is to invest both in stocks and bonds.

Balloon loan. An installment loan in which regular monthly repayments do not fully extinguish the loan. The final required payment is significantly larger than the regular payments.

Bank card. A credit card issued by a specific bank, such as VISA or Master-Card.

Bankruptcy. A court action declaring a person free of most types of debt, due to the inability of the person to pay.

Bar chart. Chart in which measurements are depicted by rectangles of varying lengths.

Bear. A speculator who believes that the stock market will go down.

Bear market. A market in which prices are falling.

Beneficiary. A person named to benefit from property under a will, trust, or life insurance policy.

Beneficiary designation. Individual named to receive property, e.g., beneficiary of a life insurance policy or a trust.

Best's ratings. Annual ratings assigned to insurance companies by the Best organization to enable independent and objective judgments of financial stability and service to policyholders.

Beta. A statistical measure of the market risk attributable to a given stock. If a stock's beta is more than 1.0, it is expected to fluctuate more widely than stock prices generally; the converse is true for a stock with a beta of less than 1.0.

Bid price. The price at which a buyer offers to buy securities.

Blackout period. The period during which survivors are not entitled to Social Security income, beginning when the youngest dependent child reaches 16 and ending when the survivor reaches age 60.

Blind pool. A real estate syndicate in which the limited partners rely on the general partner to select particular properties after the funds are assembled.

Blue Cross–Blue Shield. A non-profit organization offering health insurance, mainly on a group basis.

Bodily injury liability insurance. An insurance policy promising to pay all the legal obligations of the insured arising out of negligence in which an injury to another person has been caused.

Bond. A security of a corporation or government bearing an interest coupon and a promise to pay the principal on a given date.

Bond fund. A type of fund that invests predominately in intermediate- and long-term bonds.

Book cost. A valuation of assets based on data found in a firm's financial statements.

Book value. Total assets minus total liabilities; net worth.

Book value per share. The net worth of a corporation divided by the number of shares outstanding.

Bracket creep. The tendency for wage earners to be placed in higher-income tax brackets as their incomes are increased due to inflation, thus causing a decline in "real" income, after taxes.

Brokers. Legal representatives of buyers and sellers of such items as stocks and insurance.

Budget. A financial plan estimating income and outgo.

Bull. An investor who believes that the stock market will go up.

Bull market. A market characterized by optimism in which prices of securities are rising.

C

Call. A financial transaction in which the holder has the right to buy a given security at a stated price within some future period, usually less than one year (see call option).

Call option. The right to buy or sell a stock at an agreed-upon price within a stated period in the future.

Call provision. The option of a corporation to redeem outstanding bonds or preferred stock prior to maturity.

Cancellation clause. An insurance clause that states the terms under which coverage may be terminated.

Capacity. A credit standard judging the borrower's ability to repay the loan.

Capital gain (loss). That type of profit (loss) that one has after selling a capital asset at a price different from its original cost.

Capitalization rate. (1) The ratio of the anticipated income from an investment to its asking price. (2) The rate earned on an investment. (3) That interest rate which when applied to the earnings of an investment determines its capital value.

Cap rate. An interest rate used in valuing the future income from an asset.

Cash refund annuity. An annuity under which amounts yet unpaid to the annuitant are refunded to a beneficiary in a lump sum in the event the annuitant dies before receiving the original cost of the annuity.

Ceiling rate. The maximum interest rates paid by a financial institution.

Character. A credit standard judging the borrower's past record in repaying loans.

Charge account. An arrangement by which one may defer payment for goods until the end of a specified period, which is usually monthly.

Chartist. A technical analyst.

Churning. Excessive trading of securities in a portfolio resulting in large sales commissions.

Clauses. Terms of a contract outlining conditions of the agreement, e.g., clauses of an insurance policy.

Clifford trusts. Trusts that transfer property irrevocably for a minimum period of ten years, after which the property reverts to the original owner.

Closed-end company. An investment fund whose shares are fixed in number.

Closed-end fund. A regulated investment company investing in the securities of other corporations. The shares represent ownership of a diversified portfolio of stocks and bonds held by the fund.

Codicil. An amendment to a will.

Coinsurance clause. The clause in insurance policies that requires the insured to bear a portion of the loss.

Coinsurance deductible. A clause requiring that an amount be withheld from benefits of an insurance policy otherwise payable in case of loss.

Collateral. Property that must be pledged as security for a loan.

Collectibles. Tangible items purchased by investors for appreciation; examples include photographs, stamps, coins, diamonds, and paintings.

Collision insurance. That form of auto insurance providing indemnity for loss to the automobile that strikes another object.

Common stock. A certificate evidencing ownership interest in a corporation.

Company card. A credit card issued by a specific company, such as Sears Roebuck.

Company risk. A type of investment risk that stems from uncertainties relating to a corporation and its operations.

Compound interest. Interest earnings produced by applying a percentage rate cumulatively throughout the life of the investment to both the original fund and the periodic interest.

Comprehensive insurance. Automobile insurance that provides reimbursement for all kinds of loss to the automobile except collision.

Conditional sales contract. A credit sale in which legal title to the property being sold is retained by the seller until the loan is repaid.

Condominium. A form of home ownership in which the responsibility for given types of maintenance and other ownership decisions belongs to an association mutually supported by property owners. Condominium owners own a proportionate share of the buildings, recreational facilities, halls, grounds, outbuildings, and other portions of the property.

Constant ratio plan. A formula plan in which the proportion of stocks and bonds in the portfolio is maintained at a constant ratio.

Consumer finance company. A non-bank lending institution making short-term loans.

Contingent beneficiary. An individual named to receive property in the event that the primary beneficiary is not living.

Contractual plan. A type of periodic mutual fund purchase plan in which sales commissions for the total purchase period are included in payments at the beginning of the period.

Contrarianism. A type of financial analysis based on crowd psychology, which urges investors to do the opposite of what the crowd is doing.

Conventional mortgage. A mortgage loan typically for a twenty-five or thirty-year period at fixed interest rates discharged on an amortized basis with equal monthly payments.

Convertible bond. A bond convertible into common stock at stated terms.

Convertible security. A preferred stock or bond that is convertible into common stock of the issuing corporation at some stated ratio.

Coordination-of-benefits clause. Clause in an insurance policy placing a limitation on amounts payable in case the beneficiary has other policies or sources covering the same peril.

Cosigning. A process in which a second party is required to sign a borrower's note and thus becomes equally responsible for the loan if the borrower does not repay.

Coupon. A document evidencing the amount of interest payable on a bond. When interest is due, this coupon is clipped from the bond and presented to a designated bank for payment.

Credit card. A card issued by a creditor representing a type of charge account with an established credit arrangement.

Credit company card. A card issued by private credit card companies such as American Express.

Credit discount. A reduction in the amount due on a debt, usually made for payment within a given time period.

Credit installment loan. A loan repayable in periodic installments, usually monthly.

Credit life insurance. Life insurance on the borrower arranged to cover the outstanding balance of a loan.

Credit line. The maximum amount of credit allowed to customers in a single transaction.

Credit risk. Uncertainty involved in granting credit. Includes the likelihood that all credit terms will be adhered to and the chance of incurring a bad debt.

Credit standard. Criterion for qualifying for loans. Credit standards are traditionally judged by the "Three C's of credit"—character, capacity to repay, and collateral.

Credit terms. Conditions of granting credit, including discounts for prompt payment and time granted for repayment.

Credit union. An organization formed to grant loans and to receive savings deposits of members who are usually bound together by some common interest, such as being employees of a single employer.

Cumulative preferred. A feature of preferred stock which requires that previously unpaid preferred dividends be paid before common stock dividends may be paid.

Current assets. Cash, inventory, accounts receivable, and other assets of a firm that can be converted into cash within a twelve-month period.

Current income fund. A mutual fund whose investment objective is to produce high current dividend yields on common stocks.

Current liabilities. All debts that are due within twelve months (short-term debt).

Current ratio. The ratio of current assets to current liabilities.

Cyclical stock. A common stock whose typical price movement varies with general market and economic conditions.

D

Dealer market. A securities market in which investors deal only with brokers or other middlemen.

Debenture bond. A bond unsecured by specific collateral of the issuing corporation.

Debit card. A bank card that transfers money directly from the cardholder's deposit to another account. No check is needed.

Debt-to-equity ratio. The ratio of the total debt of an enterprise to the owner's equity.

Decreasing term policy. A life insurance contract in which the face amount declines during the term of the policy as, for example, to correspond to a declining balance of a mortgage loan.

Deductible clause. An insurance clause that specifies that a given amount may be subtracted from amounts otherwise payable for a covered loss.

Deep discount bond. A bond that sells at a price much lower than the bond's maturity value, usually because the coupon rate is lower than current interest rates on newly issued bonds of the same quality.

Default. The failure to repay a loan within the credit period.

Defense insurance. Another name for automobile liability insurance.

Defensive investor. An investor who stresses risk avoidance in the purchase of securities.

Deferred annuity. An annuity in which payment is deferred to some future time, such as retirement age.

Defined benefit formula. The formula used in a pension plan to determine the employee's pension. It is usually a function of the number of years of service and the average income during the last few years of employment.

Defined contribution formula. The type of pension plan in which the ultimate pension amount is determined by the size of the fund accumulated for retirement from periodic contributions made by the employer, the employee, or both.

Dental insurance. A kind of health insurance offering reimbursement for specified dental expenses.

Deposit insurance. Government-mandated insurance on deposits in savings institutions to protect the depositor against failure of the institution and subsequent loss of the deposit.

Direct writing system. A system for distributing insurance without employing independent middlemen; e.g., the buyer deals directly with the insurer rather than through agents.

Disability. A peril in which a person is medically impaired so as to be unable to carry on normal work, either in whole or in part.

Disability income exclusion. An income tax provision under which a portion of one's income is exempt from income tax in the case of disability.

Disability income insurance. A kind of health insurance that pays the insured a cash income in the event of disability.

Disability income rider. An amendment to a life insurance policy that provides coverage for payment of an income to the policyholder in the event of permanent and total disability.

Discount broker. A stock broker who charges a reduced commission for buying and selling securities.

Discounted cash flow method. A method of valuing investments by determining the present value of estimated future cash flows at some assumed interest rate and comparing this amount to the cost of the investment.

Discount points. An additional charge made by lenders on home mortgages payable in cash at the time of the closing. (One point equals 1 percent of the loan amount.)

Disposable income. Income received by individuals less personal taxes.

Distribution channel. A description of the agencies expected to be utilized in moving a product or service from the manufacturer to the final consumer.

Diversification. A method of reducing investment risk by investing in more than one company or industry.

Diversified common stock funds. Closed-end companies that have their portfolios invested predominantly in common stocks.

Dividend. The portion of corporate profit that is paid to shareholders.

Dividend options. Life insurance provisions providing varying ways in which one may accept dividends paid under the policy.

Dividend reinvestment plans. A method of reinvesting dividends for stock of the same corporation free of brokerage commissions.

Dollar cost averaging (DCA). The technique of reducing price risk by purchasing stocks with equal periodic dollar investments.

Donee. A person who receives a gift.

Donor. A person who makes a gift.

Double indemnity rider. An amendment or endorsement to a life insurance policy providing that if the insured dies by accident, as defined, twice the face amount of the policy will be paid to the beneficiary.

Dow Jones Industrial Average (DJIA). Daily index of stock prices of thirty large industrial corporations.

Due-on-sale clause. A clause in a real estate mortgage that allows the lender to require total payment of the mortgage loan balance if the original buyer resells the property.

E

Earned income credit. A tax credit allowed for low-income taxpayers that acts as a form of "negative income tax."

Earnings per share (EPS). Company profits (losses) divided by the number of outstanding common shares.

Efficient market hypothesis. A stock market theory which says that the market prices of common stocks move in a random pattern and that present prices cannot be used to predict future prices. The market already reflects all available investment information.

Electrical funds transfer (EFT) card. A system by which a credit card user may receive money or conduct other financial transactions from an automated teller machine.

Elimination period. A period that must elapse before an insured becomes eligible for coverage under an insurance policy.

Employees' Retirement Income Security Act (ERISA). A 1974 federal law that strengthened the federal regulation of private pension plans.

Endorsement. (1) A process in which a second party becomes liable for a note after the lender has exhausted all normal remedies against the defaulting borrower. (2) An amendment to an insurance policy changing the terms of coverage.

Endowment life insurance. A life insurance policy maturing for its face value after a stated period such as ten or twenty years.

Equal Credit Opportunity Act (ECOA). A federal law requiring the use of objective factors as a basis for granting credit. It specifically prohibits the lender from considering race, sex, age, or religion in the credit decision.

Equitable owner. The person named to receive the benefit (beneficiary) of property held in trust.

Equity-sharing mortgage. An agreement whereby the investor contributes part of the down payment or contributes to monthly payments of the homeowner in return for a share of the profit when the home is sold or refinanced.

Equity trusts. Real estate investment trusts in which the properties are owned directly by the trust.

Estate. Property, both real and personal, tangible and intangible, that is owned by an individual.

Estate planning. A planning process encompassing all activities involved in accumulating and managing property during one's lifetime, and disposing of it at one's death.

Estate tax. A tax levied on the value of property that one owns at the time of death.

Estimated tax. A tax on income not otherwise subject to withholding regulations.

Exchange privilege. A privilege offered by mutual fund management allowing its shareholders to trade shares from one fund to another within the same mutal fund family, at minimal cost.

Exchanges. National markets on which stocks and bonds are traded.

Exclusive agency system. A distribution system for insurance in which a middleman or agent is given the right to be the only person allowed to represent the insurer in a given territory or for a given type of policy.

Ex-dividend. A date on which the right to a current dividend no longer accompanies a stock.

Ex-dividend date. A date that is after the dividend declaration date and before the dividend payment date that is used to determine whether the stock purchaser (if before ex-dividend) or the stock seller (if after ex-dividend) will receive the dividend.

Exempt income. Income that is not subject to income tax, such as interest on municipal bonds, life insurance dividends, and Social Security retirement income.

Exempt property. Property of debtors, which by law may be withheld from a bankruptcy sale.

Extended term option. A nonforfeiture option in life insurance contracts that extends the term of coverage if premium payments are stopped, providing there is cash value available for this purpose.

Extension period. The period during which one may delay the payment of income taxes beyond the due date.

F

Face amount. An amount stated on the face of an insurance policy as representing the maximum amount payable in event of loss.

Face value (par value). Amount printed on a security (bond, life insurance policy, or stock certificate) as its nominal value. Face value is not the same as market value.

Fair Credit Reporting Act of 1969. A federal law requiring a lender to explain how loan interest is calculated.

Family auto policy (FAP). A standard form of automobile insurance written to cover the insured and members of the family.

Family group policy. A life insurance policy in which each member of the family is insured for different amounts.

Family income policy. A life insurance policy in which the death benefit consists of both an income to the beneficiary for a stated period and a lump sum payable at the end of the period.

Family trust interest. A trust that controls sufficient property to qualify for the full tax credit available to the decedent. The beneficiaries of this trust are usually children or heirs other than the surviving spouse.

Financial Institutions Deregulation Act of 1980. An act permitting greater freedom of operation in major financial institutions, such as banks and savings and loan corporations.

Financial responsibility laws. Automobile insurance laws at the state level requiring liability insurance or maintenance of other proof of financial responsibility in the event of automobile accidents.

Fixed amount option. A life insurance clause giving the beneficiary the right to receive the proceeds of the policy in the form of an income of a stated number of dollars for as long as the proceeds last.

Fixed annuity. An annuity that is expressed in terms of dollars.

Fixed income securities. Investment instruments paying a fixed rate of return, e.g., bonds.

Fixed period option. Clause in a life insurance policy giving the beneficiary the right to receive the proceeds in the form of an income for a given period, e.g., five or ten years.

Flat dollar deductible. A clause in insurance policies that specifies a certain amount to be subtracted from any loss before payment is made.

Flexible rate mortgage. A real estate mortgage in which payments may vary according to changes in interest rates over the life of the mortgage, subject to certain restrictions.

Formula plan. A system of purchasing common stocks according to a predetermined formula that intends to maintain given proportions of a portfolio in selected securities. For example, a 50-50 formula will attempt to maintain a portfolio that is composed of 50 percent stocks and 50 percent bonds.

Fractional share. Investment of less than a whole share of stock.

Franchise. A legal right to use someone else's ideas or business methods.

Full replacement coverage. A type of insurance policy condition under which an insured has the right to be indemnified for lost property without any reduction for depreciation.

Fundamental analysis. A type of security analysis that stresses factors such as earnings

546

and dividends per share, growth rates, and other basic financial characteristics thought to influence stock market price movements.

Funding. A process by which money is invested to guarantee the ultimate payment of a future obligation, such as employee pensions.

G

General obligation bonds. Municipal bonds whose backing is from general tax revenues of the issuing government agency.

General partner. A partner in an enterprise with unlimited liability for debts.

Gift tax. A federal law establishing taxation on property above specified amounts given to others during one's lifetime.

Grace period clause. A life insurance clause giving the insured an extra thirty days in which to pay a premium before policy lapse takes place.

Graduated payment mortgage. A mortgage loan in which monthly payments are kept lower than under conventional loans at first, but rise in stages for a specified period, such as five years, after which payments are level until the mortgage is discharged.

Greater fool theory. An investment strategy in which one pays a price known to be "high" in the belief that another person (the fool) can be found to pay an even higher price later on.

Gross income multiplier (GM). The ratio of the selling price of property to its gross rental income.

Gross margin. The difference between the selling price of a product or service and its cost, before operating expenses.

Group insurance. A type of life or health insurance issued on a group basis for the protection of specified members of organizations, such as employees.

Growth funds. A type of fund that invests in common stocks of companies that are believed to be growing at greater-than-average rates.

Growth in earnings and sales. The compound rate of growth of earnings per share for five or ten years.

Growth stocks. Common stocks issued by a corporation whose earnings are growing at an above average rate over time.

Guaranteed period annuity. An annuity under which payments to the annuitant are guaranteed for a specified period, such as ten or twenty years. In the event of the annuitant's death, unpaid installments are paid to a beneficiary.

Guarantee insolvency funds. A fund established to guarantee payment of insurance benefits in case the insurer becomes insolvent.

H

Hazard. A condition that affects the probability of losses or the occurrence of perils.

Health maintenance organizations (HMO's). Agencies offering group health insurance and stressing preventive health care.

Hidden values. Financial worth of a company not currently reflected in the financial statements or market price.

High current income funds. A mutual fund whose investment objective is to produce relatively high cash dividends to its owners.

High liquidity. Term describing an investment that may readily be converted to cash in the open market.

Holding company. A corporation organized to own other corporation(s).

Homeowner's insurance. A type of property insurance policy designed for various risks of homeowners. Coverages include losses to the dwelling, other structures on the insured's property, unscheduled personal property, additional living expenses, personal liability, theft, and medical payments to others.

Homeowner's Warranty Program (HOW). A program in which the purchaser receives a ten-year guarantee against major construction defects in a home. The HOW provides reimbursement for the cost of remedying specified defects.

Hospitalization insurance. A kind of health insurance that provides reimbursement for expenses, including hospital room and board.

Immediate annuity. An annuity whose payments begin immediately.

Includible income. An income tax rule defining the income level to be used in calculating allowed tax deductions.

Income averaging. A method of computing federal income tax on an unusually large income earned in a particular year by treating the income as if it were earned evenly over a five-year period.

Income stocks. Stocks of companies whose dividends are relatively large and stable.

Incontestable clause. A clause in life insurance policies providing that if the insured has not died within a two-year period after taking out the policy, no misstatements, even fraudulent misstatements, made at the time of application will invalidate the coverage.

Indemnity. A legal principle that determines the amount of the economic loss reimbursed for destroyed property.

Indenture. A legal contract specifying details of the debtor/creditor relationship between a corporation and its bondholders.

Indenture contract. A formal agreement that establishes terms of a bond instrument—e.g., how the bond may be redeemed.

Independent agency system. (See American agency system.)

Indexation. A process by which an account or income is adjusted for inflation so as to preserve the purchasing power of the account or the income.

Individual Retirement Account (IRA). A retirement plan authorized for individuals, whether covered by other pension plans or not, to which a tax-deductible contribution of up to $2,000 per worker per year ($2,250 if the worker has a nonworking spouse) may be made.

Industry risk. That type of investment risk stemming from uncertainties of the industry to which a given corporation belongs.

Inflation. A rising price level caused by creation of money and credit at a rate that exceeds the rate of increase of goods and services produced.

Inheritance tax. A state tax levied on individuals who inherit property.

Insider. A director, corporate officer, or large stockholder of a corporation.

Insider trading. Trading of securities by corporate officers or others who possess intimate knowledge of corporate activities and finances.

Installment refund annuity. An annuity under which amounts yet unpaid to the annuitant are refunded to a beneficiary in installments, in the event the annuitant dies before receiving the original cost of the annuity.

Installment sale. The sale of property on installment terms, as opposed to being sold for cash.

Institutional trading. A process in which common stocks or other securities are bought and sold mainly by institutions such as pension funds, insurance companies, banks, and other corporate investors.

Insurable interest. A legal relationship one has to property such that if that property is destroyed, one suffers an economic loss.

Insurance. A contract to transfer risk. A method of combining objects exposed to loss in such a way that total claims become predictable within narrow limits.

Insurance commissioners. The individuals who regulate insurance at the state level.

Insurance dividend. A partial return of premium to the policyholder.

Interest-adjusted cost. A method of determining the cost of life insurance, which considers the cost to the policyholder of interest on lost premiums paid for coverage.

Interest coverage ratio. The number of times that the firm's earnings cover its fixed interest costs.

Interest option. A life insurance clause giving the beneficiary the right to hold policy proceeds with the insurer at interest.

Interest rate risk. Changes in the value of fixed income securities as a result of changes in market interest rates.

Intestate. The legal status of a person who has died without having established a valid will.

Investment banking firm. A firm that purchases securities from a corporation and sells them to the general public at a high price—e.g., engages in underwriting.

Investment company. A corporation that receives funds from investors and invests these funds in a large number of publicly traded securities.

Investment grade bonds. Bonds that are rated from AAA through BBB which are purchased by institutional investors because they are very marketable, and hence carry less risk.

Irrevocable trust. A trust that cannot be revoked or changed by its creator. An irrevocable trust is a way of making permanent gifts to others.

Itemized deductions. Expenses such as medical and dental expenses, interest expense, various taxes, and charitable contributions that are allowed to be subtracted in determining taxable income.

J

Joint-and-last-survivorship annuity. The form of annuity in which payments are guaranteed to two individuals as long as either one shall live.

Joint tax return. A federal income tax filing option by which two spouses combine their incomes on one tax form.

Joint tenancy. That form of ownership of property in which more than one individual shares an undivided interest in the property.

Joint tenancy with right of survivorship. That form of ownership of property in which more than one individual shares an undivided interest in the property, and if one owner dies, the surviving owner automatically becomes the sole owner of the property.

K

Keogh plan (HR-10). A retirement plan authorized for self-employed persons for whom contributions are tax deductible for federal income tax. The current limit of annual tax-deductible contributions is 15 percent of income or $15,000, whichever is smaller.

L

Law of large numbers. The mathematical basis of insurance stating that the larger the group of objects under one's management, the smaller the variation of actual from probable losses.

Leading indicators. Indices of business activity said to move in advance of general business activity.

Lease option. A contract giving a renter the right to buy the property within some time period, applying rent in whole or in part to the purchase price.

Leverage. The use of borrowed fixed-cost funds in the hope of making a return higher than the cost of the borrowed funds.

Leveraged stock. Stock issued by a corporation whose financial structure is characterized by substantial amounts of debt.

Life annuity. A periodic payment of funds to an individual for life.

Life care center. A home complex catering to the needs of the aged.

Life cycle stages. Those times in one's life that may be categorized for purposes of financial planning. They include the stages of single adult, married, family with young children, family with older children, parents alone (empty nest), and retirement.

Life-income option. Clause in life insurance contracts that gives the beneficiary the right to accept proceeds in the form of a life income.

Life insurance. A method of creating a fund or an income for the protection of dependents or other beneficiaries in the event of the death of the insured.

Life insurance programming. A plan for the settlement of life insurance on behalf of the beneficiary, frequently involving the use of settlement options.

Life insurance trust. A trust set up to receive life insurance as property to distribute to others.

Limited partner. Partner of an enterprise with liability for the debts of the company, which is limited to the partner's investment.

Limited partnership (syndicate). A partnership in which one type of owner (the limited partner) has a potential liability for partnership debts not to exceed the amount of the limited partner's total investment. A limited partnership must have at least one general partner who has unlimited liability for business debts.

Limited payment whole life policy. Ordinary life insurance contracts whose premiums are payable over a stated number of years, usually ten or twenty, rather than for the whole of the owner's life.

Limit order. A type of transaction for a security in which the purchase or sale price is limited to a specified amount and usually for a specified period.

Line of credit. The predetermined limit up to which the credit cardholder can charge purchases.

Liquidity. Characteristic of salability of an investment. The greater the liquidity, the easier it is to convert the investment to cash.

Living trust. A trust set up to operate during the lifetime of the creator of the trust.

Load fund. An investment company that charges a sales commission.

Loading. (1) The overhead or administrative costs of offering insurance. (2) A sales charge levied in acquiring mutual fund shares.

Loan values. Life insurance policy provisions stating the amount that may be borrowed from the cash value of the life insurance.

Long-term capital gain. The profit realized by selling an asset that has been held for longer than one year.

Loss-control activities. Those activities designed to prevent or reduce losses.

Low liquidity. Term describing an investment that may not be easily or readily converted to cash in the open market.

M

Major medical insurance. A kind of health insurance designed to cover very large or catastrophic medical expenses on a blanket basis with relatively few exclusions.

Making a market. The practice of offering to buy securities in order to maintain the price within a stated range.

Marginal tax rate. The percentage rate paid on your highest increment of taxable income.

Margin trading. Buying and selling securities on credit by borrowing from a broker or banker. The securities are pledged as collateral for the loan.

Marital deduction. The amount of one's estate willed to a spouse at death. The amount of the estate subject to the marital deduction is not taxable for federal estate tax purposes.

Marital deduction trust. A trust set up to receive property intended to benefit a spouse. Marital deduction trust property escapes estate taxes on the estate of the spouse, thus increasing the amount of family property that can be passed to children without paying estate taxes on the estates of the father or mother.

Market order. An order to buy or sell at the best price available on the stock exchange.

Market risk. That type of uncertainty surrounding an investment which stems from changes in the general securities market and which is believed to affect all securities simultaneously.

Marriage tax. The difference between the tax that a married couple filing a joint return would pay and the tax that those same individuals would pay if they had filed separate returns.

Medical payments coverage. A form of automobile insurance providing for reimbursement of medical losses to the driver or to third parties regardless of legal liability of the driver or owner.

Medicare. A part of the Social Security law that provides health insurance to people over 65. Medicare includes both hospital and doctor bill coverage.

Minimum period guarantee annuity. A period during which the annuity rent is guaranteed for a stated number of years, but in any event for the life of the annuitant, e.g., ten years certain, and life.

Minority shareholder. A holder of common stock whose holdings are not sufficient to control the corporation.

Misstatement-of-age clause. A clause in life insurance which adjusts the death proceeds in case the insured has misstated the age when applying for insurance.

Modified life policy. A life insurance policy arranged so that premiums are smaller for the first five or ten years and larger for the remaining years of the contract.

Money market fund. A mutual fund investing in highly liquid short-term debts of the government or leading corporations.

Mortgage bond. A bond with stated assets pledged as collateral such as real estate that may be recovered by the lender in case the loan is not repaid.

Mortgagee clause. A clause in property insurance specifying that in the event of loss, a mortgagee may receive first reimbursement under the policy.

Mortgage loan. A loan usually repayable in installments, in which the collateral is real estate.

Multiple listing service (MLS). An arangement between real estate agents that pools all properties offered into a common offering list.

Municipal bond. A bond issued by a state or local government or governmental agency on which interest is exempt from federal income taxation. Interest is also exempt from state income taxation in the state of issue.

Municipal bond fund. A type of fund that invests in bonds issued by state and local governments.

Mutual. A type of insurance organization in which policyholders are legally the owners of the firm. Also refers to investment company in which owners' investments are made continuously without set limits, e.g., mutual fund.

Mutual company. A type of insurance company owned by policyholders.

Mutual fund. An open-end investment company in which the corporation stands ready continuously to receive new funds from investors and redeem existing shares at the net asset value.

Mutual savings bank (MSB). A savings bank authorized to receive community savings and invest these funds in certain kinds of assets. Mutual implies that there are no stockholders.

N

Negligence. Failure to exercise the degree of care required under the circumstances by a reasonably prudent person. Negligence can give rise to legal liability in civil court actions.

Net asset value (NAV). The total value of the assets of an investment company divided by the total number of shares outstanding.

Net current asset value. Current assets minus current liabilities.

Net profit margin. The ratio of net income to sales.

Net worth. The owners' equity or total assets minus total liabilities of a business enterprise.

New York Stock Exchange (NYSE). The leading national marketplace for trading securities of the largest and best-known corporations.

New York Stock Exchange (NYSE) Index. A daily index of stock prices that includes all the stocks traded on the New York Stock Exchange.

No-fault laws. Automobile insurance offered in about half the states, limiting the application of common law negligence as a basis for settling specified losses.

No-load fund. A mutual fund in which shares are purchased directly from the fund with no sales or brokerage commissions charged.

Nonforfeiture options. Life insurance provisions stating what uses may be selected for cash values. Three options are (1) lump-sum payment, (2) paid-up insurance of a reduced amount, and (3) extended term.

Nonrefund annuity. Annuity under which income ceases upon the death of the annuitant with no remaining benefits to others.

NOW (negotiable order of withdrawal) account. A commercial checking account authorized under the Interest Deregulation Act of 1980 in which interest is paid on the account balance if given conditions (e.g., maintaining a minimum balance) are met.

O

Odd lot. Any stock trade of less than 100 shares.

Odd-lot broker. A broker who deals in "odd" lots (trades of less than 100 shares).

Old Age, Survivors', Disability, and Health Insurance (OASDHI). The Social Security insurance program in the United States.

Open-end company. (See Mutual fund.)

Operating expense ratio. The ratio of operating expenses to total net assets of an investment company.

Option price. A legal contract giving the holder the right to purchase real estate or other commodities or stocks at a specified price within a specified future time under stated conditions.

Ordinary life. Type of life insurance contract in which coverage and premium payments continue for the life of the insured.

Ordinary taxable income. That type of income taxed at specified rates, which are progressively higher as income rises.

Overline. Amount of credit, preauthorized by a creditor, by which a borrower may exceed a regular credit limit.

Over the counter (OTC). A system of trading stocks and bonds through dealers (other than auction markets).

Over-the-counter market. Informal market for trading securities of corporations whose stock is not listed on a major stock exchange.

P

Package life insurance. A life insurance contract that combines basic types of life insurance such as term, whole life, and endowment.

Participating insurance. Life insurance in which a portion of the premium is returned to the policyholder as a dividend if the insurer's financial experience justifies such a return.

Participating preferred shares. Preferred stock that pays a fixed dividend plus an additional designated share of earnings.

Partnership. That form of business organization in which two or more individuals jointly assume personal liability for the operation and debts of the business.

Par value. A nominal or face value of a common stock.

Passbook savings account. A common form of saving in which one's current account balance, including credited interest, is shown in a small booklet.

Payout ratio. The ratio of dividends to earnings in a particular year.

Pension Benefits Guarantee Corporation (PBGC). A federal agency that insures pension benefits to workers covered under private pension plans.

P/E ratio (price/earnings ratio or multiplier). The current market price of a stock divided by its earnings per share in some previous period, usually the last twelve months.

Peril. An event that may cause a loss.

Period certain annuity. An annuity guaranteed for life and in which a certain number of years of payments, such as ten or twenty, are also guaranteed to someone.

Personal auto policy. The standard form of automobile insurance covering an individual; it is somewhat more limited in coverage than the family auto policy.

Personal injury protection (PIP) insurance. A type of automobile insurance coverage providing for personal injury protection in states with no-fault auto insurance. It includes medical expense and loss of income reimbursement without regard to fault of the driver.

Personal insurance. Insurance covering life or health risks on individuals.

Personal savings. The difference between income and outgo that serves as the measure of personal wealth.

Physical damage insurance. A kind of automobile insurance that encompasses all sorts of physical losses to one's automobile, including collision and comprehensive.

Point-and-figure chart. A method used by technical analysts to plot significant changes

552

in stock prices without regard for a time dimension.

Point of sale terminal. A machine enabling one to obtain funds or transfer funds in payment of a charge account by inserting an authorized credit card.

Political risk. Uncertainty produced mainly by the actions of governments.

Portfolio. The many different securities owned by an individual investor or an organization such as a mutual fund.

Preferred stock. Corporate stock that has a legal right to a fixed amount of dividends before payments can be made to common shareholders. It also usually has a prior claim to assets in the event the corporation is dissolved.

Premium. The consideration paid by the insured to keep an insurance contract in force.

Premium tax. A tax levied by a state upon the gross amount of insurance premiums collected in that state.

Prepayment terms. Terms of credit specifying conditions that apply when a loan is repaid before it is due.

Present value. A financial concept expressing the current value of a sum to be received sometime in the future, given that money earns a stated rate of interest.

Present value analysis. A method of valuing common stocks that determines the discounted present value of an anticipated stream of earnings, including dividends and future capital gains.

Price/earnings multiplier. The ratio of the current stock price to the latest 12 months' earnings per share.

Price range. The difference between the high and low price of a stock in a given period.

Primary market. A market characterizing the original issuance of new common stock.

Prime rate. The interest rate charged by banks on short-term loans to their most credit-worthy companies.

Principle of loss spreading. An economic principle in which losses occurring to some members of a group are redistributed to other members of the group, usually through insurance contracts.

Probability. The chance that an event will occur, which is usually expressed as a percentage of occurrences out of all possible events.

Probate costs. Legal costs incurred in the proving and settlement of a will.

Programming. A process by which insurance proceeds are planned to be paid, usually as an income, over specified years and for specified purposes.

Progressive income tax rates. Tax schedule levied on income in which applicable rate rises with income level.

Property-liability insurance. An insurance policy that agrees to reimburse the insured for legal liability for negligence that causes damage to the property of others.

Prospectus. A document giving financial and other information to potential investors in new securities.

Proxy statement. An information sheet used by a company to solicit stockholder votes on issues affecting the corporation.

Purchase money mortgage. A mortgage loan granted as part payment for real estate as part of the purchase price.

Pure risk. The uncertainty of an event, such as a fire or flood, which can produce only a loss if it occurs.

Put. A financial transaction in which the holder has the right to sell a given security at a stated price within some future period, usually less than one year.

Put option. The right to sell a stock at an agreed price within a stated period in the future.

R

Random walk. The premise that stock prices move randomly, not in predictable patterns.

Rate of return on equity. The ratio of profits available to stockholders to the amounts invested by them.

Rate of return on total capital. The ratio of net income to total assets.

Real estate investment trust (REIT). An investment trust that owns real estate properties. Shares are similar to mutual fund shares.

Regional markets. A type of market for securities with special characteristics that vary according to the geographic region in which the issuer is located.

Regressive tax. A tax, such as a sales tax, in which the same rate applies equally to individuals regardless of income.

Regular medical insurance. A kind of health insurance in which all physicians' services other than surgical procedures are covered.

Regulation Q. A federal regulation giving the Federal Reserve Board the right to determine interest rates charged by banks.

Reinstatement clause. A life insurance clause that provides for reinstating a lapsed policy.

Rental reimbursement coverage. Coverage granted by homeowners insurance and other types of property insurance reimbursing the owner for loss of rental income or rental value in the event that the property is destroyed by the insured peril or made untenantable by an insured peril.

Retirement (OASDHI) benefits. The portion of Social Security that provides pension income for retired workers and their dependents.

Revenue bond. A municipal bond for which the source of interest and principal repayment is from revenues of projects in which bond proceeds are invested.

Reverse stock split. A technique whereby the outstanding shares of a firm are reduced in order to raise the market price of the stock.

Revolving credit. An account on which new loans are made as old loans are paid off, as in a department store credit account.

Rider. An endorsement or amendment to an insurance contract.

Risk. The uncertainty of an economic loss. Risk may be measured statistically by comparing expected results with actual results.

Risk aversion. A subjective attitude encouraging one to avoid situations in which a loss may occur.

Risk management. A formal approach to handling risk that minimizes the impact of random losses.

Risk scales. Measures of the degree of risk attributable to a given security.

Rollover. A transaction in which funds are removed from one type of investment and immediately placed in another type of investment.

Rollover mortgage. A mortgage that may be exchanged for another mortgage during the life of the loan.

Round lot. A trade of common stocks in units of 100 shares.

Rule of "78." A method of apportioning income over a period of time in which the number of the periods is divided by the mathematic sum of the number of payments.

S

Sales finance company. A manufacturer-related finance company, such as General Motors Acceptance Corporation, which finances sales of the manufacturer's product.

Sales tax. A state, county, or city tax levied on the retail sales value of specified items.

Savings and loan associations (SLA's). Lending and savings institutions originally formed to finance home ownership that now have broader powers.

S&P 500 Stock Index. A daily index of stock prices of 500 large corporations.

Savings bond. A nontransferrable bond issued by the U.S. Treasury.

Savings certificate. A certificate evidencing a savings deposit in a financial institution such as a savings and loan association, a mutual savings bank, or a commercial bank.

Secondary market. The market characterizing the sale and resale of common stocks and other securities that have been previously issued to the public.

Second deed of trust. A loan arrangement in real estate in which the lender subordinates his or her loan to another lender whose priority is first in the event of nonpayment by the borrower.

Second mortgage. A mortgage debt with a claim subordinated to that of the first-mortgage holder.

Section 403(b) plan. An individual retirement

plan described in the Internal Revenue Service Code Section 403(b) in which employees of certain nonprofit institutions may set aside funds, thus deferring current taxation until retirement.

Secured bond. A bond in which specific property is pledged as collateral.

Securities and Exchange Commission (SEC). A federal agency regulating the issuance and sale of corporate securities to the public.

Sell short. To sell stock one does not own with the intent of future delivery at a lower price; it is done by those believing stock prices will fall.

Series EE bond. A U.S. government savings bond sold at a discount from face value with tax on the interest deferred until it matures.

Series HH bond. A U.S. government savings bond that pays cash interest periodically. Interest is subject to federal income tax when received.

Settlement options. Life insurance provisions stating various ways in which one may plan to have proceeds payable: over fixed periods, in fixed amounts, held at interest, or as a life income.

Shared appreciation mortgage (SAM). A mortgage in which the mortgage lender shares in the appreciation of the value of a property when the property is sold, or after a stated period.

Share draft. A check written on an account in a credit union.

Short positions. The number of shares borrowed by those who are selling short.

Short-term capital loss. A loss resulting from the sale of an asset that has been held for less than one year.

Simple interest. The ratio of the amount charged for credit to the amount of the credit, usually expressed on an annual basis as a percentage.

Simplified employee pension (SEP-IRA) plans. Plans authorized by Congress to encourage smaller employers to establish employee pension plans with IRAs as a funding method.

Simultaneous destruction. A condition under which property is subject to loss at the same time due to a common peril, such as an earthquake or flood.

Single payment loan. A loan repayable in a single sum at a stated time.

Single premium annuity. An annuity established by the payment of a single sum.

Single premium deferred annuity. An annuity purchased by the payment of a lump sum in which the rent is scheduled to begin at some future date, e.g., at retirement age sixty-five.

Sinking fund. Cash set aside in a special account for a specific purpose such as repaying bonds as they mature.

Small Loan Act. State law limiting the terms under which small loans may be made and the interest that may be charged.

Social Security integration. The coordination of private pensions and Social Security benefits.

Sole proprietorship. A form of business organization in which an individual is the only owner of the enterprise. Sole proprietors have unlimited personal liability for the debts of the business.

Specialist broker. An employee of a stock exchange who facilitates trading by buying and selling given securities and maintaining an inventory of these securities.

Special situations. Stocks of companies whose current price is two-thirds or less of its net current asset value. May be influenced by particular circumstances such as "hidden" values not reflected in financial statements.

Specialty funds. Investment companies whose stock portfolios tend to be concentrated in stocks of companies in specific industries, such as energy, gold mining, banking, insurance, or others.

Speculation. A risky process characterized by the trading of securities generally for short-term profits.

Speculative risk. The uncertainty of an event that can produce either a loss or a gain, such as making an investment.

Speculative stocks. Common stocks considered to be risky—i.e., characterized by wide price fluctuations.

Spendthrift trust clause. A clause protecting life insurance proceeds from the claims of creditors of the beneficiary.

Split estate trusts. Trusts set up to receive the property in an estate in different segments, usually to minimize estate taxes.

Spread. (1) The difference in yield between various grades of bonds. (2) The difference between the "Bid" and "Ask" price of a stock.

Standard deduction. (See Zero bracket amount.)

Standard marital trust. A trust that gives the surviving spouse complete rights to all income and the right to use up the principal.

Stock. A share of ownership in a corporate enterprise.

Stock broker. The agent for securities buyers and sellers.

Stock commission. A charge made by a stock broker for buying or selling securities.

Stock company. A type of insurance company owned by stockholders.

Stock dividend. A dividend paid in the form of additional stock rather than cash.

Stock exchange. A marketplace where buyers and sellers are brought together to trade securities.

Stockholder's equity. That portion of the company's assets contributed by the stockholders.

Stock indexes. Measures that record the change in the price levels of specified groups of stocks, e.g., the Dow Jones Industrial Price Index, of the price changes of thirty large companies.

Stock split. A procedure that increases the number of corporate shares outstanding. Splits involve a large number of shares and require an adjustment to the par value per share.

Stock ticker (tape). A mechanism that records each transaction occurring on the floor of the stock exchange.

Stop order (or stop loss order). A type of limited order used in buying or selling common stock in which instructions are given to sell if the stock falls to a given level after its initial purchase.

Straight-life annuity. A type of annuity in which there is no refund to any other person upon the death of the annuitant.

Strike price. The exercise price of a call option or a put option.

Subchapter S corporation. A form of business organization that has the income tax status of a partnership; otherwise it is a corporation for purposes of limiting the liability of its owners.

Subordinated debenture. A debenture bond in which all other forms of debt have a prior claim against earnings and assets.

Subrogation clause. A clause in property insurance that gives the insurer the right to pursue liable third parties for losses.

Suicide clause. A life insurance policy provision stating that if the insured commits suicide within two years of issuance of the policy, the insurer may deny liability.

Supplemental Security Income (SSI). A part of the social welfare program administered by the Social Security Administration for the blind, disabled, and indigent.

Surgical insurance. A kind of health insurance that pays for surgical procedures.

Survivors' benefits. The portion of Social Security or group health insurance that provides income benefits to survivors of insured workers. Survivors' benefits may also include funeral costs and are contingent upon certain conditions being met.

Syndicate. A legal arrangement in real estate in which investors cooperate on joint projects and are liable only for the amount they invest.

Systematic risk (market risk). The uncertainty characterizing the price of a common stock that is produced by changes in the general stock market.

T

Tape watchers. Persons who observe the price of securities during the trading periods, searching for patterns of price changes believed to indicate future price levels.

Tax audit. An examination of one's income tax return by federal or state revenue agents.

Tax avoidance. Taking advantage of legitimate ways to reduce income taxes.

Tax credit. An amount that one may subtract directly from the tax liability.

Tax credit for the elderly. A tax credit granted to persons over sixty-five who earn less than a specified amount.

Tax deduction. An expense that reduces taxable income.

Tax evasion. An act, usually carrying criminal penalties, in which one fails to pay the correct tax by such means as understating income, overstating deductions, or not even filing a return.

Tax exemptions. Deductions from income granted to taxpayer and spouse.

Tax-exempt money market funds. A type of money market fund that invests in short-term, good quality municipal bonds whose income is tax-exempt.

Tax-free exchange. The trading of an equity in one property for an equity in another similar property without having to pay any income tax on the appreciation of the property traded.

Tax selling. Trading in securities with the main purpose of establishing tax losses or gains.

Tax shelter. An investment on which the current returns are deferred for federal income tax purposes until a later time, such as at retirement.

Tax-sheltered annuities (TSAs). Plans available to employees of nonprofit organizations whereby an employer purchases a non-forfeitable annuity contract, usually under terms of a side agreement with the employee, to reduce the employee's salary by the amount contributed.

Tax swap. Selling a security to establish tax gains or losses, and reinvesting in a similar security.

Technical analysis. A system of analyzing stock market values that relies mainly upon past movements of the stock's price and past movements of the stock market as a whole.

Technical analyst. One who attempts to determine stock values by studying previous patterns of price changes.

Temporary disability law. State law existing in six jurisdictions providing nonoccupational disability income on a temporary (usually six months) basis.

Tenancy in common. A form of joint ownership in which each owner possesses a divisible interest that may be sold or given to third parties.

Ten-year averaging rule. A tax rule that greatly reduces the amount of income tax due on lump-sum retirement payments by treating the payments for income tax purposes as if they had been received over ten years.

Terminal interest marital trust. A trust that gives the surviving spouse the right to income only, with principal inherited by another designated heir after the death of the surviving spouse.

Terminable marital interest trust. A type of trust set up to benefit a surviving spouse by providing the spouse with a lifetime (terminable) interest in the income from an estate, but without the right to dispose of the property upon the spouse's death.

Termination insurance. Protection given to employees' pension payments under provisions of the Pension Benefit Guaranty Corporation, in case the pension plan is terminated.

Term life insurance. A form of life insurance with no cash value that is in force for a given period of years, such as five, ten, twenty, or until a given age, such as sixty-five.

Testament. Another name for a will; a document instructing survivors how to distribute one's property after death.

Testamentary trust. A trust set up by a will to receive property per the instructions in the will.

Testator. A person who makes a will.

Three-year recovery rule. A federal tax rule governing the way in which retirement income is taxed.

Time-limit-on-certain-defense clause. A period, usually two years, after which an insurer may not raise defenses against the payment of losses or health insurance policies. (Also called an uncontestable clause.)

Times interest earned (TIE). (See Interest coverage ratio.)

Tort liability. A liability that arises because of a legal wrong that one has committed.

Total debt. Consists of both short-term and long-term debt.

Total return. Usually expressed as an annual percentage, it consists of the percentage increase in the market value of the stock plus the stock's dividend rate.

Towing and labor coverage. Clause in an auto insurance policy providing payment for the costs of towing a disabled auto under given conditions.

Trade against the wind. A stock exchange rule that requires a specialist in a particular stock to sell stock out of personal inventory to smooth out price fluctuations.

Transfer agent. The agent employed by the corporation to handle transfers of ownership of its stock.

Transfer payments. Subsidies, welfare payments, and retirement income paid to citizens by the government.

Treasury bills. A form of government debt sold at discount with maturities of less than a year.

Treasury bonds. U.S. government obligations with ten-year maturities or longer.

Treasury notes. U.S. government obligations maturing in less than ten years and bearing interest-paying coupons.

Truncation. A practice in which one's checks are kept by the financial institution on which they are drawn and not returned to the writer of the check.

Trust. A legal instrument in which legal ownership of property is given to one party for the benefit of another.

Trustee. A person given the responsibility under provisions of a trust to manage property for the benefit of others.

Truth-in-Lending Act of 1969. Federal law requiring the use of the Annual Percentage Rate (APR) method of calculating interest to be paid by the borrower.

U

Umbrella liability policy. A supplemental liability insurance contract that reimburses for losses incurred because of the negligence of the insured beyond the basic limits of other insurance contracts.

Underinsurance. (1) When the policyholder fails to purchase coverage equal to the replacement cost of the property. (2) Failing to carry sufficient insurance.

Underwriter. A firm that buys an issue of securities from a corporation with the aim of resale to investors.

Unified gift and estate tax credit. An amount (credit) that may be used under tax codes to reduce directly the amount of estate and gift taxes otherwise payable.

Uniform Small Loan Law. State law placing maximum limits on interest charges on small loans to consumers.

Uninsured motorist endorsement. Automobile insurance coverage providing reimbursement to the owner of a vehicle for losses caused by an uninsured motorist.

Universal life policies. A life insurance contract in which premiums and coverage may be adjusted periodically. Premiums not needed for death protection are invested to yield the highest available current interest income.

Unlimited marital deduction. A deduction allowed for federal estate tax purposes, whereby gifts and bequests made to one's spouse are not subject to federal estate taxes in the other spouse's estate.

Unsecured loan. A loan on which no collateral is required.

Usury law. State law placing a maximum limit on the rate of interest that can be charged on certain loans.

V

Valid will. A will that has met certain legal requirements and may be enforced by law.

Valued policy. An insurance policy under which the face amount of the policy must be paid if the property is destroyed.

Variable annuity. An annuity that is expressed as a number of units of securities, similar to mutual fund shares, whose value fluctuates with the market prices of securities in which the funds have been invested.

Variable life policies. Life insurance contracts in which the cash values and amount of death protection vary according to changes in the stock market prices, subject to stated limits.

Variable rate mortgage. A mortgage loan in which the rate of interest charged may fluctuate, subject to given limits.

Vesting. When an employee permanently owns rights to pension benefits that are paid for by the employer's contributions, usually after five or ten years of service.

Voluntary plan. A type of periodic mutual fund purchase plan in which the investor pays a commission only at the time of purchase and incurs no penalty if the plan is terminated.

W

Waiver-of-premium rider. An endorsement to a life insurance policy stating that as long as the insured is totally and permanently disabled, further premium payments are waived.

Wash sale. Selling a security to realize a loss, and then purchasing identical securities within thirty days.

Whole life insurance. A form of life insurance so arranged that premiums and coverge in force continue for the insured's entire life, if desired.

Whole life policy. A life insurance contract under which lifelong protection is provided. Whole life encompasses both ordinary and limited payment life insurance contracts.

Wiesenberger Investment Service. An investment service publishing periodic statistical results and investment analysis of investment companies.

Will. A written document that specifies the details of one's wishes regarding the disposition of the estate at death.

Withdrawal plan service. A type of service offered by an investment company allowing owners to withdraw periodic amounts from their accounts.

Withholding tax. Amounts deducted from gross wages by employers and paid to the government as part payment of employees' income tax.

Workers' compensation. State-mandated insurance providing benefits for workers who incur occupational accidents or diseases.

Wraparound mortgage. A type of mortgage financing in which different types of mortgage loans are combined under one financing instrument.

Writing covered options. The practice of selling options on stock that you already own.

Y

Yield. The financial income or return usually expressed as an annual percentage of the assets invested.

Z

Zero bracket amount (standard deduction). An amount you may subtract from income otherwise subject to tax under federal income tax laws, in lieu of itemizing deductions such as medical and dental expenses, property taxes, gifts to charities, casualty losses, educational expenses, and job-related costs.

Zero coupon bond. A bond that is issued at a discount and repaid at its stated maturity value with no periodic interest payments during the life of the bond.

SUGGESTED READINGS

This list of suggested readings is arranged according to the parts of this text to which they pertain. Of course, there are many overlaps, so sources are sometimes listed more than once.

The reader is also referred to current issues of several periodicals that often contain articles on personal financial planning topics. The most popular of these periodicals are *Forbes*, *Barron's*, *Money*, *Fortune*, *Changing Times*, and the *Wall Street Journal*. Listings of specific articles are avoided since the subject matter is changing so rapidly and information referred to may be obsolete by the time this book is published.

PART I

Personal Financial Needs

Apilado, Vincent, P., and Thomas B. Morehart. *Personal Financial Management.* St. Paul, Minn.: West Publishing Company, 1980. 684 pages. *See especially Chapters 4–7.*

Bailard, Thomas E., David L. Biehl, and Ronald W. Kaiser. *Personal Money Management.* Chicago: Science Research Associates, 1980. 606 pages. *See especially Chapters 1–4.*

Bankers Magazine. Bimonthly. *See current issues.*

Cohen, Jerome B., *Personal Finance.* Homewood, Ill.: Richard D. Irwin, 1979. 515 pages. *See especially Chapters 1–5.*

Consumer Reports. Monthly. *See current issues.*

Directory of Federal Consumer Office. Pueblo, Col: Consumer Information Center. *Contains a listing of consumer guides in many fields, including banking, automobiles, insurance, housing, job information, credit, stocks and bonds, and taxes.*

Gitman, Lawrence J. *Personal Finance.* Hinsdale, Ill.: The Dryden Press, 1981. 672 pages. *Contains an especially thorough discussion on budgeting.*

Hallman, G. Victor, and Jerry S. Rosenbloom. *Personal Financial Planning: How to Plan for Your Financial Freedom.* New York: McGraw-Hill, 1975. *Provides a look at fundamentals of personal finance.*

Lang, Larry R., and Thomas H. Gillespie. *Strategy for Personal Finance,* 2d ed. New York: McGraw-Hill, 1981. *See especially Chapter 4.*

U.S. Bureau of Labor Statistics. *Occupational Outlook Handbook.* Annually.

West, David A., and Glenn L. Wood. *Personal Financial Management.* Boston: Houghton Mifflin, 1972. 705 pages. *See especially Chapters 1–4.*

Wolf, Harold A. *Personal Finance.* Boston: Allyn & Bacon, 1981. 700 pages. *A good general discussion of personal finance fundamentals.*

PART II

Protection of Income and Assets

American Council of Life Insurance. *Life Insurance Fact Book.* Annually.

Bickelhaupt, David L. *General Insurance.* Homewood, Ill.: Richard D. Irwin, 1979. 924 pages. *A good general treatment of all types of insurance.*

Greene, Mark R., and Oscar N. Serbein. *Risk Management: Text and Cases.* Reston, Va.: Reston Publishing Co., 1978. 630 pages. *See especially Chapters 7–9.*

Greene, Mark R., and James S. Trieschmann. *Risk and Insurance.* Cincinnati: South-Western Publishing Company, 1981. 548 pages. *See especially Chapters 10, 11, 16, 20, and 24 for coverage of auto, homeowners, life, and health insurance.*

Huebner, S. S., and Kenneth Black, Jr. *Life Insurance,* 10th ed. Englewood Cliffs, N.J.: Prentice-Hall, 1982. *See especially Chapters 2, 4, 5, 6, 18, and 19 for coverage of life and health insurance.*

Mehr, Robert I. *Life Insurance: Theory and Practice,* rev. ed. Austin, Tex.: Business Publication, Inc., 1977. *This publication contains a detailed discussion of life and health insurance.*

Mehr, Robert I., and Emerson Cammack. *Principles of Insurance.* Homewood Ill.: Richard D. Irwin, 1980. 737 pages. *See especially Chapters 1 and 2 for coverage of risk management.*

Mehr, Robert I., and Bob A. Hedges. *Risk Management: Concepts and Applications.* Homewood, Ill.: Richard D. Irwin, 1974. 726 pages. *See especially Chapter 2 for a discussion of the objectives of risk management.*

Rejda, George E. *Social Insurance and Economic Security.* Englewood Cliffs, N.J.: Prentice-Hall, 1976. 493 pages. *See especially Chapters 2, 5, 7, 10, and 13 on the mechanics of OASDHI and social health insurance.*

Riegel, Robert, Jerome S. Miller, and C. Arthur Williams, Jr. *Insurance Principles and Practices.* Englewood Cliffs, N.J.: Prentice-Hall, Inc., 1976. 619 pages. *See especially Chapters 7 and 18, for discussions of fire and auto insurance policies.*

Social Security Bulletin. Monthly. Current issues.

Tobias, Andrew. *The Invisible Bankers.* New York: The Linden Press, 1982. *A popular criticism of the insurance industry and its practices.*

Williams, C. Arthur, Jr., John G. Turnbull, and Earl F. Cheit. *Economic and Social Security.* New York: John Wiley, 1982. 608 pages. *See especially Chapters 1-10.*

PART III

Guides to Successful Investing

Amling, Frederick. *Investments: An Introduction to Analysis and Management,* 4th ed. Englewood Cliffs, N.J.: Prentice-Hall, 1978. *See especially Chapters 16 and 18 for an analysis of market indicators.*

Bellemore, Douglas H., Herbert E. Phillips, and John C. Ritchie, Jr. *Investment Analysis and Portfolio Selection: An Integrated Approach.* Cincinnati: South-Western Publishing Co., 1979. 656 pages. *See especially Chapters 15–20 for a discussion of fundamental analysis of markets.*

Board of Governors of the Federal Reserve System. *The Federal Reserve System: Purposes and Functions.* Washington, D.C., 1981. *Good explanation of how the system works.*

Bolten, Steve E. *Security Analysis and Portfolio Management.* New York: Holt, Rinehart & Winston, 1972. 510 pages. *See especially Chapter 19 for a description of technical market indicators.*

Brown, Harry, and Jerry Coxon. *Inflation-Proofing Your Investments.* New York: William Morrow & Company, 1981. 512 pages. *See especially Chapters 26–32 for a good discussion of creating an individual portfolio.*

Christy, George A., and John C. Clendenin. *Introduction to Investments.* New York: McGraw-Hill, 1982. 784 pages. *A broad view of investments and techniques.*

Coates, C. Robert. *Investment Strategy.* New York: McGraw-Hill, 1978. 588 pages. *See especially Chapters 1–4 for a good description of fundamental investment concepts.*

562

Cohen, Jerome B., Edward D. Zinbarg, and Arthur Zeikel. *Investment Analysis and Portfolio Management.* Homewood, Ill.: Richard D. Irwin, 1982. 946 pages. *A thorough and widely used book on investments.*

Commerce Clearing House. *Federal Tax Course.* Annual.

Dougall, Herbert E., and Francis S. Corrigan. *Investments.* Englewood Cliffs, N.J.: Prentice-Hall, 1978. 599 pages.

Dreman, David N. *Contrarian Investment Strategy: The Psychology of Stock Market Success.* New York: Random House, 1979. *A good overview of stocks as investments, especially when they are "unpopular."*

Floyd, Charles F. *Real Estate Principles.* New York: Random House, 1981. *See especially Chapter 15 on real estate financing and Chapter 17 on real estate as an investment.*

Francis, Jack Clark. *Investments: Analysis and Management, 2nd ed.* New York: McGraw-Hill, 1980. *A widely accepted advanced undergraduate book.*

Freund, William C. *Investment Fundamentals.* New York: American Bankers Association, 1966. *A good detailed discussion of securities as investments.*

Herzfeld, Thomas J. *The Investor's Guide to Closed-End Funds.* New York: McGraw-Hill, 1980. *A practical guide to closed-end funds for the individual and institutional investor.*

Kahn, Sanders, and Case. *Real Estate Appraisal and Investment, 2nd ed.* New York: John Wiley, 1977. *See especially the discussions on guides to appraising real estate.*

Kau, James F., and C. F. Sirmans. *Tax Planning for Real Estate Investors, rev. ed.* Englewood Cliffs, N.J.: Prentice-Hall, 1982. *An excellent treatment of how taxes should influence the real estate investments.*

Lasser. J. *How You Can Profit from the New Tax Law.* J. K. Lasser Tax Institute, Fireside Books, 1981.

Malkiel, Burton J. *Random Walk Down Wall Street, 2nd ed.* New York: Norton, 1981. *The entire book should be read. It has an especially good treatment of closed-end funds.*

Moody's Handbook of Common Stocks. New York: Moody's Investors Service, Inc. Annually.

Porter, Sylvia. *1982 Income Tax Book.* New York: Avon Books, 1982.

Quinn, Jane B. *Everyman's Money Book.* New York: Dell, 1980.

Ritter, Lawrence S., and William L. Silber. *Principles of Money, Banking, Financial Markets*, 3rd rev. and expanded ed. New York: Basic Books, 1980. *An elementary and easy-to-understand book on a complex subject.*

Security Owner's Stock Guide. New York: Standard & Poor's Corporation. Monthly.

Sharpe, William F. *Investments*, 2nd ed. Englewood Cliffs, N.J.: Prentice-Hall, 1981. *A modern and sophisticated book based on random walk theory.*

Shenkel, William. *Modern Real Estate Principles.* Dallas: Business Publications, 1980. *A good general discussion of real estate principles.*

Shulsky, Sam. *Sam Shulsky on Investing.* New York: New York Institute of Finance, 1980.

Smith, Adam (George P. Goodman). *Paper Money.* Summit Press, 1981.

Soble, Ronald L. *Smart Money in Hard Times.* New York: McGraw-Hill, 1975. 188 pages.

Steiner, Berry R. *Pay Less Tax Legally.* NAL/Signet Books, 1982.

Stevenson, Richard A., and E. H. Jennings. *Fundamentals of Investments*, 2nd ed. St. Paul, Minn.: West Publishing Co., 1981. *A well-written undergraduate text on investments.*

U.S. Treasury. *Your Federal Income Tax.* Publication 17. Washington, D.C. Annually. *See also specialized tax guides available free from offices of the Internal Revenue Services.*

The Value Line Investment Survey. New York: Arnold Bernhard & Co. Weekly.

Van Caspel, Venita. *Money Dynamics for the 1980s.* Reston, Va.: Reston Publishing Co., 1980.

Wiesenberger Investment Companies Service. New York: Warren, Gorham and Lamont. Annually.

PART IV

Retirement and Estate Planning

Allen, Everett T., Jr., Joseph J. Melone, and Jerry S. Rosenbloom. *Pension Planning.* Homewood, Ill.: Richard D. Irwin, 1981. 423 pages. *See Chapter 5 for a good discussion of pensions and inflation; Chapter 14, on savings plans; and Chapter 22 on tax deferred annuities.*

Arthur Andersen & Co. *Estate and Gift Tax Strategies under the Economic Recovery Tax Act of 1981.* Chicago: Arthur Andersen & Co., 1981.

Barnes, John. *More Money for Your Retirement.* New York: Harper & Row, 1980. 320 pages.

Best's Flitcraft Compend. Morristown, N.J.: A. M. Best Co. Annual.

Buckley, Joseph C. *Retirement Handbook.* New York: Harper & Row, 1977. 357 pages.

Calvert, Geoffrey N. *Pensions and Survival.* Toronto: Maclean-Hunter Limited, 1977. 167 pages.

Clark, Robert L., and Joseph J. Spengler. *The Economics of Individual and Population Aging.* New York: Cambridge University Press, 1980. 211 pages. *See especially Chapters 4–8.*

Institute for Business Planning. *Estate and Trust Practice and Fiduciary Responsibility.* Englewood Cliffs, N.J.: Prentice-Hall. Current volume.

Oldson, Lawrence, Christopher Caton, and Martin Duffy. *The Elderly and the Future Economy.* Lexington, Mass.: D. C. Heath and Company, 1981. 195 pages.

Rosenbloom, Jerry S., and Victor Hallman. *Employee Benefit Planning.* Englewood Cliffs, N.J.: Prentice-Hall, Inc., 1981. *See especially Chapter 13, on individual retirement plans.*

Stephenson, Gilbert T., and Norman H. Wiggins. *Estates and Trusts,* 5th ed. Englewood Cliffs, N.J.: Prentice-Hall, Inc., 1973. *See especially Chapters 6–10 on how to use different kinds of trusts, and Chapter 21 on estate planning.*

INDEX